AF674149

DEMOCRACY AND POLITICS IN MODERN INDIA

DEMOCRACY AND POLITICS IN MODERN INDIA

DR. N.S. GEHLOT
Former Professor of Political Science
M.D.S. University, Ajmer (Rajasthan)

DEEP & DEEP PUBLICATIONS PVT. LTD
F-159, Rajouri Garden, New Delhi - 110 02

DEMOCRACY AND POLITICS IN MODERN INDIA

ISBN 978-81-8450-410-1

© 2012 N.S. GEHLOT

All rights reserved with the Publisher, including the right to translate or to reproduce this book or parts thereof except for brief quotations in critical articles or reviews.

Typeset by RAHUL COMPOSERS
358, Pocket-B, Phase-2, Sector-16B, Dwarka, New Delhi - 110 075

Printed in India at MAYUR ENTERPRISES
WZ Plot No. 3, Gujjar Market, Tihar Village, New Delhi - 110 018

Published by DEEP & DEEP PUBLICATIONS PVT. LTD.,
9, Rajouri Garden, New Delhi - 110 027 • Phone : 25435369, 25440916
E-mail : ddpubs@gmail.com • ddpubs@yahoo.com
Shawroom :
Ansari Road, Daryaganj, New Delhi - 110 002 • Telefax : 23245122

Contents

PART IV

ON FOREIGN POLICY/STRATEGIC FRONT

Preface

The very purpose of writing this volume is to highlight the key developments of the Indian political system and the role of public functionaries of our Constitution in a coalition-model era, which has become a permanent phenomenon of our governance since 1989. Due care has been taken to discuss the critical issues of contemporary politics that relates to the era of politics of fragmentation and polarization. At various places some important cases have been cited to make events more clear understanding. The study also covers the event of confrontation between the Executive and Judiciary as well as between the Union and State Governments, involving both the leading national parties—the Congress and BJP. It is believed that the work is based on simple language to meet the needs of the students and readers engaged in advanced study or preparing for competitive examinations. Some new events/ developments have been included in the Appendix.

I shall be failing in my duty, if I do not record my gratitude to my family members who have shown patience while writing the book. I should be thankful to my publisher, M/s. Deep and Deep Publications (P) Ltd., New Delhi who managed to release the book in record time.

DR. N.S. GEHLOT

PART I

Conceptual Framework

CHAPTER

1

Functioning of India's Democracy

Meaning of Good Governance and its Relevance

The present glamour and glamour of Liberalization, Privatization and Globalization (LPG) is the product of the international funding agencies/lending agencies (namely the WTO, the IMF, the World Bank, etc.) of the Western countries, which sought to promote and perpetuate the existing inegalitarian order of things in the world. The concept of good governance was basically promoted by the UN General Assembly declaration on the established of a New International Economic Order (NIEO) in 1974 and the adoption of charter of economic rights and duties of state in UN General Assembly.

The main attributes of good governance are consisted of rule of law, accountability, equality, decentralization, responsiveness, transparency, honesty, merits, etc. in the public management. The concept emphasis on the independence of judiciary and human rights. In context with the states, these concepts are not new, as they have all been propounded and projected by the thinkers like Hobbes, Locke, Rousseau, Paine, John Mill, Karl Marx, Gandhi, John Rawls, etc. to contain the coercive power of the state. The new development ideology derives from the fact that the state cannot be a social agent of change. The LPG discourse is largely based on the 'corporate model' and capitalism.

Good Governance, however, is not a finished product. It must be the agenda of the social and economic milie. It is a dynamic concept demanding periodical re-thinking and remodeling the key institutions of governance, in order to evolve a development matrix to facilitate proper understanding of the role of state for social discourse in the present market and non-market contexts. But enhancing accountability and transparency are the very core basis of the concept. It needs enlighted citizenship and public vigilance.

In India, self-governance and good-governance (common good) was the core-basis of our freedom struggle. After attainment of Independence, 'good-governance' became and synonymous through the Constitution of India under the caption, *'We the people of India'*, or through the guiding star, the 'Preamble' of the Constitution. Since then, the search has been on for the seemingly elusive goal of good governance by setting up various committees and commissions to revitalize public administration. However, despite all these efforts, we have failed to make a significant impact on public psyche against the institutional deterioration and decline of values in general, because of lack of Dharma, common good, and our leadership. In fact, our political system could not promote and to sustain common good of the governed during the last 55 years.

Indian political system has been facing the problem of carving out of new states (like Chhattisgarh and Jharkhand) or smaller districts, as is the case in UP. Its purpose has been to make good administrative sense and to maintain law and order along with nurturing micro communities, who are economically and socially backward. It is a part of decentralization and development. But the decision of the UP chief minister to denotify Gautam Budh Nagar, while merging it with Ghaziabad has raised a number of administrative issues. It has set a bad precedent projecting as if it is based on a political vendetta against arch-rival of present CM's predecessor. The disbanding exercise of nine districts was taken on 13th January 2004, to save Rs. 37 crore on administrative management, though Rs. 80 crore has been spent. On the contrary, it is alleged that the creation of new districts/states involve enormous costs to the exchequer with the setting up of infrastructure and officialdom.

In its report on currency and finance for the year 2002-03, the Reserve Bank of India—RBI has sounded, if not alarm bells, a note of serious caution over the shabby state of Centre's finances, which the RBI is worried not so much about the Government living beyond its means by the fact that it is increasingly spending money on wrong kinds of things, namely staff salaries, subsidies, interest payments and the pre-poll sops announced by the Central Finance Minister on the eve of the 14th Lok Sabha elections.

This scenario has badly affected to our productive capacity of economy in the era of globalization and liberalization and has created the most different form of deficit to contain. This inevitably hurts the productive sectors of the both in terms of profits and competitiveness.

AREAS OF OUR AILMENT

The Constitution of India is the oldest functioning legal in the third world and we may feel proud of the country's achievements. Yet there are numerous major ailments that have afflicted the functioning of political system India. They are: Proliferation of political parties and political instability; criminalization of politics; steep fall in values and degeneration in politics, unaccountability of bureaucracy, allocation of undue perks and privileges to elected legislators with numerous discretionary powers; Annihilation of caste system, absence of pre-requisites of the British system; Prevalence of problems relating to poverty, illiteracy, backwardness, over-population and the shortage of food and drinking water, etc.; Lack of administrative and judicial accountability and work-culture, no strategic accountability of market and customers, lack of efficient grievance redressal machinery, inadequacy of the administrative justice system (despite the Malth Committee report, 1989-90). There has been effective land reforms and social Legislation. Short decline of moral values and norms in 1970's through the Licence-Quota-Permit Raj and evaporation of spirit of national service resulted into the rise of criminal gangs.

The Abdual Karim Telgi's multi crore fake stamp paper empire has highlighted how it relied on inherent flows in the system such as unemployment, corruption, election funding and establishment of corporate principles and entrepreneurial vision on the wrong side of the law by involving top level bureaucracy. Likewise, the justice-on-sole involving Ahmedabad Metropolitan Magistrate, M.S. Brahm Bhatt for issuing bailable warrants against the President of India, the Chief Justice of India and others on January 15th by the Gujarat High Court as well as the acquittals of all victims in the *Best Bakery case* v. *Zahira Shikh* have exposed the functioning of Indian Judiciary. Yet our political leadership proudly has been claiming of India 'shining' (भारत उदय).

Today, India is shining, of course, but it is shining for the privileged few. The rest are mired in darkness. If it was brought about an agriculture resolution. Our poverty line is the most austerely defined in the world the position of the country. India shall have to make concerted efforts to overcome the problem of food security and decentralization is the key to food security. Arming Panchayati raj institutions with legal, financial, technologies and managerial resources will help us to solve our basic problems of rural life. Until the aforesaid problems are solved, there can be no 'genuine feel good factor', (अधिक सुखद अहसास), nor can India boost of becoming a developed country by the end 2020 which is the vision of our President, Mr. Abdul Kalam.

In short, these drawbacks and loopholes have been responsible for the crises of governance for which both the system and its operators are responsible.

The cure for these aliments lies in the demand for systematic change such as ensuring minimum political instability as it found in the German Constitution (A provision for a constructive vote of confidence) and the time-bound President's rule at the centre under Article 356; Effecting internal democracy in political parties, audit of their funds and state-funding of elections, enforcing the right to Information for openness and transparency, etc. In short, a package of remedial measures will have to be evolved with building our social infrastructure.

The functioning of India's parliamentary democracy needs a holistic and fully integrated approach to political reforms for a clean and quality governance. The governance has to become citizen-friendly, otherwise people would loose faith in the democratic system itself. It is a healthy sign that the voting-behaviour of electorate in 2003 elections to the four state assemblies of north India concentrated on *'Development'* and *'Governance'*; and that the NDA-led government brought about a ban on political defections through the 91st amendment Act. Yet much has to be done to transform the system for qualitative governance. Perhaps the best blue print for reforms (or action plan) lies itself in Article 37 of the Constitution, where the Constitution uses the term 'governance' under the Directive Principles of State Policy. This Article speaks of certain principles being fundamental in the governance of the country. Developmental goals, economic and social renewal objectives and administrative upgradation strategies can be achieved only through decentralized pattern instead of 'centralized' pattern of planning. It must be based on popular consent and democratic consensus. Fortunately, we have the Sarkaria Commission report as well as the recommendations of the Constitution Review Commission to repair our ailing democratic set-up and to meet the challenges being used by the fallout of LPG.

In Indian context, good governance was a casualty due to the absence of mission or vision and lack of leadership. It become totally perverted by pervasive and incisive corruption in every department of social life, in general, and political life, in particular, for which our brand of socialist pattern of governance. The canker of corruption in top 'echelons' of government systematically destroyed the entire fabric of social, economic and life in this country, but caring little of bearing responsibility and throwing in winds the ethical values of public life. The result is that people are compelled today to 'eat corruption, sleep corruption and drinking only corruption'.

This was scenario, which the Vohra Committee's findings on triangle nexus as amongst politicians, bureaucrats and criminals focussed.

STRATEGY TO RETRIEVE INDIAN ADMINISTRATION

The key question is how to retrieve of the dismal situation our political system as cited above. Of course, the country needs a change. We need to jettison most of our bad 'belongings' that have made our system worse. This reform needs in the five areas; namely, (a) Political reforms; (b) Judicial reforms; (c) Administrative reforms; (d) Socio-institutional reforms, and (e) Human reforms. The first three involve our ailing systems and sub-systems. The fourth involves the entire gamut of plural society and diversity of institutions, and the fifth deals with the man, his mind, his character and psyche as well as moral values. Our original sin in governance lies in the fact that we never de-colonized our set-up while designing democratic-super-structure of the independent Republic. It was the blunder of the highest magnitude that the west-minister model has proved unworkable in the changing India. Indeed, the time has come to jettison the ideology—idiom and procedural jungle of administration and to peopleise the power of government through participation. Real democracy means real empowerment of the people; government is not a business, it is a service, born in sympathy and empathy. All this need is the will to fight the ailments.

The Role of NGOs

The world bank and the Organization for Economic Cooperation and Development—OECD first laid emphasis on the role of the NGO's through the new dimension of liberalization viz. good governance, thus rolling back the role of the State. On account of the neo-liberal account, withdrawal of the state should make room for voluntary services, namely, NGOs on one hand and free market forces, on the other. This shift to NGOs has frequently been justified as an expression of the emphasis on popular participation and participatory development. This has been favoured by multi-liberal agencies to deliver good services in to enhance represent human values.

Hence, in Indian reference, an explicit distinction must be drawn between 'government' and 'governance', and obviously, 'governance' is wider term than that of 'government'. Of course, the government is the most powerful and coercive 'institution' in governance, which believes in concentration of authority, whereas the NGOs lay emphasis on decentralization, free market, contracting out of good service, de-regularization, sustainable development, employment and result-oriented outputs. That is why these NGOs are becoming increasingly important elements in governance in the new era of LPG.

The emergence of the role of NGO's represents 'corporate sector' which includes both national and trans-national cooperation of public important. So far as India is concerned, her economic reforms need to give good bye to the regulatory regime which is known as the Licence-Permit Raj—in order to strengthen the participatory role of people in sustainable development and to entail accountability in our democratic set-up. For democracy to be successful at the national level, the grassroots organizations have to be make stronger for the cause of good governance as participation warrants every kind of citizens' intervention in administrative action. It involves a factor of determination and decision-making. To ensure people's participation, the 73rd and 74th amendments to the Constitution (i.e. a third tier of representative governance) is a good beginning, but it needs further changes in terms of their powers, position and resources. These local bodies are still not accountable, effective, responsive and efficient to the local people. The fear is that these bodies might not become the victim of corruption.

In the recent phase, our media talk of *Shining India*, notwithstanding the losing the factual reality that India remains a developing country, and it is still one of the world's poor on an array of growth as well as quality of life indicators and with the largest number of abjectly poor living within a single national boundary. Even though the country has begun to climb impressively out of economic oblivion. But the country can not (should not) shut its eye at the ban of the US on outsourcing of her MNCs, notwithstanding of the smooth fabric of US-India relations and increasing cooperation on civil nuclear space and high technology areas what we call as "strategic partnership".* However, our leadership cannot sideline the basic need of 'reforms package' to make India a competitive country in the globalized world. India must now concentrate on "insourcing" rather than on "outsourcing" to strengthen her economy. India cannot shine till the 40 percentage of its population remain below the poverty line and till the nexus between the criminals, bureaucrats and politicians remain in operation in our polity. Our achievements are numerous but our lowest strata of society—poorest of the poor—have no partnership in making India shining.

Broadly speaking, goodness of governance emerges from positive developmental roles of functionaries, underpinned with a summation of positive values—including morality, ethics, accountability, transparency, etc.—in a Weberian model of public administration operating in a democratic context. A true democracy visualizes decentralization and delegation of beneficiaries of all administrative activities relating to law and order, development, social welfare, etc. Assertion of this angle is clearly visible behind the demand for enforcement of people's charter.

Persistence in negative tendencies, in a gradually increasing proportion over the decades, had caused serious and widespread damage not only to the capability of Indian administration to be an effective vehicle of 'good governance', but also its very credibility to discharge even the minimal functions of regulatory nature. The situation is desperate and any peace meal or patch-work approach will not work. Hence, recasting Indian administration in a new mould is the caying need of the hour.

NEED FOR REFORMS AND PEOPLE'S PARTICIPATION

Therefore, a package of remedial measures will have to be

* This ban on outsourcing business on US companies was approved by the US Senate on January 23rd, 2004. This a sign of American policy of economic protectionism and against the norms laid down by the WTO v/s. openness). The ban exposed the US policy of globalization and liberalization.

evolved incorporate huge investments in building our social infrastructure (i.e., removal of illiteracy, educating the masses about their rights and duties, education, health, employment, shelter, welfare, empowerment of women and weaker sections, etc.), simultaneously with equally demanding needs of economic and physical infrastructure (i.e., power, communication, industrial development, technological development, availability of high quality consumer goods, rising level of exports, increasing per capita income and level of living, etc.)

While the existing administrative apparatus will need to be subjected to in-depth administrative reforms, including electoral reforms on an extensive scale to cover comprehensively procedural, structural and attitudinal aspects, there is also an urgent need to enlist active involvement of NGOs and voluntary groups and people's cooperative bodies and such other forms of associative democracy in carrying out functions of administration on an increasing and widening scale, thus ensuring a smooth roll-back of administrative expenditure. For the surest way of realizing good governance is, through promoting more and more people's participation, both at policy formulation level as well as the implementation level, even though it is through a wasteful process of trial-and-error.

In the 21st century, let the people themselves decide what they want, when, how, where, how and in what proportion and let public administration restrict itself to a mere enabling role and pot guiding them or leading them in their onward march to realize their socio-economic and development goals.

To conclude, in this age of information and technology, ideas spread across the world quite rapidly. And when they come with an aid package, resisting them becomes even more difficult. 'Good governance' emerged as a powerful idea when multilateral and bilateral aid agencies, like the World bank, UNDP, OBCD, ADB, etc., blessed it after a realization dawned on them that project success depended quite substantially on conditions of governance in the aid-receiving countries. This has been underlined in the report of World Bank, 1994; UNDP,

"A UNDP Policy Paper: Strategy on Governance". (draft paper), New York, United Nations, 1995.

After a series of evaluation studies of the project it assisted, the World bank underlined that since a country's capacity to implement carefully planned projects was a critical determining component of project success and sustainability, 'good governance' was a concern worthy of attention in considering projects for assistance. It emphasized three significant dimensions of governance namely: (1) political regime character, (2) organizational process by which authority and control are exercised, and (3) institutional capacity to plan and implement policies and carry out functions. Seven specific areas of developing countries' Public Sectors have been targeted for improved governance by the World Bank and the Development Assistance Committee of the OBCD. These are : (1) public sector management, (2) accountability, (3) legal and regulatory framework, (4) transparency and information, (5) human rights, (6) participatory approaches, and (7) military expenditure. It is worth recalling that these guides of the world aid agencies were meant for the Third World countries or developing countries after the disintegration of the USSR.

Reforming governmental structures of Third World countries which sought development assistance has no doubt been an old concern of aid-givers. Unlike the present approach, however, their initial strategies to improve governance focussed basically on public sector reforms, which deal with civil service, personnel pay and promotion, tax administration, budget, finance, etc. Gradually, one witnessed a shift away from these to issues of technical efficiency and economic soundness of development projects and programmes. Governmental structures received far less attention as the focus shifted to substantive policy areas; and this remained so till about the beginning of 1990s when, as mentioned before; 'governance' came to be perceived as an extremely significant determinant of economic performance and institutional capacity investment choices by both public and private sectors.

The World Bank has been actively advocating for adoption by other Third World countries the East Asian model of governance, providing considerable room for government-private sector collaboration—which was considered responsible for their high economic performance. Structural adjustment and economic reforms programme, consisting of liberalization, deregulation, privatization and State withdrawal from many economic sphere, has been a crucial component of the agenda for 'good governance' which comes from such sources.

SETTING UP OF AN ECONOMIC COUNCIL

The major problems facing the country's economy are black money, subsidies, loss-making public sector units and mounting government expenditure, apart from widespread poverty, illiteracy and the population explosion.

The long-term perspective requires a consensus on the priorities, as well as the means and resources to achieve the desired results, Resources are dwindling with the budgetary deficit increasing every year. But with a number of national and regional parties cropping up in the recent past—and each getting at the other's throat—arriving at a consensus is a formidable task by itself. Therefore, the functioning of our coalition model has weakened.

One way to accomplish this is by establishing a National Economic Council, comprising representatives from all major political parties, eminent economists and social workers, bureaucrats, representatives from industry and other economic sectors. This council should build a broad framework for the formulation of the budget. It should monitor economic progress periodically and suggest remedial measures. Unless some tough measures are taken, one can foresee the economy collapsing, as has happened in Indonesia and South Korea, and is imminent in Pakistan. We should have to take lessons from the collapse of the USSR.

Against this background, the role of Planning Commission based on the Nehru Model should be recast on new priorities basis of development in the era of globalisation. Its role of 'Super Cabinet' is no more relevant, instead its concern should be to lay down new norms of market economy and investment to prevent the habit of deficit budgets and focus the new areas of economic growth and development. Our new economic policy warrants a ban on "Politics of Populism" against depending on deficit budgets in fact, there is a need to review the role of constitutional institutions and processes and procedures thereof to procedure the benefits of LPG. As the on party rule era has ended and the era of coalition culture has become a reality, the inevitable need is of laying down new norms of coalition governance.

It is worth recalling the Comptroller and Auditor General—CAG's report about India's disinvestment process that has raised objections about the functioning of the process. It has always been subject of controversy. In its report of February, 2004 the CAG's report estimated that there was a loss of nearly Rs. 146 crore to the exchequer from the sale of Centaur Hotel of Mumbai on account of low valuations and rental. This observation underlines the lack of transparency and inherent corruption in the disinvestment process, which Disinvestment Minister Arun Shourie initially dismissed the findings as "idiotic" though later on he unreseveredly apologised his remarks; but maintaining that the methodology and inferences used by the CAG was "peculiar". Truth is that the question of valuation of public assets versus the choice of buyers has cropped up time and again in the disinvestment process on a variety of grounds—whether be it the sales of BALCO to Satellite for Rs. 500 crore, or the VSNL which was cought in the controversy of over Rs. 2,000 crore. There can be no denying that the Government despite a decade of privatisation process was adopted to the health of our economic reforms, has been unable to tend transparency to the exercise, which is one of the key features of good governance in the western countries like the USA. The CAG has a crucial watchdog role of play in the disinvestment process. The process itself should be credible in the eyes of others.

Secondly, the Government has to answer for whether the strategic sale of Public Sector Undertakings is really a superior option, as the Government has prioritized the sale of profit-making over loss-making PSUs and the Government has not earmarked the money for social and physical infrastructure. Sadly, the Government of India has not routinely answerable to institutions such as parliament and CAG on such matters, and the minister concerned was seen in patience about the system of checks and balance. Good governance demands accountable governance and against this background, the Supreme Court of India has directed the Union Government to obtain parliamentary approval for the sale of Hindustan Petroleum and Bharat Petroleum Public Sector Undertakings. There is no place to shortcuts which undermine the credibility of the Institutions like Parliament CAG. (*see, 'come to Judgment', editorial page of The Times of India,* 21/2/2004, p. 14)

The analysis of the past 56 years performance of our governance reveals that in India's context the roles of politicians, civil servants and the peoples in achieving good governance have brought to the fore many problems so far as globalisation and self-reliance is concerned. In fact, our system under the Nehruvian model of development could not recast a balance between the rights and responsibilities of individuals and of Government for achieving the target of good governance, though the issue of social justice emerged as an important ingredient of good governance, wherein our political system failed to transfer mass poverty into mass prosperity, nor could it re-order the balance of rights and responsibilities between individuals, Private corporates and Government agencies. The model proved ill-digested, dishonest and cumbersome. A lot of debate on the centre -states relations was there, but hardly anybody cared to undertake note of the administrative incompetence, political partnership, checking huge untaxed black money, etc. which frustrated most of our fiscal policies.*

In brief, the minimum requirement for achieving good governance include rule of law, decentralisation of governing authority, governmental accountability and responsiveness, and transparent administration.

Unfortunately none of these has been satisfactorily established even after more than half-a-century since Independence. India has failed to create a vibrant civil society capable of transforming mass poverty into mass prosperity. Unless there is a close and honest rapport between the government and civil society including private business sector, it is next to impossible to alleviate economic poverty of the

* Jayanta Kumar Ray, India in Search of Good Governance (Calcutta, K.P. Bagchi & Co., 2001).

Indian masses. At least, this is the lesson of developmental experience of West Europe, United states and Japan and the modem East Asian countries. Today, globalisation forces are irresistible and it will be futile to try to check the globalisation process on grounds of doctrinaire and ideological purities. A far more pragmatic approach will be to engage in intense and honest bargaining for deriving the maximum advantage of globalisation in technology and finance in order to serve India's basic national interest in turning mass poverty into mass prosperity. It would be necessary to conciliate conflicting labour and capital interests for exploiting the growth potential associated with globalisation and liberalisation. In the 21st Century context, India does not have the option of achieving economic development through regimented political system; the civil society conscious of its rights and privileges would not simply allow it. The challenges to good governance in contemporary India are formidable indeed. Good governance is not an ideological luxury nor is it a lolly-pop which we can dangle before a lisping child; it has today become an inexorable necessity like an oxygen cylinder to a suffocated patient.

References

See the World Bank's report on 'Governance: The World Bank's Experience', (Washington, DC, 1994 and the UNDP's Policy Paper on 'Strategy on Governance', New York, UN, 1994, and *Asian Development Bank Report*, Manila, 1994. They have emphasized on the key components for ''Good Governance".

The special number on 'Towards Good Governance', IIPA, New Delhi, Volume XLIV, No. 03, July-September 1998, and Also see the Issue of IIPA's Administrative Reforms—Revisited, July-September, 1985, for Administrative Reforms.

Chapter 14th of my volume, 'New Challenges to Indian Politics', (New Delhi, Deep & Deep Publications Pvt. Ltd., 2003,) pp. 212-20.

The edited book of Prof. C.P. Bathwal, 'Indian Administration Since Independence' (Lucknow, Bharat Book Centre, 2003).

Ram Ahuja, 'Social Problems in India' (New Delhi, Jaipur, Rawat Publications, 1997).

Special Issue on Globalization and the State of *The Indian Journal of Political Science*, Volume 62, No. 3, September 2001.

CHAPTER

2

Prime Minister's Position in Coalition Politics

Assessing the Functioning of the UPA Government

The results of 14th Lok Sabha elections, 2004, once again confirmed the continuance of minority/coalition government at the Centre. The results presented a gloomy political picture of governance. With the exit of the BJP-led NDA government, the Congress-led UPA assumed the office under the leadership of Dr. Manmohan Singh as P.M. in May, 2004 of the country. This is a new avatar of the grand Old Party under Mrs. Sonia Gandhi. The Congress, which had lost power in 1996 under the leadership of P.V. Narsimha Rao, then found in disarray to reconcile itself to sitting in the opposition, nor it was then not prepared to have coalition like mindset to collaborate with regional parties. But the completion of BJP's led NDA government compelled the Congress culture to accept the harsh reality of the emergence of coalition culture and the rise of multi-party system. Not only the BJP, the Congress along with national parties willy-nilly accepted the idea of coalition government. It is worth-recalling that since 1989, a gloomy political picture for our governance presented the picture of 'hung parliament' and a strong signal of the rise of multi-party system in place of the dominance of one-party system in which the role of regional parties like the TDP, DMK, AGP, TMC, RJD, etc. has been assertive and dynamic. It is a healthy sign that our national parties have accepted their identity in governance of the affairs of the Centre, but they altogether have failed to guide the nation to have a stable government. Truly, our politicians have accepted the idea of coalition not on the basis of an identical views but purely out of a desire to share power at the Centre without a concern of political stability.

WEAKNESSES OF A COALITION MODEL

The framers of a Constitution consciously and rightly adopted the British model of parliamentary democracy with a cabinet Government, with its attendant concept of collective responsibility, as best suited to the genius of India. They had a deep faith in this model because of its successful operation in England. However, it is significant to point out that on all occasions in this country when general elections have failed to produce a single party majority in England, the outcome has been single-party minority government and never a coalition. Opposition leader Disraeli maintained in 1852 that England does not love coalitions. 'While addressing the House of Commons in 1924, the then Prime Minister Ramsay MacDonald said: 'Coalition are detestable and dishonest.'

It was so because a coalition is an alliance between two or more hitherto separate or even hostile groups or parties formed in order to carry on the government and share the principal offices of the state. Not infrequently coalitions in Europe have been arrangements for postponement of an unwanted election. The cabinet speaks in many voices. The sense of direction and unity of purpose, very essential for proper functioning of a cabinet, gets lost in a coalition government.

The second major weakness of a coalition is the stature of the Prime Minister's office. In the British system, the PM enjoys a unique position of power, prestige, prerogative and patronage. He leads the government and holds the ultimate weapon of recommending dissolution of the lower house. But in a coalition arrangement the P.M. remains under the constant pressure from the supporting parties of coalition. He cannot select his own team, nor can be reshuffle the cabinet at his own will. The consent of the constituent parties plays the key role here. In short, power shifts from 'cabinet' to an extra constitutional authority, like the Coordination or Steering Committee, as was the case with the NDA government or the role of NAC headed by Sonia Gandhi. Thirdly, the working of coalition cabinet leads to increasing the power and influence of the bureaucracy. Fourthly, a coalition model threatens the discipline and unity-command of the party-system. It dampness of party interests. Thus, it obscures the clear-cut choice of a two party system and causes splits in the party as well.

STATURE OF THE P.M. IN COALITION GOVERNMENT

The P.M.'s office has undergone changes in terms of strength, stature, influence and authority during the last decade because of the transformation of one-party rule to the multi-party system and the phenomenon of 'hung parliament'. In coalition governance, the Prime Minister's authority has been rendered less in the wake of the role of Steering Committee of the United Front or the Coordination Committee of the NDA, or currently the role of National Advisory Committee of the UPA. This extra-constitutional body acts or behaves like a Supreme Commander over the PM's office and the PM as the chief executive officer has to merely endure its decisions, probably because the PM knows that coalition is fragile and the denial would lead to the collapse of the government.

COALITION HICCUPS

V.P. Singh as key PM of coalition government once said

that 'coalition politics' is essentially an art of managing contradictions. Both the governments of NDA and UPA have been backed by the 'outside factor'. This has warranted now the new art of contradiction management against the members of single party rule for more than 40 years in the life of the 'Republic'. Since the UPA-led Congress Government came to power, its Big Brother's relationship with the smaller partners has been facing a number of strains—from the NPC to the Telengana Rajya Samiti to the RJD. The PM of Congress Party which used to head previously the culture of single party rule, finds it difficult to adjust to the new reality of coalition politics, specifically in Maharashtra where the appointment of S.M. Krishna as state governor was opposed by the NCP. So is the case of carving out a separate state out of Andhra Pradesh as per poll promise and pre-poll alliance with the TRS. In Bihar the RJD of Lalu Prasad Yadav has preempted by stating not more 10 seats to the national party (Congress) for the assembly elections held in Feb. 2005, in Bihar. As the flare-ups in Maharashtra, Andhra Pradesh and Bihar suggest that Congress is increasingly finding it difficult to learn the art of managing contradictions within the coalition. Again, in Jharkhand, the Congress-JMM poll alliance was based on the agreement that the former would contest more of the LS seats while leaving majority of the assembly seats for the regional partner. Congress now seems to have gone back on its word by demanding a larger share of the non-tribal seats in the coming assembly elections and the chief ministership as well. Thus the delay in taking back JMM leader Shibbu Soren in the cabinet and rehabilitating TRS leader Chandra Shekhar Rao has soured the relations within the UPA coalition.

Shibu Soren's re-induction into the central cabinet is treated as unfortunate. It reflects compulsions of coalition, in the same manner as is the case of accommodation of tainted leaders like Lalu Prasad Yadav. The UPA was under the immense pressure of electoral politics ahead of the assembly elections in 2005. The Congress led UPA has done exactly when it as an opposition used to criticize the NDA for clinging to power at all costs. Even more disheartening is to see that an honest PM was under the compulsions. He had no choice.

NO BAR ON TAINTED MPs

On tainted Ministers in the Union Council of Ministers, PM Manmohan Singh refused to buckle under opposition's pressure tactics. There up, the tainted ministers issue was petitioned by Manoj Narula on the ground that criminal cases were pending against Mohd. Maslimuddin, MA Fatimii and Jai Prakash Yadav, apart from Lalu Yadav and Shibbu Soren. When responding to the court notice, the Centre has stated before the Supreme Court that; (a) it is discretion of PM to include any MP in his council of Ministers and that the President of India is bound by it, and (b) as per Article 75, there is no limitation or restriction in the Constitution to bar MPs from being included in the Union Ministry. (c) there is a coalition government UPA with various parties which are the part of the present government. The coalition warrants inclusion in the council of ministers of various parties. The petition of Narula seeking a ban on inclusion of 'tainted' MPs in the Union Council was dismissed on July 16, 2004 .

VIOLATION OF CODE OF CONDUCT

The credibility of the PM's government was further seen lowering when union Minister Lalu Prasad Yadav as the RJD chief was caught on camera in distributing money to Dalit women in Bihar ahead of the assembly election. It was a clear case of violation of the model Code of Conduct and the election commission was compelled to direct the authorities of Patna to lodge an FIR against the Minister. The custodians of democracy and Constitution ought not to have brazenly violated the very rules and regulations that they themselves have framed. Lalu and his associates recalled how the BJP's leader Lalji Tandon distributed the saries to poor women during the 14th Lok Sabha elections in Lucknow in PM's (Atalji) constituency which resulted in a stampede.

The matter was further took a bad shape in Parliament when the Railway Minister was not in the parliament to make a statement on the train accident in Mukerian of Punjab. As per the statement of former PM Vajpayee, it was an insult of our parliament, as the railway minister went to Patna to attend the party work. The UPA government cannot absolve of the moral responsibility by saying that the matter relating to the violation of election's code of conduct was within the purview of the Election Commission.

Likewise, the decision of the UP A government relating to the reduction of troops in Jammu and Kashmir and holding talks with Naxal groups have been strongly criticized by the BJP, on the ground that such decisions would put the internal security at risk and that Natalities have no faith/respect in the Indian Constitution and democratic governance. While criticising the style of PM, BJP General Secretary Ananth Kumar on 13th December 2004, said in Raipur (MP) that it was pity, PM Manmohan Singh has become Sonia Gandhi's Sandesh Vahak (messenger), but failed to understand whose messenger Home Minister Shiv Raj Patil is? . . . . The UPA stands for un-principled alliance which runs through three remote controls, Super PM—Sonia Gandhi, CPM and DM (Dagi Mantri)—Lalu Prasad Yadav." Quoted from the *Times of India* (December 14, 2004, p. 5) This is nothing but a symbol of UPA's misrule.

Currently, the UPA government has been under heavy pressure on the price-rising issues—both internally and externally, as the supporting parties including the left parties have alleged the Congress in failing to control it, whereas the Congress has made the NDA government responsible for it. No body is prepared to own the responsibility of it, though the government is sincerely concerned of it. As an opposition party, the BJP has surrounded the UPA government on the issue such as the tug-of-war behaviour of the two ministers. The PM had to warn the duo (RJD supreme. Laloo Prasad Yadav and Ram Vilas Paswan) to end the embarrassing war of words and the Bihar satraps had to heed the advice of the PM, as their war might have the adverse fall out on the assembly poll prospects of the ruling coalition. Of course, the Laloo-Paswan spat brought down the functioning of Lok Sabha on 10th December 2004. It was a violation of collective responsibility.

The arrest of Kanchi Seer Jayandra Saraswati by the TN police has shocked the BJP in particular and Hindus in general. Keeping in view the sentiments of Hindu community and in accordance to the religious status position of Seer (pontiff) PM gracefully wrote a letter to the CM of Tamil Nadu, asking her to take all such measures to ensure the physical well-being of the arrested Seer. The PM did not like to interfere in the on-going due processes of law, as the Seer is not above the law. The way in which the Sankaracharya has been arrested by the Tamil Nadu authorities needs condemnation. But the BJP (VHP and RSS) have not been able to politicize the issue, as the PM tactfully responded rarely, that too for the cause of secular ethos.

The BJP should release that it lost the 14th Lok Sabha elections because it did too little towards governance after the Gujarat massive. The minorities voted against the NDA government. In fact, the defeat of BJP in the Lok Sabha and Maharashtra assembly election resulted in the inner clash within the BJP for coalition culture, in the sense that issues such as the growing indiscipline in it (suspension of Uma Bharti), adhering to the concept of 'back to basics' (emphasizing on Hindutva, temple building) have created apprehensions among the BJP's allies. Making L.K. Advani as the chief of the BJP and his commitment to return to Hindutava ideology has been a matter of concern for allies of the BJP, though according to the BJP leadership, Hindutva represents a broader perspective of life and there is no contradiction between "Hindutav" and "Bharatiyata".

YET A PERFECT PM

Prime Minister Manmohan Singh nevertheless, deserves to be complemented for expressing his concern about the Shankaracharya's health. He has gone out of his way to write to the Tamil Nadu chief minister to ensure the pontiffs well-being in jail. The government had earlier sought to distance itself from the controversy by asserting that the Centre had nothing to do with it. But keeping in mind the sensitivities of Hindus, he has done well to intervene in the matter. By doing so, the PM has risen in the esteem of ordinary Hindus like me.

On the part of the UPA government, the decision of our PM to reduce the Indian troops from Jammu & Kashmir has been widely welcome, including the former PM, A.B. Vajpayee who said, "it is a good move which will improve relations with Pak". This is the fallout of the policy of composite dialogue pursued by the Congress-led government. It is a right step towards the CBMs with Pakistan. The Union Home Minister Shiv Raj Patil is stated to have claimed the reduction of militant infiltration down by 60% in Jammu & Kashmir. The government of India is making efforts to make Pakistan to understand the 'ground realities of the Jammu & Kashmir and PoK viz-a-viz Hurriyat factions. India cannot tolerate any kind of interference in her internal affairs. On the Pak's Premier's contention that Islamabad was unlikely to grant MFN status to India unless the Kashmir issue itself was resolved. In that situation, the gas pipelines going through Pakistan from Iraq cannot be realized into a reality. Despite this, the PM's Rs. 24,000 crore package for J&K shows that the government is genuinely concerned in winning back the confidence of Kashmire, keeping in mind the pledge of Indian parliament that Kashmir is an integral part of India: PM's approach underlines that peace cannot imposed by force.

Prime minister Manmohan Singh's invocation of the fall of the Berlin Wall during his meeting with his Pakistani counterpart was significant in terms of that a historic divide to reunite. As in Germany, so also on the sub-continent, no one can deny the very real yearning of people on both sides of the border to get to know more about each other. India is right to ask for a bus from Srinagar to Muzaffarabad to increase people-to-people contact. From 30 visas in 2002, India has now issued 10,000 visas for Pakistanis. There have been numerous reports of the Indian government offering medical assistance to Pakistanis, especially children. All this can only serve to build goodwill for India in Pakistan. Encouraging more Pakistanis to come here will also give them a chance to see India's free and open society at work. It will help remove many misgivings they have about India. But the government is quite alert to see that freer movement (people's to people contact) does not undermine our security, as was seen in Berlin and Europe in 1980s in the foreign illegal immigrants.

The UPA government out rightly rejected the offer of the US to help in investigating the explosions in the N.E. of India, keeping in view the past history of nexus of the ISI and the

FBI, which was meant to surround the communist China, Afghanistan and Iraq in the form of anti soviet campaign. This offer came from the FBI's through the US ambassador to India, David Mulford. We have shown strong evidence to the US many a time how the Pak's ISI had been behind the Mumbai explosions or in Kashmir Valley and how the Indian Airlines flight was captured the Khalistani hijackers. (Ravi Visvesvaraya Prasad, "Most unwanted: FBI should be kept out of Northeast", *The Times of India,* November 29, 2004). It is not in our national interests to allow US intelligence agencies to develop too many ground-level contacts in the North-East region, which is volatile and which is the internal problem the Government of India is bound to resolve it at its own level.

The UPA government has been equally sensitive to the Naga problems and believes in peace negotiation initiative. Indications are that the leaders of NSCN (I-M) are willing to trust each other in the quest of peace after five decades of a bloody insurgency. The first meeting Naga leaders with our PM was held in New Delhi on a positive note. PM Manmohan Singh is first to realize that Nagaland can be the gate way to ASEAN or Look East Policy, for which the sub-nationalism has to be honoured in the process of national-building. While endorsing the NDA/government's Look East Policy, our PM gave final touch to a 'Partnership Agreement at Vientiage (Laos). Indo-Asian Pact would provide a new dimensions to India's relations with the member-states in the areas of economics, culture and security. The pact pledges to work towards a free trade areas by roll and cooperate in areas ranging from IT to highway construction. This was the third annual summit and called for cooperation in fighting terrorism drugs trafficking and proliferation of weapons of mass destruction.

Our PM should be credited for bringing a progressive right to Information Act, 2002 on the basis of the draft approved by the N.A.C. against corruption and nepotism which has spread like a cancer in our polity. The public needs full information in which is happening to revenues and expenditures. The Act must make governance a transparent affair to which the bureaucracy is stated to blocking the attempt to give teeth to the Act. It would be a self-defeating step if the Official Secrets Act, 1923 is not altered in accordance with our democratic requirements. Transparency should be the norm instead of petitions or tortuous procedures. The new draft should be upgraded into a duty to publish the bill with human face.

The first six months performance of Manmohan's rule may not impressive in terms of 'good governance', or in terms of economic reforms that he as Finance Minister of the then Rao Government (1991-96) had initiated when the fallout of L.P.G. was inevitable to adopt them. According to an analysis of Swaminathan S. Ankiesaria Aiyar, the PM with his team of Montek Singh Ahluwalia and N.K. Singh reflects the trends of continuity. It has tilted move towards the 'politics of populism'. The government's slogan of reforms with a human face implies that PM's first round of reforms in 1991-96 was somehow inhuman. In the opinion of the writer, the list of populist trends are as follows :

POPULIST TRENDS

- Job quotas for dalits and backward castes in the private sector. The Congress benefited from such reservation in the Maharashtra elections. Expect more of the same before the coming elections in Bihar, Jharkhand and Haryana. It is on the top priority list of the C.M.P. of the UPA Government.
- Free power for farmers has been decreed in Andhra Pradesh, Karnataka, Tamil Nadu and Maharashtra, expect the cancer to spread.
- State Electricity Boards were supposed to become solvent again after their debts of Rs. 40,000 crore were partly written off, partly transferred to the centre. But the Economic Survey estimates that SEBS will lose another Rs. 21,698 this year.
- The open-ended subsidy for cooking gas and kerosene could exceed Rs. 10,000 crore. A sensible attempt to raise cooking gas prices by Rs. 5 every month till the subsidy was eliminated was rolled back when the Left Front objected to it.

- The Common Minimum Programme promises to increase education spending from 3.4% to 6% of GDP; health spending from 0.9% to 3% of GDP; and a National Employment Guarantee Programme that will cost at least 1% of GDP. These are enormous sums for programmes with enormous leakages, good intentions, but dubious outcomes.
-

The UPA government should keep in mind the fiscal deficit trend in our budget and the implementation of the promised Common Minimum Programme (CMP) should not lead to fiscal disaster. India is the second largest consolidated fiscal deficit in the world.

MAIN POSITIVE CHANGES

- A new textile package in the budget has removed traditional tax discrimination against the mill sector, provided for technological up gradation, and hence laid the foundation for India Inc to take advantage of the abolition of global textile quotas from 2005.
- Legislation is in hand for appointing a pension regulator, and allowing foreign investment in pension funds. This is a major conceptual breakthrough.
- A new Special Economic Zones law is in the works; hopefully, industries in such zones will get the same quality infrastructure and labour flexibility as in Chinese SEZs.
- The budget offered school vouchers on an experimental basis. This again is a conceptual break-through.
- Six airports are to be upgraded with private participation.
- import tariffs continue to fall towards ASEAN rates.

MAIN NEGATIVE CHANGES

- The target of doubling agricultural credit in three years reverses years of banking reform. Union Minister Chidambaram should create conditions where banks can profitably lend to agriculture, instead of forcing them to lend against their better judgment.

- Supposed decontrol of oil prices has been replaces by firm control.
- Paswan has decreed, formally or informally, price control on steel and drugs.
- The proposal to allow private coal mining has been dropped, despite the growing coal shortage.
- The absurd rule in civil aviation policy continues, allowing FDI only by companies with no connection to aviation.

Despite political rhetoric, the Congress rule has more continuity than change on the economic front. India remains firmly on the neo-Hindu path of half-baked liberalization adopted in 1991-96.*

This should continue to yield the neo-Hindu growth rate of 6% per year, but not the targeted 7-8%. The government wants neither radical reforms nor backsliding. By rocking the boat only minimally, it wants to survive a full five-year term. And it will with a Populist Tilt.

Currently, the BJP-Led NDA is in disarray following the defeat of the 14th Lok Sabha elections and then Maharashtra assembly elections. The post-defeat pangs have been painful for the BJP on account of the outbursts of Uma Bharti and Aruna Smrati. Indisciplines is rampant in the BJP cadre and the fending amongst Gen-next line up is ceaseless and Hindutva, mixed up with development-economic security saffron issues, has not paid dividends to the BJP as it expected to. The NDA has miserably failed to play a role of effect opposition.

UNPRECEDENTED STRUCTURE OF GOVERNANCE

The emergence of the old Congress under Mrs. Sonia Gandhi as the Chairman and Manmohan Singh as Chief Executive Officer (CEO) and has presented a new model of

* Quoted from *The Sunday Times of India*, New Delhi, December 5, 2004, p. 15.

working for the era of globalisation. Her style of governance is quite different to that of Pandit Nehru or Smt. Indira Gandhi. Instead of taking the post of PM, keeping in view the compulsion of coalition politics, she was influenced by left of the centre and decided not to take up the PM's job. She shared some concerns with the leftist parties, which led the present arrangement. According to Prof. Pratap Bhanu Mehta, "it insulates policy-making from a lot of political pressure, and it leaves the party free to chart a political agenda unencumbered by the daily chores of running an administration.* This kind of division of labour makes coalition stronger and brighter. The prospects of investment that was initiated by the Rao government in which the present PM (then as Finance Minister) undertook a reform blitzed. Her seven new norms of Congress (termed as Sonianomics) are as follows.

SEVEN NEW MANTRA OF SONIANOMICS AND GOVERNANCE

1. *Be cool* : Impulsive action, *a la* Indira, is out. Calculated decisions are the in thing.
2. *Talk to people* : Consult colleagues on every issue, don't act unilaterally.
3. *Be prepared* : Listen carefully, take notes, be prepared with facts and arguments.
4. *Don't rush* : Many things resolve themselves even without action, be willing to wait for events to unfold.
5. *People matter* : Analyses the impact of every decision before acting. Give weightage to things that affect more people.
6. *Stick to principles* : Never lose sight of basic principles, however tempting it is to deviate in the short term.
7. *Act firmly* : Once you've decided what to do, go ahead and do it. Face up to the consequences.

---

* Quoted in 'New Grand Old Party' by Abheek Barman, *The Sunday Times*, Oct. 24, 2004, p. 10.

In short, Mrs. Sonia Gandhi concentrated on revamping the party's organization and set-up the NAC staffed by experts and professionals to sort out hassles between the left and the coalition partners. She does not recognize to centralise power, or Congress run regime as Mrs. Indira Gandhi used to.

Mother Teresa once said "He who is faultless does not care for the opinion of the others". This fits to our PM perfectly as Dr. Manmohan Singh as an academician-*cum*-economist turned politician, has stood stead against the barrage of protests from the left and right on the issues such as pulling out of Indian army; from Siachin, tackling the Manipur crisis, opening new job window for peace in Jammu & Kashmir.

It is so because he is currently the Chief Executive Officer (CEO) knows how to get in the big bucks and how to put India on the world map. Despite the opposition, our PM visited Jammu & Kashmir and Nagaland the troubled states--to canvassing road map for peace and development, but refused to bow down before terrorism. In Imphal, on 20th Nov. he said about balancing economy and coalition. Singh said, "We have to learn to work together and we have to have a cooperative attitude in order to run the economy and manage the coalition of the type that I am handling ..." "Running the economy and running the coalition require adeptness to deal with similar problems."

It is capability of our PM's leadership that the left parties made agree to accept the Patents Act, implement on Jan. 1st 2005 and VAT to be introduced from April 2005, making the left parties convinced India cannot ignore its TRIPS treaty obligations and WTO agreements signed in 1994. On many other issues of agenda, consultation and consensus has been the backbone of decisions.

In his short period, the P.M. has set free the economy to a great extent from inept bureaucratic control and set-up a planning commission took after infrastructure projects of the nation. He has eased tensions with Pakistan with his troops reduction measure and approached the US administration towards getting a permanent UNSC seat. As a result of his efforts with the MNCs, the stock market is booming and business is flourishing. In 'a diplomatic manner' our PM declined to take foreign government help laid on account of tsunami disaster of December 26, 2004. It pertinent to recall that the Bush administration appreciated the PM's strong leadership in the tsunami rescue and rehabilitation efforts. It was an indication of India's self-reliance and pride, apart from the fact that the India did not like that our southern areas (Indian ocean) to become the pawn of the Western aid in the disaster management. It might have involved our security concerns under the sign of generosity and humanity. Likewise, Indo-Iraq oil field deal is widely appreciated in terms of western hegemony over oil. The UPA's policy of granting 'dual citizenship' for pravasis has also been hailed in the country as well as in abroad. It involves about 25 million emigrants of Indian origin living in 16 countries and brightens the prospects of investment in building our infrastructure.

PM's JUST CONCLUDED FOREIGN SOJOURN

As the Prime Minister of India, he said at Oxford University on 9th July 2005 that the British Raj, despite its ills had a beneficial side. It brought *'good governance and new institutions'* that Indians value even in the 21st century. At Oxford, Dr. Man Mohan Singh quoted the notions like the rule of law, constitutional government, free press, judiciary and legal service, professional civil services, the concept of modern universities, research laboratories, our police system, etc. that have extended benefits in good governance to India.

The criticism of the statement by the BJP leaders or Marxists like Prof. Irfan Habib is uncalled for, as they themselves were a creation of the Raj, and sought the education under the British rule. India has to admit that the British Raj brought in new values and institutions shaped by the European Enlightenment. In fact, our Constitution rests on the key notions like liberty, equality, freedom or fraternity of the West and not of Aurangzeb or Shivaji. It is irony that Gandhian philosophy could not influence much to the Constitution-makers. Now the question is: can India give good bye to the values enshrined by the West under caption 'globalisation and liberalization'?

PM'S VISIT TO THE US AS THE LEADER OF NEW INDIA

Equally, the visit of Indian PM to the US and his address to the Congress (on 19th July 2005) was historic in the post-Cold War era ideology, where in India needs to secure its core interests in the world strategic certainties and wherein India has been recognized as one of the new rising power centres in the shifting world and centre of gravity. The visit of our PM was meant to prepare the new ground for the India-US relationship. No wonder that India is being sought as a partner in new global stability. Its military, economic and scientific capacity to contribute in that role is seen as an asset and not as a threat. India's future depends on its ability to engage and participate in global developments. Keeping in view the derogatory observations against Indian PM Mr. Indira Gandhi during the Indo-Pak crisis is of 1971, and aftermath the establishment of a Sino-Pak-US axis. This led India to enter the Indo-Soviet Treaty of Friendship in August 1971. There are two lessons here for India. First, narrowing the security decision-making base to a narrow cabal is fraught with danger. Second, it would be naive for India to exaggerate the Bush administration's desire to make India its strategic partner in the emergence of India as a world power, or believe that it will abandon Pakistan in the new global order. Much shall depend on the US support to India's claim in the Security Council's membership.

It is a matter of proud and pleasure for Indians that on the eve of the PM's visit, US Secretary of state Condoleezze Rice tried to abandon some traditionally held positions and accepted some new realities in a New World Order, that is, in her words: "The US recognizes India's rise as a modern democracy and we welcome India's enhanced role in international affairs".

NO THREAT TO THE UPA GOVERNMENT

So far as question of survival of the Congress-led UPA coalition government is concerned, neither angry Laloo will be destructive due to the Congress-RJD pact in Bihar politics and dissolution of the assembly there for fresh mandate, nor the left parties are going to adopt move active anti-Congress posture in view of the pending elections in West Bengal and Kerala in 2006. Of course, left parties as principal allies of the UP A government have been annoyed at the growing ties with the US on certain specific issues like the new India-US defence framework agreement, FDI in retail missile defence and India's energy security. They have predicted in advance that the US shall not support to the India's stake of UNSC seat. They have made many blistering attack) on the UP A's government's economic reforms policy relating to the disinvestments of BHEL and other 'Navratna's' public sectors as well as on increasing oil prices. They are bound to adopt a wait and watch posture till the assembly elections in West Bengal and Kerala state in 2006. As there is no credible opposition of the NDA (which has lost 50% seats in the last general elections and then lost in Maharashtra there is no threat to the Congress-led government or the PM. This apart, the BJP is currently in crisis grip on account of Advani-Jinnah controversy on 'secularism'. In terms of ideology, the Sangh Parivar cannot keep dreaming of Akhand Bharat and remained wedded to 75 year old ideology. The present coalition is India's largest ever, which is being carefully looking after by Mrs. Sonia Gandhi under the CMP agenda. It is bound together somehow by an ideological commitment to secularism and socialism with 'human face', though its partners are ideological mobile, as they cobbled up a programme after the poll as the electoral politics in the assembly elections of Bihar, Jharkhand, Haryana has presented the picture in favour of the UPA. There was a perfect combination between the Head of Government (PM) and the National Advisory Council (NAC) headed by Mrs. Sonia. The NAC was able to defuse tensions and conflicts.

The way the Congress led UPA has been handling its coalition blues has been a new model. It is, indeed, a good strategy to keep the PM away from party politics and let Mrs. Sonia Gandhi handle the messy business through the NAC *vis-a-vis* implementation of the minimum common agenda of the UPA. This has helped the PM concentrate on other important national issues like economic reforms, communal harmony, nation-building and integration process.

It is a good indication that the Congress being a accustomed to rule the country with a clear majority in the past, has made a clear and positive impact on its functioning style of coalition model.

BIHAR : A SET BACK TO PM

The decision of the Supreme Court handed down on 7th Oct., 2005 while striking down the Presidential proclamation of May 23, 2005, regarding dissolving the Bihar assembly as "unconstitutional", was a setback to the UPA government led by Dr. Manmohan Singh. The five judge bench confirmed the mala fides intentions of Governor Buta Singh in giving report to the Centre for dissolution of the lower house. This is also a 'setback' to the position of the Indian PM (along with the Home Minister) who cannot absolve the responsibility, because the union cabinet approved the contents of the report. The NDA parties were justified in the immediate recall of Governor Buta Singh. In the light of the Supreme Court's ruling on the list of unauthorized occupants of government bungalows (Throw him out) and use of force to evict squatter politicians, to was a shameful development. As per parliamentary norms, responsibility must be fixed in such matters. The Supreme Court's decision lends credence to the allegations of Governor's acting in partisan manner since his appointment. The continuance of the Governor in his office has reinforced the opinion that the office of the Governor is still an extension of the political party in power at the centre and the Congress has not learnt from the past history and the observations made by the Supreme Court from time to time.

According to the RJD supremo Laloo Prasad Yadav, "it is our victory as the apex court has not order revival of the dissolved assembly." In fact, by not reviving the dead house, the court escaped from the controversy of direct the confrontation between the judiciary and the executive and gave an interim judgment. Secondly, it was justified because of the declaration of four-phase elections (commencing on Oct.,

18, 2005) by the Election Commission and poll scheduled between Oct.-November, 2005.

As regards the present sorry state of Bihar, there seems no justification in calling Lalu Prasad Yadav as 'Vikas Purush' (man of development in Bihar). The history of speaks how he (Lalu Prasad) had been responsible for the ills plaguing the affairs of state. Since 1998, there had been no effective and clean governance. In fact, the negative perception of coalition government (alliance of national party with regional party) should be held responsible because both the NDA and UPA partners have nothing to do with ideological commitments. Their unity rests with the strategy of keeping the Congress/the BJP out of the power. Regrettably, the BJP, once a party with a difference, too has started losing its credentials of ideology and identity, because the party leadership had to follow a policy of alignments and alliances to grab the power.

On foreign policy front, the UPA government was seen heading for a confrontation with the left parties on Iran's refusal to submit its nuclear facilities to IAEA inspection, and the PM seemed to have taken a dim view of the left's attempt to inject the Shia angle into the issue. The PM was opposed to view the community prism into the foreign policy. The demand was that when Iran's nuclear is put up before the IAEA's board meeting in Vienna on 24th November, India must reverse its earlier stand. Luckily, the matter was deferred by the board's meeting under the EU pressure. In fact, India's foreign policy is still between devil and deep sea on the Iran nuclear issue. What the left front allies wanted was that India should ensure that the Iran's N-issue remains within the jurisdiction of IAEA, and, it should not be referred to the UN. The UPA government was bound to buy peace under the national interests, yet the bilateral defence cooperation between India and US is seriously taken in terms of our security concerns. Likewise, the Oil slick matter involving the foreign minister Natwar Singh has put UPA government under odd situation.

Presently, Prime Minister Dr. Manmohan Singh may not be termed as 'weakest Prime Minister' but he is, being the head of coalition government, is in a weak position. India has ever seen (so was also the case of NDA's PM, because both the

PMs have done injustice to Bihar). The UPA is like a vehicle the steering of which is in the hands of its chairperson, Mrs. Sonia Gandhi, with influencing the accelerator and the left applying the brakes on selective issues like the Indo-US nuclear deal. This reflects the functioning of two centers of power—'PM and NAC' chairman that is why Natwar Singh's portfolio was taken away under pressure in the wake of the exposure of the Volker report but was kept within the Union Ministry for sometime. This trend violates the parliamentary norms *vis-a-vis* accountability of a minister. The trend of giving outside support too has weakened the role of Opposition.

INDIAN STATE UNDER THREAT

Maoist's attack on Jehanabad's constabulary of Bihar during the President's rule's elections exposed the affairs of rule of law. Against this background, the growing Maoist politics has to take into account in socio-political context. Its influence has now spread over 150 of the country's 593 districts. These districts symbolize the failure of the *Indian State* to transform unequal social and economic relations. Democratic institutions have failed to take root there. The state is perceived by many to be aiding social forces that refuse to shed their feudal and casteist trappings. Maoists have only tapped the discontent. Maoist politics can be neutralized only if the illegitimacy of its theory and praxis is exposed. The state has to gain the trust of the people who have been left out of the processes of nation -building. This requires a vision that looks beyond the immediate concern of establishing law and order. Violence, by ultras or the state, is counterproductive and cannot usher in social change.

Institutions of governance in India are feudal and corrupt, without democracy unable to improve the system, because of our policy to Nepal's threat of Maoists, dissolution of the Bihar assembly *versus* terming it as 'unconstitutional' by the Supreme Court. Sadly, no top priority to solve problems relating to floods, unemployment, poverty, drinking water, social security, etc. have been accorded. The UPA government cannot avoid the contours of good governance, which demands re-modelling of the functioning style of police-prosecutorial method by creating an independent Police Commission on the pattern of Election Commission institution, in order to ensure police accountability and responsiveness to the people, and not to the politicians. To insulate the police from political pressure is the dire need of the hour, without which corruption and *'nexus'* cannot be minimized. The recommendations made by the Dharam Vira's National Police Commission can guide the UPA government towards the reforms not only in police establishment but also in the functioning style of the CBI and CVS. They need fixing accountability and transparency in their functioning in the era of coalition politics and globalization and privatization. The only way to tackle corruption is to improve transparency in the functioning of the government and ensuring the accountability of all public servants, including the Judges. What the privatisers are suggesting will lead to the dismantling of all institutions of governance, and take us back to Hobbes' state of nature. The only difference: Instead of the state, private global corporations will rule the world.

CONCLUDING OBSERVATIONS

The intriguing phenomenon of Indian politics is that electoral behavior has been baffling right from 1991 to 2004 as both the minority and coalition governments have become inevitable for the governance of our system. The change has caused political instability, despite growing political awareness among the voters. The factors like factionalism, religion, caste, money-muscle power, regionalism and or the Dalit politics, have preponderantly influenced the 'transition period', in which personality cult, dynastic family rule, centralization, electoral wave etc., have lost relevance in the era of coalition politics. The Congress, the BJP or National Front as well as regional parties have hitherto been the major political formations to fulfil the goal of political stability at the Centre with the commitment to national agenda. In order to avoid the risk of horse-trading and the dislodging of a coalition government the regional outfits have shown interests in wider coalition-form of government. In West Bengal, Tripura and Kerala, the coalition governments have provided political stability. If the national parties build a principled programme, based on clear-transparent rules with commonly agreed agenda, the coalition model could inaugurate a transition to a workable paradigm. As per the behavioural characteristic of Indian voters, the first-past-the-post (FPTP) electoral system can provide us a stable and viable coalition minority government, provided there is polarization of ideological inclinations and the opportunistic power-seeking alliances after the elections are discouraged. Ideology/policy-based alliance must be the basis of governance in the era of globalization.

There is considerable talk on electoral reforms and references are made to various steps to reduce the effect of money and muscle power. Our concern is that, to have a better rapport between the elected members and the people and their accountability, the first past-the post (FPTP) system of election may be taken away with from the Representation of People Act, as it has caused division and disunity of our votes in caste/religious diversity and political parties have to rely heavily on vote-banks to get their candidates elected on caste/ community religious grounds. The new clause should be provided that no election would be valid unless 50% of the electorate cast its vote and candidates to be declared elected should get more than 50% of the valid votes polled. This experiment can be introduced at the grassroots level to clean up our electoral system. This will help elimination of caste-based politics and ensure the proper nurture of the constituencies.

Though India's Constitution has the provision of an independent Election Commission for conducting fair and free elections, a provision for a neutral and caretaker government on the eve of the elections may be made to ensure that the ruling minority/coalition government may not misuse and abuse its authority for electoral purpose. The spirit of the 13th Amendment Act of the Bangladesh Constitution, 1966, providing this kind of neutral interim government, can be followed in India.

CHAPTER

3

No-trust Vote Against the UPA-I Government

Some Implications

The beleaguered ruling coalition battled hard on 22nd July, 2008 to secure the numbers (272) to remain in power. The fate of the Government rested over the India-US nuclear deal. Both the ruling UPA and a disparate opposition were vigorously engaged in wooing still undecided independent MPs as well as small parties to reach the crucial figure of 272 in the 545 member Lok Sabha. One MP seat was vacant and one M.P. was barred from voting. The decision of 61 Left MPs to bring down the multi-party UPA strength in the 545 seat Lok Sabha reduced the strength of the UPA Government to 226. But political analysts were confident that the figure 226 would go up to 265 with the declared support of the SP having with 39 MPs. The UPA, however, lacked 07 short in the tally of 272 MPs needed for a majority. The Left was bitterly criticized over the timing of their decision to withdraw the support when the PM was in Japan. The BJP was happy at this decision as the 'unholy alliance' crumbled on its own. It demanded the PM to seek a vote of confidence in Parliament (Lok Sabha). Happily, the UPA Government won the crucial confidence vote in the Lok Sabha with 275 votes in favour of the motion, 256 against the Trust Vote. July 22, Tuesday 2008 would be historic for the Congress-led UPA Government, as this political standoff highlighted the worst aspects of politics in India. Every political party was apprehensive of cross-voting despite party whips. As is known, 28 MPs from both sides defied their parties during the Trust Vote, dramatically altering the equation. 13 MPs voted in favour of the motion, 8 remained absent and 7 voted against the ruling UPA Government.

The way the beg of cash was produced dramatically in the well of the House by the BJP MP from Morena at the end of the debate seems to have confirmed the public's dim view of our politicians. It was really unprecedented act of the Morena MP. It was, indeed, a new low of standard in the history of Indian democracy. Yet Indian voters cannot dismiss Parliament as a charade. They still have faith in our parliamentary system and democracy. Somnath Chatterjee's expulsion from the CPM may be called another 'historic blunder' committed by the party, but it offers a historic opportunity to the moderate Marxists, particularly of West Bengal, to rise against the Stalinist diktat of the politburo.

A party line that is intolerant of dissent, lacks a human face and treats a loader of Chatterjee's stature like ordinary cadre is untenable in parliamentary democracy, commitment to an ideology that does not change with changing times invites political isolation. Liberal Marxists should crystallize the restlessness within the CPM and break into another fragment, naming it CPD : Communist Party Democratic. They should redefine their ideology in the context of ground realities and imbibe democratic principles in their party, shunning US phobia and accepting the need for capitalist expansion of the economy.

It was shocking that the CPM leader Somnath Chaterjee the 10 time MP and a close friend of Jyoti Basu—was spelled from the party on account of his refusal to obey party directive to quit the post of the Speaker. This was against the dignity of the office. The office is above the party interests.

Ideology may have triumphed when the Left pulled out of the UPA-Left coalition on the nuclear civil deal issue. But did the Left leaders have an inkling that they would be forcing to prop up Mayawati as a prime ministerial candidate and share platform with politicians like Chandrababu Naidu and Deve Gowda? Do these leaders practise or even agree with the Left's distinction between secular and communal parties or between anti-Americanism and the socialist pattern of development?

The support of the CPM and other Left parties to the Congress, in fact, has been to oppose, slow down and destroy the economic reforms. It had been primarily adversary to the Congress culture. The left has successfully thwarted the planned reforms of the UPA, denigrated its existence and performance—be it the deal with the US or the secular credentials, or the India's approach to China. Domestically, it weakened the coalition Government since the PM signed the N-deal in the USA in 2005. It is unfortunate that the Congress surrendered to the CPM's blackmail, forgetting that the target of the communists is the US imperialist hegemony they imagine. It was, in fact, the Congress party and the reforms it had originally planned to carry out. The communists' aim was at promoting a Third Front Government, which they hope to dominate central politics. In this effort their primary impediment was the Congress party. In brief, the Congress should take note of the fact that:

(a) The left's objective was holding India's foreign policy hostage to communal politics via linking the N-deal with the Muslim support.

(b) The present ruling Congress party of China is only communist in name. It is a capitalist party and uses the communist label to sustain its single party totalitarian rule in China.

(c) The CPM and other parties of India are of double standards in its working in context of the globalization trends. Their professed ideology is a farce after the demise of the USSR.

(d) The Congress should go ahead with shaping the N-deal a reality on the basis of national interests.[1]

Facing the biggest political crisis in over four years, the PM won the Trust vote on 22nd July, 2002. On the India-US nuclear deal, the Indian Parliament debated the matter for two days. The Government had to seek a trust vote/motion at a time when the country was facing the problems such as controlling inflation and terror, apart from other issues affecting to the welfare of 'aam adami' (common man)

On the eve of withdrawal of the left support to the UPA Government over the N-deal, the role of the SP's support was appreciated. It not only helped salvage the deal but saved the country from holding a mid-term Lok Sabha elections.[2]

The national events, from 20th to 22nd July, 2008, regarding to win the trust vote on 22nd July, 2008, proved that law cannot put a check on horse trading because of not evolution of constitutional morality. Therefore, to prevent this evil, it was suggested that the RP Act should be amended to make a provision for registering pre-poll alliances with the Election Commission in order to reduce the susceptibility of splinter groups to horse trading. There were six MPs in jail belonging to various parties. The law allows an MP to hold his seat until his appeal against sentence is deposited of. Meanwhile he enjoys right to vote and other privileges as an MP.

How Law Makers Stand in Lok Sabha (as on 14th July, 2008)

(In favour of UPA Government) Total Seats : 545

Indian National Congress Congress I (including Mohan Delkar, associate member. Plus two nominated members)	154	Telangana Rashtra Samiti	2
Samajwadi Party	37	Independent (Babulal Marandi)	1
Rashtriya Janata Dal	24	Samajwadi Party (break away faction)	2
Dravida Munnetra Kazhagham	15	All India Forward Bloc	3
Nationalist Congress Party	11	Revolutionary Socialist Party	3
Pattali Makkal Katchi	6	Independent (Sebastian Paul)	1

Lok Janshakti Party (1 in Jail—Suraj Bhan Singh)	4	Total	258
MDMK (break away faction)	2	Undecide	
JD(S)(break away faction)	1	Jharkhand Mukti Morcha	5
Telangana Rashtra Samiti (break away faction)	1	Independents	4
JK People's Democratic Party	1	Janata Dal (secular) (official faction)	2
Muslim League Kerala State Committee	1	Rashtriya Lok Dal	3
Republican Party of India	1	MDMK (official fraction)	2
All India Trinamul Congress	1	J&K National Conference	2
National Loktantrik Party (Baleshwar Yadav)	1	Kerala Congress (One other MP barred from voting)	1
Sikkim Democratic Front (Nakul Das Rai)	1	Mizo National front	1
Total	261	Nagaland People's front	1
		All India Majlis-e-Ittehadul Muslimmen	1
		Total	22
		Abstain	
		Total (261+258+22+1=542)	
AGAINST THE UPA GOVERNMENT		Vacancies (Bellary Meerut)	2
Bharatiya Janata Party	130	One MP barred from voting. One to abstain	2
Communist Party of India	43	Effective strength	541
Bahujan Samaj Party	17	Majority Mark	271
Shiv Sena	12	We will meet on July 19 to decide (Shibu Soren JMM)	
Communist Party of India	10	We will decide one day before vote (—DEVE GOWDA JD(S)LEADER)	
Biju Janata Dal	11		
Janata Dal (United)	8		
Shiromani Akali Dal	8		
Telugu Desam Party	5		
Asom Gana Parishad	2		

During the recent phase of political instability at the Centre, it was due to a coalition of ideologically desperate parties of UPA-Left coalition formed in the post-election period. The question was raised seriously considering a presidential system of governance on the ground that the coalition era is not suitable to the Prime Ministerial model of governance followed by us from the West ministerial model and India's Constitution was conceived of a Union of States, and we have borrowed a lot from the American constitution. The evolution of 'weak Centre' has subverted the goals of the Constitution, and India lacks a pan-Indian leadership. A strong Centre with a President and states with more federal powers is the way, forward for India. A Presidential system will ensure that the head of the nation is elected directly by the people with a mandate for a fixed term. Of course, he will be accountable to both Houses of Parliament during his term. This would ensure stability in Government and prevent horse-trading in politics.

On the crucial vote in the Lok Sabha, MPs belonging to the splinter parties kept both sides ruling and opposition camps gusting in deciding the fate of the UPA Government led by Dr. Manmohan Singh. This political bot boisler of national capital targeted the regional leaders like the CM of UP. Many leaders sneaked up to other side because rich and attractive offers were given to them, even the visits were made in jails to allure the convicted MPs to get as many votes as possible. In an era of coalition Governments, every single vote has mattered. And this immensely increased the bargaining power of MPs belonging to splinter parties. On this occasion a deal of discord was seen with UNPA-left leaders combine aiming at to topple the UPA Government. Even Left and the BJP too joined to vote against the Congress-led Government. This was a surprise as they all had one point programme. The red flag and Lal Krishna Advani were one without the ideological basis.

They all hit out at the support of the SP which has 39 MPs in the Lok Sabha. For the Leftist parties—earlier an ally of the UPA—the BJP was not as a greater evil than the nuclear deal. On the other hand, hectic activities decisively stoked the Prime Ministerial ambition of Dalit icon Mayawati 14 months after she swift UP polls in May 2007, with a regional party swearing by the first even non-BJP and non-Congress rule, toasting her as their choice for PM. It was thought that a pan-India role for Mayawati could fire the imagination of dalits across the country. She is no doubt, the first dalit CM of the country. But the BJP did not like the Pan-India role of Mayawati.

For the first time in the constitutional history of India, Speaker Somnath Chatterjee was asked to resign by the CPM High Command. In the opinion of CPM General Secretary Prakash Karat, the Speaker is not 'apolitical' and it was silly to think that the Speaker was partyless, as by holding the post of the Speaker, a person does not cease to have political affiliation. He demanded the resignation of the speaker after the ratification of withdrawal of CPM's support to the UPA Government.

It was a sad and shocking development that parties like the CPM and the SSP confidently certified that an overwhelming majority of the Muslim masses opposed the Indo-US accord on nuclear cooperation. They attempted to misguide the community and communize the N-deal. It was the CM of UP who first said that the UPA Government's decision to proceed with the deal had angered the Muslims. With the support of some religious leaders and clerics, she termed the deal as anti-nation. Her attack was due to shifting of Muslim votes? It was unfortunate that the episode was not exposed in a way to convince the Muslim community that the deal has nothing to do with Muslim vote politics or Muslim veto in the country, as the deeply religious Saudi Arabia has established close alliance with the US. Even Iran and Pakistan have been trying desperately for such an accord with the US. The country is fortunate that Muslims in India have begun to accept that in a plural society no party would do anything to promote any sectional interest—religious, linguistic economic or other at the risk of losing a majority support.

It may be recalled that Pt. Nehru committed a blunder in Kashmir, the once of which India is still paying. He stopped Indian forces chasing Pakistani invaders midway, took the matter to the United Nations and made it an international issue. Had he let Indian forces complete the job, there would have been no PoK and no Kashmir problem. Noorani's contention of "secular politics" is also misplaced. It is no secret that the so-called secular parties pursue communal politics for the Muslim vote. Communalization of nuclear deal by the Left and the BSP is the latest example. Linking the deal with Indian Muslims was a political ploy of those parties to garner support of the Muslim votes ahead of the general elections.

It is worth-recalling that of the 37 Muslim MPs currently in the Lok Sabha, 26 were in parties that were part of the UPA, openly declared support for the UPA Government. They voted for the N-deal with an anti-Islamic. The four Muslim MPs of the BSP clearly said to vote against the Government.

The current political scenario has, admittedly clearly displayed the murky nature of Indian politics. The criminalization of Parliament is only the most visible aspect. But it doesn't have to stay this way. This, at least, is a problem that can be easily fixed with legislation. The challenge is getting our politicians to do it. The question is of public morality and needs an amendment in our Cr. P.C. and R.P. Act, 1951. It is terribly wrong that the fate of a country's Government rests in the hands of the elected one who have been convicted of committing serious crimes.

ISSUES BEYOND THE VOTE

In the aftermath of the UPA Government winning the trust vote, many questions remain unanswered about the charges of bribery raised so dramatically by three BJP MPs in Parliament on Tuesday. The truth behind the allegations must be thoroughly investigated and exposed. However, the shock waves that the incident justifiably generated should be tempered by the fact such things are not unknown in Indian politics. Fifteen years ago, four Jharkhand Mukti Morcha (JMM) MPs, including Shibu Soren—who was once again a key figure in boosting the UPA in Parliament—were given money to help defeat a no-confidence motion against the Narasimha Rao Government. More recently; 11 MPs were expelled for accepting money for raising questions in Parliament.

As per Article 105(2) of the Indian Constitution, MPs enjoy immunity, of course. The Supreme Court reiterated in this regard in 1998 in the JMM bribery case that bribe takers were immune from prosecution where as bribe givers had no such immunity.

It is questionable whether the immunity given to MPs was meant to shield them from bribery charges. Indeed, the minority judgment in the JMM bribery case said that immunity could not be extended to MPs who had taken a bribe. Several constitutional experts believe that in spite of the charges; by the BJP MPs being made inside Parliament, this should be the subject of a criminal investigation. They say that an FIR could be lodged under the Prevention of Corruption Act since the Supreme Court has clearly, said that MPs are 'public servants'. Therefore, this Article with immunities needs a change as elected members cannot be allowed to take bribery in open.

Speaker cannot be forced to resign from the office after his expulsion from the CPM. He can be removed, under article 94 of the Constitution, from the constitutional post only by a resolution passed by the Lok Sabha. It may be recalled that he was unanimously elected as speaker in 2004. On his own, however, he may resign. Our 10th Schedule grants exemption to the Speaker and confers on him the judicial functions of adjudicating disputes related to disqualification of MPs on the ground of defection, provided the concerned party has lodged a complaint.

To establish his independence from all parties, the provision also specifies that the Speaker shall have "the right to speak in and otherwise to take part in the proceedings" related to any resolution for his removal. For its anger at his display of independence, the CPM cannot seek Chatterjee's disqualification from the House for defying the party's direction. For, its direction to him to quit prior to the Trust Vote cannot come under paragraph 2 (b) of the Tenth Schedule which is limited to disqualifying those who vote or abstain from voting contrary to the party whip.

Those who cross-voted and those who abstained are equally liable to be disqualified under paragraph 2(b) of the Tenth Schedule which penalizes any party MP who "votes or abstains from voting in such House contrary to any direction issued by the political party to which he belongs." The only circumstance in which a whip-defying MP can escape the liability of disqualification is in the unlikely event of his obtaining "prior permission" of his party and his voting or abstention also being condoned by it within 15 days of the event. Regarding Speaker's jurisdiction, the Supreme Court in 1987 in *Prakash Singh Badal* vs. *Union of India* said: "The Speaker is supposed to be a non-party man and has been entrusted with jurisdiction to act judicially".

In the Lok Sabha, there have so far been three major instances of MPs being disqualified on the ground of defection. The first was in 1991 when eight Janata Dal MPs were disqualified by the then Speaker Rabi Ray for siding with the Chandrashekhar Government. In the second instance, Speaker Shivraj Patil disqualified four MPs from Ajit Singh faction of Janata Dal, which backed the Narasimha Rao Government in 1993. In the latest instance, three BSP MPs were disqualified last year for defecting to the Samajwadi Party.

The role of Speaker is still doubtful about the cashgate that hit Parliament's dignity for the first time. Experts are of the view that any action after the scam is improper. The Trust Vote should not have taken place after the sensational disclosure use of bribes. The Speaker should have investigated the complaint and taken a decision before proceeding with the vote. Though there is no such provision for such deferment Speaker, legally speaking cannot defer the trust vote on the ground of taking bribes by MPs. Still it is a fit case for police investigation.[3]

Faced with the trouble over the civil nuclear deal, the situation exposed the style of functioning of many political leaders, specifically of the leaders of the Left parties, who did not pay heed to national interest. Here the S.P. did a good job by taking the opinion of none other than former President Dr. Abdul Kalam. It endored the deal in public and survived the Government from the fall. The Congressmen were delighted at this as they were terrified of an early Lok Sabha elections. The SP afforded to support the UPA Government because the Congress has become irrelevant in UP. It is now a party to be used, not feared. The only parties that matter now in UP politics are Mayawati's BSP and Mulayam Singh's SP with the

BJP and Congress playing minor roles. Mulayam Singh in this scenario can use the Congress to harass CM Mayawati by pursuing corruption and tax cases against her more vigorously. He can hope to come back to power in UP in the next assembly elections by having the Congress as a very junior ally. Therefore, the SP has refused to join the UPA Government and supports it from 'outside'.

For most of regional parties, their main foe was the Congress Party. Hence, they were willing to support the BJP simply as their enemy's enemy. The TDP, AIADMK, BLD, Samata Party and others joined Vajpayee's NDA Government. The very fact that the BJP was so weak in their respective states meant they faced no threat from it locally, and that made it a more attractive partner in New Delhi. Despite this, the BJP suffered a lot in the defeat of the Trust Motion, because of cross-voting and abstention by 08 MPs. The involvement of one BJP MP in the vote for cash scam lowered BJP's image (with a party of difference).

The Trust Vote scam in Parliament has activitated several NGOs in a bid to file Right to Information (RTI) about making the video-tapes of the sting operation 'public'. The purpose is to prosecute the bribe givers and to uphold the dignity of nation's highest forum (Parliament).

CONCLUDING OBSERVATIONS

The UPA Government should see the Left's withdrawal of support as an opportunity. A few parties and MPs, in fact, wanted an early elections, they somehow helped the Government in mustering 'numbers' at the voting on a No-Confidence Motion. Now the PM should seize the opportunity to use the remaining term to push reforms in economy and control the trend of inflation, though the current phase of inflation is a global phenomenon. It is he who as the former Finance Minister of the Rao Government initiated the major reforms in 1991 through 'policy reforms'. Aam Adami, expects from the PM to aggressively do the needful. So is the need to stop the rising trend of terrorism and naxalism.

The country is convinced that the N-deal is essential for the country's energy security and development. But the ruling party has to convince and explain its importance to voters. The party has yet to face the opposition from the CPM and BJP who have spearheaded a stiff opposition against the N-deal. It may be recalled that it was the BJP who initially contributed to the making of the deal when it was in power. But the Congress failed to expose the part's subsequent double game.

The decision of Left comrades to withdraw the support to the ruling coalition once again committed another historic blunder, in the way the CPI led by B.J. Ranadive did in 1947, or it was done so in 1998 by denying Joyti Basu from becoming the PM. Infact Prakash Rat as a leader of Marxist theory has provided irrelevant after collapse of the USSR. Karat's blunder was that he sought the support of the BJP against the enemy of Congress in defeating the UPA and to capture the power at the Centre, that too against the party (Congress) with which the CPM spent four years and accommodated some reasonable and some grossly unreasonable demands placed before it, while extending the support from outside to the UPA Government. In short, Left parties should not allow them become a prison of the ideology that prevent them from making realistic assessment of ground situation. The CPM has forgotten the need to balance the theory and practice since it has joined parliamentary democracy.[4]

Expulsion of Speaker from the CPI-M was the bone of saddest day of the Parliamentary history because his, election was unanimous. No party can be treat speaker as its member are being elected to the post. As speaker of the Lok Sabha, he has rightly suggested in his six page note that, on his being elected to this post of MP should temporarily resign from his party, so as to prevent the repeatation of the above cited situation. A law may be enacted to this effect, or reconvention may be developed after the consensus of all-party meeting.

In order to prevent the social fabric of India from being wrecked, India should adopt stringent measures followed by the UN Security Council's anti-terror resolutions 1368 and 1373.

The run-up to the trust vote highlighted the role of money power and shady deals in Indian politics. The situation warrants introducing greater transparency in how parties and elected representatives raise funds on the line of the federal Election Commission of the US that maintains detailed records of campaigning financing.

By winning the Confident Vote, the era of nuclear apartheid has ended against the country. However, as per the text of IAEA safeguards agreement, it would be more honest to admit that the Indo-US civil nuclear deal is a three-in-one document comprising a civilian energy cooperation agreement with the US, *defecto* NPT and *defact* CTBT. Efforts would be made by the NSG to bring India into the ambit of non-proliferation regime. The west will oversee the supply of fissile material by other countries. All shall depend on how diplomatically Indian engages the West in fulfilling the national interests.

Notes and References

1. The nature of the Indo-US Nuclear (Civil) Deal is discussed in a separate chapter of this study.
2. For details read the article A.G. Noorani, 'Myths about Muslims', *Ibid.*, July 9, 2008, p. 14.
3. The seven member Lok Sabha panel was constituted to look into the involvement of three MPs in bribe allegations. It was appointed by Speaker Somnath and is headed by Congress MP V. Kishore Chandra Deo.
4 The two major left parties, CPI-M and CPI have announced not to support the DMK Government in Tamil Nadu, because the DMK has an allowance with the Congress, Left parties have 15 MLAs.

CHAPTER

4

Motion of Confidence in the Basic Law of Germany and the Decision-making Process

The Bonn Constitution adopted in 1949, contains a number of salient features. One of them is the political stability with accountability in national politics. It presents a model of consensus democracy. The Federal Cabinet is headed by the Chancellor. There is a provision that the constructive vote of no-confidence can be brought against the Chancellor, but the condition is that such a motion must follow an alternative candidate. This has strengthened stability and accountability to the Bundestag or the lower house of Germany Parliament. The party system in Germany is based on coalition politics. Ministers usually enjoy a relative autonomy in the policy formulation of their ministries. The decision-making process rests upon 'collective' rather than 'oligarchical' or 'hierarchical' system. The German ministers are more activism and professional experience. These features, notably the provision providing a constructive vote of no-confidence against a Chancellor have attracted our politicians and statesmen to overcome the problem of political instability prevailing in Indian political set-up.[1] The Constitution Review Commission has taken note of the provision and favours its adoption.

The National Review Commission while reviewing the working of the Constitution has seriously thought of delinking the No-Trust Motion against the government in the Lok Sabha, with a provision for the simultaneous election of an 'alternative leader' of the House. According to the its chairman, Justice M.N. Venkatachaliah, this is inevitable in, view of the growing fractionalisation of coalitions in past two decades. The German Constitution provides for the election of such an alternative leader by the lower chamber when it takes up a no confidence motion against the Chancellor. The Commission is of the opinion that a similar provision in India's Constitution may help attain the purpose of political stability. This requires to be a part of electoral reforms. The Commission in its meeting of 29th December, 2001, at New Delhi reviewed the functioning of the constitution strictly within the parliamentary form of Government. It ruled out to consider any aspect of the Presidential Model or tempering with the basic structure of the Indian Constitution.

Against this background, the present paper attempts to trace out the factors that have been responsible for accountability and durability of the Government in German federal set-up, and to study the functioning party-system in Germany that presents a model of consensus democracy.

The present Constitution of the Federal Republic of Germany was adopted in 1949. The Bonn Constitution of 1949 was drafted under the tutelage of the Western occupying powers. According to the will of the German framers, the draft constitution was put up for referendum for its ratification. The Basic Law of Germany is exclusively based on decentralisation. Most of the principles of the Weimar Constitution of 1933 were followed, with two major changes. First, the government was no longer dependent upon the power of the President, who was alone responsible for the policy of the Empire. Second, the link between the parliament and the government was, strengthened, so that the parliamentary majority has the power to dismiss a Chancellor by a 'constructive vote of No-Confidence' (in German language it is called 'Konstruktives

MisBtrauensvotum), provided that an alternative candidate is nominated by the Parliament.* This procedure protects against unstable parliamentary alignments. In German politics, as we have witnessed in Indian political system, the multi-party system has been a prevailing feature.

NO CHANCELLOR'S DEMOCRACY

The Constitution of Germany (The Basic Law) emphasises hierarchy rather than collegiality among government ministers. Accountability to the Bundestag-(Legislature) is mainly channeled through the Chancellor.[2] He answers to the Parliament and the ministers answer to him. The strong position of the Chief Executive derives from the Basic Law of the Federal Republic, which makes the Chancellor removable only by 'constructive vote of no-confidence to dismiss the Chancellor.' The 'Bundestag' must elect his successor, yet the federal cabinet has a weak collective character, because Ministers there tend not to question the decisions of other departments and many matters are despatched after discussion in the German federal cabinet. The Ministers conduct the affairs of their respective departments within the Chancellor's guidelines, though in practice the Chancellors have shown regard for the experience and expertisation of ministers. It will be an exaggreation to say of functioning 'Chancellor's democracy' in Germany. However, its cabinet is certainly more hierarchical and somewhat cohesive than its British counterpart.[3]

A MODEL OF CONSENSUS DEMOCRACY

In Germany, the executive authority is shared among members of former or informal coalition. The Executive does not dominate the legislature, as it acts under majority democracy. There is a multi-party system, rather than two party system. Elections are held under proportional representation rather 'first past the post' electoral system, as is

* 'Bundesrat' is the upper chamber and 'Bundestag' is the lower chamber of Parliamentarische (Parliament) in the German set-up.

prevailing in the U.K., New Zealand or in India. This consensus model features federal and decentralised, a strong second chamber in Germany.

The Basic Law (Constitution) of the German Republic leaves no doubt that the Chancellor enjoys the right to name his own ministerial team (cabinet), but in practice, party and especially coalition, considerations restrict his freedom of choice. Unlike as in U.K. and India, the German Ministers are appointed to posts suited to their professional trainings and experience, though the Cabinet needs to be carefully balanced by the ruling party/parties. Coalition Governments in Germany have been relatively as stable and durable as is witnessed in a majority party rule in Parliamentary democracies. It is due to the fragmentation of party system and the dependence of government more on the inter-party bargaining in the assembly than on election results.

The party system here is based on coalition model. The major parties, namely, the Social Democratic Party, Conservative/Christian Party, and small middle-class Liberal Party usually keep hold the balance of seats in Parliament. That is why the Christian Democratic Party rules in coalition with the small Free Democratic Party until there was a 'Grant coalition'.

In German Federal Republic since 1980s,the vote of No-Confidence was attempted twice; once in April, 1972 against Chancellor Willy Brandt but the motion failed, and second in October 1982, when an absolute majority of members of the Parliament voted against Chancellor Hemut Schmidt and replaced him with Helmut Kohl. Since 1949, Germany has been governed by fifteen cabinets so far. The ministries have been thus fairly stable during the tenure of over more than ten legislatures.

In Germany, the executive powers are shared between the Chancellor (Kanzlerprinzip), the Cabinet government (Kabinetts prinzip) and the ministers (Ressortprinzip). Consequently, the power structure in the German set-up is

---

* As per the Basic Law of Germany, the post-Communist East Germany was readmitted to the German Republic in 1990, and the Landers (regions) of East Germany were reconstituted according to the law.

dispersed collectively rather than hierarchically arranged. According to Article 65, the Chancellor conducts the business of the government in accordance with the rules of procedure adopted by it and approved by the President of Germany.

The government in the Federal Republic of Germany is drawn from a parliamentary majority. The Head of it is. the Chancellor, who forms his Cabinet. The ministers are appointed and can be dismissed by the Chancellor. With the exception of the Finance Ministers, all other ministers have equal rights in the cabinet meetings. According to R. Mayntz, the Finance Minister enjoys a superior position to his counterparts. He has the power to veto all decisions of financial importance, including all legislative proposals, with the implications for public spending, provided the chancellor sides with him on policy decisions[4] Parliamentary secretaries participate in the cabinet meetings but only the Chancellor and his ministers are entitled to vote.

FACTORS BEHIND POLITICAL STABILITY

The style of cabinet decision-making in the Federal Republic of Germany depends on a set of structural and behavioural variables. So far as the structural pattern of the cabinet is concerned the council is concerned, the council of ministers lays down formal rules. The working of the Cabinet ministry in the federal Republic is influenced by party coalition as well as by parliamentary fraction discipline, and accordingly the formal rules/guidelines are laid down and implemented.

Likewise, personality characteristics such as the charisma of the Chancellor (Head of the Cabinet) and individual ministers have an impact on the function of cabinet system. Among behaviour variables, the leadership style of the Chancellor seems to be the most important factor behind the political stability in German case, because decision-making in the cabinet depends very much upon the way a Chancellor coordinates the cabinet work. This task relates to bureaucrats, his party and parliamentary fraction, his coalition partners and the media. Furthermore, the effectiveness and efficiency of cabinet decision-making depends upon how much ministerial autonomy the cabinet ministers relatively and politically enjoy. Of course, the Chancellor's primacy, is well-established under Article 65 of the German Constitution. The Chancellor determines and bears responsibility for the general policy of the government, and with this policy his/her ministers conduct the affairs of the departments individually and independently under the Chancellor's responsibility. Each minister under the German parliamentary set-up enjoys some degree of autonomy in conducting the departmental policy.[5]

The ministries in Germany have been stable because of the increasing number of activities of the modern states and declining the role of Parliament (Parliamentarische). This led to grow the political influence of top civil servants and the elite of parliamentary party. Secondly, cabinet decision-making has become increasingly dependent on a consensual bargaining process of a political administrative character, and the demands of departmental secretaries and ministers are well-integrated in the form of national policy.

In Germany, the political structure of a government is composed of two or more parties and the Liberal Party (F.D.P.) has been longest in Government about 35 years—since the post-war of West Germany, despite the fact that the numerical strength of the party representation was low, in relation to that of the Christian Democratic Party and the social Democratic Party. Thus, a 'collective' rather 'oligarchical' or 'hierarchical' structure in the cabinet-formation and decision-making remains intact in Germany. It is worth-recalling that both the Chancellors, namely, Helmut Schmidt and Konrad Adenauer, had a comfortable majority in the Cabinet, yet the basis of decision-making was collective. The bargaining style relatively prevails there because of the narrow support base in the Bundestag or in the lower chamber. They have been considerably more consensual, centrist and compromising oriented than the British bare-majority or single party dominance.[6]

German political parties, in general, try to coalesce with their ideological counterparts. For example, the Christian Democratic Union with the Christian Social Union have unitedly joined hands in securing a parliamentary majority. There were only two occasions in Germany's history in-1963 and 1982—when the state experienced of a minority government for about a month. Thus, the coalition constellation has been closely related to the party strength in the cabinet. Here, it should be pointed out that leadership style of the Chancellor plays a key role in the cabinet making and decision making. During the period of 'Grand Coalition' (1966-69) of the Christian-Liberal coalition, the cabinet meetings fulfilled major functions in preparing the cabinet matters.[7]

Ministers in the Federal Republic often have autonomy to initiate policy proposals before the proposals are officially dealt with by the cabinet. Such proposals are well discussed between the personal advisers and civil servants of ministerial departments, and sometimes informal meetings are held between a minister and the Chancellor to prepare a policy proposal and to try to formulate compromises. When an agreement is reached on a proposal only then it is sent to the Chancellor's office formal approval. If there is no agreement, the matter is then referred to a cabinet committee, which is chaired by the Chancellor and the minister concerned take the responsibility for the issue under discussion.

Contrary to the parliamentary democracies working in England or in India, where the committee system plays a crucial role, the German Federal Republic makes a limited use of committees in decision-making and coordinating bodies. There have been a few exceptions of *ad hoc* committees in operation, but they did not play any major role in the cabinet decision-making.

In sum, it can be concluded that the cabinet is the only central arena for real debate. On issues concerning ministerial departments, each proposal is approved by the Cabinet before going to Parliament. Most of the problems arising in any department are resolved prior to the submission to the Cabinet meeting. In case of any conflict between a minister and the Cabinet, the Chancellor has the right to formulate a policy on the basis of the majority's views of the Cabinet. Formal voting in the cabinet is very rare. The study shows that the major problems are resolved by consensus, rather than by the Chancellor's intervention, through detailed, comprehensive discussions among ministers in cabinet meetings, where ministerial bureaucracy is actively engaged. Federal ministers have to rely on the expert knowledge of the civil servants.

During the period of the Grand Coalition in 1966-69 , a higher degree of problems solving by consensus was recorded in the German political system. A conclusion can be drawn that Ministers of Cabinet often feel a sense of collective responsibility for final Cabinet decisions, even though there is no norm for collective decision-making in the Cabinet, when the decisions are submitted for the approval of Parliament (Parliamentarische). Therefore, the possibility of exercising the constructive vote of no confidence against the Chancellor or a minister remains dim there. Individual ministerial autonomy is there. Cabinet Ministers in Federal Republic do enjoy a wide degree of autonomy in the decision-making at departmental levels. Every minister has to ensure that there is inter departmental coordination on policy formulation issues the prior to the submission to the cabinet meetings.[8] His or her satisfaction is must. It is worth-noting that Ministers often have a vested interest in neither interfering with nor criticising the proposals of fellow ministers and expect colleagues to behave in the same way when proposals for their own department/ministry come to the Cabinet. In this way, each minister protects his/her own autonomy.

The on-going trends indicate that there is more activism among German ministers in Cabinet meetings. Secondly, in terms of formal relationship between the ministers and the Parliament (i.e. Legislative-Executive relationship), it has been noticed that more than 2/3 of ministers have been the members of the Parliament, and had the specialised experience in the party cadre prior to becoming Ministers. They have acted in close cooperation with the party executive:[9] Therefore, the party in Parliament is inclined to trust the policy formulation prepared by its ministers. This apart, the members of the Parliament also maintain close contacts with ministers during the course of policy formulation which help in seeking consensus on policy issues. So far as the ministerial autonomy is concerned, the trend shows that ministers from the Christian Democratic Party feel more degree of autonomy from their party executive and Parliamentary fraction than ministers belonging to the Social Democratic Party.

Notes and References

1. Merkl, P., *The Origin of the West German Republic* (New York, Oxford University Press, 1963).
2. Ebenstein, William, *The German Record : A Political Portrait* (New York, 1955), pp. 152-53.
3. Johnson, Nevil, *State and Government in the Federal Republic of Germany* (Oxford, Pergamon Press, 1983), pp. 326-29.
4. Gorlay, J. Ford, *The Founding of the Federal Republic* of *Germany* (Chicago, Chicago University Press, 1958), p. 158.
5. Smith, G., *Politics in Western Europe* (Aldershot, Gower, 1989), p. 35.
6. Ferdinand Muller-Rommel, 'The Role of German Ministers in Cabinet Decision-making", *In Cabinet Ministers* and *Parliamentary Governments*, (ed.) Michael Lavey and Kennetha Shepsle, (Cambridge University, 1994), Cambridge University, 1994), Chapter 10, pp. 150-52.
7. Muller-Rommel, "Federal Republic of Germany: A System of Chancellor Government", in Jean Blondel and F. Muller Rommel (eds.), *Cabinets in Western Europe* (London, Macmillan Press, 1998).
8. Braunthal, Gerard, *The West German Legislative Process* (New York, Cornell University Press, 1972).
9. *Ibid.*, pp. 155-56.

CHAPTER

5

Some Key Features of Our Contemporary Politics

India is a democracy with a written Constitution. Indians are proud of their constitution and therein is the democratic set-up with institutions' like Parliament, Supreme Court, President, Army, the office of Governor, Speaker, so on and so forth. India is a true democracy where these institutions are actually functioning and the people as voters are engaged in its operation. Our Constitution-framers were not elected of course, nor did they think of fighting the future elections. Therefore, they did not bother about patronage net works and fully concentrated on long term aims, ideals and objectives of democracy. They created independent institutions that would provide checks and balances by limiting the discretionary powers of politicians and bureaucrats. Sadly, our Republic in operation has presented a revise picture contrary to the dreams of those founding members. Instances are given below:

Once Condoleeza Rice said that 'salavery is the birthmark of the US politics, which has disfigured the country. Likewise, India's birth mark is the partition politics, which has similarly disfigured the country's politics since Independence. The Congress Party has called itself a party with secular ethos. But it has to please the Muslim minority, despite the partition. According to the analysis of Meghnand Desai who is currently the member of the British House of Lords, 'communalism is the enemy and politics is constructed along the lines of coalition, secular parties against communal parties.[1] The development since 1981 to 2004 (with the formation of the UPA government) reflects this reality. The study includes a separate chapter on how ideologically desperate the left parties joined the coalition to keep the BJP out of power on the communal ground.

In the backdrop, the events of how late Rajiv Gandhi had permitted the installation of Ram Lalla idol in Ayodhya (UP), how Muslim women in the Shah Bano case were betrayed and how the Babri masjid was destroyed by the Rao Government Muslims of the North India therefore, were compelled to abandon the Congress party HRD Minister Arjun Singh was committed to secure 27% extra reservations for GBCs but no one cared about the Sachar Report (concerning the welfare of Muslims).

Dr. Lohia should be credited with laying the foundation of a social revolution in Indian politics. He raised the voice against the personalized Congress and family affair. He put caste as a central theme of radical change but not class. He saw the Congress as a Brahmin party and proposed anti-Congressism alternative as the basis of opposition party. The result was the rise of V.P. Singh and Mandal politics in Indian political system.

The ignorance of Muslims and reservation politics of Congress gave birth to the regional outfits in UP and Bihar and the rise of the BJP in North India. The SP snatched the captive Muslim votes from the Congress, and the BSP has taught dalits to reject the Congress patronage. The UP assembly elections of 2007 is the case in point.

- The Nehru Gandhi dynasty was further encircled by the Left friends (in the form of UPA) who have been against the economic reforms and soft to pro-China on the Nuclear deal. The UPA government thus is faltered with the N-deal and became a prisoner the left allies till the vote of trust on 22nd July, 2008. On the other hand, in its jealous guarding of dynastic secession, the Congress leadership discouraged a second tier of leaders from coming up. This is given birth to faction politics within the organization. Thus, anti-Congressism and anti-incumbency vote more or less helped the BJP to rise and revive. The Karnataka poll is the patent example.

- Caste disparities, caste rivalries and caste alliances have become a new phenomenon of contemporary politics and it is likely to dominate the 21st century even against the mini-set of Pt. Nehru who believed that his new generation genuinely would believed that democracy and development would bring a new social order that would free Indians from the shackles of caste. Today, the caste is not a matter of religion and ritual, as was in the past. It is of both social inclusion and exclusion on the grounds of purity and pollution which is due to mainly competitive politics education and employment. This scenario has given rise' to an middle class, which . . . believe in caste rather than 'class'. They oppose the dominance of a few castes who have been in power since last 100 years. Indian democracy, thus, cannot expect to be free of this paradox. Of course, the Raje's government of Rajasthan pulled off a coup by providing 14% reservation. His strategy was to please to all castes and communities.
- Today, the institutions, that command the most respect are the Supreme Court the Election Commission and the Army, as they all are unelected and do keep a check precisely on elected politicians. The Bilkis case is an example of our constitutional democracy enabling a fair trial being denied by popular democracy. A majority rule does not guarantee equality before the law but unelected institutions (Supreme Court and High Courts) insists

on a fair trial. This generated a tug of war between parliament and judiciary on the issue of patronage network and discretion. Likewise, the Election Commission, too, has strived to limit the abuse/ misuse of political power, against efforts to create vote banks subsidies, reservation and quota system.

- Not only the Nehru Gandhi dynasty, others Indian parties are hobbled by the concept of dynastic politics as well as anti BJPism, to some extent. Now most of political parties are caste cum religion based. Even political dynasty has developed into other regional outfits like the SP, DMK, National Conference of J&K, Shiv Sena to Maharashtra and others. Ideology has nothing to do with these parties. Family life and caste have mattered.
- The emergence of the third force as an alternative to the Congress and BJP has proved to be a dreadful option because of absence of ideology and an unstable concoction of egos of leaders and fragmentations. There is no political ideology except coming to power and staying in office. But the BSP's supreme Mayawati successfully made the first innovation since Lohia by constructing an alliance not just with, ritually 'near' castes but looping the top and bottom together. She needs some political ideology to convince ordinary voters. She has asserted that affirmative action should be on the basis of objective measures of deprivation and not caste labels. Her political strategy proved successful in the UP assembly elections of 2007. It is yet to strategy work outside UP.
- For the first time, Indian Parliament, Opposition and regional parties have been engaged in discussion on the international affairs. The specific point is of the Indo-US Nuclear Deal arrived at with the USA by the UPA government. It is a healthy sign of functioning of our democracy. The role of the CPM as an ally of the UPA at the Centre of course, helped generate a national consensus about the need of the N-deal, Likewise, Indo China ties, *viz-a-viz* the PLA's

border incursions were also debated in Indian Parliament.

Gujarat and West Bengal are ideologically and geographically poles apart, but their politics has rested on something in common, i.e. their winning formula has banked on sub-nationalism. According to Professor Dipankar Gupta of JNU, New Delhi, Jyoti Basu gave the CPM a distinctive appeal when from the early 1960s he fused left with an anti-centre posture and developed its own economy. Likewise, Narendra Modi as C.M. made a public declaration that the Gujaratis consider not paying any central taxes as all the money Delhi soaked inform this state goes elsewhere.

The state contributes Rs. 40,000 crore, for people but it gets only 2.5% of it for state development.[2] Despite this, Gujarat's development was linked up with the Hindutva appeal. When election campaign witnessed the attacks against him on the killings, he cleverly turned the game by making the assault on Gujarati pride. This was a masterstroke. He thus become a Gujarati icon overnight during the poll campaign. All this would have been impossible without Modi's subtle anti-Delhi posture. But this formula cannot help the BJP at national level.

- The defeat of the Congress in Karnataka taught a lesson to the Congress leadership to reshape its poll strategy, by setting up a panel headed by AK Anthony. The top panel recommended that candidates for the Lok Sabha elections, 2009 should be announced three months before the notification of the Election Commission, so as to give them a good chance of preparing and winning. The BJP too is set to trigger a race with the Congress it is emerging as a feature of future big battle amongst the political parties.
- Judicial activism (critically known as judicial intervention) has also become a feature of the contemporary political system. Its overreach is often criticized to disturb the delicate balance of power amongst the three organs of government. But

overriding judicial encroachment through PILs has helped greatly to decide certain policies in favour of democracy, namely in the areas of crime, corruption, police reforms, disruption of law and order, suppression of civil liberties and of human rights, etc. Hence, judicial activism seems to be a necessity in view of failure of Executive. It is required in public interests and against some draconian laws.

- In our cabinet system, the NAC (National Advisory Council) functions like a form of new parallel power. Its recommendations and suggestions to the PM and cabinet are seriously taken by the Council of Ministers. It was set-up to monitor the implementation of the CMP whose chair person is Mrs. Sonia Gandhi. She enjoys the ranks and status of a cabinet and enjoys the powers to have access all the cabinet papers and files. This hybrid model or semi-presidential system is not known to our Constitution. This is a departure from the conventions governing a cabinet system. The left parties supported the coalition from 'outside' bearing no accountability. On many occasions, the hybrid model is created hurdles in the decision-making because there is no apparent division of powers between the PM and NAC and chair person. The NAC in fact, acts as a 'super cabinet'. In short, this hybid model has proved fatal to our democracy.
- Indian politics is the politics of criminals. The nexus of criminals and politicians has become a very common feature. There are a number of MPs whose past records is linked with criminal activities. Despite this, our Parliament is not prepared to make any law to stop criminals from contesting elections inspite of the fact that the Parliamentary Standing Committee on Personnel, public grievances and Law and Justice in a report submitted in 2007 that the MPs with criminal records should be disqualified from contesting elections. Earlier our Election Committee also wrote a letter to the PM demanding to amend the section 8-9 of R.P. Act of 1951, which

prescribes disqualifications for certain offences. It is to be done in consonance with Article 102(1)(e) of our constitution. It may be recalled that the National Commission to Review the Working of the Constitution also made a similar recommendation in 2002. Unfortunately, our political parties are not prepared to cleanse the system. Therefore, our judiciary, media and the Election Commission have joined hands to SG criminals from becoming legislators.

SOME GLARING EXAMPLES OF MISUSE OF THE POLITICAL AUTHORITY

1. The CM of Uttar Pradesh took the decision to suspend four senior IAS officers for praising Rahul Gandhi and his family's role in a book, whereas as per services rules, they cannot be suspended without the Centre's nod. The state Governor refused to execute her arbitrary action. The CM was reminded how these officials had attended the BSP rallies and raised the funds for her birthday bashes, which was not justified. The officials had written about the role of the elected representatives in the past. That was not a crime.
2. Declining the credibility of Parliament, in the wake of violent postures and walkouts, has been a matter of deep concern. The number of Lok Sabha sittings has come down from 124 (34%). This scenario not only undermines the credibility of Parliament but also a colossal waste of the tax payer's money.
3. The dreaded MP, Ateeq Ahmed, facing 177 criminal cases, remained set free from the police clutches for about three years. He is accused of killing BSP worker in 2005 and then was expelled by the SP of UP. He was arrested after eight months in New Delhi.
4. The Right to Information Act has been implemented but the CIC as well as SICs authorities are hardly serious about providing required information. The

bureaucrats are opposed to release the information. It is regretted that ex babus dominate RTI panels working in the states. Most of them are retired IAS/ IPS officers, who have vested interests with the establishment. They are against the RTI Act.[3]

5. The Office of Profit controversy dominated the Indians scene through the active role of the Election Commission. It wanted the invoked MPs/MLAs and ministers to be disqualified under section 10 of the RP Act. But the party in Power managed the affair to have legislative changes and exempted some posts from the preview of office of profit. Therefore, the Election Commission could not take steps to disqualify the involved politicians.
6. The CBI has brought to fore some defence scams in the purchases of defence goods. But no strict action has been taken against the brokers and against involved officials in Kickbacks rackets.
7. Violating the model code of conduct on the eve of the elections through decision making, promises or announcements to influence the voters has very common misuse of official machinery is very common despite the warnings served by our Election Commission.
8. The Central Government has introduced the National Rural Employment Guarantee Act-NREGA. But corrupt practices prevailing these have corroded the democratic structure, social and it and the rule of law.
9. Haj subsidies as well as the subsidy to Christians have been officially granted against the tenets of Indian secularism. On the other hand, the 800 year old Jagannath temple does not permit entry of the non-Hindus. The ban was imposed by the British rule in 1805, yet it continues to exist under the caption 'Sanctity'. No political party can dare to speak against this social discrimination.
10. Tainted bureaucrats are 'not needed to attach a list of property nor the investigating agencies can prosecute them without the government's sanction. Likewise,

the elected members/ministers too are 'above the law' of the land. There have been numerous cases of 'abuse of power' and 'misuse of authority' which is due to the existence of privileges and immunities meant for the ruling elite. Sadly, no powerful ombudsman has been constituted to examine the cases of criminalization and abuse of authority by against ruling elite class.

To conclude, managed democracies like Russian model shall have to deliver clear governance, stability, development economic growth and a host of other desirable objectives for its survival. Democracy is no longer a western construct now-a-days. It has to hold fair elections for democratic process supported by independent institutions such as an Election Commission, Judiciary, a free media and protection of minorities' rights, etc.

CONCERN AT THE FUNCTIONING OF PARLIAMENT

The Budget session 2008 was not an exception. The number of sittings of the Lok Sabha came down from a yearly average of 124 in the first decade 1952-61 to 81 between 1992 and 2001—a decline of 34 per cent. This has meant that much of the discussion of legislation goes on behind the scenes in parliamentary committees, while the floor of the House is used for shouting and heckling. This is according to our speaker, subversion of the parliamentary process and democracy.

The Vice-President of India recently proposed that Parliament sit for a minimum of 130 days a year. Speaker Somnath Chatterjee, who has presided over a fractious Lok Sabha for the past four years, too suggested that MPs who disrupt House proceedings be docked a day's pay. But these proposals have unsurprisingly been ignored. If this situation continues, a statutory warning should perhaps be attached to the telecast of Parliament sessions. School children who see MPs in action inside the House should know how not to behave in public. The anguished Speaker, therefore, had to repeatedly make requests to maintain decorum. For him, the basic problem was : the absence of debate in Parliament. He was deeply concerned of the disorderly behaviour of 32 MPs from the opposition parties of the 14th Lok Sabha.

The country's highest public forum has almost come to standstill due to bickerings, interruptions walkouts and internal disturbances in the House. On the basis of the performance of India's parliamentary democracy, it seems as if its future is bleak in the era of coalition culture which has became a reality. Parliament's prestige has been eroded due to the conduct of members cutting across parties. For example, the record speaks that both Lok Sabha and Rajya Sabha work for less than 50% of their schedule during the Monsoon session of 2007. The Lok Sabha lost its 42 hours due to interruptions and that four bills were passed in the highest people's forum without any debate.*

Table at a Glance : Monsoon Session 2006 *versus* 2007

(a)	Working hours	22-17
(b)	Lok Sabha hours	124-65
(c)	R.S. Working hours	113-52
(d)	Bills passed	17-11

Disruption of legislative business by our elected members in Parliament/state assemblies has resulted in mindless wastage of tax payers' money. It is a great dis-service to the country and its democratic order our speakers after speakers have expressed deep concern over the declining legislative and deliberative standards of Parliaments and assemblies (Each minute of Lok Sabha 11th session cost Rs. 26,000 to the public exchequer).

The above-cited trend is highly disappointing as the Parliament functioned for an average three hours compared to its schedule. In 2007, out of 23 sittings planned, only 17 sittings could take place on account of issues relating to appeasement towards minorities, terrorism, social evils black money's role and contract killings. The house divided into two groups—the

* This is based on a study conducted by PRS Legislative Research Group and Published in the *Times of India*, New Delhi, dated Sept. 14, 2007, p. 10.

righteous and the wrong. That is why the UN Security Council report has criticized in dealing with terrorism effectively and efficiently. This a sad and satire development on the functioning of our democracy for which the factors like the rise of regional outfit nexus between police politicians and bureaucrats, the role of black money in electoral politics and appeasent policy towards minorities are responsible.

Why 'the Zero Hour Turned into a Torture Hour'?

The incidents of April 24, 2008, which saw opposition members storming—the well shouting slogans without paying heed to the Chair (request Somnath Chatterjee). Following repeated disruptions in the house. Speaker had to say that 'the zero hour turned into torture hour' for him. He had no options except cracking the Whip against the 32 Lok sabha members. They all belonged to the opposition—the BJP. The matter was referred to the privileges committee, Sadly, the panel refused to draw up a comprehensive code of conduct, saying that it needs to be done by an all India-party meeting. Unfortunately, our parliament neither could define 'misconduct' nor could it lay down the guidelines to control the behaviour of MPs. We have ample records in coalition politics when the members have misused or abused their powers, privileges and immunities/rights and facilities given to them. It is a matter of concern that on April 16, 2008, the burning issue of inflation and price-rise, was to be taken up, the MPs demanding for discussion were not present on that date.

On crucial issues like the N-deal and the Tibetian protests against China, the Left role was seen unjust, unfair and unpatriotic. The left, being the ruling UPA alliance did insult to the cherished values of democracy and national interests. Even on Chinese intrusions in Arunachal Pradesh, Left role appeared to be unpatriotic.

The conduct of PMO earned the bad name when the sons of the Union Shipping Minister and DMK leader TR Balu was discussed in our parliament. There was clear evidence that Baalu lobbied for his sons' firms. Thus, the Minister was founded guilty of misusing his office to push the case of his children. Yet the PM could not take action against the Minister as it involved the risk of antagonizing a crucial DMK—the regional ally of the UPA.

The Baalu affairs confirmed that regional parties have been the biggest beneficiaries of coalition politics. They have few MPs and their influence is restricted to one or two states, but that has not prevented these parties from exercising influence in the government far exceeding their strength. The DMK, AIADMK, Telugu Desam and Lalu Prasad's RJD have negotiated with the NDA and the UPA leaderships to gain crucial ministerial slots at the Centre and influence public policy to their liking. These parties blindly protect their representatives when questions of propriety are raised against them. Regional parties should recognize that coalition governments call for collective responsibility and accountability. They should not become a liability for parliamentary democracy.

The report of the Lok Sabha Committee of privileges was released at time, when the Lok Sabha was witnessed expulsion of ten member in the affair of Cash for Query scam, and scams in MPLADS and human trafficking. Yet the panel ruled out codifications of privileges of MPs.

Political Parties are Bound to Disclose IT Returns

Ever since it came into effect, the Right to Information (RTI) Act has forced the Indian state, notorious for its, stonewalling ways, to open up. Now political parties are facing the heat. In a recent order, the Central Information Commission (CIC), which oversees RTI, has declared that all political parties should disclose their income tax returns. The reason given by the CIC is that information on the funding of parties is a "democratic imperative and is in public interest". We agree entirely.[4] Even in the US, for instance, the Federal Election Commission, an independent regulatory body, keeps records of campaign finance and enforces laws on the limits and prohibitions on contributions. Anyone can log on to their website and access the latest campaign finance information on presidential candidates or on those running for other offices. One can also find out the names of individual or corporate fund givers about, how much they have donated and to whom.

The Indian electoral system, by contrast, is opaque as the funding of political parties and candidates have been unregulated due to a huge amount of black money. But since a PIL was filed in the courts to disclose the source of funds, they—political parties and candidates are—bound to disclose the sources of contributions—be that in the form of 'gifts' as BSP's supremeo Mayawati claimed about the party funds. In short, disclosure of tax returns could be a first step towards making political parties a little more transparent and accountable, and funds should be for public scrutiny to keep a cap in the root of corruption. When the MPs and Executive stake for greater transparency in Judiciary in terms of postings, appointments and assets of judges, they too should too be transparent and accountable in the aforesaid affair, on the ground, that they influence the exercise of political power/ authority and funds is given in public interest.

No Speaker in recent times has pressed as much concern Somnath Chatterjee over the declining institutional standards in the. Lok Sabha, In August, 2007 he Proposed 'no work no pay' for legislators for wasting parliamentary time by disrupting proceedings. He warned: "We are increasingly being criticized, we are losing credibility as an institution". This inspired India's Vice-President and Rajya Sabha chairman Hamid Ansari to voice his concern on the functioning of both Houses. Chatterjee's latest action comes in the wake of public concerns expressed for over a decade about the wastage of parliamentary time due to disruptions, sloganeering, walk-outs and other methods of 'street politics' within Parliament.[5]

It could be argued that Political Parties and MPs are using agitational politics to appeal to their constituencies in redefining accountability in the era of virtual politics. It helps them in a way to cut costs, time and efforts to organize protests. The NDAs human chain within the precincts of Parliament against price rise is a good example. However, we must remember Dr. B.R. Ambedkar's concluding speech at the penultimate session of the Constituent Assembly on November 25, 1949 in which he warned: "If we wish to maintain democracy not merely in form, but also in fact, there are first things in my judgment, we must do to hold fast to constitutional methods of achieving our social and economic objectives. It means that we must abandon the methods of disobedience, non-cooperation and Satyagrahha where constitutional methods are open; there can be no justification for these unconstitutional methods. These methods are nothing but the grammar of anarchy and the sooner they are abandoned, the better for US".[6] His comment strikes a chord today when hardly any significant issue is discussed ill Parliament without sloganeering, sit-ins and walkouts by the opposition.

Unlike the UK, from where we draw the model and inspiration for our parliamentary system, the role of opposition is constructive. The possibilities of switching benches on changes in popular mood and mandate are built into it however, we have displayed a total aversion to reforms in the functioning of Parliament. In such a situation time wasting and confrontations within the House are unavoidable.

Making the Meetings of House Transparent

In the post RTI era, a Rajya Sabha member, supported by Speaker Somnath Chatterjee and some young MPs, to bring part of the in cameral proceedings of Parliament's standing committees in public view through telecast or CD recording. If successful, the effort would open up yet another door shut to public scrutiny but the opposition to the move is said to be substantial. Likewise, Independent MP from Karnataka, Rajeev Chandrasekhar, after writing to Speaker Chatterjee and Rajya Sabha chairman Hamid Ansari, appealed to UPA chief Sonia Gandhi, BJP leader L.K. Advani and Congress MP Rahul Gandhi to support the cause, which would ensure greater accountability of the standing committees and also put those under public scrutiny.

The Left parties are in favour of the "opening up" but—a similar attempt made by Chatterjee as a simple MP a few years back had been unsuccessful. Proceedings of similar parliamentary institutions are open to public in the US and UK. He said; "Parliament has two roles—legislative and over-seeing the executive. With the opening up of parliamentary proceedings to the people, the role of Parliament as a legislative body is open for all to see.

Prime Ministers' Position

Dr. Manmohan Singh is well known as an economist manager. But he also has political savvy. As an economist-bureaucrat he has been a close observer of and collaborator with generations of Gandhis. When he was made PM, he knew what the dynasty needed from him. Mrs. Sonia Gandhi, never keen on politics, had taken over simply to keep the dynastic business intact for her children to inherit. The dynasty most certainly did not need an aggressive newcomer asserting himself as boss. It needed a number two to hold the fort, one who had no ambition of becoming number one. Viewed in this light, Manmohan Singh is taken less a PM than a regent, keeping the dynastic seat warm till the new generation takes over. Regents are welcome to launch new initiatives and policies. But they are not expected to take risks that might jeopardise the dynasty's prospects. On the contrary, they are expected to focus on continuity, avoid conflicts, and keep the inheritance intact in the interests of the party.

Our P.M. seems to have grasped this reality, and is acting accordingly. That is one reason why the regent always goes the extra mile to accommodate the Left Front as well as Laloo Yadav: this political scene buys time for the emergence of Rahul Gandhi or 'Yuvraj' as young leader. Once the opposition leader L.K. Advani accused him of being an invisible PM and Dr. Singh smilingly took this as a compliment. Prime Minister's main strategy can be summed up as: "do not displease the Madam and the Left. Don't test the limits of the power and concentrate on survival. The nuclear deal confirmed the reality.

The quality of politics cannot be raised without drastic steps to reduce its criminalization. Yet Manmohan Singh inducted into his cabinet a long list of MPs with criminal records. Obviously, he had to offer a top ministry to Laloo Yadav, despite that worthy's involvement in the Bihar fodder scam. But he could have refused to appoint others with criminal records. Alas, he not only ushered in the criminals but strongly defended them, saying they must be considered innocent till proven guilty beyond all appeals. Contrary to it, Mohd. Taslimuddin, it may be recalled, was dropped from the Ministry in 1986 when Deve Gowda was the PM.

Dr. Manmohan Singh frequently talked of the need to improve governance, to reform the dys-functional administration, police system and judicial system. Yet we see no sign of action, only suggestions to set-up a new committee on administrative reforms. This is waffle. Umpteen committees have given umpteen recommendations on reforming the administrative and judicial system. We need action, not more committees. So is the fate of Lokpal Bill, Women Reservation Bill or of the 86th constitutional amendment. His governance has done little to change the quality of politics.

The reshuffle of the UPA government was done in the first week of April, 2001 this was necessitated due to the compulsion of parliamentary elections due in 2009 and due to the expiry of Rajya Sabha term of many ministers. This included young MPs and experts like M.S. Gill, the former C.E.C. as sports Minister. He could have revived the tradition of Pt. Nehru who tapped talent outside of political arena to beef up the government's capabilities, as the upper house of Parliament is devised largely for this purpose. It was good that after four years, Gen. Next (Scindia and Jitin) found berth, but MP Sachin Pilot from Rajasthan missed the chance, probably due to the on-going Gujjars' movement in Rajasthan and pending assembly elections in Nov. 2008. Had he been made a Minister, the Meena community would have been upset, but his non-inclusion displeased the voters of Dausa constituency.

The inclusion of Mr. Gill in the ministry pointed to a missed opportunity for the prime minister. Why could he have not inducted more such people into the ministry? There was a need to address compulsions of electoral politics, of course. But that need not stand in the way of including a few non-party professionals in the government.

It is not that the UPA government was averse to seeking help from people outside electoral politics. The National Advisory Council (NAC) was set-up with Sonia Gandhi as chairperson as a link between civil society and the government. However, the experiment yielded mixed results, though the NAC members are credited for initiating radical public policies like the Right to Information Act, 2005, and the National Rural Employment Guarantee Act. The trouble with the NAC was that it sought to influence the government without being a part of it which was against the norm of Cabinet system. Its authority was derived from the proximity of its members to Sonia, not because of any institutional authority. Such an arrangement is unsustainable in a parliamentary democracy.

The solution is to incorporate the idea of the NAC into Parliament and government. It is necessary to have professionals with expertise in social and economic affairs in government. These people could bring new ideas to administration. The challenge is to get the right mix of politicians and government. This ought to have been the big idea of the reshuffle; it would have compensated for the is inevitable demise.

Image of the UPA Government

The UPA Government completed four years of its five year tenure in office and rating of its performance was, by and large, 'good', but not 'very good'. The survey report confirmed that Indian politics (first family with Sonia and Rahul Gandhi) has a positive impact on the coalition politics. Its prominence both in Government and party has been positive. Apart from all this, certain features should be noted. They as follows:

(a) Never before the Congress-led a coalition government was backed by regional parties at the Centre and, its choice was limited to Dr. Manmohan Singh as Indian PM who is hardly a charismatic politician/leader. But he could save the coalition from disaster on many occasions.
(b) The unity of UPA coalition was based on a single goal formula, i.e. keeping the BJP out of office. Now the Congress is poised to float broad secular front. Yet the BJP won the elections in Gujarat, HP and recently in Karnataka on its own.
(c) The Telangana Rashtra Samiti and the MDMK did not find pleased with the role of UPA managers and broke the ties. So was the case with the DMK, followed by the BSP in June 2008.
(d) The Left Front successfully dominated the dynamics of UPA governance and shaped the priorities of the

government, without bearing any responsibilities. However, the UPA may claim reasonable success in keeping the promises made with CMP, which is largely stressed on social sector. To its credit, the key measures like National Rural Employment Guarantee Scheme NREGES and the Right To Information—RTI have been good.

(e) There was no big corruption scandal to taint the image of government. So is the case in maintaining communal peace.

(f) The Government of course, faced impasse on economic reforms and handling the Nuclear deal with the US. It earned bad name on the issue like price rise and inflation. The Government sadly allowed itself to be bullied due to the Left pressure. Yet the public support has been with the honest image of the PM.

(g) The UPA Government failed to enact a law on the Women's Representation Bill and the Right to Education to all. Nor could it bring a bill on Lokpal to cape the rising trend of corruption in public life.

(h) The Government constantly faced the assault of Indian Judiciary on a number of issue.

Facts About State Being Bullied

On the US-Indo Nuclear deals the Congress-Left ties were exposed as the UPA Government has been dependents on the support of Left allies. Any strong reaction on Tibet would have jeopardized the already strained relations between the Congress and the Left, who have; traditionally been anti-Indian and pro-Chinese. Even after China's comments on Arunachal Pradesh, the Left was seen silence, which shows what kind of nationalist party they are. But then communists have always struggled with the concept of a nation state. In fact, the concept of national pride comes only when the people at the helm of affairs do not depend on confused coalition partners like the Left on critical issues. With there being no signs of an end to this mess, in future we may see more such insults heaped upon us.

On the Indo-US nuclear deal and the stance on the right to protest by Tibetans in the country against China's offensive treatment of their brethren in Tibet, sent the message that our government is weak and timid in its approach to matters of national and international importance.

As regards China, it has an abysmal record of human rights and has always had a policy of using brutal force to quell any uprising against its oppressive policies. The Chinese government should remember that even more important than material progress is respect for all human beings and treating them with dignity and equality. Similarly, the Left Front led by the CPM should have seriously concussed of the panchayat results of West Bengal keeping in mind of Parliamentary elections. These panchayat poll results indicated that the past record of implementing land tenure reforms are linked with the organizational muscle of the CPM. The way the events of Singur and Nandigram in acquiring the farmer's lands for SEZ were dealt with, exposed the CPM's authoritarian politics resulting in alienating the mass voters. The Left Front's drubling in these panchayat polls should be read a vote against the CM's industry policy and his autocratic approach.

TO SUM UP

The PM of our coalition Government (known as UPA) is not the master of his own house; he manages a motley coalition through the form of parallel power centre like the National Advisory Council-NAC and left parties supporting the Government from 'outside'. Whenever any kind of challenge is posed or hurdle is created, the NAC sends off letters to the PM, signed by Mrs. Sonia Gandhi who is the chairperson. The NAC was setup to monitor the implementation of the C.M.P. Mrs. Gandhi enjoys the rank and status of a cabinet minister. She and the council have access to all the cabinet papers and files. This political scenario is a departure from the conventions governing a cabinet system.[7] NAC appears to function as a Super Cabinet in our political system, whose influence on the cabinet is significant. This system of hybrid model is very much different to the pure models of parliamentary or presidential executive, whose reference is not traceable in our constitutional law.

The most interesting phenomenon is that the both the NAC and the left parties have been performing the role as 'veto-players', non-institutionalised role, even not legitimate vote players in terms of policy process, India is strongly displaying both rigidity and volatility as seen in some decisions. The Nuclear deal is a case in point.

A Lesson from Italian Coalition Politics

Italy, since its unification 63 years ago, installed its 62nd government in April 2008 within two years, the new government led by Silvia Berlusconi was sworn in for third time. It came to power, with the support of Northern league party. Thus, political stability has remained in question.

Much has been written about the similarities between coalition politics in India and Italy. Certainly the compulsions of coalition politics have resulted in similarly hobbled economic and social policies in both the countries. But while Italy due to its industrialized status, was for long able to afford this disconnect, India has never been in a position to allow its policies to be disrupted by frequent changes in government. Nevertheless, every time a new government is formed, the long-term policies of the incumbent are jettisoned. The damage done to both countries' economic progress due to this disjuncture is immense.

Perhaps political parties in both India and Italy should arrive at a consensus whereby the broad outline for economic and social policies are discussed and agreed upon. The Japanese, who were also plagued with unstable governments, have created an elite administration tasked with managing policy issues to ensure that there are no radical breaks in policy between successive governments. As a result, the Japanese economy has managed to survive an increasingly uncertain domestic political climate. India—and for that matter Italy could benefit from such a system.

Secondly, the US primaries may provide us a salutary lesson in the virtue of giving the grassroots members an active stake in the party. Both the Congress and the BJP desperately are in need to embrace this philosophy beyond mere tokenism.

The practice of imposing decisions by the High Command must be given good bye, for claiming pan-Indian ambition status. In the functioning of American system, these primarilies are of vital importance in the federal structure. Ours is also a federal set-up. Hence India should take a lesson in this regard to strengthen our party system structure and an active involvement of regional parties for future stability and development.

Notes and References

1. *'Bereft of ideas'*: The Congress has no clear cut Ideology and Policies, *Ibid.*, May 27, 2008, p. 14 and also see, It's a Family Affair, *Ibid.*, Oct. 31, 2007, p. 14.
2. Read his Observations in the Article, 'The Winning Formula', *The Times of India*, New Delhi, June 28, 2008, p. 4.
3. See N.S. Gehlot, RTI Act: A Review of its Implementation', South Asia Politics, Feb. 2008, pp. 18-24.
4. The ruling of the Central Information Commission was given in April 2008, in an appeal of an NGO—Association of Democratic Reforms. The 24 page landmark decision of bringing political parties in the ambit of RTI Act is blimps opposed by our political parties.
5. Read the observations made by Prof. Ajay K. Mehra, 'Don't waste time', *The Times of India*, June 16, 2008, p. 14.
6. Prof. Ajay K. Mehra, *op. cit.*
7. For the performance of the UPA Government, see the separate the matter under a separate sub-Heading in this volume.

CHAPTER

6

Threats to Multi-Culturalism in India

The Indian Constitution is unique in adhering to the concept of secularism as it emphasizes the diversity of religions, languages and cultures. It enjoys a trans-cultural and inter-faith potential which many secular nations do not have that spirit, specifically in terms of religious tolerance and liberty. One of the classic features of Indian Constitution, therefore, is that the state does not persecute any individual on grounds of religion, until he/she poses a threat to national interest or social welfare security. (Article 25) In fact, the rights of religious minorities are related to citizenry rights on equal footings. In this sense, diversity and democracy in India has been functioning together since 1950.

For a country like India with a multi-cultural society, secularism based on rule of law, is an important requirement for democratic functioning. In India, secularism does not mean non-religious, but neutrality of state towards religion that is, the state neither promotes or discriminates nor does it take up any religion as state religion. India's multi-cultural society is based on 'tolerance' and 'accommodation'.

India is essentially a multi-religious society. It has not only given birth to new religions (Buddhism, Jainism, Sikhism etc.) but has accommodated other world's religions on account of power of coexistence, tolerance and accommodation. It resulted in rich heritage of multi-culturalism, cultural assimilation, ideological diffusion, synthesis and co-existence. Of course, it faced inevitable competition, conflicts and tensions in the socio-economic-political spheres, due to the fallout of colonialism, missionary activities, Islamic conquest and the dark era of partition of India.

The secular concepts were ingrained in the Indian society long before independence and the adoption of a secular constitution, its history can be traced in the philosophical thoughts of ancient India, namely *Vasudhav Kutumbkam* (the world is one family) and *Sarva Dharma Sambhava* (Equal regard for all religions). Therefore, the demand for multi-culturalism all over the world is not a new concept for India. India is a diverse society because of important traits like tolerance, non-violence assimilation, absorption, peaceful co-existence and harmony. The Great kings and emperors like Ashoka, Akbar encouraged those ethos and evolved our compose culture. Long before multi-culturalism became a fashionable word India had already put it into practice. The bewildering diversity has been our strength, not our weakness. We have been pluralist and diverse from the ancient period and we should be proud of this pluralist heritage that earmarks the Hindu policy of 'live and let others live'.

India is a Hindu Rashtra (Nation), but it never attempted to become a theocratic state, because the Hindu Rashtra and a secular state are synonymous. Even according to the BJP's philosophy, the concept of a Hindu rashtra is not a political philosophy, but it emanates from the fact a majority in India are Hindus and Hinduism collectively represents the culture and the basic ethos of the country. As per a classic Judgment of the Supreme Court, Hinduism is not a religion but a way of life, meaning thereby that this Hinduism is very much different from other forms of worship that have originated in India. As such Hinduism is purely a geographical term, i.e. one who lives in India is a 'Hindu'.

The phrases likes minority appeasement Pseudo-secularism, cultural nationalism or soft Hindutva have been extremely controversial and debatable among both the national parties—the Congress and BJP notwithstanding that Indian secularism stands for universal brotherhood, equal respect for all religions, protection of religions and linguistic minorities. Because of this nature, India is still a multi-religious society.

There is hardly any think like pure Hindu culture and pure Muslim culture; our culture is mainly composite culture. We should be proud of this composite cultural inheritance. However, this is being increasingly de-emphasised, and that too at our own peril. Some talks more of our own variety of clash of civilizations in the light of partition politics, violence, separatism, caste politics and the politics of minoritism. It is true that politics of minority *versus* reservations, new appeasement policy towards Muslims as earmarked by the Sachar Committee and the rise of Dalit politics, have shaken the bonds of multi-culturalism in India. Today, politics of extremism has become a great challenge to national unity be it in Gujarat or Kāshmir or North-eastern India. The rise of naxalism is a new phenomenon against diversity and pluralism.

Against that background, the politics of 'pseudo-secularism' and minority appeasement has been generated by the power-hungry politicians for their narrow gains. Yet a large number of newly converted Muslims follow Hindu rituals along with the Islamic ones. This is the message of Hindu-Muslim unity and this was witnessed even in feudal and pre-feudal era of history. Thus, India's democracy is well-rooted to diversity and plurality. It is coined on the slogan—*'unity in diversity'*. This represents the real spirit of our model. Its spirit can further be strengthened if the governments of the day focus on people's issues (like poverty, illiteracy, unemployment and health care and drinking water facility) rather than identity politics based on caste and community. The globalised world can help to solve these massive problems relating to infrastructure facilities which are essential for modern life. To enable to establish a strong and stable secular polity, we have to give more emphasis on socio-economic and political development without the prejudices of majority-minority divide.

Conversion is a process by which a person changes her/his 'faith' or ideology to another. It is both theological as well as sociological. It is an age-old practice. It both voluntary and non-voluntary and it is adopted for a better social outcome against exploitation, oppression and discrimination. Mass conversion led by Ambedkar or recently organized by Udit Raj are the glaring examples. They wanted, through an attempt of conversion, to create an ideology of equality using materials from Buddhism for Dalits.

Current controversies on religions conversion in India has really posed a big challenge to the nation's unity and communal harmony. Likewise, rising incidents of communal clashes and violence too have raised serious question about the efficacy of religious tolerance enmeshed in our cultural values. In fact, religious orthodoxy *vis-a-vis* religious freedom has given birth to the misconception/misinterpretation of the word 'propagate', as contained in the list of fundamental rights in Indian Constitution [As per Article 25 (1)].

In India, most of the conversions among Dalits whether to Christianity, Islam or Buddhism are a kind of genuine response to oppressive caste ideology and social exclusion, as reports of Meenakshipuram (1981) is an illustrative case. Poverty, illiteracy, negligence and ill-treatment by upper caste members as well as atrocities and humiliation are cited as reasons for such conversion amongst dalits in India. Current controversies of conversion are related to the politics of Hindutva, leading to enactment laws to prohibit forced conversion by allurement or by any other fraudulent means. At present India needs a balance between the freedom of religion and the right to conversion.

Prof. Samuel Hunting forecast in his monumental work, 'The Clash of Civilisations', that the next round of fight will be between Islam and the West.

Today's religious crusades appear to be a response of a theory of clash of civilisations, as Islam organized suicide squads to target innocents across the world and in turn the Christian powers have made them ready to rain all kinds of bombs and missiles. The twin towers of world Trade Centre in

New York on 9 Sept. 2001 and an anti-Taliban war in Afghaistan, followed by anti-Saddam war in Iraq mutely tell the woeful tale of cash of civilisation. Regrettably, religion has become a dark force of our age. Even Godhra incident has presented an ugly picture against most credible record of religious tolerance. The Western imperialism (and now known as neo-imperialism) is bent up to strengthening the authoritarian culture in the Muslim world against the culture of basic human rights, democracy, openness, freedom and human values. It was the West, especially America, who has thwarted every move by Muslims to modernize and reform themselves. It encouraged the emergence of religious extremism/fundamentalism during the Cold-War era as a bulwark against Communism. Therefore, there is no ideological basis for civilisational clash between Islam and the West.

The era has become the history of past, when Islam was often seen as the West's other religion or depicted as a mono-cultural and intolerant religion in European civilization for centuries. In globalised world, we all are concerned with the concept of multi-culturalism, as ideological pluralism is the only a platform which provides the people an environment of dialogue and mutual respect. Unfortunately, the notion of dialogical pluralism has failed to impress upon the Muslim community because of hard reading of Islam through madarasses and lack of proper modern education in its society. Therefore, in the era of knowledge, the Muslim world has to establish the peaceful coexistence based on religion and legal principles against views of Islamic fundamentalism.

Recently, some Muslims living in Allahabad undertook to a holy dip where the Ganga and Yamuna meet and performed pooja. It is an act of solidarity with thousands of Hindu devotees gathered there for celebrations of Ardh Kumbh held in Jan. 2007. These Muslims describe this an act of Ganga-Yamuna Tehjeeb, and Tehjeeb, of course, is enjoyed by religion. The two religions are not in contradiction as has been projected by the West. This example confirms how Indian secularism is classical in nature—a very different model of the West which works for co-existence between different religions in India.* Again, it is an ideal example set by the Ramji

Mandir of Dakor in Gujarat where a Mahant married off his adopted Muslim daughter in a ceremony performed by a Kazi in the Temple. The Kazi recited the Koran (Nikah) in the said temple premises. This is an example of Hindu-Muslim social unity. (*Ibid.*, January 13, p. 9).

Today, Hindutva "Bharatiyata" has become a sectarian political doctrine with a self life of less than 80 years. It has nothing to do with the हिन्दुत्व (dutifulness) because of the contemporary politics. Hence, certain conclusions can be drawn to strength the spirit of multi-culturalism. First, Indian Muslims must face the irrational choice they made in 1945-47, when four-fifths voted for Pakistan, but four fifths stayed in India. Now, they must playa clearer role by taking the lead against Islamic fundamentalism and showing no response to appeasement tactics of vote bank. Second, the Nehruvian secularism is meaningless and non-existent as a political force in the light of appeasement policy. A spiritualism that is a synthesis of Nanak, Kabir, sufism and Bhakti might be a better bet than soulless, opportunistic secularism. Third, Hindudom has the choice of either Savarkar, Hedgewar and Golwalkar or Vivekananda, Aurobindo and Tagore. In the long run, I think choosing the latter would be better since they were liberal and global in their outlook.

IMPLICATIONS OF SACHAR COMMITTEE

Addressing the Dalit Minority International Conference on 27th December, 2006, Prime Minister Dr. Manmohan Singh said that his Government was committed to removing inequalities and imbalances faced by the Muslim community which has been deprived of an equal share of development benefits. He noted that the plight of Muslims has been established by data provided in the Sachar Committee report which has thoroughly studied the social, economic and educational status of Muslim community across the country. He was equally concerned about the Dalit's untouchability and discrimination with apartheid. Accordingly, the UPA govt. has

* "Salaam Ganga: Muslims join Hindu for a Holy Dip at Ardh Kumbh", editorial of *The Times of India*, New Delhi, Jan. 8, 2007, p. 12.

promised to implement the Sachar Committee report on the status of minorities including reservation for Dalit Muslims, with emphasis on the 15-point programme announced by the PM. Further, the report of the working group also contains a number of proposals for educational, social and economic development of minorities. The group set up by Planning Commission has favoured to put the scheme into the 11th plan (2007-11).

The Sachar Committee report has given the recommendation of re-categorisation as MBC's of Dalit Muslims to provide reservations and quotas. The panel has unbundled many perceptions spawned by the Mandal Commission report of 1980 to ensure the 'Muslim voice' in governmental bodies and even in local self-governmental bodies. On he contrary, the political outfits of Muslims, regrettably, hardly talk of raising voices of protest on real issues pertaining illiteracy, human development, infrastructure facilities, education, or on an amendment in the Muslim Personal Law to ensure the citizenry rights of backward Muslim women against social evils like Fatwa and Talak as issued by clerics from time to time.

According to the BJP, the decision to implement the report in totto reflects UPA Government's Muslim appeasement policy under cover of equal opportunities for the community. The 'minority *versus* the rest' approach reflects its vote-bank politics.

THE CONSTITUENT ASSEMBLY AND COMMUNAL RESERVATION

The question of reservation of seats on the basis of the communal electorates was considered in detail by the Advisory Committee appointed by the Constituent Assembly. The Advisory Committee, which was chaired by H.C. Mookerjee, himself a Christian, recommended for the reservation of seats for the minorities, including Muslims, on the principles of proportional representation in terms of population to be elected by joint electorate and not on the basis of communal and 'separate electorates'. It must be mentioned here that the Muslim League was also part of the

Advisory Committee and the Constituent Assembly. The decision to do away with the separate electorates was taken by an overwhelming majority, near to a national consensus. The Committee resolved that : "That the system of reservation for minorities other than Scheduled Castes in Legislatures be abolished."

The Committee had already rejected the proposal of reservation in the services for any community except for the Scheduled Caste and Scheduled tribes. In the words of Jawaharlal Nehru; "Now, all of us here, I believe, are convinced that this business of separatism, whether it took the shape of separate electorates or other shapes has done a tremendous amount of evil to our country and to our people. We came to the conclusion some time back that we must get rid of separate evil. . . . " What is most shocking is that the Sachar Committee has suggested is the same remedy which was based on two-nation theory that finally led to the unprecedented human miseries in 1947.

The Sachar Committee report, seen in the light of the Prime Minister's statement that the "Muslims have first right on the resources of the nation", has put not only the principle of 'equality' and 'equal opportunity for all', irrespective of caste, creed and religion, on a burner but also the whole Constitution being put into the dust-bin.

Let us not forget a simple but brutal fact that those who ignore their history are destined to become very soon the part of history. This is what is going to happen to India and the Hindus. Today, India is a 'secular' country just because it has more than 86% Hindu population. All those who chose to live in this country chose the primacy of the Constitution of India based on *'Sarvadharma Samabhava'* with no place for the religion in the formulation of Government's policies and State polity.* It is our solemn duty to see to it that this cardinal principle is adhered to in letter and spirit and the meaning of

* The proposed 'Surya Namaskar' programme that was officially announced by the BJP's Governments of MP holding in all governments run schools in Jan. 2007 under the Yoga Programme, the M.P. Court stayed order its implementation on the plea that it would not be compulsory, but only voluntary. The Islamic outfits feared that the 'Yoga Policy' might whip-up communal passions in schools, as it is based on Hindu rituals and is performed with chanting 'Hindu mantras'.

'secularism' is not reduced to appeasement of any particular community or caste.

In this context, it would be worthwhile to recall that when Pakistani PM Liaquat Ali visited New Delhi in April 1950, he tried to succumb the Indian PM again for separate electorate in the Legislatures and reservations for the Muslims in service. Since the issue was based on communal lines, Sardar Patel turned down the proposal. In Patel's words: "I am quite sure that the party will not accept it and the country will not swallow this bitter pill. We have conceded one Pakistan; that is more than enough." Later, on the issue of the reservations, Jawaharlal Nehru wrote to all the Chief Ministers on 27 June, 1961:

> "I dislike any kind of reservation, more particularly in services. I react strongly against anything which leads to inefficiency and second rate standards. I want my country to be a first class country in everything. The moment we encourage the second-rate, we are lost".
>
> . . . "The only real way to help a backward group is to give opportunities of good education; this includes technical education which is becoming more and more important. Everything else is provision of some kind of crutches which do not add to the strength or health of the bodyif we go in for reservations on communal and caste basis, we swamp the bright and able people and remain second rate or third-rate."

The vote-bank politics consisting of the Muslims, SCs/STs, Yadavas and Dalits have shaken the roots of communal and social harmony as politicians usually nurture sectarian and caste loyalties and divide the society into factions which are hostile to each other. The reservations on communal lines is most dangerous policy than persuaded by the imperial policy of 'Divide and Rule'. It goes against Article 325 of the Constitution which provides no reservation on the basis of religion.

Amidst strong opposition from the Muslim groups and Catholic Church to the proposed 'Surya Namaskar' programme that was officially announced by the BJP's

Government of MP holding in all Government run schools in Jan. 2007 under the Yoga Programme, the M.P. High Court stayed order its implementation on the plea that it would not be compulsory, but only voluntary. The petitions claimed that the 'Survya Namaskar' was part of worship system of sun in Hindusim and it is forbidden to certain religious communities. Therefore, it should be voluntary. The Islamic outfits feared that the 'Yoga policy' might whip-up communal passions in schools, as it is based on Hindu rituals and is performed with chanting 'Hindu mantras'. The controversial programme was proposed by Yoga guru Ram Dev Maharaj, The court upheld the ethos of secularism enshrined in our Constitution.

In short, managing cultural diversity is one of the central challenges of our time, specially in multi-cultural, multi-lingual and multi-religious country like India. Different castes and communities make demands, which are often difficult to accommodate. Before independence Muslims and Dalits had demanded their share but now several caste and communities are making their demands for reservations in jobs and education. Earlier caste-based parties did not exist. Today several caste-based parties and political-*cum*-regional parties have come into existence and only alliance of these regional parties can form a government at the Centre. No single party appears to be in a position to rule over India. It is all because functioning of democracy brings more and more awareness among people of diverse origin and they begin to assert their respective identities and organize themselves to acquire greater and greater share of educational opportunities and jobs.

In India, politics is not based on issues but on identities, it can prove highly divisive. Politicians are tempted to appeal to primordial identities rather than to solve problems. The former case proves much easier. The medieval society in India was thus more religiously tolerant as it was not competitive. The modern Indian Society, on the other hand, has proved to be more divisive as it based on competition. This competition becomes more acute if development is uneven and unjust. Development, therefore, is the only way to strengthen the concept of plurality, national integrity and social unity. Focus on strengthening infrastructure shall have been given.

India was agonised by what happened in a crass UK reality show (The Big Brother Show) and the comments said to our 'representative' Bollywood participant, star Shilpa Shetty. This scene exposed the mindset of colonial history of Britain and cultural ethos based on liberal democracy. It shows that after the collapse of communism on in Central and Eastern Europe fifteen years ago, the West was not prepared to accept the egalitarian-social-democratic ethos of pre-war Czechoslovakia and Poland where the politics of values is based on moral order and popular legitimacy. The clash of popular legitimacy with constitutionalism was a good indication for the rise multi -culturalism in U.K. Racial equality shall have to be followed. The respect and understanding should be given to all cultures and religions.

Against the above-cited example, India, too, cannot claim be a country of free racist behaviour. In the words of Manchala Deenbandhu, a noted dalit ideologue, "There is a racism in India although not in the way it is experienced in parts of the world. Casteism is the synonym for racism in India, because caste is a system of hierarchy by which people are put into rigid social categories. Caste, therefore, is a culture that ensures powers and privileges to the dominant groups through the subjugation and exploitation of the lower castes".* In short, all kinds of racism should be condemned in order to strengthen the values of equality and human rights.

REFORMING MADRASSA SYLLABI

It is truly held that the absence of modern/secular schools in poorer countries has created a ·hazardous void and that is filled by madrassas that have been providing the religious education relating to obscurantist/militant view of Islam. Lack of educational opportunities forces Muslim children to join madrassas and militant Islam. Even though in India, the Muslim children have better educational opportunities under our set-up, the poverty prevailing in the Muslim families, particularly in India, coerces parents to enroll their wards in madrassas. The above cited system has weakened our vision of secularism.

* Anand Soondas's paper, "India is Racist", *The Times of India,* New Delhi Edn., Jan. 22, 2007, p. 14.

It is unfortunate that the government has not done anything concrete to translate the ideal of free and compulsory school education into reality. In its absence, there must be appropriate reforms in madrassa education. However, the proposed reforms in madrassa curricula may not yield the desired results. First, such a move will open a Pandora's box as the mullahs will raise the bogey of intrusion in religious affairs and most likely a number of writ petitions will be filed. The judiciary may uphold their plea on the fundamental rights to freedom of religion and educational and cultural rights.

Second, out of political expediency no major political party, perhaps with the exceptions of the sangh parivar outfits, may support such a move. Third, even if government succeeds in designing the curricula for madrassas, there is no guarantee that it will be imparted to students in the true spirit. Fourth, the proposed revision of the madrassa curricula does not intend to revise the interpretation of Islam that is taught in these madrassas. The problem of revising the Madrassas syllabilies in moderate interpretation of Islam and linking scientific education yet remains in tact.

Having said this, the crucial issue remains : Who will bring about these changes in madrassa education ? The current patrons of madrassas, viz Wahabis of Saudi Arabia and individuals, who are committed to promote a regressive and fundamentalist mode of Islam, will naturally cease funding the reformed madrassas. At the same time, it would be naive to expect any financial assistance from the government. The Muslim community in India will have to find out its own sources to finance reformed madrassas to set them in modern education. A source of funding could be the wakf properties. unfortunately the wakfs are perhaps the most mismanaged institutions. It should be the responsibility of the Ministry of Minority Affairs to coordinate with the wakf boards and allocate revenue generated by the properties only for education of Muslims.

TO CONCLUDE

Pluralism in India has been a valuable source of its integration and secularism. It is important for two distinct reasons. First, tolerance of heterogeneity is central to democracy and second, practice of pluralism produces a culturally rich society. But diversity can not survive if special immunity is granted to certain communities which violates the concept of equality and justice. Our focus is related to personal laws governing marriages and property. Such asymmetries should be re-examined as this asymmetric feature has damaged. Out concept of secularism as well as the practice of pluralism.

Secondly, the fall out of liberalization and globalisation of Indian economy and the socio-economic and political change has brought in sudden upsurge of religious chauvinism, religious intolerance and fundamentalism, which is widely coined a 'clash of civilization.' It has become a worldwide phenomenon and has shaken the roots of peace and social harmony. So long as religious or ethnic intolerance exists in the world (and in India as well) there would be communal conflicts and disturbances. We have, therefore, to root out this intolerance factor and sow seeds of tolerance and brotherhood in the minds of men and community/ethnicities through education spreading the concept that God is one; entire world is one family (Vasudhav Kutumbkam) and one universal God belongs to the entire world (Devanam Adidera Ekah).

In Indian context most of terror attacks are handiwork of misguided youth by Islamic outfits. This kind of terrorism can be tackled effectively only by strengthening criminal justice system, which is century-year and old. Terror should not be treated as an ordinary crimes. Law enforcement machinery has to be geared up.

Followers of multi-culturism may draw lessons from the ruling Justice and Development Party—AKP led by Abdullah Gul of Turkey which has proved that Islam and democracy are compatible and Turkey's secular character is safe. Secularism ought to be a handmaiden of liberal democracy. At present, under the AK Party's rule, Turkey has enjoyed spectacular export-led economic growth in the last decade. Its efforts to make Turkey's integration with the European Union has enhanced the prospects of Turkey's democratic consolidation as well as the growth of free market economy. Against the reversion of Islamic agenda, the AKP regime has reconfirmed and defended the minority rights (Christian and other ethnic communities) as well as freedom of opinion. Turkey stands today as an example to the world that Islam and democracy are compatible and it would send a powerful message to Islamic parties of Muslim world who are willing to adopt a constitutional path to achieve their democratic goals.

Therefore, it is imperative that the government of day try and dampen ethnic tensions by trying to depoliticize ethnicity and minorities through establishing and maintaining rule of law, democratizing police system, favouring broad civil rights protections over specific minority rights initiatives, supporting secularism over the establishment of religious dogmas, respecting linguistic diversity and promoting multi-lingualism by means of sharing political power among ethnic groups. The great strength of consociationalism is that it insures minority participation in governmental deliberations.*

It is shocking that three MLAs of Ittahidul Muslim in Hyderabad gate clashed into the book-release function of Taslima Nasreen on 9th August 2007, one of the Calcutta-based Imam issued a fatwa to pay Rs. 50,000 if some one blackens Taslima's face. They do not have the deep study of Quranic teachings that Prophet and Islam do not permit to attack a woman. The madness incident was condemned as attackers were not bothered about their status. This reflected India's image of 'soft state'.

If we want to enjoy fruits of secular democracy we must shed all forms of partisan feelings. Politicisation of religion in our social democracy has already done enough damage to our multi-culture ethos. Democracy cannot succeed without following Rule of Law and promoting zero sum tolerance towards any act of violence. No provocation or violence justifies, ideologically or otherwise, the outrageous behaviour of the elected members who are bound by oath 'to bear true faith and allegiance to the Constitution of India'. Ours is a secular, democratic republic, unlike totalitarian regimes.

As regards the absence of modern/secular schools in poorer countries has created a hazardous void and that is filled by madrassas that have been providing the religious

* See the views of Prof. Rajni Kothari in Kumar David and S. Kadirgamar (eds.), Ethnicity, Identity and Crisis (Hongkong, Arena Press, 1996), p. 31.

education relating to obscurantist/militant view of Islam. Lack of educational opportunities forces Muslims children to join those madrassas and militant Islam. Even in India, the Muslim children do not have better educational opportunities under our set-up and the poverty prevailing in the Muslim families, coerces parents to enrol their wards in madrassas. The above cited system has weakened our vision of secularism. The Sachar Committee has taken note of its.

It is unfortunate that the government has not done anything concrete to translate the ideal of free and compulsory school education into reality. Therefore, absence, there must be appropriate reforms in madrassa education.

The crucial issue remains : Who will bring about these changes in madrassa education? The current patrons of madrassas viz. Wahabis of Saudi Arabia and individuals, who are committed to promote a regressive and fundamentalist mode of Islam, will naturally cease funding the reformed madrassas. At the same time, it would be naive to expect any financial assistance from the government. The Muslim community in India will have to find out its own sources to finance reformed madrassas to set them in modern education. A source of funding could be the wakf properties.

Unfortunately the wakfs are perhaps the most mismanaged institutions. It should be the responsibility of the Ministry of Minority Affairs to coordinate with the wakf boards and allocate revenue generated by the properties only for education of Muslims.

References

Rekha Dwivedi and Salahuddin Ansari, Religious Conversion in India (New Delhi, National Foundation for Communal Harmony, 2006).

रेखा द्विवेदी एवं राजीव दुबे, सर्वधर्म–समभाव : एक विश्लेषण (नई दिल्ली, राष्ट्रीय साम्प्रदायिक सदभाव प्रतिष्ठान, 2004)।

N.S. Gehlot, Politics of Communalism and Secularism in India (New Delhi, Deep & Deep Publications, 1993).

S.A.T. Rizvi and Rekha Dwivedi, Politics and Communalism (*Ibid.*, 2005).

Makkhan Lal, "The Meaning of Sachar Committee-II", in South Asia Politics, New Delhi, January 2007, pp. 18-22.

SMAW Chisti, "Secularism in India: An Overview", *The Indian Journal of Political Science*, Meerut, April-June 2004, pp. 183-98.

CHAPTER 7

The Role of Governor as a Chancellor of Universities in a State

The tug-of-war between the two constitutional functionaries the state Governor and Chief Minister has been one of the features of India politics, not only in the era of one-party rule dominance but also in the coalition period from time to time. The role of governor as chancellor of the universities in the state too has deteriorated relationship to such levels that the CM in public used to allege that the Governor as an agenda of the Centre has been creating hurdles in discharging his (CM) constitutional duties. The former demanded the governor's recall. The on-going tussle between the chancellor of UP (Governor T.V. Rajeshwar) and the CM is a classic example in point to cite wherein the chancellor has refused to heed to the advice of the Council of Minister in the appointment of a minister as 'Lifetime Pro-Chancellor" of an Urdu, Arabic and Persian University in the state (proposed to be known as Mohammed Ali Johar University in Khan's hometown, Rampur). Not only this, Raj Bhavan-virtually crossed swords with the Government by forcing it to withdraw the bill seeking to set-up a University. Raj Bhavan's tough posture (pleasure) has become a matter of public discussion raising the issue if the governor as chancellor has any independent role to play.

The present controversy surrounds about the issue whether the state governor in his capacity as a chancellor of the university administration enjoys marginal discretion like that of his discretion to be used during the British time practice of keeping the university under control through 'vetoing power' of the governor.

HISTORICAL BACKGROUND OF A CHANCELLOR

The practice of Governor's becoming the Chancellor of a university is inherited from the British rule. For the first time when the three universities were set-up in India in 1857, the British governors were vested the visitorial powers as Chancellors. But the British Government had enough control over the university's activities through a 'vetoing power'. Under the Indian Universities Act, 1904, the Chancellors were given more powers. But in practice, the British administration rarely exercised this power in the affairs of Universities. Those institutions used to enjoy autonomy in the real sense. Rare examples would be available when the Government did interfere in the matters of academic pursuits. Of course, the model of those universities were in conformity with the British policy, and the University financed used to operate under the supervision and control of the provincial Governments, whose purpose was to ensure that the money was properly spent. So far as the real executive powers of the university were concerned, the Vice-Chancellors (the Chancellor's nominee of a university) were to exercise without any kind of political pressure. Both the then Chancellor and Vice-Chancellor of a university were sensitive to preserving the autonomy of the institution. They were above the on-going politics of the Province.[1]

On the eve of framing the new constitution for independent India, the office of Governor was largely and deliberately discussed in terms of Centre-State relations, but the role of Governor as a Chancellor of Universities was hardly discussed hoping that the traditional convention of governor becoming the Chancellor of the University would be observed by the successive Governments of a free India, *inter alia,* the concept of University autonomy would be respected for academic pursuits.

Once a President of India Dr. Sanjiva Reddy while acting as visitor of a university was caught in such a controversy. He sought the opinion of the Attorney-General on the matter, who referred to judgment of the Allahabad High Court. The weight of legal opinion was in favour of the Chancellor's functioning in an independent capacity. But the President of India admitted in his book *'Without Fear or Favour'* that practically no Chancellor can function in terms of his individual discretion, as it would invite the possibility of litigation against the Governor. He concludes that the legal implications of any governor's acting independently of the Government need a careful examination.[2]

So far as the powers and functions of the Chancellor is concerned, the present pattern is almost the same as used to prevail during the British Raj. However, the Indian constitution contains no provision relating to the position of the Governor as Chancellor. Therefore, it is presumed that the Governor, being the constitutional head of the state, is bound by the ministerial advice, because a Chancellor cannot be a Chancellor unless he is the Governor and, as per the convention the governor comes from outside the state, it would be proper for him to be guided by the advice of his Council of Ministers. In that sense, it is presumed that, in order to avoid a tug-of-war, the chancellor should also act as a 'figure head' in the affairs of University. On the contrary, the report of the Administrative Reforms Committee on state administration favoured the chancellor to exercise his discretion in the affair of the University. But the Kothari Committee noted the idea of abolishing the post, i.e. making the Governor ex-officer chancellor of the University. The President of India is a visitor of the Central Universities and it may be noted that other institutes.

There are numerous example to cite where the governors-*cum*-chancellors of universities acted on their own discretion and the CMs did not blame to question their role and wisdom. To name a few, Dr. K.M. Munshi, G.S. Pathak, R.R. Diwakar, Dr. Zakir Hussain, and G.S. Bajpayai who were the top ranking academicians and educationists of their times and were above party politics and had towering personality. Sadly, most of the chancellors of Northern Universities have been controversial during the 1960s onwards. Appointing the educationists/ academicians as Governors has now become an out-dated fashion in our political system.

IMPACT OF CHANGING CENTRE-STATE RELATIONS

The fast changing scenario of centre-state relations, wherein the dominance of one party system has witnessed the rise of regional parties along with the emergence of BJP as strong opposition, the concept that the Governor being outsider, would be above party politics and would be able to prevent political interference in the affairs of university, has diluted due to local politics of groupism based on the factors like politics of casteism and regionalism, plenty of' issues relating to students' union elections, examinations, results or appointments have brought the CM in confrontation with a chancellor. Need not to mention here the role of our governors, as 'agent' of the Centre as is of the role of Goa's governor in February 2005 is in point to mention. As in most of the cases, the vice-chancellors of Indian Universities are appointed on party lines, the chancellors and the CMs have been seen at war path, because the state Government recommends the names of favourable persons in the panel of the appointments of vice-chancellors, whereas most of state Governors are practically from the rank of politicians and bureaucrats. Consequently, the concept of University's autonomy has suffered.

In one of the classic examples, the Chancellor of the M.D. University, Rohtak (Haryana) Dr. Hardwari Lal acted independently in the affairs of the university, whose decision was called in question in Haryana High Court. While setting aside the act of Chancellor, the court held that his actions were not immune from being challenged in a court of law as provided in Article 361(1) of the Constitution.

'NO' TO SETTING UP A NEW UNIVERSITY

UP Governor TV Rajeshwar is probably the first Governor *cum*-Chancellor of the state universities, who refused to give his consent to the setting-up of controversial Maulana Mohd. Ali Jauhar Urdu University at Rampur, which was passed twice by the state legislature. It was referred to the President of India. According to the Bill, the state Government planned to appoint state Urban Development Minister Azan Khan as its (Urdu University) pro-chancellor for life. Reacting to this development, the state Government resolved to set-up a private University which would go a long way to ensure higher education for all, irrespective of their religion. The Bill was referred to the President of India for consideration under Article 200.

The Governor as Chancellor objected to the draft ordinance for setting up the Mohd. Ali Jauhar Urdu University, at Rampur (UP), despite the approval of the cabinet headed by CM Mulayam Singh on the ground that it authorized state's parliamentary affair minister Azan Khan to be its pro-chancellor for life time ignoring sharp criticism of this issue by different political parties including the Congress and the BJP. The draft ordinance (under Article 213 of the Constitution) is probably the first kind of example in the academic world to have a pro-VC for life long, It smacked of communal appeasement to minority community by the ruling S.P. Secondly, it might have led to communal divide and frenzy on the issue of 'minority status', as was the case of AMU, which had been restored to it after a prolonged agitation.

As such, there is no justification of having yet another Urdu Varsity in the state, on the ground that with more than 30 percent seats in post-graduate courses in Urdu, Arabic and Persian were still found lying vacant in 2004 as was shown in the admission process at Lucknow University (LU). Thus, the state Government's decision to open an Urdu University has baffled educationists. According to LU post-graduate admission cell, of the 130 seats in MA (Urdu), only 105 application forms were received. In the case of MA (Persian) only 15 of the 20 seats could be filled and 22 of the 28 seats in MA (Arabic). In the case of MA (Arab culture), seven seats are still vacant. Further, many seats remained vacant in courses offered by department of Oriental Studies in Persian.

Lucknow University authorities have now re-advertised for the seats and invited fresh applications. However, so far the response has been poor. In such a scenario, teachers and students at Lucknow University are unable to digest the state Government's decision to invest Rs. 100 crore on the proposed Urdu University. Teachers by and large admit that such courses cannot be closed down and need funds to promote research and academies. They are of the view that, instead of opening a new university with heavy expenditure of 100 crore, the state Government could strengthen the departments of Arabic, Persian and Urdu. Therein a new centre/institute of learning in the Lucknow University could be set-up. At present, all these departments are in a bad shape.

The UP governor was further set to hot up with the SP-led Government when he reserved the bill for pending after being passed by the both houses of the state legislature. According to the Governor, he was not bound to give accent on each and every bill sent for his consideration, as there is no time limit fixed under the constitution. On the contrary, the CM cited the examples of Raja of Banaras and Maharshi Mahesh's appointments as pro-chancellors in Varanasi and Chitrakoot. But the Governor refused to relent. The Governor is constitutionally not bound to give his assent to the Bill. More so, the Bill sent to him earlier was not returned by him. If it is again sent to him, he has no obligation to give his assent.

In short, the fate of the much-trumpeted Rs. 150-crore Maulana Mohammed Ali Jauhar Urdu University in Rampur continues to hang in balance in spite of smooth passage of the Bill to this effect in both Houses of state legislature.

The above cited controversial bill, thus was sent back to the SP Government by Indian President with posing some questions which the state Government has to duly reply to. The Human Resources Development Ministry has sought to know whether the bill was in any way violative of the constitution, whether it has violated the University Act in any way and what was the aim behind the settling up of the proposed university?

In the eyes of Muslims, the proposed plan of setting Maulana Mohd. Ali Urdu University at Rampur, is a game-plan of the S.P. to phase the Muslim voters of U.P. The Shahi Imam of Jama Masjid asserted that the current Congress-S.P. spat on the proposed university, is a *siyasi iadai* (political battle) between them and their intentions about the Urdu language are unclear. He argued that the SP's decision to appoint Azam Khan as life-time pro-VC was "unwarranted", and the Governor as Chancellor has done right by holding back the bill. He asked the CM not to insist on it, because the CM alone as an individual does not represent the welfare of Urdu language or of the Muslim community as a whole.

SOME UNHEALTHY TRENDS

This apart, saddened with a tirade of education with power politics, the VC of Bundelkhand University, Prof. R.C. Chandra, hit at all the successive CMs and coalition Governments that could hardly spare time for improvement of higher education. Political uncertainty has been so prevailing in the state for years that CMs have been seen in pre-occupied with political equalitions to survive opposition designs. Even the Chancellor is helpless in promoting higher education. No proper financial assistance is being given to state universities.

The appointment of Somanahalli Malliah Krishna, the former CM of Karnataka, as Governor of the state was opposed by the state's opposition parties. The Krishna's appointment on the border row between the two states and the appointment was further opposed by the NCP saying that it was not consulted about his appointment.

Likewise, the Chhattisgarh Government on 9th December, 2004, removed Jose Vergheese from the post of vice-chancellor of the Hidyatullah Law University. Pankaj Dwivedi, principal secretary of general administration department was appointed as the new vice-chancellor on political grounds. Prof. Vergheese' three years term was to expire in 2006. He was made vice-chancellor of the university by the Ajit Jogi Government of Congress on April 26, 2003. He was the third vice-chancellor to go since the BJP Government came to power. Professor Vergheese said that his premature removal was unconstitutional and he would approach the High Court for relief.

More recently, the stand off on between the chancellor and the chairman of Bihar service commission on the appointment of 1,300 lecturers in different contituent colleges came to limelight in which serious irregulars and favourism were pointed out. The Governor directed all the VCs of universities not to accept the appointments. He also sacked the chairman of commission while writing to the vigilance department to probe the appointment process. Thereupon, the chairman S.D.N. Singh was arrested. The state Government stepped in and criticised Singh's dismissal. Both the state governors, Vinod Chandra Pandey and M. Rama Jois gave go ahead for appointments, but vigilance department found their illegal. (Based on the news published in the *Times of India,* dated Sept. 6, 2004, p. 8).

It is pertinent to mention that during the period of deteriorating relationship between the AP's Governor, Dr. M. Chenna Reddy and Chief minister Ms. J. Jayalalithaa, the Madras university was without a Vice-Chancellor for more than a year. The prolonged cold-war between the two related in a loss in the academic pursuits.

Likewise, some of the Rajasthan's universities too, have taken the similar sad experience due to the ideological differences between the Governor-*cum*-Chancellor and the party in power. Consequently, no panel of search committee could be set-up and in that event, the university reign was handed over to the IAS Vice-Chancellor. These bureaucrats hardly took interest in the functioning of university or enhancing the academic values. The latest example is of the newly born Ajmer University, which has seen the governance of sixth IAS Vice-Chancellor since its inception in 1987. During the take over the charge of the university by an IAS Vice-Chancellor from 29th March 2003 to 15th March 2004, the divisional commissioner as Vice-Chancellor visited the campus twice during this period, and that too with heavy police force with the apprehension that he might have to face the resistance of university staff in favour of their demands. The most unfortunate development on his part was the suspension of the Teacher's Association President, Dr. B.P. Sarawat, at the behest the Congress Government, who was an active leader of the VHP and there was a ban on holding the meeting of the VHP to be organized at Ajmer. In this meeting, Dr. Pravin Togadia of the Hindutva campaign was to welcome through a function of Trisul distribution. The teacher was allegedly charged to have taken part in that function. A fake charge sheet of anti-national activity was served on him by opening the office on Sunday. His suspension, in fact, was carried out hurriedly to please the party in power by the VC without examining the university rules or the norms of natural justice. Upon joining the new Governor, N.C. Jain, directed the Vice-Chancellor to revoke the suspension order, which the VC did without bearing a sense of accountability and answerability. It is a matter of serious concern that till this date, no charge sheet against the sacked teacher has been submitted in the court of law, nor any action has been initiated so far at the misdeed of the IAS Vice-Chancellor. The entire episode reflects the biased attitude of the Vice-Chancellor.

It is very distressing that we talk of safeguards like accountability, performance monitoring, efficiency and citizen's redress against bureaucratic mal-functioning through the Lokpal institution, yet our leadership is not prepared to do away with the inexplicable Section 197 of Cr.P.C., which was enacted way back in 1898 and was amended in 1973. It still bears the unmistakable imprint of our colonial master. This is known as a 'single directive', i.e. a bureaucrat is above the law. This section provides that a civil servant above the rank of joint secretary can only be prosecuted with the prior sanction of higher authority of the Government of India, if the alleged officer has committed a mistake while acting or purporting to act in the discharge of his official duty. In fact, under these three mischievous words (purporting to act) enable errant bureaucrat to escape from any action.

The present state Government of Mrs. Vasundhra Raje, of course, is deeply concerned of the poor plight of the state universities. It plans to reform the system which is riddled with irregularities, corruption, scams, red-tapism, etc. specifically concerned to the J.N. Vyas University, Jodhpur and the M.D.S. University, Ajmer. To maintain the autonomy of university, the BJP Government is advised to make an amendment in the University Act not to hand over the charge of a University to any bureaucrat as and when needed. Instead, it should be given to a committee consisted of senior teachers of the university concerned. Higher educational institutions should be governed by a set of ethos and norms based on autonomy and accountability. The administration must be responsive and answerable. In this regard, the recommendations of Sarkaria Commission should be studied.

SARKARIA COMMISSION'S OBSERVATIONS

It may not be out of place to refer to what the Sarkaria Commission has to say on the subject. It makes three main points. One, even though the Governor is the Chancellor *ex-officio* and the tenure lapses when he ceases to be the Governor, it does not necessarily follow that the functions assigned to him as Chancellor are to preformed by him in his capacity as Governor. Having taken this position, the commission draws a distinction between the powers vested in him and those vested in the state Government. Since the two are distinct and separate in most cases, the Governor is expected to function on his own. The Commission, then goes on to affirm that what the Governor does as Chancellor cannot be regarded as 'business of the Government of the state under Article 166(3)'.

Does this pronouncement settle the issue? Presumably not. An answer has to be found to the issue raised by Mr. Sanjiva Reddy that if the President or the Governor becomes a party to a dispute in a court of law, it takes away something from his dignity. In fact, if the Governor is generally the Chancellor, it is not so much to ensure Governmental control over the university as to confer prestige. What the Governor by becoming the Chancellor of the university does is to bring weight and authority to the office. This should also mean, in a manner of speaking, that what he does should be above the board and free of controversy.

The root cause of all controversies lies in the fact that the office of the Governor has been politicized. This has lowered the dignity of the office and their role has precisely become suspect. The intention of Governor, therefore, is questioned. In this context, the Sarkaria Commission summed up the matter when having reiterated the merit of the existing practice, it has made two interrelated recommendations. One, wherever the University Act provides for mandatory consultation between the Chancellor and the minister (or the chief minister, if necessary) that would have to be done. The second suggestion is that in those cases where consultation is not mandatory, it can still be done on a voluntary basis. This is what would ensure tension-free functioning.

How is it that no one has chosen to challenge the President in a court of law? One reason is that so far he has not taken any decisions on his own though he is known to have influenced the Government in certain directions in a few cases. Why should not the same practice be followed by Governors? One reason, referred to already, is the decline in the stature of governors. The second, perhaps an equally important one, is the absence of close and meaningful consultation between the Chancellor and the minister. It is time that certain conventions should be established in the new unfolding phase of Indian political life, where the coalition type governance has become inevitable.

The Supreme Court of India is currently seized of a controversy of removal of four state Governors by the UPA Government, and for this purpose, the matter has been referred to the full bench of Judges to settle the scope of situational discretionary powers of state Governor. It is expected that the ruling of the SC bench would cast a line on the role of Governor-*cum*-Chancellor while dealing with Article 361(1) of the Constitution.

NOTES AND REFERENCES

1. See the 8th chapter, "The Governor as Chancellor" of my book, State Governor's in India; New Delhi, Gitanjali Publications, 1985.
2. Quoted from Professor Amrik Singh's article published in, *The Times of India,* New Delhi, 2nd February, 1989, p. 16.

CHAPTER

8

The Office of Governor in Indian Federalism

Image and Reality

With the coming to power the Congress-led United Progressive Alliance (UPA), the expectations and calculations of media were ripe that same Governor with and RSS background would get worse treatment if they failed to tender their resignations to the President of India. The Center, on July 2004, sacked the four Governors of UP, Haryana, Goa and Gujarat on the' ground of safronisation. The BJP, the opposition party accused the Congress of politicising the Governor's post. The central Government acknowledged that "a different ideology" from that of the UPA Government was the core ground for their sacking.[1] It was its a precautionary measure. The BJP's protest was lavid, accept that the fact that the party itself was guilty of the very same politicisation when it was in power. The BJP while claiming to be 'a party of difference' never cared to uphold the ethos of India's Constitution. In this regard the appointment of S.S. Bhandari, an RSS leader turned Gujarat Governor, faced no problem with Modi's handling of the communal riots is the case in point.[2]

The removal of Rajasthan's Governor Madan Lal Khurana, was very much on cards and he was indirectly pressurised to put in his papers, as the Governor's role too has been of pro-active in terms of managing *Gharib Sunvayi* programme through the Raj Bhawan. The Governor has become an eyésore for hearing the problems of the poor. The Congress ever since he started using the Raj Bhawan. The Governor publicly reiterated not to resign on his own, giving the ground, "what wrong I have done so that I must stepdown".

The Lucknow bench of Allahabad High Court is presently seized of a PIL challenging the dismissal of Vishnu Kant Shastri from the post Governor of UP on the ground that it was against the basic structure of the constitution and violation of the Center-state relations. The new incumbent T.V. Rajeshwar Rao has already taken the oath.

As regards the implementation of the UPA Government's imminent plan to remove some Governors of a RSS background appointed by the Vajpayee Government, the former President of India, R. Venkatraman is reported to have reacted that the PM's advice to the President on the recall of Governors "is binding". He has cited a 1981 order of the Supreme Court of India which has given the ruling that removal of Governors cannot be challenged in the courts on any ground. Such exercise has been treated as decision of political nature. Likewise, while initiating a discussion on the issue in the Lok Sabha on 13th July, 2004, the leader of the opposition, L.K. Advani vehemently castigated the UPA Government that the removing of four Governors on the basis of ideology was an outrage on the parliamentary system and it would "weaken the federal structure". He demanded a "review of the decision with an open mind", urging the Government to accept the recommendations of the Sarkaria Commission. The procedure for removal of Governors should be the same as that of their appointment as was suggested by the Venkatachalliah Commission.

When Venkatraman was President, the V.P. Singh Government, propped up by the BJP and the Left, had removed many Governors appointed by the previous Congress regime. The other notable removals of Governors took place when the Janata Party Government took over after the Emergency and later when Mrs. Indira Gandhi returned to power in 1980. Even the NDA regime recalled two Governors. Sacking of Ms. Fathima Beevi is the most glaring case.

"The Article 156 of the Constitution specifically declares that the Governors hold the office during the pleasure of the President. *"Pleasure of the President"* is not of the individual but on the advise of the prime minister. The President can't recall or appoint a Governor without the recommendation of the PM. So long as the person is the Prime Minister, his advise to the President on the issue of appointing or recalling the Governors is binding. Our president APJ Abdul Kalam is reported to have consulted his advisors and constitutional experts as the UPA Government has conveyed to him its intention to recommend recall of some Governors. And he acted accordingly despite the strong protest by the BJP-led NDA.

On whether Governors can be recalled before they completed their five-year term, Venkatraman said: "Even the appointment of Governors to a five-year term is clearly subject to the provision that they will hold the office during the pleasure of the President". Brushing aside BJP's protests, the Centre asserted that it could replace Governors. The Government also said that the NDA should not have appointed RSS activists to Raj Bhavans. "If anyone says that replacing of Governors was not within the ambit of Constitution, then they should go and seek a refresher course about the law of the land". It was stated minister of state for home Sriprakash Jaiswal in a Press Conference. On the other hand, the former PM, A.B. Vajpayee in his blistering attack on the Government said in Lucknow on 3rd July 2004 that the UPA Government's exercise of sacking of four Governors has reduced the position of Governor to that of a daily wages work. It is a blow to democracy.

MEANING OF THE 'UNION'

A study of the institution of Governor should lead us to more fundamental questions, like the location of states in the Indian Union and, the rationale, role and location of Governors on the Indian politico-constitutional stage. In our assessment of the role of Governor, many of us are guided by the belief that India is a federal polity. Even if one avoids the Wheareian cliche of terming India a quasi-federation, it is difficult to define the Indian political system in strict federal terms-incorporation of the principles of autonomy of states and division of powers in the Constitution notwithstanding. The eschewal of the word federation for *"Union"* to define Indian polity in the Constitution was not inadvertant but deliberate. The framers of the Constitution should not be faulted for visualising a strong Centre and relatively weak states in the Union of India as their aim was to dispel the centrifugal forces that might have been encouraged by Partition. According to the constitution experts, India was a federal polity with unitary features or a unitary polity with federal features. Dr. Ambedkar had put all doubts to rest by declaring in the Constitution Assembly that howsoever the Indian polity was defined, states in India were indeed subordinate to the Central Government.

Second, the Indian federation, unlike the US, was formed not through a treaty among the federating units, but through devolution of power upon the states by a powerful Centre. Thus, this very process had rendered the states, as Ambedkar had rightly conceded, subordinate status.

Once a subordinate position of the states was conceded in the Constituent Assembly, it is difficult to accept that the decision of their head of state was not guided by this fact. It would, at the same time, be unfair to the framers of the Constitution to deny that they still struggled hard to create an institution of head of state that would be dependent more on the Constitution than on the Centre for the discharge of its functions. The Constituent Assembly debates clearly reflect this concern. T.T. Krishnamachari, for example, aired the sentiments of most members of the Assembly, cutting across party lines, when he explicitly disclaimed that "we in the House want the future Governor who is to be nominated by the President to be in any sense an agent of the Central Government, I would like that point to be made very clear because such an idea finds no place in the scheme of Government we envisage for the future".[3]

It is pertinent to mention that both the Governors, S.M. Krishna and Sushil Kumar Shinde, have expressed their keen desire to re-enter into politics. Edged out by rivals and the consequences of assembly elections in Karnataka and Maharashtra, the Congress High Command rehabilitated them by making the Governors of Karnataka and Maharashtra, respectively. These former Chief Ministers are not happy with the ornate Raj Bhawans. Sadly, both the leading national political parties have followed the same pattern in the Governor's appointments.

The debates in the Constituent Assembly are only reflective of the concern of the members, it is more important to see what actually emerged out of these debates. Not only was appointment of Governor to be through nomination by the President (read Central Government), the process of selection of persons for the office was kept informal and flexible. Though the Constituent Assembly was unanimous that eminent persons not likely to play party politics would be selected for this office, no formal procedure, with built in safeguards against possible abuse was provided.

And while the Constitution laid down elaborate procedures for the removal of the Attorney-General and the Chief Election Commissioner from office, a Governor, the constitutional head of state, could be easily removed by a Presidential decree. In fact, the Indian National Congress, the largest party in the Constituent Assembly, seemed to be in a mood to force issue on the question of nominated Governors. The motive behind this procedure was to maintain the national integration. That was a different history that the Congress leaders in power essentially favoured a subordinate Governor in order to dominate the states from New Delhi. In fact, the impact of partition led the Congress party to opt for weaker states *vis-a-vis* the centre. And, a nominated Governor fitted in well with this scheme. The Constitution Assembly debates reflected a deep concern over possible misuse of this institution in future knowing well the inherent weaknesses behind the role of Governor, as a custodian of the Constitution in the states. There is no need to mention of the key instances of misuse of the office in 1952 in Madras state and Kerala in 1959 as bad precedents. The post-1967 scenario is different from those two instances only to the extent that the abuse of the institution of Governor became more brazen in the face of crumbling Congress hegemony. This trend setter unfortunately, was followed by the non-Congress Governments in 1990s including the NDA Government in spite of the fact that the coalition politics era has taken roots.

PRO-ACTIVE ROLE OF RAJASTHAN'S GOVERNOR

Governor Anshuman Singh decided not to remain confined within the portals of Raj Bhawan and would visit more and more drought hit areas of the state to know about the miseries of people. He held, "My visits will be frequent now and all of them would be surprise visits with the district administration not knowing about them. It is part of my job to oversee welfare of the people and nobody should try to read between the lines. Surprise visits give you an opportunity to interact with people directly". The Governor, an appointee of the BJP Government, surprised the Ashok Gehlot Government by visiting villages of Jaipur and Tonk districts on November 9, 2002. His visit coincided with the Congress chief ministers' conclave at Mount Abu where the Centre was criticised for not providing adequate assistance to the drought-hit states.

The Governor said, "I have been telling that over dependence on Centre for assistance will not solve the problem. The state will have to generate its own resources to fight the drought and provide work in the relief works started by the Government". The Governor revived the Governor's Relief Fund after 26 years. The fund started receiving donations under this head from generous people and organisations. Maintaining his image of a pro-active constitutional head of the state, the state Governor continued his 'surprise visits' to several drought-affected villages in Jaipur, Bikaner, Tonk and other areas to personally supervise the implementation of famine relief works being run by the state machinery. Defending his activism of visiting famine relief works, the Governor maintaines, "my activism is nothing like that, whether it was Gujarat earthquake, Kargil war or Rajasthan famine I always extended my cooperation in mitigating people's sufferings. My visits make official machinery remain active and officials remain vigilant in performing their duties of helping the people in distress.

It may be recalled that the Governor revived a parallel a Governor's Relief Fund since 1975 for which he organised a '*Ram Katha*' by star preacher Murari Bapu in Jaipur to collect Rs. 1.50 crore in January 2003. In his comment on the revival of a Fund, the Governor in a public conference said that the fund had reduced his dependence on the state Government in helping the people in distress. As such the '*Ram Katha*' was reported to have been linked with the assembly results of Gujarat poll, 2002.

There was a hue and cry at the organising the '*Ram Katha*' by the Governor as this was the breach ethos of secularism followed by India's Constitution. The NGOs like the PUCL and Sarva Seva Sangh demanded that the Governor be 'sacked' for 'promoting Hindutva' and compromised the secular character of the Constitution. The draught relief was the only excuse to hold '*Ram Katha*' to promote Hindutva. To this effect, a resolution was passed on 29th December 2002, demanding dismissal of the Government.

Rajasthan's chief minister Ashok Gehlot, who was said to be against the idea of Governor Anshuman Singh co-hosting the *Ram Katha* recital, organised by Raj Bhawan, made a surprise appearance at the *Amroodon Ka Bagh,* the venue of the *Katha.* Two of his ministers—Shanti Kumar Dhariwal and C.P. Joshi—also attended the discourse. The chief minister listened to a discourse of the Ramayana by well-known religious preacher Morari Bapu along with the Governor. Later, he congratulated Morari Bapu and participated in the *aarti* ceremony. Vice-President Bhairon Singh Shekhawat also attended the discourse. He appealed to the people to donate generously in the *dan patras* put up in the *pandal.* The chief minister attended the *Ram Katha,* despite opposition by various NGOs and the Left parties.[4]

In fact, the Congress did not wish to annoy the devotees of Lord Ram (all the Hindu voters), after experiencing the humiliating defeats of the party in the Gujarat elections and the loss of all the three seats in the by-elections in Rajasthan. He was to face the assembly elections of 2003. After Gehlot's visit to this religious discourse, a large number of Congress leaders and workers attended the *Ram Katha*, taking the impression that every person has right to follow any religion under Article 25 and the Governor is a person who enjoys this kind of liberty. Hence, the '*Ram Katha*' should not be linked with the poll results of Gujarat 2002.

Likewise, the state Governor also appealed everyone including NIRs to contribute for the protection of cows and other cattle population of the state and inspected a number of gaushalas and cattle-camps for fodder camps to ensure their conservation. On the part of Governor, efforts were made to distribute food grains and blankets to the poor and infirm.

N.C. JAIN : 'NOT A RUBBER STAMP'

In June, 2003, the state Governor Anshuman Singh retired and the name of N.C. Jain as the Rajasthan's new Governor was announced by the NDA Government. The Governor designate of Rajasthan, said in Jabalpur (M.P.) on 5th June, 2003, "I shall not cross the *Lakshman Rekha* while discharging my gubernatorial duties", but he made it clear to the Times News Network that "I will not be a rubber stamp upon the whims and fancies of the state Government." He further asserted that he being a legal luminary in the MP High Court, he was not averse to using his good contact with PM Vajpayee and Dy. PM L.K. Advani to help the state by facing the drought related problems. (*The Times of India*, New Delhi, 6/5/2003). They were his role models to the 'Trishul diksha' in Rajasthan. He said : "The trishul episode is a cultural question for VHP leader Praveen Togadia and the law and situation is the responsibility of the state Government". The issue in his opinion, was outside the purview of the powers entrusted in the Governor by the Indian Constitution.

CENTRAL RULE UNDER DURESS (?)

In an interesting development, Arunachal Pradesh Governor VC Pande, who had recommended central rule (Article 356) in the state after dissolution of the assembly on 7th July, informed President A.P.J. Abdul Kalam that he had signed his recommendation "under duress" and sought its withdrawal. In a letter to the President he said, "I regret to say that the signature in the said report was obtained under duress. Not only myself but also all my staff including the secretary were put under tremendous mental and physical pressure by all ex-MLAs and their political workers who stormed into my chamber and remained there gheraoing me for more than five hours". Pande further said, "A prepared report was placed before me and I was asked to sign the same. I therefore request his excellency to ignore the earlier report purported to have been sent under my signature".

The 60-member assembly in Arunachal Pradesh was dissolved on the recommendation by BJP-led United Democratic Front (UDP) coalition Government headed by Apang. This step was taken to stem possible desertion from its ranks in the wake of the downsizing of the ministry which set off churnings in the ruling coalition. The Governor of the state, therefore, had to recommend imposition of President's Rule in the state. But in a new turn of political crisis, the former CM of the Congress party, Mukut Mithi demanded removal of the physically unfit Governor, V.C. Pandey. The issue caused a storm in Parliament on the constitutional status of Governor, as hijacking of the Raj Bhavan by some agitated legislators who gheraoed the Governor and his staff, presented yet another case of politics of criminalisation of our time. The Governor was forced to sign a letter to the President recommending central rule after he had to dissolve the assembly of Arunachal Pradesh.

This is not a new development as in the past, some Raj Bhavans have witnessed hostile and abusive outbursts by dissatisfied legislators who staked their claim to rule, but the Governor concerned did not budge. Even former President B.D. Jatti was subjected to ridicule during a political turmoil. Till now, only legislators with uncertain loyalties were kept as hostages before a party was to seek a confidence vote. But they were kept in comfortable confines and offered luxuries of their choice. However, the Arunachal example has given a new, though strange direction, to an ever accused politics which surely demonstrates not only criminal impatience but unparliamentary temperaments of the law-makers. The incident, has to be seen and resolved through the aid of the

Constitution. Can the Centre accept the recommendation of the Governor made under duress? Or, should it ignore it?[5]

The Centre was seen in a dilemma. The Governor's "recommendation" to impose Article 356(1)(c) stipulates partial President's rule which does not have the 356 effect. It says: "The President may by proclamation make such incidental and consequential provisions as appear to the President to be necessary or desirable for giving effect to the objects of the proclamation, including provisions for suspending in whole or in part the operation of any provisions of this Constitution relating to any body or authority in the state." The Centre cannot ignore the circumstances under which Pande accepted the minority chief minister's advice to dissolve the assembly three months before its term was due to expire.

Under the circumstances created by the downsizing of the cabinet, the Governor could have either allowed political forces to decide who would be the CM and or how long, or in order to preempt bargaining of portfolios and perks three months before the election, dissolve the assembly. The dissolution of the assembly has no doubt upset the Congress. The CM, now in a minority, would head the caretaker administration when elections take place in the north-eastern state. It must be remembered that being the CM at the time of elections does not necessarily pay. We have seen the fate of the chief ministers of Rajasthan, Madhya Pradesh and Chhattisgarh during the December 2003 assembly polls. They had to go.

In political outset of federalism, the office, used efficiently, can be a tool for monitoring and fixing state policy. The Governor after all, is the Executive Head, and this role cannot be left to the state's Chief Secretary. Both in terms of Governor as the head of the state and the chancellor of universities he should be made accountable for his actions and role. The office offers the opportunity to seed up development and clear up the Augean stables of babudan, for which the downsizing of peons, army of servants, drivers, malis, etc. attached with the Raj Bhavan should go. The word 'Raj' should be taken away with, which, we have borrowed from the British rule. During the British Raj, the Governor was the Centre's representative in the province. He used to reign over the provenance as the Centre's agent in a regal splendor of Raj Bhawan. Our past experience has justified that the office is still an 'agent' of the Centre and he has always been a threat to the federal character of the state, specifically in the shift of coalition model. The current crisis in the Arunachal Pradesh is the latest example of the 'lynchpin of the constitutional apparatus in the state' being accused of being partisan. The Sarkaria Commission recommended that the post should be occupied by persons who have not taken too great a part in politics and, particularly in the recent past is still relevant. In this regard two aspects are pertinent to point out that in the era of L.P.G. and the rise of regional parties (i.e. the multi-party system and coalition politics), our federal polity has witnessed a change in which the Centre-state relations could be harmonious, provided the office of the Governor is further democratized and made accountable. It must honour the state 'autonomy', guaranteed in the Constitution. As per the ruling of the Supreme Court (AIR 1979 SC 1109) *in the Hargovind versus Raghukul Tilak* case, the office of the Governor is not under the subordination of the Centre. It is constitutionally an independent office. It is wrong notion to regard him as an 'agent'.[6]

MAKING GOVERNOR ACCOUNTABLE

As the BJP's President, L.K. Advani was the first non-Congress leader who favoured to moot an amendment in the Constitution to make Governors answerable to parliament, or to the state assemblies. In his opinion, this was only office in the Constitution which is not yet accountable to any representative forum. The President of India can be impeached, vote of confidence can be brought against the Prime Minister, Judges and Election Commissioners can be impeached, but the Governors are immuned from it. This anomalous situation needs to be corrected constitutionally so as to restore the dignity of the office which was conceived by founding fathers of the Constitution. In fact, the conduct of the political Governors in the past years have devalued the institutions of the Governors.[7] Any delay in reviewing the issue might further hurt the dignity of the office of the Governor, because the very word 'Governor' smacks of British colonialism and sounds undemocratic status.

To conclude, as per the Indian Constitution, the Governor is the chief executive of the state appointed by the President of India as per Article 156 of the Constitution, subject to the pleasure of the president, the Governor shall hold office for a term of five years. Whatever reason the Union Government may invent in this regard, the recent sacking of four Governors is unwarranted, malafide, perverse and unconstitutional. The said Governors have done nothing wrong to lose the president's pleasure. It is reported that those Governors have been sacked for their RSS background. But the RSS is not a banned organisation. Besides, it is puzzling that the same Congress party which is running a coalition Government in Kerala with the Muslim League cannot tolerate Governors with an RSS background. It reflects the example how Mrs. Indira Gandhi had superseded judges and defended her act by saying that she wanted to have a committed judiciary. Now the UPA Government at the Centre wants committed Governors. Will the Centre also remove vice-president Shekhawat for the same reason?

The present tendency to appoint politicians who have been defeated at the hustings as Governors is not a healthy practice. It is not advisable to appoint Chief Ministers/ Ministers as Governors or *vice-versa* after defeat in the elections. Once a person has held the post of a Governor, he should not be considered for the re-appointment either as Chief Minister or a Minister.

In order to seek the malaise, the Sarkaria Commission suggested to appoint non-party Governors who have a long experience of public life and administration. The Sarkaria Commission on Centre-state relations was convinced that much of the criticism against the Governors could have been avoided had a fool-proof selection procedure been laid down. Most of the complaints that reached the commission related to the quality and standard of those appointed as Governors. The commission observed, "Discarded and disgruntled politicians from the party in power in the Union, who cannot be accommodated elsewhere, get appointed. Such persons, while in office, tend to function as agents of the Union Government rather than as impartial constitutional functionaries".[8] Though the Indian political scenario has undergone many changes since Justice R.S. Sarkaria commented on the matter, the suggestions made by him are still valid and relevant and could, if adopted, go some way towards restoring dignity to the stature and office of the Governor. The Commission was of the view that a Governor should be an eminent person from outside the state and without an active political career at the time of appointment.[9]

Against the background, that the Governor is expected to preserve, protect and defend the Constitution. The Sarkaria Commission argued for continuing with Governors, but clarified that they should be "persons who have not taken too great a part in politics generally, and particularly in the recent past". A decade later, the National Commission to Review the Working of the Constitution supported Justice Sarkaria's recommendations with the observations; "By and large, the picture has not been an inspiring one. This is because very often active politicians, politicians defeated at the polls and men lacking in integrity and fairness and individuals not possessing an understanding of the constitutional system, persons who were more interested in their personal career than public good were chosen for this office".[10] For the revival of the old glory and dignity of the office, it has recommended to change the mode of his appointment, thus doing away with the impression that the holder of the office become Centre's man. It has proposed to form a committee consisting of the President, Vice-President, Prime Minister, Chief Minister and such other key persons in order to choose the Governor.

OUR GOVERNORS : NOT CENTRE'S AGENT

The Governor's rule during the single party rule hardly stirred controversies. But the rise of coalition politics during 1970s onwards set the constitutional limits of our Governors drastically against their discretion, confirming the truth that our Governors are the eyes and ears to the Centre, but not the agent at all.

The way political developments in Meghalaya presented the malaise role of Governor S.S. Sidhu in the formation of new Government against the spirit of our federal system *vis-a-vis* the rise of regional parties as players in state politics. His role recalled the events of Nagaland, twice in Goa and Bihar that tarnished the image of Governors. As regards the role of S.S. Sidhu, he administered the oath of office and secrecy to the leader of Meghalaya Progressive Alliance (MPA) on 19th March, 2008, as the next new CM in the wake of resignation of Congress veteran, D.D. Lapang. Lapang stepped down ahead of the scheduled trust vote in the 60 members state assembly, having failed to, muster majority support, admitting that the Congress could not gather the necessary support of 31 members in the House and therefore he decided to resign without the floor test. He drove to the Governor's residence after a meeting of the Congress legislature party.

Lapang's resignation given to Sidhu ended one of the shortest terms by any Government in Meghalaya, and paved the way for the MPA, headed by the Nationalist Congress Party (NCP) and the United Democratic Party (UDP) to form the new Government with the support of 31 members. It may be recalled that the Congress had emerged as the largest single party in the March 3 poll, 2008, bagging 25 seats, and had enlisted the support of three independent members. Still, the party fell short of three legislators.

Of course, Meghalaya misadventure sullied the image of Congress leadership for blatantly manipulating the Raj Bhavan in the formation of Government. A similar situation cropped up in Jharkhand in 2005 when Governor Sibtey Razi ignored the strength (Numbers) of the BJP, JD(U) and invited JJM Chief, Shibu soren to form a new Ministry. He also failed to prove his majority and Razi had to invite BJPs Arjun Munda to form the alternative Government.

It may be noted here that the role of the Governor in this state was challenged in the Supreme Court of India by the king maker of Meghalaya politics (P.A. Sangma) but the court refused to take up matter on the plea that it was related to a political nature arbitrary decisions of Governors have been challenged before the Supreme Court. It delivered stinging judgments, setting them aside. The answers to such questions were provided by the Supreme Court in no uncertain terms in *Har Govind Pant* v. *Dr. Raghukul Tilak Judgment* [(1979) 3 SCC

458]. Despite conceding that a Governor was appointed by the President on the recommendations of the Council of Ministers headed by the Prime Minister, the apex court had said, 'It does not make the Governor an employee or servant of the Government of India'. In this context, probably former President A.P.J. Abdul Kalam, while addressing the conference of Governors in June 2005, said: "While there are many checks and balances provided by the Constitution, the office of the Governor has been bestowed with the independence to rise above the day-to-day politics and override the compulsions emanating either from the central system or the state system." Governors who rise above the day-to-day politics and overcome the guidance from the Centre, however, are a rare breed as it is extremely unlikely that a present day Governor would share the SC's view in the above cited *Raghukul Tilak* case, that he is not amenable to the directions of the Government of India nor is he accountable to them for the manner in which he carries out his functions and duties. He is an independent constitutional office which is not subject to the control of the Government of India". In fact, the general willingness of the Governors to give up independence and succumb to the diktats of the Centre stems mainly from the manner in which they are rewarded with the constitutional post. Barring honourable exceptions, posts have been given either as largesse to retired politicians or as favours to pliant and superannuated bureaucrats or generals from Armed forces. The history of previous decade speaks the truth. Probably, the deficiencies in those traits or display time and again, have made the Supreme Court read malafide motives into the decisions of Governors, starting from P. Venkatasubbaiah, who dismissed S.R. Bommai in Karnataka in 1989, to Buta Singh, who prevented the Nitish Kumar-led coalition from staking claim in Bihar in 2005.

An Activist Role

Rajasthan Governor Shailendra Kumar Singh, who was on a visit to border districts of Jaisalmer and Barmer paid a surprise visit to Bhadrej village in Barmer where people were opposing rand acquisition for a lignite-based power project. He was to visit Munabao from where Thar Express train to

Pakistan operates, but his visit to Bhadrej was not scheduled. He decided to go to Bhadrej after villagers in Bothia and Bhadrej submitted a memorandum to him at the Circuit House on Monday opposing acquisition of 5,70,000 bighas of land for mining activities for setting up a power plant by a private company. At Bhadrej, Governor met officials of the private company and asked them about what rehabilitation packages were offered to villagers whose land was acquired. He asked officials of the company to ensure that villagers get proper price for the acquired land.

At Barmer, Governor inquired about land deals in border areas that took place in recent months. He sought details of the land deals from the district collector and sought to know how land in border areas was sold without knowledge of the district administration. The Governor on a visit to Jaisalmer surprised the district administration as well, when he went to the sub-registrar's office without any prior notice to see for himself papers and documents relating to recent large scale land deals in border district. Of course, the Rajasthan Government had ordered an inquiry to probe how large chunk of land were bought by private parties. Revenue minister Ram Narayan Dudi expressed surprise over the way the Governor went to the sub-registrar's office in Jaisalmer to check the records of land deals in border areas. The Minister said the Governor was aware of the fact that the state Government had initiated inquiries into the sale of land in Barmer and Jaisalmer. The land agitators and NGOs appreciated such an initiative by the Governor against the sales of border land, putting our security concerns at risk.

Visitor's Constitutional Immunity

The Supreme Court of India held on 13th Feb., 2007 that the President of India, who is also visitor of eminent Indian universities, is not answerable to a court of law for his actions, but he would have to adhere to the principle of nature justice while sacking a professor and the minimum the visitor would have to do is to issue a show cause notice to the person proceeded against so as to bring the action in consonance with the principle of nature justice.[11] The writing petition is related to BHU, UP which was moved the apex court by filing a special leave petition after the Allahabad High Court dismissed the writ petition of sacked teacher, Ashok Sonkar.

While the President acts as Visitor of reputed universities, the Governor, by his office, is the *ex-officio* chancellor of all the universities functioning in the state. Both these constitutional functionaries, by virtue of Article 361 of the Constitution, have been made immune from court proceedings. For instance, Article 361(1) says : "The President, or the Governor or Rajpramukh of a state shall not be answerable to any court for the exercise and performance of the powers and duties of his office or for any act done or purporting to be done by him in exercise and performance of those powers and duties". Further, Article 361(4) says, "No civil proceedings in which relief is claimed against the President, or the Governor of a state, shall be instituted during his term of office in any court in respect of any act done or purporting to be done by him in his personal capacity, whether before or after he entered upon his office. . . "

While under Article 361(1) one can debate that the immunity was restricted to the acts done as President or Governor. Article 361(4) appeared to clinch the argument in favour of the constitutional heads when it makes them immune from civil proceedings even for their personal acts. For example, Section 5 of the Banaras Hindu University Act, 1915, says, "the President shall be the Visitor of the University" and vests in him supervisory powers.

The Supreme Court verdict would be important keeping in view the question that arises in the case—whether the President acting as Visitor could claim immunity for his wrongful decisions from civil proceedings under Article 361 of the Constitution.

Visitor's Constitutional Immunity

The Supreme Court of India held on 13th Feb. 2007 that the President, who is also visitor of eminent Indian Universities, is not answerable to a court of law for his actions but he would have to adhere to the principle of nature justice while sacking a professor and the minimum the visitor would have to do is to issue a show cause notice to the person proceeded against so as to bring the action in consonance with the principle of nature justice. The writ petition is related to BHU, UP which was moved the apex court by filing a special Leave petition after the Allahabad High Court dismissed the writ petition of sacked teacher, Ashok Sonkar.

While the President acts as Visitor of reputed universities, the Governor; by his office, is the *ex-officio* chancellor of all the universities functioning in the state. Both these constitutional functionaries, by virtue of Article 361 of the Constitution, have been made immune from court proceedings.

Article 361(1) says, "The President, or the Governor or rajpramukh of a state shall not be answerable to any court for the exercise and performance of the powers and duties of his office or for any act done or purporting to be done by him in exercise and performance of those powers and duties".

Further; Article 361(4) says, "No civil proceedings in which relief is claimed against the President, or the Governor of a state, shall be instituted during his term of office in any court in respect of any act done or purporting to be done by him in his personal capacity, whether before or after he entered upon his office. . ."

While under Article 361(1) one can debate that the immunity was restricted to the acts done as President or Governor, Article 361(4) appeared to clinch the argument in favour of the constitutional heads when it makes them immune from civil proceedings even from their personal acts. Section 5 of the Banaras Hindu University Act, 1915, says, "the President of India shall be the Visitor of the University" and vests in him supervisory powers.

The Supreme Court verdict would be important keeping in view the question that arises in the case—whether the President acting as Visitor could claim immunity from civil proceedings under Article 361 of the Constitution.

Notes and References

1. See the Proceedings of the Lok Sabha dated 13th July, 2004.
2. N.S. Gehlot, New Changellenges to Indian Politics (New Delhi, Deep & Deep Publications Pvt. Ltd., 2003), p. 410.

3. Vide Ajay K. Mehta's article, "The Governor's office is Constitutionally a Political One", *The Times of India*, April 6, 1989, p. 16.
4. Manoj's comments in *The Times of India*, New Delhi, Jan. 19, 2003, p. 3.
5. Rakesh Bhatnagar, "Is Recommendation Made Under Duress Acceptable?", *The Times of India*, 12th July, 2004, p. 9.
6. N.S. Gehlot's, State Governors in India, *Trend & Issues*, New Delhi, Gitanjali Publishing House, 1985.
7. It was stated in a press meet programme at Hyderabad, AP., *The Hindustan Times*, New Delhi, Jan. 9, 1990.
8. L. Faria and R.I. Menaria, Sarkaria Commission Report and Centre-state Relations, Agra, Sahitya Bhavan, 1990, Chapter 5, p. 57.
9. J.C. Johari, Indian Government and Politics, (Jalandhar, Vishal Publications, 2001) 17th Chapter, p. 407.
10. Nirmalendu Bikash Rakshit, "Constitution Review Committee and the Governor", *Economic and Political Weekly*, Mumbai, April 13, 2002 (Volume xxxv/15), pp. 1397-98.
11. *The Times of India Views*, New Delhi, 15.2.2008, p. 13.

CHAPTER

Threats to Independence of Judiciary

Need for Reforms

Focusing on a keen tussal between Judiciary and Political Executive (wherein the latter, according to the author, seems to be making concerted efforts to clip independence of the former and retaliatory steps thereto emanating from both the camps), the author covers in his discussion a chain of events. These start from controversy on powers of Chief Justice of India (CJI) regarding appointment of Judges to superior courts (two cases decided by Supreme Court on it in 1993 and 1998), admission of Public Interest Litigation cases by Supreme Court, selection of CJI and his tenure, accountability of judges, move to set-up National Judicial Commission, etc. The author argues in the epilogue the need to safeguard Judiciary's independence as well as creativity and endorses the line of action delineated in the Jodhpur address of the present CJI.

INTRODUCTION

"The subjects that loomed largest in the minds of Assembly members when framing the judicial provisions", said Granville Austin, "were the independence of the courts and two closely related issues, the powers of the Supreme Court and Judicial review. The Assembly went to great lengths to ensure that the courts could be independent, devoting more hours of debate to this subject than to almost any other aspect of the provisions. If the beacon of the judiciary was to remain bright, the Court must be above reproach, free from coercion and from political influence".[1]

Are the hopes of founding fathers fulfilled today or there is gradual and constant effort to cow-down judiciary? Courts today have to function with neglected dimensions, in atmosphere of criticism and threats. Our judicial institution on which lies the basic fabric of democratic norm is crumbling. Collapse of judiciary is due to both external and internal pressures. Obviously the former is much more greater.

Indeed, the Indian judiciary was seen to be an arm of the social revolution, upholding the equality and dignity of men that the people of India suffered long during the colonial days, but it has not been gained as yet.

Appointment of Judges

Chief Justice's Role in Appointment of Judges

The BJP's coalition Government led by Atal Behari Vajpayee raised certain doubts on the *modus operandi* of appointments of judges in the Supreme Court and High Courts and the case was referred to the Supreme Court for opinion. It was made clear by the apex court that whatever the nine judge bench said in 1993 was the law (i.e., laying down the guidelines for appointment and transfers of judges) and that the court was not going to review or reconsider the 1993 judgement. The Union Government through Article 143 of the Constitution has sought the court's opinion on nine issues. Important issues awaiting the court's opinion are: (a) Whether the Chief Justice of India (CJI) is not obliged to comply with the norms and requirements of the consultation process in making his recommendation to the Government; (b) whether any recommendation made by the Chief Justice of India without complying with the norms and consultation process are binding upon the Government; (c) whether the expression "consultation with the CJI" in Articles 217(1) and 222(1) requires consultation with a plurality of judges in the formation of the opinion of the Chief Justice of India or does the sole individual opinion of the Chief Justice of India constitute consultation within the meaning of the said Article. The decision incurred the displeasure of the political class. It was seen against the supremacy of Parliament.

The purpose of this article is to paint a picture as to how the Indian judiciary is under attack, and how it is moving towards collapse, because the Rule of Law is in danger and thereby the judiciary is surrounded by threats—both by internal and external factors.

JUDICIARY-POLITICAL EXECUTIVE TUSSLE

In the previous decades, politics of supersession in April 1973, in which Justice A.N. Ray was superseded by his three colleagues while appointing him as Chief Justice of India, appointment of *ad hoc* Judges *vis-a-vis* non-confirmation and non-revision of judges' salary, politics transfer, activist role of judiciary in public welfare, and so on marked by successfulness of the executive to terrorise the judiciary, in a bid not to dare go against the policies and philosophy of the party in power at the Centre. Many judges were punished for their strong judgements against the Executive, leading the Judiciary to fall a victim of executive-legislative control.[2] Since then, the forward looking philosophy is meant to looking forward tendency. The issues are: Should Judges follow the mandate given by the electorate to a party of majority in Parliament? Does the Constitution of India stipulate decisions of court according to the Governmental philosophy? Does the Constitution expect committed Judges?[3]

The previous experience in terms of the tussle between the Executive and Judiciary is enough to confirm that political class does not want the Judiciary to be an independent institution. They wanted such a Judiciary which agreed with their views. The same tendency has again gained ground in the wake of Judicial activism *vis-a-vis* the petitions filed against Governmental agencies through Public Interest Litigation (PIL), enabling the Judiciary to enlarge its jurisdiction over the Executive and the Legislature. The battle is between political supremacy and judicial legitimation. Judicial libertarianism launched by the Supreme Court of India has prepared a new humanitarian jurisprudence and PIL has put the Executive wing in an awkward position.

Fresh Controversy over Judges' Appointments

In 1998, a fresh controversy cropped up over appointment of seven judges to the Supreme Court of India. Of course, the approval of the names sent a signal that there was no rift between the Chief Justice of India and the President because 'merit' continued to guide those appointments. But the relationship between the two seemed to be tense over not selecting Dalit, SC and ST candidates as judges if found meritorious. President's noting was made on the file of the appointment. Commenting on the reported controversy over the President's noting regarding the need to appoint the Scheduled Castes/Scheduled Tribes and Dalit candidates as judges, former Delhi High Court Chief Justice Rajinder Sachar said, "President can make recommendation. After all he is not a rubber stamp. But such recommendations should have been made across the table".[4] He was of the view that it was a mere recommendation for giving due consideration to a section of deprived class. It should not be construed as the Presidential advice to make reservation for them in the judiciary. As a lawyer R.K. Anand said, "Only merit matters in selecting the judges. There can't be any other consideration". With the approval of those names for appointments and transfers, the competence and merit continued to be the guiding line.

The controversy regarding SCs and STs quota in higher judiciary took a new turn when the Chairman of the National Commission for SCs and STs, Dileep Singh Bhuria, raised a demand of reservation for SCs/STs in the higher echelons of the Indian Judiciary. He observed: "It is unfortunate that after 50 years of Independence, the Supreme Court does not have even a single SC/ST judge at the moment, and out of more than 400 judges in various High Courts, there are only thirteen SC and three ST judges. Obviously, the situation is not good for the country and cannot be allowed to continue".[5] It may be recalled that in the history of Independent India, there has been only one SC Judge in the Supreme Court of India (Retd. Justice K. Ramaswamy) and no ST Judge till date. India needs a more socially balanced judiciary keeping in view the instances of injustice, discriminations and atrocities on innocent, poor and backward human beings.

Choice of Chief Justice and His Tenure

Former Chief Justice of India, Justice M.M. Punchhi has suggested a longer tenure for those holding the office of the Chief Justice. Justice Punchhi said that the age limit of 55 years for being considered for elevation to the Apex Court was good enough and there was no reason to reduce it except in rare cases of men of outstanding ability as had been done in the case of Justice Mohammed Hidayatullah, Justice P.N. Bhagwati, Justice Y.V. Chandrachud and Justice R.S. Pathak. But former Chief Justice of India, Justice J.S. Varma is of the opinion that the choice of Chief Justice of India should be made at the time of initial appointment to the Apex Court to ensure that only the persons having a "flawless background" occupy the highest office. It would be a travesty to the age limit for picking up a person as Chief Justice. He does not agree with the version of Justice Punchhi that a Chief Justice of India should have too long a tenure. Rather care should be taken at the time of making initial appointment to see that the tenure is at least two years. According to him, if a person appointed as a Judge is known to have infirmities in his character and becomes the Chief Justice at a later stage by virtue of seniority, it would be very bad for the judicial system as a whole.

Accountability of the Judges

In June 1997, the Committee on Judicial Accountability (COJA) underlined certain allegations against the nature of appointment of Justice M.M. Punchhi. It raised a question in its representation that those allegations should be looked into before he was appointed as the Chief Justice of India. He was to retire in January 1998. The same concern was publicly expressed by Fali S. Nariman.[6] The controversy rested on that the Judges should be accountable for their performance, and it was supported by the Bar Association of India in its resolution. Legal luminaries too have been of the opinion that India's superior judiciary must be made accountable and there should be transparency in its appointments. To this effect, COJA has favoured a constitutional amendment to set-up an independent National Judicial Commission which will be entrusted with the matter of appointment, removal and transfer of Judges. Such a body alone can ensure independence of the Judiciary. That is the purport of the draft bill finalised by the COJA and forwarded to the Government on March 9, 1997.

The course suggested by COJA has been necessitated by past experience, including supersession of Justices Shelat, Hagde and Grover in 1973 and repeated in 1977 by supersession of Justice H.R. Khanna. The important point to note is that there were no allegations against any of those Judges. Then came the case of Justice V. Ramaswamy who was found guilty of corruption by the Judicial Committee, but saved from being removed by the Congress (I) in Parliament at a time when the impeachment resolution was to be carried out by the Lok Sabha.

It is undeniable that a person or a body of persons may bring allegations of corruption against a public functionary, including a Judge. But it is nowhere contemplated that any person or a body of persons, other than the designated constitutional authorities may usurp the authority to sit in judgment and pronounce upon the charges and clear a delinquent judge. These are matters of grave public concern. These are matters that concern the right of the people to a clean and independent judiciary. In short, both aspects, accountability of the judiciary and transparency in its functioning should be taken note of.

Judicial Idealism: A Lesson

Under the Indian Constitution, a Judge of the High Court or the Supreme Court can be removed on the grounds of proved misbehaviour or incapacity. Physical incapacity, which disables a Judge from discharging his judicial functions, is a clear case. What is the position if a Judge inordinately delays delivering judgments? Recently, the Court of Appeal in England passed strictures on Justice Harman for his intolerable delay of 20 months in delivering judgment in the case of a Lincoln shire farmer who had brought a suit for negligence against a firm of accountants. And by the time judgment was pronounced, dismissing the farmer's case. Justice Harman had lost his trial notes. Reluctantly ordering a retrial, the Court of Appeal observed, "Conduct like this weakens public confidence in the whole judicial process. Left unchecked, it would be ultimately subversive of the Rule of Law". Expectedly, Justice Harman resigned.[7]

There are some Judges in our High Courts who have deliberately shown laxity in delivering judgments. There are also instances where judgments in the Supreme Court have been pronounced after a year or two, often forgetting or misunderstanding the submissions advanced by Counsel. And review petitions are almost invariably rejected in chambers. Worse is the failure of Judges to deliver judgements before retirement, necessitating rehearing of the cases. Who pays litigants the costs incurred in such cases?

Move to Set-up a National Judicial Commission

As judicial activism has assumed significance over other organs of Government—the Legislature and the Executive—the voice is raised to revive the old debate on the need for an expert panel to perform the difficult task of appointments. It is proposed that this Commission should have five members, comprising two Supreme Court Judges, a High Court Judge, a retired Supreme Court Judge and a lawyer from its Bar. The purpose of it would be to inspire confidence in the judicial system and its credibility and independence beyond doubt. The device, according to Soli J. Sorabjee, is to discipline the Judges, by providing Executive control over judicial appointments, and transfers. It appears that the above-cited suggestion aims at reverting the 1993 verdict of the Supreme Court.

The proposal of setting up a commission was first mooted by the Law Minister in I.K. Gujral Government and it is currently backed by the BJP-led Government at the Centre. The present Government proposes to review the 82nd Constitutional Amendment mooted in 1997, in a bid to revert to the pre-1993 position in the appointment and transfers of Judges and to regain the Executive's supremacy in this regard, though present Chief Justice of India A.S. Anand has registered opposition to such a move.

Like Justice A.S. Anand, Justice S.P. Bharucha and others have opposed the idea on the apprehension that it is merely an effort to share "Judicial case". Similarly, they have opposed to alter the present procedure for removal of Judges (impeachment). The judges should have the guarantee to function, without fear or favour. As soon as the power of removing the High Court or Supreme Court Judges is placed in the hands of the proposed National Judicial Commission, the procedure would be politicised. Here, it is worth-recalling that the need to have a National Judicial Commission was felt when the motion to in support of the proven case of misconduct was foiled when the ruling party at the Centre issued a whip asking its members to abstain from voting. By not casting their votes, the Congress succeeded in defeating the impeachment motion, which can only pass through if it carried a two-thirds majority vote. The attempt is now made to simplify the procedure through this Commission. Against this background, it is suggested that a provision in the impeachment may be added that MPs on motion of impeachment of a Judge would not be asked to vote on the basis of party whip. A party whip should be constitutionally barred.

EPILOGUE

Safeguarding Independence of Judiciary

As a matter of fact, Executive interference in the Judiciary's autonomy through setting up a National Judicial Commission would be a sad development, if it is enforced without a national debate. Hence, it should be deferred till national consensus is secured; otherwise it would revive the old phenomenon of the committed judiciary projected by Indira Gandhi, and the Judiciary had to step out of the Executive's shadows to retain its degree of independence. Any piece of legislation will pose a threat to this independence of Judiciary in the affairs of appointments and transfers. Judicial independence in the background of its activist role during the last decade has been a source of deep embarrassment for the political class as a whole.

The 1993 Supreme Court judgment, making the Chief Justice of India the sole arbiter in the matter was thought to be the necessary corrective to insulate the judiciary from Executive influence. But as experience shows, with the new system, the pendulum has only swung to the other extreme, causing unease among politicians. Though in the present system, the Chief Justice of India arrives at his decisions to appoint and transfer Judges in consultation with three senior most Judges of the apex court, the judiciary has not made full use of the potential freedom this arrangement provides. The virtual reversion to the old system, Khalap as Law Minister of V.P. Singh Government, prescribed which meant basing executive decisions on considerations of caste, region or political inclination, is unlikely to evoke a positive response from the Judges and the Bar. The Government, therefore, will be well advised to entrust the Judges' selection to a body of eminent persons of integrity and with impeccable public and professional record. Representatives to such a body should be selected through a self-regulatory mechanism. Creation of an autonomous Judicial Commission—comprising the Vice-President, the Speaker, the Leader of the Opposition, and the Chief Justice of India, among others—will not only save the process of judges' selection from political interference, but also enhance prestige of the judiciary.

Needless to say that it is the judiciary which has played a vital role in the life of people. It has been striving to improve people's life through its mandates regarding basic necessities of life, like clean air, education for all, better health care and dignity. This was possible because the judiciary has realised that being an important organ of the State, it has to act for the benefit of the people particularly when the other organs—Executive and Legislature—seem to be indifferent towards their social and constitutional obligations.

Priorities of Judicial Creativity

In this backdrop, "judicial creativity" which some cynics may describe as judicial activism or judicial adventurism, has found a permanent place in the justice administration system. But in order to ensure that it does not exceed its limitation in doing complete justice in matters affecting the public interest, the judiciary has to be extra cautious. In Justice Anand's words, "With a view to seeing that judicial activism does not become 'judicial adventurism' and lead a Judge going in pursuits of his own nations of justice, ignoring the limits of law, the bounds of his jurisdiction and the binding precedents the courts must act with proper restraint and self-discipline".[8] He further says: "The danger of the judiciary creating a multiplicity of rights without the possibility of adequate enforcement is a real one. It must be guarded against. The judiciary should not become an institution or mere form bereft of substance. There are real limits to what the judicial process should attempt to accomplish and the judiciary should resist the temptation to cross those limits. The decisions of the courts should be within the zone of juridical legitimacy".

However, the judiciary has to decide its agenda on the basis of the priorities. It has to be ready to deal with the requirements of the 21st Century. Clearing the backlog of staggering arrears in all the courts across the country need to be given its due attention. "Human hope has its limits and waiting endlessly is not possible in the current life style". If the judiciary fails to appreciate the human aspiration of quick justice, there is an imminent danger that the consumers of justice may resort to 'extra-judicial methods' to settle scores and seek redressal of grievances". For quick disposal of the pending cases, it is urgent that the judiciary must have its own financial autonomy to manage its own affairs and not look for Executive's help. It is equally important for its independence, because the biggest litigant of it is the Government. If the Government continues to have control over judiciary, administrative functioning of the judiciary is likely to be eroded. For clearing the backlogs, the need of the hour is to appoint adequate number of judges in various courts.

Judicial Activism sans Adventurism

Judicial activism has been an object of criticism during the last decade. Nevertheless, Chief Justice of India Adarsh Sen Anand, defended its role by stating "courts must respond to the knock of the oppressed and the downtrodden for justice with a positive response . . . in my opinion, judicial activism reinforces the strength of democracy and reaffirms the faith of the public in the Rule of Law". However, he added that judicial restraint was important as follows: "There are real limits to what the judicial process should attempt to accomplish and the judiciary should resist the temptation to cross these . . . be within the zone of juridical legitimacy . . . no civilised system of justice can permit judicial authoritarianism and therefore, Judges at all levels are expected to be circumspect and self-disciplined in the discharge of their functions".[9]

Right Direction to Pursue

Speaking on August 29, 1999 at Jodhpur, at the Golden Jubilee celebrations of the Rajasthan High Court, Chief Justice of India Adarsh Sen Anand said that courts in India do function to the satisfaction of a majority of citizens and observed as follows: "The (citizen) wants unpolluted expeditious and inexpensive justice. In (its) absence . . . he may be tempted to take law in his own hands . . . the lack of a speedy dispute resolution mechanism has a direct impact on the level of lawlessness in our society."

He added that both, Judges and the Executive, should share blame for delay in disposing cases. Judges should only grant adjournments when warranted and keep control on proceedings and the case file, said the Chief Justice of India. And Judges should be accountable. Besides setting high standards of conduct, they must ensure their actions are transparent. Unless these things are always done, there won't be judicial credibility. It is a pity that political will of the Executive is missing to change certain old-aged laws, which are static. It is the responsibility of the Legislature to amend a few important statutes to benefit the masses at large, as per the need of ground realities.

Many of these decisions have not involved the interpretation of the law; the courts have merely directed the Government to effectively carry out what Parliament had earlier enacted. Disillusionment with politicians, disgust with Government apathy and the ability of the courts to respond, have all led to the acceptance of an enormous *de facto* enlargement of the powers of the courts and almost constituted courts into a super legislature and a super Executive. A working democracy no doubt requires an independent judiciary, it also requires an effective Executive and a responsive Legislature. The Legislature and the Executive represent the people who periodically elect them; Judges are appointed and are thus not representative.

Notes and References

1. 'Granville Austin, *The Constitution: Cornerstone of A Nation,* Oxford, Clarendon Press, 1967, pp. 164-65.
2. The illustrative examples are of the cases of Bank Nationalisation, Privy Purses, Bihar blinding incident, Fundamental Rights cases, *Habeas Corpus* case, in which the apex judiciary gave its decisions against the Government which annoyed the Government. See *India Today,* New Delhi, December 15, 1982, pp. 108-10.
3. Anirudh Prasad, *Democracy, Politics and Judiciary in India,* New Delhi, Deep and Deep, 1983, Chapter 12, p. 163, for a detailed discussion of these aspects.
4. Quoted in the analysis of Rakesh Bhatnagar and Prakash Nanda, *The Times of India,* New Delhi, January 22, 1999, p. 4.
5. *Ibid.,* December 21, 1998.
6. *The Times of India,* New Delhi, December 12, 1997, p. 10.
7. These are the views of Soli Sorabjee, *The Times of India,* February 26, 1998, p. 13.
8. These views were expressed while inaugurating the Golden Jubilee of the Jodhpur High Court on August 31, 1999.
9. Views expressed at the Golden Jubilee of the Jodhpur High Court, *op. cit.*

CHAPTER

10

Functioning of Indian Judiciary

Some Aspects Need Introspection

Very often, Indian parliament has witnessed a clash over supremacy of Parliament against the proactive role of Indian judiciary in the affairs of the Executive. The very basis of it is that our Parliament represents the 'will of the people' and 'enjoys the mandate.' On numerous occasions, a warning has been recorded that judicial activism or proactive courts might have a way to 'despotism', if not checked the on-going trend of the functioning our Judiciary. In the latest debate of Lok Sabha, on 4th December, 2007, for instance, a number of MPs wanted the courts to be subjected to the same scrutiny as legislators, so as to have harmonious relations between the Executive and the Judiciary. The reference issue was related to a probe into the allegations of corruption involving the son of a former Chief Justice of India Mr. Y.K. Sabarwal. Earlier too, on the issue of OBC reservations in central institutions and higher educational institutions, the demolitions and sealing issue in the capital, the judiciary was attacked by political heavyweights. They disliked the functioning of judiciary as third chamber.

The question is: does our Parliament really represents the 'will of the people', as very few elected representatives gets more than 50% of votes polled? Certainly not, as the first Indian PM Nehru used to claim on the question of 'Land Reforms'. A very few MPs accepted the fact that the courts have often overreacted/overstepped in the affairs where the Executive failed to deliver the basic needs to the masses, as mandated in our 'Preamble', the Directive Principles of State Policy or concerning the concept of Welfare State.

In fact, judicial activism in the product of the tardy implementation of the ethos of a welfare state concept mentioned in the 'Preamble' of the Constitution and Part IV of it. The successive Governments and political parties have miserably failed to fulfil the social obligations that are mentioned in the Part IV of the Constitution to transform the society in a modern way. The Judiciary had to overstep in the affairs of Executive and Legislature and directed the successive Governments to enforce those obligations enshrined in our Constitution. In brief, the ongoing debate on legitimacy of alleged judicial forays into the seemingly exclusive domain of the Executive and Legislature in the constitutional scheme of separation of powers is related to seeking a curb on judicial activism along with enforcement of judicial accountability.

In this backdrop the 6th December 2007 judgment of the Supreme Court Justice A.K. Mathur and Katju confirmed to consider genuine, PILs, but called for judicial restraint to prevent erosion of the independence of judiciary by the threatened exercise of political power. The nub of the decision in para 15 of the two Judges bench decision says: "The court cannot direct the creation of posts. Creation and sanction of posts is a prerogative of the executive or legislative authorities and the court cannot arrogate to itself this purely executive or legislative function, and direct creation of posts in any organization. This court has time and again pointed out that the creation of a post is an executive or legislative function and it involves economic factors. Hence, the courts cannot take upon themselves the power of creation of a post". Obviously, this is unexceptional and consistent with binding precedents.

The conclusion reached in para 39 of the order after discussing the doctrine of separation of powers, is: "We hasten to add that it is not our opinion that judges should never be 'activist'. Sometimes judicial activism is a useful adjunct to democracy such as in the School Segregation and Human Rights decisions of the US Supreme Court vide *Brown* v. *Board of Education, Miranda* v. *Arizona, Roe* v. *Wade,* etc. or the decisions of our own Supreme Court, which expanded the scope of Articles 14 and 21 of the Constitution. This, however, should be resort to only in exceptional circumstances when the situation forcefully demands it in the interest of the nation or the poorer and weaker sections of society but always keeping in mind that ordinarily the task of legislation and administrative decisions is for Legislature and the Executive and not for the Judiciary."

The Lok Sabha Speaker Somnath Chatterjee on numerous occasions warned the Indian Judicial not to overstep the 'Lakshman Rekha' and behaved in a disciplined way. His argument was that in a vibrant democracy, the two organs (Parliament and Judiciary) of Government keep the system in a healthy state. So was his concern about the loopholes of our parliamentary system which have given the chance to the judiciary to encroach upon its space. In his words: If the judiciary does not exercise self-restraint and overstretches its limits, there is bound to be a reaction from politicians. The politicians will then step in and curtail the power, or even the independence of judiciary."

The House of People's Presiding Officer was wary of the prospect of the Judiciary encroaching into the legislature's turf, if its members do not fall in line. The Judiciary was equally fearful of its independence being curtailed by the Legislature, if judges did not observe restraint. In fact, the very basis of judicial overreach was due to pilling of Public Inter Litigations (PILs) which revolutionized the new concept of justice during the period of justice P.N. Bhagwati. The flexible approach of the court drew a difference between the 'public good' and private benefit, be it the sealing drive case in the national Capital or the nursery admissions case in the schools. Of course, Justice P.N. Bhagwati, known as a pioneer of the judicial innovation of PILs also felt that our court should not get involved in the matters relating to policy-making issue. In his words, 'The courts cannot frame laws. They have to ensure that the Executive is acting in accordance with laws and policy enacted by the Government is not arbitrary'.[1] Again, the Supreme Court bench headed by the CJI K.G. Balakrishan sheered at the PIL filed by NGO "Yoga Shakti" forming it as a 'publicity stunt'. It observed on 3rd Sept., 2008 that the Centre and the Bihar Government have joined in tackling the unprecented floods caused by the cosi river (due to a breach in the embankment of Bhimnagar barrage in Nepal). The bench refused to direct the concerned Governments as they are doing its best to tackle the flood situation.

RECOGNISING SELF JUDICIAL RESTRAINT

Differences of opinion within the Judiciary on dealing with PILs on appointment of bureaucrats came out in the open in the Supreme Court on 4th Jan., 2008, with a two-judge bench taking conflicting stands. A bench comprising Justices H.K. Serna and Markandey Katju was hearing a PIL filed in 2006, that had challenged the appointment of P.C. Pandey as DGP of Gujarat, who was removed recently by the Election Commission before the assembly elections.

While Katju expressed strong reservations over the Judiciary entertaining petitions on issues like the appointment of police chief, his senior colleague Serna favoured going into the matter, asking the NGO (Citizens for Justice and Peace) which had challenged the appointment of Pandey as police chief to place before it the order of the Election Commission on his removal. In this matter, Justice Katju spoke for maintaining judicial restraint in the appointment of police chief, home secretary and others, saying that it was the domain of the state Government. He observed : "It is exclusively the jurisdiction of the state Government to appoint DGP, home secretary and others. And the judiciary has nothing to do with that." This was a similar judgement that was given on December 6, 2007. On overstepping into domain of the Executive and Legislature, Justice Katju asked, 'you are challenging the appointment of a DGP. You can even challenge the appointment of PM. Is the judiciary supposed to deal with these issues? Is judiciary going to run the Government?'

This was the first classical instance in the history of Indian Judiciary that virtually desired to lay down a *'Lakshman Rekha'* on its role. The above cited observation assumed significance when the K.G. Balakrishnan on 13th December, 2007, while taking up the rehabilitation of sex workers case (PIL) assertively endorsed saying that the observations made by a two judge bench was not binding on the apex court, Earlier, in the second week of December 2007, Justice A.K. Mathur and Markandey Katju had warned against 'judicial overreach', citing the cases where the courts have overstepped their limits or jurisdiction. Judges held, 'They must remember that judicial activism is not an unguided missible, failure to bear in mind would lead to chaos.' The judgement laid emphasis on self-introspection.

In short, the mandate given for the separation of powers should be restored. Our judges cannot create laws enforce them. The constitutional breach has to be stopped.

These remarks generated a debate about the limits of 'Judiciary/judicial activism', which in fact stemmed from PILs. No doubt, the emerge of PILs has served a useful purpose in Indian history and set in motion for reaching changes. But, the era of 1990s witnessed the danger of 'frivolous' petitions to waste the time of courts. Since then, there was a debate about the need of careful weeding out of the genuine PILs, while following the example of the US judiciary which usually decides the questions related to the constitution and federal laws. This is the only way to ensure that Indian judiciary does not come into conflict with the legislative and executive turf. A fine balance among the three branches of Government has to be maintained.

The CJI's observations to end the controversy was welcomed by both classes of jurists and politicians.[2]

WHY JUDICIARY'S POSITION PITIABLE?

The Chief Justice of India, K.G. Balakrishnan accused the Government of meting out step-motherly treatment to the Judiciary, especially when it lost no opportunity to rub it in by pointing at the massive pendency of cases. In his maiden televised address to the nation on the eve of Law Day 25th

November, 2007, Justice Balakrishnan said that huge pendency in the subordinate judiciary, which stands at 2.50 crore cases, could not be solved without the Government substantially increasing the strength of judges terming the funds allocated to the judiciary under the 10th five year Plan (0.078% total fund) as pittance, he said that the greatest institution is accorded the least attention of justice. He demanded the increase of the number of subordinate judges by five time to the present strength of 16,000 so as to overcome pending cases backlog.

NON-FILLING OF VACANT POSTS

In fact, the non-filling of vacant posts for long period has been one of the causes for delay in delivering justice. The number of cases have increased due to growing criminal activities like Jessica Lall Murder case or the Upphar cinema fire case, which took the longer period of trial.

Our PM at the Conference of Chief Ministers held on March 11, 2006, accepted non-filling vacancies as the delay factor in disposal of cases. For example, the Allahabad High Court, as on Oct. 4, 2007, had the sanctioned strength of 160 judges of which 87 were lying vacant against the pendency of 46,28,866 cases. As per judiciary's report, 26% posts are still vacant in High Court's alone and 20% in subordinate courts. Thousands languish in jail for want of verdict copy (under section 363 Cr. P.C.) As per the reply under the RTI application by the Additional Registrar, of 2,247 persons convicted by the Session Courts, only 124 (5%) convicted persons could get copies of the order/judgment in time. 995 prisoners (44%) could not get the copies even in a five years period, which is either delayed by jail authorities or by unawareness of convicts. Such a delay is violative of a prisoner's legal rights and obstacle in his access to justice. The Sanjay Dutt's bail case brought to limelight the matter. Without the judgment's copy, no appeal can be filed in higher court.

APPOINTMENTS THROUGH A COLLEGIUM SYSTEM

In a startling revelation, as many as 341 Add Judges were appointed permanent judges of different High Courts during

Jan. 1999 to July 2007, without consulting the Supreme Court Collegium. It is shocking that the Government clearly bypassed the procedure laid down by the previous Supreme Court judgements, which clearly ruled that all appointments of permanent judges should be made in consultation with the collegium. The Supreme Court heard writ petition filed by Shanti Bhushan and others. The Union Government admitted the bypassing of successive CJs in these appointments. It may be recalled that as per SC judgement of 1993, consultation of the collegium is compulsory.

The parliamentary committee headed by E.M.S. Natchiapan in its report said that judges above should not choose their colleagues, but there should be a role for the executive in these appointments. It suggested that the selection process in the Judiciary should be made public and transparent. It called on the pre-1993 arrangement as the alternative to the present system of selection. This committee also favoured to bring the judiciary under purview of RTI Act. It has come forward with the establishment of benches of Supreme Court in some parts of the country for the cause of poor and rural masses who cannot come Delhi for justice.

According to the cn's report,—the arrears increased in the High Courts from 27.5 1akh cases in 1999 to 36.5 lakh cases in 2006. In the subordinate courts, the arrears increased over the same seven year period from 2 crore cases to 2.48 crore cases. Thus, the arrears grew by 33% in the High Courts while they grew by 24% in the subordinate courts. So while the CJI made a case against the executive, facts would show that both the Government and the Judiciary are to blame. Obfuscating the distinction in the systems of appointment to the subordinate judiciary and the High Courts, Justice Balakrishnan claimed: "That takes us to the selection and appointment process where the Government how a greater role in the judiciary." In his view the performance of the in-house 'collegiums' system of selecting judges; has had far-reaching reprecussions. For instance, when the high courts proposed temporary appointment of *ad hoc* judges to help clear the backlog of cases, the Centre responded by saying that no such *ad hoc* judge could be appointed till all the regular vacancies were filled up in each high court.

The Centre similarly shot down proposals from the judiciary to increase the sanctioned strength of judges in the High Courts regardless of the performance of existing ones.

INFRASTRUCTURE NEEDS TO BE STRENGTHENED

C.J. of India, K.G. Balakrishnan, the Government has to invest move in the infrastructure of courts, because most of them in a shambles at the lower levels. The buildings need repairs expansion efficiency and responsiveness.

According to the CJI, if 1,539 new judges are added/ appointed to the existing 792 courts, all pending cases in High Courts would be cleared in a year. If in two years these are to be cleared, then 770 judges could be sufficient.[3]

FAST TRACK CRIMINAL COURTS

The judicial system is presently clogged by a rapid increase in the number of criminal cases without any corresponding courts to handle the deluge. In the light of the scenario the Supreme Court asked the Union Law Ministry to find out whether trial in all criminal cases--which are pending for more than five years, could be fast tracked. If the proposal is accepted and approved, it could potentially revolutionise the criminal justice system. At present, the major contributor to the pendency of 2.5 crore criminal cases are from the states of U.P., Maharashtra, Gujarat, Karnataka, Orissa, Bihar and Rajasthan. Hence, the SC's suggestion is significance to reduce the backlog of cases.

The order for considering fast-tracking five year old criminal cases came from a SC bench headed by Justice S.B. Sinha. At present, the 1562 Fast Track Courts (FTCs) are dealing with the civil cases. There are 72.6 lakh civil cases (upto Jan., 2008) pending before different courts. Therefore, our CJI has suggested establishing 'mobile courts' in the rural areas in order to reduce the pending cases. He urged the Centre and states to provide funds for the purpose.

It is a common practice that our courts witness repeated adjournments that are sought by lawyers in the cases listed before the bench. This is really an unhappy state of affairs as because of it the backlog situation is not diminished. In fact, more requests for adjournments are sought due to the absence of counsels or lack of preparation by lawyers, and judges allow such adjournments as a matter of courtesy. Sadly, our senior layers take kindly to this becoming the norm. In very few cases, the judges take a tough line.

CONCERNING AT GOOD GOVERNANCE IN JUDICIAL SYSTEM

On the basis of the recommendations of the M.P. High court, the state Government terminated the services of two lower judges and retired three judges in the lower judiciary, in a bid to clean the judicial system and to enhance good governance. They all were found in charges of corruption. The decision to sack them was at the full bench of the state High Court. Earlier, the BJP Government in the state also removed 22 judges in the lower judiciary on the basis of charges of corruption and other irregularities.

Similarly, three of the most eminent advocates of the country namely Fali S. Nariman, Shanti Bhushan and Ram Jethmalani—came out with a draft notice for initiating impeachment proceedings against acting Chief Justice of Chhattisgarh High-Court Jagdish Bhalla for his alleged involvement in land scams in Noida and Lucknow. This came close on the heels of a recommendation reportedly by the Supreme Court collegium to promote Justice Bhalla as Chief Justice of Uttarakhand High Court, although his candidature had been dropped just a few months ago on account of a query raised by the then President, Dr. A.P.J. Abdul Kalam, touching on the land deals. While deploring the absence of judicial accountability, Nariman, Bhushan and Jethmalani said: "There is no option left except for MPs to initiate a motion which may lead to the ultimate removal of the judges under the Judges Inquiry Act, 1968.[4]

In a bold step, the MP High Court terminated the service of Rajgarh Judicial Magistrate (1st class) Surya Kant Chauhan in November, 2007 after he was found guilty of misusing his discretionary powers and position.

On the contrary, the refusal of the Supreme Court to order a judicial enquiry into allegations of misconduct against former CJI Y.K. Sabharwal was highly disappointing and it stirred a fresh controversy against the supremacy of the Indian Judiciary. For example, CPM leader, Sitaram Yechury, asked President of India (Mrs. Pratibha Patil in November, 2007) to get the matter examined and intervene in the interests of our democratic set-up, without it, the trust and confidence of the people in Judiciary shall adversely be affected. He drew Patil's attention to the opinion of Jurist V.R. Krishna Iryer, that the president is competent to order an enquiry in this matter under the Public Inquiries Commission Act.

Indian Judiciary, too, is supposed to be accountable it was a matter of concern and surprise that the Delhi High Court took upon itself the responsibility to defend the Supreme Court and sentenced the media persons who raised allegations against the CJI. There are two aspects to be taken up. First, Article 215 of the Constitution empowers an High Court only to deal with contempt of itself; whereas in the aforesaid matter, it seems, the Delhi High Court has transgressed its jurisdiction, as Article 129 empowers the apex court alone to deal with contempt issue against itself. The Delhi High Court's order, thus, was a negation of the amendment brought to the Contempt of Courts Act, 2006, allowing truth to be used as a defence in contempt cases. Invoking the provision of contempt of court to silence the critiques of possible judicial misconduct would not strengthen the trust and faith in the Indian Judiciary.

For the first time in India's legal history a former High Court judge will face a criminal trial. A Patiala House Court found *prima facie* evidence to frame charges of corruption and criminal conspiracy against Shameet Mukherjee, a former judge of Delhi High Court and four others, including ex-DDA Vice-Chairman Subhash Sharma, in a DDA land scam case which was unearthed nearly six years ago. The trial against accused began on May 26, 2008 under the Prevention of Corruption Act for allegedly taking undue benefits and showing favouritism. The CBI framed the charges. In short, the above cited cases confirm that corruption too breeds in the functioning of Indian Judiciary.

In Jan. 2008, the Supreme Court upheld the compulsory retirement of a judicial Magistrate of U.P., Rajkumarm, for showing undue leniency to a conflict in a case of sexual assault of minor, underlining its zero tolerance approach towards rapes. He released the convict on parole under the Prohibition of Offenders Act which views raping a minor girl very serious crime and provides for a minimum ten year sentence with RI and imposition of fine. The apex bench held that such presiding officers had no place in the Judiciary, though he had a good track record but his leniency to the case showed that he violated the spirit of the law. This will serve a lesson to other judicial officers. The decision is widely appreciated.

In yet another example, the CJI recommended the removal of Justice Soumitra Sen of the Calcutta High Court for criminal mis-appreciation of over Rs. 58 million of the High Court's funds. The CJ has asked the UPA Government to initiate proceedings contemplated by Article 217(1) read with Article 124(4) of our constitution. It is meant to impeach him.

The proposed impeachment against Justice Sen highlights the need for accountability in the judiciary. A former Chief Justice of India, S.P. Bharucha, has spoken of the possibility of nearly a quarter of judicial officials being corrupt. A 2007 Transparency International report says the judiciary— contrary to public perception—is the third most corrupt institution in the country. Much of this is swept under the carpet since disciplining of judges, especially of the higher courts, is a cumbersome process. The judicial council even if it is composed of sitting judges—would go some way in bringing transparency and accountability to the judiciary. Other measures such as making the Right to Information Act applicable to the judiciary would also help. The Government should use this opportunity to ring ill changes.

APPLICATION OF RTI

The judiciary was caught in the key matter of application of RTI of course, our judiciary is an opaque institution. But a public debate sparked about the RTI application asking whether assets of SC judges should be made 'public'. In response to it, the CJI held that his office was not bound by

RTI since he was a constitutional authority. He said: 'The CJ is not a public servant. He is a constitutional authority, RTI does not cover constitutional authorities.' The CJI later on acknowledged that judges are 'Public servants and bringing them under RTI Act is debatable.[5] Against this, Speaker Somnath Chatterjee waded the debate by saying that the RTI should apply to all public servants. His logic was in favour of transparency in the functioning of the courts. On the contrary, the MPs and the Executive are not in favour of giving access information to the common citizens or holding greater transparency under the RTI because of privileges and immunities they enjoy. According to the Speaker, any matter of queries against any MP/Minister, it could be referred to the privileges panel. At a stage, therefore, the parliamentary committee favoured an amendment in the RTI. so as not bring the members of parliament under the ambit of Act.

In substance, every public institution and the authority is accountable under the RTI Act—be that the apex court or Indian Parliament, otherwise the intention of the RTI Act with objects of transparency and accountability would be defeated. At present the act is a powerful watchdog of our democracy. It can keep a check on corruption.

It may be recalled that the Bar Association of India, too, favoured declaration of assets by judges averring that it would greatly enhance their dignity. Likewise, the former CJI, justice J.S. Verma, is of the opinion that in a democracy, no one is 'unaccountable' for its functioning. The judiciary or the CJI is no exception to this rule.

TRANSPARENCY THROUGH DECLARING ASSETS

Amidst mounting pressure on judiciary to reveal judges' assets through scores of RTI queries in the recent past, Chief Justice of India K.G. Balakrishnan shot off letters to the CJs of all 21 High Courts to give practical meaning to an II-year old apex judicial resolution judges must declare their properties. The main features of 16-point guidelines, reiterated by the CJI are:

- Judges should not waver from the path of

impartiality, the core value on which the people repose faith in Judiciary.

- A judge should not contest election to any office of a club, society or other association, except those connected with law.
- Judges not have close association with advocates.
- Any immediate family member, who is a member of the Bar, should not live in the judge's residence, even if he/she is the spouse.
- Do practice a degree of aloofness consistent with the dignity of a judge .
- A judge should let his judgments speak for themselves, should not give interviews to media on judgments
- A judge shall not speculate in shares, stocks or the like.

The CJI has sent along with the letter a copy of the 'Restatement of Values of Judicial Life', a 16-point set of guidelines on the do's and don'ts for judges, to the all Chief Justices of the HCs, requesting its circulation among all 600-odd judges and its diligent observance to make the Judiciary stronger and respected.

The apex judicial resolution, attached with the letter, said: "Every judge should make a declaration of all his/her assets in the form of real estate or investments, held by him/her or spouses or dependants, within a reasonable time of assuming office. "This is also applicable to sitting judges." It was further clarified that such declaration made by them shall be confidential, or would not for public consumption, which is a must for politicians while filling the form of affidavits for nomination at the hustings.

JUDGING THE HONESTY OF LAWYERS

In an extraordinary ruling, the Delhi High Court on 21 August, 2008, found L.V. Khan and R.K. Anand—two high profile senior advocates of the Supreme Court—guilty of not only obstructing justice but also of colluding to bribe a witness in the famous 1997 BMW hit run and hit case in which Sanjeev

Nanda was accused. The sting operation confirmed that the said advocates staged a demand of Rs. two crore to change testimony of Sunil Kulkarni—main eyewitness. On the basis of the telecast, the apex court took *suo-motu* cognizance of the matter and recommended that the lawyers be stripped of their designation and barred from the practice for four months. They were slapped with a fine of Rs. 2000 each, as they did a serious crime of course, they deserve punishment.

However, the ruling is being protested by a number of bar associations of India's High Court on the plea that the suspension was legally not tenable under the Advocates Act 1961, and only the Bar Council of India or the State Bar Council can initiate action against a lawyer and, that too on lodging a complaint. The response seems to be disappointing. Instead of a strike, the bar associations should have taken a hard look at the allegations against two of its senior members. Once the sting was telecast, the local bar council should have initiated an inquiry into the veracity of the claims and taken action. By not doing anything, the lawyers' fraternity runs the risk of reputation getting seriously tarnished.

RELEVANCE OF IMMUNITIES

Indian judges have not descended from heaven but have come from the same society which produces corrupt politicians, bureaucrats and babus. This is a harsh reality. Former CJI of India S.P. Bharucha had stated some times ago, that '80% of judicial officers are honest'. It seems true in context with Rs. 23 crore P.F. scam. Dealing with the famous case, a five Judges Constitution bench on August 14, 2002, unanimously approved some comprehensive guidelines for judicial officers saying that these were 'sufficient to protect the independence of judicial officers'. These are :

- A judicial Officer can be arrested for an offence under intimation to the district judge or CJ of the HC.
- If immediate arrest of a judicial officer of the subordinate judiciary is necessary; a technical or formal arrest may be effected. Arrest should be

immediately communicated to the district judge and Chief Justice of High Court as the case may be.

- Arrested judicial officer will not be taken to police station without prior directions from the district judge.
- There should be no hand-cuffing of the arrested judicial officer. But if he turns violent, and there is a danger to life and limb, he can be hand-cuffed with intimation to district judge as well as to the CJ of the HC concerned.
- If the hand-cuffmg and arrest are found to be unjustified, the police officers concerned will be suitably penalized by the HC concerned.

Notes and References

1. *The Times of India News,* New Delhi edn., December 13, 2007, p. 6.
2. The apex court is likely to lay down guidelines for governing public litigations. The PIL filed by an NGO, Prajawal is being heard by it.
3. *The Times of India News,* New Delhi edn., dated 1-12-2007, p. 6.
4. *The Indian Express News,* 18th Nov., 2007, p. 7.
5. *Ibid.,* April 21, 2008, p. 10.

CHAPTER

11

Significance of Veerappa Moily Panel Proposals

The Second Administrative Reforms Commission has made some path-breaking recommendations. This article discusses importance of these recommendations touching upon sensitive areas of country's administrative set-up. It takes an overview of Commission's proposals pertaining to appointments in higher judiciary, status of Lokayuktas, corruption in high places, reservation issues and accountability among civil servants. It ends on an optimistic note that the recommendations shall be implemented with a strong political will.

It is often said that India is a flawed democracy, the flaw being the inability of its institutions to be accountable, responsive and efficient in their functioning. It has nothing to do with "good governance". What holds back governance in the country is a deficit of trust. In order to plug this gap, members of the legislature, executive and judiciary have to be seen to be above board. The 263 page report of the second Administrative Reforms Commission; headed by Veerappa

Moily, the former Chief Minister of Karnataka submitted to the PM on February 12, 2007. Contains a slew of suggestions to plug the failures of our administrative system, in order to match the needs of the era of globalisation and liberalisation. Some of the suggestions are as follows:

- *Rashtriya Lokayukta* be set-up, but the PM should be kept out of its jurisdiction.
- Disqualification of MPs/MLAs on charges of defection should be decided by the President or Governor.
- If a party in a ruling coalition re-aligns midstream, its members in the House will have to seek a fresh mandate.
- MP and MLA Local Area Development Schemes MPLADS/MLALADS be abolished.
- A National-Judicial Council with the Vice-President as Chairperson be set-up for appointment of judges.
- Prior sanction will not be necessary for prosecuting public servants for possessing assets disproportionate to their known sources of income.
- A Serious Frauds Office be set-up to investigate financial embezzlement of over Rs. 10 crore or having widespread public concern.
- Setting up of a collegium headed by the PM and consisting of the Lok Sabha speaker, Law Minister and Rajya Sabha Deputy Chairperson for appointment of the members of Election Commission. In the wake of the recent controversy over expulsion of MPs for misconduct, the Commission said that it may be desirable to comprehensively spell out circumstances under which MPs can be disqualified by enacting a new law.
- Suggestion of partial state-funding of elections, tightening of anti-defection law, code of ethics for ministers and a law to define office-of-profit.
- The proposal to set-up a National Judicial Council (NJC), which will decide on the appointment and removal of judges, is an improvement on the Judges

(Inquiry) Bill drafted by the Union Law Ministry. The Law Ministry Bill has called for an NJC constituted exclusively of members of the judiciary. The Moily commission wants the council to be more broad-based; it seeks to include members of the legislature and the executive besides judges in the council.

Two other suggestions proposed by the Commission are valuable:

(i) The proposal to do away with the necessity for official sanction in order to prosecute bureaucrats, in cases of possessing assets disproportionate to income, should be implemented immediately. The provision has been misused by corrupt bureaucrats to evade punishment. There is no evidence that prosecution in such cases will be a hindrance to governance. On the contrary, corrupt *babus* have held back India's social and economic progress.

(ii) The suggestion to bring private sector entities that provide public utilities and NGOs receiving substantial funding under the Prevention of Corruption Act, is also welcome. Public utilities are no longer a state monopoly. Private sector, as independent agencies and in partnership with state entities, is increasingly a major player in providing public services. It should not desire immunity from the most crucial law that seeks to curb corruption and improve efficiency. Similar is the sentiment behind the call to cover NGOs under the anti-corruption law. The definition of the 'public' should no longer be limited to the state and its agencies; it has to include all entities that function in the public sphere.

About abolishing the MPLAD/MLALAD schemes, the committee emphasises on accountability and the Chairman has coined a new definition for "corruption and monopoly + discretion – accountability = corruption."

About keeping the PM office outside the jurisdiction of the *Rashtriya Lokayukta,* while it covers all CMs and Union Ministers, Moily's arguments is that it is a political decision and in a democratic set-up, the PM's office cannot be made, 'vulnerable to attacks'. When the PM is questioned the whole system will collapse. The matter should be left to the prerogative (wisdom) of Parliament.

The suggestion of the panel to scrap the Members of Parliament Local Area Development Scheme—MPLADS, is worth-considering, as it has been controversial since its inception in 1993. Critics have pointed out that the scheme which places Rs. 2 crore at the disposal of every MP annually to fund public works, subverts the basic tenets of grassroots democracy as well as the principle of federalism. A study conducted by the Institute of Social Service (ISS) too has noted that the scheme is not accountable and undermines the role of Panchayati Raj Institutions (PRIs).

The basic tenet of parliamentary-democracy is that Parliament sanctions money for schemes approved by the House and legislators supervise and control the executive on the use of the funds. But the MPLADS distorts the role of the legislators. It is the job of the executive to implement a sanctioned project. When Parliament sanctions a project, it is a collective effort. Again, it is one individual who decides on the use of public funds. Not just that, MP even has the authority to get involved with the implementation of the project. This obviously means that the MP cannot be objective about the quality and utility of the work. This is perhaps the reason why parliamentary committees have not bothered to look at the audit reports of the MPLADS.

Infact, the audit reports of CAG have made damaging remarks about the mismanagement of public funds. They have said that there is no proper accounting system in place for this scheme. The nodal ministry at the Centre sends money directly to the district collector who after getting the sanction from the local MP gives the money to the implementation agency. After that, there is no monitoring of the work in progress. In the regular public works, the money allotted for a project has to be returned to the Government if it remain unspent. With the MPLADS, this is not the case. Audit reports observed money lying around in the collectorate for years. Utilisation reports (of the sanctioned works) are not submitted. Guidelines for the scheme say that a district collector can implement a scheme only after the MP sanctions it in writing. But there are number of cases where the money running into crore of rupees—has been spent without authorisation. The guidelines very clearly say that money from the MPLADS can't be spent on works related to place of religious worship. But in practice, nearly 40 per cent of it is spent on construction of temples, mosques and churches, to strengthen the vote-banks.

Secondly, the MPLADS has created a kind of parallel planning system. Our current system envisages planning at three levels—Centre, state and district. In the MPLADS, funds emanate from the Centre and to the lowest level through one individual. When the scheme was introduced in 1993, it was part of the Central planning. Two years later, the funds for it started coming from the Central assistance to the states. The states haven't objected to this. Such a diversion of funds is against the letter and spirit of federalism. There is no constitutional provision to give money to MPs while it exists for PRIs. The scheme was introduced with undue haste. The amount should be used by PRIs. The scheme should be discontinued, because it has given instances of corruption and irregularities as recorded by the reports. Even the final report of the National Commission to Review the Working of the Constitution has said that the scheme militates against the demarcation of responsibilities between the legislature and the executive and should be immediately discontinued since the scheme is not consistent with the spirit of federalism and the distribution of powers among the Union and the states. It also encroaches on areas under local Government institutions.

The Administrative Reforms Commission (ARC)-II, in its report on ethics in governance, has called for the simplification of procedures adopted for the initiation of disciplinary proceedings against errant officers. This is meant to check the growing tendencies of corruption amongst *babus* through a fast track probe. The report has further recommended the deletion of Article 310 (which deals with the tenure of office of persons serving the Union or a state), and Article 311 (which lays down the ground-rules for the dismissal, removal or reduction in rank of persons employed in civil capacities under the Union or the state).

The ARC, instead, has made out a case for introducing legislation under Article 309, which relates to the tenure of Government officials, in an attempt to secure an expeditious trial of recalcitrant *babus* by doing away with the case laws. The scrapping of Articles 310 and 311, in the ARC's assessment, will expedite the process of disciplinary action against officials—a proposal which, if implemented, will force the bureaucracy to fall in line. The existing provisions, according to ARC Chairman Veerappa Moily, were not just insufficient but incapable of bringing the 'black sheep' within the bureaucracy into the disciplinary net.

Existing provisions in the Constitution follow the principle of natural justice, and give tainted officials an opportunity to present their side of the story over a period of time after disciplinary proceedings are initiated against them. Unlike other countries which follow a single inquiry system, disciplinary proceedings tend to drag on for long, and give enough room to the accused to plot their survival. Article 311 details the exit-route of such civil servants. Though all Government servants other than Supreme Court judges, the Auditor-General, High Court judges and CEC hold office during the pleasure of the President/Governor, two procedural safeguards have been prescribed for the civil servants.

While the first asserts that an official shall not be dismissed or removed by any authority subordinate to that by which he was appointed, the second one points out that no dismissal, removal or reduction in rank shall be ordered against a civil servant unless he has been given a reasonable opportunity of being heard in respect of the charges framed against him.

On the line of ARC's reforms in judiciary, the Judges (Inquiry) Bill was introduced by the Law Minister in December 2006 to deal with the complaints of judicial misconduct which is a positive development in the direction of ensuring judicial accountability. Earlier, a similar Bill was presented by the NDA's Law Minister Arun Jaitley to fix judicial accountability like that of the members of Executive and Legislature. Infact, the ARC of Veerappa Moily envisages doing away with altogether with the impeachment process provided in our Constitution. Likewise, on the appointment of judges, the ARC has favoured Jaitley's proposal of overturning the 1993 judgment by the Supreme Court through which collegiums of senior judges have appropriated, 'primary' in selecting candidates.

According to the ARC, the composition of the council needs to be broad-based and its powers enhanced so that it can exercise the necessary over-sight of the judiciary. Equally significant, it added that the same council be entrusted with the task of selecting judges as their appointment should be with "the participation of the executive, legislature and the Chief Justice and it should be a bipartisan process above day-to-day politics. Referring to the more transparent system of appointing judges in advanced countries such as US and UK, the ARC has proposed that the proposed council, "in-line with universally accepted principles", be headed by the Vice-President and consist of the Prime Minister, Speaker, Chief Justice of India, Law minister and leaders of the Opposition in the two Houses. Admittedly, the impeachment provision is cumbersome (signatures of at least 100 Lok Sabha members are needed to initiate the process) and has proved to be ineffective (on the only occasion it was invoked in 1993) against Justice Ramaswamy. The ARC has declared that, "the impeachment process for removing errant judges has failed." As a corollary, the proposed council should be empowered not only to impose minor measures but also recommend removal in serious cases of judicial misconduct. "Such recommendations should be binding on the President".

MOILY'S RECOMMENDATIONS ON OBC QUOTA

The Veerappa Moily-led Oversight Committee has also recommended to provide the 27 per cent OBC quota proposal but it should not apply to institutions primarily engaged in Research and Development (R&D). The panel further recommended that quota be implemented only in institutions that are now providing seats to SC/ST students. Another significant recommendation is that the IIMs need not have OBC reservation for fellowship programmes, executive development programmes and faculty development courses. OBC reservation will be restricted to the two-year PG diploma course and equivalent programmes that lay down work experience or sponsorship as eligibility criteria.

To ensure that IITs, IIMs, IISc, AIIMs and other such top institutions retain their brand equity, the Committee has recommended that the threshold for admission be determined by the institutions, as is done now. On cut-offs too, the Committee restored autonomy. Except in IITs/IIMs/IISc/AIIMs, the cut-offs for admissions may be placed somewhere midway between those for SC/ST and the unreserved category, carefully calibrated so that both equity and excellence are maintained. In the words of Moily, "The issue of creamy layer is being considered and a view will be taken in the final report".

The decision of the Oversight Committee on "five yearly review of OBC quota", was contested by pro-quota votaries. The objection was on the review statement of Moily because it was seen as part of an attempt to balance competing claims and solve upper caste anxiety over OBC quota in the Central Institutions. The doubt was whether the affluent 'backwards' under the ambit of quota would be kept under the new OBC quota policy.

Planning Commission member B.L. Mungekar, who is also in the Oversight Committee, has contested Moily's decision. In his view, "The review spoken about is on logistics and tools of implementation and not about the quota policy *per se*". OBC satraps like Railway Minister Lalu Prasad took exception to the review promised by Moily and insisted on a 'clarification', the matter was set to snowball into a larger controversy. Similarly, G. Mohan Gopal, Director of National Judicial Academy, Bhopal also questioned the implementation of the new policy. According to him, preserving opportunity for the 'forwards' at the expense of the backward classes even in the intervening years, "is not consistent with the Constitution or the spirit of the 93rd Amendment". The Committee's "first duty is to honour and implement the letter and spirit of the Constitution". "We will also agree that the implementation of the Constitution cannot be held at ransom by threats of violence by a section of the population, howsoever, strong or the fear of loss of electoral support. That would be setting a most dangerous precedent".

It may be noted that the Oversight Committee's report was to be submitted on June 26, 2006. (This was presented in last week of July, 2006). But the HRD Ministry, in a symbol of the ultra-zealous approach, circulated a cabinet draft on the reservation policy to win the sympathy of OBCs.

The submission of resignations by the two members (Dr. Sam Pitroda and Prof. Pratap Bhanu Mehta) of the National Knowledge Commission over the OBC quota issue, was unfortunate because the Government, overlooked Commission's objection and went ahead with reservations in higher educational institutions. They wanted a broader mandate to work on. In their views, the proposal was incompatible with freedom and diversity of institutions. On the other hand, captains of Indian industry favoured OBCs uplift, but did not want it at the cost of competitiveness, merit-based quality of professionals. The emphasis was on skills, alongwith the affirmative action for under-privileged classes which is necessary at the primary and secondary levels of schools. There should not be any compromise on the standards of functioning of Indian industries.

In fact, the report of the sub-panel of management panel headed by Samuel Paul was against 54 per cent increase in seats at one go roll out. He agreed to only 25 per cent expansion possibly from 2007-08.

Amid initial unanimity and bickering between the UPA and the NDA, "the 104th Constitution Amendment Bill was moved. The Bill clearly widened the scope of reservation by extending it to all aided/unaided Private Educational institutions, requiring the states to come up with such legislations. The Bill visualised the future politics of reservation.

A five judge Constitution bench of the Supreme Court has been set-up to review the constitutional validity of the controversial law providing 27 percent quota for OBCs in elite central educational institutions. Earlier, on March 29, 2007 an interim order had been issued by the two judges bench to stay implementation of the law enabling OBC reservation, i.e. the Central Educational Institutions (Reservation in Admission

Act, 2006). That has done on the ground that data based on 76 year old census; cannot be determinative factor for such affirmative action.

A Fresh Look at Women's Participation—Meanwhile, the suggestion of Vice-Chancellor N.R. Banerjee that a provision is being made to help bring more women candidates in the country's technical colleges while creating more seats for SCs/STs/OBCs within the fold of technical education—attracted the attention many. Addressing a plan group of Planning Commission, the VC said in his letter that, "very few women are making it to engineering institutions. We want to ensure their larger participation (who are meritorious) as per male-female ratio on the technical campus, keeping in mind that they do not suffer because of lack of experience and expertisation".

Amids the on-going controversy the Congress Government of Karnataka, as per its poll promise (2001), decided to reserve four per cent of Government jobs and seats in state-run educational institutions for 25 socially and educationally backward classes among Muslims. The Government ignored an edict issued by Islamic seminaries against any division of Muslims into castes for providing such reservations. Earlier the courts have set aside the Government order of providing five per cent reservations to the entire Muslim community. As per 2001 census, Muslims constitute 9.2 per cent of the 77 million population of the Karnataka state.

Two Models of Affirmative Actions

Affirmative action in one form or the other is a universal phenomenon. For instance, the US has used two instruments to provide protection against discrimination and also to give fair access and equal opportunities to African Americans, Hispanics and women. Under the Equal Opportunity Act, the minorities get legal protection against discrimination in employment. The US also has policies to provide fair access to minorities in Government contracts in employment and admission to educational institutions. Besides, the private sector adopts voluntary measures to ensure fair participation of minorities.

Since there is no evidence to show that SCs, STs and OBCs are inefficient, arguments of merit and efficiency do not hold much water. It is essentially a conflict of interests. On the one hand, a small elite class is fighting, to perpetuate its monopoly; on the other, vast sections of society are aspiring for a legitimate share in these privileges. In a highly inegalitarian society like India, protective policies are unavoidable for inclusive development. The only substitute to quotas and reservations is to create a more egalitarian social order guaranteeing equal opportunities to all and simultaneously, to fight against all sources of inequality, exclusion and discrimination.

India can follow the South African model of affirmative action as well, i.e. under the Employment Equality Act authorised by Nelson Mandela administration in 1998, forbid quotas or reservations even as it requires all "designated employers" in public and private sectors with 50 or more employees to adopt an array of affirmative action measures.

Section 15 of the Act clarifies that those measures "include preferential treatment and numerical goals but exclude quotas." It also lays down that no affirmative action measure can force an employer to establish "an absolute barrier" to the employment or advancement of people who are not from "designated groups". Here, designated groups encompass "black people", women and people with disabilities. Black people, incidentally, is "a generic term which means Africans, Coloureds and Indians". The bar on quotas in South Africa is despite a stipulation in the same Act that designated employers must make "reasonable accommodation" for people from "designated groups". Reasonable accommodation is defined by the law as any modification or adjustment to a job or to the working environment that will enable a person from a designated group to have access to or participate or advance in employment.

Given the exclusion of quotas, the South African model of affirmative action is said to be ushering in diversity in the post-apartheid scenario without necessarily compromising merit. Affirmative action measures are designed to ensure that "suitably qualified people, from designated groups have equal employment opportunities and are equitably represented in all occupational categories and levels in the workforce of a designated employer.

Section 20 of the Employment Equity Act further lays down that a person may be considered "suitably qualified" for a job not only because he has formal qualifications, prior learning or relevant experience but also due to his "capacity to acquire, within a reasonable time, the ability to do the job". Every employer is required to prepare an "Employment Equity Plan" spelling out objectives for each year of the plan and numerical goals for achieving equitable representation.

This radical law also has teeth. It empowers labour courts in South Africa to award compensation or impose fines for violations of the affirmative action obligations cast on employers.

It may be noted that, reservation alone can not equip to face competition and empower students from the socially disadvantaged classes without the first course of a special training programme for enhancing their employability. Such programme will help them to get access to good quality high education. This kind of training is being given by Bangalore-based Special Training Programme—STP for SC/ST students to make them competitive. This placement is based on purely merit and choice of the students.

In brief, the above-cited proposals are most welcome and must be carried out to make the institutions, accountable and efficient in their functioning, as these constitute as the key factors of "good governance". They are pragmatic, more academic. Without their implementation, cleansing the system and bringing the institutions under public scrutiny cannot be hoped. To claim that the nation-states concept is going to whether away in the era of globalisation, is a myth. Of course, the existing nation-states, regardless of their size and strength shall have to cope with the transition of a new imperial age of advanced technology, free market economy, European experiment of boundary-less entity and information capabilities (Kenichi Ohmae, a Japanese scholar is of the view that the four forces namely, capital, corporations, consumers and communication—have combined to usurp the economic power once held by the nation-states and these factors have helped to all freely cress cross national border.[1]

An international economic integration and the reality of a borderless global economy has assumed importance in terms of the Four (Investment, Industry, Information and Technology and the individual consumer) but in the light of re-emergence of ethnic nationalism and clash of civilisation, the concept of nations-state is bound to take another form in the new millennium and this change shall concentrate on the concept of 'good governance' as discussed earlier. Only those states shall progress and develop who shall adhere to the components of governance given by globalisation.[2]

SOPS IN UPA'S BUDGET

The UPA Government has selectively endorsed the Sachar recommendations, while some are still under consideration. For instance, the suggestion to set-up an equal opportunity commission on the model of the UK Race Relations Act, 1976, or to set-up a national data bank are yet to be taken up. Both measures have the potential to serve Indian citizens across communities, castes and regions.

A growing consensus is, however, emerging on the urgency to address issues of Muslim backwardness. This is apparent in the policy initiatives of organisations such as the United Nations, the Department for International Development and the Confederation of Indian Industries. Some state Governments have also attempted to extend reservation to Dalit Muslims.

But the approach to the Sachar report in the past two budgets is identical : It is about raising the allocation of funds. The corpus for National Minority Development Financial Corporation has been hiked to Rs. 75 crore this year from Rs. 63 crore in 2007-08 and Rs. 16.5 crore the year before. The allocation for the ministry of minority affairs was raised from Rs. 500 crore in 2007-08 to Rs. 1,000 crore this year. In addition, an allocation of a multi-sector development programme in districts with high concentration of Muslims was taken up in last year's budget.

Furthermore, the eleventh draft five year plan expressed its commitment to further minority programmes and sought to cover more Muslim students in the Sarva Shiksha Abhiyan with an allocation of Rs. 13,100 crore in this year's budget. There is also provision for scholarships to needy minority students amounting to Rs. 1,900 crore. While each of these initiatives signal good intentions, their implementation remains a matter of grave concern. Without some evaluation mechanism and a strategy to monitor their implementation, these programmes—like the National Rural Employment Guarantee Scheme—might not reach their intended target. More importantly, separate initiatives are needed for Muslim girls, who have been dual victims of India's flawed development strategy and regressive interpretations of Islam. In this context, establishment of a national data bank and an independent assessment and monitoring authority becomes vital.

Some people like Gujarat chief minister Narendra Modi have argued that separate policy intervention for minorities is communal budgeting. In fact, Gujarat does not have separate policy initiative for minorities. This view reflects a flawed understanding of development strategy for a pluralistic society. Minority rights are now a universal language because there is an inherent danger of the numerical majority in forcing minorities to stay backward.

The Sachar report presents robust evidence of such trends for Indian Muslims. Minority rights in its expanded shape—defined not just by religious category—have the potential to serve India's diverse population. A separate plan for minorities could very well remain distinct at the policy level but could certainly promote togetherness at the national level.

Another finding of the Sachar report is the absence of proactive civil society groups with a focus on Muslim advancement that could play a role in the implementation and monitoring process of various Muslim-oriented programmes. This challenge could be addressed by encouraging Muslims to set-up civil society groups and offering select masjid committees to take over this role until a full-fledged civil society group emerges in the locality. But this decision needs to be carefully made so that such initiatives do not result in empowering the Muslim clergy known for regressive interpretations of Islam. The intervention needs to have enough space for education of Muslim girls, without which addressing Muslim backwardness would be entirely impossible.

The budget response to the Sachar report has not been encouraging. The please-all character of the budget has laid stress on symbolic gestures aimed at elections.

—Mujibur Rehman, teaches at Jamia Millia Islamia

STOP ACQUIRING PRIME LAND FOR SEZs

Seeing a deep link between land alienation and Left extremism, the Administrative Reforms Commission has called for a ban on special economic zones coming up on prime agricultural land.

In its latest report, the ARC recommended that the SEZs come up in backward and less fertile areas, "Use of prime agricultural land should be avoided in establishing SEZs,"

> The report, submitted to Prime Minister Manmohan Singh by ARC chairman Veerappa Moily, also proposed that keeping the agrarian crisis and resultant conflicts in view, the member of SEZs be limited.

"The proportion of land that is permitted to be used by promoters of SEZs for non-processing activities should be located only in areas earmarked for the purpose and in the land-use plans," the report said.

The recommendations of the commission have acquired political significance in the context of bloody resistance put up by villagers in Nandigram to proposed industrial estate.

Taking a serious view of the spreading Maoist movement across a huge swathe of Indian territory, the ARC at the same time advocated strengthening the security forces to "act effectively and firmly".

It also recommended setting up and reinforcing police stations in the affected areas along with introducing community policing.

However, the ARC argued that there was an urgent need to examine the root cause of the ultra-Left movement.

It called for breaking the nexus between illegal mining and forest contractors on the one hand and transporters on the other: this, the report said, provided the much needed financial support to the extremist groups.

In an interesting observation, the report focused on the trend of identity politics and called for consensus among political parties to keep it within permissible limits of the democratic framework.

"There should be consensus that identity politics would be played within the space provided in democracy and not be allowed to develop into intractable conflicts leading to violence," it said.

Notes and References

1. Vide this book : The End of the National State : The Rise of Regional Economics.
2. Gurmeet Kanwal, "Imagined Homelands : Globalisation Will Force National States to Change", quoted from *The Times of India*, New Delhi, February 23, 2007, p. 14.

PART II

Crisis Management of Indian Politics

CHAPTER

12

Crisis of Good Governance in Indian Policy

The term 'good governance' is the gift of the Western world, which has come to the 'Third World' now known as 'developing countries' in the form of Liberalization, Privatisation and Globalization (LPG), after the disintegration of the USSR, who was the champion of socialist pattern of society and controlled economy. Since then, the term is regarded as essential for human development of any country or for sustainable development. Though no country can claim to be achieving 'good governance' in its totally, but efforts could he made to come close to it. In fact, good governance contains factors like efficiency, responsiveness, sensitiveness, accountability and people-friendly administration, which is very much against the public administration given by the colonial rule to the third world countries. As such the state 'has failed to discharge the duties of a welfare state, relating to inequalities, protection of weaker sections in the field of health care', education, housing, elimination of poverty, unemployment and population growth. India, too, witnessed ills like scams and scandals, bureaucratic cult, lack of planning, perversity, political arbitrariness, undue delay in decision-making and lack of accountability. Against this background, the concept of 'new public administration' was developed so as to be responsive and accountable to the development of masses at large. The people as such have lost the faith in the governance process established by the British rule.

Most observers and students of public administration have perceived that Indian administrative scene is suffering from malignant sickness due to the following five major crises of the political processionally, first power struggles at the top are fragmenting and tearing apart the Governmental system. Its institutions as provided by the constitution and the moral

Factors Responsible for Inefficient Administration

Inefficient	*Irresponsive*	*Insensitive*
Recruitment	Lack of Accountability	Lack of People's Participation
Attitude and Aptitude of the administration	Lack of Co-ordination	Lack of Professional education
Inefficient Planning	Red Tapism	Insensitive Police Structure
Financial Constraints in Management	Lack of Supervision	Nexus between bureaucrats and Politicians
Over and Less Workers	Lack of Performance Appraisal	Defective Social set-up
Lack of Techniques	Low Perks and Allowances and Moral	Lack of Redressal of Grievances like Lokpal
No time management	—	Lack of Coordination
Complex laws/ procedures of British era	Electing criminal background	Inefficient Planning
Inadequate Working Condition	Bundhs and Strikes	Lack of Discipline
Lack of Integrity and Motivation	Prerogatives and Privileges	—
Centralised Power Structure	Superior-inferior Complex	—

fiber it inherited from the freedom movement. Secondly, deep-rooted social turmoil is drawing in traditional institutions like caste and ethnicity on the one hand and the needs of modern structure on the other. The result is tremendous turbulence of a psycho social type, ungrowing schemes between communities, regions and identities. Thirdly, centralized Government and the power structure's ideology of national unity from above all costs are clashing with growing demands for pluralism, self-determination of each ethnic identity, human rights and equality. Fourthly, a total lack of consensus on the meaning of justice and a just social order of equity and diversity. And lastly, the emergence of the nexus between bureaucrats and politicians has equally effected the administration. It has proved to be a curse.*

There are certain other factors which appear as a threat to administration and result in inefficient, irresponsive and insensitive administration.

WORLD BANK FORMULATION ON GOOD GOVERNANCE

The World Bank, another donor agency, has identified a number of aspects of Good Governance which have been enumerated in various documents issued by it. Some of the aspects identified by it are:

- Political accountability, including the acceptability of political system by the people and regular elections to legitimize the exercise of political power.
- Freedom of association and participation by various religious, social, Emperor Company, cultural and professional groups in the process of governance.
- An established legal framework based on the rule of law and independence of judiciary to protect human rights, secure social justice and guard against exploitation and abuse of power.

* The Administrative Reform Commission headed by Shiv Charan Mathur, in its report of May, 1999.

- Bureaucratic accountability ensuring a system to monitor and control the performance of Government offices and officials in relation to quality of service, efficiency and use of discretionary power. The related determinants include openness and transparency in administration.
- Freedom of information and expression needed for formulation of public policies, decision-making, monitoring and evaluation of Government performance. It also includes independent analysis of information by the professional bodies including the universities and others needed for a civil society.
- A sound administrative system leading to efficiency and effectiveness. This, in turn, means the value for money and cost effectiveness. The effectiveness includes the degree of global achievement as performance the stated objectives and also the administrative system which is able to take secular and rational decisions and the system which is self-propelling to take corrective measures.
- Co-operation between the Government and civil society organizations.
- From the above formulation it is clear that Good Governance cannot be achieved only by the efforts of Governmental organizations. Other NGOs have to play a role in this direction.

FORMULATION OF OECD COUNTRIES

Like the World Bank, the OECD countries have also laid down same conditions of good governance for giving developmental aid to the developing countries. They have tried to link development assistance with participatory development, human rights and democratization. The main aspects of Good Governance as identified by GECD countries are :*

* Shefali Kalia, Good Governance and Development (New Delhi, New Century Publications, 2004) pp. 17-18.

- Legitimacy of Government;
- Accountability of political and official elements of Government;
- Competence of Governments to make policy and deliver services; and
- Respect for human rights and the Rule of Law (including individual and group rights and security, a legal framework for economic and social activity and participation).

In the above formulation, the main emphasis appears to be on the competence, accountability and legitimacy of the Government and its institutions. Of course, a new component of human rights and Rule of Law have been added to emphasize the participation of citizen groups.

GOVERNANCE IN INDIAN ADMINISTRATION

The Indian Constitution provides the 'Preamble' and the Chapters on Fundamental Rights and the Directive Principles of State Policy. These clearly indicate the values that should guide the actions of the Government and other social institutions. The basic theme is to have a democratic Government. We should respect the fundamental rights of the citizens and promote social justice by taking special care of the disadvantaged groups or the society. The country has held regular elections and the political system has the legitimacy which is the fundamental requirement of Good Governance.

Attempts have been made through development plans to remove poverty and to provide basic minimum needs to all sections of the society, especially the disadvantaged groups like those living below the poverty line and the Scheduled Castes, Scheduled Tribes and other Backward classes. It was felt that to ensure socio-economic development of the country it was necessary to reform the administration system to meet the challenges of the development paradigm. The process of administrative reform has, therefore, been going on since Independence.

As early as in 1949, N. Gopalaswami Ayyangar suggested improvements in the transaction of Government business. As a result of his recommendations Organization and Methods Division was set-up in the Central Government. In 1951, A. D. Gorwala suggested the reorganization of administrative machinery to ensure greater speed; effectiveness and responsiveness. He suggested that there should be more Junior Officers than clerks. Paul H. Appleby submitted two reports in 1953 and 1956 and made suggestions to reform the administrative system through O&M Organization. He also made certain suggestions about improving the recording and filing system. He laid stress on citizens' satisfaction. On his suggestion, the Government of India set-up 'Indian institute of Public Administration'. In 1954, Ashok Chandra suggested ways to remove delay in execution of projects. T.T. Krishnamachary report dealt with training of IAS officers and improvement of State Administration. K. Santhanam's report (1964) dealt with corruption. In the meantime, the Balwant Rai Mehta Report (1957) led to the setting up of Panchayati Raj Institutions in the country.

In 1966, a high powered Administrative Reforms Commission was set-up under the Chairmanship of Morarji Desai (subsequently chaired by K. Hanumanthaiya). It produced twenty reports about various aspects of administration. Ashok Mehta Committee (1977) made important recommendations about improving the Panchayati Raj Institutions. Sarkaria Commission (1983) made several suggestions for the improvement of administration in the context of Central-State relations. The Economic Administration Reforms Commission under L.K. Jha (1983), emphasized the need for accountability. Greater importance was given to performance than mere adherence to rules and procedures. G.V.K. Rao Committee (1985) also made several recommendations to improve administration. The Planning Commission, the Estimates Committee and the Committee on Public Undertakings have also been making recommendations to improve the administrative system and to apply modern techniques of management in public organizations.

The year 1990 witnessed a significant shift in the 'Development Paradigm'. The Structural Adjustment Programme brought new economic policies. Globalization, Privatization and Liberalization (LPG) became important guiding principles. It was realized that new economic policies cannot be successfully implemented unless corresponding changes take place in the Administrative system. During this period, it was also felt that, to be responsive to the people, the administration has to be decentralized and taken as close to the people as possible. This resulted in 73rd and 74th amendment of the Constitution which strengthened the local Government institutions like Municipalities and, Panchayati Raj bodies. Mention may be made of the latest-report of the Administrative Reforms Commission II, headed by Veerappa Moily.* It is meant to meet the requirements of the New Public Administration under the fall of LPG.

NEED FOR GOOD GOVERNANCE

The last two decades of the present century have witnessed a great deal of structural adjustments and a new type of state intervention to seek co-operation and help from community organizations and empowerment of citizens. Most of the countries have attempted to limit the role of the state, viz. Down-sizing bureaucracy, devolution of authority, cost reduction, contracting out some of the operative functions of the Government, developing and designing result-oriented appraisal system, commercialization as well as market-orientation of the Governmental activities accountability. The new administration is apparently moving from systems to enterprise, obedience to reward, inaction to action, centralization to decentralization and from the duties of administrators to the rights of citizens, so on and so forth.

David Obsborne and Ted Gaebler** in their work, 'Reinventing Government', have indicated some of the requirements of good governance, Emphasis on catalystic Government, mission-driven Government and market-oriented Government has been given in their book. During the last few

* N.S. Gehlot, "Significance of Veerappa Moily Panel Proposal", in *Indian Journal of Public Administration*, New Delhi, Volume Liii, No. 3, July-Sept., 2007, pp. 466-75 .

** D. Osborne and Ted Gaebler, Reinventing Government; How the Entrepreneurial spirit is transforming the Public Sector (New Delhi, Prentice Hall, 1992).

years a considerable reorientation of the administrative system have been done in the United Kingdom. In 1979 the Prime Minister, Margaret Thatcher introduced a system of financial scrutiny and financial management set-up under the reforms called 'Next Steps' so as to decentralize some of the operational aspects of administration to an autonomous authority and accountability for the results only. Attempts have also been made in reforming the traditional politico-administrative system in China, Japan, Indonesia, South Africa, Surinam, Canada, New Zealand, Malaysia and others in the recent past. New Zealand has ushered reforms process towards corporatisation and privatization: The established principles of private sector organization efficiency and market competition have been incorporated in the Public Sector.

In Canada, the reforms in the federal public service was initiated in 1989. The reform process is to provide high quality service and increased client satisfaction. The public services have been made more open, more visible and more consultative.

OTHER FEATURES

The Concept of Good Governance contains eight major characteristics. These are participatory, consensus-oriented, accountable, transparent, responsive, effective and efficient, equitable and inclusive. It follows the rule of law. It assures that corruption is minimized the view of minorities are taken into account and that the voices of the most vulnerable in society are heard in decision-making. It is also responsive to the present and future needs of society. The other factors are :

(1) *Participation* : Participation by both men and women is a key cornerstone of good governance. Participation could be either direct or through legitimate intermediate institutions or representatives. It is important to point out that representative democracy does not necessarily mean that the concerns of the most vulnerable in society would be taken into consideration in decision-

making. Participation needs to be informed and organized.

(2) *Rule of Law :* Good governance requires fair legal frameworks that are enforced impartially. It also requires full protection of human rights, particularly, those of minorities. Impartial enforcement of law requires an independent judiciary and an impartial and incorruptible police force.

(3) *Transparency*: Transparency means that decisions taken and their enforcement are done in a manner that follows 'rules and regulations'. It also means that information is freely available and directly accessible to those who will be affected by such decisions and their enforcement. It also means that enough information is provided and that it is provided in easily understandable forms and media.

(4) *Responsiveness:* Good governance requires that institutions and process try to serve all stakeholders within a reasonable timeframe.

(5) *Consensus-oriented:* There are several actors and ,as many view points in a given society. Good governance require mediation of the different interests in society to reach a broad consensus in society on what is in the best interest of the whole community and how this can be achieved. It also requires a broad and long-term perspective on what is needed for sustainable human development and how to achieve the goals of such development. This can only result from an understanding of the historical, cultural and social contexts of a given society or community.

(6) *Equity and inclusiveness:* A society's well-being depends on ensuring that all its members feel that they have a stake in it and do not feel excluded from the mainstream of society.

(7) *Effectiveness and efficiency :* Good governance means that processes and institutions produce results that meet the needs of society while making the best use of resources at their disposal. The concept of efficiency in the context of good governance also

covers the sustainable use on natural resources and the protection of the environment.

(8) *Accountability*: Accountability is a key requirement of good governance. Not only Governmental institutions but also the private sector and civil society organizations must be accountable to the public and to their institutional stakeholders. Who is accountable to whom varies depending on whether decision or actions taken are internal or external to an organization or institution. In general, an organization or an institution is accountable to those who will be affected by its decisions or actions. Accountability cannot be enforced without transparency and the rule of law.*

In a speech delivered at the University of Tilburge in the Netherland on 9th June 2007, Congress President Mrs. Sonia Gandhi explained that only centrist democracy suits: the mood and temperament of the country. She said, "I am convinced that India can flourish only as a centrist democracy". Her argument was based on the diversity of the country in which a narrow insensitive approach could only result in serious social discards. India's many identities, languages, faiths and customs cannot coexist peacefully if anyone assumes dominance, or if the collective will of the majority denies rights and space to any minorities. Her focus was the principle of unity in diversity. On the other hand, the country has witnessed the emergence of coalition culture since last two decades.

The passages of Right to Information Act, 2005, is a historic development in the field of transparency and accountability. But the manner in which secrecy is shouded by bureaucratic-*cum*-executive fiat is a matter of concern. It is done under the Commission of Enquiry Act, taking the plea that the Parliament has not taken action, that is why reports of many commissions/committees, constituted under the above

* N.S. Gehlot, "Meaning of Good Governance and its Relevance in the Functioning of Indian Democracy : South Asia Politics, New Delhi, June 2004, pp. 14-16.

Act, including Law Commission Report, have not been made for public scrutiny. Our concern is of making 'public' the report of Law Commission which is only recommendatory in nature. According to the experience or advocate; N.M. Ghatate, the Law Commission report in 1998 was made 'public' after intervening its chairman Justice B.P. Jeevan Reddy and persuading the Vajpayee Government at the Centre.*

But when the 16th Law Commission was constituted, the law ministry inserted a clause, which deemed the reports of the Law Commission as confidential until they are tabled in Parliament. This clause was repeated when the 17th Law Commission was constituted in September 2003, despite former Chief Justice A.S. Anand and Justice G.B. Pattanaik having spoken against bureaucratic secrecy. The secrecy clause has also violated a fundamental right which guarantees freedom of speech and expression. This right cannot be restricted unless "in the interest of sovereignty, integrity of India, the security of the state, friendly relations with foreign states, public order, decency or morality or in relation to contempt of court, defamation or incitement to an offence". By no stretch of the imagination do reports of the Law Commission qualify for the exception. Furthermore, there is no law passed by Parliament introducing this secrecy clause. It has only been introduced by an executive order.

Moreover, now that the Right to Information Act, 2005, is in place, it is the duty of the Government to make public reports of the Law Commission. Since these reports provide a basis for enlightened discussion in the media, amongst intelligentsia, as well as in Parliament, there is no reason, whatsoever, to keep Law Commission report hidden from public scrutiny. Such an executive order, not backed by any law, has no place in the democratic constitution we have adopted. It is, therefore, in the public and national interest that such an executive order is withdrawn by the Government. Failing this, the Supreme Court should strike it down.

The role of CISs of almost all the states has been positive and active in dealing with public complaints against irregularities and others charges. But Chief Information

---

* All this Secrecy is Misplaced, 22/12/2005.

Commissioner, Justice M.A. Khan came under a cloud following changes of corruption and favourism due to the judgment he had delivered. The complaint against him was made to the state governor T.V. Rajeswar as the CIS of UP has been apathetic to information seekers under the RTI Act and he recruited staff without following the rules Mr. Khan was appointed by the previous Mulayam Singh Government soon after his retirement. He was very much in limelight for his dissenting judgment and upholding the split in BSP.

Corruption is a jaded theme in Indian politics. In 1970s, JP Narayan's anti-corruption agitation, called Nav Nirman brought down the Chimanbhai Patel Government in Gujarat. Likewise, Rajiv Gandhi lost the 1989 Parliamentary elections over the Bofors scam. That was the gain of the opposition's anti-corruption campaign. Thus, the ruling Congress Party was identified with corrupt practices and non-performance. Sadly, the BJP initially projected itself as 'a party with differences' to create a corrupt free society, too, could not kept itself away from the fallout of scams and scandals during the NDA regime at the Centre. Need not to talk of the rest of political parties as they are savvy about making money. Anti-corruption campaign can evoke a chord if it connects with a larger vision of reforms in the system of governance, which must come out from the grass-root levels. The institution like Ombudsman is the need of the hour.

The Centre is planning to initiate to change the Anti-Corruption Act, 1988, formally empowering the spoken of Parliament and state assemblies to grant sanction to prosecute MPs and MLAs for graft. Hence, Section 19 of the Act is being proposed to amend to tap the growing tendency of corruption in our politicians. If materialized, it would keep a check on corruption.

It is relevant to mention that the proposal to amend the Prevention of Corruption Act has come nearly nine years after the Supreme Court in a 1998 ruling on the JMM MPs' bribery case held that MPs and MLAs are "public servants" within the meaning of the Act. A subsequent executive order granted presiding officers the authority to grant sanction to prosecute members of their respective houses.

POLITICISATION OF CBI

The agency has been accused of shielding politicians in the past as well. Its failure to press charges against the powerful in society has been interpreted as the agency's failure to guard its professional autonomy and integrity. Even if this criticism is misplaced, the CBI can't afford such a perception. Given the extent of politicization of state institutions, it could be difficult for the CBI to fob off such charges. The Prime Minister has said that the Government is committed to preserving CBI's independence as an investigating agency. Such promises aren't enough. An administrative mechanism that guarantees autonomy is essential to safeguard the credibility of the agency. At present, the CBI is the investigating wing of the central police force and functions under the Union Home Ministry. Like other wings of the police force, it is also prone to politicization.

The Supreme Court directive on police reforms has recommended the creation of a national security commission at the Union level to insulate central police organization from the Government. Such commissions have been suggested for states as well. They are expected to be constituted of eminent people, including those in the Government. Such a buffer will help to maintain a healthy balance between the Government and the police. Countries like the UK have a similar system in place. State Governments, while accepting the spirit behind the call for police reforms, have been slow to act on the apex court directive. They have maintained that political interference in police administration is minimal. The Centre should take the lead in initiating the reforms. It could start with the CBI, which would be the first step towards good governance.

Sentencing jails to either JMM chief and former minister Shibu Soren as well as Salman Khan or Sanjay Dutt both from the film fraternity projected the high image of our judicial system. In a democracy, the judiciary is the final defender of rights guaranteed by the Constitution. The set of rules is applicable to all citizens, irrespective of their position in society and in public institutions. On the contrary, the acquittal of JMM leader is the latest case of once shaken the image of

CBI, now being called the Central Bungling Agency* as it has failed to provide a foolproof evidences before the court against a high profile politician.

WHY TO BREAK UP STATES?

The current demand for creating new states does not seem to be justified, as mushrooming of states will boost centrifugal forces, specially parochial forces. The mooted idea of breaking up of states into smaller units of facilitate decentralization and good governance. It is accepted that greater decentralization in India's case might lead to good governance. I, however, do not endorse the idea of breaking up of states to bring about such decentralization. The move will lead to formation of more states, and separate bureaucracies for each state. This would create a greater burden on the state exchequer and ultimately on the taxpayers. The second Administrative Reforms Commission in its report has recommended the promotion of local democracy and effective devolution of various spheres of the Government. Therefore, effective and efficient governance is possible without breaking up of states through delegation of authority and empowerment of local bodies. Even after this if devolution of power doesn't occur, such break-up would have done nothing more than to increase the public burden.

Hence, the states must be given more economic autonomy for rapid development with communication means Good Governance is a matter of character and patriotism. In a country where half population is deprived of the basic amenities, escalating the establishment expenditure is tantamount to betraying the nation. On the contrary, we have miserably failed to keep check on growing the politics of corruption and criminalization.

CONTAINING THE RED SCARE THROUGH GOOD GOVERNANCE

More than 150 districts have been affected by Maoist

* "CBI Bungles Again", *The Times of India*, New Delhi, 24, August, 2007, p. 4.

violence. Maoism is doubtless, a threat to our internal security and peace. In fact, these regions have been outside of the national mainstream due to poverty and backwardness. Our political and electoral process has been ineffective in these areas. The Government, therefore needs to make itself visible in these regions, for which revamping the police force is the basic priority. Likewise, schools, hospitals, communication facilities and access to markets should be treated as a priority in these areas. At present, few among the local population have a stake in state institutions. That must change.

Maoism can be exposed for the mindless cult of violence that it is only when the merits of a democratic alternative are accepted by the people. A coordinated set of policy options must be put in place to help people relocate to the democratic mainstream even as security measures against Maoists are efficiently tightened.

The events and developments relating to Nandigram, Naxal and Maoist insurgencies in Kashmir, Manipur and communal riots in Gujarat and other northern states, drive us to conclude that we, the people of India, are living in a state of 'unlawness', as we are ruled by decrees, whims, diktats, military and muscle power in electoral politics. India must take inspirations from the English who gave themselves the Magna Carta. We must pen our own charter, one that guarantees liberty, property, freedom to trade by land and sea, and civic self-Government, something that the Parliament of the day cannot amend, whatever be the majority disposition. This is a necessary precondition for the rule of law. In other words, the Government itself must be placed under the law if the rule of law is to prevail over the rule of arbitrary rulers. The 'unlaw' we suffer from today is entirely because of the fact that the sovereign's ministers, bureaucrats, judges, policemen and soldiers are above the law, and are breaking it with impunity by virtue of immunities and privileges. It is time now for the birth of a new league of Indian Liberals.

As regards corruption in high place, the CBI has demanded a legal framework and coordinated international cooperation to put in place effective mechanism for recovery or assets accumulated through corrupt means. It made a strong pitch for scrutinizing wealth/assets of highly influential person in the country who have made huge deposits in international financial centres like Swiss banks. They have taken protection under strict privacy laws which is against the concept of 'rule of law', which is the basic feature of good governance. Concluding Remarks: The country faces a crisis of leadership as well as governance. Both factors have collapsed from public administration whereas 'New' Public Administration demand the operationalisation of the concept Good Governance—the mantra of globalization, contrast to features prevailing like corruption, indiscipline, red tapism, etc. The malaise—collapse of governance pervades both in urban and rural administration.

India fares abysmally on the global corruption meter. According to transparency International, 20% believe Government does not fight corruption at all; 39% think its fight against corruption is ineffective; and 15% say that far from fighting corruption, Government actually encourages it. This is a difficult place for businessmen to function. A global survey ranks India among the worst countries for doing business. Whether it's starting or closing a business enforcing contracts, paying taxes, or registering property—every procedure take an inordinately long time.

In India, the emergence of the concept of 'Good Governance' has strengthened the movement of dissatisfaction with the state of the discipline of Public Administration. As a result of globalization, New Public Administration (N.P.A.) emphasized in 'public administration on the classical factors like efficiency, economy, productivity and decentralization'. The NPA talks of relevance, values, social equality, change and participatory initiative. For this change, the second Minnobrook Conference of 1988 should be credited which launched a 'movement' against the 'big role' of Government in public administration and in favour of managerialism and privatization in policy-making. And since then, as a discipline, public administration has moved away from political science discipline. The NPA talks of less burden on Government and public sector organization. In short, Good Governance is a normative concept, which is close to NPM, acknowledging the due place in public administration, the features like: (a) Accountability; (b) Transparency; (c) Rule of Law; (d) Human Rights; (e) Social equality in terms of gender, ethnic-age groups and religion, (f) Ethical and honest behaviour; (g) Greater Decentralization, delegation and De-bureaucratization; and (h) Budget cuts on ministerial and military expenditure.

Most of Indian writers and teachers have devised the new strategies of good governance for corrupt-free sustainable development for which emphasis on ethical, moral dimensions, efficiency, managerialism, people's participation, responsiveness, transparency and accountability as well as autonomy have been given to modern states in the new millennium, because the era of LPG has reduced the importance of the 'state'.*

It is wrong to say that the 'missionary role of the State is rolling back, through the era of a centralized state has gone. Without the state, the competitive role of 'free Market/ economy' shall fail to the age of I.T. Therefore, administrative system should be flexible, constalative result-oriented, creative from the bottom to the top, for which Article 311 of the Constitution (in terms of the rights and privileges and status of civil services) warrants a drastic change. State is yet to play a vital role in ensuring social cohesion, social justice while combating social inequalities. Focus shall have to he given to basic amenities.

The state is still an important organ of administration in the LPG era where its contracting role has emerged to ensure efficiency and managerial capability. India can not be an Asian 'power' without infusing principles of accountability and transparency in public administration while making the centre flexible, responsive and accountable.**

In Indian political system, the rule of coalition governance since 1980s has contributed nothing except witnessing a spell of unstable coalition Governments. At present, the Congress-led UPA Government too is facing the same situation in the light of the *Indo* v. *Nuclear deal and its ally*—the left has threatened to withdraw its support if its concerns and

* See R.B. Jain, Corruption Free Sustainable Development: Challenges and Strategies for Good Governance, New Delhi, Mittal Publications, 2004.

** S.R. Maheswari, Administrative Reforms in India, New Delhi, Macmillan, New Delhi, 2002.

(implications of the deal) are not taken seriously. The deadlock between the Congress and Left has created the possibility of fresh election to the Lok Sabha. The instability of Government has shaken the very roots of our economic grow in the era of globalization. In fact, hard policy options are not adopted by any unstable coalition Government, as they are bound to follow the populist policies to appease the supporting political parties.

Since coalition Governments seems to be inevitable in our governance, but we have yet not been able to debate on possible institutional reforms that many facilitate more stable governance against the trend of fragmentation and the rise of small-caste-based political parties in our democracy.

According to Professor Bhaskar Dutta, one of the possible solution to the inordinate degree of fragmentation in our legislatures is to modify the method of proportional representation (PR) to elect their legislatures. The pure form of PR actually tends to increase fragmentation. However, typically PR is supplemented with the stipulation that only those parties that win a minimum fraction of the total votes cast say 5 percent can gain representation. This will drastically reduce the number of parties securing seats in the legislatures. In principle, there is no reason why this "minimum votes required" principle cannot be tagged on to our "first past the post" electoral system.*

In fact, two-party system is a logical development of multiparty democracy. In a multiparty system, coalitions are forged outside the election process. In due course, these coalitions evolve a common platform and unite to form a single party. Once this process is established, only the two largest and well organized parties see recurring success. This is because the entire state will mature to support either of the parties based on their agendas for the state, instead of encouraging regional voting based on caste, religion and other divisive factors. The most advanced democracies of the world have generally evolved to have a two-party system.

A two-party system would be in keeping with India's

* Unstable Coalition Hurt, From the editorial of *The Times of India*, New Delhi, Sept. 7, 2007, p. 14.

present growth paradigm. At a time when the country is witnessing phenomenal economic and social transformation, the Government has to be ready to take quick decisions. It is unfortunate, hence, that with changes in voting patterns, multiparty coalitions have became a regular form of Government in India.

In an attempt to overcome the impasse of instability, the Weimar Republic of the new German constitution adopted in 1949 prescribed that votes of no-confidence must be "constructive". This meant that a chancellor, who is the head of Government, could only be dismissed by parliament if a new chancellor was elected simultaneously. The system of constructive no-confidence increased the durability of subsequent German Governments since the existing one could no longer be brought down by a combination of disparate forces who were not themselves interested in forming a Government. Of course, another advantage of the system is that it ruled out the necessity of any mid-term polls by providing an in-built mechanism for the smooth transition of power. Our Constitution probably did not envisage the possibility of governance by coalitions. Our current rules and norms are clearly incapable of promoting stable governance in fragmented legislatures, whereas, coalition Governments have functioned reasonably efficiently in several countries. It is important to scrutinize the best features of comparative political systems and modify them to suit our own needs.

Recently, some cases have brought the Indian judiciary in clash with the jurisdiction of the Right to Information Act with regarding to furnishing information of complaints against some judges. It is well known that the Delhi High Court *suo motu* initiated contempt proceedings against Mid-day Operation of journalists for publishing a story of biased acts of former Chief Justice of India Y.K. Sabharwal. This episode discredited a lot to the integrity of the Indian Judiciary in the same way as politicians and bureaucrats have lowered the image of administration. (governance).

Other cases involving Justice Shamit Mukherjee, Justice Jagdish Bhalla and others have already shaken the faith of ordinary people of India in Judiciary. The application or contempt of court against the exposure of corruption/

allegations by media is not justified. The functioning of Judiciary itself should be above suspicion and adhere to complete transparency in it would certainly enhance the dignity of the institutions such as CJI. Rather it would have been more judicious if an independent inquiry in Mid-day exposure against the CJI could have been set-up. The entire Mid-day issue *vis-a-vis* acts of former CJI underlines the fact that our judiciary lacks accountability and transparency. The Judiciary cannot/should not claim to be kept out of RTI jurisdiction. Even contempt powers of the courts should be subject to scrutiny.*

It is worth-recalling that against the above-cited background the Government of the day has brought the bill 'Constitutionality of Judges (Inquiry) Bill 2006 and the proposed National Judiciary Council Bill seeking to make the Indian judiciary more accountable in the functioning. On the other hand, a warning of serious consequences of Parliament's sanctity has been given on account of disturbances' adjournments or disruptions in Parliament's Houses, which in technically constitutes a ground for breach of privilege. In the words of Speaker Somnath, unless the ills plaguing the system are heeled, the people will lose the faith in the highest democratic forum and there would be a possibility of the Judiciary to encroaching upon its space.

* For this, see the views of Arvind Kejriwal, 'Contempt for the Pen', *The Times of India*, Sept. 18, 2007, p. 12.

CHAPTER

13

Functioning of Panchayati Raj Bodies

The state legislative assembly passed the Rajasthan Panchayati Raj Act on April 23, 1994, in accordance with the 73rd constitutional amendment, while giving subjects to be governed by these grass-roots bodies. The state had the rich experience of the functioning of these bodies prior to the passage of the above cited amendment by parliament. Need not to mention, Rajasthan was the first state of the country which laid foundation of the process of de-centralisation and panchayat raj system in 1959. As per the Act, 1994, the state has successfully conducted the two elections or the three tier system since 1994, one by the BJP-led Government headed by B.S. Shekhawat in February, 1995 and the other by the present Congress headed by Ashok Gehlot in the year of 1999. Both the regimes have shown the faith in the process of decentralisation and democratisation of these grass-root bodies. They have accorded importance to women empowerment as well as reservations to the weaker sections of society, along with the autonomy of these bodies. The Act has defined the functions and powers of these bodies, but it is silent about the executive powers of Panchayat Raj institutions in regard to recruitment, appointment of staff and the control under them. As per the census of 1991, the process of delimitation of those bodies were undertaken by the Government in 1994. Consequently, the number of village Panchayats, Panchayat samities and Zila Parishad increased to 9,187,237 and 31, respectively. There were 9,185 panchayats. Thus the entire rural Rajasthan was brought under the umbrella of Panchayat Raj system. It is being strengthened.

Rajasthan had 27,000 women panchas for the first time. Of the 9,173 panchayats, 3,058 panchayats were women sarpanchas. The state had 237 panchayat samities. The elections for the three tier panchayati raj institutions were held in phases. The elections were held on party lines as there is no restrictions in the Act on the basis of the understanding among the political parties. The elections of the pradhans were held on political lines in the state. The sarpanchas will not become members of the panchayat samities and the pradhans will not become members of the zila parishads. The MLAs and MPs cannot contest panchayat elections.

Rajasthan is the first state to introduce the two-children restriction on the candidates contesting the panchayat elections. However, relief has been granted to the candidates having twins. Where the couple have only one child on the date of the commencement of the Act and thereafter, any number of children born out of a single subsequent delivery shall be deemed to be one entity. Those convicted of an offence punishable under the Rajasthan prevention of Mrityu Bhoj Act, 1990 will be disqualified from seeking the panchayat elections. However, there is no disqualification for those encourage child marriages. The Government, however, on the eve of the civil elections in Rajasthan, waived the condition till November, 1995.

The state Government has drawn up many special trust on employment and training for women with the purpose of securing equal rights and empowering the rural women. These include the Anganwari plan, the support to Training and Employment Programme (STEP), the Employment-*cum*-Income Generation-*cum*-Production Units NORAD and the Indira Mahila Yojna—IMY Programmes of Education, etc. The aim of these schemes is to change he social attitude to facilitate equal participation of men and women and pave the way for harmonious social growth, to create a conducive environment for the advancement of women in Rajasthan. The state has also taken steps towards setting up commissioner for women's rights in accordance with the goals of National Policy for the Empowerment of Women and the advancement of gender equality. The State's budget 1995-96 contained special clause for it. On the other hand, the Government of Rajasthan has strictly enforced the two children condition for the elected members, and numerous elected candidates both men and women have been disqualified on account of the violation of the clause of the Act. Its purpose is to restrict the growing rate of population in Rajasthan.

On being challenged Section 19 of the Rajasthan P.R. Act, 1994, and Section 26 of the Rajasthan Municipalities Act, 1994 providing for disqualification of elected representatives for routing the two children norm, the Rajasthan High Court on August 30, 1997 held the norm laid down in the legislation constitutionally valid. According to the division bench of the High Court, the provision is in the national interest. This is one of the pioneering steps to check the growing rate of population in the state. This norm can be followed by other states also for their elected members.

EDUCATION : THE BASIS OF STATES GROWTH

The present Government's attempt has been to expand the basic education network. For it, education is the foremost condition for development, which can only help in checking the growing population and ensuring economic prosperity. The Government has launched many such measures and projects to enlighten the people about their rights and duties.

They are: Shiksha Apke Dwar, Lok Jumbish Shiksha, Shiksha Karmi, DPEP, etc. The experiment of opening Rajiv Gandhi Swaran Jayanti Pathshalas on the Madhya Pradesh pattern in strengthening the education sector in the state has earned popularity. Over 12,000 buildings for such pathshala (schools) have been constructed under Famine Relief Programme. Under this school system, educated youth of villages are employed for imparting education. For this purpose, it may be recalled, the Shiksha Darpan Survey was carried out in 2000 to identify the urban and rural children who had not been enrol led in these schools. Over 23 lakh such children have been identified who were deprived of basic education. Today, hectic efforts have been made to enroll over 12.35 lakh children, and about 10.65 lakh children are yet to be enrolled in schools. Most of these children belong to SCs, STs, minorities and other backward classes. This programme today is carried out under Shiksha Apke Dwar campaign. If it is successfully implemented by officials, Government employees and school teachers, it would bring the state in the category of the developed state of the country.

Likewise, the state Government has given top priority to strengthening the road network in the state. In this direction, a sum of Rs. 600 crore has been sanctioned on upgrading 24,000 km. roads in the state. The Government is serious to see that the Pradhan Mantri Gram Sadak Yojana is fully implemented to connect all villages of over 1,000 population. The cooperation of Panchayats is currently sought to ensure that the target of expansion of basic amenities including roads, power, education, medical health and drinking water in the rural areas of the state is achieved by March end of 2003, or before the next assembly elections. The ruling party has in its mind the fallout of anti-incumbency factor, which finished the BJPs base in the 1998 elections.

Notably, Chief Secretary Inderjit Khanna in a many meetings of top brass has directed officials concerned to lay special emphasis on completing the basic amenities in the rural areas as per the schedule. Stress is being given for the effective implementation of all those programmes as cited above. Congress President Mrs. Sonia Gandhi, too, has asked all the Congress Chief Ministers to implement the Party's poll manifesto in totality in their respective states in the Gauhati session of the party. She has taken the three meetings with the CM of Rajasthan to see that the dalits, minorities women and backward classes are properly cared of through the development programmes. The state Government has taken many steps to strengthen the working of Panchayat Raj bodies in the rural areas.

ABOUT RAJIV PATHSHALAS

When the Chief Minister took over the reigns of the state, he directed the officials to follow the manifesto of the Congress party like 'Bible' and accordingly he shaped the policies and projects to achieve the mission. The CM is determined to raise the literacy rate by providing education at the door step. His slogan Pani Bachao, Bijli bachao, Sabko Padhao (save water, save electricity and teach all) has earned popularity and the World Bank has even appreciated the slogan. But so far as the employment sector is concerned, it has not been able to generate many jobs. Instead of providing jobs, the state has surged to 12 lakh employees. The only consolation for the educated youth is the Rajiv Gandhi Pathshalas. These Pathshalas impart primary education and appointment of the teachers are done through Gram Sabha—the lowest tier of the rural administration.

Each gram panchayat has a woman teacher and by appointing 32,000 such teachers, eight lakh children who were deprived of basic education are now likely to get education. The teachers of Rajiv Gandhi Pathshalas get an honorarium of Rs. 1300 per month. Opposition leader Bhairon Singh Shekhawat blamed the Government for opening an avenue for the Congress cadre and paying them Rs. 1300 per month through the Rajiv Gandhi Pathshala scheme.

The Gehlot Government is finding it tough to implement the recommendations of the Fifth Pay Commission to abolish 10 per cent of posts in various Government departments on an annual basis. It is so because the state Government has signed an MoU with the Union Government to this effect. However, the state Government feels that large scale abolition of posts will not be practical and it would cause a setback electorally. The Government is unable to abolish posts in the health, education and police departments though a sub-committee or the cabinet had suggested that 6,000 posts should be abolished. Against the recommendations of the sub-committee, only 3,000 posts have been abolished. The present work force of Government employees are six lakhs and those working in the Panchayat Raj is about a lakh.

The state is finding it difficult to disburse salary every month.

ROOTING OUT CORRUPTION

As regards rooting out of corruption in the state, the state Government has appointed a Chief Vigilance Commissioner (CVC) to weed out corruption of high places. The state's Anti-corruption Bureau has booked a number of cases against high officials including some collectors. As first CVC R.K. Naiyar received over one thousand complaints against officials, but no action was taken. There is a growing trend corruption at the Panchayati Raj level too. The sad thing is that the role and powers of the CVC has not been properly outlined and sarpanchas ate taken out of the purview of the CVC. The Personnel department has not given the CVC powers to book state Government employees. At present there is a Lokayukta institution headed by justice M.C. Jain, but it has proved to be a teethless body.

LAND ALLOTMENT CAMPAIGN

According to official figure, the state Government claims to have allotted land to 57,000 families through the camps known as 'Prashasan Gaon ke sang' and 'Prashashan Shaharo ke Sang' (प्रशासन गांवों के संग एवं प्रशासन शहरो के संग).

According to the Government "over 57,000 families of different categories have been allotted the land worth Rs. 200 crore during camps organised under land allotment and regularisation campaigns in different parts of the state. Under the campaign, over 27,000 families of general categories have benefited from the allotment and regularisation of 42,414 acres of land worth Rs. 72.22 crore it is claimed that in these camps, nine thousand acres of land, costing 28.92 crore has been allotted to 7,716 families of scheduled castes and 23,509 acres of land, costing Rs. 72.22 crore to 22,247 families of scheduled tribes. Over 50,000 families have been allotted agricultural land under the land allotment and regularisation campaign in the state. It includes 7,165 families of Ajmer division, 1,455 families of Bikaner, 6,966 families of Jaipur, 1,041 families of Jodhpur, 10128 families of Kota and 24,305 families of Udaipur. As many as 6,507 scheduled castes families, 21,344 scheduled tribe families and 22,210 families of general categories have been benefited under the campaign.

Similarly, land of 6,898 families has been regularised, including 1,209 families of scheduled castes, 903 families of scheduled tribes and 4,786 families of general category.*

IMPLEMENTATION OF FAMILY PLANNING RULE

Rajasthan is the pioneer state to adopt the family planning concept at the Panchayat Raj level and as per the provision of 39(2) of the Act, the born of a third child of any elected member is a crime. Rajasthan is the first state to adopt this rule. Accordingly, the state officials have been very much serious about the implementation of this provision. A number of elected members from Pradhans towards have been disqualified in 2001-02, after a through investigation by Divisional Commissioners, though in most of cases, local level feuds have been the cause of complaints by villagers. Third child has practically proved to be a curse for these elected members at the grass root levels.

The administration has instructed all official is to ensure effective implementation of 'Shiksha Aapke Dwar' campaign and mid-day meal programme in all districts. Most of the primary schools have been involved in this mission. The rural administration bears the responsibility of enrolling children under the Shiksha Aapke Dwar campaign, so as to achieve cent percent target or literacy. As regards arrangement of the mid-day meal programme rural officials have been asked to ensure that wheat should not be rotten. Tehsildars have been made incharge of this programme.

The present Government has taken up the Anti-poverty project at district/Panchayat level to benefit those families who are below poverty line. It is meant to eradicate poverty. This programme is being carried out with the assistance of the world Bank. The CM has very much serious about the proper

* *The Times of India*, New Delhi, ed., July 7, 2002, p. 3.

implementation of the school children nutrition programme (Mid-day food) and to effect the CM has written a letter to the Centre on July 13, 2002 to ensure the supply of a good quality of wheat being provided by the FCI for these poor and dalit children. This is meant to avoid any health hazards to children. This state administration has received numerous complaints about the poor quality of wheat. Even many parents have directed their children not to consume the mid-day food (Gughari)

In Rajasthan, the polity is gradually changing. The ruling party has started giving importance to 'good governance'. The Chief Minister emphasised all efforts to project the right image of his Government, so that it can return to power next year. The party has picked up cudgels in advance to keep the anti-incumbency factor away. The grit and determination has been shown 15 month before the party faces the next assembly elections falling due in 2003.

Among other priorities, the ruling Congress in Rajasthan has been giving top priority to supply of potable water in the far flung areas of Rajasthan, and the CM has sanctioned to increase the capacity of the Rajiv Gandhi lift cancel to benefit more villages. For this purpose Rs. 108 crore has been sanctioned. The CM is concerned of the constant lowering of the underground water level in the state. To fight the current curse of famine seems to be a serious challenge for the state Government both administratively and electorally. The second top priority of the CM is power sector reforms. The power production has been improved/increased due to power reforms. The CM has laid the foundation stone at many places to erect more grid sub-stations, in order to ensure adequate supply of electricity in the rural belt. The Congress party has launched many other campaigns to bring respite to the common people. For example, over 66 lakh rural population had been benefited under the 'Prashashan Gaon ke Sang campaign' and 12 lakh urban population under the 'Prashshan Sehron ke Sang'. Under these campaigns many land regularisation and allotment of land has been carried out. This approach has yielded positive results. Now the Government has initiated to open cyber kiosks in many villages.

With a view to bring about improvement in the nutrition and health level of children and women, the state administration has initiated 66 child development projects under the ICDS III project of the state. They commenced in the year 1999 and shall be continued till 2004. Under this programme, over 9,648 new anganwari centres would be opened. At present, 9,240 such centres are already functioning and the centre has earmarked over Rs. 190.68 core for this purpose. Likewise, the CM plans to spend Rs. 120 crore for nutrition programme to benefit school children in the state.

CONCLUDING OBSERVATIONS

The pattern of decentralisation of administrative machinery has reduced the role of the bureaucracy and local autonomy and accountability have been strengthened. But the apprehensions are expressed that the devolution of this power under the new act may create a sense or deep frustration among bureaucrats, who are now expected to work under the elected representatives in panchayats, and they may handle the new assignment half-heartedly, against the spirit of democratic decentralisation. The danger at this moment is that if the euphoria is generated about the 'power to the people concept', the bureaucracy may be seen as friend to the PR system. This is possible only if it ensures the freedom to these bodies in terms of their flowers entrusted under the constitution Amendment Act, 1992. The question is—how to motivate the bureaucracy to make the PRIs successful? It is proposed that periodic conferences/seminars or meetings or various heads of departments and elected members local bodies may be convened to highlight the roles to be played by the civil servants in making the scheme a success. These conferences/ meetings should be addressed by the Chief Minister and the role of bureaucracy *vis-a-vis* the elected members should be clarified in the era of globalisation and liberalisation. A motivated bureaucracy is as necessary condition for the success of the nascent democratic polity at the lowest level of PR system.

The slogan 'power to the people' shall have to be linked with the past mischievous and demagogic experiences in which the real powers are yet to be transferred to these people. It may be recalled that our colorial hangover system of district administration remains intact and it is responsible for the failure of our PR system. It may negate the potentiality of the reforms even today. Therefore, there will be need to ensure under the new changes in the act that the measure does not suffer in the course of implementation. The state Government will have to provide adequate funds to empower these grass-roots bodies to raise them. Care will have to be taken to ensure that the new decentralised system does not become the prey of our societal structure, backwardness, illiteracy and the culture of poverty, coupled with caste, communalism and the other group rivalries in the majority of the villages.

It is heartening that the ruling Congress party is sensitive to the power to the people's concept, or the functioning rural democracy in Rajasthan. It is gradually reducing the powers of the bureaucracy to ensure the concept of autonomy, transparency and accountability of these bodies. There is no doubt that the middle classes and peasants as well a woman have been enlightened by programmes and policies carried out by the state Government. However, the state leadership is supposed to take into account the following :

(a) The grass-root bodies should not be allowed to suffer from the paucity of funds.

(b) The interference of the party in power in the state should be minimal and the role of the collector and his jurisdiction should be finalised in respect of the running the self-Government. He is still the symbol of imperial rule on a republic base. The trend of politicisation of the local administration through the bureaucratic staff should be discouraged as the state had the experience or it before the enactment of 73rd/74th Amendment Act. The need of the hour is to have a proper coordination, both vertical and horizontal between the popular and bureaucratic elements. There is also a need for change in the psychology of the Government servants. The voice of elected members must have primacy over the bureaucratic element, and for this a proper training should be provided to the administrative personnel.

(c) The proliferation of caste-*cum*-trends at the grass-root level must be prevented in order to boost up egalitarian trends contributing towards the socialistic pattern in our rural economy. Care has to be taken that new economic order of the country with the market-oriented forces does not become a source of exploitation of poor/rural masses of the state through the dominant caste superiority or rampant factionalism. Real rural leadership should be allowed to merge in place of forged linkages between caste and politics.

(d) The practice of child labour is still widespread and our children are employed in local factories, small industries and farm fields. The mission of curbing child labour can be achieved by rapid growth and expansion of primary and secondary education at the grass-root levels.

(e) Social mobilisation is vital for the removal of poverty and the success or poverty alleviation programmes hinges crucially on social mobilisation, which will in turn lead to greater efficiency in the use of resources. But it has been seen that no state has so far set-up any machinery under the new legislation enacted through the 73rd Constitutional Amendment relating to Panchayati Raj. Our concern is that social mobilisation *vis-a-vis* poverty alleviation programmes should be linked with the grass-roots level planning process and the efforts should be made by our Planning Commission to involve non-Governmental organisations (NGOs) for the success of the programmes and plans. A top bottom approach without adequate participation has been mainly responsible for the failure of such programmes. In this process, the district should be the basis to deal with the issues like illiteracy, land degradation, continued population growth, gender inequalities, food security, application of technologies, maintenance of rural health, etc.

CHAPTER

14

Rural Development Through Panchayat Raj Institutions

Decentralisation is "a new mantra of governance", but in Indian context, it is narrow in the administration of poorly governed northern states, as decentralization would lead to more powers in the hands of a feudal elites at the grass-roots levels. That is why centralized planning still prevails in our federal set-up against the very spirit of 73rd amendment. The 'Centre' with funds and bureaucrats has not disappeared or its charates has not changed in the administrative devolution of power. What is needed is replacement of it with decentralization and with intellectual pluralism as a guiding principle of planning for development.

This contradiction calls for a rethink of the planning process. The solution lies in decentralizing the process. States have their planning boards, which can coordinate work at the grass-roots. Panchayati Raj institutions should be asked to work on localized plans. Problems and concerns specific to a particular area will then get enough attention. This will also make the process more democratic and inclusive. The People's Planning exercise initiated in Kerala in the 90s offers lessons for a decentralized and participatory approach to policy-making. If backed by sufficient funds and judicious redeployment of bureaucrats, grass-roots planning could help states to cut down project costs and maximize benefits to the people. At present, planning is an exercise undertaken by a small group of *babus* who follow state economic models handed down by 'experts' and 'consultants'. This boxed approach only alienated people (*aam admi of India*), the intended beneficiaries. Development is after all a political problem and it needs the involvement of the people at large.

HOW TO HAVE A RESPONSIVE ADMINISTRATION?

The conference, convened by Cabinet Secretary B.K. Chaturvedi on 19th July, 2006 discussed the changes for making the administration more responsive to the requirements of 21st century. It was particularly concerned about the procedural bottle necks that keep the poor and dalits from accessing a ration card or copies of land record and other kinds of documents. The focus was rightly concerned on the implementation of schemes like Rural Employment Guarantee Programme; National Rural Health Mission, Right to Information Act, the Bharat Nirman, poverty eradication, the mid-day meal scheme, etc. which shall definitely have a vital bearing on country's aspirations for double digit growth rate. Herein, the Panchayats shall have to be recognized as 'agency' to increase the reach of the schemes to the downtrodden, keeping in mind to arrest the ongoing trends of corruption, caste politics and violence.

STRENGTHENING A PARTICIPATIVE DEMOCRACY

There was much discussion on increasing the strength of Lok Sabha seat on the basis of population. In order to avoid North-South divide, a better solution was proposed to have favoured to keep the inter-state allocation of Lok Sabha seats intact while read just constituency boundaries to reflect population changes. The same arrangement applies for Legislative Assemblies as well. In order to have a balance between rural and urban areas and to maintain arithmetical parity in terms of population, the Panchayats and Municipalities, 1992—a third tier of governance under the 73rd and 74th Constitutional amendments should be given due representation in the state assemblies/Parliament or by creating Legislative Councils for states (at present the council exists only in five states in our federal structure). Today, we need our Panchayats and Municipalities as much as we need our assemblies and Parliament and it is suggested that the voice of the people should be heard to strengthen a participative democracy, instead of adding a few hundred more MPs in parliament to represent increased population which shall increase expenses to the tax payers.

On the other hand, our democracy needs functional reforms to make it more accessible to ordinary people to be more say in them. According to Harsh Mander,* more number of powers are needed not in Parliament but in panchayats and municipalities. Many critical decisions have far-reaching effect on the lives of ordinary people and they have no say in them. For example, the economic policies of globalisation, for which we need deliberative forms of democracy such as referendums and citizens' juries. We need to strengthen the rights of citizens to hold Governments and their representatives more accountable. The Right to Information Act has done more for Indian democracy than the creation of a thousand new MPs. It should not be possible for Governments to suppress democratic freedom and popular discontent with armed forces or anti-terror laws. Democracies are as much about the rights of minorities as it's of majorities, and therefore religious minorities, Dalits, and women, need to be defended and strengthened.

The elegant circular structure that the house of lower Parliament in Delhi does not need to be populated further. The defence of democracy requires greater powers for the real rulers of this land, the people themselves. Until this is done, farmers will continue to extinguish their lives unheeded, and Sharmila from Manipur may refuse food and water for another six years but still never be heard by those she and her people elect.

---

* "RTI can do more for Democracy than a thousand MPs", *The Times of India,* New Delhi edn. Oct. 15, 2006, p. 18.

REVIVING RURAL INDIA

We have confirmed statics of suicide by 25,000 farmers since 1997. About 80 percent of India's population still lives in rural areas where consumption has actually declined in the last fifteen years. In fact, we have a sub-Saharan African in our mindset. How can we talk of marching forward or of a software park in the conditions of shortage of onions; rising price commodities like gas, milk, petrol, wheat, etc. This kind of depressed situation must be stopped and farmers' class should be made to live in a decent condition, for which the Government must change their mindset by restoring a bold and revolutionary approach. The Government should depute a team of 10 to 12 young officers of rural background to every block of villages as 'developers' with a mandate to act as change agents. The team should be led by a project leader who must be empowered to achieve desired results in the given time frame and budget.

The responsibilities of the team should be the following: Undertake watershed development, construct check dams and tanks, dig wells, popularize drip irrigation, ensure safe drinking water supply and prevent soil erosion; motivate farmers to sell their produce directly to urban consumers and construct cold storage facilities; obtain help from agricultural universities to improve farm productivity and to train farmers.

There is also an urgent need to abolish outdated laws like APMC Act which force farmers to sell their produce only to market committees controlled by influential politicians. Farm produce should be allowed to be sold freely across state boundaries. The Government should protect our farmers' interests in WTO negotiations or in building SEZs. We must prevent developed countries, which give huge subsidy to their farmers, from dumping their farm produce on us at cheap prices.

Finance Minister P. Chidambaram budgeted Rs. 50,000 crore for the Bharat Nirman programme in 2006. But Rajiv Gandhi had famously observed that only 15 percent of development funds actually reaches intended beneficiaries. The Centre also depends on a matching effort by the state

Governments. State Governments need to strengthen the delivery mechanism.*

We need an economic revolution that starts in villages, not one that bypasses them. And we need a creative solution for such a revolution.

BHARAT NIRMAN PROGRAMME

The Central Government led by U.P.A. has announced massive programmes for the renewal of Urban Centre for Bharat Nirman, for which guidelines and monitoring system have been laid down to implement programmes. The major objectives of the programme are as follows :

> (a) One crore hectors of un-irrigated land will be irrigated; (b) All villages whose population is 1000 or more and 500 or more in hilly areas will be connected with roads; (c) Over 60 lakh houses will be built in villages; (d) 74,000 habitants which do not have access to safe drinking water will be provided these facilities, and (e) Each and every village will have at least one telephone connection. This programme if enforced honestly, has tremendous potential to solve the problem on unemployment, abolish poverty and create a new wheat policy for the country, provided proper planning is made and care is taken of investment and people's involvement is ensured. It needs huge money to spend.

It may be recalled that the Indira Awas Yojana has been introduced by the Central Government since several years. Any survey of the houses constructed under Indira Awas Yoj ana would virtually reveal that most of the houses have been dilapidated, as they were constructed without any norms or standards. Besides, the Government should reconsider the existing policy of construction houses for the people from Scheduled Castes, Scheduled Tribes or minorities at a distance from the habitants. This may perhaps keep them away from the national stream and perpetuate the existing caste system.

---

* Arun Firodia, "Reviving Rural Indian", *The Times of India*, July 6, 2006.

Before constructing 60 lakh houses in a random manner, according to Dr. Mohan Dharia,* a long term plan should be undertaken to reconstruct our villages. It is well known that various tribes created their own habitations and housed were built from the point of view of security. Naturally no care was taken of health or sanitation. On this background restructuring the whole village habitation providing all possible amenities should be considered by the Government.

Programme of restructuring 6 lakh villages is, indeed, a Herculean task and enormous investment may be required for the same. However, if we plant species like Bamboo, Casuarinas, Poplars, Teak, etc. on a massive scale in the earnmarked area, within next 10 to 15 years such plantations would share maximum part of the expenditure required for reconstruction. With a visionary approach the farmers staying in the villages may be asked to reserve about 4000 to 5000 sq. ft. area from their field only for plantation of tree species, to erect a house in future. It may be possible to have small house with all amenities, cattle shed and storage for food grains along with kitchen, garden. This will also require perfect planning for every village. The Government should reconsider the whole programme of constructing houses without such planning. Similarly, National Agencies or Missions as suggested above should be constituted to effectively implement objective) of the programme. It would be advisable to get these objectives scrutinized from the Planning Commission before introducing the programme with proper planning and adequate mechanism to monitor the same and to keep them away from competition.

POSTING DOCTORS IN RURAL AREAS

In 2006, the Health and Family Welfare Ministry proposed compulsory rural postings for all MBBS students but due to stiff resistance the plan was shelved. But the ministry once again, after discussion of the matter with Medical Council of

* Dr. Mohan Dharia is President of Vanarai, Pune and former Deputy Chairman of the Planning Commission and has given his reflection on the programme, South Asia Politics, Feb. 2006, pp. 6-7.

India and other professional bodies, has made up the mind to have a legislation making it mandatory for all doctors to undergo one-year rural posting before they get a permanent registration. And the steering group *National Rural Health Mission* has approved it. It is like that of the Chinese model where it is mandatory for all doctors to undertake the fresh job at rural areas. This policy should be the basic part of infrastructure facilities to look after the health of rural masses. Around 26,000 doctors are posted at the health and community centers, but about 30 to 40% of doctors do not report for work. The compulsory postings would ensure better health facilities for people living in the rural areas. The manner in which cases of dengue fever have been reported in Sept.-Oct. 2006 in the country, underlines the need of such a law. Though it was epidemic yet it is matter of concern. We need to create masses awareness through young doctors while roping schools in this mission to contain such diseases.

Government health services are pathetic, with either employees or drugs missing from primary health centers on most days. Only one-fifth of all medical services are supplied by the Government, the lowest proportion in the world. What is the way out? First, some states should experiment with education and health vouchers given directly to households, who will have the option to use these in Government or private schools and clinics. The ensuing competition will raise standards. Second, we must end the license permit raj that strangles private school growth. Third, we should devolve budgetary powers to panchayats so that they can directly hire doctors and teachers, and not have to depend on unshakable staff from state capitals. Fourth, local Governments should have the power to withhold the wages of staff that are absent on any day. Fifth, private universities must be encouraged rather than banned, and foreign universities should be allowed to open campuses in rural sector. Such reforms will be just a starting point. We have a long way to go.

A LESSON FROM SINGUR LAND ACQUISITION

The UPA Government has enacted the SEZ Act, which needs changes in its rules (Special Economic Zones), specially on land acquisition, tax concessions and labour laws. The way the Trinamul Congress supreme launched movement against Tata Motors plant in Singur (West Bengal) underlines the flaws ill the land acquisition procedure for industrialization. Even Land Acquisition Act, entacted by British India in 1894, no industralization should be allowed at the cost of cultivators' land which is fertile. The matter needs to lay down new national guidelines.

In the light of liberation and globalisation *vis-a-vis* the spate of farmer's suicide in the recent years, our agri-trade policy needs to be reshaped in a way that the SEZ initiative adds new dynamics in the food security because, agriculture sector in India has long become economically unviable. Probably against this backgrounds, the UPA Government endorsed Congress President Sonia Gandhi's concern on acquisition of farmer's land for industrial purposes including creating SEZs. The Centre has directed state Governments to ensure that SEZs are built only on wasteland or in fertile fields and farmers should be rightfully and adequately compensated for acquiring such land. The concept of economic development should not be carried out at the cost of farmers and peasants. At present, India has approved 164 such zones to boost exports and economic growth, aiming to attract petro-chemicals, auto parts, IT, bio-technology, jewellery and electronics firms with investment of at least 22 billion over three years.

That the above cited crisis does not get aggravated further, the prevailing practice of controlling food trade by middle men to procure crops should be broken down to ensure the role of FDI in food retail. The structure has to be reshaped. The Government should incentivise retail companies to procure directly from the fields, particularly from farmer cooperatives. Policies, especially related to credit, should be put in place to encourage the latter's formation on the lines of self-help groups. Women self-help groups should be encouraged to take up local procurement of farm produce, if need be. Cooperatives have been successful, most famously in the dairy sector, and to some extent in sugar and plantation crops. It is time we explored this option in the case of food grains and with food majors, including multi-nationals. The retailers, in turn, could help farmers access not just the market but also technology and credit to boost productivity. Such a relationship could work not because of any altruistic reasons but for sound business reasons. Geography and climatic variations offer India the possibility to be the world's food basket. On the other hand, declining productivity and low prices have been the bane for agriculture in India. The entry of food majors could open up new markets for farmers, drive out middlemen and fetch producers better prices. Assured business would also empower farmers to risk diversification of crops. Besides formulating policies that would encourage a healthy retailer farmer arrangement, the state should step up public investment in irrigation and electricity. Now Jai Kisan slogan should not continue to be an empty slogan.

While keeping in view the events of West Bengal *vis-a-vis* SEZs, the Apex Chambers like C.I.I., Ficci and Assocham have agreed to compensate to farmers for their land cost as per market rates and the members of the displaced families be given alternative employment. According to our President A.P.J. Abdul Kalam, India can be move into 10th position (now holding 43th position in global competitiveness), if following important factors, namely—knowledge, technology, innovation, resource investment, customer loyalty, quality and value of products, employee productivity, working environment and a creative leadership—are taken into consideration. Rehabilitation, not displacement should be the focus of new SEZ's policy. It needs a carefully study and its implications on social sector.*

ACCOUNTABILITY OF NGOs

In a globalised world, it's not just the Government that affects the lives of people, but NGOs too. So if the Government can be held accountable to internal and external stakeholders, why not NGOs? This is a debate that's now seeing some

* In West Bengal, forcefully acquisition of farm land at Singur for TATA Motor's proposed project of small car unit, triggered mass movement because of not paying adequate compensation to farmers. This was led by Trinamul Congress supremo Mamta Banerjee and attacked by the police. Now the Left Government had to suspend the scheme.

fruition. Over the last decade, NGOs have proliferated in India, while remaining relatively unregulated. There are an estimated 12 lakh NGOs, over half based in six lakh villages. But many do good work, but lack of accountability has allowed less-credible NGOs to undermine the work of the credible ones. This has led to a dilution of trust between donors and beneficiaries. In order to celebrate good work and raise confidence, Credibility Alliance of London (CA), an initiative by voluntary organizations to enhance good governance within the sector, was stated in 2004.

For this accountability and transparency, the public mobilization shall have to be streamlined at the village level. They should have to standarise their accounts, reports and other things. We cannot effort to a sliding of public morality.*

ACCOUNTABILITY OF CIVIC BODIES

Urban Development Ministry's Model Municipality Disclosure Bill, to be adopted by states pitching for funds under the Jawaharlal Nehru Urban Renewal Mission (JNNURM) to revamp the crumbling infrastructure, calls for municipalities to put in public domain details of services being offered and their quality. The civic bodies also have to provide details about their financial health on a quarterly basis. "The move will empower people to demand better quality of services as promised by civic bodies in their disclosure details." The model Bill, aimed at injecting transparency and accountability into various municipal administration, will require CIVIC agencies to disclose their financial statements within two months of the end of each quarter and for the full year within three months of the end of the financial year. In fact, the purpose of it is to put a check on growing tendencies of competition in these bodies, to evaluate the civic agencies' performance and enforce accountability on officials and staff. The bodies will have to maintain and publicize official records of subsidy (programmes) while revealing decisions made by their bodies" councils/committees. This should be applicable

* Surendra Mushi, Biju Paul Abraham, G.G., Democratic Societies of Globalisation (New Delhi, Sage Publication, 2004).

to Panchayat Raj institutions which need to undertake systematic rural reforms. As such no system of governance is effective without accountability. Gram Sabha should be permitted to hold Panchayats accountable and responsive.

In UP, the elections to the local bodies were held in Oct. 2006, in which Minister Sanjay Garg resigned due to the excesses committed by the police on minorities in his own constituency. Such events/developments can be prevented if the range and scope of the Election Commission of India is further enlarged and brought in its preview to ensure that the entire state level electoral machinery does function under its command and supervision. The grass-roots level democratic institutions shall have to be strengthened while keeping control over mal-practices involving caste politics, etc. Without this, the fruits of good governance can not be procured at grass-root level.*

RURAL DEVELOPMENT THROUGH NCAER**

In a first of its kind estimation of infrastructure deficit in rural areas, the National Council of Applied Economic Research (NCAER) has estimated an investment of Rs. 1,58,310 crore in telecommunications, power, roads and transport, water and sanitation. Pointing to the fact that rural India faces more acute shortage of infrastructure, the *India Rural Infrastructure Report*, released in December, 2006, made a strong pitch for decentralizing and localizing the provision of these services in addition to seeking newer financial instruments. Today, rural areas 23.98% minorities in and 30.41 % urban areas are living below poverty line.

* In a classic but first-ever judgement, the court of India ruled that the state Election Commissions can under no circumstances postpone elections to Panchayati and Municipalties after the completion of their 5 year term. The only exception to timely holding of elections could be man-made calamities, such as riots and breakdown of law and order or natural calamities. This ruling will strengthen grass-roots democracy. The petition was related to holding the elections of the Ahmedabad municipality and the pressure was put on the Government to hold the timely elections. *The Times of India*, New Delhi, 21 Oct., 2006, p. 7.

** NCAER's India Rural Infrastructure Report, released on 31.12.2006.

According to the Report, The capital needed to build infrastructure is a small percentage of the total expenditure that would be needed to be incurred by states (for operation and maintenance). Nor do the capital costs include central funds that would be needed to be spent on administrative expenses and subsidies. Probably, this is the first time that the focus has been stressed on Rural India, and that too on strengthening infrastructural facilities through the 11th plan. Much shall depend on the concept of 'good governance' and the priority of local administration.

INDIA NEEDS ANOTHER GREEN REVOLUTION

Our former President, Dr. A.P.J. Abdul Kalam has stressed the need for a 'second Green Revolution' based on practical applications of latest technological innovations in the age of globalisation to meet the future food needs of common man necessitated by increasing population growth. It needs to focus on agriculture sector, which is still backward. The President said so while inaugurating the Global Forum on Agricultural Research—GFAR.

Of course, 'water' could not lead wars in the near future, as per UNDP's report, but hydrologists have pointed out to exploit earth water plant net (Oceans) that has 97% of its water, as water needed to grow food, support industries and maintain the environment. As per the UNDP's Human Development Report 2006, by 2025, over billion people across the world over would be facing water crisis.

TO CONCLUDE

Democracy in India has to move from elections to development and the same has to be extended to all organizations and institutions. Our family, religious institutions, political parties, educational institutions and development organizations have to be democratized. As there is no democratic spirit in our institutions, the organizations have to be democratic accountable and respossive in its functioning. Many of our constitutional provisions are not operationalized because they are countered by the practices of the communities. As our activities are in a feudal mode, community practices are taking upper hand to sabotage the provisions of the Constitution. There are numerous examples to mention where the caste Hindus has not allowed the Dalits to contest in the Gram Panchayat elections. Thus, communities have totally pushed the constitutional provisions away from the grass-roots. It is a paradox that the caste based communities have reservoir of energies, talents, skills, knowledge, capacity and capability but they are not being harnessed, and instead in the name of expansion of Government they are annihilated and allowed to die. But there are certain practices which are antithetical to democracy which are being allowed to survive. As a result, the anti-democratic feudal elements have perfectly buckled with our electoral politics and bureaucratic development activities.

To overcome these problems, late Rajiv Gandhi when he was the Prime Minister, took the initiative to introduce series of reforms and of which economic reforms and political reforms were phenomenal. In political reform he intended to deepen democracy, change the character of our democracy, bring the development initiative from below by changing the total paradigm of development and made it an inclusive and gender-sensitive democracy. This would create a change in our society and show the way to other societies in the world by involving the people as stakeholders. The reform which he initiated in economy has paid rich dividends to those who have enhanced their capability and skill. But the poor and the unskilled are still marginalized.

The reform which he initiated on decentralization has brought the marginalized to the central stage for governance. But handling power by them has yet not taken a shape. The Dalits have come forward but caste politics and discrimination have presented them. The people who are marginalized now have to build their capacity and negotiate for power and resource to develop themselves on their own. New forces are emerging. The Panchayati Raj system, therefore, has to be freed from the clutches of political parties by declaring the grass-roots institutions non-party-based context. The new forces of youth groups have to actively involve themselves in the grass-roots institutions. The civil society organizations have to build the capacity of the local body leaders. Along with the capacity building, people have to be mobilized to participate in Gram Sabha meetings. Constantly providing support to the Dalit and women Panchayat leaders to manage the Panchayats is the need of the hour. By supporting and strengthening the constitutional Panchayats, the customary and traditional Panchayats have to be democratized and a synergy has to be established between the traditional Panchayats and constitutional Panchayats. All activities, especially, development initiatives have to be undertaken. With the active participation of stakeholders delivery of services will be done effectively. Grass-roots empowerment is more important than grass-roots development. A new citizenship culture has to be created at the grass-roots. By doing so the self-dignity of the poor, marginalized, women and Dalit will be restored. They should have a feeling that they can decide their destiny on their own. All major changes in the electoral politics came after Rajiv Gandhi through the Panchayati Raj Institutions have created revolutionary changes, but this new arrangement is yet not properly shaped to function with autonomy. Today, forces are working against the devolution of powers, inclusion of women and Dalit in governance. To overcome this kind of barriers and obstacles, a movement from below has to be initiated which will strengthen grass-roots democracy.*

TAKING E-GOVERNANCE TO RURAL AREAS

In a bold step, the BJP Governments of M.P. and Rajasthan have shown assertion to take e-governance to rural areas and ensure villages 24 hr. service of electricity. The plan is good but would face a cropper if power supply in rural areas is not improved. It is yet not clear how will computes work without power supply? These states have been facing a power shortfall since last two years. Even farmers in villages are troubled over the non-availability of electricity, apart from the crisis the student community faces the power crisis during examinations. The idea of e-governance is good for bringing

* "Indian Democracy: A Re-thinking" in South Asia Politics, New Delhi, Dec. 2006, pp. 30-31.

transparency and good governance as it would connect the Government Secretariat to the key villages. The reality is that more than 50% of the states' websites are either defunt or not up-dated in the wake of power-crisis. The states shall have to prioritise the supply of power before the e-governance is to be introduced in the rural sector for development. Without ensuring power supply no development is possible. The farmers have already protested and blocked the offices/ highways against power crisis and faced bullets also.*

Unfortunately, our Budget 2007-8 claims to be dedicated to the Kisan cause but it has little to say about the crisis of rural infrastructure, particularly power. Instead, it talks of fertilizer outlay/subsidy which helps the industry rather than the farmers. Besides, fertilizer than the farmers. Besides, fertilizer cannot be more important than bizli, sarak, panni, housing, telecommunications. If rural infrastructure is overlooked in any budget, all poverty alleviation programmes shall withhold the overall growth plan, namely the Bharat Nirman or other schemes. Both the power and agricultural sectors are equally important.

* The issues relating to institutional structures and dynamics of global governance, the fallout of gender, caste class, ethnicity and religious political processes have been thoroughly discussed in the book, Manorajan Mohanty, Richard Baum and Rong Ma (ed.), Grass-roots Democracy in India and China: The Right to Participate (New Delhi, SAGE Publications, 2007).

CHAPTER

15

Human Rights Movement and the Role of Indian Judiciary

The human rights movements in India is steadily gaining impetus. It is the fallout of the three declarations issued by the United Nations in 1948. The adoption of the human rights resolutions by the UN is, not new for our country, because the Part III of India's Constitution entails an elaborate list of fundamental rights for its citizens. Due safeguards to the identity of cultural, ethnic and linguistic as well as religious minorities have been provided therein. However, the Government of India appointed the National Human Rights Commission (NHRC) for the protection and safeguards of human rights of the down trodden and unprivileged classes of the citizens. It is a different story that the implementation process of courts decisions has been both slow and tardy, and minorities still appear to be frightened of the police atrocities, army carnages or ruthless suppression of a minority caste/ religion by the majority ones.

The new theory of social rights would never have taken birth In India if the media/press would not have brought to the limelight some petty instances of injustice and exploitation of poor and tyranny of the local issues at national level and the Judiciary would not have taken fundamental rights like Article 14 (right to equality) and Article 21 (the right to personal liberty), which had been converted into positive rights by activist interpretation of our

Judiciary. The new concept was first confirmed by the apex court in the Municipality Council of Ratlam (MP) *vs.* Vardichand case (AIR, 1980 SC 1622), where the court shifted from 'traditional individualism of *locus standi* to the community orientation of public interest litigation (PIL). From here law was no more viewed a closed shop of a few privileged, rich and mighty persons of the Indian society. The above-cited court's judgement laid down the foundation of active judiciary to provide them an easy access to justice and free legal aid to the coming millions. As a result, new dimensions of state liability under Articles 13, 32 and 226 were sought out. The duties of the state were re-defined through the Social Action Litigation or PIL to serve the cause of the destitutes. The basis of it was Article 14 and the concept of Social Justice.

In terms of human rights movement in India, Public Interest Litigation-PIL has stirred the style of functioning of the Government of the day. PIL was pioneered largely by the former Supreme Court Judge, Justice P.N. Bhagwati in the mid-1980s. In the later years, it was activated by a number of courts to make human rights/fundamental rights available to the poor, ensuring that the Government fulfils its constitutional and legal obligations. The purpose of this trend has been to fix the accountability of the Government. The ambit of PIL has practically increased while covering every aspect of public administration. Thanks to the intervation of the apex court in tackling the classic cases of pollution, cleansing Yamuna rivers from industrial wastes, allowing a sensitive hearing in camera to a rape-victim, directing the states to solve the cauvery water dispute or providing mid-day meal to poor children of schools, role of the Indian Judiciary in making human rights significant is beyond doubt. There are numerous instance where the Judiciary has made political leadership accountable for its actions and performance, though it is ironical that one pillar of democracy (Judiciary) has shattered public faith in another pillar (Executive).

The National Human Rights Commission has done a commendable exercise in highlighting those areas which needs drastic reforms in our system. The 4th annual report for 1996-97 is of special significance, as it has made several such far-reaching recommendations in the direction of civil liberties, rights of children, administrative system of Justice. It emphases on making free and compulsory elementary education a 'fundamental right'. It lays a duty on both the Doordarshan and AIR to help generate human rights awareness against the nexus between the Police and Jail authorities and between politicians and criminals. It also talks about the special training and freedom to be given to doctors who examine the cases of lock-up deaths or torture by the policemen of the army. It has been deeply concerned of the safeguards of the rights of SCs, STs, Women, Dalit, Children and girl-child.

The present paper includes the following sub-headings : (a) Emphasis on ensuring the Basic Education as provided in Article 45 of the Constitution: (b) The faith in 'Indian State' has shaken because of human rights violations by its role and shirting trends from state controlled economy to the western capitalistic economy-based on open market forces. (c) State Terrorism is flawed as it has led army atrocities in manu parts of the country, nor the investigating agencies such as CBI is autonomous, accountable and responsive for their performance. (d) As the present the prison system has lost the humane face. Hence, the whole management of Jail system of the country should be reformed and it should be governed by a single Uniform Jail manual. (e) The structure of the Enforcement Directorate should also be democratised and made accountable for its functions. (f) Some suggestions are also proposed to curb the cases of human rights violations.*

IS JUDICIARY A THIRD CHAMBER?

While the judiciary appears to be the only beacon of light

* Taking note of the 700 cold wave deaths. The apex court under the PIL has issued to the Centre and 13 states, alleging that lives were lost due to failure of Governments to provide shelter and relief and honour the fundamental right of he poor under Article 21 (the right to life) of the constitution.

amidst the darkness that has engulfed the country, any imbalance of power raises valid questions on the attendant dangers of such a situation. If viewed in the larger context, is judicial activism, a dangerous trend? Are we increasingly heading towards a situation in which the country is governed by the apex court?

There can be little doubt that circumstance has expanded the scope of judicial review far beyond what the framers of the Constitution had in mind. Despite the repeated warning by Jawaharlal Nehru of not allowing the judiciary to become a third chamber, today the apex court is increasingly becoming the last resort of those seeking to safeguard their basic rights. There are a host of other issues that plague the Judiciary : For example the, appointment or judges, corruption, salary structures. Judges' sex scandals, transfers, privilege of contempt, etc. have tarnished the image of it. But, perhaps, the most pertinent is the accusation that increasingly judgements relating to public interest litigation have a populist bias. The court, it is felt, addresses convenient issues and skirts the thorny ones. There are numerous cases pending for final disposal which have been hanging fire in the Supreme Court for over a decade. The functioning of India Judiciary warrants some changes while making it accountable too. Dr. L.M. Singhvi rightly writes that "all horses of our state's chariots should pull together, not in different directions, and they should be in a robust shape and form. The health of our lends strength to another, and if one begins to drag its feet, the performance of other cannot reach the peak of excellence".

In short, an archiac legislation like the Contempt of Court Act, should be taken with to make the Judiciary accountable. As a first step, the Union Government should ask the Law commission/an independent panel of jurists to examine the relevance of the Act in the 21st century. The entire legacy of British Raj should be reviewed as the whopping pendence of cases, undue delay in the justice delivery mechanism, the granting stay after stay or bail discriminately, remaining Supreme Court closed for 143 days (about five months) in a year process of filling and summons, huge backlong have practically lowered the dignity of the Judiciary. The year 2002 was an eventful one for the Judiciary which daced many allegations of corruption and scandal. The Judges cannot and should not be above the law. The Code of Conduct for Judges should be strictly enforced to reinstate the values of judicial life. Recommendations of removal of Judges made by the National Commission to Review the Working of the Constitution should be implemented in the light of the 'Jaipur Declaration' adopted unanimously at the Ninth SAARC—Law International Conference, which has called for evolving panel and self-regulation for ensuring a good corporate governance, an effective dispute resolution mechanisms and making justice principle in accordance with the current needs of the society.

To conclude, the role of the Indian Judiciary or Judicial Activism has been significant in upholding the values of human rights *viz-a-viz* human administration. To strengthen the spirit of the NHRC further, its administrative and financial constrains must be taken away with. The suggestions of Professor Amartya Sen, the Nobel Price winner of 1998, that the Western model of economics and globalisation should be linked up with the social security-net at the grass-root levels, must be seriously pondered with. It needs to generate awareness about the human right values. It should be the key agenda of the 21st century before the nation.

The decision of L.K. Advani to set-up a Review Committee on the POTA's implementation is widely welcomed, as the committee shall be headed by a retired High Court Chief Justice and it will take a comprehensive look at the way the Act has been misused and suggest remedial measures. The development shows that the POTA has been abused/ misused by the parties in power, and most of them are the allies of the NDA itself. The NDA allies have settled political scores from Jayalalitha's arrest of Vaiko in Tamilnadu to Mayawati's vendetta Raja Bhaiyya, in U.P. Such detention, indeed, violates the letter and spirit of the law as well as the human rights. It is easy for any ruling party to use it for political motives. In the Parliament, it was assured that POTA was meant to deal with terrorists, not ordinary criminals. But the examples given below present a reverse picture.

In Jharkhand—a state not known for terrorism—it has been used by BJP chief minister, Babulal Marandi, "to bring to book" dozens of people—from a 12 year-old boy to an 81 year old man. In Gujarat, another party notable, Chief Minister

Narendra Modi, has unleashed the fully fury of POTA on more than a hundred accused in the Godhra train tragedy, but refused to invoke it in the case of any of the thousands involved in the post-Godhra carnage. Elsewhere in the country, POTA enthusiasts have zerored in on Kashmiri Muslims as an easy target. The implicit assumption is as clear as it is dangerous. Depending on religious affiliation, a suspect can either be described as an ordinary criminal or an enemy of the state. The point is not only that a law is only as good as those who implement it. It is also that terrorism is increasingly being identified with a particular community. One can only hope that the review will question this warped mindset. But beyond that, there is a more fundamental question still. Do we really need a legislation like POTA to counter terrorism or is the IPC enough to deal with the menance .

The Jharkhand Government has announced to withdraw 83 POTA cases against the people. The CM Arjun Munda announced on 4th April 2003, confirming that out of 130 cases registered so, 83 persons involved in the POTA cases found innocent by the review committee. He promised not to misuse of POTA in future. It was done so under the instructions received by the PM and Dy. PM of the NDA Government. The withdrawal cases confirms the misuse of the POTA by police authorities. It was one of the reasons that led to out the former chief minister of the state. It is meant to tackle the acts of terrorism only. In short, The Union Government being driven to take such untenable and contradictory positions on the detention of Mr. Vaiko and the Uttar Pradesh MLA Raja Bhaiyya, is conclusive evidence of POTA being bad in law and its sweeping provisions a tool for repression. Instead of setting up a review committee to check the 'misuse' of POTA, the Centre should scrap the law, because it has no defined 'use' that is legitimate and in conformity with democratic norms. ('Trial & Eeror', *The Times of India*, New Delhi, April 3, 2003, p. 12).

OVERCROWDING OUR JAILS

As a result of increase of rate of crimes in the previous decades, Indian Jails are overcrowded by under-trials on petty criminals. There are numerous case where pendence of cases take two to three years in final disposal by courts. Thus, the Indian criminal justice system tends to ignore the plight or under-trials and convicts languishing in the country's 1,155 jails. According to former SC chief justice M.N. Venkatachalia, 'the jails are penal dustbins'. Another former chief justice, A.S. Anand, dubbed the criminal justice system an engine of oppression.

The population of jails is fast increasing despite Justice Anand's landmark judgement ordering release on bail of all undertrials who committed "petty offences" and had spent over a year in jail. Delhi's prestigious Tihar jail has, for example, 12,000 inmates against a capacity of 3,700. Chief Justice V.N. Khare assured Tihar inmates that steps would be taken to decongest the prison. Justice Khare, who visited the jail on the eve or Republic Day, 2003, favoured enlarging the jurisdiction of special courts dealing with cases carrying upto three years jail term.

Overcrowding of jails is as much a violation of the right to life as denial of speedy trial. Nearly 75 percent (about 2 lakh) of the about three lakhs prisoners in the country's jails are awaiting trial by over-burdened courts. With a backlog of three crore cases, unless the pace of fast tracks courts is accelerated, they are likely to languish in jails for years. Noted jurist and former SC judge V.R. Krishna Iyer said: "Prisons are built with the stones of law". The tragedy is that they are increasingly being occupied by law makers, enforcers of law and those who are expected to, check lawlessness. The Supreme Court Bar Association president R.K. Jain felt that the special courts should be held frequently and favoured a "liberal approach" in granting bail to petty offenders.

SOME UNIQUE FEATURES

Rajasthan has presented an ideal example of "open jails" known to be a campus for jail inmates/convicts who have served one third of a life sentence. Such inmates are eligible to be sent to such open jails. It is meant for those who have shown good conduct during the jail-tenure. The highest number of 141 prisoners are lodged at Sampurnan and open jail at Sanganer of Jaipur. It is meant to ensure the dignity of every prisoner, through reforms and rehabilitation. The theory is to ensure better efforts and measures for both protecting the rights and dignity of prisoners.

Prisoners in these jails work to earn their living. The prisoners are allowed to keep their earned money and spend it on food and house. There are some who make enough for themselves and send some money to the kith and kin. Married inmates are allowed to live with their families. In Sanganer open jail, several families are living together. The unique feature of the open prison is that the inmates work on the farms of the agriculture university as agriculturists, construction workers, industrial workers or in other related trades. Loans are arranged for the prisoners to enable them to establish their own trade. It many benoted that the Sanganer open camp is a village within a village. Sanganer is known for its distinct fabric printing where factories provide employment to skilled and unskilled workers in printing and dying. Sanganer open camp, has been working for almost in years and in mates here live as they would in their own villages and their children go to schools. They do a variety of jobs for their living and some as even employed by businessmen and traders as they have special skills. Some inmates have even built their own houses in the camp, have TV sets and have their own farm animals.

The state Government has initiated a scheme under which the children of the poor convicts are given scholarship. A corpus has been formed and 25 children of the convicts have been given scholarship worth Rs. 12,550. This year, 33 such children will get scholarships. The other Indian states can follow the pattern to ensure the human rights of jain inmates.

CUSTODIAN DEATHS

The NHRC has ways expressed its deep concerns about rising incidents or custodian deaths both police and judicial, but the commission has failed to do justice with the rising such incidents, nor its directives have properly been followed by the state authorities so far as the compension is concerned. For example, the NHRC cleared 163 custodial death-case between

April 1, 1999 to March 31, 2000 and 121 cases in the same period in 2000-01. The figure rose by leaps and bounds to 3,645 cases between April 1, 2001 and March 31, 2002. At the same time, the figure for the number of cases in which the NHRC gave relief has come down substantially from 266 cases between April 1, 1999, and March 31, 2000, to just 73 between April 1, 2002 and January 17, 2003.

Rationalising NHRC's action, one of its senior officials anonymity said, "With five officers and 70000 cases, what do you expect the Commission to do"? Yet, he justified, the NHRC's action by saying, "Ninety percent of deaths in judicial custody are natural deaths". How? Most inmates die in hospital after which the magistrate's report is prepared. We look into it and in cases where the magistrate has cleared the cases. The commission has no option except to close the cases, because the body does not have the wherewithal to prove the charges against officials. (Based on *The Times of India* news dated 27th March, 2003, p. 4). Likewise, the NIIRC, the All India SC/SC Commission and the National Commission for Women severely indicted the Antony Government of Kerala for the in human repressing the tribals leading to the police firing on Feb. 19, 2003.

The exact number of deaths in the February 19 police firing is a bone of contention with the Government claiming that just one person had died while the media and other independent bodies have pointed out that a large number of tribals are still missing.

The police had fired at the tribals who were occupying forest land in Wayanad district in protest against the Antony Government reneging on its promise of giving five acres to the landless tribals who over the decades were outsed from their homeland by the electorally powerful settlers. The tribals had killed a policeman, which, according to the Government, led to the police firing.

The NHRC has *'prime facie'* rejected the state Government's report and ordered a CBI inquiry. The SC/ST commission had recommended a magisterial inquiry while the New members, after meeting tribals in jail, a large number of women were molested. But confirmed that the matter is being resolved through the interference of the Congress leadership.

CHAPTER

16

Human Rights Movement in India

A Plea for Women Empowerment

HISTORICAL BACKGROUND

The human rights movement in the country is steadily gaining impetus. It is the fallout of the three declarations issued by the U.N. in a span of about 45 years. On December 10, 1984, the UN General Assembly had adopted a declaration for all kind of basic human rights, irrespective of the numerical strength and size of the respective religions, linguistic or ethnic groups which they belonged to. Again on November 25, 1981, the UN proclaimed a specific declaration on the elimination of all forms of intolerance and discrimination based on religion and belief which virtually warned the human race that no kind of discrimination/exploitation by any state, institution and group of persons on the ground of religion or other beliefs of a particular ethnicity would be tolerated. Again after a decade, the UN on December 18, 1992, adopted a declaration for the promotion of human rights, especially for the minorities. It was seriously concerned of safeguarding the identity of cultural, ethnic and linguistic and religious minorities. That changeover is not new for India as Part III of India's Constitution contains enough protections for human rights. Accordingly, the Government of India appointed the commissions like the National Commission for Minorities and the National Commission for Women or the NHRC to protect those rights. That is a different story that the implementation process has been tardy. There was no effective implementation of all the safeguards provided for the minorities in the Constitution or recommended by the commissions in their respective reports.

SIGNIFICANCE OF THE 4TH NHRC'S REPORT

The National Human Rights Commission in its annual report for 1996-97 has done a commendable exercise to highlight those areas which need drastic reforms. The Commission has made several such far-reaching recommendations in the direction of protection of civil liberties, rights of children, police and prison reforms and for streamlining of Criminal Justice administration system, including the emphasis on making free and compulsory elementary education a 'fundamental right'. The Commission in the end of the report, lays a duty on both Doordarshan and AIR proactively help in enhancing greater human rights awareness against the nexus or collusion between the police and jail authorities. The report was tabled in the Rajya Sabha by the Union Home Minister, L.K. Advani on 10, 1998.

The NHRC's fourth annual report 1996-97 is remarkable, not because of the coverage it gives to violations of human rights by the state and its agencies, but because of its commitment "to protect those who are the most vulnerable: the Dalits and Scheduled Tribes; women and children, especially marginalized by 'growth.' and change (propose of construction of big dams) so that some may cease to be less equal than others".

EMPHASIS ON BASIC EDUCATION

Another area which has been neglected by successive governments, and even by social activists relates to the treatment of the child and illiteracy. India has the largest illiterate population in the world, exceeding the population of the US, Canada and Japan 35 million children in the six to 10 age group do not attend primary school. While the all-India figure of female literacy is 43 per cent, it is 25 per cent in Rajasthan, 29 per cent in Bihar, 32 per cent in UP and 34 per cent in MP.

It is against this background that the NHRC's report is significant and unique. The NHRC is now convinced that child labour can never be eradicated unless compulsory primary education up to the age of 14 is implemented. This should have been accomplished by the State within the first 10 years of the commencement of the Constitution, but it has not been done even after fifty years. As such no NGO has drafted legislation binding the State to eradicate child labour by sending children to their brightfull place, school. The NHRC has taken the lead. It gives the utmost importance to a positive movement to "send the child to school" rather than depending solely on well-being but negative, and therefore futile, programmes of eradication of child labour through legislative measure and through foreign commercial interventions being encouraged by NGOs in India. The NHRC seems to realize that such a negative approach is bound to fail.

WOMEN EMPOWERMENT

The women empowerment issue has been a matter of serious debate since the UP Government mooted a plan to provide some reserved seats for women in the Parliament and the state assemblies, notwithstanding of the fact that educationally backward and politically corrupt country like ours, the plight of women, in every walk of life is the worst. We have been boasting about their empowerment. But can a handful of women solve the problems of the majority of working women? Equality for women remain a distant dream. In this context, two categories of women have made an entry into politics. First, women from well-to-do families. Second, women who have their husbands in a political party, such as Mrs. Rabri Devi. They are neither politically independent in their thinking not socially conscious about the conditions of women in the countryside.

The first priority of women legislator should be to educate women and liberate them from religious orthodoxy, ignorance, and superstition. Unless educated women come forward with honesty and sincerity to alleviate the sufferings of the poor and illiterate women, empowerment of a few women will not lead to progress. Equality can be brought about or sustained only by ensuring equal opportunities for all. Men have failed in this process. Now it is the turn of women as a class.

In terms of social transformation, the role of the Supreme Court of India and its Hindu and Muslim wives have been landmark to strengthen the position of women in society, *vis-a-vis* the existing personal laws of the respective communities. In all the rulings favouring women, the apex court has sought the application of existing legislation on gender issues and to modernize them on the basis of the principle of equality before the law. But our political parties have shown scant respect to these verdicts *vis-a-vis* the women's legal rights. Assuming the role of the Supreme Court as social reformer has evoked protest in political circles. An eventual uniform, civil code, therefore, remains a distant dream in our political set-up. Women's non-violent movement can only stir a wave against the prevailing feudalism, casteism and traditionalism in society.

The status of women in society is not decided by the number of seats they occupy in the legislature. In the advanced countries hike the US, Japan and Singapore is 11%, 8% and 3% respectively. But the status of the condition of women in these countries is well and good because of education and development. Likewise, it is also not proven that only women can strive for amelioration of the conditions of women. Mrs. Indira Gandhi was the Prime Minister of the country for seventeen years. But what did she do for enhancing the status of women is well known. Unless social attitudes towards women change radically, spurt of violence against women can not be stopped. The attitude of police personnel and judicial officers cannot be expected to be different from the very society they come from. Therefore, what really needed is for women to be educated and economically self-reliant. There is a need to have 'code of crime' against women approved by the Parliament, and job opportunities should be provided for women in the services like police and judiciary alongwith the simplifying the procedures of system of administration of justice.

For the women empowerment, I am of the opinion that grass-roots women's movements in India should be synthesized with the social movements theory, development theory and theories of the State. For this, the urgent need is to mobilize resources for poor women and to facilitate their participation in the development process. With the help of the new economy policy, investment through MNCs and market economy, the leadership of grass-root activism should be linked with Socio-economic problems facing the rural India.

PANCHAYATI RAJ INSTITUTIONS ARE STILL MISGOVERNED

Fifty years after Independence, India has shown remarkable reliance in working its democratic system. What is more important is that India has now embarked upon a historic change in its institutional framework of governance after the 73rd and 74th Amendments to the constitution. This has heralded a system of multilevel governance from the Union to the State, to the district, to the Panchayat Samiti and finally to the village panchayat, besides the municipal bodies. There is no other parallel in human history where over three million elected representatives operate the political system of the country including one million women. In fact, the decentralized process has been set into motion, but the structural and procedural mechanism have eroded the spirit of the 73rd and 74 Amendments Acts. Our political parties are least interested in the empowerment of citizens, especially the women class, at the local levels. They do not like to see them coming to power.

As regards the functioning of our Panchayat Raj system, the mention of the two major social failures is important. One concerns gender inequity, i.e. disparity between women and men and this extensive gender based inequality can be seen even in the elementary matter of health care and nutrition in many regions of the country. By and large, the rural Indian women today do not see their situation as one of painful inequity and do not pine for reform, even though the process of politicizing of rural population has set in. They still do not value the importance of their freedom or status to their counterpart (men). The second failure relates to illiteracy prevailing in India. Since Independence in 1947, India has made a considerable progress in higher education, but remarkably little in elementary schooling. In the last census, in 1981, only 41 per cent of the adult population was found to be literate while the proportion of literacy among women was only 28 percent. Elementary education has never received quite importance that other social objectives have enjoyed in Indian public policy. For example, the reservation policy. Despite this, it has been observed that the India illiterate is not acutely unhappy about being illiterate, and seeing education is not one of the more intense desires of the deprived Indians. Against this background, John Rawls's theory of justice, which has contributed greatly to radical regeneration of modern political philosophy and ethics or importance of individual freedom and safeguard the priority of primary goods appear to have lost the meaning, because of the variations in sex, age, inherent characteristics, environmental differences, etc., that are prevailing among and within the groups of people.

One of the reasons for derailment of the women's reservation Bill 1998, is insecurity among men. Men have started seeing the impact of women panchayat leaders in local bodies. Thanks to the one-third reservation for women in Panchayats, making them capable of battling age-old prejudices at home. Even then, elected Panchayat women leaders are facing un-recordable obstacles and challenges such as physical threats, harassment, character assassination from male colleagues, etc. They are sexually exploited by male officials when they approach them for work. Uncomfortable at dealing with women leaders, the BDOs or other officers often brush them off saying, 'As you are illiterate, send your husband. Likewise, in most cases a category of mail members have conspired to bring a No-confidence motion against women "Pradhans and sarpanches, threatening then to not as they (male) want to operate the accounts of Pass-books. Caste discrimination still prevails at the level of gram Panchayats, because of the failure of the system and proxies for men. The SC/ST women are doubly humiliated and discriminated against by their male colleagues and officials".

The democratic decentralization process has taken its roots, of course, through the 73rd and 74th constitutional amendments. But the ground reality is that the grass-roots administration has virtually collapsed in the most of the country. The administration is unresponsive to the basic needs of the masses. Fifty years after the Independence, our most villages are without the drinking water, schools without teachers and health-centres without doctors. The bureaucracy is not prepared to handover their powers to the elected members at the grass-roots level. The interference of the state government is a constant phenomenon in the affairs of appointments, postings or transfers. Consequently, our mission to mobilise panchayats and Anganwadi's pans for the implementing of the schemes and programmes of girl-child education, eradication of poverty and illiteracy has not fairly fulfilled. The grass-roots bodies, therefore, are in a shambles in the absence of the administrative and financial antonocy to be granted to them. Mass-empowerment has yet not been geared up against the trends of centralization casteism and feudalism. Without autonomy, no accountability can be laid down.

India have some lessons to learn from the historic Scottish referendum in which Scotland's district identity and culture has been honoured in social sector against the direct control of imperial Government of England. Now Scotland enjoys full autonomy to deal with the areas like primary education, health, law and order-police system and other ethnic issues. It is a fit case of devolution against over centralization.

GOALS FOR 21ST CENTURY : A FUTURISTIC VISION

Given prognosticative analysis, India needs to re-define its goals and objectives for the next century on the long term basis. For the task of social, economic administrative goal setting, we have to re-look at our Constitution to remove the anomaly and the prevailing inner-contradictions in the constitutional law, which adversely affects our developmental goals. The contradiction is in between the interests of individual, group and social order. Our social and economic goals should be so set to harmonise with administrative task and responsibilities.

In terms of developmental goals in the era of capitalist economy and liberalization, the various facets of economic development such as growth, GDP-GNP, per capita income, national income, growth of trade and industry, the role of public and private sectors, distribution system, etc. must be linked up with Equality, Justice and Welfare. Focus should be on removing inequity, poverty and unemployment so as to enhance societal quality. Banishing poverty must be our main goal as poverty and unemployment have causal relation. All the developmental objectives have to have and time dimension in terms of goal achievement and their effect on society.

It is distressing that after a half century of Independence and having adopted the process of democratic development, we are still faced with the question of poverty, illiteracy, unemployment, the very strange form of coalitional politics and government incapacitated to handle the emerging challenges. In fact, our planning policy has been based on short-term goal; it is still defective and centralised. There have been overlapping in objectives and processes, and no proper attention has been given to tribal, rural and agricultural development. Therefore, in years to come, agricultural growth, labour intensive, manufactured export and regional disparity must receive utmost attention; landlordism must go and more incentives to agriculture be given. Infrastructure development in terms of road, water for irrigation and drinking, primary health, education and facilities, schooling, power supply, etc. must receive quick attention for the 21st century.

Sadly, there is all round decay of ethics, morals and values because of the impact of westernization. Our family-system is under severe strains. Caste and religion politics has hampered or development and growth, for which the factors like exploitation, illiteracy, scarcity, corrupt practices, excess population, poverty, etc., have been responsible. Therefore, on crucial question is as to how to ensure protection of the family as basic human and social institution for welfare, happiness and peace of individual members within the group and the society in the 21st century. If the 'family unit' is strengthened, India shall be able to preserve its cultural heritage and traditions and resist the impact of westernization on our values, ethics and morals, which are rapidly in decay. Hence, policy-makers must protect individual citizen interest through family group. With the help of the 'state system' and democratic processes, social security or concerns must be our vital goal in the next century. Here, the empirical studies made by Professor Amartya Sen, the Nobel Prize winner in economics in 1998, needs utmost attention. His theory of economics believes that the goal of the welfare of the poor can be achieved by the western model of economic growth. Globalisation can be a major force for prosperity only if it is backed by adequate national policies in a conductive social and economic environment; otherwise globalization would be counterproductive for the country's economy and social security net. Our policies plans, goals and objectives should cautiously marry with the process of globalization and liberalization of western model. In short, our economic reforms, which are still sadly, in a state of unfinished agenda, must be put in the top list of priority for our development and growth.

CONCERN OF SELLING 'FRUITS OF THE WOMB'

Because of its poverty, backwardness and scarcity, 'child-prostitution' is slowly rising at an alarming speed like a flourishing industry in Rajasthan, where traditional nomadic-entertains tribes are raking in huge profits from selling their 'fruits of the womb' by the tribes/castes Banjaras, Rajnats, Kanjars, Bedia and Dehrendar in and around Jaipur. This "pink triangle" of sex trade, as is described the author, Joseph Gathia, of the Centre of concern for Child Labour (CCF-CL) New Delhi, is higher in Rajasthan, say at least between 45 and 55 per cent girl-children are prostituted in this profession. The principal reason for this is that the prostitute practice is family-centered with women members adopting the trade of sex as profession and male members including fathers and brothers have been acting as pimps or procurers. The survey claims that the profits are enormous. The major clients are transport operators (Drivers and cleaners) migrant labourers, young students and tourists.

According the study, the problem of child-prostitution in the 'pink Triangle' area is serious among 15 districts of Rajasthan comprising Jaipur, Alwar, Ajmer, Udaipur, and Jodhpur. This commercial child prostitution area is linked with certain national high-way routes through the hotels and Dhabas. The study cautions that the trade phenomenon will soon surface in the districts of Baran, Bundi, Banswada, Dausa, Dungerpur, Sawai Madhopur and Sirohi. The main reasons of its flourishing is that only source of livelihood in the name of tradition. Monetary compulsions have compelled the child-girls to adopt the commercial sex trade. In fact, awareness of the legality of child-prostitution is law among these traditional and backward communities. Income-generating activities may help them to set free from this sex trade. The Study on "Child Prostitution in India" is based on survey conducted by the author. See, *The Times of India*, New Delhi, Edn., November 12, 1998, p. 5.

TO CONCLUDE

It is a tourism that women have greater social mobility—be they from the Hindu caste or from other poor classes. Therefore, the final test for the progress or development of the country should be tested on providing the quality of women's education. The country has made tremendous strides in women's education during the last 50 years of Independence, the final goal of providing education for all women is yet to be realized. There are many good schools in the country but not many women have access to them. In the rural sectors, the conditions of schools is still in the grip of social evils and the impact of the western culture. No society can be reformed without the quality or education for women and the background of its cultural heritage.

Poverty, social isolation, family breakdown, cultural myth, poor percent child relations, rape incidents bonded child labour, migration and unhealthy environment are the major factors responsible for compelling children to enter into the flash trade/prostitution. All these issues can be solved if the effective empowerment of women education of the girl child and proper care of mother-child health are ensured in the era of globalization, which can further help change socio-economic conditions, provided. India is capable of exploiting its human resources and its lion's share of the central budget is spent for the development of the deprived sections as a priority. It is distressing that we have celebrated the golden jubilee year of India's Independence, forgetting the harsh reality that the half population of women is still marginalized economically, socially or otherwise. Illiteracy, ignorance, exploitation, still prevail.

In terms of sex crimes, rape cases and child abuse, etc., the statement of the Union Home Minister, L.K. Advani that the rape cases now would invite the death penalty does not appear to be as important as is to have useful changes in our law on the patterns of California or Bosnia. Death penalty will have minimal impact, as criminology studies reveal that deterrence in any crime should be based on three factors. In order of significance, those are firstly—the certainty of punishment, secondly, the time it takes to punish, and finally, the penalty. In India, unfortunately, only four percentage of FIRs resulting convictions in cases of violations of human rights, because prosecution usually takes a four years period or more. So, increasing the penalty from life imprisonment to death will have imperceptible effect. To fight such cases, the better alternative is certainty of punishment and no delay in prosecution. Finally, there must also be training and licensing of forensic doctors and nurses on how to not lose evidence.

It is an unfortunate aspect of our system that the deterrence still rests on the Police Act enacted in 1861, whose primary focus was law and order so that the property of the British rulers against the Indian masses could be protected. Those rulers have left India in 1947, but the same laws are enforced to protect the vested interests of the ruling class. In this regard, the finding of the National Police Commission report were made in 1979. But they have not yet received proper attention towards the basic reforms to have a more professional, responsive, accountable and educated force. No attention has been given to specialization and training as per the societal needs. Mention may be made of the section 155(4) of the Indian Evidence Act, which prevents women from coming forward to go to the court because of its nature being harassment. The US has already put together a new evidence code dealing with sexual conduct of the victims (the Declaration for Basic Principles of Justice for victims of crimes was adopted in 1994). India is sadly not keeping the modern trends of progressive democratic nations.

In India socialism as a political philosophy has not died nut only suffered setback, due to exploitative an inhumane behaviour of our politicians and the bureaucracy. The rise of 'crony capitalism' has made the state ineffective and distorted in its intervention. The past experience of two decades has proved the un-viability of both liberal democratic market commanded systems and the Stalinist authoritarian administrative command system, in which the socialist cause was badly ignored. The Nehru's strategy of mixed economy, combining planning development and democracy can still be a good alternative.

It is reliably learnt that the much touted legislation to make the right to free and compulsory elementary education a fundamental right is still lying in the cold store of H.R.D. ministry of Delhi, though the U.F. Government had pushed it ahead in Indian Parliament to ensure its passage. A special committee set-up by the UF Government had estimated that the Centre would require Rs. 40,000 crore over a period of five years to the academic and administrative provisions for implementing the proposed plan into action. Since then, no sincere attempt has been made to revive it as yet. The BJP led coalition has also made a similar provision for making elementary education a "fundamental right", but no serious thought has been given to it.

It is irony that India has been under tremendous pressure from the international community, particularly donor agencies, to make elementary education a fundamental right since they believe that such a legislation would help check the growing problem of child labour. It is argued that though 14 states and four Union territories have enacted compulsory education Acts, these have remained unenforced due to socio-economic compulsions that keep the children away from schools.

Besides, it is also feared that the compulsion contemplated in the legislation is a compulsion on the state rather than on the parents. A section in the HRD ministry believes that the country is not yet ready for such a legislation, which will make elementary education a justiciable right, as it would only give rise to endless litigation, as people will be liable to take the state to court if they eel they are being denied their right to education.

In fact, regulation like this should not be introduced when large number of children do not attend school, because they do not have access to schooling, In such a case, it is said, that legislation may well result in a situation where there may be more parents in jail than children in school. Other ways and means, therefore, should be searched to promote the spirit of schooling amongst children belonging to rural cum backward regions.

CHAPTER

17

The Importance of Women Police with the Administration of Criminal Justice

At present, India has near about 500 million women, a big number if we think of it as a cohesive whole. But across the country, women are subjected to discrimination, harassment, rape and violence within the household, at work place, in the fields, on the road and everywhere in the country. Illiteracy and poverty along with patriarchal Indian milieu coupled with suppressive customs and traditional mindset have place women in a position of perpetual disadvantage, in spite of the fact that we believe in the concept of 'Sakti' (Power) or Divine human power in our myths, our police women officers, like Mrs. Kiran Bedi, Magsasay Award winner, has enriched the quality of life of prisoners of central jail, Delhi.

The 73rd and 74th amendment Acts, have led to the empowerment of women, of course, and women have begun to occupy high position in the grass-root politics. Yet the practice of gender bias and gender-based violence continue to prevail due to the ideology of patriarchy and western impact.

It is a pity that as per ratio of country's population only 2% of women are in the civil police.

At present violence against women (i.e. molestation, rape, dowry, murder harassment to married woman, trafficking in women, rape of girl child, etc.) has increased. Even some times police men themselves become the reason to custodian rape, molestations and other offences. Therefore, the need of hour is to have more attention towards women rights.

In the light of critical juncture when the country has convulsed by lawlessness of unprecedented magnitude, the importance women in police system cannot be over-emphasized. The dignity and credibility of the police force will enhance if changes in the structure of police force are carried out by inducting women at senior and junior levels, treating them on par with their male colleagues. The process has been attempted to, but is a slow. For the betterment of society and police functioning, adapting women in police management cannot be overlooked. Unfortunately, due to a variety of reasons, mainly social, legal, administrative/managerial, the women police do not enjoy adequate support and confidence of the society. If we want to make the police more humane, effective and approachable, induction of educated, intelligent and socially aware women in police service is significant. They should be provided special training relating to crime against women. They can prove to be sensitive in solving such problems. Constitution of special women cells/police stations, training, etc. is the need of hour.

A shift in the whole paradigm-from colonial policing to democratic one and its procedure set out by Lord Macaulay as the coercive arm of the Britishers to suppress Indian subjects, has to be undertaken on the mind set not as 'force', but as 'service' to the society. A gender sensitive police force is inevitable to improve the image of the police structure.

Women in police can properly understand the problems of women victims or their witnesses/interrogations in courts. In detection of crime done by women, a male police officer finds very difficult to deal with such criminal women at all stages of interrogation, search, arrest, nor the women can discuss freely before the male officers of their cares relating to rape and molestations, etc.

Various empirical studies and surveys have confirmed that women as police do their work better than men police and women can perform all types of police duties exactly same as men. Yet studies confirm that, women in policing (i.e. in matters of selection, recruitment, training etc.) remains the same due to colonial mindset and police being the agency of a 'state subject' no serious efforts have been made to attract the women for police jobs.

If we look in to the "strength" of women police, as many as 18 states have a strength of less than, 1000 each including Rajasthan (before the pass out of new batch of constables consisting of around 200 in Oct., 2004). The share of women in armed police is 0.39%. They exist only in a few States, namely Madhya Pradesh, Himachal Pradesh, Jammu and Kashmir, Assam, Goa and Delhi. There are not enough police women for investigation.[1] Women police were appointed mainly to deal with women and children as victims and criminals. The growth and strength of women police has not been satisfactory, taking into account the increase in the number of women and juvenile criminals and victims of crime or increasing their ratio of illiteracy. One of the major drawbacks is the absence of proper man-power planning. There is lot of adhocism and lack of proper policy with regards to the growth and strength of women police.[2]

In spite of so much publicity of women police and the creation of the women police stations/women protection cells allover the country, the strength of women police has not increased satisfactorily. Women police at present constitute near about 2% of the total police force. The National Police Commission and 8th Financial Commission recommended increasing the strength to 3% of police force, taking into consideration the conditions prevailing around 1980's. Even after passage of 23 years, there is no serious thought to implement them.

We are already in the 21st century, but the above mentioned recommendations of the National Police Commission are not fulfilled even today. If we increase the strength of women police in the country depending on the recommendation, i.e. up to 3% right now, that may hardly give and results due to the growth of population and changing scenario of crime involving many women as criminals and victims. It is suggested that a fresh commission should be formed to evolve the conditions in giving due place to women in police administration so as to contain the crimes perpetuated against women and children.

NEW RECRUITMENT METHODOLOGY

At no stage in the process of development and modernization of police, the women are taken into confidence. Due to many reasons besides above the government is facing the problem of attracting the educated women from respectable families for the police service, especially in view of the stigma attached to it. The crux of the problem is not only the willingness to recruit women but how to encourage women to join the force to demarcate jurisdictional areas between men and women and judiciously utilize their services. Women, by and large, do not still fancy the enigmatic life of a police officer, some of the present women police officers notwithstanding. Secondly, and especially at lower levels, there IS a tendency to overlook the existence of a women force for serious jobs.

To tackle the above situation, it is suggested that:

(i) Media, i.e. news papers, radio and TV should be used to highlight the significant role which women can play in law enforcement.

(ii) Efforts should be made to attract the girls of NCC, sports champions and the girls of degree/diploma holders in social, psychology and criminology subjects in to the service.

(iii) To attract women into the service police should be given reservations (Rajasthan state providing 30% reservations at present), special privileges by way of incentives, such as a fixed quota in schemes like housing, personal loans, etc.

As regards the 'educational qualifications' of the women candidates, the present educational qualifications prescribed, knowledge in the subjects like sociology, psychology, be made mandatory for both lower and higher level of categories. For higher levels, i.e. SI and above, degrees/diplomas in sociology, psychology, criminology and juvenile related subjects should be made mandatory for women students. The knowledge in the above subjects should guide women police in right way while tackling the problems of women and children.

The recruitment is the cornerstone of personnel management. The quality of the force largely depends on the type of candidates recruited. This in turn requires that the methods of recruitment should be such as to ensure induction of meritorious persons into service. Hence, recruitment policy needs to be streamlined. Besides to combination of different methods such as examination, interviews and physical fitness tests, the methods of recruitment should be revised such as:

1. More objective and emphasis should be given on the aptitude of the candidates for the police service. It is essential that no relaxation should be shown to women either in eligibility or in the methods of testing the merit of the candidates.
2. As the recruitment of women police is made on the lines similar to men police, the methods prescribed for tests also are the same without giving any consideration to test the special feminine qualities of woman such as patience, endurance, sympathetic and helpful attitude, etc. which are mostly required qualities of women police. Consideration should be given to test the above qualities as a must while recruiting women in to police.
3. Neither there is any effort to test the aptitude of women for policing, nor is any preference given to those who have acquired special qualifications in social work and in the subjects like sociology, psychology, child psychology, etc. Moreover, these requirements are not made for the recruitment of lower categories who are basic roots of the police organization. Efforts should be made to consider the above requirements for all categories while recruiting them not only on paper but in practice also.

4. The recruitment procedure especially of the constables has been highly subjective and gives a lot of scope for favourism.

So far as the 'Post entry training' programme is concerned, all police persons are supposed to have a rigorous training in view of the nature of the functions allotted to them. But various studies have confirm that the police departments of various states have not paid proper attention to the training of women police-whether it is related to indoor or outdoor training programmes.

SUSTAINABLE TRAINING PROGRAMME

Generally the functions of women police relate to mostly women and children, whereas the training do not even touch any of these aspects and give them just the same training as their male counter parts without covering the training any subjects like investigation in rape cases, harassment, dowry death, bride burning and juvenile-related crimes, etc. Here the observations made by the Committee on Police Training (1974) while highlighting the need for greater involvement of police in social defence work, it recommended the scope of invaluable services that units of women police could render. In this context, the Committee recommended that women police should be given sustainable training in recognized institutions of social work education.[3]

Highlighting the need for above mention areas, the National Police Commission also recommended: "The effectiveness would be greatly enhanced if they receive special training in social work in an institute of social science to qualify them to diagnose and treat social ailments. They should also be put in special courses in schools of social work to perform their special role in relation to women and children, intensive training should be imparted to them in the enforcement of special Acts relating to children and vice and also in the technique of search of women and their belongings."

It is therefore, suggested that there is need of drastic changes in the contents of training syllabus. Women police needs training on specific subjects having a bearing on her job. Subject like human psychology, handling of women suspects, i.e., criminal, juvenile delinquency, investigations of sexual harassment, rape, unnatural death, dowry deaths, recording FIR's and dying declarations, extracting information pertaining to social evils, curbing immoral trafficking, etc., should be necessarily included in the training curriculum.

Making police women rough and tough seems inevitable so that the women police can face the hazardous task of police life. Women police are made tough to handle the criminals. The use of force, abusive language, use of third degree methods, suspecting every person to be a criminal, is some of the characters acquired by police personnel. There is hardly any attempt to inculcate feminine qualities such as patience, politeness, sympathetic and helpful attitude and respect for the individuals. When the women police are also given the same type of training as men do, women police forgets that she is a woman, as all the time she is reminded that she is a police and she should behave like wise by losing the feminine qualities and turns to be a tough police, which defeats the purpose of the existence of women police. In this regard, a look into the recommendation of the National Police Commission is the need of hour, i.e.

> "Basic training course should be same as for their male counterparts and women should be trained at the same training institution where men are trained to ensure uniformity in recruitment and training. However, certain modification may have to be made in the physical training programme for women recruits. Instead of toughening their physical strength, training should be directed to instill a sense of physical self-confidence and equip them with physical safety techniques. Mastery over, tactics of unarmed combat, such as judo and karate, in addition to special instruction to deal with agitations and mob upsurges in a humane and sensitive manner".[4]

In short, women police should be treated as an agent of social change. Their basic qualities different from men should be kept intact. The training programme should enable women police to understand human behaviour and develop special skills in dealing with particular problems relating to women and children. Their social structure training should be sounded to understand social problems.

This has been noticed that a very few women police are posted at the police stations which results into frustration and stagnation. In this regard, the National Police Commission emphasized importance of women role, i.e. "Women police have great potential to be cool, defuse and de-escalate many situations and therefore, greater use should be made of them than at present. In non-combative roles requiring restraint, patience and endurance they can be employed with advantage. They are especially needed in areas where police come in contact with women, so as to obviate complaints of indignity and misbehaviour towards women. The presence of women police in police stations will greatly help in creating confidence and trust in the police set-up. Women police can also helps in giving better attention to service aspects of police work.[5] Women police can play a perfect role in different areas at par with male counterparts. If is worth-mentioning that the President's Commission on Law Enforcement and Administration of Justice, 1967 recognized that police women can be and invaluable asset to modem law enforcement and favoured to broaden their role in staff services like planning and research, training, intelligence inspection, public information, community relations and as legal advisors. And the women police officers like Kiran Bedi, Kanchan Choudhary, Badam Bairwa have proved their capabilities of handling hazardous and dangerous situations.

To conclude, the role and position of women police (in terms of their functions and duties) has to be re-oriented in the light of the impact of globalisation and the increase rate of crime in social life. In most of the cases; functions like investigations of crimes, cases of sexual abuses eve-teasing, rape, dowry deaths, crimes committed against women, immoral traffic of girls, etc. have been kept out of their purview. Women police only assist male police whenever needed they do not enjoy to act as an independent entity.

In fact, areas efficiencies of women police has not been utilized properly. Police department lacks an effective policy to utilize them accordingly. All investigation work including interrogation and recording of statements of women accused, criminals and victims of crimes, etc. is mostly carried by men police. This defeats the very purpose of which women are recruited in the police service. Therefore, the involvement of women police in all law enforcement duties against the 2% of total women police force is necessary and women police should be employed in more strength on a priority basis for specialized work, concerning women and children. It is a welcoming decision that some of states have come out with a new policy to inspire and boost the confidence amongst women.

A FEW SUGGESTIONS

1. The recommendations of National Police Commission should be implemented fully taking into consideration the changing circumstances and scenario of society and crime situations.
2. Women police should involve in the important functions like investigation of crimes relating to women and children and can also be employed on intelligence work connected with such crimes. Therefore, Women police constables/officers should be utilized in a large number for arresting and interrogating women suspects, escorting and guarding women convicts and accused, conducting personal search of women suspects, etc.
3. In the changing socio-economic conditions, preventive force relating to crime, if they are given an opportunity, women police can play an effective role in preventing many social ills and crimes such as juvenile delinquency, drug addiction and eve-teasing, etc.
4. Each police station should have a cell with female staff to look after matters relating to crimes against women. This will reduce the atrocities of male police towards women clients as well as counterparts.
5. Women police should be entrusted with the duties of tracing missing women and children, assisting

women commuters at airports railway stations and bus stands and places of pilgrimage. Likewise, Women police should be used for regulating processions, meetings and demonstrations where there are large numbers of women participants.

6. Besides to above duties, women police should be involved in night patrolling, riot control duty, raids, etc. and do all other dangerous/risky jobs which are usually done by their male counterparts—to serve better and to raise confidence in the women population.
7. With proper training in specialized skills like karate, judo etc. women police can be utilized as 'spies' to prevent social ills and crimes such as immoral traffic among women, eve teasing etc., women police with determination can definitely find out ways and rescue the women/girls from the clutches of such person and try to arrest this social evil to some extent. The involvement of women police in this area request the links between ill reputed male police and criminals.
8. Setting-up of police stations headed by women will go a long way in providing justice to the innocent victims and putting up an end to the problems of custodial rapes. The sensitive areas concerning the detection of crime on or by women can be handled with much ease at all women police stations which will provide fearless atmosphere for interrogation and investigation. This will also enable women victims to lodge their complaints without embarrassment and fear.
9. The modem trend of education, IT, etc., and economic compulsions are making women to come out more and more. Even though she feels insecure due to various reasons like teasing, exploitation of women by anti-social elements, etc. A common phenomenon observed in places near schools and colleges located on thorough fares is the presence of gangs of anti-social elements indulging in

harassment of young girls. If women police are deployed in these areas they can reduce this practice to some extent. Therefore, the women police should be deployed to do patrolling during the day at all sensitive places like schools, colleges, market-places, and picture halls, etc. the presence of women police at these places will work as a deterrent of crime control method.

In brief, Services of women police should be utilized to improve the image of police and also to develop better police-public relations, as recommended by the National Police Commission to curb the rate of crime against women.

The suggestions of President Dr. A.P.J. Abdul Kalam that Police Department compile a nation wide database of criminals available in all police stations and its data be updated continuously, should be put into action. India cannot ignore the need to establish a police e-governance grid through high bandwidth network, for this an action plan should be prepared for progressive induction of IT police forces. This idea was proposed by the President while inaugurating the 37th All India Police Science Congress at Bangalore on June 6, 2006.

He advocated: "To attract and retain talented youth in the police force right from constable to officers, what we need is to design attractive service conditions with suitable pay packages, career planning and advancement, housing, leave, children's education, healthcare facilities and self-upgradation schemes".

The pay package must be attractive enough to see that police personnel at all levels do not succumb to extraneous considerations at any cost and exhorted the police to be people friendly, corruption free and responsible.

Notes and References

1. *The Hindu*, Madras, 1st Sept. 2002.
2. The Ph.D. Thesis (2005) of G.S. V.S.S. Subrahmanyam, submitted in the Deptt. of Political Science, J.N. Vyas University, Jodhpur (Raj.) has highlighted in depth all these aspects.
3. M.S. Gore Report on Police Training (1973), Ministry of Home Affairs, Government of India, New Delhi, pp. 107-08.

4. Aruna Bhardwaj, Women in Uniform: Emergence of women police in Delhi (New Delhi, Regency Publications, 1999).
5. 5th report of the National Police Commission (1981), p. 77.

References

Amarji, Mahajan, Indian Police Women, New Delhi, Deep & Deep Publications, 1982.

Aruna, Bhardwaj, Women in Uniform : Emergence of Women Police in Delhi (New Delhi, Regency Publications, 1999).

Radha, Kalyani, Police, Crime and Human Rights (Jaipur, Pointer Publishers, 2003).

Jayanto, N. Chaudhary, "Policing India in 2005: Challenges and Issues Ahead", *The Indian Police Journal*, Jan.-March, 2003.

Mohd. Umar, "Role of Police in Curbing Violence against Women : A Critique, *Supreme Court Journal*, III volume, 1999.

CHAPTER

18

Empowering Weaker Sections of the Society

Image and Reality

The role of science and technology has considerably changed the lives of Indian masses in general and the Scheduled Castes and Scheduled Tribes (SCs and STs) with Dalits in particular. The planned investment and planning of the Government have provided the weaker sections sustainable livelihoods and dignity. Despite all these good development, both the Centre and States since Independence, continue to spend crores of rupees for providing loans, training and creating jobs for Dalits (the economically and socially deprived classes of the society) so as to rise above deprivation. The National SC Finance and Development Agency has been providing to them funds, training other facilities relating to income generating activities. The long-term mission of our welfare state is claimed to be impressive and progressive.

A review of the state corporations, done by the National Institute of Financial Management—NIFM in 2006 paints a shocking picture against the above cited claim of the

Government. As per the report, there has been a wide spread irregularities in selection of beneficiaries, as 'Table' given here has recorded. Most of state corporations have not given accounts since last six to sixteen years. Loan recoveries are about 45% with some states like Assam having Iowa rate as 14%.

Another problem is decline of allocations and even lower utilization. In the past decade the central government spending of SC/ST and OBCs. declined from a tiny 0,005% of the total non-plan revenue expenditure to 0.004%. Plan expenditure for this purpose from 2.4% to 1.6% over the same period.

For raising Dalit families above the poverty line, there is a Special Component Plan (SCP) under which each Central Ministry and all state governments are supposed to allocate funds in proportion to the Scheduled Caste population. According to the Mid-term Review of the 10th Five Year Plan (2002-07), only 14 out of 37 Central Government ministries had complied with this. All state governments had made allocations but excepting a few like Assam, Haryana, Punjab, Sikkim, Tamil Nadu and Uttaranchal. They all were below the required proportion. Delhi, for instance, has about 16% SC population, yet it has allocated about 7% under SCP.

The Ministry of Social Justice and Empowerment is charged with implementing schemes for welfare of Dalits and other disadvantaged sections. For the Ninth Year Plan it was unable to spend nearly Rs. 1000 crores from the allocated Rs. 6028.23 crore. The Central Government allocated Rs. 5786 crore for welfare of SCs in the 10th Plan, but it utilized only about 42% in three years.

Are, Dalits receiving bank credit to run their own businesses and not depend on government charity? Data from Reserve Bank shows the opposite results amount of credit per capita received by Dalits Rs. 495 in 1993 to Rs. 285 in on welfare 2001 and further to Rs. 225 in 2004. In fact, the number of small borrower accounts of Dalits declined from 77 to 23 per thousand. It is not surprising that in this world declined of unkept promises hope has turned to despair among dalits. They see all these schemes and plans as an elaborate charade carried out year after year. Add to this the ever-present social exclusion they have to bear and the transition to anger is not surprising.

TABLE 1

% Share of Union Government Expenditure on SC/ST/OBC Welfare

Year	*Of Non-Plan Revenue Expenditure*	*Of Plan Expenditure*
1998-99	0.005	2.4
2002-03	0.004	1.7
2007-08	0.004	1.6

Amount of Bank Credit (Rs./Capita)

Category	*1993*	*2001*	*2004*
Dalit	495	285	225
Non-Dalit	708	756	936

Numbers of Dalits Provided Job-oriented Training

Years	*Number*
2002-03	1484
2003-04	1367
2004-05	2345

Source : *The Times of India*, New Delhi, December 4, 2007 p. 11.

Ministry of Social Justice and Empowerment

	Rupees in Crore
9th Plan Outlay	6,028
Expenditure	5,039
Unspent fund	989

Infact, they do not teach an official curriculum to students to face the challenges of modern living, learn other languages. The intention should be to equip the grass-root students with skills and tools needed to negotiate the demands of modern technology and democratic polity. India needs a legislation to regulate the functioning of such institutions.

The decision of the Supreme Court on August 12, 2005, while banning registration in unaided Private Professional Colleges has stirred up a new controversy as to whether such reservation in these institutions should be governed through a new legislation, keeping in view the objectives of social justice. {The Supreme Court ruling on reservations in private education institutions is the fallout of *P.A. Inamdar* v. *Government of Maharashtra,* followed by the ear Her Pai Foundation Judgment given in 2002}. The core issue is providing education to the disadvantaged social and economic sections of society, because private education institutions—aided or unaided, have proved to be better at providing quality education. In comparison to Government-run institutions, these bodies have failed to come up with capabilities necessary for competing in the job market.

Today, the weaker sections are facing double jeopardy, i.e. they can not afford any education in the private schools and are bound to send their wards to Government schools. Consequently, these students of schools can not compete in entrance test and enroll in private professional colleges. However, those few who somehow cross the merit barrier are unable to pay high fee that private professional institutions charge. This scenario hits the concept of Social Justice *vis-a-vis* the role of private institutions. The Government can offer to meet the cost of admitting reserved category students.

On the other hand, it must be admitted that the private professional institutions/colleges are largely guided by profits and commercial considerations. They have nothing to do with the objectives of social justice/services. In the light of the above-cited scenario, a new public-private partnership needs a serious consideration for the cause of promoting social justice to the disadvantaged sections, and under the new model of norms, the state and the management of private colleges/

institutions should enter into a burden-sharing arrangement. This requires political and social will.

The development of rural segments depends on building basic infrastructure to lure investment. It is regretted that due to the resource crunch of the Government budgetary allocation for 'infrastructure' (which is basically part of 'Good Governance') has been reduced. Now the new guidelines under the Planning Commission should be issues inviting private sector involvement shaping infrastructure, in order to eradicate poverty and unemployment. In its implementation, bureaucratic delays should be avoided. The development efforts have to proceed in the manner to contain the problem of unemployed and under-employed in the rural areas. Likewise, Public Sector Health Care system is faced with resource problems and infrastructure gaps. It should too be taken care of.

EMPOWERMENT OF WOMEN

To counter Patriarchal ideology and male-dominance or to weaken social structures and institutions that perpetuate gender discrimination, there is a need to bring about change in these settings so as to be helpful in empowering women. One of the ways to do a way with discrimination would be: (i) Improving education status of the child-girls at school levels and women at higher educational levels; (ii) Reservation can be introduced and (iii) Strengthening the hands of those who want to start their own enterprise by making financial easily available to them; (iv) Empowering women by giving them choice to decide the family-size which needs education and training programme to make them aware of their rights.

The National Integration Council {NIC} met in New Delhi 31st August 2005, after a gap of almost 13 years. It promised to deal with firmly communalism, in urgency violence/ divisive forces or separatism. Our Government is committed to provide a humane Government as our democratic set up permits any annoyed desperate section to address their grievances through democratic means. The meeting had an agenda of communal harmony, education and media, apart from the concept of secularism and gender justice. A national consensus is needed to redefine these concepts in the light of our multi-culturism and the ongoing tends of globalization. NIC's regularity should be evolved. National integration is not a house which could be built by mortals and bricks it; the consciousness which awakens the people at large through social harmony. But the gulf between haves and have not must be minimized with the help of the Directive Principles enunciated in our Constitution.

Mention may be of the so-called progressive legislation like Women's Reservation Bill, the symbol of women empowerment. Our political leaders, specifically regime outfits, speared headed their strong opposition/resistance on the basis of a shrill advocacy for separate quota for OBCs and Muslim women within the proposed quota {33%}. On the contrary, the UPA-led Congress refused to agree to the demand for "quota within quota", because it would create a precedent for caste/community-based reservations in legislatures. Therefore, the Bill failed to get the national consensus amongst political parties.

This apart, the Human Rights Movement through the school to Higher Education should be launched to make the backward/weaker sections of rural India aware about modernity and globalization. They should be taught about the initiatives taken by the State/Central Government from time to time to "take away a host of irrational notions, social biases, superstitions, etc. that have been responsible to foment communalism. Hence, NCER's National Curriculum should be linked with the curriculum of Indian Universities/Colleges Institutions through the UGC, New Delhi, stressing the need on local knowledge as well the knowledge of globalization. With the change of a Government in states and at the Centre, there should be no fallout of ideological dogmas of Left/rightist intellectuals on it. Emphasis should be given on professional and technical courses based on new technology. The draft National Curriculum Framework (NCF), 2005 is, indeed, the first national policy document that pushes us into understanding the ways in which the child can be nurtured. Yet the recommendations Yashpal Committee (1993) should be taken care of. The text book writers should be asked to abide by the guiding principles and values of the Constitution, instead of obscurantism and irrational historical references or social inequalities. Rather, school knowledge should provide a lens through which children can develop a critical understanding of their social reality.

To conclude, our educators and policy-makers should stick to the basics of our national culture, i.e. The N.C.F.-2005 as well as the framework for high Education syllabus must vigorously include factors like exclusion of religion from education, enriching pluralist approach, diversity and developmental issues relating to social science disciplines and others. While following to a shift from development to a normative post-development approach, the text-book writing works on local knowledge should not avoid the question of why poverty, social privilege and inequalities of all kinds have persisted in our social structure. Without this approach, our normative concerns such as equality, social justice, human dignity or economic development in rural India would be irrelevant and meaningless. According to Prof. Zoya Hassan, educational materials under whatever pedagogic approach must be produced within the framework of the Constitution. The key issue is the lack of monitoring and scrutiny of textbooks. Good quality books should not be prepared in a hurry.

This apart, it is suggested that the Government should take away the obsolete laws enacted during the British regime, such as the Press and Registration of Books Act of 1867 or the Indian Telegraph Act, 1885, as these are grossly inadequate to deal with the challenges of Globalization and Privatization.

In a major initiative to promote education among girls, the decision of the Union Government that every single girlchild would be eligible for free education from VI to XII, should be hailed as the fee waiver scheme will boost the girl-child education. It is likely to have a positive impact on the status of women in the society. Likewise, U.G.C. too would launch graduate and post-graduate scholarship scheme for the single girl-child. The scheme aims at promoting education for girls. But sadly, the new schemes/scholarships will by pass girls belonging to the poorer families who generally drop out by high school. The government, therefore, may think of providing a small scholarship of Rs. 100 from middle school onwards for girls from an economically weak background of rural belt. It would help keep them in school, much like the mid-day meal scheme. But the scheme will have the desired impact only if the government of States and Centre improves the educational infrastructure and makes schools more accessible and education more meaningful.

It is a good precedent that some women I.A.S. officials are working towards ensuring that every child goes to school, gets at least one day-meal and no adult remains illiterate. Under the Government of India, the first ever 'womanned Department', the three Secretaries, namely Mrs. Kumud Bansal, Vrinda Swarup and Vandana K. Jena are reported to have launched the ambitious programme of worth Rs. 7,000 crore under 'Sarva Shiksha Abhiyan'. Because of their three decades experience with education and professional jobs, the Government's education-drive programme is expected to succeed.

Here, it would be worth-mentioning of changes that have been made by the Centre in the Right to Education Bill 2005, which would make it tougher for states-aided and unaided schools to escape the responsibility of providing free and compulsory education to children between the age of 6 to 14. This was circulated during the CABE meeting in July 2005. There has been no change in the provision that at least 25% children of weaker sections be given free education by partially aided—schools and unaided schools. State schools would have to provide free education to all admitted children. Likewise, according the new change, schools have been barred from taking capitation fee and conducting screening fee. If it is done by any managing committee, it would have to pay a fine which may more than to ten times the capitation fee is charged or a fine of Rs. 25,000. Thus, the Bill gives clear an important role to Central and State Governments in ensuring standards in elementary education and access to every child. At present, according to the HRD Ministry's information, 14% to 15% schools in India are run by private management and less than 5% are unaided schools. The said Bill (with changes) shall be tabled in the winter session of Parliament after getting comments from the State Governments. If the Bill is carried out by the Parliament it would have far reaching effects on the elementary education.

CHAPTER

19

Empowering People with Right to Information

A Review of Some Successes and Concerns

CONSTITUTIONAL BASE OF THE ACT

Right to Information Act, 2005 was passed by both Houses in the summer session of the Parliament and received the assent of President on June 15, 2005. The Bill was passed after about 150 amendments were introduced in the original draft. The Act replaced relatively all the weak and ineffective legislation *'Freedom of Information Act, 2002'*, passed during NDA regime. The legislation confers on all citizens a right to seek information and correspondingly makes it the duty of the public authorities to disseminate information for better governance and accountability. The law has widest possible reach covering Central and State Governments, Panchayati Raj Institutions (PRI), local bodies and recipients of government grants but would not apply to the intelligence and security organizations except if the information related to the allegations of corruption.*

SOME FACTS FROM HISTORICAL BACKGROUND

The last decade witnessed great deal of activity over RTI. RTI legislation has been enacted in as many as nine states, namely, Rajasthan, Maharashtra, Karnataka, Tamil Nadu, Goa, Delhi, Madhya Pradesh, Assam and Jammu and Kashmir. In states such as Tamilnadu, very weak laws were enacted which remained largely on paper. Elsewhere, citizens have been able to use the RTI in a relevant and effective manner. In some states, RTI is in operation at the panchayat level or in some government departments. In Rajasthan, RTI Act, 2000 does not have independent appeal mechanism, nor a penalty system. Penalty is decided on the basis of civil service conduct rules.

India's grass-roots experience in invoking RTI to strengthen democratic institutions and improve governance attracted global attention. The work of Mazdoor Kisan Shakti Sangathna (MKSS) in the villages of Rajasthan has been particularly inspiring in this context. Villagers use RTI to obtain official records like bills, vouchers and muster-rolls from the panchayat or block office. They compare the records with development work at the actual site, or with the experience of workers employed (according to records) at the rural employment or drought relief works.

The strengthening of grass-roots democracy is perhaps a more significant contribution of the law than the reduction of financial irregularities. It is encouraging that such efforts are spreading to new areas, as is evident from recent reports from Nokha (district Bikaner of Rajasthan) and Bharavan (district Hardoi of Uttar Pradesh) areas. In Janawad Panchayat, Kumbalgarh block of Rajsamand district, MKSS held one of its public hearings in 2001. It came to light that out of works of Rs. 1.20 crore, Rs. 70 lakh were ghost works. The rural campaign was led by social activist Aruna Roy. She empowered the rural populace. A government committee,

* Sapna Chadah, "Right to Information Regime in India", in *Indian Journal of Public Administration*, I.I.P.A.; New Delhi, Jan.-March, 2006, pp. 8-13.

thereafter, corroborated this fact. In Bhim block in Rajsamand, payments amounting to Rs. 30 lakh were made to a fraudulent company, which existed in the form of a bank account of a block-level employee's wife. This was exposed at a public hearing. The campaign enabled people to overcome caste and class barriers, and came together against irregularities.

In the urban context, efforts made by *Parivartan* and *Satark Nagrik Sangathan* in Delhi had been encouraging. Instead of making several complaints, a citizen can submit an application under the new RTI legislation of Delhi, seeking information on the action taken on previous complaints, the officials who handled the file(s) in question and the action to be taken against them for not acting upon a genuine complaint. The results of the RTI law were startling.* Complaints not attended to for years were redressed within days. In some cases, the applicants received thinly veiled threats from officials. Several organizations have incorporated RTI in their work in the slums and resettlement colonies of Delhi. The law has been widely used in Delhi and Rajasthan to expose corruption in the public distribution system.

In the light of the aforesaid fallout of the RIT, the UPA Government followed the same path. The Right to Information Draft Bill, 2005, was enacted as a law by the centre after taking into account a set of proposed amendments to the Freedom of Information Act, 2002, though not notified nor it came into effect. It was passed on June, 21, 2005. The National Advisory Council (NAC) played a very important role in shaping it, though a handful of officers were against it on account of penalty provisions as well as an independent system of appeal, as the Act would not only exposed corruption in public life, but also encouraged people to actively participate in development processes. No doubts, the startling results of the RTI laws applicable in states were a lesson for the NAC. It was expected then that the new draft would overrule the official Secrets Act, 1923 and it would be more effective control law. It is worth-recalling that Mrs. Aruna Roy, the committed activist of MKSS was the member of the NAC.

* Bharat Dogra, "Power Shift : Information Law Will Empower Citizens Against State", *The Times of India*, New Delhi, December 15, 2004, p. 14.

In short, the tenets of economic reforms and the Enron project controversy; the May 2004 Lok Sabha election verdict, pro-poor policies as well as the role of the existing laws in some states inspired the Centre to undertake the right to information as the right to life in governance. The RTI came into force in Oct. 2005.

PURPOSE OF THE ACT

As per the Preamble of the Act, the aim is :

- to provide the citizens right to information which will enable them to have access to information under control of the public authorities which will promote transparency and accountability in the working of every public authority; and
- to provide for the constitution of a Central Information Commission and State Information Commissions. Thus, the Act ensures every citizen of India to have a Right to Information on under Section 2(f) of the Act.

The Act will extend to whole of India except the state of J&K.

DEFINITION OF RIGHT TO INFORMATION

Right to Information under the Act means as the right accessible under this Act, which is held by or under the control of any public authority and includes the right to :

(i) inspection of the work, documents, records;
(ii) taking notes, extracts, or certified copies of documents or records;
(iii) taking certified samples of material; and
(iv) obtaining information in the form of diskettes, floppies, tapes, video cassettes or in any other electronic mode or through print-outs where such information is stored in a computer or any other device.

THE APPOINTMENTS OF CIC AND SIC

The Act provides for creation of the Central Information Commission and State Information Commission at Central and State levels. The Central Government shall constitute Central Information Commission consisting of Chief Information Commissioner and Central Information Commissioners not exceeding 10 in number. They should be appointed by President on recommendation of committee consisting of Prime Minister as Chairperson, Leader of Opposition and Union Cabinet Minister nominated by the Prime Minister. The Chief Information Commissioner (CIC) and Information Commissioners (ICs) shall be person of eminence in public life with wide knowledge and experience in law, science and technology, social science, management, journalism, mass media or administration and governance. CIC shall hold office for a term of five years or till he attains the age of 65 years which ever is earlier. IC shall also not be eligible for reappointment as IC but he may be considered as CIC provided his term of office on appointment, as CIC shall not be more than five years in aggregate as IC and the CIC. Salaries and allowances and terms and conditions of the CIC shall be the same as that of a Chief Election Commissioner and the IC as that of an Election Commissioner. CIC and IC can be removed from office by the order of the President on ground of proved misbehaviour or incapacity. This can be done after an inquiry made by the Supreme Court on a reference made by the President.

Similarly, every state government shall constitute State Information Commission, which shall consist of State Chief Information Commissioner and State Information Commissioners not exceeding 10 in number. The appointment shall be made by the Governor of the state on the recommendation of the committee consisting of the Chief Minister who shall be the chairperson of the committee, Leader of the Opposition, the Chief Minister. The State Chief Information Commissioner (SCIC) and State Information Commissioner (SIC) shall be person of eminence in public life with wide knowledge and experience in law, science and technology, social science, management, journalism, mass media or administration and governance, and he shall hold office for a term of five years or till he attains the age of 65 years which ever is earlier and not eligible for reappointment other terms and conditions are same as cited above.

SCIC and SIC can be removed from office by the order of the Governor on ground of proved misbehaviour or incapacity. This can be done after an inquiry made by the Supreme Court on the reference made by the Governor. The duty of the Central Information Commission and State Information Commission have been mentioned in sections 18 to 20 of the Act.

PROCEDURE FOR SUPPLY OF INFORMATION

A person who desires to obtain information has to make a request for the same in writing or through electronic form. It can be in English, Hindi or in the official language of the area in which the application is being made. Such application shall be accompanied with prescribed fee. The application is to be made to the Central Public Information Officer; or State Public Information Officer of the concerned public authority, or Central Assistant Public Information Officer of the concerned public authority or Central Assistant Public Information Officer or State Assistant Public Information Officer as the case may be. The particulars of the information required must be specified in the application. No reasons or personal details are required to be given for seeking information. The application must either be decided within a period of 30 days or the request be rejected for the reasons as specified under section 7 of the aforesaid Act.

RESTRICTIONS ON RIGHT TO INFORMATION

The Information under the Act can be denied under sections 8 and 9 of the Act; namely,

- Disclosure prejudicially effects sovereignty and integrity of India, security, strategic, scientific or economic interests of the state, relation with the foreign state or lead to incitement of an offence;

- Publication of the information is expressly forbidden by court of law or tribunal and disclosure constitute contempt of court;
- Information disclosure of which, causes breach of privilege of the Parliament or the State Legislature;
- Information includes commercial confidence, trade secrets or intellectual property and disclosure would harm competitive position of the third party unless the competent authority is satisfied that the public interest warrants disclosure of such information;
- Information available to the person in his fiduciary relationship unless the competent authority is satisfied that larger public interest requires disclosure of such information;
- Information received in confidence from the foreign government;
- Information whose disclosure endangers the life or physical safety of any person or identifies the source or assistance given in confidence for enforcement of law or security purposes;
- Information which would impede the process of investigation or apprehension or prosecution of offenders;
- Cabinet papers including records of deliberations of the Council of Ministers, Secretaries and other officers. However the decisions of the Council of Ministers and the reasons and material on which the decisions were taken shall be made public after the decision has been taken, provided it is not covered under any of the exemption clauses mentioned.
- Personal information which has no correlation to any public activity or interest or which causes unwarranted invasion of the privacy of the individual unless larger public interest justifies the disclosure of such information;
- Providing information involves an infringement of copyright subsisting in a person other than state.

PENALTY

If Central Information Commission or the State Information Commission at the time of deciding a complaint or appeal is of the opinion that the Central Information Officer or the State Public Information Officer has:

- without any reasonable cause refused to receive application for information or has not furnished information within time specified under section 7(1); or
- malafidely denied request for information; or
- knowingly gives incorrect information, incomplete or misleading information; or
- destroyed information which was subject of request; or
- obstructed in any manner in furnishing information.

It shall impose a penalty of Rs. 250 each day till application is received or information is furnished, however the total amount of penalty shall not exceed Rs. 25,000. Further it shall recommend for disciplinary action against the Central or State Information Officer as the case may be under the service rules applicable to him/her. Sections 19(3), 20(1) and 20(2) are related to the penalty.

SOME PREVAILING TRENDS (LEAVE-ME-OUT PLEASE)

Information is power and those who wield power know it. That is the reason that the key-agencies of administration are in the long queue seeking exemption from the ambit of the RTI Act, 2005. Even our judiciary, too, is in this race. Despite sustained campaigns by various civil society organizations, including of few political parties, a section of the bureaucracy have been blocking attempts to give the teeth to the Act, as they are afraid of becoming accountable to the public. It is a matter of concern that even the central law will not supersede the state or Panchayat Raj system's Right to Information Acts. Yet, the RTI Act, is, 'progressive' in terms of making governance a transparent affair.

In the euphoria of Independence, we have forgot to address the contradiction of continuing with a bureaucracy that was tailored to implement the British Empire's agenda. Democratization of the political process should have ideally transformed the character of the state. But that has not been the case. Laws like the *Official Secrets Act,* 1923, have made instruments of state a law unto themselves our politicians and bureaucrats. The result is that we are a democracy that functions within a legal and administrative framework that is essentially autocratic. Such a self-defeating system is an enemy of open society, as it tends to work against any measure—be it opening up the economy or enforcing social security initiatives like the public distribution system: that tends to upset the applecart. It is ironical that we gloat over India's information technology prowess but refuse to insist on measures that will make access to information regarding public affairs a right of the citizen. The essay in hand presents certain cases that go against the spirit of the RTI Act, 2005. For example,

- The Right to Information Act is supposed to give people access to information that was hitherto not available. But the way the Union Public Service Commission (UPSC) interprets the law, it turned out that even information that was publicly available earlier is now being treated as not for disclosure. The Times of India put in an application to the UPSC under the RTI in Sept. 2006, asking for information on the domicile, educational background, gender and such details of candidates selected for civil services. After almost the full 30-day period given under the RTI for the concerned body to respond, it got a list of those selected without any of these details. The reason cited : All of these are, according to the UPSC, "personal information" of the candidates. The 'privacy' of information was the basis of the denial.*
- Mission Netaji, a research group, asked the home ministry for the records on June 23, but this was summarily declined on the ground that the

* *The Times of India News,* New Delhi, 16 Sept. 2006, p. 4.

documents were classified. The group then appealed to CIC for the documents on July 29, 2006. The deputy secretary in the Union Government, M.M. Chopra, was quoted as writing to CIC: "The matter happened more than 20 years from the date of request and as such, it is refused."* A week before Gandhi's murder, Gandhi remembered Netaji in the midst of communal holocast. He missed Netaji. If Netaji had came back, the history of India would have turned different. But people of India must be assured that it was murder. Following Three Reports were release on Netaji :

(i) Shahnawaz Committee, 1956
(ii) Justice J.D. Khosla Commission, 1970-74, and
(iii) Justice Mukherjee Commission of Inquiry, 1999. The Report was submitted in 2005.

Till this date, all three reports are contradictory in findings, witnesses and statements, but non-availability to public.

The Delhi High Court on 27th November, 2006, stayed a CIC order to disclose the information, on the ground that releasing such information would entail the violation of provisions of the Official Secrets Act, 1923 and harm the integrity of the UPSC, that is, it would undermine the entire examination procedure as well as would lead to violation of intellectual property.

- 'Leave-me-out-please campaign' was joined by the Central Bureau of Investigation (CBI) and the Central Vigilance Commission (CVC) soon after the RTI Act, 2005 was put into operation. Sadly, the Union Government, too, sought their exemption. It wanted that the CBI and the CVC agencies to be included in the Right to Information Act's Second Schedule

* 'Did Netaji Died in a Plane Crash' or Was He Eliminated? South Asia Politics, New Delhi, Sept. 2006, pp. 2-3.

which lists 18 intelligence and security agencies that have immunity from the Act. In fact, the Second Schedule includes agencies like the Research and Analysis Wing (RAW), Intelligence and Bureau (IB), Narcotics Control Bureau, BSF, Assam Rifles, and the Directorate of Revenue Intelligence. The bogey of national security and the sensitive nature of investigations these organizations undertake-have been cited to seek exemption.

There are already provisions in the Act that exempt information from being provided where disclosure affects national interests, if forbidden by any court or tribunal or may be contempt of court, trade secrets or intellectual property where disclosure would harm competitive position, endanger life or physical safety or identify confidential source of information or assistance, impede the process of investigation or apprehension. Why then should any public body or authority seek to be protected from a process that will go a long way in making our public space more democratic? Surprisingly, only these high profile public authorities, as cited above, the four PSUs—BHEL, Rashtriya Chemicals & Fertilizers Ltd. and National Building Construction Corporation, too, have sought exemptions from the RTI's purview. Likewise, the Chief Justice of the Supreme Court, too, has sought the same kind of exemption.

The Central Information Commission has asked University Grants Commission (UGC) to disclose cut-off marks of its National Eligibility Test examinations and provide question papers of past exams along with answers to applications. Passing the order, Information Commissioner O.P. Kejariwal rejected UGC's plea that disclosure of such information were always regarded as confidential and hence, can't be provided to applicants under the Right to Information (RTI) Act. The Commission directed UGC to disclose last five years' cut-off marks of the NET examination for lectureship in colleges. The order came on the basis of an appeal filed by one Ravindra Kumar, a resident of Ghaziabad, who was denied the access to previous five years' question papers along with model answers. The Commission asked the UGC to consider its order in their meeting and provide cut-off marks and other information to the applicant. Kumar had approached the public information officer of UGC, seeking information about selection process in NET exams along with details regarding cut-off marks.

The CIC had earlier directed the Union Public Service Commission, it may be recalled, to disclose the cut-off marks to unsuccessful civil services candidates which was hailed as a move towards achieving transparency.

- The lawyers of Supreme Court Bar, Association, in its a majority resolution, demanded that the Judiciary should not be exempted from the purview of the RTI, Act. The resolution, though expressed regards for the judges debunked to the Supreme Court's claim that Section 25 of the RTI Act could hit the independence judiciary, if applied, or tend to interfere with the functioning of justice administration. The CJI's decision has proposed to have 'reforms' in the application of the RTI Act. The appointment issue relating to Justice Vijendra Jain of the Delhi High Court who had been promoted as CJ of the Punjab and Haryana High Court was probably the background for exemption of the RTI Act.
- According to Shailesh Gandhi, the RTI Act has empowered the citizen and it has bombarded the Maharashtrian Government through NGOs, in spite of the fact that the Government has appointed only one Information Commission, instead of four, resulting in a pile of appeals. It has spread into a rural areas through the role of socialist activist Anna Hazare. A number of fictitious muster-rolls of the

National Employment Guarantee Scheme have caught under the Act.*

- Twenty years after CBI charge sheeted an employee in a corruption case, a 73-year old former staffer of Food Corporation of India (FCI) succeeded in gaining access to two official reports which may help him 'conclude' the long pending matter. Central Information Commission (CIC) directed FCI to allow its former official ML Kohli to inspect two vigilance investigation reports on him in its custody. He (Kohli) sought inspection of the files which relate to a period 20 years before the date of his application under the Act, but according to Information Commissioner Padma Balasubramanian FCI cannot deny the information. The order was passed on the appeal filed on March 23, 2006.
- The Calcutta University has finally crumbled under the weight of right to information, agreeing to show answer scripts to an examinee. It had tried everything to prevent this from calling itself the guardian of the candidate, to saying the examiner's life would be at stake, but nothing worked.

The West Bengal Information Commission quashed all the appeals of the university. As the custodian of the Right to Information Act, 2005, in the state, the Commission, in an order dated January 15, 2007, told the University that any candidate can demand to see his or her answer script. The University Registrar was unhappy to open a floodgate of such demands and he asserted that RTI Act had been interpreted by the candidate. The commissioner Arun Kumar Bhattacharya rejected all those reasons. The credit for this victory goes to the commission.**

Thus, in the light of the experiences of the working of the RTI Act, 2005, the Government of India came under the tremendous pressure to make certain amendments/ clarifications and provide guidelines to the Act, specifically the

* *The Times of India* news, 1st Oct. 2006.

** *The Hindustan Times* news, New Delhi, 18-1-2007.

substantive file notings, and some sensational sting operations. Currently, the Act contains a list of 10 exempted categories a strong. A strong lobby is behind the amendment move to enlarge the exemption scope of section 8 of the Act, 2005.

> In a bid to restore a balance between free speech and fair trial, the 17th Law Commission came up with a set of controversial proposals to rein in what it called *"Trial by Media"*. Reacting to aggressive coverage of crime stories, the Commission recommended that the media be barred from reporting anything prejudicial to an accused, right from the time he is arrested in the course of the investigation. This is a far cry from the existing situation in which the contempt law kicks in only after the investigation is completed and the accused chargesheeted.

It said that its recommendation to render the media liable to contempt right from the stage of arrest was in keeping with a Supreme Court judgment of 1969, *A.K. Gopalan* v. *Noordeen*. The report seeks to incorporate the Supreme Court verdict in the law. In views of the commission, judges, despite all their training and experience, are vulnerable to getting biased because of the media. If carried out, it would affect the ambit of the RTI.

IAS officials, usually opposed to applications filed under Right to Information (RTI) Act, too, have found it to be a useful instrument in digging out information. Some in the IAS lobby have decided to pierce the iron curtain shrouding their annual confidential report (ACR), which is a leash in the hands of politicians to ensure that bureaucrats tow their line with the help of RTI. For, just one adverse remark on their ACR could ruin their bureaucratic stint or their hopes for a promotion. While some have now begun using RTI Act to get a copy of their ACRs, others have even gone to the extent of demanding specific file notings made by their seniors in the confidential reports. For instance, honourary secretary of the IAS association in Gujarat, Arvind Agarwal, has demanded a copy of his ACR from General Administration Department (GAD).

Mr. Agarwal claims that as a member of his association, he wants to set a precedent for his juniors that it is their right to know their overall grading in the past 10 years and what has been the 'nature of their performance'. According to him, these are two basic issues that determine the promotion of officers. We have the right to know how we have performed in our careers. Knowing where we stand will help us improve the administration system as a whole.

RTI Report Released on Jan. 5, 2007

In the latest example, the UGC was fined Rs. 25,000 for delaying scholarship to the student/awardee of Meerut, Charumita, by C.I.C. in November 2007. She won the scholarship in Nov. 2005, but the UGC did not released the amount, despite writing a number of letters. He was falsely informed by UGC that the amount had been credited in the ICICI bank, Meerut, UP.

In a historic decision, the CIC held that citizens cannot question government by utilizing the RTI. This is the right of the Parliament and the Ministry is responsible to it.

TABLE 1

Public authorities that have received at least 50 RTI requests but rejected none		*The Ministries/depts. that have received the most number of RTI requests*	
Authority	*No. of Requests*	*Ministry/Dept.*	*Requests (with percentage)*
• DDA	1,988	• Ministry of Finance	4,770 (19.5%)
• Hindustan Shipyard Ltd.	1,203	• Ministry of Railways	2,665 (10.9%)
• Ministry of Social Justice and Empowerment	152	• Ministry of Urban Development	2,504 (10.2%)
		• Ministry of Comm. and IT	1,722 (7%)
• Department of Tourism	120	• Ministry of Shipping, Road Transport and Highways	1,680 (6.9%)
• National Highways Authority of India	118		

CONCLUDING OBSERVATIONS

The Right to Information Act, 2005, was one such promising start that the UPA government has made. One of the most progressive laws of its kind in the world, it is meant to be one of the UPA government's finest legislative achievements. Championed by civil society groups and pledged in UPA's common minimum programme, the RTI Act promised to reform the functioning of government. The Act espoused transparency and accountability in the functioning of public institutions. It sought to rescue governance from colonial laws like the Official Secrets Act, 1923, which gave unbridled powers to the Indians bureaucracy. It raised hope that the people will finally have access to the workings of the state. The euphoria has been short-lived. The bureaucracy has intervened and convinced the government to accept its 'right' to stonewall queries about decision-making. A proposed amendment to the RTI Act plans to exclude notings made by senior government officials on files in all areas, except social and development sector projects, from the purview of the law.

By and large, the RTI Act has made the government officers to realize that this rule is meant for common man. It is very much related to our 'swaraj' concept. It is now applicable for our rulers. The Act has come as a true empowerment of citizens and its fullest implementation would make ours a true participatory democracy. The awareness is going to be slow, but it would soon grow rapidly nationwide through media and NGOs.

The UPA Government has decided to conduct a detailed evaluation of the RTI Act, which it has admitted, won 'immerse response from public'. But it has to be evaluated on professional basis, taking into account a genuine cross-section of the people who are partners in the Act's implementation. The study has to be full democratized, totally transparent and participatory.

The Act has to be viewed in the context of the reforms process. Transparency and accountability in the functioning of institutions that are integral to good governance—is a must if economic reforms are to have any meaning. Of course, an Act is just a legal measure, it can only mediate between the *babu* and the public. Political agencies and civil society groups need to maintain pressure on public bodies to abide by the provisions of the RTI Act. The bureaucracy should view the Act as an agent of social change rather than as a challenge to its role in governance. The state's watchdogs like the CVC and the CBI should take the lead in effecting this change and arresting the trends of corruption.

If the proposed plan is meant to have amendments to the RTI Act, including not to disclose of file-notings (except in social and developmental issues), it would, if carried out, render the Act 'limp and infracterous', or making it a mockery of the Act. According to O.P. Kejariwal*, Commissioner of CIC, if the nuances of corruption involved in the file-notings would not be revealed, the amendments to it would throw back to an age of darkness after experiencing a fresh hope of transparency, openness and accountability in the administration/public life. As we know our position in the list of most corrupt countries of the world is quite high. But the RTI has given us a chance to bring down our ranking in this regard. Let us not throw it away. (by seeking more exemption than the ten exempted categories in the Act). Of course, there is a need to check on 'frivolous RTI applications'.**

Today, because of RTI, some aware people have taken the RTI route to get basic amenities, install road or get admissions in schools. The 80 old lady Laxmi Devi of Delhi could, for example, get her pension from MDC. There are many who have got their passports, pensions, ration cards and IT refunds, etc. Thus, this credit goes to 'Satark Nagrik Sanghathan', an NGO which has been organizing camps to aware the masses about the importance of the RTI. The poor practically find it difficult to access their entitlement because of lack of information about their rights. SNS has tried to help them by using the RTI Act through holding camps in big cities like Mumbai or Calcutta. It has received tremendous response.

On the contrary, a trend of misuse of RTI Act has been noted by the CIC itself, whose purpose (seekers of

---

* O.P. Kejariwal, "File of the Matter", *The Times of India*, New Delhi, Sept. 12, 2006, p. 14.

** "The Editorial, Bending before Babus", *Ibid.*, 14th Oct. 2006, p. 14.

information), has been for 'harassing the public authorities'. Because of its misuse, CIC office is currently flooded with RTI applications. They have forgotten the limitations and the basic objectives of the Act. The CIC observed that Hyderabad based K. Gopinath alone (who was suspend on disciplinary grounds) for examples, put in as many as 67 applications to JNTU, AICTE, UGC for diverse pieces, of information. This kind of practice should be checkmated and penalized, in order to set free the public institutions/offices from the burden of petitions and applications.

CHAPTER

20

Right to Information Act

A Review of its Implementation

The enactment of the Right to Information Act, 2005, has ushered in a new era in the history of Indian democracy, which is meant to protect citizens' right to information. The right to inform and to be informed is enshrined in the constitutions of many countries. But in India's Constitution, it not explicit on this point, though it has been recognized in general as part of the right of freedom and expression under Article 19(1)(a) of the Constitution. Credit should be given to the NGO-Mazdoor Kisan Shakti Sangathan—MKSS of Rajasthan for carrying on an agitation in 1994-95 against the government to make available information of the work done in their villages under the funds sanctioned for various development project and to sensitize the rural people about the need for it (the right to information). The slogan was : *Hamara paisa, hamara hisab: our money, our account*. The Rajasthan Government ultimately introduced a version of an access to information Bill in the assembly. MP then followed it. Likewise, thanks should be given to the U.F. government that it initiated under the Common Minimum Programme, the right to information in dealing with the widely prevalent corruption in Indian Public Life as it will increase transparency in the government and its administration.

The new Right to Information Act, 2005 is a radical improvement of the Freedom of Information Act, 2002. One of the outstanding features of the Act is the provision for the set-up of Information Commissions which are said to be independent and high level bodies. It is a commendable step to ensure an open democracy as it would give the public at large an opportunity to participate in Government activities. However, the Act has brought to limelight many cases of clash between the people's access to information and preserving confidentiality in public interests.

Since this law was put into effect, it was hoped to ensure transparency and accountability in the working of public institutions which have been plagued by the growing politics of criminalization and corruption. The Right to Information Act which is a radical and refined version of the Freedom of Information Bill, 1997 and Freedom of Information Bill, 2002—is meant to make the public informed, open and accessible to Indian citizens about the functioning of our government, which hitherto have been kept 'secret' and 'confidential'. This is a new right of citizen to know about 'governance' and to ensure meaningful participation of people in the working of democratic institutions, as the Act required public authorities to respond to queries within a stipulated period (30 days) failing to which they may face penalties.

CIC's ROLE

Under the RTI Act, the Chief Information Commissioner CIC is the delivery system at the apex. It was expected that the CIC would act as a quasi-judiciary body. It is currently, headed by CIC Wajahat Hubibullah. The two groups of NGOs Parivarthan and Delhi Right to Information Manch-headed by Magsayany award winner, Arvind Kejariwal, came out to record people's experiences who have been dissatisfied of the C.I.C.'s style of functioning. By the end of Jan. 2007, as per CIC records, there were 2,371 cases of complaints and the CIC office failed to redress grievances as per expectations of the

Act. Their complaint was based on the scope of Section 8 of the Act that has exempted from being made 'public'. It demanded to widen the scope of the Section 8 itself, as many complaints have been dismissed on that basis, i.e. the information asked for was of a 'fiduciary nature', or hurt the personal or institutional interests of the organization.

Some of the previous developments and verdicts given by the Central Information Commissioner (CIC) has been hostile in dealing with RTI applicants and aggrieved parties, leading to RTI activities to knock at the doors of High Courts of the country. Naturally, they would be more frustrated in getting justice in view of the disposal rate of pending cases in these courts. This has increased an additional burden on our judiciary. The question is: Is the CIC's is a quasi-judicial body under the RTI Act? Unfortunately, high courts have entertained writs against the CIC decisions, whereas, according to the member of CIC, the office lacks the infrastructure to effectively fight its cases in these courts.* This situation has under mined the common man's faith in the Act. The fact is that till this date, the CIC office has shown no presence in any court at the time of admission against its divisions. Therefore, the CIC should review its own cases and provide cover to public authorities to reinstate the faith in the Act.

Secondly, the media has played up the charges even without taking the commissioner's point of view. While the media has covered important CIC decisions, it has not woken up to the potential of the Act to introduce elements of transparency and accountability in administration and contain corruption. It has refrained from bringing widespread corruption to light. If properly utilized, the RTI Act can perhaps work as effectively as sting operations. In fact, the media has failed to take up social issues which could result in bringing about systemic changes, which is one of the major objectives of the RTI Act. The law is arguably the single most powerful piece of legislation enacted in independent India.

RTI has raised the hopes and aspirations of people. Applications under RTI law have increased in almost

---

* O.P. Kejariwal, "For your Information", *The Times of India*, New Delhi, 18 July, 2007, p. 12.

geometrical proportions. If CIC continues to be under siege from activists, courts and the media, it will only serve the bureaucracy's purpose of crippling CIC by creating a jungle of hurdles.

In the absence of proper support from the government, the CIC may well tread on a path that would render the RTI movement ineffectual. A controversy cropped up in the affairs of Municipal Corporation of Delhi (MCD) and the Jamia Hamdard University, New Delhi, in Sept. 2006 about the lenient view of the CIC on imposing monetary penalties on them. The penalty matter exposed a schism between the CIC and CIC member on a waiver of a fine, raising the question: Is CIC just a paper tiger?

RECORD OF ITS IMPLEMENTATION

The study conducted by an NGO Centre for Civil Society—examined all states except Jammu & Kashmir to judge how many were complying with Section 4 of the RTI (termed as duty to publish or DTP) that makes it compulsory for States to give *suo moto* certain information relating to the functioning of the administration. The findings of it reveal that a handful of states have sincerely put the RTI Act in operation. Even the states with high literacy levels like Kerala, Mizoram and West Bengal have not make use to it for proper awareness, nor they have given of appropriate infrastructure to the offices of CICs. They legged behind in RTI compliance. This is all due to the 'design' that most of the Information Commissions—though independent appellate authorities are packed with retired bureaucrats, whereas the Act has provisions to include professionals and representatives of Civil Society groups in its set-up. Thus, these RTI bodies have not been able to function as watchdogs of the state machinery. This picture has brought for the conflict interests and overcrowding heap of files, as examples given ahead justify it.

- The campaign for an RTI Act was started by grass-roots movements. The idea was to empower people with a legislation and an administrative apparatus that would keep a check on sarkar. Our RTI Act is considered to be one of the best in the world, but it will be effective only if the independence of RTI commissions is maintained. The attempt to block access to file notings was defeated by a sustained people's campaign. A similar effort may be needed to preserve the autonomy and independence of information commissions. An overhaul of information commissions is necessary. They have to be rid of the *babu* mindset. The penalty clause meant to haul up officials refusing to give correct information has to be effectively used. It is revealing that the Central Information Commission has not one case to show where an erring official has been penalized. The commissions have to put in place a transparent mechanism where complaints are heard so that decisions are not made on arbitrary or subjective grounds. Proper reporting of the proceedings at the information commissions would ensure accountability. It is in the collective interest of the nation that RTI becomes an effective tool to ensure good governance.

Unfortunately, the implementation of the RTI could not inject an element of transparency to governance in a way that was imagined at a time of its enactment. Now it has become a weapons in the hands of bureaucrats. A host of Government institutions like the Supreme Court, UPSC CBI, Delhi Metro, etc. have now sought exemption from RTI.

❖ The Supreme Court's application for exemption is at odds with its role. The courts are meant to be a sentinel of democracy, providing a check on the other organs of government. It has stood up for citizen's rights against encroachment by the state. But the Supreme Court is chary of disclosing information about how judges are appointed as well as the status of complaints against particular judges. The apex court is already under the scanner for an application under RTI about a complaint against a High Court Chief Justice. The SC's logic that it must be exempt from RTI on the grounds that its authority would be undermined holds little water. The court must be the most accountable institution in any democracy because of its vital role as a watchdog. In fact, judges must be held to standards that are higher than other government officials. There is little known in the public domain about the appointment of judges as well as the status of complaints against them. This can change if RTI is made applicable to the Supreme Court. That will ensure that the court, like any other institution, is accountable to the people.

- It is strange that in a landmark decision, the CIC has ruled that judicial proceedings of all courts and tribunals are beyond the purview of the RTI Act. This judgment was given in Sept. 2007. Likewise, the Supreme Court has asked the Government of India to amend the RTI Act to take out of the purview of CIS which is too is an autonomous body and provide a provision that CJI can stop any release of information. This approach is tantamount to violation of RTI Act, as such exemptions and privileges would put a veil on the transparent functioning of judiciary in public interest. It is further regretted that most of the High Courts have not yet appointed Public Information Officers—PIOs as required under the RTI Act. This is clearly a violation of Section 8 of the Act.
- In many cases involving the People's Union for Civil Liberties PUCL versus the Union of India, the apex court has supported the plea of the state dispensation not to release the desirable information under Section 8 (1) of the RTI Act, 2005. It is power in the hands of the government wings, because of phrase 'Secret' confidential activity, national interests. In dealing with disclosing marks of aspirants in institutions like CAT, IIMS, UPSC, the Central Information Commission (CIC) has favourably responded to RTI applications under section 25(5) of the Act.

- A thick curtain of secrecy and bureaucratic mindset of functioning in RAW and IB has weakened to meet the growing challenge of internal security—both within India and in its neighbourhood due to the existence of the Official Secret Act, 1923. It helps to suit politicians to play politics with intelligence. In fact, their recruitment, training promotion and performance needs to be made transparent so as to strengthen the spirit RTI Act. Unfortunately, the administrative culture of secrecy in India—a colonial legacy of the British rule— still prevails. That is why the right to information has not been effect in checkmating the widely prevalent corruption in public life.
- In a daring move, the Bihar is the first state to introduce/launch helpline service for RTI applicants. Now, instead of writing an application for seeking information under the RTI Act and submitting its concerned departments, all one has to do a dial a specific member where an attendant processes the request and sends an application to the concerned official. According to CM of Bihar Nitish Kumar; the purpose of the RTI helpline to empower people and bring transparency as well as accountability in the Bihar's administration. It operated from 29th Jan. 2007. He is not bothered about opening a Pandora's Box in a problematic state by launching this helpline. His plea is that the people of the state have a right to know about the fate of on-going projects, reasons for delay, amount spent or status of loan applications, etc. He hoped that the helpline will act as a deterrent against corruption in public life.

SOME EVENTS OF TRUTH TRIALS

The CIC under the RTI Act is still in its learning phase in dealing with the government and the citizenry. It has developed into an instrument of confrontation between one section of the society and another because of awareness.

- At present our RTI law is among the most liberal in the world, as allowing access to file notings in social and development sectors keeps vast areas under the RTI. But the top echelons of bureaucracy have dug in their heels over the need to restrict access to official notings and feel that the RTI Act be amended with some curbs. As such the bureaucracy does not appear prepared to surrender its claims in the politicized areas. Official is set against a see-all law and demands the Act for further 'review' as the following cases have proved it.
- The CIC asked (in July 2007) the Union Home Ministry to make public within three months various secret documents relating to the mystery-shrouded death of Subhash Chandra Bose in 1945. However, the CIC gave the ministry the liberty to examine those documents which could affect the country sovereignty and integrity, if they were disclosed such documents would be exempted from disclosure. This decision came in response to an application by Delhi-based resident Sayantan Dasguta.
- In a landmark decision, the full bench of CIC ruled that facts relating to the appointment of judges can not be kept 'secret' and beyond the purview of the RTI act. This broadened the scope of the Act and expended the frontier of transparency to the Judiciary. The verdict was given 27th March, 2007, directing the law ministry. The application was related to the appointment of justice Virendra Jain as CJ of Punjab and Haryana High Court. It may be recalled that the member of SC collegium objected to the appointment of justice Jain as CJ of the aforesaid High Court and the President of India returned the file to Law Ministry on the basis of the dissent.
- In many cases, the CIC has ruled in favour of the aspirants, who have faced his preliminary examinations of USPC/state level Public Service Commissions, specifically under the 'scaling formula' and asked the authorities give the criteria and marks

to aspirants. The startling results of the Chhattisgarh Public Service Commission were in flash-light.

- In yet another landmark order, CIC directed the Centre (PMO) to disclose details of the PM Relief Fund. As per the order, it is a discretionary Fund with the PM but is accessible to the citizens under the RTI Act. It is not exempted under Section 8 of the Act. The order put to rest claims of babus that the records of disbursements from the Fund cannot be made 'public'. Order was given in response to the RTI application filed in June 6, 2006.
- According to the Chief Information Commissioner, W. Habibullah, associations including companies and other corporate entities should be considered on a par with citizens in their quest for seeking information under the Right to Information Act. "We direct that an application/appeal from an association or a partnership firm or a Hindu Undivided Family (HUF), or from some other group of individuals constituted as a body or otherwise should be accepted and allowed", chief information commissioner Wajahat Habibullah said in a recent order, observing that the RTI Act's objective is to secure access of information to all citizens to promote transparency and accountability. The Commission referred to a number of Supreme Court decisions which did not reject applications from corporate bodies on grounds that they were not natural citizens under the law. He said: "It is a fact that all superior courts have been admitting applications in exercise of their extraordinary jurisdiction from companies, societies and associations under the provisions of the Constitution of which the RTI Act, 2005 is a child".
- The Judiciary should be credited to have shown positive indication in tackling RTI cases. The Delhi High Court, on 17th April, 2007, for example, upheld the CIS order/directive asking V.P.S.C. to disclose individual candidate's scores marks/cut-off marks of

civil service preliminary examinations, 2006. The plea was that disclosing UPSC's scaling system involves large public interests and it does not infringe upon the intellectual property right of the Commission. The approach of CIC (Wajahat Habibullah) in this matter has been in corrective perspective.

- Contrary to the above-cited cases, the CIC heard an RTI application of J&K resident, B.R. Manhas, who had sought from the CBI information on various counts on the 'Purlia Arms Drop case'. But the CIC rejected the RTI plea stating that disclosure of such information/identities would impede the prosecution process. The CBI's case, thus, was exempted under the provisions of the RTI Act.*
- Likewise, the CIC ruled that when it comes to white-collar crimes such as tax evasion, a private citizen cannot seek access to official records even after the investigating officer in the given case had submitted his report to the competent authority. This is a departure from the RTI norm that public authorities are obliged to disclose information related to any criminal case once the investigation is completed. The plea was based on section 8(1)(h) of the RTI Act, pointing out that disclosure of such information would impede the process of investigation. It was a major setback to RTI.
- In Madhya Pradesh, the RTI exposed the top official's fraud Swaraj Puri, who was ejected, from the post of Madhya Pradesh director-general of police (DGP), is the first major casualty of the one-year-old Right to Information Act in the country. On the basis of the information obtained under the RTI Act, a special court in Indore, directed state government to register a case of corruption, forgery and cheating against Puri. The complaint alleged that Puri had filed a false certificate in order to obtain

* *The Times of India* news, dated 30th July, 2007, p. 5.

admission for his son in 2001, under 'NRI-sponsored quota' in an engineering college of MP.*

- RTI helped Pak migrates to get the passport. Dr. C.V. Acctra, the principal of a pharmacy college in Ulhasnagar, won the battle. He got the passport after a wait of almost five years. He wrote a number of letters to the ministry of External Affairs and Union Home Ministers, but in vain. Thane is decided to use the RTI.
- Delaying any information promised under the Right to Information Act has proved costly for any government official. Cracking his whip, Maharashtra Information Commissioner, for example, imposed a fine of Rs. 10,000 on the divisional joint registrar of Cooperative Societies for a 39-day delay in providing information. The State Information Commission (SIC) asked the commissioner of cooperation to recover the amount from the officer's salary.** This is, of course, an unprecented decision in the history of the Act. The order should serve a lesson to all governmental agencies not to take the RTI lightly. The case was filed in Jan. 23, 2006 by Andheri-based C.A. Tarun Ghia the penalty was imposed in December 2006.

In the same manner, Karnataka Information Commission in December, 2006 imposed fines in one case Rs. 500 for not giving information and in other case Rs. 5000 for giving misleading information under the RTI Act. The penalty amount was to be deducted from the concerned officials' salaries.*** In April, 2006, the C.I.C. slapped under the RTI Act Rs. 25,000 on the possible penalty for not furnishing information to an applicant within 30 days. He was informed after 86 days. This is the first instance where the CIC levied the maximum penalty.****

* Based on the report given by Manjon Mitta, in *The Times of India*, dated Sept. 27, 2006, p. 5.

** *The Times of India* news, New Delhi, 30 December, 2006, p. 13.

*** *Ibid.*, December 9, 2006, p. 10.

**** *Ibid.*, 24-1-2006, p. 4.

HOW TO STRENGTHEN THE ACT?

The RTI is a new law and it has not yet reach the rural areas to the extent that it should have. In the functioning of government, the 'mindset' has not changed so far to strengthen the act. Most of the cases in fact, come from public institutions and the response is not properly given. That is why the people have to wait for 30 to 45 days to file a second appeal, at the regional commissioner office's level.

Secondly, the law needs to be given a 'human face', because it is all about empowering the common man, or Aam Admi in words of our PM. It is in accordance with the Preamble "We, the People of India". Hence, bureaucracy should be made sensitive to human sufferings. As per the background as cited above, its performance in meeting objectives of it during the last two years has been half-heartedly, successful and it needs some more modifications. The Act must insist that people/institutions give reasons for seeking information and people having ulterior motives in demanding information must be penalized in case of non-compliance of the CIC's directives. Therefore, there must be a new penalty provision and no officials/heads of public institutions be allowed to shirk responsibility.

Thirdly, the RIT needs to create more public awareness and more people's involvement. There is no corrective mechanism to deal with information received through the Act. So it should ensure corrective action in a specific time-frame.

In many cases and references, as cited above, the attitudes towards sharing information under the Act have hardened, under section 5 of the Official Secrets Act, on the ground of secrecy, national security or public interest. This has help strengthened a source of bureaucratic corruption.*

In this regard, the Chief Information Commissioner suggested that the RTI Act should be amended to do away with the conflict between the Official Secrets Act (OSA) and

* It is worth-recalling that American expert Dr. Appleby who was invited by Pt. Nehru to study Indian Administration commented that the new Government had not got away from and arbitrary secrecy depriving Indian University professors and citizens in generally of desirable information. The same mindset still prevails. (See Prabhat Dutt, India's Democracy: New Challeges (New Delhi, Kanishka Publishers, 1997) p. 18).

the RTI Act, as the OSA has no place in a democracy set-up. The OSA was enacted way back in 1923 to serve the interests of power. Unfortunately, it is still a tool in the hands of bureaucrats, who with the alliance of their political bosses guard their interests at the cost of democratic ethos. In fact, the QSA has been a big hurdle in rooting out corruption by the country's premier agency—CBI. It is necessary for democracy to set free the whistle-blower (CBI) from the shadow of the OSA. Even the Second Administrative Reforms Commission, too, has asked the government for scrapping the OSA, taking the plea that the privileges of the citizens' 'the right to know' over the public officials' 'right to secrecy' should not be subjected.* Hence, there is a need to give the teeth to the RTI Act.

The Act is meant to give voice to the civil society and to create a watchdog independent of the state, which is possible only if Information Commissioners are representatives of the diversity in society, instead of the exclusive domain of bureaucrats. At the movement, they in the states as well as at the Centre—have become parking lots for retd. bureaucrats. This nature of appointments has defeated the purpose of the RTI Act. Therefore, professionals should also be included in the list of appointments.

According to social activist, Anna Hazare, the RTI Act has become a powerful tool for the people of Gram Panchayats and bloc levels. They have started demanding information on issue that are concern to the areas like Government projects and financial aids to educational institutions. But in rural areas, they find it difficult to get court fee stamps and many times elected members are unable to file quarries. Therefore, he has urged the Centre to issue a special stamp to be affixed to applications under the RTI Act which is mandatory under the RTI Act, 2005.

The CIC has proposed to have 'paperless affair', i.e. E-administration of government's departments so that public records are accessible online and can be used to provide information under the RTI Act. When implemented, this would

* Recently, the OSA was invoked against a former RAW official for writing about corruption in the CBI but the material relating to it was not disclosed on the ground of 'classified information'. See the editorial 'Secrets and Laws', *The Times of India*, New Delhi, Oct. 17, 2007, p. 14.

mean that a person can file an RTI application online, and the department's Public Information Officer would be able to access Government records on the internet and send a reply, thus reducing delays and increasing transparency within the system. Bihar is said to be the first state to take a step in this direction by accepting RTI applications on phone. At present, the CIC is the only agency that receives online appeals under the RTI, but because of rudimentary information it continues to face delays.

This suggestion carries significance in the light of the missing files of Dr. B.K. Mishra, a resident of Bihar, who filed 32 appeals in CIC office of New Delhi, which got mysteriously lost from the office. Likewise, several applications have been reported missing. Today, disappearance of such files from the office is problematic issue, which is due to the lack of infrastructure staff and the negative role of the staff. As per *The Times of India* news carried out on 8th March 2007, the CIC office gets about 600 appeals in a month but it is able to hear only six cases a day, which means piling up of work at CIC's office. Similarly, numerous sanctioned posts are yet to be filled up. Increasing work load of the Commission is currently in big problem.

References

Prabhat Datta, India's Democracy: New Challenges (New Delhi, Kanishka Publishers & Distributors, 1967), Third chapter, p. 1522.

Ruchitta Priyanka, "Right to Information", South Asia Politics, New Delhi, Volume 5, No. 6, Oct. 2006, pp. 46-49.

Subhash Tripathi, "Right to Information : Making Democracy Meaningful", *Ibid.*, August 2006, pp. 26-30.

Sapna Chadah, "Right to Information: Regime in India: A critical Appraisal", *The Indian Journal of Public Administration* (IIPA), New Delhi, Volume 11, Jan.-March 2006, pp. 1-17.

The RTI is the product of progressive interpretation by our courts of Article 19(1)(a) : State of UP *v.* Raj Narain (1979) 4 SCC 428; S.P. Gupta *v.* Union of India, (1981, SCC 87) and Dinesh Trivedi *v.* Union of India (1997, SCC 306), where-in the apex court laid stress on disclosure of information as an ordinary rule against secrecy and government's claim of privilege.

For the first time, the Mathew Commission Report (1982) recommended an amendment to Section 5 of Official Secrets Act, 1923 to strengthen the need of the right to know and the V.P. Singh's National Government initiated in this regard.

CHAPTER

21

Reflection on the Latest Developments

This chapter deals with the latest developments and issues that have concentrated the attention of our governance. The first part is concerned with the developments of Indian government and politics and the second part is related to the foreign affairs.

TACKLING RED TERROR

Naxalites continued the killing spree by shooting innocent persons. In context with killings in Jharkhand and Chhattisgarh, P.M. Manmohan Singh described the Naxalities as the most serious security threat facing the country. They are well-connected with the extremist movement in the North-East, or fundamentalist terrorism across India's borders.

According to a home ministry assessment, 160 districts are Naxalite-affected, which is more than one-quarter of the total number of districts in India. Given the magnitude of the problem we should address it much more, instead of brushing it under the carpet. Local mobilization drives such as Salwa

Judum or Nagrik Suraksha Samiti were stepped up as ways of privatizing the response to Naxalism by struggling off the state's responsibility. They doomed to fail as Salwa Judum separated and arms anti-Naxalite villagers. But, besides encouraging thuggish behaviour, it makes anti-Maoist groups easy to identify and attack. There's still a need for a concerted strategy that coordinates among beleaguered states and draws maximum assistance in fighting Naxalite terror from the Centre. The Naxalite movement typically recruits as its foot soldiers poor tribal living in forested areas, where the topography makes it possible to set-up armed camps and conduct guerrilla warfare. It's necessary to be clear-headed here. While many may be swayed by the Robinhood-like image of Naxalites, they in fact indiscriminately murdered a number of civilians. Violence has no place in a democracy. The first job of the state is to establish its authority, short of which people will do the Naxalites' bidding simply out of fear.

But the state is not just a punitive presence. It has to be a positive and enabling presence as well. Naxalite pockets, mainly tribal inhabited areas, lack roads, electricity, schools, hospitals and commerce. So long as the state fails to facilitate these, Naxalite hubs will continue to thrive on the resulting discontent. Failing to check the Naxalite threat could make a chunk of India go the way of Nepal.

HOW TO OVERCOME THE FALLOUT OF NAXALITES

The report, prepared by a high powered panel set-up by the Planning Commission has for the fifth time, admitted that Naxalism is political movement with a strong base among poor peasantry and adivasis (tribals). It has suggested some very important proposals to the Naxal problems spreading in India.

The key observation of it are as follows:

- The committee, set-up in 2006, was headed by D. Bandopadhyay, a retired IAS officer who played a key role in dealing with Naxalites in West Bengal in the 1970s. Among the members are Prakash Singh, former UP DGP and an expert on Naxal issues; Ajit Doval, former director of Intelligence Bureaucrat; Sukhdeo Thorat, UGC chairman and K. Balagopal human rights lawyer. The committee submitted its report earlier this month.

The report said that while policy documents admitted direct correlation between extremism and poverty, in practice, the government treated it as a law and order problem.

- Naxalism is linked with poverty and under-development. The Gul should not treat it as law and order problem .
- A policy should be laid down to allow small, marginal farmers to lease lands in land with rights. The landless farmers must be given pattas.
- It has asked for immediate winding up of Salwa Judum against Naxalities as it has delegatiomised politics and dehumanizes the people and degenerated the role of the state itself.
- Dialogue diplomacy negotiations are the only democratic way to resolve the conflicts. In the previous years, the government of India talked to extremist outfits in Nagaland and Jammu & Kashmir in Mizoram has yielded peace. We know how the Nepal Maoists agreed accepted to join the multi-party democracy.

The panel has also suggested that talks should be backed by other policy decisions like debt relief for people in distress. Debt relief may be bad economics but it is a practice followed by the government for political reasons. The aim, however, should be to build a formal banking system in backward regions. This is necessary to curtail the influence of moneylenders and build a modern credit-based economy. The panel has exposed the unconstitutional nature of Salwa Judum and the civil war it has triggered off in Chhattisgarh. Stale-sponsored militias are not substitutes for a professional police force. Political problems call for political solutions. Talks are the first step toward that.

CONGRESS SHOULD STAND BY ITS IDEOLOGY

It is a matter of concern that the Left is enjoying power without accountability in the UPA Government. The party with the UPA on the Indo-US nuclear deal has weakened the PM's position through the game of toppling the government. Leading a coalition is the only option to attain power once should not have shown the behaviour like a power out of water when the party is out of power. The Nuclear deal have proved that the Congress is unfit to protect its political agenda/ideology. The party should at least learn to sacrifice power instead of giving up party objectives on the issue that was initiated by the BJP when it was in power. To develop the weapon programme was its agenda as per the resolution adopted in 1996. BJP never opposed to closer its ties with the US. But as the key opposition party of parliament it has refused to support the Nuclear deal.

It was a good gesture that the Congress reiterated to build organization under the young leadership of Rahul Gandhi—yet a symbol of the Nehru Dynasty or a family-run enterprise. Consequently, talented and meritous have failed to seek the due place. It is yet to be seen how young Rahul shall be able to attract the new allies in competitive politics. Failure to run a coalition government at the Centre is an example in point. The Congress of the past was a coalition of various social groups. Since then political outfits that address the concerns of each of these groups have emerged. It is futile to hope that the Congress can revive its brand of identity politics. The party can only hope to build electoral coalitions with the new political forces. This ought to be achieved without compromising the core ideals of the Congress party, primarily the belief in a secular and democratic republic. But how much of a democratic outfit is the Congress party? The party has not had organizational elections for many years now. Nominated members have replaced elected leaders in the Congress. This had encouraged cronyism in the party. The decline in the party's organizational poll is directly linked to the absence of inner party democracy. How can new leaders emerge from the grass-roots if the party fails to conduct organizational polls?

Rahul should address this issue if he is serious about transforming the Congress into a democratic party.

INDIA NEEDS A FEDERAL AGENCY

The task of combating terrorism cannot be "effectively discharged by single agency of any particular state" as the prime minister pointed out. He, therefore, urged the acceptance of the concept of "federal crime" and establishment of a separate agency to investigate crimes with "multi-state aspects" such as terrorism and white-collar crimes.

In India, the state police investigate into violations of central as well as state laws. There is a single hierarchy of courts to try all such offences. In the US, in contrast, the FBI investigates offences created by federal laws or federal crimes. Only deferral courts can try such cases. The state's courts cannot.

The stark reality is that terrorism has truly become globalised. In almost every affected country, terrorists draw inspiration and sustenance from outside while sleeper cells dwell within. The menace can be fought only if intelligence.

Is our constitutional system incapable of devising a solution, which meets the needs of the times yet respects the ståte's sentiments? The Constitution itself suggests the solution. The entry on "police" in the state's list is qualified by a proviso: "Subject to the provision of entry 2A of List One" (The Union List). Entry 2A was inserted in 1976 to empower the Centre to deploy the armed forces or the paramilitary "in any state in aid of the civil power". The Centre is charged with a clear duty by Article 355 "to protect every state against external aggression and internal disturbance. . . ." If a state is unable to quell the disturbances, the Centre is bound to step in. Cannot the entry related to police be amended on similar lines to enable the Center to check international terrorism ?

The encroachment, if at all, will be a strictly restricted one and the Supreme Court will enforce the restriction. The states will be unwise to object. "Defence of India" is a central subject. If the penal code is amended by the Parliament to create the offence of international terrorism and a special squad is set-up; to fight that menace, the Supreme Court might well hold that "defence of India" includes defence against new forms of aggression such as international terrorism.*

In the light of the May 13 terror attacks following suggestions are :

- It's incumbent upon the central government to take a holistic view of the situation in coordination with all state governments and conduct a well-chalked-out war on terror. The image of being a soft state should be dispelled by enacting tough laws and dealing strongly with illegal immigrants.
- As standard methods of political are not effective and they (laws) failed. Therefore, extraordinary laws are also now required to face this scourge of terrorism. It is fine to create an FBI-like federal agency. It is equally necessary to put POTA-like laws in place, revamp the intelligence gathering and collating system and enhance policing ability. The argument of 'misuse' of the law is untenable in the context of safety and security of the citizens, more so when we know that every law in the country is misused.
- As the battle against terrorism should not be held hostage of the spirit of federalism, the country needs to have some anti-terror laws to eradicate serious crimes from society.

  The law should act as a deterrent to criminal activity and then be used to trace, nab, prosecute and punish the culprit. Global terrorism cannot be fought with laws meant for general crimes. We should heed the call of the Chief Justice of India for a strong anti-terror law to deal with the problem. In the aftermath of 9/11, the UN Security Council adopted Resolution 1373 and called on all member-states to adjust their national laws to ratify the existing international conventions on terrorism. Instead, the UPA repealed POTA more for political reasons than anything else.

---

* See the leading lawyer and constitutional expert A.G. Noorani, "We Need a Central Agency", *Ibid.*, May 27, 2008, p. 14.

Are our existing criminal laws and procedures of dealing with global terrorism commensurate to those of US and UK, who have succeeded in preventing any major terrorist attack after 9/11?

- For a central agency (like the FBI working in the US), a constitutional amendment to invest the union with power to combat terrorism, is require its ratification by state legislators (by one half of the states), because the CBI falls within the Union List, whereas the police and law and order issue falls within the ambit of the State List. The states have been reluctant to curtail their powers. This is exclusively a Central-State issue to be handled with confidence and consensus. But it should be an independent body on the lines of the Election Commission.
- Alternatively, the Centre on its own form an autonomous nodal agency while defining 'terrorism' to tackle it, which shall coordinate with other agencies working in the states. Then there is no need to have a constitutional amendment.

FALLOUT OF GLOBALISATION

Globalisation has left impact in many ways along with the reform of the state. For example, a new concept has come up, that is 'Multiculturalism'. This a both sophisticated naive idea because ever culture has the ultimate right to determine its fate regardless of what is the culture of the rest society. It underlines the need for a common basis for all cultures, a common law for democracy. The Western World has been highly affected of the fallout. Today, multiculturalism overrides the principles of nationality and the principle of general citizenship, a common framework of respect for individual rights. It emphasizes on the deep commitment to reconcile different cultures. In that sense it has affected the nation-state system, though it is not going to disappear in the near future. According to Anthony Giddens, a great UK socialist and the member of the House of Lords, the nature of the nation state is changing dramatically due to globalization and liberalization. It is reducing the importance of concept of sovereignty of the nation with respect to global events which we need collaboration and trans-national institutions to deal with. Globalization also has a push-down effect which promotes local autonomy and local cultural difference. This has a double impact. On the one hand, it creates somewhat noxious forms of local nationalism. On the other hand, it also opens new opportunities for civic participation and it is not accidental that there is a renewal of participatory democracy around the world, partly a result of globalization itself but partly a result of new technologies, which make it easier to have local interactions, or even, in some cases, national interactions organized through electronic media. So we're in a state of flux in these things.

FALLOUT OF NANDIGRAM VIOLENCE ON THE LF GOVERNMENT

The camaraderie between CPM and its three major allies in the ruling Left Front of West Bengal (the RSP, Forward Bloc and CPI) surfaced after "the Calcutta High Court's verdict against the police firing at Nandigram on March 14, 2007. The UF held the judgment as 'wholly unconstitutional', as the court directed the state government to pay compensation to the dead, injured and rape victims. But the FB and the CPI welcomed the judgment as 'people's opinion' and asked the government to respect the judgment. By any angle, the court verdict was a slap on the CPM, specifically on Sitaram Yechury who defended the police action in Nandigram.

The clearage within the LF reflected the 'Big Brother Syndrome' of the CPM over other parties/allies. They were not treated equal partnership in a coalition culture. In fact, West Bengal CM Buddha Dev Bhattacharjee was held responsible for weakening the coalition culture built by his predecessor, Jyoti Basu, as the CM did not deeply discuss the partners the proposal to allot the land to Tata Motors at Singur. His arrance and concept was seen dominated since the party came to power in the assembly elections of 2006 (with 49% votes secured). As regards resentment among other allies of the CPM, the farmer's cadres began to encircle Nandigram to make their life hell and added fuel to the fire, by inviting the

Mao elements. It ignored the people's movement/resistance, visible causing worry to Jyoti of CPM's the Big brother attitude, as the prevailing mindset may destroy the unity of LF experiment. It was Basu's efforts that the 7th LF Ministry came to power in the state. This is the world's record in itself.*

In short, Nandigram was one of the darkest chapters in the CPM's history and the name of SEZ (the event of 14th March 2007 killing 14th people). Nandigram witnessed the CPM's campaign of armed violence to regain control of the areas. No police force was sent there. Ultimately, the CRPC forces had to rush in to defend the masses in general. The motive was to teach SEZ opponents 'a lesson' (i.e. anti-CPM Bhumi Ucched Pratirodh Committee—BUPC). Thus, the incident exposed the rot that has set into the West Bengal CPM in the form of criminalization, pro-rich policies, corruption, and reliance on muscle power and arrogant towards its own allies, who publicly held that the CPM alone had been responsibility for the Nandigram violence and it must re-think of its policies and politics.

The recent Panchayat poll (held in May, 2008) results exposed the CMP's fortress could crumble. The poll behaviour further exposed the CPM's authoritarian politics and anti-people approach in tackling the developments at Singur and Nandigram versus the implementation of industrial policy for SEZ.

It is tempting to read the Left Front's drubbing in Singur and Nandigram as a vote against Buddhadeb Bhattacharjee's industry policy. However, implementation of the policy rather than the policy itself is to blame. People didn't want to give up land for industrialization and the autocratic approach of the government and the CPM only strengthened their resolve. In places like Burdwan and Purulia where land had been acquired for industrial projects without alienating local people, Left Front candidates have won. Fertile land is a scarce commodity in West Bengal. Farmers will not part with land unless they are adequately compensated. It is undemocratic on the part of the government to force farmers off the land. The

* Sankar Ray, "Big Brother Syndrome", *The Times of India*, New Delhi Edn., November 22, 2007, p. 14.

CPM should recognize that dissent has a place in a democracy. Development models can't be forced on people and administrators need to take people into confidence before setting out to implement the state agenda.

SEZ : A SYMBOL OF NEW ZAMINDARS

Special economic zones came in for criticism in the Rajya Sabha with CPI MP D. Raja saying it was a king of "land grab" which had created new and "modern zamindars" and it had debased the life of farmers, tribal and agricultural workers who are being deprived of their land.

Stating that the government was yet to make any assessment of the impact of SEZ policy on society. Raja demanded a review. When the SEZ idea was mooted, even some Left party members had supported it "as it looked very naive initially. But once rules were framed, the devil was out of the bag". He felt that 40% of the land acquired for SEZs belonged to tribal, adding the government "had sanctioned 600 SEZs". "There is no limit to it. And all this land is being used to build malls, theatres and cinema halls. It's kind of land grabbing". In fact SEZs are only benefiting big business houses and MNCs who are getting various exemptions from labour laws and tax rules. The policy is based on the assumption that it is conducive for faster economic growth. "The question is the government made any assessment about this and about its impact on those whose life it was debasing. The Act must be amended.

UPA—LEFT RIFT ON SURFACE

Apart from the events of violence in Nandigram, the Alliance partners were seen clashed over a number of issues. The Taslima Nasreen versus the brand of Indian secularism was the latest one. For example, Taslima Nasreen, as writer became the latest victim of the paralysis of coalition politics. Her plight should shame the leaders who invited her and who crow loudly about Indian tolerance. Taslima did not know that she was just one more link in the elaborate chain of coalition politics disasters, which have beset the UPA government since the summer, 2007. First, there was the stalemate over the US nuclear deal where partners in the coalition had differences. After threatening to proceed unilaterally and hold mid-term elections in late August 2007, Congress lost its nerve and backtracked into a negotiated surrender. Then came the retreat over Ram Setu. Again another coalition partner had differences about the issue, but it was never resolved whether the government believed M. Karunanidhi or L.K. Advani on the existence and significance of Ram. So the Supreme Court had yet another issue to crowd its already long list of outstanding cases. But then the TADA court in Mumbai had issued its judgment and Sanjay Dutt apart, most convicts were Muslims. So there was a threat to implement the recommendations of Srikrishna report to get a few Hindus behind bars. That would have assuaged Muslim vote. But then Shiv Sena was in a love fest with NCP, a UPA coalition partners, so that was quickly dropped. The Sachar report was dusted down and noises followed that something would be done. The UPA, reportedly, was much concerned of the minority vote, not of Taslima's fundamental right, or international law obligations on the Government.*

PERFORMANCE OF UPA'S GOVERNMENT

The survey conducted by the Times of TNS, India, in August 2007 rated as 'poor' or 'average', because of the following factors. The impasse on Indo-US "Nuclear deal and periodic confrontations between the UPA and its Left "allies weakened the position of coalition government. Poor outcome of Congress in the UP assembly elections with projecting of Rahul Gandhi as vote-catcher, BJP's relentless attack on the policies and performance of the Government, the Sethu Samudram issue (the blunder over that the Ram does not exist) handling of the Nandigram violence versus anti-land acquisition agitation, Muslim factor and the Taslima Nasreen issue as well as wide-ranging incidents of corruption involving MPs and ministers, etc. projected the coalition Government as weak and weak.

* Meghnand Desai, 'Just Another Power', *The Times of India*, Nov. 30, 2007, p. 14.

PRESIDENT'S RULE IN KARNATAKA AFTER 5 WEEKS

Karnataka was on 20 November, 2007 brought under president's rule for the second time in little over a month and the Assembly was kept under suspended animation. President Mrs. Pratibha Patil signed the proclamation bringing the state under Central rule after the Union Cabinet accepted governor Rameshwar Thakur's recommendation in this regard and advised such a course of action. The Centre's action came a day after the first-ever BJP government in the south collapsed following coalition partner JD(S)'s decision to vote against the government on confidence vote in the Assembly on 18th November. The PM said that government would seek the approval of Parliament for imposition of Central rule in Karnataka and dissolution of the State Assembly at the "earliest opportunity."

Karnataka was under Central rule for 34 days from October 9 to November 12, 2007 after the fall of the JD(S)-BJP coalition government headed by H.D. Kumaraswamy and the state Assembly was kept under suspended animation. The BJP-led coalition was first in South to fall. The CM had to resign after a week. When JD(S) as ally decided to vote against the confidence motion in the House.

Hopefully, Karnataka's first experience/experiment in coalition politics won't be repeated after the fresh elections of the assembly. The leaders betrayed their partners. It was a worst example of desecration of coalition drama. As national party, the BJP cut a sorry figure because its CM, BS Veddyurappa remained in power for seven days.

LAYING OUTLINE FOR PRESIDENT

On the eve of the Gujarat assembly election, 2007, clemency President Pratibha Patil was under immense pressure of a PIL, moved by M.K. Balakrishnan who alleged that, (a) hundreds of persons, despite spending 14 years in previous are still languishing in jails and sought their release, and (b) over 50 mercy petitions including those convicted in the Rajiv Gandhi assassination case are pending. In the light of the PIL, the Centre (i.e. the Home Ministry) was compelled to make 'public' the secret guidelines that influence the decision of the President to commute a prisoner as death to life imprisonment under Article 72 of the Constitution. Till today, there have been 50 mercy petitions laying pending since 1990, only two persons have been saved from the gallows and allowed to serve life imprisonment.

The Home Ministry stated in its clarification in Nov. 2007 that the President's clemency under Article 72 could not be circumscribed by any statue, rules or a ruling of the Supreme Court. However, there are general guidelines which have been evolved over a period of time regarding disposal of mercy petitions. They are :

- Personality of the accused (age, sex or mental deficiency) or circumstances of the case such as provocation or other similar justification.
- Cases in which the appellate court has expressed its doubt as to reliability of the evidence but nevertheless decided on conviction.
- Cases where it is alleged that fresh evidence has come to light.
- Where the High Court has reversed on appeal on acquittal by a session's judge or has on appeal enhanced the sentence.
- There is any difference of opinion in a Bench of two judges necessitating reference to a third judge of the High Court.
- Consideration of evidence in fixation of responsibility in gang murder case.
- Long delays in probe and trial.

PART III

Analysis of Electoral Politics

CHAPTER

22

Assembly Elections of Rajasthan, 2008

Voting for a Change

Raje Government was not able to steer clear of the corruption charge against her ministers and gave ammunition to the Congress against the BJP. In some constituencies, the BJP rebels and growing indiscipline in the party was also said to have spoiled the chances of the party. The leadership was critical of some of the bold decisions, like fielding more women candidates in the fray.

The just concluded assembly elections to six states have offered the hope of change. It is also meant to punish individuals/parties that have ignored the cause of 'aam aadmi' in the way of governance. Therefore, the very first common pattern witnessed in these elections was the high voter turnout, extending from the country's western borders in Rajasthan to its eastern extremities in Mizoram and from the northern extreme of J & K to deep within the heart of India in

Madhya Pradesh and Chhattisgarh. This high voters' turnout indicates a hither interest in the elections believed to be specially so among urban, middle class youth, particularly first time voters and Dalits as well. The same common pattern has prevailed in the electoral politics of Rajasthan.

Voters in Rajasthan voted on 4th December, 2008 for electing its 13th state assembly. Caste, religion and similarity of background were considered more important here than in other states that went 10 the polls. It witnessed around 66% poling over 36 million people including 17.2 million women, that were eligible to vote. There were 2,193 candidates in the fray including 154 women. The Congress fought all 200 seats while the BJP fielded 1930. The BSP fought in all but one constituency. The BJP had the strength of 121 legislators and the Congress 53 in the 2003 assembly.

The Congress emerged as the single largest party by winning 96 seats out 200. The BJP stood second by capturing 78 seats. It was a setback to the BJP leaders as it was confident of coming back to power in Rajasthan. In fact, it was Ashok Gehlot, who spearheaded the poll campaign across the state by holding maximum (over 100) rallies and meetings against the BJP rule.

TABLE 1

Party Position (Total Seats 200)

Party	*Seats won*
Congress	96
BJP	78
BSP	06
CPI (M)	03
JD(U)	01
LSP	01
Independents	14

Cutting across castes, religions and party affiliations, skyrocketing prices, unemployment, the urban rural divide, law and order situation, police crime visibly played an important role in comparison to works done by the BJP Government (such as beautification of Garden and other developments).

JAT LOBBY AGAINST GEHLOT BECOMING THE CM

With the clearance of the poll picture, the Jat lobby in the Congress insisted on making a Jat the next new CM even though former CM Ashok Gehlot reportedly could mustered the support of a majority of legislators the Congress won in the assembly elections. There were 16 elected candidates from Jat community, but 10 Jats with others who won from Jat dominated areas were not against Ashok Gehlot becoming the CM. Their second option was of the PCC chief, Dr. C.P. Joshi, who had lost the poll by one vote from Nathdwara. Mr. Gehlot, at this critical stage, never favoured of projecting a list of seventy MLAs nor did he make a visit to New Delhi for seeking blessings of Mrs. Sonia. He had a feeling that the party cannot afford to buy the displeasure of Jats in view pending the Lok sabha elections. Therefore, the central observers decide to use the slip system amongst the newly elected legislators of the Congress. The matter was, therefore, left for the High command to decide about who would be the next CM of the Pradesh. Despite all this, it was a truism that the Jats failed to put up a united front in favour of leadership. But their pre decided strategy was to subrogate the prospects of Ashok Gehlot in becoming the C.M. again.

FACTORS BEHIND THE BJP'S DEFEAT

The ruling BJP lost the poll-battle mainly because of the Gujjar ire, though it did manage to gain some seats in the Gujjar domains of eastern Rajasthan i.e. Bharatpur and Alwar regions. The party failed to hold on about 13 seats from Tonk, Ajmer and Dausa districts. In fact, a strong section of Gujjar community was against the Vasundhara Raje government's failure to ensure an ST status to the community, despite her promise during the last assembly elections. It may be recalled that Gujjars had held a 21-day long stir and protest for getting an ST status in which 70 Gujjars were killed in police firings. The most violent agitation was at Sikandra, Bandikui and Dausa. Likewise, the BJP was wiped out from Tonk and Sawai Madhopur districts. In Ajmer, where it had seven out of the nine seats last time, it has managed to clinch just three out of a total of eight seats. Here too the Congress gained four seats.

However, in other segments of eastern Rajasthan, the BJP seemed to have done well despite a Gujjar presence specially in the Bharatpur and Alwar regions, largely because of a strong Jat presence who voted for the BJP, besides the BSP having eaten into Congress votes. In these two districts, the BJP gained six seats thrashing the Congress there. In the other Gujjar-dominated district of Karauli, it had just been a single seat's loss for the BJP. However, notable in the eastern region was a total victory of BJP in the Dholpur region with the party wresting all of it from the Congress. Only the Bari constituency was clinched by BSP's Girraj Singh.

FALLOUT OF THE RSS' DISPLEASURE

While taking the command of Rajasthan politics by state BJP Chief Om Mathur, a number of leaders with the RSS brand were against the deo who grabbed powers and neglected the RSS lobby. A number of RSS leaders were against the style or functioning Raje Government. The BJP leadership failed to note this pulse. Therefore, the BJP had to pay a high price for the Gujjar-Meena tussle and the behaviour of Jats. The Congress could race closer to the power. The Congress yet could increase it vote share by 1.2% which the BJP shed 3.7% over the 2003 polls.

It is argued that when the state had thrown its lot with Meenas, it was upto party and central leaders to broken peace with Kirorilal Meena. It laid bare the rift between party and CM since then, the Jat conundrum remained to be understood the BJP swept Bharatpur and Dholpur and held on in Churu and Bikaner, but the Congress came up trumps in Jhunjhunu, Sikar and Barmer.

The Gujjar-Meena-Jat trio held the key to the electoral battle. For BJP, while wooing back Gujjars and Meena as in such a short time was tricky, the party should have to check its emphasis on Jats lest it further consolidated minor OBCs behind the Congress.

Likewise, the BJP's excessive focus on terrorism backfired in Rajasthan. This is a clean reflection that state elections have their own dynamics like local factors the selection of candidates, governance issues and the role of caste.

FEATURES OF POLL STRATEGY

Continuing its 2003 strategy of fielding new faces, the ruling BJP once again reposed faith in first timers. The party nominated more than 70 new faces this time. Last time, the party fielded about 135 new faces and nearly 50% of them emerged winners. Therefore, it clinched with the same experiment hoping to repeat its previous success. This was, in fact, a compulsion for the BJP leadership in the wake of delimitation of constituencies and due to the underway rise of anti-incumbency factor. Axing of a number of sitting MLAs whose performance was not good in the public was inevitable. Also for those ministers who had been facing the charges of misuse of their official position.

The BJP high command projected Vasundhara Raje as the future CM. The party fielded the largest number of women and changed a record number of sitting MLAs to beat the threat of anti-incumbency and the fallout of the corruption charges against ministers. But these initiatives boomeranged, resulting in the largest number of rebels in the fray. Karorilal Meena is the key example who damaged a lot the BJP in the Meena belt.

IRE OF JATS

The results of assembly elections presented a picture of 'fractured mandate', for which the Jat community's rebellious posture was responsible. It stood against once the process of ticket distribution began. The senior most leader of Jats, Parasram Maderna was the most vocal opponent to stage a protest to Mrs. Sonia Gandhi. His strategy was to oppose Ashok Gehlot's role in becoming the CM, if party wins a majority. Unfortunately, the Jat lobby was not united in their ambitious mission and the BJP looked for an opportunity to take benefit of their protest. The BJP too failed to exploit this situation. The poll results thus, expressed the resentment of the Jat community. In fact, the voters did not accept that sons and relatives of Jats were projected in the hustings. Therefore, powerful leaders like Harendra Mirdha, Richpal Singh (from the Nagaur and Degana constituencies, respectively) were rejected. Mahipal Maderna, the son of Parasram Maderna, managed to win from the Ossian constituencies with a close majority.

This kind of Jat resentment against the Congress was clearly seen in the Bilara and Bhopal constituencies (Reserved) of Jodhpur District where the BJP could mange to win the seats. There were 28,000 and 55,000 Jat voters in these reserved constituencies. Similarly, the victory of another Congress rebel and Jat candidate, Dilip Chaudhary, from the Jaitaran constituency of Pali district clearly showed that Jats voted against the party as he was a strong claimant of party ticket.

But with Hemaram Choudhary the story was different. Despite being a Congress candidate, he did manage to win from the Gudhamalani constituency of Barmer district, another Jat dominant district. Col. Sonaram Choudhary of Congress too managed victory from the Baitu constituency of Barmer. But according to observers, this is the time when both the parties, especially Congress, will learn a lesson and try its best to appease the Jats in the wake of the Parliamentary elections ahead.

The BJP had fielded six Jats in this division, out of which two won. Out of the five Congress fielded, four Jats won. Many feel that if Congress had not resented the community, it would have had a clear majority.

The BJP's performance in the Hadauti region, which used to be considered the stronghold of the BJP, remained gloomy. In this election, the BJP could retain only 7 seats out of 17 in this south-eastern region of Rajasthan. Hadauti region is consisted of four districts, namely Kola, Bundi, Baran and Thalawar. The main reasons for SIP's defeat here was the infighting within the BJP's stalwarts and miscalcutions in the allocation of seats. This weakness of BJP proved to be a boon for the Congress because the BJP rebels disturbed the caste equation. Sadly, the outgoing CM could retain only two seats in her home district (Jhalawar) while the two constituencies went to the Congress.

KIRORILAL MEENA'S ROLE : A DENT IN THE BJP VOTES

Kirorilal Meena, when he was dropped from the SIP list of nominees for the assembly polls, he instantly, reacted saying 'Dhool chata denge' (will inflict a crushing defeat). Apparently, he vowed to ensure the defeat of SIP's candidates and teach its leaders (the CM and Mathur) a lesson. SIPs defeat may not solely be attributed to Meena's revolt but he certainly played a vital role in saffron party's downfall, as cited above, in same of 13 constituencies of Meena dominated districts (eastern Rajasthan) where the BJP had swept in poll in 2003.

The voting pattern in these elections reveals that the anti-BJP stand taken by the Meena community and the Bhil-Meena community in the Mewar region resulted in the win of the Congress in as many as 18 seats. Out of the 25 reserved seats for STs, the BJP lost in 20 seats. For this anti-BJP tirade, Kirorilal Meena was a sole campaigner. In the 30 general seats where the population of STs ranged between 4.80% to 27.66%, the Meena-Bhil community helped the Congress (and other parties also) to win at the cost of the BJP. In the last assembly, there were 22 legislators belonging to the BJP. CM Gehlot was well aware of this ST factor while forming his Ministry. In view of the pending Lok Sabha, this was a compelling factor for him to provide a ministerial seat to the wife of Kirorilal Meena.

The outcome of 2008 assembly polls confirmed that it was mainly the flowed ticket distribution in the BJP which cost the party dear. The case of Kirorilal Meena is the best to exemplify it. The party reports have accepted that deserving candidate in the BJP were ignored. In the post polls, Meena has emerged stronger due to the victory of non-BJP candidates who won with his support—12 in Congress, 4 BSP and 4 Independents.

The reports further highlight that it was an inherent fight between Raje and Mathur that left a sour taste behind the BJP.

These assembly elections are being regarded as Raje *versus* Congress but Mathur's way of putting pressure on the High Command put the CM in defence. As a matter of fact, the disagreement between former chief minister Vasundhara Raje and state party president Om Prakash Mathur. Once again exposed after the poll outcome. The central leadership took a week to manage a truce between the two. M. Venkaiah Naidu, who was entrusted with the job, however, reportedly found it difficult forcing BJP president Rajnath Singh and BJP's prime ministerial candidate L.K. Advani to intervene to manage a truce between the warring leaders.

Mrs. Raje, who always viewed Mathur as her rival, was unhappy about his interference in poll-related activities, while Om Prakash Mathur had complained that Raje was autocratic which led to severe discontent. Individually, both the leaders held each other responsible for the discontent and a high number of rebels, resulting in the poll debacle of the BJP.

IMPORTANCE OF TENDER VOTES

It was the first time in the history of Rajasthan's assembly that the PCC Chief C.P. Joshi's another claimant for the CM post, lost the Nathdwara seat by a single vote to the BJP's Kalyan Singh. They got the 62,215 and 62,216 votes, respectively. The case of tender vote is related to the ten votes that snatched a victory of Joshi. According to a Supreme Court ruling; "In any state assembly election if the number of tender votes can affect the counted result in anyway, then the party concerned has the right to ask for counting the tender votes, but only after filing a plea with state High Court". The number of tender votes were 10.

On December 4, when polling for the 13th assembly formation was on, 10 bogus votes were cast in Nathdwara. When the real voters arrived and proved their identity; they were allowed to vote under the Tender Voting System. According to the EC guidelines these votes are to be kept in a sealed envelope and be a part of the counting process, till not needed. According to Sub-Rule 6 of Election Conducting Rule, 1961, if anyone else votes instead of the real voter; then the polling officer; after identifying the real voter may allow him to cast a tender vote. Tender votes are never a part of the normal voting, if not required. If the number of tender votes has any impact on the result, the concerned state High Court can ask for the counting of these votes.

THE ROLE OF MUSLIM FACTOR

The Muslim votes played a decisive role in the victory of both the BJP and the Congress as well. They proved to be an angel's gift to these parties. For example, the BJP candidate Vasudev Devnani from Ajmer (North) won the seat due to the support of Muslim votes, defeating the Congress candidate, Dr. Srigopal Baheti, by 785 votes. Similarly, Naseem Akhtar won the Pushkar seat by getting the traditional Congress votes. Likewise, Muslim voted for Habibur Rahman of the BJP who defeated Harinder Mirdha (from Jat Belt) of the Congress. This seat is used to be considered of the Congress fiefdom with the combination of Jats and Muslims. Muslims came out to vote their candidates enmass without caring the party ideology. The BJP fielded only 04 Muslim candidates whereas the Congress put up 14 candidates in the fray.

In short, the voting behaviour of Muslims has shown the spirit of 'Ganga Jammni Tehzib' of Hindu-Muslim solidarity that seems to be drying up in UP and Bihar. Muslims have did not take towards any centralized religions leadership for guidance in political matters, as Deobandi and Barelvi schools of thought in UP used to do in shaping the Muslim opinion on the eve of elections. In Rajasthan, Muslims have looked at the integrity of candidates, other things like religious beliefs were secondary. Most of Muslims (Cheeta-Mehrat communities) are influenced by the philosophy of Khwaja Moinuddin Chishti. This is a clear cut of reflection of secularism. There is a unique composition heritage. It emphasizes assimilation of Hinduism. That is why Muslims in Rajasthan are not as determinedly against the BJP as is witnessed in North Indian states.

CONCLUDING OBSERVATIONS

The 13th assembly elections of Rajasthan have represented the picture of two party system in the governance of

Rajasthan. The emergence of 'hung assembly' is not a new phenomenon for state politics, as on several occasions the voters have given their mandate to a single party. For example, in 1962, 1967, 1977, 1990, 1993, the trend of an absolute majority was broken and the single largest party had to form coalition governments with the help of independent MLAs. Despite this, the trend of two-party system continued to remain, inspite of contesting elections by some regional parties. As per past history, the role of the Independent MLAs have been significant in formation of coalition governments.

Voting patterns in the previous assembly have confirmed that voters in general have been casting votes on the basis of caste and religion. But the 13th assembly elections, after the delimitation of constituencies) has revealed that caste factor got diminished and the issues like, corruption developmental works—candidates' merits and integrity mattered. Therefore, projecting new faces by BJP/Congress did not payoff. The voters, in general, were hell bent on not promoting on a particular caste against the other. The voters refused to accept the supremacy of any particular caste be it Rajputs, Jats, Gujjars or Meenas.

Thirdly, the excessive for us on terrorism by the BJP (it is in the light of Mumbai terror strikes) backfired. It is no surprise that the voters did not appreciate the BJP's attempt to exploit the situation at a time when the country was really in need of unity though the Mumbai seize was a tragic incident.

Fourthly, after the BJPs poll debacle, the party is yet in a dilemma over the charismatic leadership to replace ex-CM Vasundhara Raje. It is now in a divide house with Mrs. Raje versus the rest.

Fifthly, the Congress-led Ashok Gehlot must have to be cautious of the support of Independents, specifically of Kirorilal Meena, who revolted against the BJP rule and made a dent in the BJP's Meena vote bank. Kirorilal Meena may try to unite the Bhil-Meena of Mear region to become a force to reckon within the Congress circle.

And lastly, the Raje Government was not able to steer clear of the corruption charges against her ministers and gave ammunition to the Congress against the BJP. In some constituencies, the BJP rebels and growing indiscipline in the party was also said to have spoiled the chances of the party. The leadership was critical of some of the bold decisions, like fielding more women candidates in the fray.

DEADLY ATTACKS ON MUMBAI (26-27 November, 2008)

On November 26, 2008, the country faced another terrorist attack, the worst it has ever suffered that exposed our intelligence failure and administrative lapses. The jihad took lives of nearly 200 innocents in Mumbai.

The carnage in Mumbai marked a new phase of the terrorist war against India. The monthly bomb blasts in one major city or another have now been escalated to a full-fledged commando strike at the heart of India's commercial capital. The politicians have continued to dish out their usual platitudes, either making alibis or pointing fingers at each other, while the intelligence apparatus and the security czars have proved themselves to be utterly incompetent in coping with the challenge. It is high time to bring in new people and new ideas on, how to win the war against terror, because the promise of solid action against terrorists in Pakistan by the Pakistani government seems insincere. Islamabad is not ready to hand over the captured people to India. Muslim communities around the world have failed to must understand that the choice of jihad as a way to air grievances is wrong. Jihad does not mandate the killing of innocent people. In fact, these terrorists have no religion; they only understand the language of violence. Therefore, India must retaliate in the same way to root out the threat. It is within India's rights to pressure Pakistan to hand over these terrorists and to strike terrorist camps operating in Pakistan if this is not done. If the US could do so in Afghanistan for the same reason, why not India?

WAS A WAR REALLY AN OPTION?

On at least one occasion in the recent past-after the attack on the Indian Parliament in December 2001, India appeared serious about exercising the military option against Pakistan.

Apparently our politicians were energized only when they were directly targeted; as if, the deaths of thousands of other Indians—mostly by Pakistan sponsored terror groups—weren't reason enough. But the only chance to hit Pakistan with swift air attacks was in the immediate aftermath of the attack on the Parliament. Technically; Pakistan-occupied Kashmir (PoK), where many of the terror camps were located, is a part of India. Since India claims all of the erstwhile state of Jammu and Kashmir, hitting terror camps within it can thus be justified. This opportunity was lost as the Vajpayee government dithered..Deploying the army for almost a year thereafter along the Indo-Pak border was of no use. The Vajpayee Government gave in to Washington's pressure not to distract the Pakistan army from supporting America's 'war on terror' on the Pak-Afghan border; as if India's war was not against terror. Pakistan today is using the same argument now to slip out of its current predicament by threatening to shift its forces from its western border with Afghanistan to the Indo-Pak border. And the Bush administration as well as the British Government counted on India back down, as a full-fledged war against Pakistan like that of the 1971 or on the lines of American invasion of Iraq.

ISI TO BLAME FOR ALL ATTACKS

Before the 26th Nov. carnage, the Government of India was silent over Pak links in a number of terrorist attacks. But it got strong evidence of involvement of the ISI in the terrorist incidents through the capture of terrorist alive. Though the Centre spoke of the role of Pakistani elements in the 26/11 Mumbai carnage after getting clear evidence against banned outfit Lashkar-e-Taiba. It had earlier preferred not to talk about any Pakistani linkages in the case of terror attacks in UP courts (November, 2007), CRPF's camp in Rampur (January 1), Jaipur (May 13), Bangalore (July 25), Ahmedabad (July 26) and Delhi (Sept. 13) So, whatever the government told the Upper House was clear indication of linkage of Indian Mujahideen (IM) with ISr.[1]

These attacks have exposed the role of ISI III Pakistan's civilian administration. The elected government in Pakistan is, of course, in power but it has little power *vis-a-vis* the Generals and ISI. The ISI (Army also) is functioning a state within a state of Pakistan. The Americans know it with the identification as the global hub of terrorism. Therefore, India should not walk into the trap of the west, but it should let the US to clip the ISI wings through diplomatic pressure.

Sadly, we have still a Nehruvian hangover diplomacy, i.e. our military structure—is not outside of India's policy-making. The lack of understanding of national security issues amongst the Neta Babu set up in Raisina. Hill is still alive.

Indian Muslims across the country have given a strong message to protest against terrorism/radical Islamic ideology. They occupy a unique position. It is a symbol of secularism and unity. For example, just after the attack, Eid all over India was not celebrated. Even Imams of several mosques stood united against terrorist attacks. It was a slap in the face of hard core Muslim groups operating jihad against India. Therefore, Muslim scholars should speak against the misinterpretation of those who have given definition/ideology of terrorism under the name of God or Islamism as a religion to prevent the scourge of terrorism.

In this eventuality, the military option against Pakistan was not an option at all, because of the history of the protracted wars that the world's greatest military powers have fought, but they never won-be it the case of Vietnam, Iraq and Afghanistan. Pakistan can be influenced and pressurized through diplomacy of IMP funds, that is, Aid to Pakistan should be tied to dismantling existing terror groups on the soil of Pakistan. The leverage can be done with the help of both China and Saudi Arabia—the two of Pakistani's closest and richest friends. Both the countries have been serious about terrorism concern. Likewise, India must now work towards a UN Security Council resolution to permit strikes against terror camps functioning within Pakistan. But this strategy needs the support of the international community and veto-wielding powers.[2]

The past history of Pakistan has contradicted the odious religion-based two-nation theory that led to its creation. The birth of Bangladesh only added to its sense of insecurity, as the rulers of Pakistan have failed to develop a fully functional state. That is why the fundamentalism with the help of Army and ISI had flourished in Pakistan. The ISI with the support of now acts as a state with the state (Pakistan) that has waged a proxy war (attacks) throughout India.

Both the events—the Kargil war and the 26/11 have happened unexpectedly and broke the peace process initiated by the Pak's civilian leaders. Today, President Asif Ali Zardari has little experience of good dialogue with India. Therefore, skepticism prevails over the move taken against L-e-T and other terrorist organizations by the civilian Government of Pakistan. Therefore, New Delhi must prepare for all eventualities while tracking carefully Pakistani's crackdown on terror. And it is a responsibility of the international community to strengthen Pakistan's fledging democracy by supporting the civilian government firmly while enabling the Army and ISI to become genuinely professional forces willing to take on terror groups that threaten Pakistan, India and global peace. It is high time for India to pressurize Pakistan to have over the terrorists to trial in India, as they committed crimes in India.

Terrorist cadres recruited for jihad believe that they are destined to win as a civilization though individually they may become martyrs. The jihadi fanatic poses threats to Russia and China as well. The stabilization of Afghanistan is in the interest of not just the US, NATO and India, but also of Russia, China and Central Asian republics and most of the Islamic world as well. In this context, the war against terrorism—of which Pakistan is now the epicentre—has become a global war. The attacks on Mumbai, Ahmedabad, Jaipur, Hyderabad and other Indian cities fall into the same category as those on New York, Washington, Bali, Madrid and London and constitute a jihadi offensive—against civilized nations and their democratic values.

A major mistake was committed in the global war on terrorism by attention being diverted to Iraq. The beneficiaries of this mistake are the supporters of jihadi terrorism. New President Obama has advocated that Afghanistan and its neighbourhood should receive primary attention in battle against terrorism. The crucial need today is for him to build a coalition including NATO, Russia, China, India and moderate Islamic countries to contain terrorism in the Pakistan—

Afghanistan region and then lend global support to Pakistan so that it can salvage its much mauled democracy.

After decades of terrorism and ten of thousands killed in the blasts, India as the emerging global power, has finally responded to set-up the FBI model like agency in India. After the Mumbai carnage, the Congress-led UPA Government brought forward the National Investigation Agency (NIA) to deal with the fallout of terrorism. It a tough anti-terrorism law, though it is not as tough as the US has done to prevent attacks after 9/11. This apart India still has to create a Deptt. like that of the Ministry of Homeland Security in U.S.A. with a separate budget (The US spends $ 650 bn on Defence alone). The agencies like National Security Council created under the new NIA would be dysfunctional without a new category of federal crimes that are related to terrorism, organized crime, narcotics, money laundering, etc., which are happening across state international borders. It requires a statutorily status. We need skill investigators. According to Ajai Sahni, an expert in security affairs,[3] it is astonishing that the very political formation that has been vociferously arguing that Pota was ineffectual in containing terrorism, is now offering a tough anti-terrorism law as a solution. It is, of course, obvious that opposition to Pota : was inspired by electoral calculations and these have changed dramatically after Mumbai.

Regrettably, the half-truth of that original argument remains inescapable. A counter-terrorism law is as tough as its implementing mechanism. Within the degraded policing and internal security environment in India, and the equally debilitated justice system, a tough law will be entirely toothless. That is the core reality that needs immediate attention.

It is high time to think of local administrative responsibility which remained helpless in lack of appropriate powers during the city crisis *vis-a-vis* evacuation operations after the attacks. The local Government then was non-existent. The city policy was ill-equipped to resort to any rapid response. The military and the NSG commandos were flown from Delhi to clear the hotels.

In brief, our staff response stems partly from concern about weakening the brittle civilian democratic Government *vis-a-vis* the military rule in Pakistan. India should shield its soft approval to Pakistan. The post 26/11 required withdrawal of our envoy, calibrated economic sanction, travel for restrictions and demand that international economic assistance be curbed.

The key issue for any ruling party is governance, and effective governance is not the job of politicians alone, it of the bureaucracy also, which needs both administrative and political accountability. After 26/11 attacks, it was difficult as to whom to blame for it—the CBI, the navy and the coast guards, local police or the party in power in Mumbai? Why a Home Minister, a CM or his deputy have lost their job? Why not the bureaucrats advising them to act? Administration officials should too be held accountable for effect governance.[4]

During these horrible terrorist attacks, a new theory was projected by Ameresh Mishra saying that a joint operation by the RSS and MOSSAD of Israel was there to avenge arrest of Hindutvadi Sadhvi Pragra Singh, the self-proclaimed Sankaracharya Pande, Lt. Col. Purohit and others. They were to eliminate the ATS Chief Hemant Karkare and his team. But this theory appears to be incredible and baseless.[5]

CONSTITUTING A NATIONAL INVESTIGATION AGENCY

The government has at last—after the country and its people have paid a heavy price—come up with a proposal to constitute a National Investigation Agency Act, 2008 (NIA) and given more teeth to anti-terror laws. The NIA is "to investigate and prosecute offences affecting the sovereignty, security and integrity of India, security of state, friendly relations with foreign states and offences under Acts enacted to implement international treaties, agreements, conventions and resolutions of the United Nations."

The UPA Government cleared the formation of a central terror agency, christened National Investigating Agency (NIA) and tightened the relevant laws to allow wiretaps to be used as evidence in camera trial and fast track special courts to deal with terror cases. The new law gives greater teeth to the centre it has taken some features contained in now defunct POTA and in Maharashtra Control of Organized Crime Act (MCOCA).

The NIA is to be entrusted with the investigation and prosecution of offences falling under the Anti-Hijacking Act, Suppression of Unlawful Acts Against the Safety of Civil Aviation Act, the SAARC Convention on Suppression of Terrorism Act, Weapons of Mass Destruction Act, Atomic Energy Act, Unlawful Activities (Prevention) Act and offences against the state mentioned in Chapter VI of the Indian Penal Code.

The concept is excellent. That such an agency was urgently required goes without saying. But the framers of the Bill have made two cardinal mistakes. The first is the creation of the plethora of law enforcement agencies, which would take time to grow and to operate : Our CBI is there to have inter-state linkages. The Government should have enlarged its additional powers, alongwith the replacement of the Delhi Special Police Establishment Act, in place of strengthening the provisions of the Unlawful Activities (Prevention) Act, 1967 (UAPA). Our Supreme Court, vide writ petition (Civil) No. 310 of 1996, has already suggested to entrust the CBI with more powers, so as to nab the activities of mafia groups with international linkages. Secondly, the UPA Government should have endorsed the views of the NHRC, the Sorabjee Committee and the Bureau of Police Researches Development. The Government of India should have done on the pattern of US model the—Department of Homeland Security structure is single unified body.[6]

There is no harm if a terrorist as per article 22 of the Constitution might have been given the right to get a lawyer to defend himself during the trial. This would have a chance to comment that our justice delivery system has not been vitiated trial. The CJI K.G. Balakrishnan has endorsed this view. Likewise, with the enactment of NIA and amendments in the UA(P) Act it has to be ensured that the move does not trample the citizen' civil liberties, nor does it terrorize the states that the Pan-India federal agency might curtain their powers to maintain law and order by being in conflict with the state police. This concern must be looked into and addressed by allowing an all Party Parliamentary Committee to periodically ensure that the NAI is not abused. Also, we need police judicial reforms to match the changing profile of current crimes.

Today, India is facing the security challenge from 'within' due to extreme ideologies—be it regional chauvinism, religious bigotry or a wrapped sense of Indian Tradition and ethos inspired by Hindu groups like Shiv Sena and the Sri Ram Sena.

DELHI LOSES LOTUS

The third consecutive victory of the Congress in Delhi under the leadership of CM Sheila Dikshit, is both historic and rewarding for her development. The Congress won 42 seat in the 70 member Delhi assembly, while the opposition BJP had to be content with 23 seats. It is a setback to the BJP leadership which had project Prof. V.K. Malhotra as the CM in waiting. It is a moral victory of the Congress. The rout of the BJP was due to excessive projection of the Mumbai terrorist attacks (26/11) and the Malegaon incidents during the poll campaign though Terrorism was a key issue here. The BJP failed to beat incumbency in Delhi, despite the ten year rule of the Congress. The BJP alleged the Congress rule for being 'soft' on jihad is which lacked credibility because of the NDA record on this issue. The anti-UPA sentiment projected vigorously by L.K. Advani, the PM in waiting, had no impact on the voters, by and large. In fact, the BJP suffered due to its embedded factionalism and unilateralism. The party looked like a maze of conflicting camps fiercely suspicious of each other. The process of ticket distribution as well as complaining style was not satisfactory for the party workers.

FRACTURED MANDATE IN J&K

The assembly elections in J&K declared on 25th December, 2008, threw up a fractured mandate with no single party getting the 44 legislators out of 87 seats needed to form a new Government. The NC emerged as the single largest party with 28 strength, the Congress got 17, the PDP 21.

This is the victory of the regional National Congress which won 28 of the assembly's 87 seats. It is a setback to our national parties that were in the fray.

The poll results compelled the Congress to agree to rule the state through coalition/alliance. Both these parties have been secular nationalist, Pan J&K forces. It is a good development for J&K's developmental road map.

A number of sitting MCAs of both the ruling Congress and PDP faced anti-incumbency, as they were charged with corruption, but rarely investigated.

Both the parties—BJP and the PDP gained in terms of seats and vote share and contributed to the decline of the Congress tally. Therefore, the Congress had little option but to go along with the NC. This scenario materialized the NC-Congress alliance. This would diminish the poll prospects of both the PDP and BJP in the forthcoming Lok sabha elections due in April-May, 2009. The NC-Congress would be unbeatable.

Table A

(All figures in Lakhs)

LS Seat	*NC + Cong*	*PDP*	*BJP*	*Rest*
Jammu	5.18	1.11	2.82	3.26
Udhampur	3.99	0.30	1.94	3.08
Anantnag	2.15	2.11	0.08	2.30
Srinagar	1.92	1.20	0.04	1.23
Baramula	2.37	1.35	0.04	2.15
Ladakh	0.58	Neg	Neg	0.46

These poll results were meant for democracy, economic development and social peace. It is a lesson to be learnt by our neighbours. The events like Amarnath land transfer row or poll boycott calls and terror threats hardly had an effect on the verdict. Voters' final verdict is a robust blow against ideological extremism and is meant for a change in J & K.

The BJP has reason to be satisfied with the success in Jammu where land transfer row led by the Sri Amarnath Sangharsh Samiti helped to win 11 seats. The separalist opposed the transfer of land for Amarnath pilgrims and saw it as a plot to set-up 'Israeli style establishment', though the move was meant for temporary structure in view of hostile weather conditions. The protest lasted for about 40 days, it was really a people's agitation that was won by the BJP. of 37 seats in the Jammu region, the BJP won 11, the Congress 13, the NC 06, JK Panther party 03 and independents 02.

So far as the empowerment of women is concerned, only three women could win the poll and got the entry into the assembly. 67 women contested the elections. They were Mehbooba Mufti (PDP), Shameena Firdous and Sakina Yatoo—both from the NC.

Table B

Total seats : 87 Total electorate : 649375

Voting : 71%

Parties	*Seats won 2008*	*Seats won 2002*	*Loss/Gains*	*Voting%*
NC	28	28	00	2008 : 71.66%
PDP	21	16	(+)5	2002: 43.70%
Congress	17	20	(-)3	1996: 58.92%
BJP	11	01	(+)10	1987: 74.88%
Independents	04	15	(-)11	1983: 43.24%
Others	06	07	(-)1	1977: 67.19%

It is worth recalling that these elections in J & K were held during the President's rule clamped on 11th July, 2008 in the wake of withdrawal of the PDP from the Congress coalition government. Earlier, President rule was imposed from 26 March to July 9, 1977; 6th March 1986 to 7th Nov., 1986, 19th Jan. 1990 to 9th Oct., 1996 and 18th Oct., 2008 to 2nd Nov., 2002.

To conclude, the J&K poll results have produced a hung assembly with the NC as a single largest party. The fractured verdict needs a fresh thinking and mindset towards the successfulness of coalition government in the state, hoping that the Congress would be able to neutralize the separatists of the valley. The victory of the BJP in the Jammu is due to the fallout of the Amarnath land low. Its performance should be seen as an expression of the regional aspirations of Jammu rather than religious sentiments.

The Congress—NC tied up for power sharing agreed to form the Government in J&K under NC Chief Omar Abdullah on 6th Jan., 2009, with equal member ministry from both the parties. Their focus is largely on developmental issues, like education, power, water, employment, eradication of corruption and militancy.

The high turnout of voters in the recent elections in J&K is being seen as a rejection of Kashmiri separatists' boycott politics. But it is too early to declare the azadi movement dead, because of the coalition politics in the state and the role of Pakistan (ISI and Army) in the background of the Mumbai attacks and the diversion approaches between India and Pakistan on terrorism. As the public is fed up of the movement to self-determination, they may demand de-militarization and repeal of the Armed forces Special Powers Act from J&K. They want normalcy to restore the NC would like near autonomy if not total autonomy.

In the light of these elections, the Union Government (MEA) should attempt to 'internationalize' Kashmir issue by projecting how India's democratic and secular credentials are rich and how an enthusiastic turnout of voters cast a ballot for peace, prosperity and development, i.e. for Bijli, Sarak and Paani, against Talibanization, bigotry and separatism. Kashmir (India administered Kashmir) doesn't need plebiscite or referendum, nor is it now a 'disputed area'. The recent state elections is a testament to India's pride in telling the fact to the world that Pakistan-occupied Kashmir has never gone to the polls.

Notes and References

1. The arrest of the Pakistani terrorist Mohd. Ajmad Kasab has disclosed all these things to the police during the interrogation. But Pakistan refused to accept his nationality, saying that she owned no responsibility of non-state actors.
2. Jug Suraiya, 'Indistan Zindaba', *The Times of India*, Jaipur edn., December 6, 2008, p. 10.
3. *The Times of India* news, *Ibid.*, 19th December 2008, p. 5.
4. Raju Santhanam, 'Bell the Babus', *Ibid.*, December 23, 1908, p. 12.
5. Quoted through Secular Perspective, edited by Dr. Asgar Ali Engineer Mumbai, December 16-31, 2008, pp. 1-2.
6. Prakash Singh, 'Too Many Cooks', *The Times of India*, Jaipur, December 31, 2008, p. 12.

CHAPTER

23

The Results of the 15th Lok Sabha Elections in Rajasthan

The election results were almost a dream-come-true for the Congress leadership, specifically for CM Ashok Gehlot, who, on the basis of performance, bolstered the victory, winning 19 out of 25 Lok Sabha seats. The party had coined 'Target 25' slogan, hoping to win all the 25 seats. This was Congress's second best performance in the state after 1984 polls when it won all 25 seats in 1994, although the 'sympathy wave' after the assassination of Mrs. Indira Gandhi was the key factor behind that victory. In Rajasthan, it was a positive vote for the UPA's performance at the Centre and good coordination between the party machinery and the government.

VERDICT SHOCKING AND UNEXPECTED

The BJP never expected of such a strong undercurrent wave in favour of the Congress, specifically at the defeat from Jaipur because the saffron party had won the seat for six consecutive terms and another win for the party was seen as a foregone conclusion. Congress's Mahesh Joshi defeated BJP's Ghanshayam Tiwari by 15,000 votes, an outcome belying all speculations in the Pink City of Jaipur. The BJP in Rajasthan is sadly restricted to four seats. The blame game is given to the RSS embarrassment. In fact, declaring Advani as the next Prime Ministerial candidate of the BJP (and also of the NDA) proved disastrous for the BJP. The NDA allies were not happy when some BJP members cited the mention of N. Modi, the Chief Minister of Gujarat, as the P.M. candidate in 2014. This was one of the important causes for the BJP-led NDA's defeat in Rajasthan which witnessed emergence of the 2-party system in state politics. Modi's projection was a mistake. In short, the BJP should admit that the era of hard-line Hindutva (as well as Mandal and Kamandal politics (relating to OBC reservations for Hindus) is over. Voters preferred to vote fer positive issues like development, education, security and employment.

The recent assembly and the 15th Lok Sabha elections witnessed the sons and daughters of many prominent leaders of the Congress and BJP joining the political hand wagon. But the CM of Rajasthan kept his 28 years old son, Vaibhav Gehlot away from the hurly burly of electoral politics so far. There was a rumour of his son being contesting the Lok Sabha seat from Jodhpur or Tonk, Sawai Madhopur. But it did not happen. Of course, he actively campaigned for some Congress candidates.

Other prominent Congress winners from the state: include PCC chief C.P. Joshi. (Bhilwara), Girija Vyas (Chittorgarh), Sachin Pilot (Ajmer), Chandresh Kumari (Jodhpur), Sisram Ola (Jhunjhunu), Ijjeyaraj Singh (Kota) and Jitendra Singh (Alwar). In fact, the pro-Congress wave was so strong that the candidates, who lost the recent assembly polls in December, 2008 won during the LS polls. Prominent among them were PCC chief CP Joshi, Mahadev Singh (Sikar), Lalchand Kataria (Jaipur-rural). Likewise, the BJP camp had many casualties, the most prominent being the defeat of senior party leader was Jaswant Singh's son, Manvendra Singh from Barmer, who lost to Congress nominee Harish Choudhary. The only solace for the saffron brigade was the over 52,000-vote victory for Dushyant Singh, the son of Mrs. Vasundhara Raje.

It is believed that the CM's 'social engineering' helped the Congress to win all seats of Marwar, barring the Jalore Lok Sabha seat. Despite the fact that Jats from Nagaur and Pali, after delimitation were opposed to the Congress but the Congress maintained a recorded victory with huge margin. From the Pali Lok Sabha constituency, the Jat dominated areas, Badri Ram Jakhar clinched his biggest victory by a lead of 1,96,717 votes. This is attributed to the CM's efforts to improve relations with Parashram Maderna, the eminent Jat leader, in the post-delimitation time. So is the case of Jyoti Mirdha who scored a huge margin of 1,55,137 votes, defeating the BJPs Jat candidate and BSP's Muslim candidate from Nagaur. Here the Mirdha legacy was a major factor behind her victory. In Banner, Harish Chaudhary's victory was due to appeasement policy of the CM towards the Muslims and offering a cabinet post to Sheo's MLA, Amir Khan.

The victory of Sachin Pilot from the Ajmer Lok Sabha seat too sprang surprise, because it was BJP's fort for the last twenty years and former MP Rasha Singh Rawat used to represent it. The cause of the victory was to due to the voting on caste-line and the youth card that the Congress played at the hustings. The youth broke across caste line while changing the previous voting trends in general and particular in Ajmer. He won the seat with a margin of 76,000 votes, defeating— Mrs. Kiran Maheshwari (the MLA from Udaipur) who was the BJPs candidate. The post-delimitation factor changed the caste lines.

The BJP was all set to play the 'Jat card' against Sachin Pilot, the Congress candidate from Ajmer Lok Sabha constituency after adding new areas in delimitation. Earlier the BJP ruled on the Gujjars votes and Rasa Singh Rawat have been winning the seat consecutively for five times. This time Rawat was shifted to Rajsmand where huge Rawat votes were with the Beawar and Masuda areas. Clearly, there was a strong contest between Jats and Gujjars. (Gujjar votes were two lakhs) alongwith the Rajputs and Dalits. The problem facing with Pilot was the 'outsider factor'. This was noted by the Congress High Command while declaring his name, as Vishnu Modi and Jagdip Dhankar were outsiders but they won the seat.

Likewise, dissidents within the party too were a challenge for young Pilot.

JAT FACTOR NOT HOSTILE TO THE CONGRESS

This time, the political equation of the Jat with the Congress was favourable. It was not so strain as was seen in the 2003 assembly elections when the old Jat guards raised a pitch for making Jat CM and they were opposed to making Ashok Gehlot as Chief Minister of Rajasthan.

In the 1996 elections, the Jat's support for Congress was promised on the assurance by Ashok Gehlot to make Parasram Maderna CM with providing reservation for the Jat community. But Gehlot reneged on both his promises, which angered the Jats. This led to Jats supporting the BJP in the assembly elections of 2003. The Jats still remain a decisive force with five ministers in each cabinet. There are only three districts where Jats have no influence, namely, Sirohi, Dungarpur and Banswara. Armed with the OBC status, the Jat because strongest community among other OBCs to stage a demand for the CM post.

It should be noted that today, every third MP from the state is a Jat, barring one veteran Sis Ram Ola, who raised the voice for a Jat CM. The rest are rallying behind the CM. These elections have reaffirmed the hold of the Congress on the approximately 70 lakh Jat votes in the state and acceptance of Ashok Gehlot as 'leader in the community. The party fielded six Jat candidates in the Lok sabha elections, compared to three by the BJP, and all of them managed to win the seats. This reflects the maturity of the Jat voters. They quickly learned from the assembly polls' defeat that saw many senior leaders losing their seats. This time relatively a new factor was that the results have brought the new faces as Jat leaders, like Lalchand Kataria and Mahadev Singh Khandela (both of whom had lost the assembly elections of 2008). But today they are stronger in the Jat community. The new brigade of Jat is not all about the caste namely Jyoti Mirdha, Harish Chaudhary and Badri Ram Jhakhar. The voting behaviour reflects as if caste and dynasty politics have a short life span. Jyoti Mirdha's victory may mark the foray of Jat women in Rajasthan's politics.

RE-EMERGENCE OF RAJPUTS IN THE ELECTORAL POLITICS

Before Independence, Rajasthan was ruled by princes. With the dissolution of these kingdoms and the abolition of royal titles and privileges in 1971, many of the royals have become entrepreneurs, hoteliers diplomats or soldiers. But many others have forged a successful career in politics and this year's polls have seen some of Rajasthan's most powerful aristocratic families throw their hat into the ring for instance, the royal families of Alwar, Dholpur, Jaipur, Kota, Jhalawar, Bikaner, Bharatpur, Jodhpur and Dungarpur are active in politics. Five royals were in the fray for the 15th Lok Sabha elections.

The scion of Alwar royal family Jitendra Singh, Chandresh Kumari, daughter of late maharaja of Jodhpur Hanwant Singh, Dushyant Singh, son of Opposition leader Vasundhara Raje and the scion of Kota royal family and son of Maharao Brijraj Singh; Ijjeyaraj Singh and Divya Singh, who was given a Congress ticket from Jaipur.

Jitendra Singh, who is a secretary in AICC and has been very close to Rahul Gandhi did not contest the Vidhan Sabha elections as he had made-up his mind to contest the Lok Sabha polls.

During the era of Mrs. Indira Gandhi, the princes lost their importance and with each elections the number of those princes elected to parliament/assembly came down in view of enlargement of democratic process, and common man like Girdhari Lal Bhargava (Jaipur) was able to defeat the five-time Jaipur MP and the former prince of Jaipur.

In the past, the royal families distanced themselves from active politics, but this time surprisingly, they were forced to join politics. For example, the grand daughter Siddhi Kumari of Bikaner royal family was given the BJP ticket for the Bikaner's North Assembly seats in December 2008 and she won it comfortably. In fact, delimitation process compelled the BJP and Congress to field the members of royal family, be it Dushyant Singh of the Dholpur royal family, or Ijjeyaraj Singh of Jhalawar royal family or Chandresh Kumari of royal family of Jodhpur. All the three have direct closeness with Mrs. Sonia

Gandhi. This is probable the first time that the royal's have flirted with the Congress in Rajasthan. The erstwhile ruler of Jodhpur, Gaj Singh, it may be recalled, had been a BJP supporter of all years, but he changed equations on the basis of Rajput card, which the Congress needed to win the elections in Rajasthan.

All the royals fielded by the Congress won convincingly. Mrs. Chandresh Kumari (Jodhpur) moved in from Himachal Pradesh (from where she had won twice) won by 98,326 votes. Jitendra Singh, AICC Secretary and scion of the Alwar family managed a victory by over 1.5 lakh votes. Likewise, Ijjeyaraj of Kota royal family won by a margin of 80,000 votes. Dushyant Singh (BJP) held his Jhalawar Baran seat again by a margin of over 50,000 votes. But Siddhi Kumari of the Bikaner royal family (BJP) lost the seat to the Congress candidate, Arjuna Ram Meghwal.

CLOUT OF KIRORILAL MEENA AT STAKE

On the eve of allotting party ticket, the relations between the minority Government led by Ashok Gehlot and its supporters including Kirorilal group got soured. Kirorilal Meena, the MLA from Todabhim, was considered as the most decisive factor in the defeat of the BJP during the assembly polls. The reason behind the strain was due to demanding seven seats for Lok Sabha elections, in-spite of the fact that his wife Golma Devi and Parsadilal Meena were made ministers in the cabinet. This was a flexible approach to Meena's clout. But the CM refused to bow down at any cost, taking the plea that Congress tradition does not give party tickets without his inducting into the party. Indications then were that Kirorilal might field his Independent candidates to show his strength/ clout; though in his address to a meeting at Bassi (Dausa) on 21st March, 2009, he made it clear not to have any confrontation with the Congress and his primary aim was to defeat the BJP in Rajasthan. The Congress was worried of a division of Meena vote-bank mainly in the eastern constituencies, as his clout proved instrumental on the victory of nine independents during the assembly polls. Truth was that Meena community was guided by his leadership.

No other Lok Sabha constituency in Rajasthan drew the attention of voters and political parties as Dausa in the post-delimitation period. After being declared a reserved seat for STs, Kirorilal Meena, former BJP minister, filed his nomination paper against the Congress nominee, Lakshman Meena, a former IPS officer while nursing ambitions to move beyond the state politics. It was he who played a crucial role for the BJPs defeat in the assemble polls. The coveted seat was earlier won by the Congress ten times. This time it witnessed 'multi-cornered fight'. BJP's candidate was Ram Kishore Meena (former Minister), alongwith Qamar Rabbani Chechi, a leader of Gujjars. As independent leader, Kirorilal Meena was poised to teach a lesson to the Congress, specifically the CM, who refused to offer the seat for him in his bargain tactics. The total strength of voters of Dausa constituency was 13,14,917, consisting of about three lakh Meena, two lakh Gujjars, a little over two lakh Brahmins, two lakh SC voters and around 75,000 Muslim voters.

In a U-turn, the tug of war between the Congress and Kirorilal Meena ended when he filed his nomination as an independent candidate from Dausa constituency, but declined by withdraw on April 22. The CM campaigned for Laxman Meena who was the Congress candidate from Dausa. The CM was concerned of polarization of Meena votes here. He was not sure of win of Laxman Meena.

During his campaign in the Meena belt, specifically at Chaksu on 25th April, 2009, the CM lashed out at Kiroilal Meena, that independents hold no value and wield no influence in his Government, as they have no policy and the voters, thus, should only vote for those candidates with a party behind. This was the first occasion that the differences between the CM and Kirorilal Meena were made public.

SOME OTHER HIGHLIGHTS OF ELECTORAL POLITICS

During the assembly elections, the BSP contested all the 200 seats in Rajasthan, but managed to win six seats only. The party was considered a major factor in making a dent in the Congress seats as the BSP candidates cut into the Congress vote's across the state.

In a surprise move, the horse-trading development on the eve of these elections blew the Mayawati's big dream. As the Congress was afraid of BSP's rise in the state, Chief Minister Ashok Gehlot ended it with completely wiping off the BSP from Rajasthan politics with all its six MLAs joining the Congress. The leadership of those MLAs was given to Rajendra Gudha on 4th April, 2009, who accused the BSP leadership of laundering in ticket allocation. They all were unhappy with the money transactions that occurred during the assembly elections. These MLAs in fact, fought the election against the BJP's misgovernance and won the elections comfortably. The BSP, however, termed the defections as 'treachery'. The BSP was embarrassed as it lost its bargaining power with the Congress government, both in the state and at the Centre.

The six MLAs of Mayawati-led party were Rajkumar Sharma, Rajendra Gudha, Giriraj Singh, Ramesh Meena, Murarilal Meena and Ramkesh Meena—This was virtually a coup by joining the Congress just before the general elections, leaving their party high and dry, while taking the tally of ruling party to 102 in a House of 200 seats. The prime motive of these MLAs was to stabilize the Congress government and put to end all the uncertainties that might crop up against the government. The immediate fallout of this event was that it closed the doors for Kirorilal Meena to bargain the Congress High command in getting Lok Sabha seats. His wife and minister resigned from the Ashok Ministry in humiliation.

The petition against this defection (joining the Congress) was filed by Jaswant Gurjar, taking the plea that the six BSP MLAs violated article 191 of Constitution, read with the 10th schedule. They contested the elections on a national party and voluntarily gave the membership of BSP (parent party) to form the Congress, whereas the 10th scheme does not permit to do so. They therefore, should be liable to be disqualified. There was no margin as such. The matter is still pending with the Speaker's final nod.

On the contrary, Kirorilal Meena was also angry at this development, as he lost the bargaining power due to the switchover these MLAs ahead of the Lok Sabha elections. He could have cut into the dalit vote-bank of the Congress.

- The Jalore Lok Sabha constituency after delimitation was termed as Jalore Sirohi SC category Buta Singh as a senior Congress leader was interested in getting the Congress ticket but was-denied and in his place Sandhya Chaudhary was given the Congress ticket. This was the key factor behind losing the seat by the Congress.
- Many villages of rural belt recorded a low turn out because of 'Chitra and Swati nakshatra yog' on the polling day, on which day a large number of marriages took place both in urban and rural areas. On the eve of the elections in Rajasthan, the people chose to attend weddings rather than using their voting rights in the rural areas of Rajasthan. Marriages, thus, took centre stage in rural areas. That day was auspicious for wedding ceremonies. Secondly, the temperature went up to 38 degrees Celsius, voters did not like to come out to vote.
- So far as the Muslim voters are concerned in Rajasthan, it was an important development; in the sense that their various organizations relating to Darul Uloom Deoband appealed the Muslim voters to come out, irrespective of their political leanings, and utilized their vote correctly. The 'fatva' was not in favour or against any political party. The spirit was that no vote must go waste. The campaigns launched by them made an impact in rural belt regions and the large number of voters came out on the polling day. The scenario testimonies that India is virtually a secular democracy.
- The victory of Namonarain Meena from Tonk Sawai Madhopur Lok Sabha constituency was significant, because of the defeat over his BJP rival, Coln. Kirori Singh Bainsla, who came to limelight by spearheading the statewide Gujjar agitation in 2008. And because he (Meena) won it with a narrow margin of 317 votes he set a record in this Lok Sabha polls by winning with lowest margin in the country.
- This time, the election outcome erased stigma of being 'outsiders' of the four candidates who won the

parliamentary elections from the Marwar region, namely, Jodhpur, Pali (M), Nagaur and Jalore, The outsiders were: Jyoti Mirdha, Chandresh Kumari, Badri Ram Jakhar and Devji Patel. They all were new faces in their constituencies, despite having birth root here. The youth wings of the Congress did not oppose their candidatures because the CM convinced the voters during the poll campaigns to keep the larger interests of the party on the top. The delimitation process the fact, helped them to win the seats. It is however, worth recalling that it was the CM who played an important role in the land slide victory of the Congress in the Marwar region, (barring Jalore seats), he persuaded Parasram Maderna and his son Mahipal (Minister) to share dias during the election meetings in Pali district. The Jat community was neutralized in favour of the Congress enjoys its hold.

- Unlike the previous elections, caste and good governance prevailed over the inflation and price rise. The sky rocking prices of eatable materials of economic recession, etc. did not influence voter choices. Instead, their vote went on a hot of other issues with caste and community considerations. Voters chose for good governance. Price rise almost remained non-issue.
- A number of winning young candidates like Sachin Pilot acknowledged that the Rahul phenomenon worked wonders for the party who in this campaigning said that the nation's interests were supreme. The voters in Rajasthan were looking for a change in the leadership. Rahul proved his charisma as he spooked for country's development and the cause of underprivileged.

TO CONCLUDE

The CM successfully grappled with his competitors and rivals who had in the past posed a serious challenge to his leadership—be he C.P. Joshi, Sisram Ola or Girija Vyas. Today, he stands as 'unchallenged kshatrap' in Rajasthan, who has none to challenge his supremacy in state politics. As per his strategy, he gave the party ticket to another Jat leader Mahadev Khandela to dilute the influence of Ola and to keep in tact the Jat vote-bank. At this insistence, Khandela of Sikar was included in the Union Ministry, Ola won the Jhunjhunu LS seat. Likewise the CM was instrumental in fielding Nathuram Mirdha's grand daughter, Jyoti Mirdha from Nagaur, in a bid to downgrade Harendra Mirdha's influence in Nagaur. According to many poll analysists the recent victories in the Assembly elections, 2008 and the LS polls 2009, has definitely elevated Gehlot's statuture in state and national politics. He has opened a new chapter in the Congress culture. On the contrary, the BJP fared poor performance in these elections due to internal differences between former CM and O.M. Mathur and wrong selections of candidates. The BJP has yet to come up with a new approach and a new image of non-communalism to gain women turn in state politics. The issues affecting the concerns of masses should be taken up to secure the lost grounds.

Rajasthan's share with its 25 MPs in a House of 554 may be small (4.5%), but it holds a special significance for both the BJP and the Congress, as the contest here has essentially been bipolar in which 'caste' has played a very significant role. That is why differences of seats acquired by each party.

CHAPTER

24

15th Lok Sabha Elections 2009

A Mandate for Change (Some Highlights at a Glance)

The verdict of the 2009 Lok Sabha elections should be read as *'a vote for a change, stability and continuity'*. The voters rejected a number of regional political parties/outfits that bargained the UPA-led government at the Centre under Dr. Manmohan Singh. The voters rewarded those parties/candidates that offered a positive agenda for governance. They opted largely for the two-national parties and their local allies, decisively rejecting regional players with national pretensions. The significant increase in the UPA tally has come mostly at the expense of regional parties, some of which were either part of the alliance or supported it during its first term in office. The emerging picture is that of two constellations—with the Congress at the heart of one and the BJP of the other. Regional parties had the choice to align with either of them.

The BJP, while losing ground in some states that it swept in 2004, maintained its national profile. However, it seems to have failed to attract new voters. This holds true of the Left also. Why did the BJP and the Left fail? Because their ideologies did not reflect the aspirations of the voters and the tactics they followed during the campaign alienated even supporters.

The victory of the Congress-led UPA was based on its performance, which helped the Congress increased its allies in the 545-member Lok Sabha from 145 seats it had won in 2004 to an invisible 185 seats in 2009. The UPA poised to win 254 seats-just 18 seats short of the half mark needed to form a Government at the Centre. The people of India preferred to have a stable and secular government under PM Dr. Manmohan Singh. On the contrary, the NDA won 161 seats. The worst sufferer was the Third Front, made up by the communists and regional groups who had sought to topple the Manmohan Singh government in 2008 over the Indo-US nuclear deal. Its leadership has admitted that the pullout of the support of the UPA government was a mistake, and it is one of the factors behind the poll defeat.

This election saw the emergence of Dr. Manmohan Singh, as a true politician who had been a 'good professor', as he silenced his rival and BJP's prime ministerial candidate L.K. Advani who made the PM's weaknesses as a major campaign issue. Having got a renewed lease to govern the country, the PM enjoys considerable good will and confidence that the Congress President Sonia Gandhi reposed in him. He is now perceived to be a strongman in the UPA.

MYTH OF A THIRD FRONT

The Left parties, specifically the CPM faced the humiliating defeat due to the 'Big brother' behaviour and it admitted the failure of the strategy, i.e. projecting before voters a 'Third Front' as an alternative to the Congress and the BJP. In fact, this Front was nothing but a pre-election coalition of convenience consisting of parties with disparate agenda like the AIADMK, TDP, the Biju-JD or other regional parties. The voters rejected the myth of the third front because of non-committing to lead/join the government. The electorate was aghast about the possibility of an unstable coalition led by over ambitious leaders seeking key offices. Consequently, the left tally came down from 61 seats in 2004 to 24 seats in 2009. The CPM itself lost 27 Lok Sabha seats.

These parties need self introspection and humility in their behaviour keeping in mind that the left ideology of 20th century has lost relevance in the national politics of 21st century. In brief, these results exposed the. Prakash Karat's stewardship of the left stand with the UPA government.

Apart from the existence of NDA and UPA, the 15th Lok Sabha elections witnessed the emergence of a Third Front, which was a myth with potency, powering the trajectory of most of non-JP non-Congress political parties giving a race to post of PM. It was a similar what happened in 1996-97, when a humble farmer HD Deve Gowda resumed the country's most power office for nearly ten months with the support of national party Congress. In this race, the leaders of regional parties, namely the NCP, SP, BSP, RJD and AIDMK were ambitious to become the prime minister. The sad thing was that the key-two national parties, the Congress and the BJP have been unable to co-opt. and contain this churning, whereas regional parties were in a stage of consolidation and expansion, with the motto to finish off the Congress party at the state level. This picture explains the urgency for national parties to become more federal, more representative with greater space for regional leaders and an end to the High Command culture.

The results of the 2009 Lok Sabha elections are new like that of the 1991 mandate, as the UPA has managed to garner significantly higher numbers in these elections. Having tasted a number of coalitions and their after effects, these results are yet the clearest signal that India is tired of coalitions of the past. In fact, such experiments have failed, leaving the negative impression in the minds of the people and causing considerable damage both socially and economically. Therefore, the results are startling similar to the 1991 mandate when the Congress felt short of a majority, but no threat to stability. The mandate is meant for the country's stability. Now with the new mandate, the PM is supposed to take forward the initiatives left behind in 1991 when he was the Finance Minister. But for him, the challenges are many. There is a lot of works to be done, in the field of education, health care, infrastructure, power generation etc.

The emphasis on an inclusive pluralist secular platform was a factor behind the Congress victory. There was an overwhelming evidence that its performance lay in its projecting itself as an advocate of the caring state on a broadly left of centre or social democratic platform through the NREGA, farm loan waiver and other progressive schemes including the Right to Information Act. These schemes affected the voting patterns in Rajasthan, Tamil Nadu, Punjab, AP, Maharashtra and Delhi. Clearly the new mandate was a vote for a change in favour of the under privileged popularly known as 'aam aadmi' in the words of our PM.

State-wise Voting Pattern : A Glance

Turnout (%)	*2009*	*2004*	*Turnout (%)*	*2009*	*2004*
Nagaland	90.2	91.77	Uttarakhand	60.8	48.07
L'dweep	86.1	81.52	Karnataka	59.4	65.14
Tripura	83.9	67.08	Chhattisgarh	58.2	52.09
Sikkim	82.0	77.95	Goa	55.4	58.77
Manipur	79.8	67.41	Himachal Pradesh	55.0	59.71
W. Bengal	73.9	78.04	NCT	51.8	47.09
Kerala	73.3	71.45	MP	51.3	48.09
AP	72.4	69.95	Mizoram	50.9	63.6
Assam	69.7	69.11	Jharkhand	49.8	55.69
Haryana	67.7	65.72	Maharashtra	49.2	54.38
Punjab	67.4	61.59	Rajasthan	48.5	49.97
Arunachal Pradesh	65.0	56.35	Gujarat	47.9	45.18
Chandigarh	65.0	51.14	UP	47.2	48.16
Meghalaya	64.4	52.69	Bihar	44.3	58.02
Orissa	63.4	66.06	J&K	40.0	35.2
Tamil Nadu	62.0	60.81			
Punducherry	60.0	76.07	**India**	**56.7**	**58.07**

The BJP leadership at the national level has admitted that the party did not get the expected Muslim votes and in future the party must ensure that the Muslim do not become the cause of its defeat. The Muslim leaders like MA Naqvi and Shahnawaz Hussain referred to the Pilibhit brand of Hindutva, which too led to the electoral loss. They were against the adaptation of hardline hindutva. The BJP's biggest drawback was projecting L.K. Advani as 'PM-in-awaiting'. Likewise, the name of Narendra Modi was floated as PM in during the poll campaign also backfired.

For the first time, a record 61 women MPs have been elected to the 15th Lok Sabha—the highest since independence. A majority of these MPs 23—belong to Congress. The BJP has contributed 13 women to the House. Uttar Pradesh has sent more women to parliament—13 than any Indian state and West Bengal is in second place with electing seven women MPs: That is a different matter that about 70% of them have been chosen and got party tickets because of their strong political background. Therefore, there are high hopes from these female MPs in the 15th Lok Sabha, specifically in passing the 33% women reservation in Parliament and changing the panchayat poll-parameters. The Bill was introduced in Parliament 13 years ago. It is believed that there would be a positive change in regard to the issues directly related to enhancing the lives of less privileged women of the country.

It was the first occasion that the Kashmiri Pandits, classified as. 'Migrants' by the Election Commission, did not vote. They boycotted these elections taking the protest that they are not migrants. This was a kind of discrimination as they were forced to leave their lives in the Kashmir valley. Therefore, the Election Commission did not received a single 'M' (Migrant) form. They all unitedly did not respond to it, though arrangements for their voting in Delhi were made. It may be recalled that some 300,000 Kashmiri Pandits were forced to fleed the Valley since 1989 when militancy was at its peak.

In northern India, the pattern of results show that young voters rejected those parties who were dabbling in caste politics or whipping up communal passions. Even in Rajasthan too, the impact of caste factor was weak. The voters, by and large, favoured a viable leadership, stable government at the centre and a new change in governance.[1]

BJP

The BJP, of course, gained seats compared to 2004 Lok Sabha elections but it secured votes it had ceded ground in every state except in the two states—Karnataka and Himachal Pradesh, inspite of the fact that it was a minor partner in an alliance with the dominant regional players namely the TDP, the AIADMK, the Trinamnol Congress and BJD of Orissa. The Table given ahead reflects the trend.

BJP's-Vote Share (%) at Glance

State	*2009*	*2004*	*Change*
All India	18.8	22.2	-3.4
Uttar Pradesh	17.5	22.2	-4.7
Maharashtra	18.2	22.6	-4.4
Andhra Pradesh	3.8	8.4	-4.6
West Bengal	6.1	8.1	-2.0
Bihar	13.9	14.6	-0.7
Tamil Nadu	2.3	5.1	-2.8
Madhya Pradesh	43.5	48.1	-4.6
Karnataka	41.6	34.8	6.8
Gujarat	46.5	47.4	-0.9
Rajasthan	36.6	49.0	-12.4
Orissa	16.9	19.3	-2.4
Kerala	6.3	10.4	-4.1
Assam	16.2	22.9	-6.7
Jharkhand	27.5	33.0	-5.5
Punjab	10.1	10.5	-0.4
Chattisgarh	45.0	47.8	-2.8
Haryana	12.1	17.2	-5.1
Delhi	35.2	40.7	-5.5
Jammu & Kashmir	18.6	23.0	-4.4

Uttarakhand	33.8	41.0	-7.2
Himachal Pradesh	49.6	44.2	5.4
Arunachal Pradesh	37.2	53.9	-16.7
Manipur	9.5	20.7	-11.2
Tripura	3.4	7.8	-4.4
Goa	44.8	46.8	-2.0
Pondicherry	2.2	35.7	-33.5
Chandigarh	29.7	35.2	-5.5
Andaman and Nicobar	44.2	36.0	8.2
Daman and Diu	65.5	48.4	17.1
Dadra and Nagar Haveli	46.4	15.6	30.8

Source : The Times of India, Jaipur, May 21, 2009, p. 14.

OUR POLITICIANS ARE SHINING ECONOMICALLY

These elections reflected the picture that Indian society is 'affluent', not poor or backward, as there were at least 193 millionaires were among 1715 candidates in the fray. Truly, Indian Parliament has never been a club of the poorest of the poor. To put the trend in perspective, the average assets owned by an MP in the last Lok Sabha were Rs. 1.6 crore millionaires in the fray in extremely poor parts of the country. It raised the question : can the common man dare to enter into the electoral process, despite the best intentions of the nation's founding fathers and the institutions like the Election Commission. Against this disturbing trend, the answer lies in reforming campaign finance so as to reduce the cost of elections. A possible way out is, as is in Europe, to explore state funding of election campaigns. It is, therefore, necessary that campaign donations be made transparent and accountable, making it clear who has funded whom. The recognized parties should only be allowed to use technology to reach out more voters and cut down on travel expenses. Leaders, instead of hopping across the country in choppers, must reach out to voters through the mass media.

Our general elections got underway amist sporadic violence. It was meant to disturb the electoral process which is a unique phenomenon in the democratic world on the basic of size of its electorate (714 million). The Maoist violence first disrupted the poll process in pockets of Chattisgarh, Jharkhand, Bihar and Orissa. Since the Maoist groups lacked a mass base to enforce a poll boycott, they used hit and run tactics to scare poor votes. Surely, security forces were there to ensure their right to vote, it is the primary duty of the elected representatives to ensure the effective delivery of public service in a bid to reinforce the trust of the people in democracy and marginalize violent groups. Like that of the Maoist threat, the Hurriyat Conference also gave a boycott call. The impact of threat was poor in view of reasonably high polling. As these threats to elections were largely from external players, like Maoists, it is the duty of the new government at the Centre to nab their activities and people's problems are properly addressed to.

CONCLUDING OBSERVATIONS

The mushrooming of political parties in India is not a sign of healthy and mature democracy. Most of these parties are formed with a single point agenda that is acquiring power by any means and at any cost. Sadly, these parties do not have leaders of national stature and lack the vision and motivation to achieve genuine good. If the trend is left unchecked, it will only weaken national unity, acting as agents of fragmentation. Therefore, steps should be taken in the direction of encouraging a two-party system instead of multi-party system, as smaller partner/groups have no vision, no ideology of accountability. This scenario needs an amendment in our Constitution to define the existence of party system. The proliferation of regional/communal parties with a narrow perspectives has to be checked in the interests of national unity and security.

The growth of regional parties—or regional parties as their number seems to be legion has been a process parallel to that of the formation of new, smaller states, Smaller states were—largely welcomed as they would lead to a devolution of centralized power—and provide for more responsive local governance, which is the aim of genuine federalism. But with the proliferation of parties representing purely parochial interests and the make-or-break clout they can wield in government formation at the Centre, the question increasingly being asked is : if such regionalism will lead to the balkanization of India. Already Bal Thackeray—whose Shiv Sena is competing with nephew Raj Thackeray's MNS for the vote of the Marathi manoos—has urged other region-based parties to formulate and pursue their own sons-of-the-soil policies. A seditious precept, which if put in practice would inevitably lead to the break-up of the Republic.[2]

The demand to introduce negative voting needs attention as it would help cleaning up politics and cause frustration among party leaders. This will compel to parties fielding more good candidates, leading development of the nation and checking the rising trend of criminalization. This will empower our electorate to choose a better quality of candidates at the hustings. It may be noted that as many as 150 tainted MPs have managed to win the polls. This is based on the survey of the National Election Watch.

Efforts should be made at the legal executive level to disclose the wealth of Indian money in the form of black money deposited, in western banks. The right to information should be made accessible to it. The total amount in foreign bank was reportedly 2.6 brillion in 2001, which has gone upto 5.7 trillion in 2007 (This amounts to Rs. 285 lakh crore).

Certainly, these results were for 'stability' and 'good governance' and against divisive caste politics. Indian voter overwhelmingly preferred Manmohan Singh to take over the second term as India's P.M. It is a strong indicate of the arrival of the 'youth' and the good bye to communal/regional politics. The voters did not like the way the provocative attacks were made on the P.M. during the poll-campaign were made, or the projection of Varon Gandhi by the BJP. We cannot claim of demise of regionalism but its role has been marginalized by the return of national parties in the 15th Lok Sabha elections.[3]

We are a nation surrounded by a failed state like Talibanised Pakistan. (Hillary Clinton—statement about Pakistan abdicating to the Taliban is unprecedented and also an alarm bell for New Delhi). Bangladesh where jihad churns, Nepal where the Maoists are messing around with the system, Sri Lanka which is mishandling the Tamil issue and, above all,

China which looks over our shoulders. Add these factors to internal terror wars. If, despite these problems, we have not only survived but a small section has marched ahead, the credit must solely go to the resilience of the Indian people.

Though the Congress is by instinct a left-of-the-Centre party, but it would emphasize on rural development, social' spending and poverty eradication under the Common Minimum Programme (CMP). It would increase its Budge in spending on education, health, employment guarantees and rural development. It is a matter of pleasure that the Congress went well by this with its own 'Bharat Nirman' programme under the CMP. It has promised affirmative castes and tribes reservation in the private sector through training and skill development. All this would be under the name of Rahul Gandhi—a future strategist a smart management guru, to complete the unfinished agenda of his late father Rajiv Gandhi.

The BJP's stunning defeat in the 15th Lok Sabha sent a message that BJP's iron man L.K. Advani has no scope of getting the nation's top job in light of his age (81 year old) and the party agenda. The Hindutva card has weakened the party. He is no more a secular mode of the BJP. Therefore, while questioning the BJP leadership over poll debacle, veteran leader Jaswant Singh has correctly demanded for making it (BJP) *'a current party and not of a party of yesterday'*. He also underlined the need to redefine the concept of Hindutva. There is a need for ideological distillation of thought.

Sadly, the BJP has yet not been able to come to grips with electoral defeat. It has been largely low-key in its role as an opposition except for belligerence of the issues like composite dialogue with Pakistan. There is so much hostility within the party itself that it is unable to play the role of a strong opposition to play a reasonable role in Parliament, it must resolve its internal differences.[4]

It was a matter of concern that our politicians indulged in the worst form of personality battles and offer little by way of substance pertaining to a blue print for future governance and issues of national importance. The US Presidential elections and the victory of Barak Obama is a lesson for those who were aspiring for prime ministerial candidates in the fray. There was hardly any political party that would claim of ideological assertion and functional democratic inner party norms. Today, India needs more than coalitions without ideological contours as well as a Pan Indian attitude in governance.

Notes and References

1. Rajiv Desai, 'The Decency Option', *The Times of India*, Jaipur, May 21, 2009, p. 12.
2. *The Times of India* News, Jaipur, May 19, 2009, p. 5 and also, *Jug Suraiya*, 'Negative Democracy', *Ibid.*, 16-3-2009, p. 10.
3. As of Oct., 2005, there were 730 parties registered with our Election Commission, many of them were unrecognized. But they have been useful in making public awareness among the masses, which is essential for diversity.
4. Wilting Lotus, The editorial of the *Times of India*, July 20, 2009, p. 12.

CHAPTER

25

Red Surge in West Midnapore

The Lalgarh's siege of Maoists once again reminded us of the Naxalbari uprising of the 1960s in which a number of tribals and policemen were killed. Maoist looted 30AK 47 rifles and other types of guns and amunication from the security forces. The Centre was reminded of it by governor Gandhi when the Nandigram carnage in 2007 took place when a large section of CPM supporters brook ranks and sided with Trinamul Congress to oppose the Maoist violence was a backlash against 32 years of cadre raj enforced by the Marxists. Against this scenario, the UPA II Government imposed a ban on CPI (Maoist) across the country, under the unlawful Activities. (Prevention) Act, 1967. It was resisted by the West Bengal government. The outfit is already banned in Andhra Pradesh, Chhattisgarh, Jharkhand and Orissa. According to the Home Ministry of India, there are 27 indigenous terror groups operating on our soil, making to the largest number of domestic terrorist organizations in the world. The CPI (Maoist) is the 34th terrorist organization banned under the unlawful activities (Prevention) Act, 1967.

The security forces conducted combating operations against the Maoists in the Lalgarh area of West Midnapore

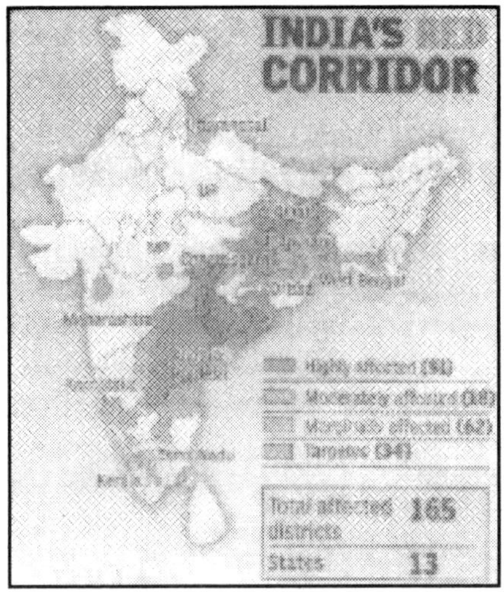

district. The security forces liberated all 47 Lalgarh villages of falling under the control of Lalgarh police station.

There is no doubt that the 32 years rule of CPI (M) in West Bengal is a proof its performance, which never implemented the schemes and development activities such as water, roads, electricity, etc. in the backward districts. There have been starvation deaths. There is no scope for RIT and the Forest Act.

The massacre of 30 cops in Chhattisgarh's Rajnandgaon district in July 2009, was a grime reminder to the Governments of the centre and the state that India has failed to learn lessons from the Naxal strategy of multiple ambush, through the Union Home Ministry has claimed to appoint a military committee to prepare an Action Play to deal with naxal affected states. Parallel governments have sprung up in the Naxal affected states where as much as 50% of development funds pass into the hands of Red ultras. Sadly, the government has not taken a leaf from the AP model of fortified and specially designed police stations.

LATEST RED TERROR AT A GLANCE

- Total number of incidents: 1,130 highest in the past

five years. During the same period last year, 766 incidents were reported.

- Paramilitary personnel deployed 37 battalions over 37,000 personnel.
- Deployment in Chhattisgarh 16 battalions (over 16,000 personnel).
- Bihar, Chhattisgarh, Jharkhand and Orissa have collectively report over 82% of the total incidents and over 77% of the total casualties.
- Casualties in 2009 : 485 (including 230 security personnel).
- Chhattisgarh 178
- Jharkhand 122
- Maharashtra 057
- Bihar 043
- Orissa 040

Security personnel killed (year-wise)		*Civilians killed*	
2005	153	2005	524
2006	157	2006	521
2007	236	2007	460
2008	231	2008	490
2009	230	2009	255

Naxal attacks:

2005	1608
2006	1509
2007	1565
2008	1591
2009	1130

CHAPTER

26

Mrs. Vasundhara Raje Scindia's Appointment

The Game Plan of Shekhawat to Oust the Congress Rule in Rajasthan

The Former the Union Minister, Mrs. Vasundhara Raje was appointed as President of the BJP unit of Rajasthan on Sept. 12, 2002. The decision was taken and announced during the two day north zone states' meet of the BJP, by BJP President Venkataiah Naidu. Barely 15 months left to go before the Vidhan Sabha Poll in (2003) Polls, the heavy responsibility was given to her, the party decided to restructure the organisation because after the exit of Bhairon Singh Shekhawat from active politics, the state unit of the BJP was in vacuum in terms or leadership. Alter the elevation or Mr. Shekhawat as Vice-President of India, who successfully carried the burden of the party for over half a decade, the replacement was inevitable. The then Union Minister was chosen because the state units was sick of internal rifts and dissidence, she belongs to the young generation of Jat community and she has been an uncontroversial face to lead the party and to attract the rural women voters of the State. The former CM still enjoys effective political clout on state politics.

JAT BAHU : BJP's POLL CARD

During the deliberations of North Zones States' meet at Jaipur the saffron brigade prepared a 'Maha Plan' to win all the elections railing due to in 2003 and 2004. The forum was deliberately used by BJP leaders to put a check on the internal feuds and dissidence. Before being elected as vice-president, Mr. Shekhawat had chosen Mrs. Vasundhara as the new leader. But the idea was opposed by all senior leaders. Shekhawat, however, had his own reasons for choosing Vasundhara, who is a member of Lok Sabha from Jhalawar. She is the daughter of late Vijayaraje Scindhia and is wedded into the Dholpur royal family. It was Shekhawat who roped the former socialite in the state politics by making the contest the Vidhan Sabha elections and then made her contest the Lok Sabha election from Jhalawar. She won all the elections comfortably.

From among senior leaders like national treasurer Ramdas Agarval, the then state unit Chief Bhanwarlal Sharma, former deputy Chief Minister Hari Shankar Bhabhra, Lalit Kishor Chaturvedi, Raghubir Singh Kaushal and Ghanshyam Tiwari, Shekhawat's game plan was to introduce an uncontroversial face who could be acceptable by all. As B.S. Shekhawat thought that she would inspire the young cadres, knowing well that most of his detractors would not like her. However, she was' chosen to procure the Jat votes, because Mrs. Vasundhara Raje is the former Maharani of Dholpur's Jat principality and she was initiated into politics by party partiach B.S. Shekhawat in 1985 Vidhan Sabha elections. She represented both the Dholpur and Jhalawar constituencies. Her popularity in Jhalawar, another principality of Jat belt, among masses in both effective and immense. Although she has not been active in organisational matters her new appointment as the BJP's President of Rajasthan is expected to fill the void in the absence of B.S. Shekhawat. The BJP hopes that as a 'Thakurani' she will be able to cash in, on her identity as the Maharani of Jat principality.

Her appointment is a well planned strategy of the BJP to use the caste base to propagate her as *'Jat Ki Bahu Rajput Ki Beti'* and *'Gurjar Ki Saas'*. Though a true Rajput does not accept the Scindias as Rajputs, she is being projected as a woman from the royal ruling class. Her image as Dholpur's Jat Bahu and the marriage of her only son Dushyant Singh to the daughter of a big Gurjar landlord of Uttar Pradesh are the factors, which according to BJP analysts, would bring in the votes of Rajput. Jat and the Gurjar communities. There is no answer to this in the Congress Camp. Suddenly, the Congress camp found itself in a quandary and realised the appointment of Mrs. Vasundhara an imposing challenge. The Congress camp felt that the present PCC chief Girija Vyas would not be able to deliver the goods and a new PCC leader would have to be found to take the party to electoral success.

In Rajasthan, the BJP is deeply divided into the three camps. B.S. Shekhawat is a senior Rajput leader. But he is opposed by Ramdas Agrawal (Baniya), the treasurer of the BJP and incharge of the BJP state unit. He represents an anti-Shekhawat camp. The other unit group is led by Harishanker Bhabra (Baniya). To top it, Mrs. Vasudhara Raje Scindia is blessed by the Shekhawat camp. She is being projected as the chief ministerial candidate in Rajasthan. Against this background, the central leadership of the BJP is worried about this infighting. It knows that reviving the Hindutva agenda to will not serve the purpose encash the anti-incumbancy factor in Rajasthan.

It is for the first time that battle lines had been drawn for the Vidhan Sabha elections ten months ahead to lock honors with the Gehlot government on the drought front and the state government will have to inculcate extraordinary skills to counter the BJP attack.

There was already a demand for having a Jat as PCC Chief. The two main contenders among the Jats are veteran members Sis Ram Ola, a Lok Sabha MP and Harendra Mirdha, the PWD Minister. The Chief Minister, Ashok Gehlot will have a real testing time as he is considered to anti-Jato The Jat community, for example, inspired defeat, of the Congress Party in the last Lok Sabha election, is still fresh in the minds of people. The Congress leadership knows that the Jat community cannot be ignored, it can inflict deep wounds which could take long to heal. The Congress has realised that the BJP will play its cards on casteist lines and would not spare any opportunity to woo the Jat votes because of the presence of Mrs. Vasundhara. The BJP would definitely convince the Jat community that if Mrs. Vasundhara becomes the Chief Minister, the card will be in the hands of the Jat community. Adding to the caste factor, her being a woman and that too a charming woman may click with the masses to the great discomfiture of the Congress.

After the elevation of Bairon Singh Shekhawat, Ashok Gehlot tried to woo the Rajput community. The Rajputs had solidly backed the BJP only because of Shekhawat and caste reasons. The number of Rajput voters in the state is estimated over 15 lakhs and their presence matters in more than 60-70 Vidhan Sabha seats. The agitation launched by BJP MLA Devi Singh Bhati and Lokendra Singh Kalvi demanding reservation for the Rajput community is providing to be a thorn in the flesh of the Jat community. Therefore, The Congress High Command cannot ignore the fallout of this fierce battle of the Rajput community. It needs to counter the campaign as well as the BJP's soft Hindutva plank.

RESERVATION FOR UPPER CASTE POORS

For the first time, the Social Justice front-SJF organised its first ever huge rally at Jhunjhunu in October 2002, to raise a demand for the reservation of Upper Caste poors on the eve of election year. The sufferers among those seeking reservation and those who are for the name sake beneficiaries of reservation, expressed the feelings that they would vote for a party which, would bring them the benefits of reservation. The Social Justice Front, while demanding, protection to the reserved class in the OBC, has been also demanding reservations for the upper caste poor. The Front has identified Rajputs, Vaishyas, Sindhis, Kayasthas, Jat, Sikhs and Rajpurohits for providing them redressals. They are also demanding reservations for all those communities which have been ignored. The Social Justice Front's brain trust is Satyanarayan Singh, the former secretary of the State OBC

Commission. Mr. Singh, who belongs to Mali community knows how to do the homework well. He has carved out a doctrine on the basis of which benefits of reservation can be demanded. In his words, "Reservation is not given on the basis of caste alone, rather it's given on the basis of traditional occupation, economic conditions, educationally backward and those classes who did not find representation in government jobs. Caste is not the whole basis for reservation". In fact, the main cause of reservation is economic backwardness.

The Jhunjhunu rally was attended by people from all communities. There were a number of speakers who blamed the Gehlot government for the reservation given to Jats, but Satyanarayan Singh clarified that Gehlot is not the culprit, as after the announcement of Atal Behari Vajpayee of giving reservation to the Jats, Gehlot also had to follow the suit. The Jhunjhunu rally was targeted against the inclusion of the Jats. But Lokendra Singh Kalvi, Devi Singh Bhati and, Satyanarayan Singh insisted that the OBC should be categorised as *"backwards"* and *"most backwards"*. It worked on the principle that there could be comparison only when there are similarities and two entirely different communities cannot be expected to contest. The idea was that a healthy person should not be pitted against a physically handicap person.

For political considerations, the ire was that the Jat community which was basically a prosperous farming community was given reservation. Thus, under the guard of "farmers", the community was given undue, benefits, while other farmer communities were left behind. Now farmers, who are comparatively less fortunate or those belonging to professions, which do not pay well, should be listed separately. According to Satyanarayan Singh, the Supreme Court in its judgement has also suggested the preparation of two different kinds of lists. The Supreme Court is also for backward classes and more backward classes. The two lists are a must, otherwise those of the backward classes who are little more advanced might walk away with all the seats. The apex court has clarified that there is no constitutional or legal bar to a state categorising the *"backward classes"* and *"more backward"*. In other words, the Rajputs who are spearheading a battle will have to make the power managers understand that the government should form a separate group of farmers and then categorise them as *"backwards"* and *"more backwards"*. Kalvi has categorically stated that the sufferers would vote for only those who care to listen to their demands. This constituted an alarm to the Chief Minister.*

Infact, these communities have been opposed to sweeping the plum jobs by Jats under the OBC category. The purpose of the S.J.F. is to create the adequate pressure on the Government to revise the reservation policy or the ruling Congress face turbulent time in the next assembly elections. This agitation is based on caste lines. The front has organised several such rallies to attract a sizeable crow as a part of its strategy to condemn the faulty reservation policy. The, Front chose to organise its huge rally at Jhunjhunu—the constituency of heavy weight Jat leader Sis Ram Ola who floated the idea of reservation for the Jat community in Rajasthan and they got reservation during the BJP rule in 1998, whereas Chief Minister Ashok Gehlot was opposed the reservation to the Jats. He had to bow before the pressure of the Congress high command, as he visualised that the State's OBC's commission recommendations, if implemented on categorisation of the other backward communities, would resulted in a 'class conflict'. Unfortunately, the trifurcation of the OBCs categorised the prosperous Jats, Ahirs, Bishnois and Gujjars into "backward" group with a six percent reservation facility. They all belong to the agriculture communities constituting 80% of the total OBCs population.

According to the report of the Rajasthan Public Service Commission, the Jat community has swept numerous jobs of OBC's category. In his essay, the former Chief Secretary, M.L. Mehta, revealed that the Jat community procured maximum benefits of reservation given to the OBCs. For example, before the reservations given to the OBCs in Government jobs, there were 82 Jats RAS officers out of a 'flat cadre of 681 in 1999'. Out of 162 OBC Officers in RAS, 50 'percent belonged to the Jat community'. So is the case in other service such as Account Services, Engineering Services, Police Services, etc. Even in Medical and Engineering Colleges, they cornered all most

* *The Times of India*, New Delhi ed., 25th October 2002, p. 3.

35.74 percent seats. This percentage has further increased. Even the Jat community's own journal (Jat Surya), 52 Jats were 'selected, 72 in RPS, 16 in Rajasthan High court services' and 19 in judicial services. The revelations in R.P.S.C.'s report of 2000-01 are startling as one particular community has cornered 50-70 percent seats while depriving the benefits of reservations of other OBC's, thus nullifying the philosophy of reservations. In the state's RPSC, the percentage of reservation for QBC's is 21 percent, in comparison to Centre's 27 percentage. It is worth calling that these benefits are deprived by the people of one community from the districts of Jaipur, Sikar, Jhunjhunu, Hanumangarh, Nagour, Bikaner and Churu, because the Jats are economically prosperous and educationally well-being.

In short, the main purpose of the Front is to get included other castes in the reservation category as on Oct. 19, 2001 and there should be categorisation of OBC as 'backward', 'Very Backward', 'Extremely Backward' and precariously positioned backward, as is done by the UP Government. The Front's movement is basically targeting the Jats, the new beneficiaries who are called the new OBC in Rajasthan. According to Kalvi, "We are demanding reservations on the basis of poor economic conditions for all those castes which were left out, when new castes were included under the OBC for giving them reservations benefits". Kalvi lamented that under the garb of poor peasants, rich farmers managed to get reservations while those who were really poor were left out. Kalvi's grouse is against the rising influence of the Jat community and he has enough evidence to prove that the Jat community after the Panchayat elections has cornered most the posts which were reserved for the OBCs in the Panchayat Raj elections. The Table given here shows the truth. The new OBCs managed to get themselves elected in 75 percent of the reserved seats for the other backward classes. Apart from this, they also managed to get 30 percent of the general category posts also. All other castes which could have benefited under the reservations, are now forced to become backbenchers because of the domination of one caste in the OBC category. The Front feels that it is a very dangerous situation and may result in a class conflict. Both Devi Singh Bhati and Kalvi with Satyanarayan Singh as the front's patron have been organising rallies in the state and at present, the response to these rallies is overwhelming. The October 20 rally at Jhunjhunu, which had been organised by the Samajik Nyaya Manch of Jhunjhunu, is a clever move of the non-Jat communities to show their collective strength to the Congress MP from Jhunjhunu, Sis Ram Ola. The hidden agenda behind the Jhunjhunu rally is to send a message that if all other castes join hands together, the Jat candidate could be defeated. The example is cited how Bhim Singh Mandawa, a Rajput from the Thikana of Mandawa won the assembly election as a Janata Party candidate amidst strong Congress wave. He defeated Sis Ram Ola in a triangular contest.

TABLE 1

	Position before the last Panchayat elections	*Position after the last Panchayat elections 2000*
1.	Six Pradhans of Kumawat community	None Now
2.	Two Zila Pramukhs and eight Pradhans among Jangids	None Now
3.	Saini (Malis) had nine Pradhans	None
4.	Three Yadav Zila Pramukhs and seven Pradhans	Only two Pradhans now
5.	Three Gujjars Zila Pramukhs and nine Pradhans	One Zila Pramukh and three Pradhans
6.	Five Uhakars as Pradhans	Only two Pradhans now

According to Satyanarayan Singh, "The OBC is not confined to one community, it's a strata of society who for thousands of years have been economically backwards. The inclusion of the community will have negative effect on others. The endeavour was to divide the backwards, but what we are demanding is patronage with reservation."[1] He said that states like Andhra Pradesh, Tamil Nadu, Bihar, Haryana, Karnataka have identified OBCs under two categories. One category is of backward people and the other economically very backward castes. He demanded that the same formula should be adopted in the state and very backward castes be covered under the new provisions.

The Social Justice Forum (SJF) intensified its a campaign, for including all those communities in the "Other Backward Classes" (OBCs), which have been denied the privilege of reservation in Rajasthan. They have been demanding the recognition or Rajputs, Rajpurohits, Brahamins, Vaishyas and Kayasthas as OBCSs. These castes, of course, belong to the upper castes, but some of families are still poor and economically backward. The purpose of the movement is to counter the impact of reservations to OBCs by the Gehlot Government, specifically, the Jat community which has politically blackmailed the Congress Government in the state.

The Forum is committed to create political awareness among the electorate to seek social redress before the next Vidhan Sabha elections to be held in 2003. BJP's leader, Devi Singh Bhati, as an M.L.A. from the Rajput community, is behind the movement. It demands that reservation should be on the basis of poor economic conditions for all those castes as mentioned above. Infact, a dangerous situation has cropped up due to managing reservations for rich farmers/castes in place of poor peasants. In the present social strata, many castes have been truly economic backwards for thousands of years. The Government has taken cognizance that, the negative impact must be taken away with, while following the patterns of other states. Lokendra Singh Kalvi, another Rajput, is the convenor of the Forum, too has drawn the fierce battle by organising a number of rallies for the reservation at various district headquarters.

On the contrary, the State Government experienced of caste discrimination in Chaksu at Phagi, 40 Km. away from Jaipur, where the Dalits (Bairwas) were denied access to a pond for drinking water and an entry in temple by the upper castes. The demonstration of Dalits led to a clash with the Police, resulting in injuries of the policy and the Dalits. It reflected the caste domination and warned the government at caste discrimination. The Social Justice Front insists that the OBC should be categorised as "Backwards" and "Most Backwards", for which the clauses 14 and 16 of Articles of the Indian Constitution should be amended. It has balanced both the BJP and the Congress for not linking the backwardness with educational and economic factors for those belonging to upper caste poor category.

JOB QUOTA FOR BRAHMINS

As a result of the SJF's campaign, other communities like Brahmins, Gurjars, Rawats, etc. have started their agitations to demand for job quota. On 12th January 2003, thousands of Brahmins participated in the Brahmin Arakshan Rally in Bikaner. The rally was attended by leaders cutting across party lines, including present and former ministers. It was the second such rally organised by the Rajasthan Brahmin Mahasabha to press for the demand of reservation for the community in government jobs. It will be organising four more such rallies. The first rally was held at Sikar. Addressing it, Mahasabha President Bhanwar Lal Sharma appealed to the community members to fight for their rights. He cited the example of Parashuram in this context. Sharma, a Congress MLA from Sardasahar, appealed to approximately 60 lakh Brahmins of the state to vote for the candidates belonging to their community only, in a bid to strengthen their political case. For example, senior BJP leader and former Deputy Chief Minister Hari Shanker Bhabada said that the present reservation policy was faulty and it should be 'changed immediately to accommodate Brahmins in it. He said that Brahmins today are a deprived lot and they deserve the benefit of reservation. According to him, the descendants of Parshuram are the Brahmin community, whose number is over 50 lakhs in the state. They demand reservation of the basis of economic status. According to Kalvi, "The Mahant of Nathdwara, Kankroli, Mehandipur Ka Balaji and Jaipur's Govinddeoji temple have been given the benefit of reservation, then why not an ordinary Brahmin who is the priest of a small village temple be given the same benefit?" Kalvi advocates the case of Brahmins who hardly own five percent of the land holdings of the state and make their living by doing odd jobs. The poor Brahmins have traditionally been economically backward and are not educated. They are not known for their skills in business and have been earning their living as small time farmers and livestock keepers. The offerings at the temple also do not come to the Brahmins necessarily. Those educated Brahmins, who could study with great difficulties have no jobs and even after getting 85 percent marks, higher education remains a problem with them because of the faulty reservation system.

In response to these developments, the CM has shown his helplessness to go beyond by 49% reservations. Only the Central Government can remove the limit laid down by the Supreme Court of India.

LOSING BY-ELECTIONS : A SETBACK TO CM'S LEADERSHIP

The state leadership was perturbed at the electoral reverses that the party suffered in the Vidhan Sabha bypolls held in December 2002. Though the CM was confident that all was not loss and the fallout of Gujarat experiment would not be allowed to repeat in Rajasthan. The CM's lobby was fully confident to seek the new fresh mandate in the next Vidhan Sabha elections under his leadership. However, his key detractors mostly the Jat leaders didn't miss the opportunity to exploit the situation against Ashok Gehlot's leadership and raised the demand for leadership change. His well known detractor, MP from country's largest constituency of Barmer, Col. Sona Ram Choudhary hosted a dinner in Delhi on 22nd December, 2002 night in which invitations were sent to all Congress MPs. The aim of the dinner party was to build a consensus to seek the leadership change in the state. But only five MPs attended the dinner. Most of the MPs attended the dinner hosted by a general secretary of AICC in Delhi. This dinner party was attended by PCC president Girija Vyas. Four other members of Parliament opted to skip both the dinners.

Most of Gehlot supporters viewed the loss of at the three bypolls as a result of the Hindutva wave which flowed during the Gujarat poll. They felt that it was a failure of the organisation and not Gehlot's which let the party down. The final decision of fielding the party candidates was taken by the High Command.

As the traditions supporters of the Congress, Jats are a very powerful lobby in the State politics. They have been feeling marginalised, as in the past 50 years nobody from the community could become chief minister. In the last Lok Sabha elections, the anger of the community cost the party heavily and the Congress could win only nine out of 25 seats. The ire was at making Ashok Gehlot as the CM of the state.

Although on its own Jats may expect to capture 42 seats because of the support of the community, but there are many claimants for the post of CM in the community. Prominent among them are: Col. Sona Ram Choudhry, Sis Ram Ola, Speaker Paras Ram Maderna, Minister Kamla and Ram Narayan Chaudhry. Under such circumstances other communities might prove stronger in getting Chief Minister of their choice. In a nutshell, the purpose of hosting the dinner politics was to bring a Jat leader as CM of Rajasthan on the eve of the assembly elections (2003). As a result of this game plan, the tug of war in the organization and the government continued with other alternative options to put a hault on it.

It was a pity that senior Congress leaders, of old generation, have unitedly demanded the ouster of the C.M., while exploiting the defeat of the party in the assembly by-elections. The CM was personally stunned at this development. Two former CMs, namely Shiv Charan Mathur and Heeralal Deopura, and other senior leaders like, former Union Minister N.K. Sharma, Buia Singh, Sis Ram Ola and P.C.C. Chief and Mrs. Girija Vyas met the High Command to rejuvenate the state level organization in the light of lost of three Vidhan Sabha seats in the by elections. They all together camped New Delhi to save Dr. Girija Vyas. The CM received a jolt to know that these leaders expressed their dissidence at making B.D. Kalla, the Minister confidence of the CM, as New PCC Chief of Rajasthan, while impressing upon party chief, Mrs. Sonia Gandhi that mere removal of Dr. Vyas would not lead to rejuvenation of the party, nor any caste equation could affect any change in the fortune of the party. They demanded the removal of the CM as well, taking the plea that Mr. Gehlot was incapable of leading the Government and he would not be able to prevent the repetition of the Gujarat experiment. These leaders reportedly suggested the name of Senior Jat leader, Natwar Singh, presently the Rajya Sabha member. The whole game-play was to please the Jat community at the cost of OBC leadership. It is worth-recalling here that it was Natwar Singh, who suggested that the senior Minister of the Gehlot Government, B.D. Kalla, another strong Brahmin leader of Bikaner be made PCC president.

JATS AGAINST KALLA AS PCC CHIEF

At a stage the Congress leadership cleared urban development minister Bulaki Das Kalla for the Pradesh Congress Committee (PCC) presidentship in place of Girija Vyas; the Jat community wanted to have its own representative to head the PCC. The leadership is also learnt to have recommended that senior minister in the Gehlot cabinet, Mrs. Kamla, who is from the Jat community, should be made the deputy chief minister. But the Jat lobby in the caste ridden state Congress forcefully insisted that a Jat should be made the PCC president. It was also averse to Mrs. Kamla being made the deputy chief minister as she is a liberal and does not believe in caste-oriented politics. Reportedly, the Jat lobby headed by MP Sis Ram Ola sent feelers to AICC general secretary Mrs. Ambika Soni that Kalla should not be imposed as the PCC chief. But the Jat leaders followed the diktat of the Jat Mahasabha and its leader Gyan Prakash Pilania told Jat leaders not to accept the positions of PCC president and deputy chief minister. He said that a Jat getting the chief ministership is long overdue. G.P. Pilania, who is considered a father figure in the Jat community and led the anti-Congress agitation during the last Sabha elections, categorically demanded that somebody from the community should head the government as it has been backing the Congress for over half a century now. This will have a positive impact on the peasants and the party could return to power under a Jat leader. As the Jat leaders lacked consensus over the name of Mrs. Kalla Beniwal as Dy. Chief Minister, nor they agreed to the name of B.D. Kalla, the Congress High Command referred the crisis till the assembly elections, without the change, but by constituting a review committee consisting of all the leaders of 'old generation'. The manner in which the Congress High Command reacted to the BJP's victory in the Gujarat assembly polls on 'soil Hindutva' came to an end. It was a wise step that

Mrs. Sonia Gandhi did not follow the illustratous example of Maharashtra (change of leadership) in Rajasthan.

At present, Ashok Gehlot facing the drought striken Rajasthan relatively seems to be safe, because the Congress leadership has felt that any major organisational change may fuel dissidence within the party and such attempt may prove to be counter productive just ten month before the Assembly elections. Hence, CM's outer campaign by senior party leaders was tackled with elevation of Jat leader, Mrs. Kamala Beniwal as Dy. Chief Minister and the expansion of the State Ministry on 10th Jan. 2003. While including the two designated Dy. Chief Minister Kamala Beniwal and Banwari Lal Meena, the reinduction of Ram Singh Bishnoi into the Cabinet proved beyond doubt that the party has acted on caste lines aimed at pleasing the caste configuration in the election year. It should be noted that Mr. Kamla is from the Jat community while Berwa is a Dalit. Interestingly, Kamla dropped her surname Beniwal over a decade ago and is happy to be identified just as Kamla Chief Minister.

Ashok Gehlot admitted that he had to abide by the decision of the party leadership to have two deputies like in Madhya Pradesh, but he refused to admit that this would in any way dilute his powers. In his words, "I would say the appointment of two deputy chief ministers would only repose confidence in different communities that they have been properly represented in the Government."

Asked why Bishnoi was reinducted into the cabinet when his son Parasram Bishnoi was allegedly involved in production of narcotics in his factory and was absconding for several months, Gehlot said Bishnoi resigned on moral ground when his son's factory premises was raided. But even after nine months his son had not been charges heated. According to political observers, the appointment of two deputy chief ministers has been a tactical victory for Gehlot. He was reportedly against making only a Jat as the deputy chief minister. Gehlot was of the view that if one community was given over importance, the idea would backfire and any other communities. But political observers here feel that the little changes in the Ministry were only cosmetic in nature and would not serve any long-term purpose. Senior leaders of the party, however, managed to stall the removal of PCC President Girija Vyas. The coordination committee formed by the central party leadership would serve as the "watch dog" to appraise the performance of the Gehlot government.

On the contrary, Mrs. Vasundhara Raje has been relieved from the Union Cabinet to strive to bring together reverse people of different opinions on the basis of 'Good Governance Mantra'. She has been directed to fierce battle of campains against the Congress rule. But state unit is ridden with strong opposition of senior party leaders like Hari Shankar Bhabra and Ramdas Agrawal, who have now stressed for the inclusion of their men in the party's executive since she had been imposed. Those leaders may not let her sit easy till their men are not included in the party executive. Their dominance is likely to matter on the eve of election year.

Likewise, the state politics is caste ridden and various castes and communities have been staging rallies demanding reservation. Rajputs arid Brahmins have been particularly vocal in their demands and have even threatened that the communities would support only those parties which take up their cause. These castes had been supporting the BJP, which since the days of Jan Sangh, was led by Bhairon Singh Shekhawat. In his absence, the party will have to project a Rajput of eminence as its leader. Infact, Mrs. Vasundhara comes from the royal stock and is the former Maharani of Dhoplur principality. She is seen both as a Jat and a Rajput, a factor may which work in her favour.

Here now the new executive will have to reflect caste representation as this is election year and the result the three Vidhan Sabha elections proved that the caste card plays an important role. Keeping it in view, Jas Kaur Meena of Rajasthan has been brought into the Union Cabinet to lure, the Meena tribal community. This community counts a lot in the electoral politics. She is the daughter of a farmer of Mandawari village of Dausa district of Rajasthan. She is expected wield political clout in Jaipur, Kota and Udaipur divisions.

TO SUM UP

The previous history of state elections bears the testimony that the two party system is one of the key features of state politics, despite the strong undercurrent waves of caste politics. On many occasions, attempts to form a third front were made in the state but they proved in vain against the well-rooted existence of the Congress and the BJP on caste/feudal order. Despite this, the Congress party has strengthened the secular forces in the state against the fallout of communal forces since the demolition of the Babri Masjid in December, 1992. The fatwa politics hardly lured the Muslim voters. They have been with the Congress culture. Presently, the CM is firmly committed not to repeat the Gujarat model in state politics on the eve of election year of the assembly, though the events like the desecration of Rao Shekhaji and Baldev Ram Mirdha's idols have taken place, deliberately to rouse the caste-based emotions. In contrast to Gujarat's Gaurav, Rajasthan's Gaurav (pride) is unique, as it believes in secular ethos and peaceful coexistence. It is well reflected in the performance the three-tier Panchayat Raj System. In the light of the current drought, the CM is well alert of the fallout anti-incumbency factor in the due election where his performance as well achievements shall be tested in the people's court. He knows that the drought management would play an important role in this electoral politics. He recalls how the allegation of mass hunger, instead attributing some deaths to an unspecified disease was framed to blame the name of Rajasthan, because the state is ruled by the opposition party at the centre. On the other hand, the state Government has provided food free of cost to the poor and needy people through Annadaan Yojana Kosh Scheme/Annadaan scheme by various NGOs and donors.

The current state politics is polarised between the Dalit and Jat factor *versus* the BJP's soft Hindutva plank. The state unit of BJP too has shown the interests in Dalit votes by reshuffling the Union Ministry in which MP Jas Kaur Meena of Rajasthan has been inducted into the BJP-led NDA ministry. The concern question is : will the BJP's Hindutva card be able to attract Jat and Dalit voters on the basis of such changes? or the strategy followed by the Congress will be capable of stopping the repetition of the Gujarat experiment in Rajasthan, MP, Chhattisgarh and Delhi, where the assembly polls are due to in the Year 2003 ? The fact is that the Congress and the BJP have nothing to do with Gandian principles, ethos of socialism and secularism or the values of Indian culture. They are inevitably concerned with the battle lines caste-equation to win the polls.

Note and Reference

1. The figure is based on Prakash Bhandari's observations and comments published in Rajasthan Plus, *The Times of India*, Jaipur, 18th Oct., 2002, p. 1.

CHAPTER

27

Some Lessons from the 14th Lok Sabha Elections

Even after 56 years of Independence, we have not been able to make any meaningful reforms in our electoral systems, despite several sensible and practical suggestions have been offered by various commissions and committees including the Election Commission of India. The reality is that almost all the political parties have been able to sustain the single point agenda *'to win the election'*. The impact of the landmark judgement of 2 May, 2002 (disclosing the information of qualifications, criminal antecedents, financial assets of candidates at the time of filing nomination and of the 13th March 2003, was seen on the 14th Lok Sabha elections. The judgement created a ray of hope for good governance, yet this right to information is not sufficient to keep the criminals away from the arena of elections. Other steps have been to be taken to stop the growing clout of money power and violence to retain the lost credibility of our electoral system.

As regards, the electoral verdict 2004 is concerned, it is being analysed in a diverse ways from the past verdicts. Despite tremendous evasion in the healthy party system *vis-a-vis* the people's apathy towards the political processes,· the voters demonstrated a rational option for the two major national parties-the Congress and the BJP-as legitimate force to govern the country. Their share of vote the respective parties is: 26.7% and 22.2%. The sad aspect for them is that they are continued to be black mailed by criminals petty local politicians and small parochial parties supported by caste-*cum*-communal background. The elections 2004 have put the all political parties on warning that mass rural poverty of India cannot·be ignored. The verdict is meant for good governance through the experiment of coalition government. This has supported to the Riker-Lawrence Doddy theory coalition formation (i.e. multi-party parliament).

The last Lok Sabha elections are widely interpreted as a revolt of rural masses by-passed by the Information Technology (I.T.) revolution. They voted for a new regime with a human face, which is led by the UPA government. This theory owes much to the defeat of the regional parties in many states like Andhra Pradesh, Karnataka and others. But the fact is that new regimes have risen to power on the basis of murder, loot, terror and false voting. On the eve of elections, the local warlords and mafia launched a veritable regime of terror in the area to have the poll results in their favour. This scenario can be taken away with if police-judicial reforms are made. Unfortunately, all parties now have so many thugs and warlords with criminal records, who as MPs would never be interested in reforms with a human face. They are today known as *'trained ministers'*, to which the Chief Justice Ramesh Chandra Lohoti, has ruled out to do anything against trained ministers. Only parliament is competent to take the final decision through making a law while seeking consensus amongst all political parties. It requires a strong political will.

GIVING VOTES POWER TO REJECT

The proposed *'None of the Above'* button may be the most radical step the Election Commission has taken in recent years. For the first time in India's electoral history, voters are to be given a choice to reject all candidates, by pressing a reject button on the EVM's list. What makes this option crucial is that if more than 50% of the voters push this button, the election will be cancelled. When re-election takes place, the earlier candidates will be barred from contesting. However, the second time round, the *'None of the Above'* button will be removed. But our political parties do not seem to be serious about the 'Push-Button Plan' mooted by the Election Commission of India. (*The Times of India*; 3 March, 2004, p. 3). Media and NGOs can take up the matter to educate the masses and inform them to discard a group of unwanted politicians. It is a good way to protest and say that a voter wants better candidates.

Former Chief Election Commissioner Dr. M.S. Gill suggests other way of adopting the protest, i.e. the first past the post system of election should be replaced by a *'run off election'*, as is the case in France. (*Ibid.*, 7/3/2004, p. 14). In his view, on the first day, field all the eligible candidates in a constituency. Two days later, the top two can fight it out once again. Only one of them can win and win with a clear mandate. So, instead of having a constituency represented by someone who has say a mere 22 or even 33 percent of the electorate's vote; you can be represented by a person who has a clear majority. His plea is that this would go a long way in reforming our caste and class-based politics to one that is issue and development based. For, to get such a mandate, both the political parties and the candidates will have to rise above sectional politics and reach. This can only be done by addressing real time problems, by planning development programmes and then implementing the promised programmes in time. This is possible only through legislation, which needs a concerted and combined effort from the political parties and civil society as a whole. This will enhance the merit basis in place of caste-based voting pattern.

AMENDING THE ANTI-DEFECTION LAW

The Ninety-first Constitution Amendment Act, which received the President's in Jan. 2004, was historic in terms of banning defections by elected members and ceiling the strength of ministry. It takes away the protection that was provided to group defections on the ground of party splits and

1/3rd of the members' of the party defecting. But the other group defection under the merger clause still continues to be protected under the new amended law, i.e. if a group of 2/3rd of the members of a legislature party decide to defect to topple a government to get a share in the ministry or in return for other material benefits, they can be saved from disqualifications by claiming to have to merge their party with some other party. Thus, the principle that group defections are as bad as individual defection or that a crime whether committed by one person or by a group of persons has not been accepted fully in the Act.

Secondly, the decision in matters of disqualification on grounds of defection is still left in the hands of the Presiding Officers and the experience thus so far has been large disastrous. They can misinterpret the Tenth Schedule. And thirdly, the latest amendment does not say anything about the validity of the vote of defections. The adverse fallout defection was experienced in Haryana and Arunachal Pradesh in June-July 2004. Hence, all those illusions of the reform must be taken away with to strengthen our parliamentary system. The question of removing *'tainted ministers'* has largely loomed in Parliament.

GLAVANISING THE STEEL FRAME

Babudom (Lord of Files) was once an honorific in India but today its style of working has become horrific and derogatory. In his first address to the nation, UPA's Prime Minister Manmohan Singh lamented that the government's "delivery mechanism has failed quite abysmally". Ironically, the idea behind adopting the British model of bureaucracy with security of service tenure was to protect the civil servants from political influence. But due to the growing a culture of sycophancy in professionalism and interference of political leadership, the model witnessed the decline favouring the idea of *'a committed bureaucracy'* rather than a *'neutral bureaucracy'*. The perceived ideological predilections prevailed during the Indira Gandhi regime.

In this regard Cabinet Secretary B.K. Chaturvedy admits that the main problem his with bureaucracy itself, which lacks commitment and proper training. Over the years their ability to withstand pressures has also declined. (*The Times of India*, 25.7.04, p. 8). In the era of LPG' idea of a neutral civil servant is unthinkable because of postings, transfers and promotions, with liberalisation and WT coming into play, down-sizing the staff, out sourcing and performance may be the answer.

JP's Loksatta (an NGOs working on electoral and administrative reforms, suggests that the monopoly of civil servants on key positions must end, with open system to everyone on the basis of vision, merit and plan of action. Premature removal (as the Rajasthan High Court has given compulsory retirement to its 7 judicial officers whose C.R. was bad) must be on the basis of proven incompetence/corruption. As regards accountability and transparency, the concept of decentralization should be the very basis at the lowest level, and India can learn from the False Claims Act operating in the US, which allows citizens to file a case against a public servant who has given wrong information. The offending official shall be liable for excessive use of authority. But no amount of reforms in the bureaucracy will do the trick unless the polity too is cleaned up.

WHO IS RESPONSIBLE FOR MISSING NAMES IN ELECTORAL ROLLS?

Lok Sabha elections, 1904, in India were among the largest events of its kind in the world. But one of its fundamental flaw was missing the name of voters in the electoral rolls, for which the Election Commission was singled out for blame. Nay, the blame should be borne by all the stakeholders, namely voters, the political parties and the Electional body. Though the primary task of preparing and revising the rolls rests with the EC, it is as much the responsibility of political parties, and the voters, to ensure that the margin of error is kept as low as possible. Once the electoral rolls are ready, they are made widely available to the public so as to remove the mystery of missing names today had, in other words, plenty of opportunity to rectify the lapse earlier.

Besides, part of the blame must go to our political parties, who are known to manipulate the official machinery to exclude inimical voters. Rather than putting the blame at the doorstep of the EC, we must take a closer look at the negative role played by other interested parties. Indeed, the EC deserves credit for weeding out lakhs of bogus voters as it did in Andhra Pradesh from the rolls. Let no one forget too that the EC operated on a skeletal staff. It has to essentially rely on the cooperation and support of local administrations, prone to parochial and party biases, to complete the electoral paperwork. The need of the hour is CIVIC participation and involvement of all stakeholders. This is basic part of electoral process and right to vote. Alas, the urban voter is more of a cynic than a citizen. It is time we had a more honest assessment of the ground realities rather than look for easy scapegoats.

It is easy to blame the system of the statutory body for flaw, but why we forget that the holding an early elections by the BJP-led NDA government, indeed, did not provide the needed time to revise and finalise the electoral rolls. Hence, both the political class and civil society should share the blame for the missing names of voters.

POLITICS BEHIND FREE POWER

The popular declaration pertaining Free Power for farmers in the Lok Sabha elections, many Chief Ministers (Andhra Pradesh, Tamil Nadu and Maharashtra) appear to have amazed. But the question is was it an irresistible voter demand? No. Many cynics have a theory to justify that a swing of just one percent in the popular vote means the difference between victory and defeat in elections. The politicians do not wish to take risk antagonising a single section of population far fear of losing that is vital (one percent of the vote). They have no concern of empty treasury. They know this is short-sighted and unsustainable, as voters seen myopic enough to prefer suicides to sustainable development and it is not the popular wish of people. Democracies should be based on populism, but not on bankrupt governments. Politicians and educated voters should know that electricity is not like rain that drop from the heavens free of charge. It involved costs of producing, transmitting and distributing. If the farmers do not pay the cost for it, it has to be paid for the tax payers.

Today, bankrupt state governments cannot maintain roads, cannot provide textbooks to schools or medicines to dispensaries, cannot undertake rural development. Giving free power to farmers means less money with the state government. It should be taken as a part of corrupt practice. That translates into fewer schools, medicines, roads, and jobs. So, free power for farmers is not free at all: it is paid for through greater illiteracy, ill-health, unemployment and lack of road connectivity for the poorest, remotest areas.

INDIA SHINNING BACKFIRED

Breaking his silence after NDA's debacle in the Lok Sabha polls, 2004, former deputy prime minister L.K. Advani admitted that the twin phrases of *"feel good"* and *"India shining"* cost the party dear. He also attributed the party's defeat to anti-incumbency against the state governments and party candidates, besides the caste factor. He further asserted that while the BJP considered as its strength the ideology of cultural nationalism and Hindutva, "our ideological struggle will continue against those who seek to project it narrowly.

Conceding that the outcome of the elections had gone "completely against our expectations", he told a press conference at the BJP headquarters in New Delhi saying, "I would like the Congress-led coalition government not to misread people's fractured verdict as a decisive mandate for any alliance, much less for any single party and certainly not for any individual". Anyway, 2004 verdict was not exception as since independence India the country has always been governed by minority regimes. They all have projected pitfalls of First-past-the-post-system.

Similarly, BJP's senior leader, Murli Manohar Joshi, too admitted that the foreign original issue did not click. He also obliquely criticised Gujarat CM's Narendra Modi's outbursts against Mrs. Sonia Gandhi accepting that the language used by Modi was a mistake. (*The Times of India,* dated May 25, 2004,

p. 11) Modi had said that Sonia was not capable of being recruited for even a "clerk's job". The voters did not like this kind of language. It was against the Indian tradition. But both the leaders still accept that non-inclusion of ideology in a proper way in the electioneering had cost the party dear. The poll results confirms that spending luxurgerious on mass campaigning through media did not lead to victory. The BJP-led NDA government made an unprecedented use of mass media to influence the Indian voters. On the contrary, Congress President Mrs. Sonia Gandhi's aggressive road shows and pad-yatras helped the party to explain the voters the party's manifesto. It is learnt that all political parties spent close to Rs. 500 crore on their communication during the three months.

In the light of the verdict-2004 the following electoral reforms may broadly be considered :

- Under the present system of *"first-past-the-post"*, a candidate can get elected even on a minority of votes. No candidate should be declared elected unless he or she secures *more than 50% of votes cast*. In case no candidate gets this, it should be followed by a run-off election. With electronic machines, it should be possible on the next day. The Push-button Plan may help to solve the problem.
- Any person standing for a public office should be required by law to file an affidavit giving this *particulars of movable and immovable assets* owned by him/her or dependent members of his/her family. If elected, he or she should file similar returns every year.
- Women constitute almost 50% of voters in the country, but a very small percentage of the elected candidates are women. To rectify the imbalance, the strength of Lok Sabha and also of State Legislatures should be increased by 10 percent. *All these seats will be reserved for women*. They will be elected by the members of the Lok Sabha and Vidhan Sabha in the same manner as laid down for election to Legislative

Council for the seats earmarked in Vidhan Sabha as provided in Article 171(d) of the Constitution.

- Persons *convicted of criminal offence* by any Court irrespective of any appeals pending should be debarred from contesting elections. Those guilty of electoral offences should not be allowed to contest elections for at least ten years. We can learn from the 'Tainted Ministers' drama of Parliament staged by opposition parties.
- If a person against whom *criminal charges have been framed by any Court,* punishable by imprisonment for more than one year wants to contest an election, the case may be referred to a special tribunal which should give interim decision ill regard to disqualification or otherwise.
- In. the light of experience gained, there should be strict provision for checking the menace of *post election defections* by candidates. The defectors should lose the membership of legislature and must be made to seek fresh mandate.
- *State funding of electoral expenses* should be done to the maximum extent possible in kind through special facilities provided. Countries like Sri Lanka, Malaysia, Japan, Germany, South Korea and several others do have the system of state funding of electoral expenses.
- The *election expenses should be reduced* and limits strictly enforced. The TV Channels may be allowed to be used for purposes of campaigning. The rallies of all political parties can be done at a common platform after the announcement of election. Common meetings may be arranged by the Election Commission. The campaign period may be reduced to seven days only. Newspaper advertisements may be allowed as common advertisement for all candidates in a constituency and funded by the State. The number of words for each candidate may be fixed.
- In terms of reforming our party system, an important aspect of electoral management *is*

registration and recognition of political parties or pre-poll alliance of parties. A party/pre-poll alliance should have the status of national party only if it secures 10% of votes ill at least 50% of the states in a parliamentary election. Similarly, a state party/pre-poll alliance should secure at least 10% of votes in the Assembly Elections to be recognised as such. This will put a check on the rise of caste-*cum*-communal-based smaller parties.

- Prescribe a higher educational qualification for the membership of the legislative bodies. Education helps in ensuring the quality of proceedings in the Legislature.
- The Election Commission should have statutory *authority to deregister any party* for undemocratic and unconstitutional conduct. This step will go a long way in reducing the proliferation of political parties which has contributed to post-election opportunistic coalitions and unstable governments. The proposed law should define the conditions for registration and deregistration. All parties must be organised on democratic lines with regular inner party elections in order to be eligible for registration. The proposed law should ensure inner party democracy in every political party.
- Only an *all India or a pre-election alliance of parties* should be eligible for contesting Lok Sabha elections. Similarly, *parties recognised as state parties* besides all India parties should be eligible to contest elections to the houses of the State Legislature and the Rajya Sabha.
- *Each party should have its accounts audited* and must reveal the source of its funds and details of expenditure. The duly audited accounts should be published for public scrutiny soon after the election. It should be the part of Right to Information.
- There is widespread concern about unstable government at the Centre, because hung parliaments have become common since 1989. Due to fragmented party system and emergence of many small regional

parties, strong union governments have either not emerged or not survived for long. There is a case for changing constitutional provisions for Indian parliament by adopting the German system of *"constructive vote of no confidence"*. The Prime Minister should be elected by the Lok Sabha and can be voted out of office only if the same motion identifies a successor who can assume office within the same Parliament. It is a must for the stability of government in the era of coalition politics.

- Although Panchayati Raj Institutions have been provided for in the 73rd and 74th amendment of the Constitution, the laws made by State Governments do not fall in line with the spirit of the Constitution. It is imperative that the Panchayati Raj Institutions are strengthened in the spirit of Constitution. There has to be some *monitoring mechanism* such as inter-state council to ensure this goal. The right to know doctrine must be introduced at the grass-root level to weed away the impact of politics of crimination and money power. For this, tribunal on Zonal/regional basis should be set-up for the speedy disposal of election disputes and cases.

The Election Commission in its latest report submitted to PM Manmohan Singh, has sought the need to containing the fallout of politics of criminalisation. In a more aimed at expediting the procedure for disqualification of a person found guilt of corrupt practices, the Election Commission has suggested that its secretary could be specified as the authority to refer cases of disqualification to the President. As per report, "What is required to be done is to ensure that a decision on such questions of disqualification be rendered expeditiously, as the period of disqualification in such cases cannot exceed six years from the date of order of the High Court or the Supreme Court". This is one of electoral reforms submitted to PM Manmohan Singh.

Under the existing provisions of the Representation of the People Act, 1951, the case of a person found guilt of corrupt practice was to be submitted to the President by the authority specified by the central government. The government by its notification has specified the secretary general of the Lok Sabha of the Rajya Sabha and the secretary of the state assembly, or the legislative council as the authority to submit cases of disqualification to the President. According to the report, the commission is seriously concerned of inordinate delay in referring the matter and in setting the matter by the courts. Hence, it wants the procedure to be simplified to contain the fallout of corrupt practices.

Likewise, for the mushrooming of political parties, the Commission has suggested that a clause could be introduced in the Representation of the People Act, 1951, authorising the Commission to issue necessary orders regulating registration and deregistration of political parties with a view to strengthening the party system in the country.

In this regard, mention may be made of the blueprint of the P.L. Hota committee. It is for bureaustroika, i.e. how lethargic bureaucracy can be made citizen-friendly, while weeding out corrupt and lazy officers. The committee consisted of 16 members contains 64 recommendations made to the Union Government. It is headed by former UPSC Chief, P.C. Hota. It was set-up by the previous NDA Government to suggest ways and means to make the civil service transparent, account and responsive in the era of Liberalization, Privatization and Globalisation (LPG) and to keep the bureaucracy away from wrongful pressures politicians and ministers. In short, catch them young is the panel's recommendation. To mould young entrants, it favours age eligibility to lower from 21-30 years to 21-24 for the general candidates and a five-year concession for ST and SC candidates.

The panel suggests 'rigorous review' after 15 years of service. It says, "If an officer is not honest and performance-oriented, he be weeded out of service,". A similar review should also be carried out subsequently at periodic intervals to determine if performance level of an officer has fallen sharply or if there are allegations against his integrity.

It advocates formulation of rules under the Benami Transactions (Prohibition) Act, 1988 for attachment/forfeiture of the ill-gotten property of corrupt public servants. The committee also wants amendment to Article 311 of the Constitution for dismissal of officers charge sheeted in corruption cases. The report suggests immediate notification of the Freedom of Information Act, 2002 rules, and modification of the Official Secrets Act. (*The Times of India*, New Delhi, August 8, 2004, p. 6.)

CHAPTER

28

Gujjars' Agitation in Rajasthan

Politics Behind Reservation Demand

The unrest in Rajasthan led by the Gujjar community for inclusion in the ST category, spread like wildfire in some parts of Rajasthan. Where the community was in a sizeable numbers. The agitation hit the law and order of the national capital as well as some districts of UP, Bihar and MP. The agitation was led by Retd. Coln. Kirori Singh Bainsla of the Gujjar Sangharsh Samiti, stressed on a demand shifting of the Gujjars from OBC to ST .category. Since the BJP Government come to power, the unkept promise, made in the previous assembly elections by the BJP, added to the Gujjar's ire. The agitation was so intensive and furious that the ministers of BJP-led Vasundhara Raje Government failed to desist them to take part in caste-oriented violent movement.

Today, caste factor has once again acquired a new dimension, as in Haryana, or in UP, Rajasthan's Jat success in getting OBC status, have been demanding OBC category, against the trend when the 1931 census, there was a rush among several lower castes and OBCs to be categorized as upper castes.

Rajasthan is the single largest beneficiary of quota for Scheduled Tribes despite there being many other states with much larger tribal populations. In Rajasthan, it is the Meena community that corners the biggest chunk of ST quota benefits, if their representation in All India civil services is any indication. Meenas dominate over Bhils, Sahariyas, Patellas, Koknas among others. Though tribals of Rajasthan constitute just 8% of the tribal population of the country; thanks to the Meenas, the state has a significant presence in the ST quota. The results of the civil services examination of 2006 also show that the Meena community continues to dominate the quota for scheduled tribes. Of 474 candidates selected in 2006, for example, 36 were ST candidates. Of these, 13 were Meenas, constituting 36% of the tribal quota. About 56 serving IAS officers are currently from Meena community which means that it accounts for 14% of ST quota among IAS category, apart from the fact that many of Meenas are rich peasants.

A HISTORICAL BACKGROUND

In Rajasthan, reservation has been a constitutional problem since 1971 when Indian Parliament adopted a resolution under Article 342 to add a particular caste in SC/ST category. But for the Rajasthan, the Government of India made no such change in the list of SCs/STs. In 1981, the reservation demand during Congress rule resumed a revolting importance. The Gujjars first demanded ST status in 1981 when Shiv Charan Mathur of Congress was the chief minister of Rajasthan. He looked into the matter and rejected their demand. The reason was simple that the Gujjars were primarily involved in milk production and reasonably good land holding. Besides, the Gujjars had no indication of primitive traits—that may have swung the argument in favour of an ST status—and had no distinctive cultural trait. Nor did they live in isolation and were anything but shy in their interaction with others. So, C.M. Mathur wrote to the Centre which alone has the power to grant reservation to any caste or community under Article 342 of the Constitution, saying that there was no way the Gujjars could get ST status.

For about 13 years, the whole thing remained a closed chapter. Then, in 1994, the chief minister at that time, Bhairon Singh Shekhawat of BJP, got the Gujjars categorized as OBCs. After all, this community was backing his party. Shekhawat first formed a Cabinet Committee headed by home minister Gulab Chand Kataria. The state collected data on Gujjars—their history, life style, customs and profession and made its recommendations to the Centre and thus the Gujjars got the OBCs status.

But that is not quite what they wanted. The Gujjars want to be labelled tribals because of the fringe benefits that were associated with the ST tag. Moreover, the Gujjars felt that the OBC category is an overcrowded one where the Jats (who became OBCs in 1999) any way enjoy more clout and they are not at all comfortable with this. And then thus, old rivalry with the Meenas followed. Today, the community feels that the Meenas enjoy an edge over them because they were classified as ST and prospered because of the benefits that followed thereafter.

The Gujjars feel that they should easily have done better than the Meenas because there are more educated people in their community. Also, because they have footprints in different professions—be it agriculture or animal husbandry, teaching or mining, law or transport. In fact, the Gujjars are the biggest transport operators in Rajasthan, Haryana, MP, UP and even Delhi. On the contrary the Meenas are primarily located in eastern and southern Rajasthan ranging in five districts. But for years, the Meenas of southern Rajasthan were a deprived lot and could not attain the same level of prosperity as their eastern counterparts.

The Meenas of east and south have joined hands to take on the Gujjars. The Meenas understand that if the Gujjars get the ST status, it would hit them hard and they would have to reckon with more competition.

During the Congress rule, it may be noted the Ashok Gehlot Government decided in May, 2003 (in principle) to give 14% reservation in Government jobs to the economically poor among the forward castes like Brahmins, Rajputs and Vaishyas. This was unanimously approved by the Cabinet. As this was above the 49% reservations, it was decided to refer this case to the Centre for suitable amendments in Article 342 of the Constitution. The move was necessitated in the wake of a series of agitations launched by Brahmins and Rajputs who had been demanding job quota on economic basis. The BJP then supported these rallies for political overtones. The smart decision was taken keeping in mind the general elections of 2004. Only Indian Parliament is authorized to pass a bill granting ST, SC or OBC status to any caste or community.

BASIS OF PROVOCATION

Historically speaking, the cause of caste conflict between the Meena and Gujjar communities lies in Meena's prosperity, which is due to their ST status, whereas the Meenas too are basically agriculturalists. Because of this status, the Meenas have immensely improved their social and political conditions since 1956. Today, two ministers are in Raje's cabinet and has over 1000 persons in IAS/IPS allied series and in state service. Thus holding sway over the administration. It is a force to reckon within state politics. Today, Namo Narain Meena (Formerly Addl. Director of Police) is a Union Minister. That apart, there are 24 reserved constituencies for tribals in the Vidhan Sabha and in most cases, these seats are occupied by the Meenas. They are still Zamindars and rich.

Against this background, it is worth-recalling that during the British rule, the Meena community was classified as criminal tribe under the 1924 Act. As per the various gazettes of princely states and also the imperial gazette of India, 1941, the Meena community was classified as 'Tribe'. However, the Meenas could be recognized as tribals and were included in the Scheduled List of Tribals only in 1956 after the Kaka Kalelkar Commission and U.N. Dhebhar Commission recommended their inclusion in tribal list. The die was cast in 1956 and the first Meena enjoying the benefits of reservation was selected in the IAS was given Rajasthan cadre. He was C.P. Meena, a youth from Kota. The Gujjars feel that their community would also grow if they were classified as Tribals. The Gujjars therefore feel uncomfortable being in the OBC category, as they that the presence of Jats in the OBC would not give them enough opportunities both in government jobs and in politics to procure benefits of reservations and they could perform better if they classified as 'Tribals'.

The Meenas could get the reservation pie, but the woes of the voiceless denotified nomadic and semi-nomadic tribes have gone unnoticed, and there is no body to raise the voice for these tribes, who too were once described as 'criminal' like the Meenas during the British rule. The most unpriviledged of them are the nomadic Banjaras and Gadiya Lahors. They are still unorganized. The Mathur Government in 1981 accepted their STs and sent a recommendation to the Union Government include these nomads as STs. But the centre to this date did not accept the recommendation. It is difficult to understand when the criminal tribes Act of the British era was repealed after the enforcement of India's constitution and when all the erstwhile criminal tribes got a new name as *'denotified tribes'*, why the tribes Bagri, Mogya, Naik, Bhat and Multania were not placed in the ST category under the Government's notification of Feb. 1964? They were put under the category of denotified tribes, surprisingly, the four caste of Baoris, Kanjaras, Sawis and Naths were shunted out to the Scheduled Caste one from the denotified tribe category through a notification of July 21, 1977. Similarly, three of the nomadic tribes out of the ten—Banjaras, Gadia, Lohars, Kalbeliyas—were later categorized as OBCs while two others Rebaris and Jogi Nath—out of the 13 semi-nomadic tribes found a place in the OBC category. While these tribes, should have all been categorized as STs, they met gross injustice at the hands of the subsequent governments: and were not categorized properly obviously for political reasons. In fact, the class under which they are categorized are overcrowded and they have to compete with larger number of castes. They would have been far more comfortable as STs, if they were given their due. "The erstwhile criminal tribes can envy the better lot of the STs with 12 per cent reservation and with only 12 castes to compete with hardly any other competitive caste. But they have been categorized as either Scheduled Caste or OBCs where they have to compete with larger number of castes. They deserve a place in what is now being branded as the coveted class of ST.

SOME FACTS ABOUT RESERVATION

The Akhil Bharatiya Adivasi Vikas Parishad—a national body of the tribals, came out to oppose the demand of the Gujjars getting the ST status. The opposition was based on the following grounds:

(a) Dominant castes from all over the country has been demanding to be including in the ST list and Gujjars are one of them. Provisions in the Constitution for ST are meant only to the aboriginal and hill tribes of the North East region.

(b) Various commissions and committees constituted by the Union government so far, like the Kaka Kalelkar Commission in 1953, the BN Lokur Committee of 1965 and the Joint Parliamentary Committee of 1968, the National Commission for SC/ST in 2003 and the National Commission for ST have consistently rejected such demands. It may be recalled that in 1981, the Rajasthan government had sent a report to the Union government regarding the claim of the Gujjar caste in which it was stated that Gujjars are various commissions and basically milk sellers; and cattle breeders. The response of it is still pending.

(c) They are financially well-off and suffer from no shyness of contact with people of other castes. They also do not have primitive traits, so that they could not be considered for inclusion in ST list. Likewise, the Chopra Committee also did not make any recommendation in favour of the community granting a ST tag.

(d) During the Congress regime in 1981, then Chief Minister Shiv Charan Mathur had rejected the Gujjars' demand after the state government found that the community was primarily involved in milk production and had 'reasonably good land holding' which did not fulfil the requirements for categorizing them as STs. The C.M. found Gujjars had no primitive traits or no distinct culture which are common among tribals. In his recommendation to the Union government he clearly said that Gujjars did not "deserve a place in the list of STs". However, during the BJP rule in 1994, then chief minister Bhairon Singh Shekhawat played a key role in categorising them as GBC in a bid to strengthen his vote banks.

In the past 30 years, the Union government has not added any caste or community to the existing list of SCs and STs.

(e) During the stand off between the BJP Government and the Gujjars, the Raje Government of Rajasthan through its enjoy S.N. Thanvi (Sr. IAS officer) proposed the issue of according ST denotified tribe status to the community and sought a reply from Col. K.S. Bainsla. Even the Centre too felt that the state Government may follow the Maharashtra model to give a separate quota to the Gujjar community without breaching the legal-political restrictions, meaning thereby to categorize Gujjars as a 'denotified tribe' entitled to a separate quota (with 4-6%) as a sub-category under the GBC list. Article 16 of the Constitution enables the state government to make such laws.

RECOMMENDATIONS OF CHOPRA PANEL REPORT

The high powered justice Jasraj Chopra Committee which studied the Gujjar community's demand for ST status, presented its 290 page report to the Rajasthan CM Vasundhara Raje on 17th December 2007. As per the contents of the report, the committee recommended that the Gujjar community 'may' be given special reservation with Government jobs and number of scholarships be increased for their children. At present the community enjoys the benefits of GBCs. But the committee did not favour any tribal status to it. Instead of it, it suggested incentive package relating to jobs, reservations in academic institutions and scholarship. It is well known that the Meena community has a strong tribal community opposed granting any reservation in the Gujjar community. The Committee advised the state government to take the matter to the Union government to abrogate the criteria used so far to include any class of people in the fold of STs as these have become obsolete and outdated.

The committee further felt that judging eligibility of a group for tribal status, using the established criteria is impossible. The committee found that passing judgment on the candidature of a particular group (here Gujjars) for ST status in terms of presently used criteria is very difficult. It suggested that the present criteria used so far should be replaced by quantifiable criteria that are relevant in the present context. The Committee also advised the state government to take immediate steps to set-up a board to attend to the problems faced by people living a life of abject poverty in remote areas such as ravines, forests and hills where development has not reached.

On that basis, the Raje government decided to forward the report to the Centre without any comment or recommendation of its own. A committee headed by Rajya Sabha member Ramdas Agarwal was set-up to suggest to the government on how to implement recommendations on special packages relating to road, power drinking water, education, etc.

BJP's national treasure, Ramdas Agrawal, in his reaction to the report, blamed former Congress regime for not helping the cause of the Gujjar community in terms of granting ST status in 1981. During the last 26 years, in fact, no state government respond to reply to the Centre. The BJP however, had been concerned about the light of the Gujjar community within limitations of state government in granting the OBC status.

CONTENTS OF THE FACT

The Gujjar agitation held the functioning of state machinery to standstill and ransom for 26 days. Ultimately, the state Government agreed to grant 5% reservation to the Gujjar community and 14% to economically weaker sections of the society.

As per the demand, there is no mention of ST tag to be granted to the Gujjars in this agreement. But it was decided that the matter would be reserved to the Centre of a letter of

1999 suggesting to accommodate the demand under the ST category.

The Government would recommend 4% reservation for Gujjars under the denotified nomadic tribe category. The agreement raised the quota from 49% to 68% on the line of the Tamil Nadu model. Hoping that it would be put under the 9th Schedule as some states like Tamil Nadu have done so.

In brief, the Raje Government felt a sign of relief in view of pending the assembly elections in November, 2008.

THREATS OF AGITATION BY UPPER CASTES

In objection to the recent allotment of five per cent quota to the nomadic tribes, various associations representing castes falling in the general category have decided to challenge in court the recent agreement between the state government and the Gujjar representatives. Sawarn Aarakshan Manch, a conglomerate of such associations, has warned of a massive movement across the state.

"The outcome of the Gujjar agitation has proved that the government yields only to measure tactics. Hence, it would also have to follow a similar path. This was attended by the representatives from Brahmins, Rajputs, Vaishya and other general castes. They all vowed to challenge the decision of the Government. In short, on the eve of assembly elections the 14% reservation to these caste's has failed to please these castes.

REACTIONS AT THE VIABILITY OF RESERVATION

The pact is based on the please all formula. But the legal viability of the reservation granted by the Raje Government to the Gujjars and the economically weaker sections was debated and discussed at various forums. 'Citizen's Forum of Arya Samaj' organized, seminar on it, where some former judges and legal experts dubbed the 'Gujjar pact" as unconstitution, on the following grounds:

The Constitution mentions just two categories—SC and ST to whom reservation may be given. There is no mention of any third category called 'external', backward class under which the pact has given 5% reservation to the Gujjars.

The Supreme Court has categorically said that the total reservation cannot exceed 50%. Therefore, the agreement signed by the government is a total bluff. In his address, Justice Panchnama Jain said that is only under certain conditions that the SC allows for more than 50% reservation but since Rajasthan already has 49 per cent reservation, such a system cannot be brought into it.[1]

The Gujjars will not be able to get any reservation in the Lok Sabha or Rajya Sabha under this system. Section 16(4) of the Constitution allows for such a reservation only in jobs to socially and academically backward sections of the society on the 14% reservation for the economically backward sections. Jain clarified that there is no provision for reservation in the Constitution for them. Similarly, Justice Israni also termed it the reservation as illegal and, said that it is not for the state to decide as to who is a backward caste and who is not. That is the privilege of the Backward Tribes Commission. The state can only recommend a case and in the case of reservation, it can give it only from the 21% that has been kept for the backward castes and not from share of the unreserved category.

Others present for the occasion also termed the agreement as illegal saying that it was just a ploy of the government in an election year to gamer votes. They felt that even if the state is to pass the agreement in the Assembly and recommend the case to the Centre, the Centre would not accept it.

The quota plan would face the legal hurdle in view of the Supreme Court's decision given on 11th Jan., 2007 that laws put under the 9th schedule were and subject to judicial review. A nine Judge bench headed by CN Y.K. Sabharwal gave this ruling. Thus, the judiciary may take up the pact for view under the 50% ceiling. The ceiling was paid down in 1963. This was reiterated in a 2006 ruling by the SC bench saying that reservation beyond 50% resulted in reverse discrimination.

BOYCOTTING BJP BY GUJJARS' MAHAPANCHAYAT

Angry with the Vasundhara Raje government's stand over the reservation issue, Gujjars from across 11 states have decided to boycott Bharatiya Janata Party (BJP). These Gujjars gathered in Indore on 30th December, 2007 for a Mahapanchayat (general meeting) to discuss their strategy after the Rajasthan government did not recommend to the Centre that their demand for reservation as a Scheduled Tribe be considered. Leaders said that the community would boycott BJP in 11 states, including Madhya Pradesh, Rajasthan, Chhattisgarh and Delhi where the assembly polls are due in November, 2008.

Among those present at the "Mahapanchayat were two ministers. One of them was from BJP government in Madhya Pradesh and the other from Congress government in Maharashtra. About 10 crore population of those states is currently esteemed. In this grand meetings, some BJP leaders were also present and supported the gujjars' demand for ST status. The entire community was furious with BJPs attitude towards the community in Rajasthan. This heights the role of the caste in decision-making and influencing the party in power. Both the Centre and state were concerned of the decision in the background of vote-banks *vis-a-vis* pending the elections ahead in 2008-09.[2]

A tug-of-war was witnessed between the Centre and the Raje's government on granting ST status to Gujjar community. As per the meeting of ministries of Tribal Affairs and Social Justice's Law held on March 17, 2008 in New Delhi, the Rajasthan Government did not specify where does it stand on the politically fraught demand of the Gujjars for ST tag.

Instead of sending a request for ST status to Gujjars as laid down in the procedure the Rajasthan government sent the Justice Jasraj Chopra Commission report to the Tribal Ministry. The report had rejected the demand for ST tag. Instead, it recommended a special economic package for Gujjars, including separate job quota for them in 14 districts of the state. The ambiguity was designed to help state government find a way out of the caste quandary it has been pushed into because of the resistance from the politically crucial Meenas to the Gujjars' agitation for ST tag.

Likewise, the Centre too has been obviously reluctant to carry the can for the state government. It has insisted that state government follow the procedure, and make a specific recommendation, if, it so desired, for tribal status for Gujjars rather than courier the report of a state commission.

In fact, the Rajasthan government asked the Centre to change the five pronged criteria—primitive traits, distinctive culture, geographical isolation, shyness of contact with the community at large and backwardness. But tribal ministry sources said that the criteria cannot be changed, instead the state government should follow the rules.

SOME FACTS ABOUT THE PROTEST

- Gujjars, who are currently classified as OBCs, held protests all over Rajasthan from May 29 to June 4, 2007, and again in May-June 2008, to demand their inclusion in Scheduled Tribes category with a view to getting better benefits from quotas in education and government jobs.
- Gujjars' demand was being opposed by tribal Meenas who say they do not qualify as STs.
- Mrs. Raje persuaded Gujjars to withdraw agitation and announced formation of Justice Chopra Committee to make recommendations on their demand. The Chopra Committee report submitted in December 2007, says Gujjars do not fulfil the criteria required for granting of ST status but adds that criteria for inclusion in ST list is outdated.
- Chopra report was forwarded to Centre but no recommendation was made by Raje government.
- Another panel headed by BJP leader Ramdas Agarwal was given the assignment to looking into the recommendations of the Chopra report for uplift of Gujjars by providing them with special packages,
- With an eye on Gujjar vote-bank, BSP President Mayawati extended her support to the community's

> demand for scheduled tribe (ST) status at a massive rally held in Jaipur. Mayawati said that the BSP was not averse to the demand of Gujjars for identifying them as "tribals". She added, that quota for STs should be raised, and benefits of the raised quota should be passed on to Gujjars to fulfil their just-demands. In fact, her eyes were on the rural votes. She wanted to make BSP base in Rajasthan by adopting the UP model of 'Social Engineering' (Power-Sharing between upper and lower castes), so as to replace the BJP rule. The aim of the party was to popularize the UP model of Dalit-upper caste combination that proved her a success at the hosting. The UP CM was looking at the support of Brahmins and Jats.

The BSP's ambition is to emerge as a third force by aligning the key caste leadership, in a bid to spread its wings in Rajasthan. Therefore, the BSP organized its massive rally of Dalit Brahmin solidarity on 19th August, 2007 and Mayawati's confident man, Satish Mishra was here to woo Brahmins. It was joined by key Brahmin leaders and MLAs like Bhanwarlal Sharma, she was well aware of the absolulist style of the Raje government, and the fall out of expulsion of Jat leader Natwar Singh.

Most of our political parties have begun demanding reservation in private-aided educational institutions and deemed universities as well. They demand to regulate their fee structure and admission process in higher educational institutions since 'Education sector' has witnessed increasing commercialization and racketeering.

In view of resuming dialogue with the agitating Gujjars, three BJP MLAs from the Meena community sent their resignation and registered protests against state government's failure to control the Gujjar agitation. It was a pressure tactics of these Meena leaders as not to accept the Gujjars' demand (the ST tag). It was believed, that to polity the agitators, the ST status might be granted on the basis of the Union government's letter of 1999 seeking state governments opinion for including any caste in ST list.

NOW OBC TAG FOR RAJPUTS

After Gujjars in Rajasthan adopted the path of agitation demanding a tribal status, Rajputs also joined the quota bandwagon, too.

The 'general' category Rajputs have come forward demanding other backward classes (OBC) status for their community. On 20th June, Rajputs belonging to economically deprived sections held a massive rally here demanding that the community be classified as OBCs. A large number of men and women belonging to the community turned up at the rally organized by the Karni Sena—a body of Rajputs. Women in traditional 'poshakis' (attire) showed their solidarity with the community by raising their swords along with the men and vowing to fight for the cause of the community. The Sunday's rally wasted by Kokendra Singh Kalvi. Kalvi blamed the ruling BJP for triggering fresh caste conflicts in the state by including Jats in the list of OBCs. He said though Rajputs has supported the BJP, yet they were not rewarded.[3] Criticizing the ruling BJP and chief minister Vasundhara Raje, speakers told the gathering that poor among Rajputs had no political support and erstwhile rulers had no sympathy with them.

In fact, when the Union government had decided to club the economically backward community under GBC category. Rajput leaders had refused. They felt that they were too dignified to be classified as GBCs. But now, speakers said that the mistake had to be corrected as the community had lost considerably on both political and social spheres.

In Rajasthan, there are more than 60 lakh Rajputs belonging to Rathor, Shekhawat, Bhati, Chauhan, Tanwar, Kushwaha, Kachhawa, Ranawat, Chundawat, Panwar, Rajawat and other clans. Historical records mention that they were most trusted soldiers of erstwhile rulers. Later, they served the British and Indian army under the Raj. But since Independence, their numbers in the forces had gradually declined. What's more, their lands were taken away under various land reform laws after Independence and now, they were left with little land to make both ends meet. However, Rajput youth opted to join the Army, police and other services but now opportunities has shrunk as government jobs are limited and there is no quota/reservation for them.

After India's Independence, the Rajput community formed the Ram Rajya Parishad and later under the leadership of Gayatri Devi, the wife of erstwhile ruler of Jaipur, they supported the now defunct Swatantra Party which is now defund. With the emergence of Bhairon Singh Shekhawat as a towering leader who went on to become the Vice-President, the Rajput community tilted towards the BJP. Even then a few Rajputs made a headway in politics, the community in general gained nothing and continue to remain poor.

TOWARDS RESOLVING THE GUJJAR CRISIS

The CM in an effort to pacify the on going Gujjars' agitation agreed to give the community reservation under *'De-notified Tribals category'*, i.e. it would be entitled to state level jobs and educational facilities. According to the draft to be sent to the Union Government the state Government decided to provide 4%-6% reservations to Gujjars and 23 other normadic tribes and caste living in the state. Under this classification of nomadic and denotified tribes, they will get a special package for the Gujjar dominated areas, along with reservation (i.e. opening of schools and colleges, hospitals and other infrastructure development). But the Gujjar leaders dismissed the proposal, saying that they wanted a full tribal status and depicted to go ahead for Mahapadav (huge sit in).

In between twists and turns of the events—holding the Mahapanchayats by Gujjar leaders, two important developments were of significance. First, on the eve of the expiring the term of the justice 'Jasraj Chopra (12th Sept. 2007), the Rajasthan High Court gave a new turn to the Gujjar reservation issue by restraining the state Government from issuing any letter of recommendation to the Union Government for providing reservation to the Gujjar community. There was a tremendous pressure from the Gujjar Mahapanchayat to send such a letter to the Centre and not to extend the term of the Chopra committee. Second, the Raje Government allowed the fire brand Rajput leader. Devi Singh Bhatti, to rejoin the BJP after almost five years breakup. He had served as a Minister during the B.S. Shekhawat period. He was expelled from the party in 2004 at the behest of the Madam became of his opposition to the 'Parivartan Yatra' of Mrs. Raje as part its assembly poll campaign and the role of his social forum Samajik Nyaya Manch whose purpose was to demand reservation for the Rajput community. Bhati belongs to Bikaner (Kalayat constituency). After the assembly poll of 2004, this social outfit was converted in a political party. Bhati's re-entry into the BJP was to win the confidence of the Rajput community in the state. This was a testing time of Raje government over Gujjars' demand for tribal status.

CONCLUDING OBSERVATIONS

The 'caste war' in Rajasthan should not be taken in isolation, i.e. the trouble had its roots in the stay of operation of 27% OBC quota (including the creamy layer in it) in central educational institutions. The stay was given by the Supreme Court on 29th March, 2007. The week long violence a companied by Gujjar stir was termed a national shame by the Supreme Court on June 6, 2007 and directed the Government of Rajasthan, Haryana, UP and Delhi to submit their action taken reports on the caste incidents. The court took *suo moto* cognizance of those incidents which resulted in destruction of public-private properties during the agitation.

Gujjars' demand for a demotion in their social position from other backward classes—(OBCs) to Scheduled Tribes (STs) first set Rajasthan on fire and later burnt the social fabric to erupt as a full-blown caste war in North India.

The Gujjars' craving for ST status did not godown well with the Meena community as it feared that it might have to share the fruits of reservations with—another group, shrinking its access to government jobs. On the other hand, Gujjars felt that the OBC stable is full of many a caste stallion making it difficult for them to corner as many benefits has the Meenas have done through their ST tag. Thus the Gujjars' fight for ST status and the Meenas' fear of having to share the reservation pie led to clashes between them.

To identify caste as the very basis of reservations for educational institutions is a breach of constitutional mandate to make India a casteless society. If the 'caste' is made the starting point of backward class identification the ideal of a casteless society could never be achieved. In that sense, caste cannot be the basis of a 'class'. Article 15 of our Constitution talks about a special provision for backward classes but it is strange that the party in power took it as reservation and never thought of free books, free education and scholarship for backward students. Likewise, the identification of backward classes on the basis of religion is not justified and rational, and on that ground that the Supreme Court on 28th Sept., 2007 asked the A.P. government not to make any admission in professional institutions under the controversial ordinance providing 4% reservation to the Muslims of the state.

In our politics, the reservation policy has become a necessary evil to achieve social and economic transformation, more so in the absence of other instruments of change. However, escalating caste politics could in the long run blunt the edge of affirmative action and reduce the competitiveness of the Indian economy. The way forward is to facilitate traditionally oppressed communities to set-up their own businesses and educational institutions. This has been an integral part of social justice politics in south India. A Dalit Doon School, for instance, is the need of the hour. It could inspire a revolution in education and even change the grammar of quota politics.

Barack Obama's success (who is an African American) of presidential nominee for the Democratic Party was not due to quota politics. Nor his counterpart Hillary Clinton was in this race due to feminism. They are highly qualified, talentant for the highest office in the US. By contrast, quotas mean that merit and hard work repeatedly are trumped by Sectarian identity. Hence, Obama's success should serve us a lesson as it will provide unmatched incentive to the people of all colours and races in the US politics.

And finally, the quota laws should define backwardness and stipulate a period to review mechanism to exclude those who have crossed the backward barrier. In fact, reservation is a tool to break the social backward barrier. Giving it permanency will affect social engineering and harmony. Hence, in law itself the Government should lay down parameter for identification of the backward classes. If the reservation is not time bound, it would divide the society in the form of pressure groups. Nevertheless caste should not be a relevant factor in deciding backward tag for those who are still in traditional profession or switched over to other better occupations. Occupation can be a reliable guide but not caste in ascertaining social backwardness. As per the spirit of Article 45, one who has completed 10+2 education, he cannot be counted as educationally backward sections.

It is shocking that the Government itself is becoming a victim of its own populist measures by trying to please every section of society through reservation politics and its consequent expansion of seats in IITs or by building new IITs, forgetting the truth that poor quality—without good faculty and adequate infrastructure may result in irreparable damage to the brand IITs. This approach cannot make our country proud.

It is unfortunate that both Gujjars and Gorkhas have adopted an unacceptable mode of agitation, which is against the principles of democracy. Though our Constitution provides sample scope for hartals, they are misusing it by resorting to violence. At the outset, the Gujjars claiming an ST tag is illegitimate and so is the Gorkhas' demand. Violence will not provide any solution. Hence, the government must reject their demands and the Centre should not politicise the issue to gamer mileage in the wake of elections. No party or person is above the law. It would be wise on their part to mend their ways at the earliest before the situation reaches a point of no return.

Following three events blasts in Jaipur, quota agitations by trigged by the Gujjars in North India and the Noida double murder case (Aavshi) once again underlined/stressed the need to neutralise the police force from political influence. In this regard, the Supreme Court judgment in the Prakash Singh case directed to separate investigation and law and order duties, each a specialist police job.

In this 2006 judgment, the SC had quoted a letter written by the union Home Minister on April 13, 1997 to all State Governments imploring them to understand the "great national importance" in insulating the police force from "growing tendency of partisan or political interference in the discharge of its lawful functions of prevention and control of crime including investigation of cases and maintenance of public order". Almost all police reform commissions as well as the Law Commission had, the past, suggested separation of investigation and law and order wings of police.

The latest committee, headed by former attorney general Soli J. Sorabjee, in its report, suggested establishment of an autonomous Bureau of Criminal Investigation (BCI) in each state. It is imperative in crime investigation, especially homicide cases, that the police has sufficient forensic skills to lift all possible evidence from the crime scene at the earliest before TV crew and others run over the place.*

Notes and References

1. *The Times of India* News, June 24, 2008, p. 4.
2. In this reservation agitation led by Gujjars, at lest 26 persons killed in violent clashes from May 29 to June 4, 2007.
3. In the aftermath of agreement between the Government and the Gujjars, Kalvi agreed to dissolve the Munch and thereafter he was given the ministerial post by the CM. It was necessitated to win the support of Rajput community in view of the assembly elections ahead.

* For more details see the separate chapter of book on 'Police Reforms'.

CHAPTER

29

Electing the First-Ever Women President

Some Facts Behind Politics

With the UP assembly elections over in May 2007, the attention of the national political parties turned to electing the 13th President for the Rashtrapati Bhavan, scheduled to be held in July 2007. Because of prevailing coalition politics culture and the polarization of forces between the UPA and NDA, various names were floated and preliminary discussions were held to arrive at a consensus candidate, but in vain. The Congress-led UPA government commanded around 5,15,000 votes in comparison to NDA's about 3,50,000 votes. About 2,30,000 votes were enjoyed by other smaller parties.

THE METHOD OF ELECTION

The President is elected by an electoral college, consisting of the elected members of both Houses of Parliament and state legislative assemblies. Since the presidential elections of 1997, these include the assemblies of the National Capital Territory of Delhi and the Union Territory of Pondicherry. Only elected members form part of the electoral college, not those nominated to any of the legislative bodies. For the presidential elections, there were, thus, a total of 4,896 potential electors, consisting of 543 Lok Sabha members, 233 Rajya Sabha members and 4,120 MLAs.

The Constitution under Article 53(3) lays down the formula to determine the number of votes each elector' commands. The basic principle governing it is of Proportional Representation. The formula is :

(i) $$\frac{\text{Total Number of valid votes caste}}{\text{Number of seats} + 1}$$

+ quota fixed in the first stage.

and

(a) Value of the vote of an MLA is arrived at

$$\frac{\text{Population of the state}}{\text{Total number of elected members}} \times \frac{1}{1000}$$

= value of one vote

(b) Value of the vote of an

$$\frac{\text{MP Value of votes of all MLAs from the states}}{\text{Total No. of elected members of Parliament}}$$

Thus, the attempt is to ensure that each legislator's votes reflect the population he actually represents. This is how it is done: The population of each state is divided by 1,000 and then by the number of elected MLAs in the assembly to yield the value of each MLA's votes from that state. For example, the value of each Uttar Pradesh MLA's vote would be equal to the population of the state—83.85 million, divided by 1,000 and then by 403, the number of MLAs in UP, to give 208. A similar calculation shows that the value of each Sikkim MLA's vote equals just 7. In all, the MLAs of all the assemblies put together have 549,474 votes in the electoral college.

The system also tries to ensure a balance between the value of votes of MPs and state legislators. Hence, the next part of the formula takes this number 5,49,474 and it divides it by the total number of elected MPs, which is 776; to work out the value of each MP's votes. This, after rounding off, yields a figure of 708 votes per MP. Hence, the total value of all MPs votes equals 708 multiplied by 776, which is 5,49,408. The grand total of votes in the electoral college, thus, added up to 1,098,882, a little over a million. The population figure is the relevant census tally under the Constitution. However, since the 1974 presidential elections, the 1971, census has formed the basis for the above calculation. This is because delimitation of parliamentary constituencies has been frozen since that time. Ensuring proportional representation, therefore, meant freezing population statistics too.

It should be noted that under the single transferable vote formula, the candidate should have obtained the required quota of votes (51%) in the first count. If not reaches to it then, the second round of counting takes place to declare him the winner. This time, the balance of votes between the UPA and NDA was similar like that of 1969 because of the strength of votes of regional parties which was around 2.4 lakh votes. This strength was enough to swing the balance.

SEARCHING FOR PRESIDENT

Under the scheme of constitutional law, there was no question of conferring any kind of discretionary powers on the President. However, there are so many political occasions where in the brilliant and courageous President can exercise his 'situational discretion'. The framers did not aware of the rise of multi-party system in independent India nor about of coalition politics in Indian federal system.

The quest for a consensus President has so far proved elusive. Different persons have been named by different political parties in different criteria. What criteria did the Founding Fathers have in mind? That takes us to the questions: What was their conception of the role of the President in the Indian Republic?

The Constituent Assembly debates reveal that the overwhelming consensus was for adoption of the British parliamentary system of ministerial responsibility of the Westminster model in which the President as the constitutional head would be analogous to the monarch in England. In the words of Dr. Ambedker, the President occupies the same position as the king under the English Constitution. He is the head of the state but not the executive. He represents the nation but does not rule the nation. He is the symbol of the nation. The President of the Indian Union will be generally bound by the advice of his ministers. He can do nothing contrary to their advice nor can he do anything without their advice". But Dr. Ambedkar silenced H.V. Kamath who queried whether refusal to accept ministerial advice would amount to violation of the Constitution, with the words: "There is not the slightest doubt about it". Ambedkar's enunciation of the legal position has by and large been accepted by the Supreme Court in its landmark judgement in Shamsher Singh's case.*

Founders were hopeful that the President and Prime Minister would not be at loggerheads. It was perception of all members that our President would be a man of great dignity more than PM and the people will respect the President of Indian Republic.

In the Con-Assembly, the question of the President being a party man too was debated and Ramnarian Singh moved an amendment to the draft constitution that "President must not be a party man. The amendment was not carried out saying by Pt. Nehru that it is thing like asking a fish not be in water". However, there was total unanimity that after election the President should sever all his political connections and affiliations and "should not functions as a partyman. . . but with complete impartiality when he is in high office". He should act "as the guardian of all alike", and remain in office "as a man belonging to all or to none".

Above all, "the President should be a man, who like Caesar's wife should be above suspicion". How was this to be achieved? A suggestion of one of the framers, B. Das, was that all presents received by the President or his family should "accrue to the nation and become state property". He further said : "We have to see that our future President, his wife, his

* Soli J. Sorabjee, "Merit should be sole criteron", *The Times of India*, June 16, 1992, p. 18.

daughters or his daughters-in-law are not allowed to accept such presents". K. Santhanam's proposal was that the President after his election, "must declare his holdings in any company so that the public knows". Nehru thought that an express provision to that effect in the Constitution was not necessary, but agreed with Santhanam that any person in high responsible office should make some kind of disclosure of his connections with business and of his holdings and so on. He thought "there would be an advantage in that, whether he is President, or whether he is a minister or any other person in high responsible office".

Should the President be selected from any particular caste or community or religion or any region of India? Interestingly, there was an amendment moved by T. Channiah for election of the President by rotation either from the north or the south. According to him, "there will be great discontent among the minorities like the depressed classes and Muslims, when their claims are overlooked and when their very existence is not felt sufficient either in the administration of the country or when their claim for Presidentship is not contemplated at all".

But Kamath strongly opposed Channiah's amendment because it sought to divide the north from the south. He thundered, "When we are trying to build a strong state, when we are trying to wipe away all the differences of the past, when the division of the country on a communal basis has been accepted most reluctantly, it is amazing that an amendment of this kind should be propounded". R.K. Sidhwa was equally emphatic in rejecting the amendment. He said: "We cannot tolerate the election of the President community-wise, or province-wise or from the north, south, west or east of India, or we shall elect a Parsi, a Christian or a Muslim. The best man should be elected". (Emphasis added).

In the light of emergence of communalism, multi-party system and regional forces in national politics, it is a matter of deep concern that those expectations and the choice of non-partisan President is belied. Today, the basis of religion, caste (SC/ST) and community is taken as the sole criterion for the election of the Head of the State rather than a man of sound constitutional morality. The 13th Presidential election has brought to for some glaring facts.

FIRST-EVER WOMEN PRESIDENT ELECTED

UPA-Left nominee Pratibha Patil on 21st July won in Presidential election by a huge 3 lakh margin, defeating NDA-backed Independent candidate and Vice-President Bhairon Singh Shekhawat, to become the first woman head of state in a bitterly-contested poll that saw some cross voting from the BJP. (She is also first ever woman-President as commander-in-chief-of all the three armed forces of the country).

After the verdict, Shekhawat resigned as Vice-President. In the final count, Mrs. Patil got a vote value of 6,38,116 while Shekhawat secured 3,31,306 in an electoral college of 10.98 lakh. The winner got 65.82% of the valid votes. In Parliament, she got 442 votes against 232 of Shekhawat. In states and Union Territories put together, the winning candidate bagged 2,489 votes against the loser's 1,217.

Legislators in West Bengal, Kerala, Mizoram and Tripura voted only for Patil as Shekhawat drew a blank in both the states. It was a sweep for Patil in her home state Maharashtra, where she won the support of 223 MLAs leaving 58 for Shekhawat.

It was a similar story in Haryana with her getting 74 to Shekhawat's six, Himachal Pradesh (47-20), Manipur (55-5), Meghalaya (49-6) Andhra Pradesh (223-2), Arunachal Pradesh (58-1), Assam (92-20, four votes were invalid), Jharkhand (49-28), Delhi (50-19), Goa (25-14), Nagaland (40-12), Sikkim (31-1) and Tamil Nadu (171-59).* In Karnataka, it was a close fight as the BJP's ruling ally-Janata Dal (Secular) abstained from voting. (See the Table 2)

Dashing all hopes of the BJP-led alliance for a conscience vote in favour of Shekhawat, the 72-year old former Governor of Rajasthan significantly picked up votes of the value of over 10,000 more than expected helped by cross-voting. In BJP-ruled Gujarat and Chhattisgarh. (See the Table) In the other saffron-ruled state of Madhya Pradesh, Shekhawat did not poll even the expected votes. Eleven votes were declared invalid because of writings like 'Om' and 'Jai Shri Ram', apparently indicating rebellion in the BJP voters. Patil later described her win as the

* In Rajasthan the total value vote of 200 seats was 25,800.

TABLE 1

Sl. No.	Name of the Candidate	Year of Election	Percentage of Votes	Main Rival
(1)	(2)	(3)	(4)	(5)
1.	Dr. Rajendra Prasad	1952	83.81 (1 Election)	K.T. Shah
2.	Dr. Rajendra Prasad	1957	99.25 (2 Election)	N.N. Das
3.	Dr. S. Radhakrishnan	1962	98.24	Ch. Hariram
4.	Dr. Zakir Hussain	1967	56.23	K. Subbarao
5.	Mr. V.V. Giri	1969	48.0 (initially) 50 .22 (finally-because of second preferences)	N. Sanjiva Reddy
6.	Mr. Fakhruddin Ali Ahmad	1974	80.18	T. Chaudhuri
7.	Mr. Neelam Sanjeeva Reddy	1977	Consensus candidate	NIL
8.	Mr. Giani Zail Singh	1982	72.73	H.R. Khanna
9.	Mr. R. Venkataraman	1987	72.29	V. Krishna Iyer
10.	Dr. Shankar Dayal Sharma	1992	65.86	G.G. Swell
11.	Mr. K.R. Narayanan	1997	94.97	T.N. Seshan
12.	Dr. A.P.J. Abdul Kalam	2002	89.58	Laksmi Sahgal
13.	Ms. Pratibha D. Patil	2007	65.82	B.S. Shekhawat

Source : Election Commission of India, New Delhi.

TABLE 2

States	Patil	Shekhawat	The Swing Factor
Bihar	+7	+2	SP and independents
Gujarat	+6	-6	Cross Voting from BJP
Jharkhand	+6	-8	BJP, JD (D) and Independents
Orissa	+3	+7	Smaller Parties and Independents
Karnataka	+17	-2	Some JD (S) members may have voted
Rajasthan	+2	+ II	4 INLD MLAs, 14 Independents
West Bengal	—	-30	Trinamool's absence
Madhya Pradesh	+ 11	-12	Uma's supporter's votes invalid, Congress gained from others
Uttarakhand	-2	+7	Smaller parties and Independents voted for Shekhawat
Tamil Nadu	+4	+59	AIADMK votes for Shekhawat

Source : *The Indian Express*, New Delhi edn., July 22, 2007.

"victory of the principles", which the people of the country uphold. She said: "I am grateful to the voters. . . I am grateful to the people of India, the men and women of India".

CONSENSUS NOT EMERGED

For the first time in our coalition model, the national parties in the form of UPA and NDA failed to project a consensus candidate for the country's first citizen. Strangely, the Left did not agree to the name proposed by the Congress. The NDA had already announced to prope up the then V.P. of India, Bhairon Singh Shekhawat, as an independent candidate. The final call, thus, rested with the Congress whose decision was to be influenced by the UPA's ally, the Left.

Former President Dr. Abdul decided not to context against any one for a second term because of lack of consensus. He did not want to be 'party' to a political process and damage the name of Rashtrapati Bhavan, as during his tenure his efforts were for transforming it in a 'People's Bhavan'. He did not like it to be degenerated by involving in a political process. He was to demit his office on July 24, 2007. However, the two developments should be kept in mind that did not help in emergence of consensus in his favour. First, former President Kalam disapproved the proposal to confirm Justice S.L. Bhayana as a 'permanent judge' of the Delhi High Court in view of the strictures passed on him by the same court for acquitting Manu Sharma in the Jessica Lall murder case as a trial court judge. It may be noted that the President returned the file with a query. Kalam's intervention was significant because Prime Minister Manmohan Singh had cleared the same file in Feb. 2007, despite the HC structures. The collegiums of the High Court and Supreme Court has proposed Bhayana's confirmation a month before the December 18, 2006 judgment reversing Manu's acquittal.*

Second, in a bold step, he happened to return the Bill (Office of Profit) which displeased the powerful lobby of politicians, though Indian President can do so as per the Constitution. He did so for the first time because a matter of debate in Parliament.

SOME GLARING FACTS OF POLL

- The era of coalition did not witness the need to pick up the best among available candidates on the basis of 'consensus'. Instead, compulsion of coalition politics prevailed. Patil's candidature was based on compromise formula of the compulsions of coalition politics, specifically by the left-supporting to the Congress rule from 'outside' under the banner of 'secular credentials', though it equally symbolized the respect for women empowerment.
- Presidential poll presented visible cracks in the opposition groups of NDA with Shiv Sena supporting to the candidature of Mrs. Patil. Her Maharashtrian origin prevailed over party ideology.

* *The Times of India* News, New Delhi, March 2007, p. 1.

- The prospects of President Kalam getting a second term receded due UPA-Left alliance 'No' to second term for the incumbent. Dr. Kalam wisely maintained an enigmatic silence on his re-election. His secular brownie points were doubtless.
- For the first time, the UPA and NDA campaigned a war of words and a spate of charges against the candidates ahead of the presidential poll. Political parties digged dirt on the presidential candidates. It is worth-recalling that thirty-eight years ago, a similar campaign against presidential candidate, Dr. Sanjiv Reddy, was carried out by Mrs. Indira Gandhi through a colourful pamphlet in which he was alleged to have unfair relationship with various women.* The purpose or it to ensure the victory of V.V. Giri and to tarnish the image of Dr. Reddy.
- Mrs. Pratibha Patil was categorically reported to have stated that she would not a rubber-stamp President, if elected. The moot point raised was: would she have acted as an independent governor had Rajasthan been under the Congress rule? She was yet the choice of Mrs. Sonia Gandhi, because of her credentials as a Gandhi family loyalist, though she was a compromise candidate.
- As a Governor of Rajasthan, Pratibha Patil earned the reputation of simple living; she was a woman of simple habits. There were no parties/dinner during her tenure. Raj Bhavan was a picture of austerity with expense kept to the bare minimum.
- The July 19 poll put the long-standing alliance of BJP and Shiv Sena to acid test and it really proved doom in Maharashtra when its members voted against the BJP supported candidate, Sri Shekhawat and preferred Mrs. Patil being Maharashtrian. Ideologically, it caused a rift in NDA's unity. On the other hand, the RSS too questioned Shekhawat's decision to contest the 13th Presidential poll as an

* हरिहर स्वरूप, "राष्ट्रपति चुनावः आरोप–प्रत्यारोप", राजस्थान पत्रिका, अजमेर संस्करण, 7 जुलाई 2007, पृ. 8.

independent candidate, wondering what were the compelling reasons for the Sangh Pariwar veteran to do so, despite having his long association with RSS-BJP. In fact, BJP's internal power struggle was responsible for this sideline show.

- For the first time, no opinion poll survey was conducted about the possible outcome of Presidential poll, probably because of crystal clear of arithmetic number, which was heavily loaded in Mrs. Patil's favour, notwithstanding the call for a conscience vote from Shekhawat's poll managers the BSP led Mayawati had already announced to support the Patil candidature.
- For the first time, NDA-backed presidential candidate, Shekhawat voluntary declared his assets to put moral pressure on the UPA supported candidate Mrs. Patil, even though the declaration of assets is not required by law. Shekhawat sought to take the high moral ground hoping to have a similar response from Mrs. Pratibha. But the Congress did not response to the game-plan. It was taken nothing more than hard hitting anti-Patil pitch by the Shekhawat camp.
- For the first time in the constitutional history, an incumbent Vice-President was defeated by such a huge margin.
- The formation of the Third Front, rechristened as 'United National Progression Alliance"—UNPA, on the eve of the poll, consisting of regional forces proved to be non-starter in Indian politics. This alliance initially approached outgoing President Dr. Kalam to fight the election for the second term, but he declined the offer, saying that he did not like the name of the office damaged/degenerated, which he attempted to develop as 'People's Bhavan'.

LEGALITY OF UNPA'S CALL

The appeal of United National Progressive Alliance (UNPA) to its legislators (voters of electoral college) to abstain from voting provoked a legal controversy under section 18 of the Presidential and Vice-Presidential Elections Act, 1952, under which 'undue influence' on ongoing presidential poll is legally banned. The UNPA's call was interrupted as a formal appeal. In *Shiv Kripal Singh* v. *V.V. Giri* case, the Supreme Court laid down that the expression exercise of his electoral right contained in Section 18 does not mean that a voter is to be influenced by all legal and legitimate means.

According to the Election Commission's clarification, sought by the BJP against the possibility of issuing any 'whip' by the Third Front to their members to absent from voting, the members of Electoral College (MPs and MLAs) have the freedom not to exercise their franchise in the polling for the top constitutional institution and political parties can issue any whip to their members to vote or not to vote, compulsive abstention would not attract disqualification under 10th Schedule of the Constitution. Hence, voting is not compulsory in the Presidential election, which is different from voting by an MP or MLA inside the House. Voting outside is not a part of the proceeding of the House. As per the Election Commission, the Supreme Court has already referred to the question that arose before the Supreme Court in the *Kuldip Nayar* v. *Union of India* case on whether the provisions of the anti-defection law would be attracted in the case of election to the Rajya Sabha if an MLA votes in defiance of the party's directions.*

The court had held that an elector would not attract the penal provisions of the anti-defection law for defiance of party whip in the Rajya Sabha election. The apex court further had maintained that it was not correct to contend that the open ballot system tended to expose the MLAs to disqualification under the loth Schedule since that part of the Constitution was meant for different purposes. The EC also cited the SC order in the *Pasupati Nath Sukul* v. *Nemchandra Jain* case, which held that election to the Rajya Sabha by MLAs is a non-legislative activity and not a proceeding within the state legislature.

* Voting in Rajya Sabha elections is now done in a system of open balloting.

JAILED PERSON'S RIGHT TO VOTE

Should jailed MPs be given voting rights? The logic of the apex court was that an incarcerated MP could not be quoted with a citizen barred under Section 62 (5) of the Representation of People Act from voting if he/she was in jail. But MPs/ MLAs being people's representatives are indirectly casting vote on behalf of a constituency, depriving them of this right would amount to dis-enfranchising the entire population of the constituency. The petition was related to MPs namely Shahabuddin, S. Soren and Pappu Yadav. It may be recalled that the desirability of dis-franchising a person during the period of incarceration was discussed in the past two judgments of the apex court—*Mahendra Kumar Shastri* v. *The Union of India,* 1983 and *S. Radhakrishnan* v. *Union of India* in 1999) *vis-a-vis* the purity or validity of Section 62(5) of the R.P. Act that takes away the jailed person's right to vote. In its 1997 judgement in *Anukul Chandra* v. *Union of India,* the apex court aptly said: "The objective section 62(5) is to prevent criminalisation of politics and maintain probability in elections and that any provision which furthers that aim and promotes the object has to be welcomed as sub-serving a great constitutional purpose."*

TO CONCLUDE

The striking feature of this year's presidential poll was the consensus within Congress for a party loyalist Mrs. Pratibha Patil, she emerged as the front runner because of her credentials as a Gandhi family loyalist. The reason for Congress's insistence on a loyalist is understandable with Parliament elections scheduled in 2009, the Congress wanted its own man in Rashtrapati Bhavan. The party was aware that it can't be confident of a simple majority. Recent trends indicated that the days of single-party rule are over, not only at the Centre but in states as well. In the age of coalition politics and fractured mandates, the President can decisively impact the formation of a government. A 'friendly' President

* Quoted from the *Times of India,* New Delhi, 19 July, 2007, p. 7.

may help the party in office to push its case. Therefore, inspiring factor behind Mrs. Patil's candidature was not Maharashtrian ethnicity as powerful as was the loyalist factor.

The Indian President is not a mere ceremonial head. He has to embody the idea of a secular and liberal India—that's somewhat symbolic and ceremonial—but he is also the guardian of the Constitution during political crises and stalemates. Any President ought to be a politically aware being. Previous Presidents other than Radhakrishnan, Zakir Hussain and Dr. Abdul Kalam have had a stint in electoral politics.

PRESIDENT : THE FIRST SERVANT OF THE PEOPLE (?)

In the words of Mahatma Gandhi, the President of India is the 'chief servant' of the nation. It is a good symptom that Dr. Kalam tried to transform the office- or Bhavan into 'People's Bhavan. The important point is that a good human being is brought to this office so that he/she can protect and preserve our democratic norms and federal ethos.

The word 'servant' contrasts to the fact that all Indian Presidents have lived in a house bigger than those occupied by most head of states including the American President (it has over 350 rooms as compared to the 132 in the White House) and that too is occupied by the first servant of India in the Rashtrapathi Bhavan— earlier known as the Viceroy's House before 1947, which was a symbol of British colonial power. Today, the office is a bid more than ceremonial, as the job doesn't involve real work, except the odd constitutional crises cropping up in state politics.

Outgoing president Dr. Abdul Kalam—a man of missile and music, too wanted the Rashtrapati Bhavan (spread in six acre bungalow with the Mughal Garden) to convert it for people's visits.

Taking over the charge from "People's President" APJ Abdul Kalam, President Pratibha Patil said that she would be a "political President" instead of being a "Rubber stamp". Defining it she said that a president can pass on several suggestions to the government on several critical issues and government after due consideration can accept or reject those suggestions. She was keen on addressing problems faced by rural India and the deprived classes. Her mission deserves appreciation, of course.

Thirdly, ours is a federal—parliamentary democracy. The President cannot be (should not be) taken to have a mere ceremonial role. As a non-partisan entity, he is strictly circumscribed by some implied powers and functions, which may be termed a 'situational discretion'. Our past experience indicates how, despite the passage of 42nd and 44th Amendment Acts, the President managed to play an activist role, which was not meant to bring him with the PM in conflict, but meant to avoid a national crisis. It was constructive in enhancing our federal spirit. On obtaining political situations like hung parliament, political instability or any other constitutional crisis, our President can assert his autonomous role.

The Congress High Command was very much conscious of the history's experience how late President Jail Singh turned the Rashtrapati Bhavan into 'a challenge' to the then PM Rajiv Gandhi. UPA's stress on loyalty could be understood from the history or how K.R. Narayanan, reputed to be mild, surprised his sponsors by refusing to acquaintance in the move to dismiss Kalyan Singh's BJP Government in UP in 1992. Likewise, R. Venkataraman, the choice of the Congress, is reported to have suggested for a National Government at the Centre, consisting of all political parties. And K.R. Narayanan returned twice the Union Cabinet's decisions relating to imposition of President's rule in Bihar and UP. He dared to speak against the Gujarat communal riots of 2002.* Need not to mention of Kalam's role on the office of profit issue. On nomination issue, both the Left Front and the Congress leadership was wary of a President role who can, once appointed, may develop airs of autonomy. They wanted to ensure such a person in office who can be activist as per the taste of party in power.

Secondly, the 13th presidential election indicated the decline of Congress party's nationwide clout. It had to rely

* Ruchi Tyagi, "Election of the First Woman President", South Asia Politics, New Delhi, August 2007, pp. 28-30.

upon the support of the BSP, apart from the leftist parties in getting Mrs. Patil elected. The party had to opt for a consensus candidate, though under secular credentials of Pratibha Patil who as Governor of Rajasthan, returned the Anti-Conversion Bill passed by the state assembly. Her low profile personality also attracted the BSP. In fact, the spirit behind it was to keep away the communal forces.* It was, however, a plus factor for the UPA coalition that her Maharashtrian root fetched the support of Shiv Sena an NDA ally. This is yet another indication of the decline of BJP's ideology.

* 'Checkmate the NDA', The editorial of the *Times of India*, New Delhi, dated June 16, 2007, p. 7.

CHAPTER

30

Significance of BJP's Poll Victory in Gujarat

The BJP in Gujarat witnessed an unpredicted victory under Hindutva poster boy Narendra Modi. He powered the BJP to a near 2/3rd majority for a record fourth term giving him as CM. Those elections were seen as 'referendum' on the CM and the party could successfully win 177 seats out of 282—five less than a two third majority. The Congress got 62 seats while others got three seats.

In these elections, the BSP polled just 2% votes with no seat. It was a shock the part whose social engineering brought it to power in UP. Factors like anti-incumbency and challenge from party rebels could not stop the Modi Juggernaut. Of course, the saffron party suffered reverses in central Gujarat due to the post-Godhra riots in 2002. Even then, it was not a victory of communal ideology (Hindutva) but of his performance. The CM made the state a role model by undertaking several developmental projects.

The state overall witnessed 63 to 65% voters turnout in the two-phased poll. The base of Modi mantra was to focus on the achievements and development of the BJP in the state, for which over 2000 party workers had been trooped into Gujarat from other states to work for the party's cause but a large section of local functions of the party remained indifferent to the Gujarat campaign. The campaign, thus, missed of the star campaigners due to the Modi style of functioning. The campaign was focused on Modi's development agenda and its hard-line stance against terror, as opposed to Congress' lack of focus and inconsistency in terror during the poll campaign. The failure of the Congress to launch a leader to counter the CM's leadership was a factor behind the defeat of the Congress.

ISSUES AT STAKES

- Projection of L.K. Advani as the future PM;
- Modi's highly centralized campaign to blank out local incumbencies;
- Over-dependence of the Congress on BJP rebels;
- The clean image of CM Modi and his efforts for developmental projects;
- Highlighting the poor performance of the UPA government on issues like national security, corruption, minority vote-banks and unfair treatment with Gujarat;
- The impact of the battle cry and campaign slogan : '*Jeetega Gujarat*';
- Adversely fallout of the statement of Sonia Gandhi (Merchants of death). It was taken as an insult to Gujarat; and
- A tough response to terrorism, demanding a more honest approach in combating 'minorityism'.

CAMPAIGNING STRATEGY

Till the end of the poll-campaigning, Gujarat CM Narendra Modi was hopeful that the franchise would roup home a historic victory in these elections, as the elections were being fought by the people for the victory of the state on 'development'. The Congress leadership, on the contrary, claimed for 'a change' because of the fed up of the BJP rule.

The role of the Election Commission in holding the elections was appreciable as it ensured to see that the spirit of the code of conduct was followed. The Election Commission expressed its 'deep displeasure' over the violation by the CM and Congress President Sonia Gandhi during election campaign in Gujarat and served on the notice on their controversial remarks as the speeches aggravated differences between the two communities. Their controversial remarks were alleged related to the justification of the CM of his fake encounter and killing of Sohrabuddin Sheikh and Mrs. Sonia Gandhi's comment "merchants of death" during the poll campaign. The poll body asked them to be more cautious in future, reminding the sagacious advice and high expectations of the Supreme Court over the conduct of political leaders in election campaign. Like Modi and Mrs. Sonia, the senior Congress leader Digvijay Singh, who allegedly made references to Hindu terrorism, too was accused by the Election Commission of behaving discriminatory in taking up the cases of transfers.

The poll-campaign witnessed anti-party activities with the aim to out Modi forces during the elections. The two senior leaders—former CM Keshubhai Patel and Kashiram were prominent in this regard and they were suspended from the party while serving notice to Keshubhai Patel. In fact, the former CM was sure of a new third term for Narendra Modi on the eve of elections. His appeal was related to "a change in the dictatorial regime". He had compared Modi with Hitler and said that a 'mini-emergency like situation prevailed in Gujarat in the run up to the state elections, he attempted to affect adversely the BJP's poll prospects; Modi's detractor, Rana was also accused of 'sabotaging' the party's poll prospects and hobnobbing with the rival Congress. It may be noted that former CM Suresh Mehta had resigned from the BJP. He too was against the Modi leadership.

FACTORS BEHIND THE DEFEAT OF CONGRESS

The Congress leadership/campaign managers should be blamed for the party's defeat in Gujarat because of its being 'Over-dependence on BJP rebels.' It was a matter of concern, despite the ideology of past record of politics, that the party leadership hoped from a rebel leader Shankar Singh Vaghela of RSS to get captive vote bank in Congress' favour, without the hard work of organizing workers at the grass-roots level. So was the case from Shiv Sena's politician, Narayan Rane. Of course, these leaders are popular but irony was that the Congress approved their case. This mindset of the Congress caused immense harm to its ideology and organization. Why did the Congress not revive its own base as substitute to the BJP and why it failed to promote its regional leadership, in order to undercut the influence of other regional leaders? This created a leadership crisis in the party at grass-root levels.*

It is high time for the Congress to realize that its brand of secularism does not appeal to anyone anymore. It is nothing more than the policy of appeasement towards minorities. On the other hand, the BJP must equal alarm bells, as the concept of Hindutva is fast changing to Moditva. The days of bluff and bluster are over, as well as vote bank politics. Therefore, leaders of both the national parties must show some kind of statesmanship in their functioning. They must set aside their egos and ensure that the moderates' voice is given preference with soever for caste, creed or religion. Modi's victory in Gujarat shows that week-kneed-ambivalent Vajpayee style of politics will lead the BJP to disaster. Pseudo-secularism, has no sense before the need of a decent standard of living CM. Modi succeeded because he has improved the lot of Gujaratis in terms of good policies and development. That is why anti-incumbency factor was marginalized to win the poll-battle. The mandate reflects good performance and governance implying that the voters at large including Muslims voted for Modi.

Secondly, Modi will acquire a high profile national role within the BJP, pushing further to promote Gujarat as a model state. In 2002, the CJI registered a mild, soon to be withdrawn protest against the collapse of law and order. But today, enlightened industrialists lavish praise upon the CM.

---

* Abheek Barman, "How to Spoil a Party", *The Times of India*, New Delhi, December 27, 2007, p. 10.

Thirdly, democratisation of Congress is imperative for the party's vitality and health. Mrs. Sonia Gandhi should check sycophancy and allow active participation of workers in policy-making and implementation.

And lastly, these elections have been clean, blemish free and record of zero committal and terrorist violence. People in Gujarat has given a convenient go-by to the factors like narrow casteism and creed considerations for the cause of development and communal peaceful coexistence. It reflects the rise of middle class against pseudo-secularism. In this regard, Gujarat is only a curtain raiser, as it is our politicians who have created the two worlds of communal flames.

In other words, genuine mass leaders are under threat from a coterie that claims to have the ear of the party chief. It is necessary to have strong regional leaders in a federal polity as the Gujarat elections have shown. It is not that the Congress lacks state leaders, but the central leadership is shy of promoting them. Here, the Congress should take a clue from the BJP and the CPM; as both the parties have maintained a healthy balance between national and state leaders. A Congress revival is in the interest of the national polity. We have influential right and left wing parties in our politics, but the Congress has traditionally occupied the middle ground. That space ought to expand, perhaps with more parties competing to occupy it along with the Congress, for India to remain a liberal democracy. Otherwise, one of the extremes might move into a growing vacuum.

In brief, the poll victory of BJP's under the leadership of Narendra Modi as well as in Himachal Pradesh in the assembly elections of December 2007, is viewed both 'historic' and 'significance' for 're-emergence of BJP for national politics, because these elections were fought to symbolize a battle of ideologies—a tussle between perceptions of what is and what ought to be done for India. Modi's victory would have a significant impact for the course of Indian politics. Modi's victory was not only against the Congress, but it also symbolized the defeat of the important sections of the Sangh Parivar, specifically those which had opposed him behind the scenes. His leadership defied anti-incumbency factor and defeated a rebellion within the party. The electorate was urged to vote for an agenda which he skillfully combined Gujarat's 'sub-nationalism' and 'economic development'. The men in Modi's mask flooded his rallied highlighting the party's achievements, projecting as if the elections were a 'referendum'. Truly, these were so.

For the first time, the CM as a regional leader/politician dared to project himself above the party as well as the Sangh Parivar to fight the elections on his own basis. He won the poll battle despite the cold responses from the RSS/VHP. At state level, the CM espoused a personalized brand of Hindutva politics without the influence of RSS, preventing the rebellion led by Keshubhai Patel and Kashiram Rana. The Moditva approach was viewed as a shift to move strident Hindutva tone, combined with dire warnings about terrorist threats to India. This could mark BJP's revamped ideological approach at national level.

WHY GUJARAT BECAME 'HINDUTVA LABORATORY'

According Asghar Ali Engineer, Narendra Modi combined development discourse with Hindutva Mantra and won elections hands down. He, thus, proved the *'Hindutva Laboratory'* quite successful in Gujarat. Because trade and economic prosperity has been the lifeline for Gujaratis, the CM tried to win over rich traders of Muslim community alongwith upper caste. Hindu Gujaratis under the caption 'development', and he was sure of development factor. The blame of 'Maut ka Saudagar' of Sonia ben came later on against Hindutva. Yet the Gujarat model can be effective in other states—be that state MP or Rajasthan where the BJP in power, which are yet to face the next elections.* These states cannot become Hindutva laboratory because caste and community equations are very different nor development *a la* Gujarat can be effected in these two states. Then, the caste diversity is different.

It may be recalled that Mayawati's BSP won the UP assembly elections due to Dalit-Muslim bet and the active support of a section of upper caste voters. She enjoyed

* For this comments : "Gujarat Elections and Aftermath, Secular Perspective", Mumbai, Jan. 1-15-2008.

Charisma like that of Modi. In short, BJP's dream of repeating Gujarat can hardly be fulfilled other states.

MOVING TO MODITVA

After the victory of 'Moditva' in Gujarat, the meeting of the BJP's National Council in Jan. 2008 was meaningful as the party attacked the UPA's 'Aam Admi' credentials. The BJP leader L.K. Advani, as PM in awaiting placed the Gujarat CM above the gennext ranks. Modi's victory was praised here keeping in view the polls to be held in several states in 2008 and the Lok Sabha elections of 2009 the party voiced its concern for gaon, krishi and kisan' (village, agriculture and farmer) because the UPA's rule as hurt the rural population and its economy. It criticized the PM's communal budgeting; laying stress on minorities on the basis of 15 point programme as per the 11th plan.

Infact, the real boost for the BJP came from the Gujarat's victory and party chief Rajnath Singh believed to have won the states assembly polls in 2008. He appealed to other BJP CMs to replicate the Modi model of Governance and Modi's style of management and development. Modi's development agenda attracted the Gujarat middle class in a big way through improving rural electrification, water supply, roads, implementation of pro-poor plan like the NREG Scheme, etc.

BJP's announcement here that to reserve 33% of all posts in its organization at structure for women was meant to ensure the victory of the party. This is the first step towards the women's reservations (1/rd seats) which was sometimes back suggested by the Election Commission.

An Apprisal, The Modi's victory march proved to be a Waterloo in Indian politics. As a strong leader, he was a hero of poll-campaign management and proved to be a slayer of monsters; the 'monster' that Modi created in the post-Godhra period, so as to cast himself as a protective hero. In Modi and Moditva, the true saffron Avenger has finally been found.

The statement of Sonia Gandhi 'Hindutva terrorism' and 'Merchants of death'—in the second phase of poll campaign was filled in with excitement among the BJP's youth. In fact, Modi started off focusing development issues during the early phase of Gujarat election campaign, but Sonia's 'maut ke saudagar' speech on December 1, 2007, CM Modi lost little time in latching on to it, linking it with 'Gujarat pride.' His Sohrabuddin speech re-energized BJP's cadre from the speech given on December 3, at Mangrol. The twin issues reached the election Commission's office, inviting structures against the CM. But that ensured that the issues remained centre-stage, turning out at local factors like caste (Patel's) and grievances. Despite the claim of development in the states, he had to talk, 'Moditva, using 'Gujarat asmita' more in the way of Bal Thackeray used to do. The development theme was never discarded but it was well woven into a larger 'tame Gujarat, Chcho rhetoric designed to tap into a resentment against perceived discrimination against Gujarat'. Thus, the rebels within the BJP ranks proved toothless. The Patel vote did not, as expected, go against Modi, because the development platform he initially campaigned on had a firm foundation. Yes, Sonia's accusation (merchants of fear and death) on December, 2007 backfired and wounded 'Gujarat pride', which the CM tactfully re-invigorated, so as to ensure the BJP's electoral success at the hustings. Modi's impressive show rested on exploiting the tactical mistake of Mrs. Sonia Gandhi's statement (liars and merchants of death) or the comment of Digvijaysingh about Hindu terrorism in Gujarat. BJP's landslide victory since 1989 leaves no room for ambiguity in interpreting the Gujarat verdict as BJP's West Bengal. He has led the BJP to its 4th consecutive win in Gujarat defying all types of anti-incumbency factors.

The next test of the BJP leadership will the Karnataka assembly elections—a state the BJP leadership burut its finger by forming a short-live government on the support of H.D. Gowda's Janata Dal.

CHAPTER

31

Electoral Reforms

Foremost Priority for the Nation

The May 2, 2002 judgment of the Supreme Court of India, the June 28 order of the Election Commission (EC) directing full disclosures by candidates seeking elective office and the obvious resistance to those by the political parties served a great purpose, as the issue of electoral reforms was debated and discussed at best by our political parties and about 5 per cent of Indians, has now come to occupy the centrestage. Because of the court's judgment, rarely have people come together so spontaneously on any issue during peace time as on the above cited title. Different surveys, opinion polls and ballots indicate that an overwhelming majority of the people (95-99 per cent) was in support of full disclosure of the criminal record and financial details of the candidates. Equally impressively, our parties, cutting across ideological and political barriers, have stood as one in opposing disclosures. This divergence between the public mood and the views of the political establishment, is dangerous and detrimental to our democracy. In fact, our political parties have two concerns—one legitimate, and another spurious. First, the legitimate concern. The EC's order provided for rejection of nomination by the Returning Officer (RO) for furnishing wrong or incomplete information, or suppression of any material information. Political parties, understandably, were afraid that such unfettered discretion vested in the RO, can become an 'unguided missile' in the hands of their opponents. Therefore, they opposed to strengthening the hands of the Election Commission.

Former Chief Election Commissioner (CEC) G.V.C. Krishnamurthy, while addressing a seminar on *'Electoral Reforms: Foremost Priority for the Nation'* in New Delhi, on May 5, 2002 emphethetically said that the Election Commission must gear up to translate into action the landmark judgment of the Supreme Court of India for curbing criminalisation of politics and ensuring transparency in elections. The supreme Court's ruling did a marvelous job by giving its stamp of approval to the recommendations made by the Election Commission in 1998. Since then, the countrywide public opinion from various quarters has demanded them to be urgently translated into action on the basis of the past ten year's experience, specifically making amendments in the Representation of People Act and the Code of conduct rules, 1961. Calling for a 'microscopic examination' of the electoral laws every ten years, Krishnamurthy said, "Parliament mirrors the standard of the people of the country and is its *de facto* cockpit. Thanks to the judgment, only deserving citizens can now enter Parliament. He also said that the EC's decision in 1998 making it mandatory for candidates to file an affidavit and stating their background had helped in bringing down non-serious candidates and those with a criminal past". He further pointed out that, "During the 1996 Parliamentary elections, out of 13952 candidates for 543 seats, 1500 had cases relating to crimes like murder, rape and extortion against them. But in 1998 the number reduced to just 150. Even Prime minister A.B. Vajpayee was asked to file an affidavit".

The National Commission to Review the Working of the Constitution, it may be noted, also recommended mandatory imprisonment and disqualification for spreading caste or communal hatred during election campaigns disqualification of those charged with serious offences and de-recognition of parties putting up such candidates, permanent disqualification of those convicted of heinous crimes and speed by trial of election petitions and of cases involving politicians/candidates. Also included were disqualification on conviction to apply to sitting legislators and ceiling of election expenses to be progressively raised with increasing costs but to cover all expenses by party, friends, etc.

With a view to reducing the costs of elections, the Commission recommended that, to the extent possible, state and parliamentary elections should be held simultaneously, the campaign period should be reduced, no one should be allowed to contest from more than one constituency, the code of conduct should be made into a law and its violation should attract penal action. Besides intra-state delimitation of constituencies, the Commission has categorically recommended rotation of reserved seats. None of these electoral reform suggestions call for any constitutional amendment, nor can such matters be left to courts. Amending the Representation of People Act and the rules can achieve the desired results, provided there is a strong will to act by the party in office.

The ordinance issued by the Centre on electoral reforms sadly pushed all those recommendations into dustbin. It was against the population sentiment as well as it was meant to counter the draft recommendations of the Constitutional Review Committee. The Commission made a compressive report *inter alia* on electoral reforms; but no serious attention was paid to the report by our leaders and the government.

One of the issues that contained in the report was related to 70 percent of our representatives who are elected on a minority of votes cast. The representational legitimacy these elected has usually been doubtful. The drafting and editorial committee of the Commission in its unanimous report based on decisions of the Commission, proposed that we should only have representatives who win on the basis of 50 per cent plus one vote. If, in the first round, nobody gets over 50 per cent, then there should be a run-off contest the very next day or soon thereafter between the top two candidates. With the use of electronic voting machines, the constituency would know at the end of the day whether a run-off was necessary. If so, the announcement would mention the names of the two candidates. The final results would encourage pre-election agreements among parties and lead to moderation and stability. Thus, with each successive election, the number of run-offs would be reduced. It was hoped that it would resolve the problem of representation and make it in the interest of parties to widen their appeal beyond narrow vote-banks. Issues of good governance rather than narrow identities might start to surface in the political vocabulary.

The proposal evoked a favourable response from people. It also found overwhelming support in the Commission and the general feeling was that this one proposal had the greatest potential to rid Indian politics of the scourge of casteism and communalism. In the final report, however, the recommendation was sadly diluted considerably saying that the government should examine this issue, consult parties and other interests and evaluate its acceptability and benefits.

Another worth-considering recommendation of it was making voting a 'citizenship obligation', as is already compulsory in many countries. It was suggested that this responsibility could be entrusted to the panchayats. According to one of its member, the proposal was agreed upon unanimously but was dropped in the final report.[1] However, the suggestion is still relevant.

PRESIDENTIAL ACTIVISM

The President of India, Dr. A.P.J. Abdul Kalam's decision to return the Representative of the People (Amendment) Ordinance, 2002 for reconsideration was, of course, a great morale booster for all those who sought peaceful transformation in our democratic set-up. He applied the breaks on the controversial electoral reforms ordinance, as the Ordinance was a brazen move to overturn the Supreme Court's specific directives on electoral reforms and warranted a second, unhurried look. The issue at hand is not one of Parliament *versus* the Supreme Court, as conveniently projected by the political class, but of upholding a fundamental right—the Right to Information. When the Supreme Court declared it mandatory for contestants to publicise their assets and antecedents, it did so on the premise that the common voter had the right to ascertain the background of the person he or she was going to nominate to the public domain. The court argued that the right to know was a fundamental right flowing from the right to freedom of speech and expression of Article 19th the Constitution.

The President gave the government the opportunity to gracefully resile from its indefensible position, hoping that the Cabinet would drop the Ordinance and introduce a comprehensive electoral reform Bill in Parliament providing for full disclosures and funding reform, among other. The disclosure issue was an opportunity, not a threat, to the politicians to break loose of the vicious cycle of criminalisation, excessive and unaccountable expenditure, endemic corruption and increasing illegitimacy of the political process. If the government resorts to brinkmanship and reiterates its recommendation, the President will have no other moral and constitutional option but to seek the opinion of the Supreme Court under Article 143 of the Constitution.[2]

Instead of resorting to its genuine concern in the rule 4 of the Conduct of Elections Rule, 1961, the government chose to recommend promulgation of an Ordinance whose only real intent and purpose was to substantially nullify the judgment of the Supreme Court, declaring the voters' right to information about the candidates a fundamental right derived from Article 19(1) of the Constitution. There is nothing new in it, as the government has previously introduced legislation to nullify court judgments. The court's ruling on election expenditure ceilings and the *Shah Bano case* of 1986, are two such instances. But never before was fundamental right sought to be unreasonably and arbitrarily restricted by a legislation, in order to nullify the apex court judgment. Section 33A, which this ordinance seeks to introduce in the RP Act, explicitly prohibits electing of any information from candidates by means of a Court order or the EC's directives. This is unconstitutional, and violative of Article 13 of the Constitution, which prohibits making any law which takes away or abridges the fundamental rights.[3]

ELECTION COMMISSION'S BOLDNESS IN GUJARAT

The Election Commission won its first victory when the Supreme Court gave its ruling on 2nd Sept., 2002 that "there is nothing wrong in holding the Gujarat Poll in November-December, 2002. It was the first severe setback to the BJP's attempt. The court's ruling compelled terms of compulsion of Article 174 of the constitution (six month duration is not applicable here). The Election Commission, it should be recalled, never made any recommendation for imposing President's rule, as the Election Commission was blamed for its partisan role. The reference before the Supreme Court was; "can the EC frame a schedule for the elections to any assembly on the premise that any infraction of the mandate under Article 174 would be remedied by resorting to Article 356. . ."[4] Against this background, the EC's order was historic as it did not hide behind any technicalities. The entire debate on holding the Gujarat elections had focused on the narrow question of interpreting Article 74. The EC's order refused to fall into either of the traps and affirmed that the assembly should normally meet every six months even after the dissolution of the house and the constitutional mandate to hold free and fair elections must take precedence over any technical requirements.

The EC's order, in brief is all the more important in the context of all the intimidation tactics, threats of packing the Commission with more members, rumours about possible impeachment of the CEC and so on. If all this was a chilling reminder of the pre-emergency days of Congress rule, the Commission's order itself was reminiscent of justice Jagmohan Lal Sinha's bold ruling against Indira Gandhi, 1975.

The Election Commission's Order not to take out 'Gaurav Yatra' was directly related to the law and order situation, which candidly exposed the double speak of the Government in the Presidential reference. The Election Commission's order nailed the lie of the Modi Government using his own documents relating to the post-riot situation *vis-a-vis*, the rehabilitation in the violence affected areas and the ordering of the revision of electoral rolls.

The assembly elections brought to the fore—a nadir of the politician—bureaucrat nexus. The rioting arson and burning men, women and children with their property would not have been possible but for the connivance of bureaucrats and police. This nexus was further confirmed how the upright IAS officers like Harish Mander was transferred twenty-two times in his twenty years of service. His account of Gujarat atrocities (which was worse than of what happened in 1984 in Delhi) compelled him to act as per his inner voice and resign. Against this background, the most unfortunate development was the 'Fatwa' declared by the Imam of the Ahmedabad Jama Masjid to defeat the BJP and to support the Congress at the hustings, though the Muslims blamed the 'Fatwa' for the defeat of the Congress in the poll battle. This led to react the Hindutva forces. This tendency must be discouraged as there is no room for politics in religion.

EPILOGUE

The application of adult franchise has led to the slow but steadily increasing political consciousness of the Indian voters. But it is a sad phenomenon that the Indian electorate is still heavily influenced by several irrational forces and factors like caste, sub-caste, community, religion, money-muscle power, and above all, charismatic personality and dynastic rule have assumed importance. Our electoral system is governed by a mixed political culture of traditional values (like feudalism and caste-factor) and the influence of western democratic values. The overall picture of our self-governance indicates that we are riddled with many ills. One of them is the politics of corruption and criminalisation, as has been highlighted by former Home Secretary Mr. N.N. Vohra. The Vohra report reads: "A network of mafia is virtually running a parallel Government pushing the same apparatus into irrelevance." The Vohra committee report in its severest indictment of the polity and the governance has exposed the ugly 'networking of money, muscle and criminal power'. The networking of the CBI, the PMO and the Defence Ministry relating to the Bofors Gun scam, the Hawala case and others are the key illustrations to mention. Sadly, in some cases, the CSI was supervised by the judges directly. This background has tremendously weakened the very root of democratic set-up, i.e. 'We, the people of India'. It is now known as 'We, the political parties of the country'. Consequently, the authority of the 'State' at all levels have been marginalised and its role is both evasive as well as unresponsive.

A critical study of the past experience in electoral politics, on the basis of the performance of the election commission, electoral processes and the functioning of political parties, warrants the following important suggestions to be taken into account:

(i) The manual of electoral laws should be revised so as to define the term 'political party' and its area of operation in our polity. There is a dire need to institutionalise the whole party-system structure in our constitutional law. Likewise, corrupt practices relating to misuse of official machinery, the money-muscle power, and the status of care-taker government etc., should be defined in the RP Act, 1951. The Gujarat-experience should serve us a warning to the set-up.

(ii) The Election Commission of India should have the constitutional authority to make regulations for; (a) compulsory registration of our political parties; (b) compulsory maintenance of accounts including all receipts and donations and minute book year-wise. They should be available to voters; (c) Compulsory audit of account by an agency to be named by the Election Commission itself, (d) Submission of periodic reports to the Commission; and (e) Residuary powers relating to the role of political parties. Our political parties, in short, are not above law and they are bound to disclose the sources of funding under section 77 of the RP Act.

(iii) Our Election Commission should be governed by identical constitutional provisions, as are applicable to the secretariat of Parliament, the Supreme Court of India and Controller and Auditor-General of

India. It would enable the Commission to have an electoral machinery of its choice to discharge its functions without and kind of political influences or intervention.

(iv) The Anti-Defection Law, 1985 must be reviewed and revised in the light of the functioning of coalition politics model in the country, requiring that the President of India and state Governors must be given specific powers to consult the Election Commission in the matters of disqualifying elected members, if he or she defects from the party on whose ticket he or she was elected to a legislative body.

(v) Article 326(6) should be changed so as to enable the C.E.C. to utilise the services of the polling staff on the eve of elections. This poll-staff should be accountable to the Commission for its roles and performance during the election period.

(vi) The idea of state-funding should be debated and the total outlay of about Rs. 1000 crore should be created. Ways must be found to make the electoral process more wholesome, less expensive and free from money-muscle power.

(vii) The Election Commission should be empowered to deal with the cases relating to the violation of the Model Code of Conduct for political parties under section 8 of the RP Act. It lacks teeth today.

(viii) The Lok Pal institution should be created on the constitutional basis, requiring to deal with the cases of corruption and criminalisation. Likewise, the Central Vigilance Commission and the CSI should be reorganised with an independent character.[5]

All these reforms are not new; as they have already been advocated by the former Chief Election Commissioners in their reports since 1983. The Goswami report also contains them. Because of the lack of a 'strong will' on the part of our political parties, these reports are gathering dust in offices. Hence, the country needs a 1974-type mass movement to create political awakening amongst the grass-roots people and to ensure answerability of the elected representatives.

The Mafia raj has brought to an end the working of the democratic, order of the country.* Ministerial immunity is the very root cause of the prevailing corruption in public life. What the Indian Constitution and legal system have solely Jacked all the years is any independent machinery of investigation into charges of corruption against the men of high places/positions. The Lok Pal as a constitutional body and an independent functioning of the CVC are the only answer to arrest the fallout of corrupt practices. The role of our Judiciary (known as Judicial activism) has come forward to checkmate the malady, but the lack of public activism has made the rulers/authorities to escape from the punishment and penalty of law. The remedy of the criminalisation of politics as per the Vohra report, lies in speeding up justice, stopping political interference in prosecutions and weeding out corrupt elements. It has suggested the creation of a model· agency to collect information from all sources and pursue cases against criminal elements. The resolution of all electoral cases on time-bound basis need of the hour.

Therefore, the right to information should be ensured to make all government activities open to 'we', the people of India. This warrants drastic changes in the Official Secrets Act, 1923, which is still a sign of the British colonial legacy. Self-government is meaningful only with an informed public.

Both the proposals, making fixed term of legislatures for the cause of 'stability' and simultaneous Lok Sabha and assembly elections, have not received due favourable response from even the NDA coalition partners. Many political observers have hailed the move as a great strategic master stroke of the BJP. With the opposition still bitterly divided over the issue of Sonia Gandhi's leadership, the BJP's idea is to ensure electoral gains. The party in its 'Chintan Bathak' (the strategy of Brain-Storming session) noted increasingly alienation of its coalition partners from post-Gujarat events to its core Hindutva agenda. Both the suggestions are not

* The dramatic arrest of Siwan MP (RJD Leader) Mohd. Shahabuddin presents the classic example of politics of criminalisation in Bihar. He berated the D.G.P. and threatened to fix him on arresting him, as he had been moving about scotfree for years despite several criminal cases against him.

relevant to the norms parliamentary system, specifically because of the rise of multi-party system, instead one party dominant system. The functioning of coalition model in India has become almost a harsh reality. The party feels that the Atalji *v.* Soniaji shift in focus will work entirely to the BJP's advantage, if synchonised polls are held. Therefore, the Election Commission has termed the idea as anti-democratic in nature.

Notes and References

1. Subhash, C. Kashyap, "Against Popular Will: Electoral Reforms Run-off Rails", *The Times of India*, New Delhi, September 9, 2002, p. 14.
2. 'A Little Gesture', *Editorial of The Times of India*, August 24, 2002.
3. Jayaprakash Narayan, "Fundamental Knowledge What Politicians Owe The People", *Ibid.*, August 24, 2002, p. 12.
4. Yogendra Yadav, "Free And Fair Elections", *The Times of India*, 22 August, 2002, p. 14.
5. See my paper published in CB Barthwal's, Indian Administration Since Independence, Lucknow, Bharat Book Centre, 2003, pp. 286-89.
6. P.R. Ram, "Threats to Indian Constitution", Secular Perspective, Volume 3, No. 4, Feb. 16-29, 2000, Mumbai.

CHAPTER

32

BJP's Electoral Victory in Himachal Pradesh

On the pattern of the Gujarat assembly elections, the BJP swept up a clear majority in the assembly election held in December 2007—just five days after the Gujarat elections. This was the second blow to the Congress within a week. The BJP won 4th of the 68 seats in the assembly while the Congress won only 23 seats. The Congress was victim of poor performance, factionalism, anti-incumbency wave and corruption. The BSP won one seat for the first time, while independents captured three seats. The BJP notched the Virbhadra Singh Government under the leadership of Prem Kumar Dhumal. Earlier, the Congress had begged 43 seats in the 2003 assembly election. The HP's victory sent a strong signal in the BJP's circle to win the Lok Sabha elections due in 2009, 18 months away. For the BJP, these results were taken trailers of the Lok Sabha election.

For Professor-turned politician, his (Dhumal's) victory was emphatic due to his aggressive campaigning. He was sworn in as CM on 30th December 2007 by Governor V.S. Kokje. He was popularly known as "sadak wala mukhya mantri", for a number of road projects took up during his previous tenure (1998-2003).

According to Dr. Subhash, C. Kashyap, the BJP's thumping majority in the Gujarat elections under Narendra Modi was the most remarkable event of 2007 because the triumph was received where there was a massive gang up against the CM—both from within and outside, including the Media. For his victory, credit should be shared by the party, ideology, its workers and the role of state level leadership. The following three most important factors should be taken into considerations:*

(i) The Development-oriented and largely corruption-free good governance by the CM during the tenure,
(ii) The backlash to the unashamed and overdone rhetoric of minority interest protection as part of vote-bank politics of the Congress, and
(iii) The poor election campaign management by the Congress leadership putting their supreme leader Rahul Gandhi at par and face to face against C.M. Narendra Modi.

After the stunned successive defeats; not only the Congress Party, but also other parties are bound to rethink of the role of the factors, namely, rebellion within the organization, corruption charges, excessive reliance on caste rebel factor and so on. The Gujarat outcome has sounded a warning to the Congress which relied excessively for the rebel factor. On the contrary, parties have to rest on the alliance of social base. They cannot ignore the emergence of a new class (OBCs or SC (ST)) of political clout.

As regards the Congress the defeat was humiliating for India's grand old party. It did a mistake to rely on Shanker Singh Vaghela who had defected to the Congress from the BJP. The leadership has to review the political scenario why the party in J&K, Maharashtra or Tamil Nadu, has to coexist

* The Editorial page of South Asia Politics, New Delhi, Jan. 2008 Issue, pp. 2-3.

within regional parties often uneasily with the coalition partners.

According to an analysts : If this trend continues, the Congress faces the threat of turning into India's first exclusively national party one that fights and might win federal elections, but loses every state to local rivals. Parenthetically, the BJP is the exact mirror image of the Congress: in Madhya Pradesh, Rajasthan and now Gujarat, it has won state elections. (Now in Karnataka also) but its national leadership is geriatric and the favourite pastime of its younger leaders is to stab each other in the back. Its once-popular vote catcher, Uma Bharti, has walked out of the fold in a huff.

Today, the biggest question Congress president Sonia Gandhi needs to ask is not about Gujarat, it is this: Why doesn't the Congress have stable, influential leaders in most of the states.*

It is well known that former Congress Chief Ministers lost the poll battle due to the anti-incumbency factor be he Digvijay Singh of MP or Ashok Gehlot of Rajasthan and S.M. Krishna of Karnataka. They all once were very popular leaders in their respective states. Why do these leaders spend much of their time in Delhi after the defeat, and why not they have been asked to prepare the ground for next assembly elections. Why S.M. Krishna was shifted to governor's house in Maharashtra who was once a very popular leader of Karnataka politics. It is irony of the Congress culture that it has never allowed to build regional leadership in their states. It is how quite irrelevant to stick to Mrs. Sonia or Rahul or Priyanka. They may be the person individual leaders, but cannot defeat the local leaders like Mayawati or Modi, nor can the Congress ignore the basic needs of masses, infrastructure or economic reforms.

Today, the Congress has lost the generation of powerful local leaders and organizations, which used to be in 1960s. It is worth-recalling how Mrs. Indira Gandhi centralized power to undercut the influential and regional leaders like Morarji

---

* Abheek Barmar, "How to Spoil a Party", *Ibid.*, dated December 27, 2007, p. 10.

Desai, Nijalingappa, Atulya Ghosh, Rama Rao and so on and they all had to leave the party. In the wake of this vacuum of regional leadership, the party weakened the process of the grassroot building of organization. It made the base of the rise of BJP. The grand party is losing every election of state to local rivals leaders whose clout had not been accommodated in the organization. The Indira Gandhi's strategy has lost relevance in the wake of the change in Indian federal set-up. The defeat of the Congress in Karnataka again underlines the needs to revamp the organization.

Tripura's ruling Left Front stormed back to power for a fourth straight term while Meghalaya registered a fractured verdict. These elections were held in March 2008, and were a setback to the Congress party after the polls in UP and Gujarat. In Tripura, dominant partner CPM on its own won 46 seats of the total 49 bagged by the Left Front in the 60-member assembly, while its allies RSP and CPI won two seats and one respectively. Thus, the opposition Congress managed to win just 10 seats, while its ally, the Indigenous Nationalist party of Tripura, won one. Notable winners included chief minister Manik Sarkar, who won the Dhanpur seat by a margin of 2,918 votes.

In Meghalaya, the polls threw up a hung House with Congress emerging the single largest party, bagging 25 out of 59 seats for which polling was held. The Congress party which

TABLE A

Tripura		*Meghalaya*	
Total seats	60	Total seats	60
Elections held	60	Elections held	59
CPM	46	Cong.	25
RSP	02	NCP	15
CPI	01	UDP	11
Cong.	10	BJP	01
Others	01	Ind./Others	07

Note : The Governor's role as an agent, in this state is separately discussed in the study.

led a coalition ministry in the outgoing assembly, formed a government with the support of independents and two smaller parties—Hill State People's Democratic Party and Khun Hynnieutrip National Awakening Movement. The NCP, led by former Lok Sabha Speaker P.A. Sangma, garnered 15 seats followed by UDP with 11 and HSPDP with two. KHNAM and BJP won one seat each. Independents romped home in five constituencies. The NCP, a constituent of the UPA government at the Centre staked to form the coalition government.

BJP's VICTORY IN KARNATAKA : A HISTORIC TURN

On the eve of the assembly elections in Karnataka, the BJP high command thought it fit to go alone and not to join any coalition in these elections. Once bitten twice shy the BJP declared in public to sit in opposition if it failed to get a clear majority in the legislative assembly. In the words of BJP leader L.K. Advani, "If we do not get a clear mandate to rule Karnataka, we will prefer to sit in opposition than go for alliances". In an appeal to the doctorate, he demanded a chance to form a stable government on its own ... you have given so far the Congress many a chance and also given various formations of the Janata Dal. This time, give BJP a chance to set things rights in difficult and trust us we will never betray trust.

NO PRE- OR POST-ALLIANCE

History speaks how a fractured verdict in the May 2004 general elections led to the formation of the first coalition government in the state by a defeated Congress and an upbeat JD-S, which had won respectively 64 and 58 seats. After 20 months, former Chief Minister H.D. Kumaraswamy revolted against the Congress-led government in January 2006 and withdrew support to its Chief Minister N. Dharam Singh joining hands with the BJP. Kumaraswamy formed the second coalition government in February 2006 on the condition that he would transfer power to his deputy, Yeddurappa of BJP, after 20 months rule in October 2007. But the deal was not honoured at the time of its maturity. This resulted in the invocation of Article 356. The Janata Dal (Secular) be frayed the BJP in the matter of transfer of power to BJP in October, 2007.

Karnataka was set for a three phase polling in May, 10, 16 and 22, 2008 to elect a new Government by its 55 million voters. The polls were held under President's rule clamped in November 20, 2007, after the fall of the seven-day BJP coalition government following the withdrawal of support by its coalition partner JD(S). Against this background of breach of trust, the BJP ruled out pre- and post-poll alliances. In an appeal to the voters, the votes were asked to ensure that 2004 (a hung assembly) was not repeated in 2008.

The first ever BJP government in the South was sworn in on May 28, 2008 under the leadership of B.S. Yeddurappa. The party got almost a majority (110 seats), just 03 short of winning 113 seats required for a simple majority in the 224 member assembly. The four Independents out of seven extended support to the new ministry. They were the party's rebels. The Congress won 80 seats. The JD(S) remained third bagging 28 seats. In the previous elections, the BJP and Congress had 79 and 65 seats, respectively. The JD(S) got 58 seats.

The Congress shocked a poll results and possibly for bad showing due to the open infighting. The party was lured into a false brief that elections would be set to be delayed for November due to the new delimitation of constituencies as the Election Commission also initially indicated the Congress was unprepared. According to campaign managers, the other factors that were responsible for the defeat of the Congress and the victory of the BJP were as follows:

- There was a neck to neck race between the BJP and Congress. But the much publicized return of S.M. Krishna (former Governor of Maharashtra) to politics did not respond favourably. The real leadership should have been of Siddaramaiah, the GBC leader who rebelled in JP(S) to join the Congress.
- The poll managers of Congress failed to mobilize workers of minorities this time.
- These results cemented Arun Jaitley's reputation as a Master of poll campaign manager. For him,

Karnataka presented a challenge of different sort because the party remained handicapped by 20 month uneasy power sharing with the JD (Secular). He stands now chances of being asked to look after the party's campaign in the forthcoming Lok Sabha elections.

- Party's debacle in Karnataka raised apprehensions and increased woes over the end year poll battles in Rajasthan, MP, Delhi and Chhattisgarh. It fears of a similar disaster if the clear leadership (future CM) is established within the party. The Issue like price rise, inflation, terrorism would be tested there.
- The JD(S) leadership (with the Cormer PM H.D. Deve Gowda and his son) tried a determined bid to subvert the mandate of saffron outfit and with the support of Congress for a coalition government in the state. But the move was wisely rebuffed by the Congress, keeping in view the credibility of the ex-PM in cheating the Dharam Singh Government as well as the BJP. In fact, Gowda's woes were of a split in a small party. He even proposed the name of Dalit MLA G.P. Parameshwara of the CWC to lead a new coalition government.
- The BJP campaign projected its leader B.S. Yedduruppa as its future CM, and more crucially by portraying him as the 'victim' of the grand betrayal scripted by Deve Gowda clan. This generated sympathy for the seven day tenure CM of the BJP. Apart from the anti-incumbency factor or the price rise and growing terrorism across the vindhyas. The party could fulfil its cherished dream to set-up the first ever saffron Government in the South under the farmer's family leaders. The BJP gained a new territory all the analysis of poll pundits and exit polls proved wrong. They projected a 'hung assembly' with Congress emerging as the largest party in the 224-assembly seats.
- The significance of BJPs victory lies in the reality that it sets the BJP on a par with the Congress—a

national party with Governments across the country. The Congress has lost as many as 13 assembly elections since 2004. It has to ponder over it. The Congress should wake up to the limits of its patronage politics.

- These results were not a referendum on national issue even through inflation figured in the campaign poll. The very focus was more on local governance issues, which the party as a regional outfit projected successfully at the grass root levels. There was no reference of the Hindutva agenda.
- The BJP's rise in the state coincides with the decline of Janata politics in the 1990s. Much of the Janata votes seems to have gone the BJPs way under the influence of anti-incumbency factor.
- With the BJP coming into power, the pro-Telangana forces will get a leg up and New Delhi may give the green signal to its demand for statehood ahead of 2009 Lok Sabha elections. The TRS is presently unattached and any national party would like to have an alliance with a serious promise of creating Telangana. The BJP seems fit in this regard as the previous NDA Government created the three states and it would like to take advantage of the sentiments of the movement of TRS.
- The new government took office on 30th May, 2008 with the 30 member ministry. Five of the six Independent MLA were made ministers. The ministry is based on the line of 91st constitutional amendment (i.e. 15% strength of the House).

CHAPTER

33

Fault-lines of Caste, Class and Religion versus Fury of 2007

The fault-lines of caste, class and religion in the form of *'Collective Madness'* have shaken the functioning of India's political system. The people got violent and indulge in public display of anger over certain issues, whether they are related to granting ST status to Adivasis in Delhi, Jaipur highway and Guwahati, or fuming over Taslima Nasreen's book in Kolkata or the Sun TV camera event of Chennai/the role of Dera Sacha in Batinda of Punjab. The latest example of people's fury was seen in Nandigram and farmers' agitation through Mahapanchyats in Rajasthan. (Its details are given ahead in this chapter). The furious events rendered the government and its machinery totally abdicated from their responsibilities. This picture presented the impression of utter neglect of duty by the government. In this regard, the Calcutta High Court held that the state machinery has insufficient machinery to tackle the mob at Nandigram. If the Judiciary takes congninance of these developments, its proactive and positive stand is disliked by the party in power. In fact, the crux of the problem is that the mob behaviour as (known as collective ego) is not prepared to tolerate a small scar on its ego. On the contrary, the expression 'mob violence' does figure in the statute book of Cr.P.C. or I.P.C. *vis-a-vis* the subject of public order and tranquility. The only section is 11 of the Cr.P.C. which is invoked at the time of violence and riots. But the offence is bailable. But such cases are withdrawn by party in power and punishment given under section 188 Cr.P.C. further is withdrawn under the compromise or agreement. Likewise, there is no check on the police and magistracy on being miscreants let off when situation is out of control.

Little wonder then that there is no dearth of instances when public servants have been found to have acted under the influence of their political masters in ways that are prejudicial to maintenance of peace and order. The police may, for instance, use their preventive arrest powers selectively, adding to the problem rather than resolving it.

The police reforms ordered by the Supreme Court are, therefore, designed to insulate the law enforcement agency from extraneous and undesirable influences. Independent oversight mechanisms are envisaged in each state to confer the necessary autonomy on the police to act real time in a professional manner. Amid the efforts made from time to time to combat high-profile threats like terrorism and organized crime, the state has overlooked the need to update and strengthen the legal regime against mob violence which is spreading like a wildfire in the country.

Redrawing the Map of Poll-Constituencies and the views of the Delimitation Commission—Increasing the number of Lok Sabha seats in view of versus increasing population ratio in some states, there has been a question of controversy. The states having population increased demanded to increase more seats in the Lok Sabha and those states aggressively promoted family-planning did not like to be penalized. Thirty years ago, it was decided that the number of seats in Lok Sabha would remain frozen at 543, till the census 2001 were avail. Till this date, the demographic profile of the country based on 1971 figures used to operate.

A new Delimitation Commission was set-up in 2003 under the chairmanship of retired Supreme Court judge Kuldip Singh. Its task was to redraw the map of the constituencies within a state leaving the total number of seats in the state unchanged. This would take into account population redistribution within the state but leave the balance of power between different states unchanged. The commission was also mandated to draw up uniform-sized Lok Sabha seats. It is this report of the Delimitation Commission, finalized after five years of fierce resistance from political parties, that was placed in Parliament for approval. With the notification of the report, many seats cultivated by politicians as pocket boroughs are likely to be disappear. Though most parties are now reconciled to the proposed changes, many feel that they may be deferred till after the 2009 elections. What has queered the pitch further is that the commission has recommended an increase of 10 reserved seats for SCs and STs, reducing the number of general seats. A PIL has now been filed with the Supreme Court seeking speedy implementation of the report, but the apex court is yet to hear and decide the case.

Delimitation is the process by which the boundaries of electoral constituencies are periodically redrawn on the basis of population. It is based on one man one vote dictum—the ultimate pillar of our democracy. If not redrawn regularly as per increasing population, then changes are that the constituencies will become unequal size over time. The outer Delhi Lok Sabha constituency is the example where it had 34 lakh electorates in 2004 election, whereas Lakshwadweep had an electoral of just over 39,000.*

It may be noted in 1973 that Parliament amended the constitution (31st) to strike a balance between the constituency's electorate and representation (seats). Again, 91st Amendment to the Constitution put off re-allocation of seats between the states upto 2026 under the 42nd Amendment of 1973, the delimitation was put off till 2001, that is 1971 census figure would be valid till 2026.

On behalf of NGO, Delhi Study Group—Arun Jately filed a PIL accusing the Union Government of sitting over the recommendations of the Delimitation Committee and not placing them before the President for a formal Notification to

* See the observations of Kingshuk Nage in, "Changing Poll Equations", *The Times of India*, New Delhi edn., December 5, 2007, p. 14.

make them 'enforceable' in the forthcoming elections. Inaction in this regard is taken as violation of the spirit and provisions of the Constitution and the provisions of Delimitation Act, 2002. The purpose of it was that constituencies be readjusted before the Lok Sabha election due in 2009 on the basis the recommendations of Delimitation Commission.

RE-DRAWN CONSTITUENCIES APPROVED FOR NEW ELECTORAL MAP

The Cabinet Committee on Political Affair—CCPA, approved the re-drawn constituencies proposed by the Delimitation Commission and decided to put into operation the recommendations that the next Lok Sabha elections as well as assembly polls to be held in 2008-09 would be held as per the suggestions of the Commission which is a statutory body. As per the notification by the Election Commission, the majority of top level politicians were unhappy at this decision of the UPA Government but there was no way out to defer the implementation of the report. The commission, it may be noted, submitted its report in respect of 25 states covering over 513 Lok Sabha Constituencies out of 543. The report was tabled in Parliament in December 2007. As per the exercise of the commission, 3,726 assembly constituencies in 25 states would be affected. The Commission was constituted in the middle of 2004 and completed the work in all states barring the four states (Nagaland, Assam, Arunachal Pradesh and Manipur) of North-East.

As per the report, the number of SC seats in Lok Sabha will go up from 79 to 85 and ST from 39 to 46. Likewise, for the assemblies, SC seats will increase from 555 to 610 and ST from 527 to 545 but the CCPA decided that states like, Jharkhand, Arunachal Pradesh, Manipur, Nagaland and Assam would be de-linked from the delimitation process.

The delimitation move stirred the activities of political parties and begun to seek the support of the SCs/STs, specifically in the Congress circle. It welcomed the Centre's decision as it would give them an ownership of democracy. The day after the Union cabinet decided to redraw the Lok Sabha and assembly constituencies in keeping with the rise in the SC/ST population, the Congress rushed to claim the political copyright of the government initiative. "We are enthused because the exercise will give the SC/STs a larger electoral role both at the Centre and in the states." Party spokesman Abhishek Singhvi said so.

It was evident that the next assembly elections as well as the Lok Sabha elections would be held on the basis of the delimited boundaries. But the apprehension in certain quarters was about of the implications of the Sachar report, if implemented. The report has suggested identification of the substantial Muslims presence in some of the Constituencies.

FALLOUT OF DELIMITATION OF CONSTITUENCIES IN RAJASTHAN

As per the fallout of delimitation of Lok Sabha constituencies in Rajasthan, nine out of 25 Lok Sabha seats are going to be affected. As per the Delimitation Commission, the status of several constituencies—general, ST, or SC has been changed in Rajasthan. However, the number of reserved seats will be same as before at seven four reserved for Scheduled Caste candidates and three for Scheduled Tribe candidates.

Change of status and redrawing of political map will affect seven BJP and two Congress MPs. The BJP MPs who will be affected are party vice-president and MP from Tonk (SC) Kailash Meghwal, former ruler of Bharatpur, Vishvendra Singh, B. Sushila, who is wife of former BJP president Bangaru Laxman, Ramswaroop Kohli, Kiran Maheshwari and Mahavir Bhagora. Bollywood actor-turned-MP Dharmendra, who won from Bikaner, will also have to shift to some other constituency as this general seat has now been reserved for SCs.

Dausa general constituency which was earlier represented by late Rajesh Pilot and after his death, his son Sachin has now been made a reserved constituency for STs. Meghwal's Tonk constituency was reserved for SC, but now it has been made a general seat. Sawaimadhopur reserved (ST) constituency, represented by Union Minister for Environment and Forest Namoh Narayan Meena (Congress), has been converted to a general constituency. Bharatpur general constituency has been now made a reserved constituency for SCs. Udaipur general constituency has been converted into a reserved (SC) constituency, forcing Maheshwari to look elsewhere. Salumabr reserved (ST) seat, which is represented by Bhagora, has been made a general constituency, while Jalore (SC) seat, represented by B. Sushila, has now been made a general seat.

Two new Lok Sabha constituencies have also been created Jaipur (rural) by bifurcating Jaipur seat and Rajsamand. However, the total number of parliamentary seats remains unchanged at 25. Bayana reserved (SC) seat, held by Kohli, will now be called Dholpur-Bayana reserved (SC) constituency and Sawaimadhopur reserved (ST) constituency will now be clubbed with Tonk. Salumabr reserved (ST) seat will be called Rajasamand seat.

The Supreme Court has put a rider on delimitation notifications by telling Election Commission (EC) that the number of reserved constituencies in a state has to be proportionate to the population of Scheduled Castes and Scheduled Tribes. This is the mandate of Article 332(3) of the Constitution and the EC will do well to keep this in mind while giving effect to the recommendations of the delimitation commission, a Bench comprising Justices A.K. Mathur and Markandey Katju said in a recent order. It held "this (mandate of Article 332) should be the paramount consideration of the Election Commission and not any other consideration".

This order came on a petition filed by Anand Singh Kunwar challenging the EC's decision to reserve three seats for STs in the 70 member Uttarakhand assembly, which has a 3% ST population. Singh, resident of Dharchula constituency, said that as per the census data, the 3% population of STs were entitled to two seats (2.1 being closer to 2 rather than 3) in the assembly, but the EC reserved three constituencies for STs. During the pendency of the petition, EC admitted its mistake and said it has rectified it by reducing the ST seats from three to two. With this, the issue before the apex court became an academic exercise, but the Bench went on to clarify that "the mandate of Article 332(3) of the Constitution of India should always be kept in mind. Article 332(3) mandates that the reservation must be made in proportion to the population of SCs and STs".

The court said it was not inclined to comment on the considerations that led the EC to increase ST seats from two to three but said it was totally unwarranted as it was in violation of the constitutional mandate. "The mandate of the Constitution is supreme and the EC has no scope to go beyond the Constitution", the Bench said. "We hope and trust that when any notification is issued, the EC shall confine itself to the mandate of the provisions of the Constitution of India and will not be swayed by any other consideration", it said. *Justification for Presidential System in India* : We adopted the Parliamentary system but its functioning during the last sixty one years has created unique breed of legislatures, largely unqualified to make the laws, who have election on Caste-*cum*-religion basis in order to wield the executive powers. They are more skilled at politics than at policy/performance. The system has permitted our parties to shift alliances of individual's ideology or ideals, specifically in the era of coalition governance.

According to Shashi Tharoor, the Presidential System puts two limitations on our Executive. First, only 'electable', not 'able' is chosen for executive posts. (In the council of Ministers) backed by political leaders. Second, it puts premium on defections and horse trading, despite the Anti-Defection law of 1984 now, party splits has gained significance for getting ministerial posts as the best rewards in Indian political system.

The most serious argument against the Presidential system is of risking of dictatorship. They conjure up the image of an imperious president, immune to parliamentary defeat and impervious to public opinion, ruling the country by fiat. Of course, it does not help that Mrs. Gandhi, during the Emergency, contemplated abandoning the parliamentary system for a modified form of Gaullism, thereby, discrediting the idea of presidential government. It is worth calling that Nepal is proclaiming a New Republic with adopting a mixed system of proportional electoral system in which 60% of the seats will be chosen proportionally and the rest remaining 40% through straight contests. This has been done in the light of multi-party system. The assembly has endorsed the mixed system as cited above.

The case for a presidential system of either the French or the American style has, in his view, never been clearer. The French version, by combining presidential rule with a parliamentary government headed by a prime minister, is superficially more attractive, since it superficially more attractive, since it resembles our own system, except for reversing the balance of power between the President and the Council of Ministers. This is what the Sri Lankans opted for when they jettisoned the British model. But, given India's fragmented party system, the prospects for parliamentary chaos distracting the elected President are considerable. An American or Latin American model, with a president serving both as head of state and head of government, might better evade the problems we have experienced with political factionalism.*

A directly-elected chief executive in New Delhi, instead of being vulnerable to the shifting sands of coalition support politics, would have stability of tenure free from legislative whim, be able to appoint a cabinet of talents, and above all, be able to devote his or her energies to governance, and not just to government. The Indian voter will be able to vote directly for the individual he or she wants to be ruled by and the president will truly be able to claim to speak for a majority of Indians rather than a majority of MPs. At the end of a fixed period of time—let us say five years—the public would be able to judge the individual on performance in improving the lives of Indians, rather than on political skill at keeping a governmental in office. It is a compelling case.

The most serious argument against the Presidential system is of risking of dictatorship. They conjure up the image of an imperious President, immune to parliamentary defeat and impervious to public opinion, ruling the country by fiat. Of course, it does not help that Mrs. Gandhi, during the Emergency, contemplated abandoning the parliamentary system can be distorted to permit autocratic rule. Dictatorship is not the result of a particular type of governmental system.

In any case, to offset the temptation for a national president to become all-powerful, and to give real substance to

* Shashi Tharoor, "India Should Switch to Presidential System", *The Sunday Times of India*, New Delhi, December 23, 2007, p. 18.

the decentralization essential for a country of India's size, an executive chief minister or governor should also be directly elected in each of the states. The case for such a system in the states is even stronger than in the Centre. Those who reject a presidential system on the grounds that it might lead to dictatorship may be assured that the powers of the president would thus be balanced by those of the directly-elected chief executives in the states.

Democracy, as I have argued elsewhere, is vital for India's survival: our chronic pluralism is a basic element of what we are. Yes, democracy is an end in itself, and we are right to be proud of it. But few Indians are proud of the kind of politics our democracy has inflicted upon us. With the needs and challenges of one-sixth of humanity before our leaders, we must have a democracy that delivers progress to our people. Changing to a presidential system is the best way of ensuring a democracy that works today after sixty-one years of Independence.

It is worth-recalling that Nepal is proclaiming a New Republic with adopting a mixed system of proportional electoral system in which 60% of the seats will be chosen proportionally and the rest remaining 40% through straight contests. This has been done in the light of multi-party system. The assembly has endorsed the mixed system India can learn a lesson from Nepal.

We must agree with Shashi Tharoor's criticism that Indian political system has corroded beyond redemption and it is high time for a change in it. But it is not feasible to agree with his argument to switch to the Presidential form of democracy for India. Because a number of writers and critics of the American political system has pointed out to 'temporal rigidity' and other major disadvantages of the presidential system on account of fixed term of the President, leaving no room for the continuous re-adjustments that changing events may demand. Likewise, the system operates on the basis of winner-take all rule, which tends to make democratic politics a zero-sum game. The fixed term does not give him/her incentive to form coalition/negotiate with the opposition lobbies, which is vital to deal with divisive problems. According to Professor Prajapathi of Harward University

Trivedi, a number of American writers, (namely, O.J. Simpson, Jean Elshtain, Robert Dahl of Yale, Juan Linz and so on) are not happy with the working of Presidential system and that is why democracies in Latin America have failed to work.* The American model in Philippines too is presently subject to change.

According to Shugart and Carey, the rate of breakdown of democratic regimes in developing countries in the 20th century is similar under the two systems—52 per cent for presidential system as opposed to 59 percent for parliamentary regimes. They define failure as a breakdown that leads to a replacement of the regime by a non-democratic regime. The executive-legislative deadlock leading to paralysis of the government is the first major problem that has plagued presidential systems all over the world. This is the inevitable result of the coexistence of the two independent organs that a presidential government creates. When disagreement between them occurs, there is no institutional method of resolving it—unlike the instrument of legislative vote of confidence that keeps the legislature and executive in tune with each other in parliamentary systems.

There is no denying the truth that the current state of affairs is unsustainable. So what is the way forward? We do not have to fall prey to the false dichotomy created by the choice between parliamentary and presidential forms of government. Both have outlived their usefulness. Time has come to think out of the box and completely re-imagine constitutional arrangements. Old constitutions were made by lawyers and political scientists. Hence, they focused on "due process" and "power struggle" as the underlying paradigms. The next generation of constitutions will have to focus on delivering results and effective management of complex contemporary economies. Existing constitutions seek to give us freedom and autonomy. The new system should be based on the concept of good governance.

At present, the demands for new states begun surfacing for the setting up of 2nd States Reorganization (SRC) for

* Prajapati Trivedi, "It is not Better", *Ibid.*, dated Jan. 17, 2008, p. 4.

redrawing boundaries of large states. (The first SRC was set-up in 1953 and created 14 states). Thereafter, double states were created through amendment process. Our point is how carving out new smaller states are related to administrative good governance?

The controversies over new states have also obscured the questions of autonomy of and power-sharing with local communities. Neither the Motilal Nehru Committee nor the SRC viewed state reorganization from this perspective. Centralism, which has characterized the Indian state since colonial days, ignored the communitarian entitlement of autonomy. Instead, it was the Indian state decentralizing some of its responsibilities. No wonder pockets of disaffection emerge from time to time, which have not been doused by the arrangements provided for by the 73rd and 74th constitutional amendments and various district councils. The idea of a second SRC is welcome. But it must not be another exercise in partisan politics. This opportunity must be seized to develop a consensus on issues of autonomy, power-sharing and an agreeable basis for creation of states for good governance. This is the basic requirement of globalised world.

DIPPING THE WORK-RATE OF INDIAN PARLIAMENT

It should be a matter of serious concern that in 2007, the work-rate of Indian Parliament dipped dramatically indicating that our MPs have not done their jobs. In 2007, our Parliament functioned for the least number of-days and the lowest number of total hours since 2000, with the exception of 2004, an election year. This year also saw the lowest number of bills being introduced and passed in the new millennium, again barring 2004.

Shockingly, young Lok Sabha MPs (between 25 and 40 years) and their Rajya Sabha counterparts (between 30 and 45 years) had the lowest participation rates among all age groups in Parliament debates this year. A study conducted by PRS Legislative Research, an independent and not-for-profit group, has revealed that Parliament's total working hours in 2007 were nearly 40% less than in 2006. This year, the LS met for a mere 66 days, the lowest since 2004. According to constitutional expert Subhash Kashyap, the current state of affairs does not speak well of parliamentary democracy. He remarked: "It means that there is a quantitative as well as a qualitative erosion". In 2007, Parliament introduced 56 bills and passed 46 last year was much better: 66 introduced and 65 passed. Between 2000 and 2006 (barring 2004), on an average, 75 bills were introduced every year and 65 passed. Political scientist Imtiaz Ahmed said such a development indicated a lack of consensus among political parties and the government's unwillingness to face Parliament. In his words : "It also means that Parliament now acts primarily as an agitational body rather than as a constitutional and legislative authority. The Indian exchequer lost more than Rs. 20 crore on account of disruption of Parliament during 2007. The question is how to prevent repeated uproar and pandemonium? It may be noted that disruptions cost the loss of Rs. 24,632 per minute. (See Table 1)

TABLE 1
Average Hours Worked Per Day

Year	*Lok Sabha*	*Rajya Sabha*
2000	5.5	4.4
2001	4.5	3.8
2002	5.6	4.2
2003	6.1	4.7
2004	4.5	3.4
2005	5.8	4.7
2006	5.7	4.9
2007	4.3	3.3

Source : PRS Legislative Research.

IMPLEMENTING THE 86TH AMENDMENT?

The Centre, otherwise keen to promote education, to implement the 86th amendment to the Constitution, enacted five years ago? The 86th amendment adds a new Article 21-A to the Constitution that says; "The state shall provide free and compulsory education to all children of the age of six to 14 years in such manner as the state may, by law, determine". This makes the right to education a fundamental right for children in this age group.

Simultaneously, in Article 45 the Directive Principles of State Policy on providing free and compulsory education to all children in the age group 0-14 years was rewritten limiting this provision to the age group 0-6 years. A new fundamental duty was added making it mandatory for all parents to send their children to school when they are six to 14 years of age. In deciding a writ petition by J.P. Unnikrishnan and others against the state of Andhra Pradesh in 1993, the Supreme Court for the first time read Article 45 (Directive Principles of State Policy) along with Article 21 (Fundamental Rights). It ruled that the right to education was a fundamental right, flowing from the right to life itself. This judgement stays put as the law of the land at least until the 86th amendment is notified. States may resist a central legislation that will force them to bear the cost of education of children aged 6-14 years. But shelving the amendment, apart from the obvious moral cost of such action, keeps the state's current constitutional burden much bigger and more intractable over the age group 0-14 years.*

It should be recalled that the amendment Bill was passed unanimously and without debate in both the houses of Parliament. Yet, it is awaited for its implementation for various reasons. One of them is the opposition of many poor states fearing that the notification on it would compel to bear the additional financial burden under the Fundamental Right to education. The Centre has been supportive of *Sarva Shiksha Abhiyan—SSA* and under the X plan, the states used to get 50:50 financial assistance. Despite this, why the Centre dithered over notifying a constitutional amendment passed unanimously in each House, whereas it is model amendment towards the right to education Cost effective should not come in this way.

---

* Tapas Majumdar, "Education should be a Right", *Ibid.*, December 14, 2007, p. 14.

Note : The study contains more details under the chapter some key features of our contemporary politics.

AREAS OF REFORMS

(1) People's Participation in Policy, Decision-making and Implementation

People's participation and public opinion are the basis of democracy for an efficient, responsive and sensitive administration. Efforts should be made to give more weightage to the public aspirations and opinions. An administration which tries to ignore public opinion for a best is time-bound to face impediments. Therefore, government should abridge the gap between the ruling class and the public through interaction and involvement. People should be an active part of planning. Accessibility, credibility of the agencies and motivation can encourage grass-root participation. Hence, Institutions like Ombudsman, Lokayukt and Lokpal need to play their role effectively. All we need today is a co-ordination between political, administration and social participation. As said by critics 'people's participation' in administration is a democratic rhetoric which translated into action, tends to become mere redressal of citizen's grievances.

Check and balance are the two phases of one coin. In an efficient, responsive and sensitive administration check and balance can only be sustained through temporary and accountability. Efforts and reforms should be introduced by the government which are conducive for transparency and accountability. Every right should be paired with duty, achievement with reward and guilt with punishment.

(2) Privatisation

Public administration cannot shadow private administration though even it suffers from certain bureau pathologies, but it is able to hide such things and draws attention towards its good side. Public is more prepared to give private administration, the benefit of the doubt and judge it differently. Hence, one of the suggestive measures for quick progress and efficiency is to turn all public institutions and organizations private. For private administration is more adaptive, accommodating and caring and profit-making.

(3) Judicial Reforms

The Indian judiciary has shown unprecedented initiative during the last few years. The independence of judiciary is a myth as the political environment influences the court's decision. The say of politicians in the appointment of the judges has highly effected the judicial system. Judiciary is the pillar of democracy and thus, needs to work independently and impartially, to sustain its integrity. But, unfortunately it is not so. Hence, to make the judiciary more efficient, responsive and sensitive certain reforms are required. The old saying of 'Justice delayed is justice denied' needs to be replaced by the proper functioning and by minimizing the number of pending cases. Judiciary should work in an unbiased and uncommitted manner. More and more public interest litigation (PIL) should be introduced for the redressal of public grievances and to increase accountability. Public opinion and judicial criticism should be welcomed for more social and economic reforms. All we need in reference to judiciary is the reformative judiciary. Courts occupy key position in India as regards judicial control of administrative action. Since, we adopted the concept of welfare state, it became exceedingly necessary that rule of law and conformity to the provision of the constitutions are maintained and the multitudinous administrative authorities are brought under the control of courts of law.

(4) Probity and Morale in Administration

Probity and morale go hand in hand. Probity in administration can be judged through the level of morale and *vice-versa*. Regrettably, in the present state of administration probity and morale are highly lacking. The reason is increasing corruption and low morale. All considerations of merit and efficiency are governed by the supreme test of loyalty to the political chiefs. Degeneration of bureaucracy is directly linked with political degeneration. To enhance efficiency responsiveness and sensitive, probity and moral in the administration, we need to do away with caste bias, lack of professional competence, politicization, indecision, lack of transparency and accountability. This can be done through strict implementation of anti-corruption laws, checking the use of blackmoney in election. All politicians and bureaucrats, etc.

should come under the authority of Lokpal. All these measures will be conducive for probity. In order to build high morale, devices like human relations approach, management of attitudes, incentive schemes, rotation of jobs, building responsibility into a job, employees participation in decision-making and job enrichment are suggested.

(5) E-Governance

Change is the law of nature. Every change leads to progress. In order to change our administrative framework all we need is to introduce the e-governance techniques with this aim the government needs to aim for a functional IT driven system of governance with lateral and horizontal computerization in all state government departments. All departments and public sector units (PSUs) would use the state-wide value-added network (VAN) for inters and intra-departmental communication. Communication should take place through video-conferencing and audio-techniques, and through hot lines. This will enhance the cost efficiency. To improve management and to increase accountability, all the revenue earning and public dealing departments and agencies should be fully computerized and net worked. All these measures can lead to quick redressal of grievances and reveals efficient, responsive and sensitive administration.

Performance evaluation is another important reform to be implemented to increase efficiency, discipline, responsiveness and morale boosting. Once a civil servant has been selected, indicated and trained for his post. There has to be a periodical performance review instead of permanent selection for the post. According to the response and result, he should be paid and punished. The report should be based on knowledge, output of work, quality of input, decision-making ability, interpersonal relations, communication-leadership skill and other abilities. According to Prof. Devang Mehta, E-Governance is related to 'SMART', that is 'S stands for Simple; M for Model; A for Accountable; R for Responsiveness and T for Transparency'. It is the gift of Information Technology (LT) to administration and economy of our era which is poised for globalization.

(6) Efficient Responsive Police Structure

Administration can be made more efficient, responsive and sensitive only through efficient police structure. There should be proper recruitment of impartial and uncommercial persons. People today are in need of not only duly bound police but it should be more sensitive, society-friendly, value based and with human face. Police should fulfil its responsibility of implementation of law and maintenance of law and order sincerely. In order to increase efficiency in police personal continuous training and continuous vigilance should be done.

The police today should have a belief in democracy, democratic values and should work for implementation and defence of human rights. It should work in order to win confidence of the people. The police should not be authoritarian or arbitrary. It should be free from casteism, communalism, pressure tactics and nepotism.

(7) Simplification of Rules, Procedures and Laws

To improve service delivery and transparency in the government's functioning simplification of laws, rules and procedure is essential. There should be one window system where all services would be available at one place. It is necessary to use modern management techniques to ensure that procedures are drastically simplified for the convenience of the citizens. For the proper understanding of laws, rules and procedures. There's need for the simplification of the language and forms used by administration. Communication also needs an improvement. Citizens are not well informed about rules and regulations because communication is defective. Certain administrative issues which need to be simplified are de-regulation of licences for effective working, there should be end of broker-system for ending hawalas, end of redtapism, quick procedures within time limit, clarity of laws and rules, accessibility of concerning persons and departmental heads. Improved communication and feed-back channel for clarity of laws and rules.

(8) Constitutional Reforms

Constitutional reforms are another essential requirement

for increasing efficiency, responsiveness and sensitiveness in the administration. Constitutional reforms are constraints and reflections. Therefore, their timely appraisal and review is a must. Government should make an effort to do away with the obsolete reforms and should introduce and implement the reforms required according to the need of time. All the reforms in practice should be clearly defined. Reform like de-criminalization of politics, to do away with nexus between politicians and bureaucrats, to strong them grass-root democracy, empowerment of women, clarity of powers and authorities, clarification of grey areas like care taking government and CEC, etc. should be concentrated and considered with great speed.

(9) Electoral Reforms Process

Our electoral process is suffering from some major flaws which lead to the inefficiency, irresponsiveness and insensitiveness in the administration. Certain electoral reforms to be emphasized are like, to minimize the multiplicity of parties, to cast the caste away, to make minimum education compulsory, introduction of principles in politics, say of judiciary in the contestants with criminal records, a well framed agenda for electoral reform, check on the role of black money and state funding should be there. All these reforms can lead to efficiency, responsiveness and sensitiveness in the administration.

(10) Need to Create Conditions which are Conducive for Social Justice

To practice equality and to provide social justice to all is the first pre-requisite of a democratic system. The government has to create all those conditions which are conducive for social justice to all majority and minority. To check the atrocities of upper class on the weaker section, we need. to change the mental framework of upper castes/classes through literacy, resources, empowering women education to the girl. All this needs to improve our educational pattern. Rural service should be focused to link the cities.

CONCLUDING REMARKS

The country faces a crisis of leadership as well as governance. Both factors have collapsed from public administration whereas 'New' Public Administration demand the operationalisation of the concept Good Governance—the mantra of globalization, contrast to features prevailing like corruption, indiscipline, red tapism etc. the malaise-collapse of governance pervades both in urban and rural administration.

India fares abysmally on the global corruption meter. According to transparency International, 20% believe government does not fight corruption at all; 39% think its fight against corruption is ineffective; and 15% say that far from fighting corruption, government actually encourages it. This is a difficult place for businessmen to function. A global survey ranks India among the worst countries for doing business. Whether it's starting or closing a business, enforcing contracts, paying taxes, or registering property—every procedure take an inordinately long time.

India, the emergence of the concept of 'Good Governance' has strengthened the movement of dissatisfaction with the state of the discipline of Public Administration. As a result of globalization, New Public Administration (N.P.A.) emphasized in Public administration on the classical factors like efficiency, economy, productivity and decentralization. The NPA talks of relevance, values, social equality change and participatory initiative. For this change, the second Minnobrook Conference of 1988 should be credited which launched a 'movement' against the 'big role' of government in public administration and in favour of managerialism and privatization in policy-making, and since then, as a discipline, public administration has moved a way from political science discipline. The NPA talks of less burden on government and public sector organization. In short, Good Governance is a normative concept, which is close to NPM, acknowledging the due place in public administration, the features like: (a) Accountability; (b) Transparency; (c) Rule of Law; (d) Human Rights; (e) Social equality in terms of gender, ethnic-age groups and religion, (f) Ethical and honest behaviour; (g) Greater Decentralization, delegation and De-bureaucratization; (h) Accountability for deeds; and (1) Budget cuts on ministerial budget, etc.

Most of Indian writers and teachers have devised the new strategies of good governance for corrupt-free sustainable development for which emphasis on ethical, moral dimensions, efficiency, managerialism, People's participation, responsiveness, transparency and accountability as well as autonomy have been given to modern states in the new millennium. The state should base on mere reforming internal rules and the role of bureaucracy cannot keep the administration corruption, free.* Of course, the era of LPG has reduced the importance of the 'state'.

It is wrong to say that the 'missionary role of the State is rolling buck, through the era of a centralized state has gone without the state, the competitive role of 'free Market/ economy, shall fail to the age of LT, administrative system be flexible, consultative result-oriented, creative from the bottom to the top, for which Article 311 of the Constitution (in terms of the rights and privileges and status of civil services) warrants drastic change. State is yet to play a vital role in ensuring social cohesion, social justice while combating social inequalities, focus shall have to be given to basic amenities.

The state as an important organ of administration in the LPG era where its contracting role has emerged to ensure efficiency and managerial capability. India can not be an Asian 'power' without infusing principles of accountability and transparency in public administration while making the centre flexible, responsive and accountable.**

In Indian political system, the rule of coalition governance since 1980s has contributed nothing except witnessing a spell of unstable coalition governments. At present, the Congress-led UPA Government too is facing the same situation in the light of the Indo-US nuclear deal and its ally—the left has threatened to withdraw its support if its concerns and (implications of the deal) are not taken seriously. The deadlock

* R.B. Jain, Corruption Free Sustainable Development Challenges and Strategies for Good Governance (New Delhi, Mittal Publications, 2004).

** S.R. Maheswari, Administrative Reforms in India (New Delhi, Macmillan, New Delhi, 2002).

between the Congress and Left created the possibility of election to the Lok Sabha. The instability of government has shaken the very roots of our economic grow in the era of globalization. In fact, hard policy options are not adopted by any unstable coalition government. They are bound to follow the populist policies to appear the supporting groups or political parties.

Since coalition governments seems to be inevitable in our governance, but we have yet not been able to debate on possible institutional reforms that many facilitate more stable governance against the trend of fragmentation and the rise of small-caste-based political parties in our democracy.

According to Professor Bhaskar Dutta, one of the possible solution to the inordinate degree of fragmentation in our legislatures is to modify the method of proportional representation (PR) to elect their legislatures. The pure form of PR actually tends to increase fragmentation. However, typically PR is supplemented with the stipulation that only those parties that win a minimum fraction of the total votes cast—say 5 percent can gain representation. This will drastically reduce the number of parties securing seats in the legislatures. In principle, there is no reason why this "minimum votes required" principle cannot be tagged on to our "first past the post" electoral system.

It is also worth thinking of what can be done to extend the longevity of governments once they are in office. An interesting option is a rule, which was adopted in response to the instability of German governments during the Weimar republic. Historically, majorities of the right and the left combined forces to bring down governments composed of centralist parties. But these extreme groups could not themselves formulate a common platform given their vast philosophical differences.

In an attempt to overcome this impasse, the new German constitution adopted in 1949 prescribed that votes of no-confidence must be "constructive". This meant that a chancellor, who is the head of government, could only be dismissed by parliament if a new chancellor was elected simultaneously. The system of constructive no confidence increased the durability of subsequent German governments since the existing one could no longer be brought down by a combination of disparate forces who were not themselves interested in forming a government. Of course, another advantage of the system is that it ruled out the necessity of any mid-term polls by providing an inbuilt mechanism for the smooth transition of power. Our Constitution probably did not envisage the possibility of governance by coalitions. Our current rules and norms are clearly incapable of promoting stable governance in fragmented legislatures. However, coalition governments function reasonably efficiently in several countries. It is important to scrutinize the best features of comparative political systems and modify them to suit our own needs.

Recently, some cases have brought the judiciary in clash with the jurisdiction of the Right to Information Act with regarding to furnishing information of complaints against the judges. It is well known that Delhi High Court *suo motu* initiated contempt proceedings against Mid-day journalists for publishing a story biased acts of former Chief Justice of India, Y.K. Subharwal. This episode discredited a lot to the integrity of the Indian Judiciary in the same way as politicians and bureaucrats have lowered the image of administration (governance). Other cases involving judges justice Shamit Mukherjee, justice Jagdish Bhalla and . . . have already shaken the faith of ordinary people of India. The application of contempt of court against the exposure of corruption/ allegations Judiciary is not justified. The functioning of Judiciary itself should be above suspicion and adherence complete transparency in it would certain enhance the dignity of the institutions and post such as CJI. Rather it would have been in one judicious if an independent inquiry in Mid-day against the CJI could have been set-up. The entire Mid-day issue *vis-a-vis* acts of former CJI underlines the fact that our judiciary lacks accountability and transparency. The Judiciary cannot/should not claim to be kept out of RTI jurisdiction. Even contempt powers of the courts should be subject to scrutiny.*

* Arvind Kejriwal, 'Contempt for the Pen', Sept. 18, 2007, p. 12.

It is worth-recalling that against the above-cited background the Government of the day, has brought the bill on constitutional of Judges (Inquiry) Bill, 2006 and the Judges proposed National Judiciary Council Bill seeking to make judges more accountable.

SIGNIFICANCE OF THE PM'S VISIT TO CHINA

The visit of our PM was an important milestone in evolution of the relations with China. The most important feature of it was to set an ambitious two-way trade target of $ billion by 2010. The visit was, of course, assumed a global significance in terms of mutual understanding and trust between the two Asia's big nations.

The Joint statement signed by the two sides signed as many as 11-wide ranging agreements tripling a trade target within five years and deepening a defence engagement that was unthinkable a few years ago between the two neighbours. Both the leaders decided not to let their five decade border dispute cloud the growth in their relationship, but set a deadline for arriving at an agreement framework of settlement to the problem. India, thus, was set to take up with China its attempt to wriggle out of the existing agreement between the two nations and sought the settlement of disputed borders with the exchange of maps.

The desire for a fresh collaboration was articulated by the spokesperson of the Chinese foreign ministry, Quin Gang, who tried to evoke the pre-1962 friendly spirit by raising "*Hindi Chini Bhai Bhai*" toast during a lunch he hosted for visiting Indian journalists. It is expected to be reflected strongly in Singh's address to the Chinese Academy of Social sciences. Dr. Singh, who while addressing Indian business persons stressed on the complementarily, expected to call the 21st century the century of Asia marked by vigorous trans-Himalayan partnership.

Government sources indicated that they were expecting a resolution of the fresh irritants on border issue during talks that national security adviser and special representative for the boundary talks, M.K. Narayanan, would hold with Dai Binggyo, the Chinese points person. The attempt to get China to reaffirm its pledge to keep populated areas-read Tawang valley in Arunchal Pradesh has been necessitated by indications that Beijing could be chaffing at the understanding worked out between Prime Minister Manmohan Singh and his Chinese counterpart, Wen Jiabao, in 2005. Nevertheless, Prime Minister Manmohan Singh hoped that China would support the country's bid for civilian nuclear energy at the IAEA. But he admitted he had no firm commitment from the Chinese leadership. The Prime Minister also noted that China had finally come around to share India's concerns and ready to work together on the threat of fundamentalist terror emanating from Pakistan which is now in the throes of uncertainty.

Our Prime Minister sought the Chinese support for India's bid for nuclear energy during his interactions with President Hu Jintao and Premier Wen Jiabao. The PM was also learnt to have suggested that the atomic energy commissions of the two countries meet, although without any prior commitment. Singh suggested that the first such meeting be held in India. The Prime Minister, however, admitted that while China had reached out on civilian nuclear energy cooperation, he had not got any firm and definite answer.

RECALLING THE TROUBLED HISTORY

Behind the new efforts to forge a strong relationship between the world's two biggest emerging economies the old decades of suspicion, a bloody war and political animosity comes in the way. For example—the first Indian PM Jawaharlal Nehru visited China in October 1954 and was said to have been amazed by the "tremendous emotional response" from the Chinese people. He also met Mao Zedong for the first and last time. Under Nehru and his doctrine of Panchsheel (five Principles of Co-Existence), Hindi-Chini bhai-bhai was the mantra of India-China ties. From 1959, ties became strained with border skirmishes and discovery of a Chinese road in Aksai Chin. That year, the Dalai Lama of Tibet had to fled from Tibet to India further worsening relations.

In 1960, Zhou Enlai visited India. He proposed to Pt. Nehru that China would relinquish claim on Aksai Chin if

India gave up claim on Arunachal Pradesh. India rejected the proposal. In Oct. 1962, the war broke out and Chinese troops entered deep into the Indian terrory.

Relations languished with China supplying conventional weapons as well as nuclear arms in 1976 to Pakistan. However, in 1976 there was a restoration of ambassadorial ties. There was a new thaw with Chinese foreign minister Huang Hua visiting India in 1981. Though there were few rounds of border talks between 1981 and 1987, tensions remained. In 1988, Rajiv Gandhi became the first Indian PM to visit China since 1954. He met Deng Xiaoping, Zhu Rongji and other leaders resulting in the formation of working groups for negotiating the border issue and promoting trade. The Panchsheel doctrine was resurrected.

Ties steadily improved with Chinese premier Li Peng visiting India in May 1992 followed by president Jiang Zemin in 1996 in between, PM Narasimha Rao visited Beijing and signed the Agreement on the Maintenance of Peace and Tranquility along the Line of Actual Control on the India-China border. Relations nosedived after the Pokhran blast in 1998, when PM Atal Behari Vajpayee cited a Chinese threat as a reason. During the post-2000 period, Atal Bihari Vajpayee's visit to Beijing in June 2003 and an earlier visit to China by president K.R. Narayanan paved the way for better relations. A Declaration on Principles for Relations and Comprehensive Cooperation was jointly issued in 2003.

Against the above-cited background, India should recall the experience of Tibet's forcible absorption and Burma's territory, with whom we had close historical ties with Tibet and Burma. (Till 1937, Burma was part of British Indian empire). Today, Tibet and Burma are at the centre of the India-China relationship. India should see Burma as a hedge against China's authoritarian rise. Both the small nations—Tibet and Burma's leaders—Dalai Lama and Daw Aung San Suu Kye—have received the Nobel peace price against the Chinese repressive rule through powerful resistance movements. But the autocrats in Beijing, who value Burma as an entry to the way of Bengal and then the Indian Ocean, have inspired the authoritarian rule and have strategically reached at Burma's natural resources. Beijing is busy in making roads rails links at

Irrawaddy Corridor between Burma and ports of Yuman. For India, this link constitutes a strategic concern.*

The potential for Chinese strategic mischief has to be viewed against the background that the original tribal insurgencies in the north-east were instigated by Mao's China, which trained and armed the rebels be it Naga or Mizo guerrillas-party exploiting the Burma route. During the World War II, the allied and axis powers had classified Burma as a "back door to India". Today, India shares a porous 1,378-km border with Burma, with insurgents operating on both sides through shared ethnicity. Tibet and Burma are going to stay pivotal to Indian security. The centrality of the Tibet issue has been highlighted both by China's Tibet-linked territorial claim to Arunachal and by its major inter-basin and inter-river water transfer projects in the Tibetan plateau, the source of all of Asia's major rivers except the Ganges. By damming the Brahmaputra and Sutlej and toying with the idea of diverting the Brahmaputra waters to the parched Yellow river, Beijing is poised to use water into a weapon against India.

India cannot afford to shut itself out off Burma, or elsewith an increasingly assertive China to the north, a China-allied Pakistan on the west, a Chinese-influenced Burma to the east, and growing Chinese naval interest in the Indian Ocean—it will get encircled.

BEYOND THE GREAT WALL

The visit of our PM to China in Jan. 2008 was of great significance in the sense that the two great civilizations the Elephant eyeballing the Dragon-talked on various aspects of trade development and economic growth. India obtained a great opportunity to strike bargain with the People's Republic of China, though India was not in a position to match the economy and China's gross domestic product, export or trade. The Table 2 shown below makes clear of 'unequal status' to call the shot.

---

* Brahma Chellaney, "Counter China's Design, *Ibid.*, dated Jan. 16, 2008, p. 14.

TABLE 2
World of Difference

	China	*India*
GDP (ppp $ Trillion)	5.33	2:34
GDP per capita (ppp $)	4,091	2,126
Forex reserves ($ Billion)	1,612	276.0
Population below $ 1 day (%)	9.9	34.3
Population below $ 2 day (%)	34.9	80.4
Rice Productivity (kg per hectare)	6233	3034
Wheat Productivity (kg per hectare)	4155	2688
Life Expectancy (years)	72.5	63.7
Underweight children (%)	8	47
Infant mortality rate	23	56
Maternal mortality rate	45	450
Public health expenditure (% of GDP)	1.8	0.9
Telephones (million)	910	265
Internet users (million)	185	46

Source : *The Times of India*, dated 13 Jan. 2008, p. 13.

The Tibet issue too figured in the discussion between the two leaders for the support to persuade Dalai Lama to resume a dialogue, as it has caused trouble for China and has drawn world attention. China expects from the Indian Government to tackle the Tibetans living in India China takes the Tibet issue as a *"settled issue"* since the visit of PM Vajpayee to Beijing in 2003 under the Agreement 2003, which recognized the Tibetan Autonomous Region—TAR as 'part of China'. Then, India agreed not to allow anti-China activities organized by Tibetans in India. Here, India might use the issue as a bargaining chip in dealing with Chinese on the whole of Arunachal Pradesh. The Tibet issue cropped up again on the eve of the Olympic games held in China. For this see the separate chapter of the study.

India was, of course, deeply concerned over the huge gap in trade between Beijing and New Delhi and our Commence Minister Kamal Nath wanted to bridge the differences.

Surprisingly, Chinese leaders told our commerce minister that their government was extremely keen on investing in hydro-electricity projects in India, that too in Arunachal Pradesh. This was seen in Indian circle as an attempt to establish Chinese commercial presence in the Arunachal Pradesh, known for its awesome and untapped potential of hydro-electricity, apart from other places in the country. The offer was heeded to, though India is currently in a need of energy sources like hydro-electricity, but in the light of Chinese claim over the part of Arunachal Pradesh, it was difficult for India to concede the Chinese request unless China is interested in investing in other parts of the country.

CHINA'S OBJECTION TO INDIA'S CLAIM ON ARUNACHAL

It is shocking that China has taken exception to Prime Minister Manmohan Singh's assertion that Arunachal Pradesh belonged to India and lodged a protest over it. China has conveyed to India that it was not proper to make such comments at a time when the two countries were engaged in talks over the boundary question. Dr. Singh, during his visit to Itanagar in Feb. 2008, had said that Arunachal was "our land of rising sun", in a clear message that the state belongs to India. China has been laying a claim over large parts of the state and the two countries are holding talks to resolve the issue, but without any results. Sources in the UPA government said that they were not surprised at Beijing's reaction, since China is habit of laying claims over the Indian territories.

The past events on border areas reveal that China's incursions are due to refusal to clarify the Line of Control (LoC) by the Chinese leadership. This has been told by India to China before the PM's visit. India had already complained about Chinese incurious in Arunachal Pradesh and the India-Bhutan tri-junctions after repeated instances of Chinese movements which were described as "aggressive". Sadly, Indian side did not raise the LoC breaches during the PM's visit. Therefore, differing perception upon the LoC would hardly help to strengthen the bilateral ties between the two Asian powers. The question of boundary settlement is the need of a new world order.

CHAPTER

34

Administrative Corruption in India

How to Combat Corruption?

Corruption is a global phenomenon. As per the 'Transparency' International of German,—NGO, India is the 7th most corrupt country. Of course, a vast majority of the people, particularly the underprivileged and less privileged fell that a system of non-governance characterized by rampant corruption exists in Public Administration. In the governmental set-up, the critical task of public administration is entrusted to the popularly elected politicians called Ministers and officially appointed personnel called Bureaucrats. Good conduct and ethical practices are two cardinal principles of public administration to govern. The expectations of the people for fairness and justice in public administration are the same everywhere irrespective of their race, culture and the structure of the Government.

Corruption is both a systemic and individual phenomenon. Corruption has increased violence and lawlessness in the society and in the electoral politics. It has heightened inefficiency, nepotism, lethargy and indiscipline against the norms, work culture, rule of law, good governance and merit, etc. as are stressed by the era of globalisation and liberalisation. It has nothing to do with the concept of accountability, or bureaucratic accountability. Today, both at the central and state levels, a number of ministers, MP, MLAs, top level bureaucrats have been identified to have been alleged in adopting corrupt practices and our courts have confirmed those scandals and scans. It is unfortunate that corruption still remains as a hydraheaded monster in our public administration.*

The responsibility of the Government his increased leaps and bounds with the growth of the concept 'Welfare State'. I has been perceived many a times that there is a tendency of the ruling class to protect the interests of the "haves" and ignore those of the "have nots" and deprived class. Therefore, it is essential that people should have faith and confidence in the administrative elite and at the same time be, assured that any action taken by them is for the overall development of the nation and its people. If the public servants do not resort to arbitary, capricious, discriminatory and fanciful actions, there could be good rapport between the people and the Government and consequently the greatest good for the largest number of the people could be achieved. Transparent and clear public administration is a "must" for any Government of the time and public accountability is the core and conscience of the public administration.

It is unfortunate that with the passage of time corruption in India has substantially increased. A non-governmental organization transparency International based in Berlin has come with the corruption perception index. It ranks countries according to the level of corruption. In the year 2004 out of 102 most corrupted countries, India occupies the 33rd position. For a developing country like India corruption is a scourge. It is anti-national. It seriously retards country's economic development.

---

* This paper was presented by Dr. S. Balamurugan and S.S. Varma in the National Seminar on 'Corruption in India; Origin, Causes & solutions' Held at Haridwar, 1-3 October, 2004.

The World Bank has defined corruption as the use of "Public office for Private Profit". Corrupt acts include bribery, embezzlement, etc. International anti-corruption convention of the United Nations defines corruption as ". . . promise or giving of any advantage to another person as undue consideration for performing or refraining from the performance of that person's duty, or the soliciting or accepting of any advantage as undue considerations for performing or refraining from the performance of one's duty."

The Administrative Reforms Commission was appointed on January 5, 1966 by the President of India. While dealing with one of the terms of reference, namely, "to consider the problems of citizens' grievances", it unanimously recommended that the Ombudsman type of machinery be set-up in India. The Commission recommended two types of Ombudsmen i.e., Lokpal at the Centre level and Lokayukta at the State level to inquire into allegations of corruptions against public functionaries and for investigation of authorities in certain cases and for matters connected therewith. The commission had felt the urgent need for such institutions in view of the inadequacies in the existing system and for introduction of supplementing the already existing agencies like the Courts and Tribunals which were not always within the reach of the common people because of various factors including cumbersome procedures, long delays, litigation costs, etc. In addition, the Commission found that there was a vast area of cases arising out of the unjust exercise of executive power for which no remedy was available. Again, in the context of the off-expressed public opinion against the prevalence of corruption and for ensuring the highest standards of efficiency and integrity in the public administration and for making administrative wing accountable and transparent, the commission had underscored the need to set-up 'Ombudsman' type of institutions throughout the country.

The basic idea of the Lok Pal is borrowed from the office of Ombudsman, which has played an effective role in checking corruption and wrong-doing in Scandinavian and other nations. In a climate where, to use the former Prime Minister's

Vajpayee's own words, "corruption has bred contempt for the law an additional mechanism which takes note of public grievances and can take cognizance of wrong doing in public life deserves to be welcomed". Just how effective the Lok Pal legislation will be in checking corruption in high places has been a matter of long-standing and inconclusive debate. The Lok Pal is no substitute for judicial action and by itself the institution is unlikely to magically transform the manner in which the administration works. But, as conceived in some earlier draft Bills, the scope and jurisdiction of the Lok Pal is reasonably wide and the very existence of an institution which can bring public figures to book could act as an important check on the misuse of power. Given that virtually every major party has routinely supported the setting up of a Lok Pal in their manifestos, the Bill will not fail because of the lack of political support. All it requires now-just as all it had required before—is the requisite political commitment to see the proposed legislation through Parliament.

The Government of India introduced the Lokpal Bills in the Parliament in 1968, 1971, 1977, 1985, 1989, 1996, 1998 and 2001. It had been referred three times to joint select committees of both the Houses and as many times to the Parliamentary standing committee on home affairs. They had also submitted their reports. Thus, up to now, there is no national Ombudsman in India.

The bill has failed to get Parliament's approval several times in the past due to lack of consensus among law-makers about the exact functions of the Lokpal (Ombudsman) and whether to include the office of the Prime Minister in the definition of public servant.

The UNDP Report on Human Development in South Asia, says that if corruption levels in India were reduced to those of the Scandinavian countries, the investments in the country could increase annually by 10 per cent and GDP growth by almost 1.5 per cent each year. One recent study shows that investing in relatively corrupt country compared to a relatively honest one is equivalent to additional 15 per cent profit on investment.

CORRUPTION INDEX : WHO'S DIRTY, HOW DIRTY?*

Politicians, bureaucrats, doctors, contractors, stock brokers, top cops, petty clerks, sports administrators. . . . Is everybody on the take in India? As more and more worms creep out of the nation's woodwork, *Sunday Times* zeroes down on.

- Which are the three most corrupt sectors?
- Which institution/profession is still relatively clean?

Deep Focus

- *Bureaucracy* : Their sheer numbers and years in service makes their corruption much more than their political bosses.
  Politicians : All political parties are based on corruption. They require funds for elections and therefore the scope for accumulating and using black money is much more.
  Business : Most business came up during the licence-permit raj when the scope for making money out of licenses was ample. Even after liberalisation, corruption took on new avatars : now even policies are suited so as to encourage corruption. With the involvement of private players, more scams have been unearthed. Use of IT too has lead to more corruption in the form of e-crimes. Corruption has now become part of the DNA of this sector.
- Institutions with constitutional functions like the Election Commission (EC) and the Central Vigilance Commission are still clean.

How to Curb Corruption

- Pay special attention to education, especially value education. How else will children learn to discern and discriminate? Getting into IITs and IIMs is fine,

* *The Times of India*, 7/12/2003, p. 7.

Tree of Public Life

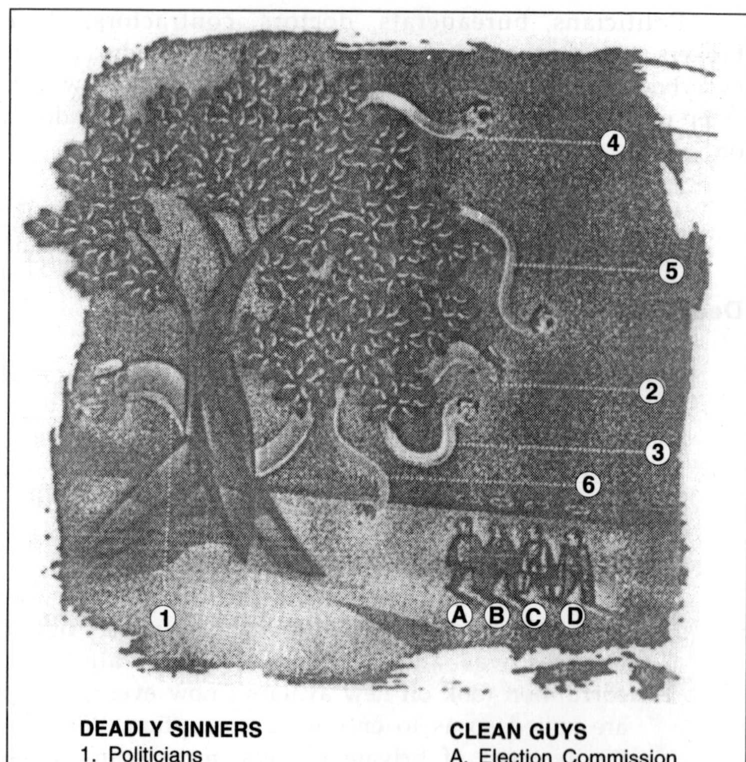

DEADLY SINNERS
1. Politicians
2. Police
3. Bureaucracy
4. Contractors
5. Arms Industry
6. Health Services

CLEAN GUYS
A. Election Commission
B. Supreme Court
C. Working Classes
D. Armed Forces

but what about making them better human beings? All schools should offer the humanities stream so that life in all its hues is imbibed. Are we producing a nation of just book-keepers and pipette wielders?

- Simplify rules and procedures. The more rules there are, the more scope for corruption. Red tape has now been replaced by green tape. All kinds of environmental clearances are now needed—all the more scope for corruption.

- Punish the corrupt. Why should law-breakers get await? The legal system has to get its act together. Discipline yourself, else the world will discipline you.
- Nothing like a committed media to expose scams. Make the common man aware of the details of corruption to start a movement against it.
- Dilute the powers of appointing and transferring officers. How about involving the public in selecting important officials?
- Enact the Lok Pal Bill and see the big fish get caught and brought within the purview of law.
- Implement the Citizen's Charter to ensure accountability and quality of services in various government organisations.
- Have an integrity pact in all government dealings

WORKING OF OMBUDSMAN IN SCANDINAVIAN COUNTRIES

The office of Ombudsman is a Scandinavian institution that has received much attention in recent years. New Zealand and Canada and several states in the U.S. and some of the new countries of Africa have adopted the idea, and the name atleast has been applied to officials in business concerns and on college campuses. The concept of an Ombudsman originated in its present form with the Swedish constitution of 1809 and it has been adopted and even extended in the other Scandinavian countries such as Finland (1919), Denmark (1953), and Norway (1962).

Bureaucracy sometimes rides brutally over the rights of the individuals, either because of careless disregard, or because regulations cannot cover exceptional cases, or for other reasons having to do with the fallibility of laws or officials. Any society that seeks justice must provide channels for appeal and correction of mistakes, but too often the procedures of complaint go through the same governmental structure as the thing objected to. Therefore, the Swedes provided for a judicial agent, the Judicial Ombudsman (JO), acting under the authority of Parliament to be a watchdog over administrative officials and acts.

The JO is a person respected in the community, with salary and position comparable to that of a Supreme Court Judge. He or she has the right to see all relevant documents and access to whomever he wishes to consult. The press checks with the JO each day, so the power of publicity is at the JO's disposal. The constitution of each country empowers the JO not only to accept complaints from individuals but also to initiate proceedings whenever he or she senses there may be injustice. Occasionally the JO makes inspection trips, visiting courts, hospitals, schools, smelling out little and big cases of wrongdoing, suggesting remedies.

The JO also makes an annual report to Parliament but is never ordered by Parliament to undertake a case or to desist from prosecution. Thus, the JO is a free agent, appointed for a several-year period and frequently reappointed. The JO has a deputy and staff of lawyers but still has difficulty handling the workload. The office of JO gives people confidence that there's someone concerned not only with the welfare of society as a whole but with their own rights as individuals. More recently, Ombudsman offices are being created in the former socialist countries of Eastern Europe (Poland, Hungary, Slovenia, Albania, Bosnia-Herzegovina, Macedonia) as well as in the Russian Federation.

During the last decade, Latin America has witnessed a process in favour of a more democratic rule compared to the tradition of authoritarianism long developed in the area. As a consequence, many countries began to include the figure of Ombudsman with different names : Defensor del Pueblo, Procurador de los Derechos Humanos, Defensor de los Habitantes, Comisionado Nacional deDerechos Humanos. Until then, just Puerto Rico (from 1977) and Guatemala (1985) had institutions like this. From 1990 on, it was created in Mexico, El Salvador, Colombia, Costa Rica, Paraguay, Honduras, Peru, Argentina, Bolivia, Nicaragua, Panama, Ecuador and Venezuela. It is also in agenda for Chile and Uruguay. All the Latin American Ombudsmen are integrated in the Federation Iberoamericana del Ombudsmen to give their efforts an international support.

Regardless the name of the office, all Ombudsman institutions respond in essence to the basic pattern of an independent investigator capable of receiving complaints from the public to make the state administration accountable for wrongdoings and facilitate redress to the victims of maladministration or violations of human rights.

Not all the Ombudsmen are however, equal since traditionally the Scandinavian and European Ombudsman has been responsible only for cases of maladministration or administrative injustice. Lately under the influence of the Spanish Constitution of 1978 a so-called hybrid model has been developed to include within the Ombudsmen jurisdiction the responsibility for human rights violations. In some cases, the enlarged mandate has gone even further as to include the protection of the environment, freedom of the press and supervision of elections.

The Scandinavian countries and especially Finland have been regarded quite highly in many international ratings of anti-corruption. What are the reasons for this fine situation? It is useful to look at some Finnish experience of combating corruption.

There have been times in Scandinavian history, too, when corruption has filled the front pages of the tabloids. Every now and then cases do emerge when an individual, a lower or a high-ranking public official, is caught red-handed committing some criminal offence. In most cases this has led to the resignation or dismissal of the person and, depending on the case also to a criminal prosecution. Yet ordinary Finns do not come across corruption in their daily lives. Recently, there was a survey done on the citizens' perceptions of public institutions. The police scored the top rating for honesty.

As noted, in international ratings of corruption Finland has enjoyed high esteem for a number of years. The corruption index by Transparency International has had Finland ranked number one as the least corrupted country for many years. A few possible explanations for this phenomenon.

The model of the present-day Finnish welfare society is widely known. It is, however, useful to point out some background facts as to its origins. In Finland, democracy and the rule of law were consolidated in the beginning of the twentieth century. In those days, good education was seen as one of the most powerful social tools. Being a nation of 5 to 6 million people, they know that everybody's skills were needed in building welfare and prosperity. Education became compulsory for everyone.

The Finnish legal norms on corruption have been basically the same for the past 100 years. The administrative principles of good governance effective in Finland, are : (1) the principle of equality, (2) the principle of objectivity, (3) the principle of proportionality, and (4) the principle that any action must be appropriate in view of its purpose. The main idea of the Finnish anti-corruption legislation is that it is never considered as a separate phenomenon, with separate laws or separate supervisory bodies. Instead, corruption is seen as part of criminality and as part of bad governance and/or politics. The prevention of corruption also involves creating and observing ethical norms of behaviour, increasing transparency and preventing procedures.

Both in state administration and in local administration, a so-called employment instruction system is being applied to new office-holders. This is a form of introduction training. If there is a great risk of corruption in the field in question, matters related to corruption shall naturally be emphasized during the introductory training. New office-holders are also given examples of some typical situations where the risk of bribery may arise. Management training, as well as other kinds of staff training in public administration are moreover planned so that they include sections on values and ethics.

According to the Finnish Constitution, some of the most important guarantees of good governance for the citizens are the right to be heard, the right to hear the grounds for decisions, and the right of appeal.

TRANSPARENCY AND OPENNESS

The transparency of public decision-making promotes anti-corruption work. Open access to public records makes it possible to apply transparency and good information practices in public activities. It also makes it possible for individuals and associations to control the exercise of official authority and the use of public finances, freely to form their opinion, to influence the exercise of official authority, and to assert their rights and safeguard their interests.

Transparency in public administration is enhanced by the obligation of the highest officials to declare their commitments, and by restrictions on secondary occupations. Training, leadership and publications increase the consciousness among civil servants of values and ethically sound proceedings in public administration. Informing partners in the private sector of the requirements of civil service ethics is a factor for promoting transparency. In local administration, a clear definition of the eligibility for office for members of a municipal executive board and other institutions promotes transparency and reduces corruption.

Finland was one of the first countries to allocate state funds for political parties. The elimination of conflicting interests and liabilities and thus corruption is also pursued through the publicity of election financing.

LESSONS CAN BE LEARNED FROM THE FINNISH EXPERIENCE

The key contacts that can be distilled from the Finnish experience and other Scandinavian countries are: 1. access to education for all; 2. well functioning democracy both at national and local level; 3. civil service based on meritocracy; 4. openness in public administration; 5. low hierarchical structures; 6. devolution of decision-making powers to civil servants in their respective fields of responsibility; 7. non-politicisation of key civil service posts, and above all, 8. the effort to defend the values of an open society.

In India, it is proposed to create one national Ombudsman with general responsibilities which will combine the characteristics of the classical Scandinavian Ombudsman model with some of the new features of its modern versions existing in the European countries, and with some adjustments according to condition in India. The most essential function of the Ombudsman institution will be to guarantee more efficiently the rights and freedoms of private persons. If the former are abused by the public authorities, the Ombudsman shall be entitled to propose measures for terminating the acts of abuse, compensating the incurred damages and creating conditions for the smooth and efficient exercise of their rights in the future.

More specifically, the Ombudsman must have the authority to monitor and control the exercise of administrative power, the organization and regulation of the judicial system's administration, as well as any other exercise of public authority. However, the subject and scope of the Ombudsman's activities must not include certain institutions, such as the Parliaments, the President, and the Judiciary.

It can be proposed that the Ombudsman be elected by a simple majority directly by the Parliament. It has been suggested that the Ombudsman's mandate should be longer than the mandate of the Parliament—five or more years. The number of the Ombudsman's mandates will be limited to no more than two. At the same time, he will enjoy immunity similar to that of the members of Parliament.

Because of its Parliamentary origin, the Ombudsman will report to the Parliament once a year which would secure a high level of publicity and transparency for its activities and the results thereof. This effect will have a positive influence on those public institutions which do not fully respect the rights and freedoms of private persons.

TYPES OF RESPONSIBILITIES AND AUTHORITY

In general, the responsibilities and authority of the Ombudsman are:

- To review petitions in any form from private persons—individuals and legal entities, whether local and/or foreign, as well as from individuals with no citizenship;
- To conduct investigations and examinations when a particular case has been referred to him;
- To make proposals and recommendations to all observed institutions with public powers or functions regarding their respect for human rights and freedoms, and to recommend possible remedies

for the infringement of certain rights and freedoms and the reasons for that infringement, notwithstanding whether the ombudsman acts at somebody's request or his own initiative;

- To act as an intermediary between private persons and public entities in order to overcome the existing infringements on private rights and freedoms;
- To request and receive timely, complete and precise information from all observed institutions;
- To have direct access to the observed institutions, including their meetings, discussions and other forums;
- To give and announce publicly his opinions on cases he has been approached with or on issues on which he makes summaries and conclusions at his own discretion;
- To approach the prosecution bodies when, as a result of his observations and investigations, the ombudsman has obtained information on a committed crime; and
- To prepare special reports, if necessary and to inform the Parliament incidentally about particularly serious cases of disrespect and abuse of rights.

CONCLUDING OBSERVATIONS

The mafia raj has brought to an end the democratic and transparent order of the country. Ministerial immunity is the very root cause of the prevailing corruption in public life. What the Indian Constitution and legal system have solely lacked all years is any independent machinery of investigation into charges of corruption against the men of high places/ holding position. The creation of the Lok Pal and an independent functioning of CVC is the only answer to arrest its fallout. Judicial activism has come forward to checkmate the malady, but the lack of public activism has made the authorities to escape from the punishment and legal penalty. The remedy of the criminalization of politics, as per the Vohra Report, lies in speeding up justice, stopping political interference in prosecutions and weeding out corrupt elements from public life. It has suggested the creation of a nodal agency to collect information from all sources and pursue cases against criminal elements. Lastly, the right to information should be ensured to make all governmental activities open to public. This warrants drastic changes in the Official Secret Act, 1923, which is still a sign of colonial legacy.

The prevention of Corruption Act came into force in September 1988. It consolidated the provisions of the Prevention of Corruption Act, 1947, some sections of the Indian Penal Code, the Criminal Procedure Code and the Criminal Law Act, 1952. The Central Government has set-up the following from departments as anti-corruption measures, namely : (i) Administrative Vigilance Division (AVD) in the Department of Personnel and Training, (ii) Central Bureau of Investigation (CBI), (iii) Domestic Vigilance Units in the Ministries/Departments/Public Undertakings/Nationalized Banks, and (iv) Central Vigilance Commission (CVC).

Various commissions and committees have been appointed by the Government of India to inquire into the charge of corruption against politicians and public companies from time to time. Corruption charges were recently leveled against Chief Ministers and ministers. At present, only eleven states of India (including Bihar, Himachal Pradesh, Karnataka, Madhya Pradesh, Karnataka, Madhya Pradesh, Maharashtra, Rajasthan and Uttar Pradesh) have set-up Lok Ayukts for investigating charges of corruption against ministers, MLAs and other public functionaries. There is no such institution as yet at the national level which may act as a watchdog body on a minister's probity. Way back the United Front Government introduced Lok Pal Bill but due to lack of political will it could not be passed. Prosecution under the prevention of Corruption Act is possible only if the complainants gets Government permission which is seldom given for obvious reasons.

In August 2002, the Supreme Court of India was seen worried of newspaper reports highlighting scandals and scams in public administration. It then suggested to the Centre to appoint a Lok Pal to look into corruption in public life. It was in reference to the allotments of Petrol Pumps to certain top level politicians against the dependents of Kargil martyrs. The SC bench then had held: "Once the Government appoint is Lok

Pal, a major headache will be over it as would first go into the issues rather than litigants rushing to the courts."*

Likewise, in the Naina Sahni murder case, after coming to highlight the Tandoor murder case, the Supreme Court asked the Centre to make the C.V.C. an autonomous and the CBI accountable in the controversial case of single Directive Provision in the CVC Act, 2003. There was a clause to restrain the CBI from inquiry against high officials without the Government's. permission.

The Government later had to change the clause as per the Judgment of 1997 in the Hawala case.** In this case, the Government had to reveal the contents of the Vohra Committee Report, substantiating the alleged existence of a diabolic nexus among the underworld, politicians, bureaucrats, businessmen and media. Then Justice J.S. Verma coined, 'Be you even so high, the law is above you'. This reflects how the executive has been lukewarm to the efforts of the court to arrest the fallout of corrupt practices in public life.

* *The Times of India* news, New Delhi, 20-8-2002, p. 4.

** *The Times of India* news, carried out by Rakesh Bhatnagar, 5-11-2003, p. 6.

PART IV

On Foreign Policy/Strategic Front

CHAPTER

35

Twists and Turns in India's Foreign Policy

In formulation of a foreign policy, both domestic and external factors are taken into account. If we look at the way the formulation of foreign policy in democratic and non-democratic countries, they mobilize national power, define their national interests, pursue effective policies, play military strategy in the light of balance of power—which is one of the basic principles of power politics game that acts to control interstate relations. However, the formulation of foreign policy is the result of its leader's capacity which gains people's support in implementing that foreign policy. A democracy cannot keep its foreign policy objectives as secret from its people (like India), but non-democratic system (like Pakistan) can avoid this procedure. Even the role of mass media, press, television are least allowed to influence the formulation/ execution of that country's foreign policy. Hence, in the game of power politics of democracy, the foreign policy suffers from certain weaknesses like openness and lack of clear thinking and courage or commitment to a line of action.

Despite above-cited description, the balance of power doctrine has been a part and parcel of diplomacy of all successful states—be they are democratic or non-democratic in nature and system, as it continues to control the pattern of world politics. In the words of Professor Morgenthau, the principle of balance of power implies 'equilibrium', i.e. it refers to distribution of power among several nations with approximate equality, as the Bush administration has done it between India and Pakistan in the emerging uni-polar world order, following the tools and techniques such as divide and rule, armament/disarmament alliance, intervention, ideological mourings, etc.

EMERGING A NEW BALANCE OF POWER

With the help of the Indo-US nuclear agreement of July 2005, the Americans are poised to project a strategy to ensure that the US remains the foremost power in military, economic, technological and cultural terms in a group of six major powers, namely the Israeil, China, EU, Japan, Russia and India. In order to implement this strategy, the Bush administration enlisted India as a 'partner', as the US has already done this with the other four powers. It is pertinent to mention that the thrust of US strategy towards China is engagement, not confrontation, containment, because China is currently as a rising capatalist nation as the US or the rest western world. The relationship of the US with the Soviet Union and China during the Cold-War era has lost the meaning, because Russia is very much close to the NATO and she shares membership with the US in the organisation of Security and Cooperation in Europe and Russia has been co-opted into the G-8 group of leading economies. The US is militarily allied to E.U. and Japan. This new balance of power is emerging in the 21st century with US as hegemon, with the thrust to ensure energy security for the whole world, which is a must for economic growth of all the major powers. Against background, the US thought it fit on making India is 'partner' and tapping into its economic and technological potential.

The very purpose of the Indo-US nuclear pact is to overcome the hostility of discriminatory and non-proliferation regime. It is good symptom that the plea of India has been endorsed by N-powers. Now India is set to play a global role in the new power equations.

On Indo-US nuclear negotiation, some odd suggestions from the US emerged, such as that India should be made to put up a 'cap' on future nuclear testing, and that if it conducts a test, the cooperation with OS would be nullified. In defence, Indian delegation has already pointed out that India has already declared a unilateral moratorium not to make a bomb. But it would not support to making it a legal condition. Further the bilateral nuclear agreement is meant for civil nuclear reactors. There is no question of signing the NPT on behalf of New Delhi.

Till this date, the UPA has assured our Parliament not to bow any US pressure over the civil N-deal of July 2005 and it shall be bound by a bilateral pact, not subject to any US laws and India will not accept any extra obligations of NPT. The transparent approach is appreciated as we have refused to accept any kind of compromise with India's strategic N-weapons programme that has run into criticism in the US Congress. Indian's concern is that our energy security should not be put in to any risk.

India's missile test (Agni-III Test) needs no criticism if it is compared with North Korea's missile programme carried out in July 2006, because our Nuclear programme has been transparent and non-threatening to world peace. These two developments cannot further be compared, as India had notified in advance the US and Pakistan about the tests. Against the North Korean test, Indian Nuclear programme never defied the set rules of international conventions. And unlike North Korea, Iran and Pakistan, India has not proliferated its N-technologies. Above all, India is a true democracy of Asia, which abides by international commitment and the rule of law while North Korea is a militaristic dictatorship.

The Leftists are justified to ask the UPA Government to explain whether the decision of the UPA Government to shut down the 50 years old circus Reactor in four years by 2010 and shift the Apsara Reactor from its present location in Barc (Bhabho Atomalic Research Centre). Our concern is whether the IAEA inspection made independently or under the American pressure. If India loses the right to reused or re-processed nuclear fuel, its shortage would be a costly affair for us in terms of our future developmental programmes.

So far our relations with Nepal is concerned, India has been strongly supporter of peace process between the Nepal Government and Maoists after a decade of civil war. They have agreed to hold Con-assembly elections to a 25 point code of conduct for further negotiation. They have also agreed to invite the UN to monitor the ceasefire. India's interests lie in the fact that the peace process is not bogged down, because a revival of anarchy shall hit New Delhi's interest, nor the high profile Indian presence in Nepal is warranted. New Delhi must keep in mind the experience of a peace-keeping force in Sri Lanka in the 1980s. New Delhi should also acknowledge its ambivalent relationship with the UN and UN resolution demanding a plebiscite in Nepal. What New Delhi could inform international interlocutors that any UN role in Nepal should be precisely defined, i.e. its role should be to facilitate the peace process rather than to take it over. Tuning Nepal into UN dependency (as happened in Kosov) would go against the strategic interests of India. India has tangible evidence to prove that the Indo-Nepal border has been used in the past by Pakistan's-trained militants to infiltrate into India and spread terror. It has to be controlled.

While India's concern about the Chinese role in Nepal is unwarranted but it needs not panic. In the light of India's improvement in relations with China, she is India's competitor but not an enemy. Moreover, in view of Pakistan's economic vulnerability and its dependence on Washington, it now appears relatively difficult for Neapl to play China or Pak card against India. Yet Indian foreign policy establishment should undertake initiative to win the confidence of Nepalese people directly. Similarity, both India and China should come forward to join hands to arrest the on-going Japanese imperialistic ambition so that regional peace and order is not thwarted.

China only wants India not to intrude into her market and allows her to develop internally unperturbed. Japan, on the contrary, wants to conquer our markets through her NGOs and companies like Suzuki, Hyundia, Toyota, etc.

It is worth-mentioning of some of the new developments in Asia, notably North Korea's long rangle missile programme, which confirms the existence of an 'arms race' across the region. Likewise, some events such as China's military build-up, Indonesia's alignment with China, purchasing new arms by Thailand, Vietnam under anti-terrorism and anti-piracy plank send the message that both the US and China are interested- in the Malacca Strait and the Andaman sea. Even both China and India are seeking to have greater influence over Myanmar as well as other South-East Asia countries who have began modernising their armed forces, while compromising their autonomy and security matters. Currently the balance of power strategy is volatile.

THE FIRST EVER-MILITARY BASE IN TAJIKISTAN

This build-up reflects India's quiet strategy to position itself as a 'player' in Central Asia. It is India's first overseas military base being set-up in Tajikistan at Ayni/Farkhor, which will have MIG-29 fighter aircrafts. This is new beginning towards playing a power ability in Central Asia to ensure regional security. The Indian base is adjoining a Russia base at Ayni. It is a new reflection of longer relationship in the area and it will be unique in the sense that it will not ruffle either Russia or the US strategy in view of India's close relationship with Russia and growing a new convergence with the USA.

Indo-Chinese trade cooperation is boosting in the era of globalisation, of course. But the presence of Chinese companies in the development of ports, specifically the Hong-Kong-based Hutchison Port Holdings at Mumbai and Channai ports is seen with risks by Intelligence Bureau and the RAW, so far as Indian maritime security is concerned, as bidding for projects would let China an entry in the Indian Ocean with serious consequences for our national security due to China's proximity with Pakistan and Bangladesh with whom Chinese companies have the similar involvement in building strategic ports in Gwardar deep sea port in Pakistan, Chittagaon in Bangladesh and Sri Lanka and Myanmar.*

India is currently poised to join hands with E.U. countries to foster her trade and economic relations, keeping in view the background of WTO's role and the suspension of the Doha rounds of negotiation. It is meant to gear up for an alternative option to enhence regional trade agreements like that of the Singapore—type Comprehensive Economic Cooperation Agreement—CECA, which has registered higher FDI Investments and services of the EU countries, giving the benefit to the ten ASEAN countries as being the members of this group. In fact, EU is obviously interested in having a greater market access for its Industrial goods, whereas India is more concerned in investments and service sector for her economic growth.

Mention may be made that the Non-Alignment Movement NAM can still rise to meet the new challenges and bring development with dignity and human face into the centrality of world politics. For this, India should evolve an agenda of national and global policy action, while assuring the developing countries that India has not given up her commitment to the cause of evoluting a new world order with equity, justice and fairness, as a New International Economic Order—NIEO emphases. India must project the principle of Independence and autonomy in decision-making as per her own national interest in the uni-polar world order that prevails today, wherein the trends of globalisation, massive liberalisation, overnight privatization, the role of WTO, etc. continue to maintain their protectionist tendencies. The WTO forum, for example, continues to be loaded with the influence of the powerful nations who often cause harm to the interests of poor and weaker countries. The NAM is, therefore, an appropriate forum in the emerging world order where the

* After close to a year of intensive debate, the Government of India decided to shut ports to Chinese companies investing in, or managing any Indian port on security reasons. This includes Hutchison Port Holdings Mega Plan play in August 2006. The decision was taken by Chinese as discrimination and biased. It is based on news released by the defence ministry news published in *The Times of India*, New Delhi, July 21, 2006, p. 6).

loud voice of sanity against perpetration of human miseries on the innocent civilians of the countries like Iraq, Iran, Lebanon can be raised.

I was, indeed, shocking and surprising that Havana's NAM summit emerged into a 'thaw' in the rocky relationship with Pakistan where the Indian PM agreed to sign a deal with Pakistan's General Musharraf for a joint mechanism on terrorism in spite of the harsh reality that the ISI was behind the 7/11 Mumbai blasts and the terrorist training camps still have been operating on the Pak's soil. This is why, there is strong resentment, within the Congress and UPA partners as to why the Indian leadership agreed to a damage control exercise with Pakistan. It is will-known that since 1991 centrality of Pak sponsored terror has hamppered India's peace process undertaken by the previous NDA government headed by A.B. Vajpayee. The pact has put India in a weaker position in the fight of terrorism in the region. The deal reflects a sense of conspiracy against India to jeopardise our strategic interests in J&K.*

One must agree with the analysis of Ajani Sahni of the Indian Institute of conflict management that the deal is 'utterly misconceived', in the sense that it is like entering into an alliance with a criminal (Islamabad). India has destroyed what we have made over the years to convince the world that Pakistan is a source of terrorism. How can India hope to get information from Pakistan about the free-lance role of terrorist groups? Indeed, India has been a victim of terrorism sponsored by the ISI and it is believed that any Pakistani cooperation on the terror front will be part of a larger context of resolving the J & K problem as per the master plan of Pakistan's foreign policy. Mention may be made how Indo-Pak dialogue on Siachen and Sir Creek ran into rough weather on account of the strength of our armed forces there to which Islamabad insists on downsizing the strength.

There is great disappointment in our domestic circle that the world's pre-eminent power (the US), which has invented the concept of pre-emption, is preaching a different mantra to

* See the observations made in the *Sunday Times of India*, New Delhi, "Will Thaw Last?", 4/9/2006, p. 8.

India, specifically in the background of G-8 meeting at St. Petersburg where the horrific blasts in Mumbai on 11th July, 2006 were discussed. At the highest level, India clarified to the US that the blasts were the handiwork of the Lashkar-e-Taiba, which is directly controlled by Pakistan's ISI, yet the US diplomat for South & Central Asia, Richard Boucher, hedged the issue, stating that "The evidence to who is responsible we have not seen yet" (?). In the light of the Middle East crisis, the rapidly rise of Taliban in Afghanistan and Iran's nuclear programme, it is futile to hope that the western powers will come forward to help India against Pak's terror, though Pakistan is currently engaged in the US's Afghan plan to eliminate the Taliban forces.* The Government of the day shall have to, in a nutshell, undertake the hard decision to strengthen external security and to combat internal terrorism on its own strength.

MAKING BORDER A BOND OF FRIENDSHIP?

China's aggressive statement taking claim to the whole of Arunachal Pradesh, days before Hu Jintao's visit in December 2006, leaves one in doubt of its intentions. This was raised by Chinese ambassador Sun Yuxi putting Indian officials wonder whether the experience was a deliberate one to put the controversial issues before the visit in advance. They can hardly be called neighbourly. There is no need for us to be afraid. On the contrary, we should be firm and stand our ground. It would do India good if she were to stand up for her territorial integrity and defend the Tibetan cause. The Chinese annexation of Tibet remains one of the most unforgivable political crimes of the last century.

On the contrary what was said earlier was contradicted by Chinese President Hu Jintao when he said on 23rd Nov. 2006 in New Delhi that Beijing would not seek "selfish gains"

* One should recall the account of the book: Bush at War in which the former Dy. Secretary of state Richard Armitage is referred to as having threatened to Pakistan to fall in the line with the US strategy after the 9/11 terror attack or face 'back to stone age' through bombings. The US then was well-confirmed of Pakistan's long history with the Taliban regime. *The Times of India* News, Sept. 23, 2006, p. 1.

in South Asia. He hoped that the China; India boundary will be converted into "Bond of good neghbourliness and mutually beneficial cooperations."

It is appropriate to mention how the dispute between the two nations originated over Arunachal Pradesh, which was formally known as Tawang China, is interested in the district of Tawang that borders Tibet and Bhutan. This Tawang is famous for its monastry built in 1681. By the Tibetan Lama Lodre Gyatso as per the wishes of the 5th Dalai Lama. It is situated near Guwahati. This is the strong evidence that China cites to claim the territory.

Like that of Arunachal, China, ahead of Hu Jintao's visit to India raised the Dalai Lama issue with India, stating that the supporters of Tibetan spiritual leader have been using Indian soil for aniti-China activities, whereas India has categorically made position clear of not allowing such activities from its soil. At present the Tibetan Government in exile has been running from Dharamasala in Himachal Pradesh for years. The matter, of course, raised by Chinese delegation was taken by surprise as the issue had never been taken up at this platform earlier.

CONNECTING THE OLD STILLWELL ROAD

Chinese President initiated a talk for a direct road link between India and China. China wants the old Stillwell road

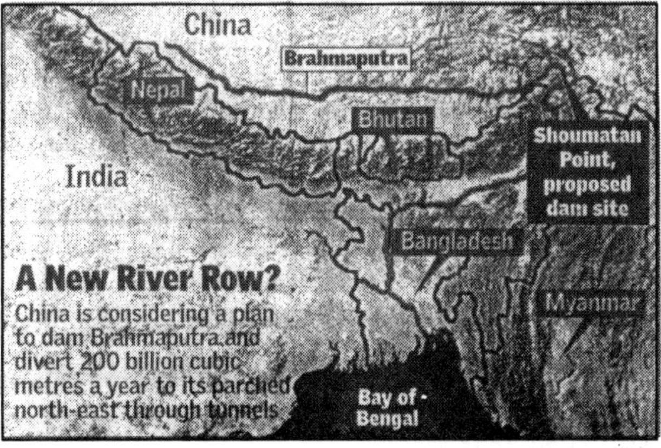

connecting Arunchal Pradesh with Yunan province in western China through Myanmar-rebuilt and reopened in order to give a new impetus to trade. It may be recalled that the Stillwell road, closed since World War II, was part of the agenda at the ministerial-level talks. India has not been very keen on re-opening this road link though it's developing another one, linking Manipur to Myanmar.

According to Sun Xiao, Deputy Director of China Council for Promotion of International Trade.* "Business will grow rapidly if this big corridor is opened up as it would reduce transportation time and cost significantly. Why should close neighbours trade through the long sea route when a land route is available?"

Construction of the road on the Chinese side has already begun, Beijing has pinned hopes on business with India to develop backward areas in western China, including the Yunan, Sichuan and Tibet provinces. As per Chinese sources, China's seriousness on this count is evident from the fact that of the 164 business executives chose into accompany Jintao to India, 66 are from the Sichuan province alone. "We want the big corridor between India, Myanmar and China to help in development of western China, Beijing is assisting Yangon in re-building the road, most of which passes through Myanmarese territory and opens at the Teng Chong border with China. Of the 1,700-km stretch, just 60 km is in India though it forms a crucial business link. India, on the other hand, is more keen on the road connecting Tamu in Manipur and Kalemyo in Myanmar. Infect, India is reluctant to have a link through Arunachal Pradesh because of the sensitive nature of the border. China's grandiose plan is to link India with the Stillwell road while building a direct corridor to Thailand from Kunming.

After the Chinese Revolution in 1911 (not the one led by Mao), the last of the Chinese dynasties, the Qing dynasty, came to an end. Consequently, China, Mongolia and Tibet became three separate countries and the Republic of China was declared in February 1912. Within a year, Tibet declared its

* It is based on the report of Saibal Dasgupta published in *The Times of India*, New Delhi, 15-12-2006, p. 6.

independence and forced Chinese troops out of Lhasa back to the mainland. In a bid to prevent the unrest from spreading into their territories, the British tried to assert the Indian boundary. A meeting was organised at Shimla in 1914, between the British and the Tibetans.

The Shimla convention ceded Tawang (present day Arunchal Pradesh) and other Tibetan areas to Britain. Later, the Chinese rejected the Shimla convention saying that Tibet had been Chinese territory for centuries and that a local government had no powers to sign any treaty. The Chinese refused to accept the border decided in the Shimla convention and further claimed that territory located south of Tibet, present day Arunchal Pradesh, too was a part of Tibet and hence belonged to China. This territory was occupied by China during the Sino-Indian war of 1962 and later returned to India at the end of the war.

Mention may be of the Macmahon line, it is the line drawn on the map attached to the Shimla convention demarcating the border between British India and Tibet as Britain tried to advance its line of control and establish buffer zones around its colony. The line extends along the crest of the Himalayas for 550 miles from Bhutan in the east to the bend of the Brahmaputra river in the west. It includes present day Arunachal Pradesh in India's (then British India's) territory. It was named after Sir Henry MacMahon, then foreign secretary and chief negotiator for the British at the convention.

It is almost the same as the Line of Actual Control that now demarcates the territory controlled by India from that under the Chinese. India regards the Macmahon line as a permanent border. However, the Chinese have stuck to their stand that it is merely a temporary line of control.

Chinese plan to damming the Brahmaputra river by diverting 200 billion cubic meters of water annually under the proposed project called, Why India worried at Damming the Brahmaputra River? to feed aging yellow river through the tributary Yangtze river, has worried the Indian Government The plan, though under serious discussion, has the backing of Chinese president Hu Jintao—a Hydro engineer by profession, whose plan is to divert water to the China's north-east Shaanxi, Hebei, Beijing and Tianjia. If the project goes through, it could strangle one of India and Bangladesh's biggest sources of water.

Not only this, the Brahmaputra Project, according to Indian experts, will change hydrological conditions available to India and Bangladesh that could spark a new dispute similar to the crisis over the Pareechu Lake that developed in 2004 and to this effect India and China signed an agreement on sharing information on Sutlej, yet India draw little comfort from this pact. The work has already been started by China in August 2006. (See Indrani Bagchi's observations published in *The Times of India*, New Delhi, dated Oct. 24, 2006, p. 6)

In fact, the idea is to dam Brahmaputra, known as Yarlung Tsangpo in Tibet, at the Shuomatan point (also known as the big U-turn) in China and divert the water to the Yellow river through a series of tunnels. China has already started a project of damming the Yangtze and Lancang (Mekong) for power projects, as the enclosed map helps us to understand the gravity of crisis. This largest river of India originated from near Mt. Kailash in Tibet. This is the Brahma's putra or son (the only 'male' Indian river).

It is a matter of concern that such 'Big U-turn' disputes cannot be settled through Judicial System nor the international law provides any regulatory organization (Like WTO) to solve such trans-boundary natural resources. Hence, such disputes can be solved through involvement of a great deal of understanding, diplomacy, expertise and negotiating skill.

In substance, the two developments should be addressed at the failure of our diplomacy. First, Shashi Tharoor as a meritorious candidate for the post of UN Secretary General had to formally bow out of the race because of the ambivalent posture of the US and China. Infact, the US has been very much familiar with South Korea, who has been a long-term usually of the US and an American protectorate against N-armed North Korea. Ban Ki-Moon suited Washington more because he shall not stand in the way of the American interests while handling any critical issue of international importance by the UN. China too did not take a confrontationist attitude because of the proximity of US-China ties-up. India failed to back Shashi Tharoor when it mattered with the PM not actively canvassing support in Havana and also missing the meeting of UN General Assembly. Likewise, the Bush administration never came out to support our claim for a seat in the UN Security Council, inspite of India being a 'strategic partner' of the US. Even China did not extend its support to our cause. As such our growing ties with the US in the strategic game plan of Asia, was seen to be an attempt to contain Chinese influence. Indeed, India's foreign policy is at the crossroads in the unipolar order. This scenario underlines the need to come out of the US 'influence'. No UPA partner wants India to see to be a junior partner of the Bush administration *vis-a-vis* India's autonomy in terms of formulating our policies—be it the foreign policy or the trade policy.

It is worth-recalling that the Chineses wanted to add Tawang rider to boundary talks as think-tank experts of China expressed their views in the conference organized by the Institute of Asia Pacific Studies, which is part of the giant Chinese Academy of Social Science in Beijing. The closed-door meeting was held of a ahead of Hu Jinto's visit to New Delhi from November 20, 2006. As per views of Chinese experts, the border problem could be solved if Indian handed over Tawang to China. But the Indian heavy weight experts opposed to the idea on the ground that Tawang is part of Indian territory and also it is strategically vulnerable in the Himalayan region, keeping in view the population factor that the people living in Tawang are Indian citizen. Therefore, the question did not arise to be discussed with Hu.* Even South Block too has admitted that India does not expect any substantive progress on the border issue, nor New Delhi thought it fit to link Hu's visit to the border issue.

Even if no solution of the border dispute is reached in near future, there are routes along the border, which would ultimately render it irrelevant. At present India needs to strengthen the infrastructure of roads and check posts, which are meagre today as the Nathu La Post trading access the border is a case in point. New Delhi ought to think of more opening up overland trade routes from China to Bengal and the North-East, as a key to reviving the moribund economics

* *The Times of India* News, New Delhi, November 11, 2006, p. 9.

of these regions. For example, land routes to China and to Thailand, Vietnam and Malaysia through Myanmar would lend substance to the 'look east' orientation of India's foreign policy. It would also resolve the north-east's political problems by ending its isolation, which cuts it off not only from the rest of India but also from India's northern and eastern neighbours. If everyone is having a party in the region it is likely that Dhaka too would, sooner or later, want to join what is effectively the only game in town. New Delhi must look more to the neglected eastern part of the country, and do all it can to facilitate border trade.*

* *India Today*, New Delhi, November 14, 2006, pp. 17-20.

CHAPTER

36

Strategic Importance of Indo-US Nuclear Deal in the World Affairs

The political bickering over the nuclear deal between the Congress and Leftist parties has paralysed governance beyond repair. Naturally, 'We', the People of India has the right to question from the Left parties that if India were to acquire the wherewithal to set-up nuclear power plans on a large scale, how would harm the nuclear deal to India interests to the extent that the issue necessitated to bring down the coalition government on the nuclear deal issue, specifically in the light of the fact that the Left support to the UPA coalition Government is only from 'outside'. This scenario necessitated to analyse the importance of the Indo-US Nuclear Deal, though the Congress has set at rest the speculation of holding an early election to the Lok Sabha. Sadly, the UPA government has decided not to operationalise the 123 Agreement, making it clear that it can not be renegotiated.

THE INDO-US AGREEMENT STILL HONOURABLE

The deal is still deemed to be 'honourable', good and

justified for India, shall enhance our national interests in the long-long. 'The nuclear deal is dead, Long live the Nuclear deal.' This is why the nuclear deal has been 'paused' and it would be revived later on in the middle of 2008. This kind of impression was construed from the visit of IAEA chief Mohd. El-baradei in New Delhi in the middle of Oct. 2007. Since India's Cabinet has signed the deal, it hasn't killed it. The Government has let it lie. The India-US ties; despite this, shall continue on fast track on technology and trade.

A NEW SHIFT IN BALANCE OF POWER STRUCTURE

At present, India can not ignore some of the new dimensions and changes in the world affairs that have immensely influenced the balance of power in Asia. For example, the creation of the Shanghai Cooperation Organisation (SCO) in Central Asia and the military exercise of Malabar 2007 in the Bay of Bengal. The SCO is widely taken up as an 'Asian NATO' to counter the US growing economic, military and strategic influence. On the contrary, New Delhi's growing proximity through the nuclear deal and taking part in the Malabar exercise 2007 has been a matter of concern for China.

Perhaps the most important change the nuclear deal will make is in the status of India. The US is willing to change its own laws and the larger nations in the NSG have come around to supporting the lifting of the embargo, not out of altruism, or because they want to reward India for being a 'good boy'. They are willing to do this because they want India to shoulder some of the responsibility for restoring order in a world that has been thrown into chaos by globalization, the end of the Cold War, the rise of terrorism and the destruction of the basic tenets of the Westphalian State system that occurred five years ago. India is being invited to sit at the global high table, not to serve as a lackey of the US, but to add a voice that is missing from the discussion—that of a large, militarily powerful, economically successful, but still fairly poor democracy, that can articulate a different viewpoint on international developments and serve as a bridge between the North and the South.*

This realization is changing traditionally held foreign policy positions of the Indian government. The Left's accusation that it is becoming a lackey of the US, when Washington itself has conceded, tacitly, that it has lost its way, reflects the Left's deep-rooted lack of confidence in the nation and therefore is opposed to the Deal.

The Indo-US 123 agreement is historic for a variety of reasons : It is a matter of deep concern that we could not learn from our nuclear outcaste position or isolation of the past decades. The debate on this agreement is a sad reflection of the level of opposition for opposition's sake. It has no meaning in foreign policy-making. Hence, there is a need to understand interrelationship between the 123 Agreement and the Hyde Act. For instance:

- Allowing India to be the first and only the country in the world to be a *de-fecto* and *de-jure* nuclear power, with supply of uranium and equipment and grant of reprocessing rights in principle but on terms is more favourable than any other country. China is the example. India has availed the facility without having to sign either the NPT or the CTBT. China has done the 123 Agreement on remarkably inferior terms compared to India. Several US laws oblige China to provide all information on non-proliferation, about human rights records. But we are exempted from such terms and conditions.
- The 123 Agreement shall help us to reduce our huge energy deficit, without which (energy security) India cannot imagine to become the world's largest third/ fourth economy. It is cheaper to the cost of an Indigenous nuclear obtained through a hydro-plant or gas-based unit. The coal-based electricity plants have proved to be costlier, as well as contrary to the present world environmental campaign.

* Prem Shankar Jha, "It's Now or Never", *The Hindustan Times*, New Delhi, Oct. 9, 2007, p. 8.

- In the changing world order and the new balance of power, our foreign policy strategy has to be holistic, multi-pronged and multi-faceted in fulfilling our national interests and developmental plans in the 21st century. The Deal will bolster India's image as a 'soft state' in the eyes of P5.*
- It seems that our decision-makers still have some misconceptions about the US Hyde Act. It is supreme for the United States of America and not for those who sign the 123 Agreement. For example, Article 6 of the US Constitution clearly declares that US treaties are as much part of the 'supreme law of the land' that is why a treaty goes back to the US Congress for ratification, as will hopefully happen to the 123 Agreement in an up-down vote in the near future. It is the same US legislature which ratifies the 123 Agreement as has passed the Hyde Act. Hence, it is "latest expression of the sovereign will" of the US. Secondly, the sections 109, 103 and 109 of the Hyde Act are meant for nuclear non-proliferation countries like Iraq and others. These sections are not binding for us, as the US President and other authorities have declared this position in writing, i.e. understanding of his country's law. The domestic law of the US can not be applied to others .
- The Hyde Act cannot be compared with the famous Pressler Amendment required the US administration to certify that Pakistan was not developing nuclear weapons and the successive American President did so, notwithstanding the fact of Pak's clandestine nuclear programme. Yet Islamabad continued to get military and civil aid from Washington. In short, India is not Pakistan because India's policies have been meeting the standards of the Hyde Act. After all we are a transparent and democratic nation. It should be recalled that in the new shift of balance of

* See the obervations made by Professor Sumit Ganguly of Indiana University, Bloomington (US); "Save the Nuclear Deal", *The Times of India*, dated Oct. 26, 2007, p. 14.

power, the US is seeking our cooperation because of ours position in South Asian region. It is up to our diplomacy how we view cooperation of the US.

- Clause 16(4) of the 123 Act mandates the implementation of the agreement in accordance with the principles of international laws, provided it fulfils the national interests. Moreover, our scientists and skilled strategists have dispel all doubts about the Hyde Act and about the 123 Agreement. Meanwhile, India should develop its own thorium reserves in producing our own nuclear power/ energy, in order to reduce our dependence.
- It is worth-recalling that since July 2005 (during 26 months of negotiation), there have been participatory spirit, which is based on transparency and open diplomacy.
- As regards our all future testing, the NDA government in Sept. 1998, on the floor of the UN House formally committed voluntary permanent moratorium. This is not a permanent and forever-binding. If national interests demands, India can go ahead in nuclear testing as Russia did in Sept. 2007, despite the 1954 Autonomic Act and the CTBT. And last but not least, the Indian Parliament is not a 'rubber stamp' under our constitutional set-up. As per Article 73(1) and Article 246, Parliament is entitled to review, scrutinize and modify of cancel any and every act/treaty of the Executive (i.e. the Council of Ministry). This is the 'prerogative power' of Parliament. The Executive is not immune from the Parliamentary scrutiny. The 123 of the US Atomic Energy Act, 1954 is subject to its review if it goes against the national interests. If it feels that the Hyde Act passed by the US Congress in 2006, is not in consonance with national interests, it can send the message to the US through the Government of the day to consider its sentiments (objects).*

* *The Hindi*, New Delhi edn., August 10, 2007, p. 4.

- The UPA is not going to be an effective Government for the rest of the Lok Sabha term, if it yields to the Left's blackmail and the government would be a lame-duck one without any credibility. This will adversely affect the outcome of the next elections to be held in May 2008.
- The Left is mainly concerned of an 'American imperialism' in the background of US nuclear deal and the Indo-US strategic partnership. The US has been a muscular-bully globally. And after the terror attack, 9/11, the alone super power has posed itself differently to the old colonialism or imperialism. But why we forget that India too has been a hegenonistic country in dealing with the developments events of the Asian region which was essential for our national interests and for our existence. For example, India resorted to military force, though regionally, splitting Pakistan into Bangladesh in 1971; India ousted the Ranas regime in Nepal by putting king Tribhuvan on the Throne; India trained the Tamil Tigers, though our diplomacy failed due to their attack on the IPKF, in the same way as the US has failed in Iraq to bring peace and political stability. Likewise, Indian troops captured the military coup leaders and restored PM Gayoom's rule in 1988; and finally India has posted a large scale military in Kashmir.
- Our internal opposition to the N-deal has emboldened the American non-proliferation lobby to block the deal, raising the question that the Bush administration gave away too much to India even without Congressional hearing to examine the provisions of 123 agreement, which it alleged has undermined the intent of the Hyde Act. In New Delhi, Henry Kissinger rightly warned that a delay would help critics better organized to oppose the deal.

In short, 123 deal is a diplomatic triumph for India as the US has agreed to support our cause without signing the NPT. It has officially recognized India as a nuclear power.

In view of opposition of the Nuclear Deal, the 15-member panel was constituted to examine the implications of the deal. The BJP's demand for a Joint Parliamentary Committee was not accepted by the UPA Government. There is no practice as such and there is no provision for a JPC on an international agreement. But Indian democracy has witnessed the emergence of coalition period—a reality of the governance. And it was the first time that above cited agreement was approved by the Cabinet, but vetoed by a committee at the Left pressure which is not responsible to Parliament. It is still a high time to ponder that such international deals are debted and discussed in our Parliament which are related to our national security and strategic importance.* Against the background of the new millennium's Great Game in Asia, the role of Parliament must be sounded in such matters. Today Asia is a multi-power continent and India should preserve its strategic autonomy.

The Left may not want a close strategic partnership with the US, and they will find others who share their misgivings. But in taking the government hostage on the nuclear deal they have picked an issue which enables three decades of technology sanctions imposed by the international community on India to be lifted. If the deal is approved it would raise India's stock and enable high-tech collaboration not just with the US, but also with France, Germany, Japan, Russia and South East Asia. It may be against China's immediate interests, but if the issue comes up at the NSB where China is a member,. it is unlikely to stand out alone in holding up the waiver if most other countries are convinced of India's case.

THE NATURE OF HYDE ACT

It represents a set of India specific guidelines, duly legislated by the US Congress. But these guidelines are not mandatory, particularly for India. Therefore, its nature does not hamper India's freedom to conduct its independent foreign policy in world affairs.

---

* Nalani Kant Jha, "Indian Parliament: A Deal Breaker or A Deal Breather", in *South Asia Politics*, New Delhi, Oct. 2007, pp. 12-14.

The fear of the Left is that the Act talks of the US taking its fuel reactors and related technologies once India conducts a nuclear test. It is irony that the same Left had criticized then Vajpayee-led NDA government's decision to have N-tests in 1998, which was a poll plank of BJP's manifesto for the 2004 parliamentary polls. Then CPM had promised to revert to nuclear policy of using nuclear energy for civilian and peaceful purposes. India has already put a parliamentary sanction/ban on unilateral moratorium on future nuclear testing when it opened fresh talks with Pakistan for a de-nuclearised environment in South Asia by then Vajpayee Government. Against this background, the Hyde Act because redundant.

As regards the criticism of the BJP on the above-cited Act *vis-a-vis* the nuclear deal, the past record of the Vajpayee Government ensures that India would always retain the right to conduct nuclear tests. In contrast, the Vajpayee government, for all practical purposes, was on the verge of signing the highly discriminatory Comprehensive Test Ban Treaty (CTBT) under pressure from the Clinton administration. The then US deputy secretary of state, Strobe Talbott has been on record that the BJP government had assured Washington that India would sign the CTBT by the end of 1999. So much so that on August 22, 1998, the BJP National Executive had passed a special resolution in Jaipur, urging its own government to exercise caution before signing the CTBT. The Vajpayee government did not sign the CTBT, precisely because the Democrats lost power in the US and the Republican Bush administration rejected the CTBT.*

On the contrary, the Manmohan Singh government must be complemented for not surrendering to the Americans the option of conducting a nuclear test in the agreement with the Bush administration.

OBJECTIVES OF CHINA'S NUCLEAR DIPLOMACY

It is worth remembering that China has been against India's entry into the UN Security Council mainly because of

* See the comments of Prakash Nanda, "Critics have lost the Plot", *The Times of India*, New Delhi, August 24, 2007, p. 14.

Japan's closeness with the West, specifically to the US. Today China is silent on the quadrangle relationship of the four as cited above. India however, cannot and should not shut her eyes at the 77 nuclear power projects on its planning board, the capability to influence nuclear diplomacy in the Western world. This globe clout will influence the Asian market. As India has a much smaller market compared to China's, that is, only 19 nuclear power projects at different stages of planning and execution. Constituently, China will have more leverage on world nuclear diplomacy than India. This is a crucial issue for India's interests and it can be sought by the approval of the 45 member Nuclear Suppliers Group through the Indo-US nuclear deal. And some of these countries are interested to see that India's commercial nuclear capability match the China's position in Asia.

It is equally important to mention that China's attempt is to gradually pushing Washington to the wall on nuclear issue by taking up the concerns of North Korea, Iran, Pakistan *vis-a-vis* the Indo-US nuclear deal. These three countries are more comfortable in China's support that of the US. In the meeting of Iranian President with Chinese President Hujintao in August 2007, assured Iran of China's support in the face of the US strategy to isolate Teharan on the nuclear-issue. Both the leader took the note of test of nuclear missiles test conducted by Russia. It is further important to mention of the Shanghai Cooperation Organisation—SCO, which is gradually emerging as an 'Asian NATO' in terms of the security of Central Asia.

Furthermore, India cannot ignore the key trend arms-race that has come to limelight. Pakistan, for example, a country about a sixth of India in size, population, economy and several other metrics, has for the first time outstripped India in purchasing military hardware and software, notching up arms deals worth $5.1 billion in 2006, as compared to $ 3.5 billion by India, to be ranked the world's largest arms shopper.

Against this, India still continues to spend just about 2.5% of its GDP on its defence requirements since 1991-92, despite our armed forces consistently is demanding that it be raised to at least 3%. Currently, China's expenditure on defense is around 4.5% of its GDP. Need not to mention that China, actively but secretly, pursues its strategy of keeping defence expenditure, arms imports capabilities, etc. which is higher than it declares in public. Official China pegs around $45 billion. Even the US is unnerved by the China's rapid military modernization and build-up in this decade and the Whitehouse is in a need of seeking a regional military balance. In future, India would not face a threat from Pakistan but from China's military capabilities and satellite weapons.

In the changing scenario of power structure and balance of power, no sovereign nation choose, to pursue an independent foreign policy. She is bound to pursue a totally or partly dependent foreign policy to advance her national interests. This happened even during the Cold War era. For example, France was part of the NATO alliance during the Cold War period, it left the NATO military structure yet it remained close to the US foreign policy. France was one of the western countries who opposed the US military attack on Iraq, while still continuing to remain in the alliance system. Likewise, even most of NAM countries attended Summits, but they pursued their national interests in their foreign policies which was in stark contradiction to the non-aligned declarations. And most importantly, how China after 1971 switched sides and joined the US camp for her development. Albania seceded from the Moscow bloc but she kept her relationship with Moscow intertwined. This does not mean that these countries did not practise independent foreign policies. In fact, they followed foreign policies which suited and promoted their national interests in a particular system/ time.

Today, the world is different. The US has to balance its policy towards China, with that of towards Japan and South East Asian nations. The US as a, major world power seeks a partnership with India because: (a) it is a fast-growing economy with an expanding market; (b) it is an IT power; (c) it is a nuclear and space power; and (d) India is a regional power because of its geo-strategic location and lastly, she is a stable democratic country of the whole Asia.

India and the US have arrived at an 'agreed text' of the Nuclear Agreement. It has yet to clear two stages, the mode of the 35 member board of governors of IAEA and NSG—the two important forums from where India can face the tough challenges in the light of the fact that India has yet to negotiate an India-specific safeguards agreements. A number of realistic diplomats feel that NSG clearance will not be an easy affair. Because of the US keen interest in the Deal.* The battle lines would be cleared on the basis of consensus. It is a plus point with us that IAEA Director General Mohd. Ebaradei has a favourable outlook for India, though he is not the final arbiter as the final power vests with the Board of Governors.

CONCLUDING OBSERVATIONS

Not putting the UPA government at stake over the Indo-US nuclear deal has been widely hailed. The Centre has taken a sensible decision. Ours is not a one issue government. Meanwhile, the government should show the maturity of parliamentary democracy on the issue how far the 123 Agreement is a perfect document and how far it would suit our national interests in terms of its interpretation and reprocessing issue. If there are some doubts about the Hyde Act's language which is said to be not India-friendly, these aspects should be discussed, keeping in mind that 'waiver' was specifically for India. But the UPA government should not be allowed itself to be blackmailed by the Leftist forces. National interests should be prioritized in international affairs.

It will be unfortunate for India's growth and progress if it lets the civil N-deal slip through its hand. The US might be wanting India to become a part of the region *vis-a-vis* China. India needs nuclear energy for various civil purposes. Hence, the Union Government should be serious to give a green signal Indo-US Nuclear to the Accord with the rider that the Hyde Act will not prove a stumbling block in implementing the deal. It is ironic that the Left parties who claim to be a champion of common man's cause is centered on the N-deal, rather than any of their problems like unemployment, price-rising, rising rate of crime, labour law reforms, land reforms, etc. mere Anti-

* Pallava Bagla, "N-Deal has Miles to Go", *The Times of India*, Oct. 4, 2007, p. 10.

Americanism is not going to help us, we need investment, technology, foreign professional education and military expertisation.

Secondly, ours is the Asian Century. The twin trends of rising Asia and politically crumbling Middle East are likely to lead to a naval emphasis on Indian Ocean and its surrounding seas, because of globalization, world trade and commerce. Therefore, the strait of Horzus, the Bab-el-Marideb of Rea sea, Malacca, etc. will become increasingly suspectable to terrorism. India shall have to protect her own tanker routes of Indian Ocean and Chinese water sea, for which India needs a naval strategy of military defence with the help of US and China against rising risk of terrorism and piracy. Getting ourself in the above cited military-*cum*-naval strategies is in no case going to affect our non-aligned policy. After the Iraq war, America is not the same as was in the pre-Iraq war *vis-a-vis* the Middle East crisis.

It should be noted that the crux of the issue raised by the Left is neither about the nuclear agreement nor about policy towards US if those were the real issues the Left should have raised its objection when the defence framework agreement was signed with US, when the Indo-US joint statement was issued on July 18, 2005 or when the Hyde Act was passed. But they waited till the UPA government finalized, to the surprise of many skeptics including the Left, the nuclear deal. Then they delivered their ultimatum.

That timing was very important. The Left allowed the government to go this far and allowed it to finalise and initial an international agreement. The Left is, in fact, attempting to demonstrate that though it may have secured only 5 percent of the national vote and 11 percent of Parliament strength, it can be a major political force in the domestic balance of power. Besides Congress and BJP and a number of regional parties, the Left has emerged as the Third major autonomous player just a year before the Lok Sabha term to win the confidence support of the regional parties before the next election. It is in New Delhi's interest, therefore, to do what it is expected to do under the July 18 deal, that is, quickly separate its military from its civilian nuclear plants, and agree to a regime of international inspections for the latter. This will not only help meet India's future energy needs, it will also bring transparency to our nuclear energy establishment which, at present, is shrouded in a veil of secrecy. Current nuclear technology is much better and safer than technology of the 1970s or earlier, which India's power plants rely on. Besides, inspections also look at safety aspects, which will ensure—an upgradation of safety at Indian nuclear power plants up to international standards.* There have been many reports of shutdowns and radiation leaks in India's nuclear establishments—nobody really knows what goes on there because the Department of Atomic Energy is not accountable to the Indian public. In the interests of democracy as well of avoiding future Chernobyls, this needs to change. We can make a virtue out of necessity by separating civilian and military establishments and opening up the former to public scrutiny.

* See 'Nuclear Democracy', the editorial of *The Times of India,* New Delhi edn., December 10, 2005.

CHAPTER

37

A Review of Indo-China Ties in the Emergence of Asia

Indian foreign policy has recently turned assertive and confident by UPA's declaration of a strategic partnership between New Delhi and Washington through the Indo-US Civil Nuclear Deal signed in July 2005. It is a sign of new shift in New Delhi's approach, which aims at entering into a strategic understanding with Washington. Likewise, Union Defence Minister Pranab Mukherjee's sojourn in Beijing has given the concept of Non-Alignment a new, positive content, which could be called Neo-non-alignment in the unipolar world against the old sense of Non-alignment in the Cold War era, when India refused to get into entangle with military alliances of super powers. Neo non-alignment is meant to have New Delhi's attempt to play an important role in Asian politics, to which China, of course, is a very important player. Neo-non-alignment in the current phase is meant that New Delhi enters into security dialogue with everyone who has interests in South Asia. These strategic alignments have nothing to do with the envisioned doctrine of containment. The Minister took a sweep visit through the meeting of

Defense Chiefs of Tokyo to Beijing and Singapore. It was very much concerned with the concept of collective security arrangements against the challenges related to terrorism and trade. The visit of Mukherjee to China in June 2006 was meant to strengthen friendship between India and China, provided the border is resolved without which they cannot act in concert in Asian politics.

INDO-US NUCLEAR DEAL

The UPA government is committed to Sign a safeguards agreement with the IAEA, keeping in view of the following developments :

(a) Domestic opposition to the N-deal is gradually softening in many quarters apart from the Left. The scenario changed after the 23rd July, 2008 when the government could survive on the issue.

(b) BJP's Brajesh Mishra, as an ex-National Security Adviser to the previous NDA Government, too, has endorsed the deal.

(c) Our former President, Dr. APJ Abdul Kalam, doyen of India's strategic missile programme and also closely involved with the 1998 Pokhran nuclear tests, has followed suit. The community of nuclear scientists many of whom earlier harboured suspicions that India's strategic autonomy would be curtailed by the deal has largely come around. But segments of the political class still cling to outmoded beliefs on the pact, forgetting that India is rapidly running out of uranium for its nuclear plants, a fact that could not be publicised earlier as it would have jeopardised India's negotiating position. Without signing the nuclear deal with the US, with the concomitant IAEA safeguards agreement and NSG waiver, would mean that India would be unable to conclude similar deals with Russia or France. It could wind up India's nuclear programme, which certainly wouldn't do much for its strategic autonomy. Not to mention that continuing sanctions on India would deny to it technology and investments in high-tech sectors.

(d) The regime change in the US next year, with the new President, India is hopeful of getting the support on this deal.

(e) China's underground unclear submarine base at Hainan Island in South China sea, with 58 launch pads for N-capable ballistic missiles apparent targeting north India and South Russia, must be a move worrying development for us. This information is based satellite pictures taken by the Federation of American scientists of the US. This is why China continues to adopt an aggressive border posture as far as India is concerned.

A TUSSEL FOR SUPREMACY

China has always been uneasy about the augmentation of India's new stature in international affairs. Currently, India's special status acknowledged by the US in the matter of proposed N-deal is a case in point. In fifties India went out of its way to advocate China's inclusion in the UN; but Beijing cannot dream of backing India's claim to a Security Council membership since it would add to its status. Pt. Nehru belatedly realized this follow during 1959-60 when the territorial claims was staked by China.

B.N. Mullick intelligence chief at the time of the Chinese incursion, wrote in his book, 'The Chinese Betrayal', Nehru said, 'It was wrong to assume that the Chinese undertook this aggression only because they wanted some patches of territory. The real cause was something else. . . . China did not want any country near her which was not prepared to accept her leadership. So India had to be humiliated'.

In the changed power status, its democracy and multicultural society are earning widespread admiration while the totalitarian China evokes more fear than respect. For another, while the world has begun to understand the complexities of the Kashmir situation, especially in the context of Islamic terrorism in the Pakistan-Afghanistan region, all the material improvement in Tibet can no longer hide the prevailing discontent there. Clearly, China believes that it cannot afford to lose ground to India either in the race to be a major power or because of the opprobrium it faces over Tibet. Hence, the reassertion of her claim to Arunachal Pradesh and the staking tension in Sikkim.

Secondly, like the Indian CPM, China does not believe in the untenable colonial nature of the McMahan Line, whereas it has made adjustment in accepting the same line in Myanmar, which is under the military rule. It is worth-recalling that the former CM of Kerala, comrade, EMS Namboodiripad held that the Chinese had entered Indian territory because they thought it was theirs and hence there was no question of aggression on the part of China. Sadly, China has still loyal allies in the Indian communist parties even after the collapse of the Soviet Union.

HAS THE RED ARMY CHANGED?

In the background of inclusions of Chinese army across LAC compels us to think of what is the message (PLA) of China to India. The Chinese defence think tank calls India 'arrogant' because we claim Arunachal Pradesh as our territory. On the Tibet issue at the time of Olympic touch arriving in India, the PLA warned India to stay away from a path of confrontation. The language it was a kin to the 'Cultural Revolution'. India cannot and should not misjudge this situation, despite the booming business between the two countries or the joint military exercise.[1]

Right from the days of Nehru, when we used to enthusiastically shouting Hindi China Bhai Bhai the Red Army began to the territorial claim over Tibet and Tibet's Dalai Lama was compelled to fled India in 1959, as well as the Chinese staked claims over large parts of Indian territory in both Eastern (Aksai Chin) and Western sector (NEFA) now known as Arunachal Pradesh and making in roads into these areas. The worse was the 1962 Chinese armed aggression. The purpose of the war was to damage Nehru's image, wrecked India's economy and humiliated a nascent democracy which was trying to stand on its own feet.

During the new phase of Sino-Indian closeness during 2007-08, when China begun to talk of 'a new partnership' with India in trade and business, the ghosts of past (territorial ambitions) did not lay to rest because of the role of People's Liberation Army is the same. There is no change in its mindset. In 2007, for example, the Chinese Army is reported to have crossed the Line of Actual Control some 140 times. Once again, China has upped its claim on Arunachal Pradesh and Beijing is lashing out at Tibetans, while asking India to contain their political activities. And once again, China is blaming India for creating tensions on the border.

Mention may be made of China's stakes in Tibet. Propelled by the desired for Asian hegemony it ruthlessly annexed Tibet bringing its military might close to the Indian border. Her next eye is on Nepal. It may be recalled that the new Maoist PM Prachanda has made his first choice to China. While attending the closing ceremony of the Olympics in Beijing, he met both Hu Jintao and Wen Jiabao for financial aid and assistance from China. On the other hand, the Nepalese PM has already demanded to review the India-Nepal Friendship Treaty because it was unequal.

Since January, 2008 Chinese toops have intruded a dozen times into Indian territory in a strategic Pangong Tso lake area in eastern Ladakh as part of Beijing's continuing aggressive posture all along the Line of Actual Control (LAC). Pangong Tso (Tso means lake in Ladakhi), two-thirds of which is controlled by China as it extends from India to Tibet, and other parts of Ladakh like Demchok and Trig Heights, in fact, are witnessing "an enhanced level of activity" by the People's Liberation Army. The sector has witnessed aggressive Chinese foot, motorized and boot patrols on March 23, 2008.

Pangong Tso, at an altitude of 4,218-metres, has become a "hot" area ever since the 1999 Kargil conflict with Pakistan, with China even constructing a "track" right up to the lake's Southern bank.

This apart, China continues to play a cat and mouse game in the eastern Himalayas, despite having implicitly accepted Sikkim to be a part of India as a *quid pro quo* for New Delhi's unequivocal recognition of Beijing's claim over Tibet. There have been already as many as 40 "intrusions" by Chinese troops across the 206-km border between Sikkim and Tibet since January, 2008. "Chinese intrusions largely take place in Ladakh, Arunachal and other parts of the Line of Actual Control but now the transgressions across the border into Sikkim are also going up. In short, China has never been honest to LAC in all three sectors Western (Ladakh), middle Uttaranchal and Himachal Pradesh and eastern Sikkim, Arunachal, (spreading in 4,057 kms.)

About the reaction of China on our position of Arunachal, it should be kept in mind that the Chinese have a long-run ambition of restoring their previous boundaries which they feel were nibbled away by imperial powers or by dissident Chinese. Thus the old British drawn borders with India still pre-occupy China. Chinese nationalism is territorialist. China was a unified state for about 2000 years of its history and became weak only in the 19th century when it began to loose out to western powers. On the contrary, India never had been a unified kingdom or state till the British defined India's boundaries. Then the basic reason to ponder is that the nature of Chinese Government is of military mindset. Chinese leaders/intellectuals have always find myriad objections to democracy even in the era of LPG.

A massive $ 5 billion river diversion and hydro electricity contract in PoK has been pushed ahead by China in Feb. 2008. The scheme involves a 42 km tunnel to divert the waters of Neelam in PoK to Jhelum, which flows through the plains of Pakistani provinces of Punjab and Sind. India which has built the Krishna-Ganga hydro-electricity project on its side of the border, has objected to the river diversion project on the ground that it does not meet some of the conditions stipulated in its river-sharing agreement with Pakistan. To it, India has registered its protest, as India plans a 'security exclusion zone' on any Indian border. India does not like the Chinese to invest in any Indian border nearby Chinese boundaries (like J & K or Arunachal Pradesh). The river is only 144 sq. km. away from Indian border and Jhelim river. The Hydro-Project on Neelam river is likely to be used as a water weapon.

On the eve of approaching the Beijing Olympics, China cracked down on peaceful movement/protests of Monks in Lhasa. It was against the Human Rights record. As per the official position of India, Tibet is a part of China and Beijing expected us not to a allow anti-China activity on Indian soil. Therefore, the ministry of external affairs intoned that no 'anti-China' activity would be permitted from Indian soil. It's an authoritarian trait to describe any protest as anti-national. India is a democracy. That principle isn't worth-go suspending just because Beijing is offended. Neither has it paid much dividend. Beijing's response to India's whole-hearted backing of Chinese claims on Tibet, but she has so far been meager in giving a clear cut recognition of India's claim on Sikkim, probably because not settling of the boundary question to its entirety. China still continues to claim Arunachal Pradesh

To conclude, the Dalai Lama, the follower of the principles of Gandhiji, has helped China tightened its grip on Tibet. Mahatma Gandhi did not go to the US or any other country to fight for India's independence. Indians were never refugees anywhere in waging struggles to obtain freedom. Here, in India, Tibetans are refugees for decades. Everything is given free to them at the cost of Indians. They have no right to talk about China. If they want, let all of them go to Tibet and continue their freedom struggle from there.

Some Facts About Beijing's Provocations Against India

- China is a system of arrogant authoritarian rule controlled by the Communist Party.
- China dared to ask the world's largest democracy to deny Tibetans the right to protest. In our Constitution, there is a mention of human dignity principle, but India did not respond to China's brutal crackdown on Tibetiean Mocks over the Olympic issue.
- China made a protest over the PM's visit to Arunachal Pradesh stating China's claim over the territory.
- Chinese forces in November 2007 provocatively destroyed some Indian army bunkers at the Sikkim-Bhutan-Tibet tri-junction. But India tried to sweep the grave episode under the rug rather than to lodge a strong protest. After four months India

acknowledged it. So was the case of China's attack in Sikkim. The tri-junction border is settled by the Anglo-Sikkim Convention of 1890.

Beijing summoned the Indian ambassador, Nirupama Roy, postnight (2AM) to register her protest against the Tibetan exiles living in India. No host government can compel a foreign diplomat to appear before it at an odd hour, that too in peace time. It inflicted self-humiliation to India but Indian remained soft.[2]

A massive $ 5 billion river diversion and hydro electricity contract in PoK has been pushed ahead by China in Feb. 2008. The scheme involves a 42 km tunnel to divert the waters of Neelam in PoK to Jhelum, which flows through the plains of Pakistani provinces of Punjab and Sind. India which has built the Krishna-Ganga hydroelectricity project on its side of the border, has objected to the river diversion project on the ground that it does not meet some of the conditions stipulated in its river-sharing agreement with Pakistan. To it, India has registered its protest, as India plans a 'security exclusion zone' on Indian border. India does not like Chinese to invest in any India border nearby Chinese boundaries (like J&K or Arunachal Pradesh. The river is only 144 sq. km. away from Indian border and Jhelim

China committed about 300 border intrusions during 2006-07 and China continues to refuse to clarify the frontline. We cannot avoid Chinese military intrusions into Bhutanese territory saying it is a matter between China and Bhutan. It must be noted that India is responsible for Bhutanese defence. Even Bhutan is the only India's friend as neighbour.

The NDA Government's decision to recognize Tibet as part of China was a gross error and our former PM A.B. Vajpayee allowed us to be bullied in 2003. India still shall have potential threats from China in the wake of her intrusions.

According to a strategic affair analysis the more power China accumulates, the more it will seek to humiliate India. It is past time India got its act together to deal with Chinese provocations deftly. Asymmetry in inter-state relations does not entail the propitiation of the stronger. Diplomacy is the art of off-setting or neutralising power imbalances. Consistency and confidence help obviate, flipping and whining. India's present slapdash approach is not only an invitation to greater trouble, but nationally demeaning.

Table 1
Nation's Nuclear Power Map

Current Capacity	*Capacity by 2008*	*Capacity by 2020*
3310 (MV)	6710 (MV)	20000 (MV)

Presently in function:

Location	*No. of Reactors*	*Type of Reactor*	*Fuel*	*Total capacity*
Tarapur	3	2 BWR, 1 PHWR	Enriched Uranium	860
Rajasthan	4	PHWR	Natural Uranium	740
Kalpakkam	2	PHWR	Natural Uranium	390
Narora	2	PHWR	Natural Uranium	440
Kakrapara	2	PHWR	Natural Uranium	440
Kala	2	PHWR	Natural Uranium	440
Total	15	2 BWR, 13 PHWR		3310

Source : *The Times of India*, New Delhi, 21 July 200, p. 9.

Under Construction

Location	*No.*	*Type of Reactor*	*Fuel*	*Generation**	*Completion Date*
Tarapur	1	PHWR	Natural Uranium	540	July 2006
Kalga	2	PHWR	Natural Uranium	2X220	Dec. 2006, June 2007
Rajasthan	2	PHWR	Natural Uranium	2X220	May 2007, Nov. 2007
Kudankulam	2	WER	Enriched Uranium	2X1000	2007, 2008

*in MW (Mega Watts)

BWR : Boiling Water Reactor

PHWR : Pressurize Heavy Water Reactor

WER : Russian version of Pressurize Water Reactor

- India will be able to buy nuclear reactors and fuel on the international market, after ratification by other nuclear countries.
- India has limited Uranium reserve but has more than a fourth of the world', Thorium reserves.

India is currently facing threats from her neighbouring countries that the authoritarian, anti-democratic anti-secular in nature in South Asia region. Their hold on nuclear weapons, too, have posed us dangers. It is a matter of concern that the South Asia region has been a source as well as a destination of proliferation of weapons of mass destruction into the hands of volatile states.

According to M.K. Narayanan, our National Security Adviser, "First and foremost are existential threats and vulnerabilities that pluralistic, secular and democratic countries such as India—with rapidly modernizing economies—face from nations in the region that are authoritarian, anti-democratic and anti-secular, approximating to failed states". He listed proliferation of weapons of mass destruction and terrorism emanating from Pakistan-Afghanistan "region" as the dangers to South Asia as well as the entire world. Credible reports suggest that the region has been both a source and a destination for proliferation of WMD material and equipment—a situation that is cause for concern if proper steps are not put in place. In his view, volatile states are Iraq, Iran, Afghanistan and Pakistan, China is least concerned of their political stability.

COLLECTIVE SECURITY IN THE REGION

The Asian countries need to build strong channels among their defence establishments and share intelligence to counter the growing challenge of terrorism and proliferation of nuclear arms. The real threat is from the Non-state actors, which are 343 in the world in number of which there are 187 in the Asian region alone. These armed outfits have no borders but have strong networks to spread their massage of death and destruction. Against this background, the US has decided to reorient her foreign policy in South Asian region, and the

Indo-US nuclear deal is a case in point to take a liberal bet towards India in view of the fact that China's emergence has significant implications for the region and the world at large. A long-term strategic shift underlines the following factors that have cropped in the post-Cold War period, namely, the rise of China as regional political and economic power with global aspirations, the rise of global Islamism, spurred by the petro dollar boom in West Asia and culminating in 9/11 strategy. Now Islamabad is no more a faithful ally of the West in containing the fallout of terrorism.

The idea behind the nuclear deal is to develop India as a hedge against being over-extended in China. New Delhi has successfully become a democratic country against Pakistan. The US would not like to see India a poor, malnourished and racked by insurgencies services as her North East region as well as some pernicious effects of global Islamic fundamentalism. The US wants India to emerge a powerful and prosperous country to face these challenges in Asia.[3] The deal should not be interpreted to mean that washing for is looking to draw New Delhi into a military alliance to contain Beijing. That sort of thinking has ended with the end of the Cold War era.

In a nut shell, India's economy poses challenges to China's aspirations to dominate global markets. China is a tough competitor. So, while Beijing keeps diplomatic channels with New Delhi open, it ensures that it keeps India on its toes by constantly heckling it. This, it does through unprovoked incursions or via statements by Chinese diplomats and ministers, which are meant to rile India. And, of course, it keeps strategic tension alive through quiet support to forces in India's neighbourhood that are not always well disposed towards this country. On the other hand, India seems to have no clear policy on how to manage its belligerent neighbour. But it is time that South Block got its act together on its China policy. Going forward, India and China will both play a greater role in world affairs, strategically and economically. It is inevitable that they will have to engage each other on a range of issues. If we do not make it clear where our lives of patience are drawn, we might as well abandon hopes of being equals in the future.

To conclude, in diplomacy, vision, consistency and tenacity are said to be good factors, and any pragmatic foreign policy has to shut out personal whim and fancies as well as too much zeal. In that background Sonia Gandhi's visit to go the Beijing Olympics was not a part of sound diplomacy, because of (a) Chinese assertiveness over Indian borders/ border incidents, (b) the post-midnight summoning of the Indian ambassador, Nirupama Rao, on the Tibet issue. India surrendered here, (c) China has publicly extended an Olympic ceremony invitations to the most powerful personalities of the West, but not to Indian President and the P.M. (why?), though such is the prerogative of country's national Olympic committee. The message is clear that Beijing does not care much of the duly-elected Indian government functionaries, but knows where actual power centre resides. Her visit, in short, was ill timed, forgetting that she has dealing with a state that replaced Maoism with nationalism as the legitimatising credo of the 60 year old communist rule, and forgetting also the advice given by the first PM that 'the 1962 invasion has became a permanent piece of education'. Sadly, despite this, the flurry of Indian officials visits to China continues. India's self-esteem is ebbing.[4]

Beijing's Olympic Games (39th) has ended with the message to the world community that the ruling community party (CP) has an organizing capacity in national life. Her nationalism is beyond doubts. This Olympic was a top political priority of China to demonstrate its hospitality and efficiency to foreign visitors. The games were, thus, an unparallel success by the CP. China also demonstrated that it is a rising economic and political power of Asia. In South Asian region's politics, the concerned states specifically India cannot and should not ignore the deepening self-confidence of China's model of development based on centralized power of authoritarian system, though the system is marked by corruption and a lack of transparency. The world has learned much about China. The games reflected the success of a state controlled sports machine by wining 51 gold medals.

SOLUTION TO GLOBAL GOVERNANCE

The current international politics is locked in impasse due to the following key issues; namely Nuclear Weapons Proliferation, dismastment, international terrorism (which has yet no definition), global pandemics, the Doha trade standoff since 2004, climatic change, so on and so forth. This global impasse is due to the clash of interests and differences between the East and the West, resulting in failure of global governance of international institutions like the UN, WTO, G-8, etc. The world has yet not evolved any mechanism of facilitating cooperation against conflict-interests in the post-Cold War era. These pressing problems, of course, need a collective approach and require global solutions. The application of coercive authority by the US—the lone super power in Iraq has failed. So is the case in Afghanistan. In fact, the global governance needs inclusion not exclusion of the following emerging new economic states for global solution. There is a lack of distribution of authority in existing international institutions. For instance, India and Japan should be the members of the Security Council and China of the G-8. Without their inclusion, no global solutions can be sought. The gap between legitimacy and efficiency has to be abridged, as the UN's unique legitimacy and authority universally applicable and recognized. These international institutions shall have to be kept out of personalized decision-making powers' ambit.

With the end of the Cold War, the very axis around the East and the West has ended and it has morphed into a North-South axis in the form of industrialized and developing countries. The global North has to listens the issues of the South global through dialogues and conversions to enhance mutual trust against the mistrust of colonial era. Likewise, G-8 should be formalized with G-8+5 (namely, Brazil, China, India, Mexico and South Africa), because G-5 has emerged as competing from and G-8 must further include a few Islamic nations to secure a guarantee solution of clasing interests.[5]

It is worth-recalling that the Myanmar's Junta Government did not allow international aid flights when the country was destroyed by Cylone Nargis near Yangan and upto 1.5 million people reported were believed to be facing the threat of starvation and disease. Yet the country's military rulers frustrated the UN efforts to aids and supplies to victims and rescue operations. It was a failure of the UN itself.

PREVENTING INDIA AS AN ASIAN POWER

The way the CPM and its left cohorts went against the Indo-US Civilian N-deal (1st July, 2005) on the ground of the Hyde Act was seen as sabotaging India's rise as an *'Asian power'*. Their strategy was meant to present India from going into a strategy alliance with the US, as such an alliance could disturb China's emerging unipolar hegemony over Asia. The Singh-Bush nuclear accord, in fact, is poised to help in creating a multi-polar Asia by involving Japan and India, so that these could play significant roles alongwith China in the 21st century. Sadly, the Comrade Prakash Karat and others termed the pact as 'Imperialist design of a multi-polar Asia'. He did not want that the US contain China's rise through India with the help of the N-pact. For the US, as well as India, China is and shall be a strategic rival. The US approach in contrast to it was manifested to propup India as a counterweight. The CPM and others thus have been more honest to fraternity of China's Communist Party (Leninist ideology) than to the cause of national interests. Unfortunately, the left was deeply concerned of China's strategic interest. Let us recalled that the CPM supported China when it attacked India in 1962. Yet the Congress Party in power could not understand the conspiracy of the CPM against India's emergence as a major power in the global matrix.[6]

It is high time for India not to get bullied by China. The dragon spews fire in totalitarian arrogance at regular intervals through border incursions and provocations. China has kept up its anti-India stance. India must face China with deft-diplomacy stemming from strength and self-respect, against Chinese cross-border activities and intrusions in Sikkim and Arunachal Pradesh.

UNDERSTANDING THE HYDE ACT

The CPM-led leftist parties issued threats against the UPA

Government at a time when India decided to go ahead for negotiating a nuclear safeguards agreement with IAEA. The slogan was either the N-deal or stay in office. It was evident or the Len blackmail. The main opposition of the Left was the Hyde Act. According to the clarification of US Assistant Secretary of State Richard Srucher, the Hyde Act was domestic legislation of the US. The main function of which is to allow the kind of cooperation in the civil nuclear field with India as envisaged under the nuclear agreement between the two countries. While the Hyde Act binds the US government, it has nothing to do with India. India is bound only by its agreement with the US.

There are a clear ruling of the US Supreme Court that according to Article VI of the American Constitution, treaties made by the US will be the supreme law of the land. The nuclear agreement will be approved by the US Congress after its clearance by the NSG. Since that would happen later than the earlier Hyde Act, the legal position will be that the nuclear deal constitutes the last word of the US, Congress, superseding what had been said in the Hyde Act.

The Hyde Act itself has three major sections: first section on the sense of the Congress, second on the statement of policy and a third on waiver authority, through Congressional approval and other incidental matters. The first two sections are not binding on the administration and are essentially meant to placate the non-proliferation lobby. The crucial bit is Section 104 on the waiver which authorizes the US President to enter into civil nuclear cooperation with any country (here India) prescribing certain conditions. Besides this, the section also deals with certain restrictions on nuclear transfers to India.

Section 106 of the Hyde Act deals with this nuclear exemption coming to an end if India detonates a nuclear device. The nuclear agreement says there will be consultation be the two parties whether the circumstances leading to the termination of the agreement resulted from a serious concern about a changed security environment or as a response to similar actions by other states which could impact on its national security. This provision ensures that if India were to conduct a nuclear test, the nuclear cooperation won't be terminated automatically but there will be consultation between New Delhi and Washington.[7] At this stage, India's attention should be on getting the nuclear passed by the US Congress after the clearance of the IAEA safeguards agreement and the NSG waiver. Once the nuclear agreement passes the US Congress, the Hyde Act provisions contradictory to the deal need not bother India. Those provisions may cause some worry when we are to negotiate contracts for US reactors. That will be another day and at that time India can press for amendments to those provisions of the Hyde Act which govern equipment supply if the US wants Indian business. In short, the Hyde Act controversy is a red herring put forward by those who had always opposed India's civil and strategic nuclear programmes. (a) The CPM is obsessed with their obsolete ideology. (b) for China's foreign policy, there is no permanent friends and foes, but only permanent interests. (c) India's cannot be a 'power' without ending nuclear isolation. (d) India never remained a 'Rogne State', like Pakistan or North Korea, who proliferated the N-technology. Even Australia has given uranium to China a trained proliferation country. But India firmly believed in non-proliferation regime. (e) The ban on India was imposed in 1978 by the then London suppliers Club—the predecessor of NSG formed as a response to the Indian nuclear test in 1974. The original founders of the Club were the US, the then USSR, the UK, France, Germany, Japan and Canada. Today, all these countries have backed the waiver from the ban of nuclear commerce. Major objections have come from the countries (namely Austria, Ireland, New Zealand, Netherlands and Switzerland are known as hardliners) who joined the suppliers club later. (f) The NPT was the product of the Cold War era and today it has lost relevance in the light of globalised economy. At present, the NPT has been signed by all nations except three nations, Israel Pakistan and N. Korea.[8] North Korea withdrew from the treaty.

Lastly, the non-plorafication community has failed to take action when nuclear weaken powers proliferated the technology in 1980s and 1990s. India's the case in point of China who proliferates N-tuning to Pakistan. As per the *New York Times* news, dated 4th Sept., 2008, China gave her nuclear technology to Pakistan in 1990, including conducting a proxy test for it was. As per a high ranking former officer Thomas Reed. It was a violation of NPT, which was fully known to the US and the West. On the contrary, India's record is unique in the sense that it never transferred its advanced nuclear technology and a fast-breeder reactors to any country, India has agreed to put her indigenously constructed civil nuclear reactors to Atomic Energy safeguards. India has declared voluntary moratorium. On the basis of the above cited record, the NSG has favoured our case (N-Deal).

A HISTORIC MOMENT

It was a success of India's diplomacy that her nuclear case got a clearance on 7th Sept., 2008 at the Vienna meeting of the 45 Nuclear suppliers Group—NSG, which welcomed Delhi's reaffirmation of commitment to non-proliferation goals and other global responsibilities. The consensus ended the country's three decade (about 34 years) long nuclear isolation, i.e. the NSG's waiver frees India from signing the NPT. Now India can import nuclear fuel and technologies from France, Russia and other countries, apart from the USA, through bilateral civil nuclear cooperation. Therefore, the BJP's fear that India's right to test had been compromised by signing/ accepting the 123 Pact, is baseless. It would not affect to our future nuclear strategic programmes. It is worth-recalling that we would have to be more alert of the Bangladesh's missile test (conducted on 1st May, 2008, near the Chittagong port) with the active participation of a Chinese group of experts. China has armed each of the South Asian nations surrounding India with missile systems and Dhaka is the latest in line Beijing's play is to encircle India.

On the eve of the Ahmadinajad's visit to India on 25th April 2008 his way to Srilanka, India was asked by the US administration to cool its ties with Iran due to the latter's Nuclear programme. In response to the suggestion, India boldly snubbed saying that India seeks to repair ties damaged by its vote against Iran at the IAEA. External Affairs Minister Pranab Mukherjee said in the Parliament that the US need to arrogate itself the role of the International Atomic Energy

Agency (IAEA) in pronouncing judgment on Iran's Nuclear programme. Sparing no words, India asked the US not to usurp the power to declare Iran a 'rogue nuclear state' since it is for the global nuclear watchdog (IAEA)—the designated authority—to decide if the Islamic Republic of Iran is developing nuclear weapons or not. It may be known that Iran is a signatory to the NPT and it has accepted same obligations to international treaties. The US posture here was taken as unsolicited advice to India. This boldness has made the India-Iran gas pipeline a reality.

IS SOUTH HEADING FOR A COLD WAR?

A number of renewed efforts have been made to achieve a global deal under Doha Round of multilateral talks by the ministers of South under Indian leadership, to bridge differences on farm subsidies and opening markets for industrial and agricultural products through the WTO—the highest decision-making body. But it has been seen that India and the US have been on opposite sides in the way of negotiation since 2004, and they could not meet the target due to differences on the issues of agriculture subsidies and market access, it may be noted that India, China, Brazil, South Africa has combined the cause of developing nations. But the US and the EU nations have been trying to get the best deal in favour of rich nations. Apart this, the Olympic torch issue versus dealing with protests over Chinese policies in Tibet (i.e. China's sovereignty) outraged the developed North over Beijing's crackdown in Lhasa involving the question of human rights. Experts of International affairs like Shashi Tharoor is of the view that the fears of a new cold war are unfounded as the North will continue to be tempted by self-national interests and the South will be alert from the world's former colonial powers to assert position that undermine their hard won and jealously safeguarded sovereignty.

DALAI LAMA IS RESPONSIBLE FOR CHINA'S GRIP IN TIBET

In March 2008, on the eve of the Olympics in China

which was held in August 2008, reports from Tibet were received how the killing of demonstrators took place in Lhasa by the Chinese Army by imposing of martial law.

By contrast, Samdhong Rinpoche, the Tibetan prime minister in exile, opened a conference in Dharamsala in February 2008, to highlight and support the Dalai Lama's policy of compromise with China. The Dalai Lama and the exiled Tibetan leadership in the early 70s made the decision to accept Tibet as a part of China. But policy change was announced publicly only in 1988. The new policy sought to gain "real autonomy" for Tibet as envisioned by the Dalai Lama, Tibet would control all areas of policy except for foreign and military affairs, which would remain . . . hands of the Chinese central government. According to the 6th chapter of Chinese Constitution, 'autonomy' has been granted to local government under which cultural and spiritual heritage can be protected. But in Tibet's case the Chinese have razed the culture. In the words of Samdhong Rinpoche the PM of Tibetan Government-in-exile, it is a 'cultural genocide', because Tibet's history and culture has been banned from teaching in schools and Monasteries. The strength of each Monastery has further been reduced.

In the years that followed, China, nimbly taking account of the Dalai Lama's political naivete and desperation, has held firmly to its position and made no substantive concessions to the Tibetan exiles. All the while the Dalai Lama and his officials have continuously ratcheted down their position: from Tibetan independence, to "real autonomy", to simple cultural rights". Now, the Tibetans are taking it down yet another not asking only for those minimum rights that are protected under China's Constitution and its law on regional ethnic autonomy.[9]

In sum, China got the goal, i.e. the Dalai Lama renounced the demand of independence which he categorically did in 1988 as a spokesperson: China's image got a boost in international strategy for handling the Tibet issue. As per the agreement, Chinese officials have got the right to handle foreign affairs and nationality issues. Here, Lama failed to understand China's interior intentions.

Sadly, in reaction to the latest demonstration, the Lama was accused of working to sabotage the Beijing Olympics, inspite of the fact that Lama declared his firm support for these Olympics, which China wanted. The Chinese fact was meant to marginalize the role of the Dalai Lama against the legitimacy. China does not care of Dalai's hardened stand on the issue (condemning the use of force by China against the Government of Tibetan Autonomous Region—TAR). Currently, China has the two options to deal with the protestors in Tibet. First is of the style of Myanmar to suppress them in the way the Buddhist monks were. The second is to offer concessions as per the Agreement and maintain peace. But China is not Myanmar; she is a global power. The world and the UN expect Beijing to deal with the issue according to the rules of international law. China is a responsible power instead of an authoritarian power. Hence, Beijing should recognize that the Dalai Lama is its best bet to settle the Tibet issue. The Chinese leadership should invite him for talks. Such a gesture would go a long way to show China in a positive light. It is fatuous for Beijing to imagine that it could sweep dissent under the carpet by enforcing a ban on foreigners in Tibet or You Tube in China.

Sadly, the Left parties which have been vociferous and vehement to the US imperialism to the Indo-US deal has never spoken against the Chinese imperialism in the region.

INDEPENDENCE OF KOSOVA FROM SERBIA : NO THREAT TO J&K

Kosova's declaration of Independence from Serbia is the 7th state to emerge from the wreckage of Yugoslavia. The ethnic Albanian majority province had existed in a limbo since 1999 as a 'UN Protectorate'. This the final act of Yugoslavia's 17th year process of disintegration to which the EU and the US were actively engaged to encourage separatist movements after the end of the Cold War. But the model existence of newest state of the world is not going to influence the thinking of Kashmiris or of the world's opinion despite giving legitimacy to it by the EU and the US. Kosova cannot be compared to Kashmir because of India's model/record of civil liberties, its commitment to democratic values and human rights. Secessionist movement in Kashmir has been well checked by the Government of India through dialogue and conferences. However, India should remain concern of Kosova's independence seceded from Serbia. It is yet to be seen if it can survive as a sovereign nation in years to come.

Likewise, Russia has formally recognized independence of South Ossetia and Abkhazia—the two enclaves of Georgia whose separatist aspirations stirred the fierce conflict. The blood shed and crimes against Russian population forced Moscow to intervene militarily. The European reactions (EU) were rapid and sharp. The action was criticized on the ground that it was a violation of the principles of territorial integration and sovereignty of Georgia. The Georgian crisis presented the first ever the post-Cold War situation in Balakan region, where the NATO proposed to play a role against the Russia, because Georgia wanted the membership of NATO.

In fact, the NATO forces have flouted the rules of international law by violating collective norms of international community against unilateral military interventions in Kosova, earlier in Iraq and Afghanistan the role of UN was setside in all those crises in view of great powers' core interests. How can Russia forget her Cold War defeat and the role of NATO closer to Russia's borders? The balance of power and the struggle for power theory is still very much relevant in international politics. However, the above cited analogy of the situations does not apply to J&K.

The way the agitation and 'Azadi' fervour was launched in J&K in July August 2008, in the wake of the Amarnath land controversy, by self-professed politicians and separatist leaders, forget that the population of the state by and large is in favour of remaining with India. It is silly to term the status of J&K with India's semi-colonialism, or compare its relationship with Junagadh. They must recall that Pakistan imposed economic blockade on Kashmir to bring a pressure on the then Maharaja to accede to Pakistan and the Indian troops entered Srinagar on October 27, 1947, after the Maharaja had duly signed the accession of instrument which was endorsed by Sheikh Abdullah who was present in Delhi. Lateron, the leaders of the NC sadly breached the national trust.[10] Anyhow, the following steps should be initiated to avoid the re-emergence of tragic situation in the valley :

(a) The Valley should be granted autonomy (not Azadi) on the very foundation of Article 370 through national consensus.
(b) Ensure the conduct of a free and fair election in the state as we did four years ago.
(c) The state needs good and firm governance, not only in Kashmir, but also in other states. The ongoing violent agitations have posed a challenge to the federal secular democracy.
(d) The rights of 300,000 displaced Pandits must be ensured to restore political stability and protect social harmony.
(e) The BJP suggests of nationalizing of road to Amarnath shrine.

Notes and References

1. Similarities to 1962, Sobban Saxena, in *The Sunday Times of India*, New Delhi, April 20, 2008.
2. Brahma Chellaney, 'Stop Beijing Bulled', *Ibid.*, April 4, 2008, p. 14.
3. See the book of R.R. Sharma, 'India and Emerging Asia' (ed.), New Delhi, Sage Publications, 2005 and also the comments of Swagato Ganguly, "Taking a Liberal Bet of the US", *The Times of India*, 25/5/2006, p. 14.
4. See the comments of Brahma Chellaney, "Sending a Wrong Signal", *The Times of India*, New Delhi, 11.8.2008.
5. Read Professor Ramesh Thakur's comments in 'The World Turns on Thrust', *The Times of India*, New Delhi, April 24, 2008, p. 12.
6. Amit Mitra, 'Sabotaging India's Rise', *The Times of India*, New Delhi, April 18, 2008, p. 12.
7. These views and comments are of a noted strategic affair analyst, Dr. K. Subrahmanyam, published in *The Times of India*, dated March 8, 2008 under title 'Don't be Afraid of Mr. Hyde.' Mrs. Hyde has recently expired.
8. As per Kyodo news, North Korea has begun reassessing its Yongbyon reactor that can make material for atomic bombs in violation of the six party nuclear agreement.
9. Elliot Sperling, 'Big Brother is Watching', *Ibid.*, 17/3/2008, p. 11.
10. Arif Mohd. Khan, 'Keep it together', *The Times of India*, New Delhi edn., August 28, 2008, p. 14.

CHAPTER

38

Meaning of Indo-US Strategic Partnership

There is no need to express concerns about the unfateful past developments of 60 years when the US used to ignore country's national interests. Today, India has risen from a poor developing colony to become the fourth largest economy of the world and has enjoyed the status of Asian power. India is now a nuclear weapon state with a space and information technology power house. India, thus, has taken the experience in conducting its foreign policy according to her national interests. We need not to recall the events like our dependence on PL 480 imports, the passage of the UN resolution by the Western powers on the Kashmir issue tilting support in favour of Pakistan or the strategic behaviour of the US during the period of liberation of Bangladesh, compelling us to become a Soviet satellite. Why not we recall India's boldness of not signing the NPT conducting our first N-Test in 1974, and later in 1998, despite economic sanctions. Likewise, we as a non-aligned country conveyed our concern to soviet action in Afghanistan or the US military action in Iraq, India faced these events with self-confidence on external front.

The world politics has changed strategically and the balance of power in Asia is not that what used to be in the era of cold war then known as bipolar world. The emergence of China as well as the rise of India has compelled the US to move to lift the technology apartheid against India. Without requiring India to join the NPT/CTBT or give its N-weapons programme. It is worthcalling that there is no evidence of India having compromised on its independent foreign policy. India's vote against Tehran in the AIEA board was perfectly justified as Iran developed a clandestine N-weapons programe from A.Q. Khan of Pakistan, which was a violation of IAEA safeguards.*

India is a strategic partner of the US on equal footings, as our democratic leadership has been accepted by the US foreign policy formulators because of our democratic success. But India has refused to be an ally (which former PM Vajpayee used the term 'naturally') of the U.S. We are in need of sustaining our strategic ties with the US to maintain the new balance of power in Asia and the world as well. This strategic partnership is the new experience of both the countries—the US and India. Both can not ignore the rise of China in Asia after the disintegration of the USSR and other follow up developments. Likewise, the US or the West alone after 9/11 can not fight the growing spectre of terrorism. Our Army's skill in counter-terrorism has earned reputation that is why the joint Indo-Chinese military exercise is gearing up to counter-terrorism and to hold its first every joint exercise in the Chengdu military region of China. It is a imperative in the light of the 9/11 terror strikes.**

The two developments in Asia—the SCO and the Malabar 2007, consisting China, Russia, Kazakhstan, Uzbekistan, Kyrgyzstan and Tajikistan (six members) and the US-led Japan, Japan, Australia, Singapore and India, respectively, are stated to be cared out their economic turfs and the preservation of supply of pipelines aimed at countering piracy and terrorism.

* K. Subrahmanyam, "Let's believe in Ourselves", *The Times of India*, New Delhi, August 20, 2007, p. 14.

** David Scott, "Strategic Imperatives of India as an Emerging Player in Pacific Asia", in *International Studies*; A Sage India Journal Publication, New Delhi, January Issue, 2007.

The Shanghai Cooperation Organisation (SCO), an Alliance with Russia and energy rich four central Asian nations (as cited above) is the making of China's strategy. It is related to putting its military and air combat operations on display against terrorism in the region as well as to prevent the growing influence of US in Asia. Its military/drill/clout was displayed in August 2007. They are, indeed, the part of grand and great game of big powers' play in Asia. The US-led Quad (India, Japan and Australia) and China led Russia and four central Asian countries as SCO appear to be locked in a strategy conflict for supremacy over Asia. The six day joint naval exercise in Sept. Malabar 07 is drawn into an alliance aimed at containing China in Asia and it has a similar role that was of the NATO after Second World War (i.e. containment of Soviet Union/communism). Therefore, Beijing views Malabar 07 military exercise a step towards the creation of an 'Asian Nato' to counter China's economic military and strategic influence.

The Indian Navy is set to participate in a multilateral navel exercise with other countries as part of sea-lane security for trade. The Malabar 07 naval exercise of Sept. 2007 of four countries (the US, Japan, Australia and Singapore) is a new symbol of military diplomacy 07 Indian ocean. This multilateral military exercise is viewed as the protection of an Asian NATO, whose purpose is to contain China in Asia. It is loosely termed as a US-led axis of democracy in Asia.

It is alleged that this is the beginning of the end for the Independence of Indian foreign policy and New Delhi is gradually being twisted into the sinister strategic designs of the new US imperialism. But this is not a new or the first time exercise that the Indian navy participated in such multilateral military exercise. In the early period of 1947, for example, India was an active member of the JET (Joint Exercise of Trincomalli) under Commonwealth navies. India at that time was the forefront of the non-aligned movement—NAM. India has revived the same link, with a cautious process, with the littoral navies and powers. The Malabar-07 is purely professional objectives exercise for mutual cooperation and military date-sharing. A similar multilateral military exercise that was conducted by China and Russia along with some central Asian Republics for nine days in August 2007 under the Shanghai Cooperation Organization (SCO) banner. Therefore, it a baseless to interpret Malabar-07 as anti-China or that India is getting drawn into a US plan to contain China, on the following two grounds: (a) China in our 'greatest neighbour' and the government of the day trying best to have cordial relations with China. And (b) the US too has been evolving its trade and other ties with China during the last two decades. Because of Russia's oil and gas revenue and China's export drive rise, the area is of strategic importance so far as the new balance of power is concerned.

In short, China, which views the Malabar exercise 07 as a step towards the creation of an Asian Nato, has formed the Shanghai Cooperation Organisation (SCO) with Russia and energy rich central Asian nations. The organization is aimed at building an axis that will give control of Central Asian energy reserves to Russia and China, which in turn will give Beijing a lot of muscle, in Asia. China has built military bases in Myanmar, Thailand and Sri Lanka to contain the growing influence of the West.

The post-Cold War era has marked new fault lines of great game of power in Asia for economic and strategic alliances. The Indo-US deal is not a mere energy or technology pact, but is also a grand design on the US part to suck India into an alliance and to give the US a new kind of leverage in the region. Japan, too, in favour of a broader Asia and urges India to become partner of the strategic global of Pacific Ocean to counter the fallout of terrorism.

Secondly, if the SCO is meant to limiting American influence in Central Asia, the quad of US, Australia, Japan and India (Singapore is an additional member) is aimed blocking China's proliferations against piracy in Malacca straits from and where world's oil passes through and prevent the proliferation missiles from China to other countries. Prevention of disruption is its key motive.

LEFT NEEDS TO EXPLAIN QUESTIONS

The Left front of UPA seemed softening its stand on the Indo-US Civil Nuclear Deal and entering into negotiations with IAEA. The UPA government has given numerous clarifications to the left against the left's fears on our strategic policies and the alliance with the US. It is a proved sign that left has okeyed New Delhi going to Vienna to sit with the IAEA, with which an India-Specific safeguards agreement is necessary for the deal to go ahead and after that the deal will go to the NSG and thereafter it would be ratified by the US Congress. But the way the left alleged the Manmohan Singh government as move pro-"active imperialist, pro-capitalist and pro-US" or making India a "pawn" in the imperialist US global power game* the country needs some clarifications from the left on the following counts:

First, why does the left think that a nuclear deal, which is a bilateral agreement between two countries and which needs the consent of all nuclear suppliers and an international supervising agency, is a camouflage for drawing India in a global strategy intended to serve US interests? Is it that the government of India, in its eagerness to have nuclear sanctions lifted, has made a bargain with US agreeing to work in tandem with America's state department and Pentagon in its global power game? If the left thinks that the government has given any such commitment, it must explicitly say so: no government has the right to remain in power if it has in fact entered into any such secret understanding that would jeopardise the country's independence.

Second, China has a similar bilateral agreement with the US (which contains many more conditionalities than the one with India). If the Left thinks that by such an agreement China has been handicapped in pursuing an independent foreign and defence policy, it must say so clearly; if, on the contrary, China has not compromised its independence in any way, then why does the Left think that India will succumb to US pressure?

Third, the Left would cry wolf when India approached multilateral agencies for temporary financial relief. The government of the day was severely criticized on the ground that, with imperialist America dominating these institutions, India would be making herself a victim to America's capitalist designs and lose her freedom in pursuing economic policies

* D.N. Ghosh, "Qestions for the Left", Nov. 16, 2007, p. 14.

that are in her interest. Nothing of that sort has happened; India has been crafting and designing her policies that strike a balance between what is required to be done in a globally interdependent world and the dictates and compulsions of her own interests. What makes the Left think that we would surrender our sovereignty in the future?

Fourth, on the strength of a similar deal, China has drawn up an ambitious plan to increase the nuclear component of power generation and, as current reports show, is scouting aggressively all over the globe for sourcing and securing supplies of nuclear fuel. This is exactly what India needs to do: diversify sources of power generation. China will continue exploiting her initial advantage while we remain a laggard, eroding fast even our existing indigenous resource. No country of India's size and potential can view this with complacency.

Are there any special reasons why these relative disparities between China and India do not trouble the Left? Since the Left is a partner in the present government, it owes and explanation to the nation for its obdurate stance.

Finally, one has to take note of the string of insinuations as to the real game plan of the Left. The long-term consequences of backing out of the deal are deeply worrying; it is bound to put India, permanently, as many commentators have argued, in a position of comparative disadvantage *vis-a-vis* China. These do not seem to concern the Left: in no case should India be allowed to do anything that, in their perception, harms China, for in the party primer on geopolitics, the interests of China are primary and those of India secondary.

Why look at only the nuclear deal? In many sectors where we have demonstrated our capability to grow fast, the Left has been consistently putting one roadblock after another; these, many argue, are precisely the areas in which China has been wise to shed the hangover of her colonial experience, openly welcoming foreign investment and technology from the US and other developed nations.*

* D.N. Ghosh, "Questions for the Left", Nov. 16, 2007, p. 14.

CHAPTER

39

India's Role in the New World Order

The year 1990 heralded the new post-Cold War era in world politics, which witnessed not only the Soviet-American friendship on nuclear weapons, but it also earmarked drastic changes in the map of Europe, significantly with the unification of Germany, the disintegration of the Communist regime from the entire Europe and the survival of NATO as political strategic alliance. No doubt, the end of the Cold War with the disintegration of the U.S.S.R. was a historic event in the international scene as change resulted into the easing of several of the regional conflicts. It brought to the fore some sea-changes in world affairs such as, grave instability due to the collapse of the Soviet Union, the rise of ethnic nationalism in Eastern Europe as well as the rise of Islamic fundamentalism in Arab world and disappearance of balance of power, etc. compelled the formulators of India's foreign policy to review and revise the basic contours of our foreign policy and diplomacy. The need was felt to re-examine the relevance of non-alignment foreign policy of India. Following the retreat of the Soviet Union in 1989-90 from Afghanistan, the world order emerged as alone 'uni-polar system' with the United States as the only surviving super power. It was a harsh reality of the world affairs. India, therefore, urgently needed to bring about the necessary adjustments in terms of its priorities and objectives of her foreign policy. It compelled us to reshape, consistent and coherent the foreign policy if she had to seek the place in the new world order. There was a dramatic shift in the tools of diplomacy as well, containing more emphasis on trade economic priority than that of military or strategic values. The future war, it was believed, would be fought in the market-places, not in the battlefields.

Our decision-makers recognized the fact that in the post-cold-war era, the Indo-Russia-relations might remain stable in view of the convergence of interests, but Russia as a successor of the USSR, was more inclined towards Europe and the United States for her rise and revival than India and the other third world nations, and India therefore, had to resolve its problems with China and Pakistan peacefully and bilaterally. In view of this change, the strategic content of Indo-Soviet relations as they were, saw vastly change. The new relationship with Russia and China, therefore, upgraded in the field of trade and economic cooperation. It was realized that India will have to really practise Non-alignment policy in her dealings with the former Soviet Republics which were independent states. For, the end of the Cold War era did not mean the end of power-rivalries between and among the regional or super powers. Evidently, the end of the cold war marked shifts in balance of power, in which it was very difficult to tell friends from foes or *vice versa*. In fact, the new world order itself was a disorderly stage, in view of the removal of the Soviet threat to the Western world allies, making the Europeans less dependent on the US protection. The possibility of Japan correcting its economic muscle into military power and the new prospects of China with its feverish economic growth were other two developments. These two states emerge super-power in Asia began to influence the formation of foreign policy.

On the other hand, the Indo-US relations registered a new sign of improvement. The old irritant of Pakistan as a factor in Indo-US relations appeared to have lost relevance since the US

Government took the decision in 1990 to cut down and suspend its military aid to Pakistan, ostensibly, in the background of the latter's nuclear weapon programme and the involvement of Pakistan in Islamic fundamentalism before the 9/11 event.

The crises around the world (namely, terrorism, racist mindset, degradation of the UN's role, regional conflicts, in the Middle-East was left the United Nations in a state of uncertainty without parallel in its 1947 history. The sea-changes in the Post-Cold international affairs have been so quick and continuous that the UN in its social and political areas found itself in a confused state. In fact, it was virtually due to the development the West's bid to weaken the sovereignty of developing countries through globalization and investment. Both Germany and Japan were on the rise for acquiring a new international status. There was a need to intensify our efforts to reshape and to re-define the aims or objectives of the U.N. to avoid a variety of disasters, specifically after the Iraq war.

The key challenge before the United States was how to defend the human rights problems facing the new world order. Inter-religious strife and inter-ethnic conflicts involving minority groups began to pose a threat to world peace, security and democracy. Such strife were seen in Somalia, India, Sudan, Yugoslavia and Cambodia and their destabilizing influence was seen on world peace and order. Their fallout threatened to reverse the progress and development made towards freedom and democracy. India, being the model of the largest and stable democracy of the world, needed to play a meaningful role against the deprivation of the rights of ethnic minorities through the UN. Against this background, there was debate over restructuring of the United Nations' charter, and both Germany and Japan as the rising industrial powers claimed to become a permanent member of the UN Security Council. The Germany's case for a permanent seat was first backed by Chancellor Helmut Kohl of Germany. The plan reflected the rise of Japan as an Asian economic power.

India then too staked its claim for the similar status in the changing international environment on the basis that she is the largest democracy of the world and its case further merited on the basis of territory, population and its importance in South Asia. But much depended upon how she pursued her diplomatic efforts in wooing the permanent members like the USA, Britain, France and China as well.

IMPORTANCE OF ISRAEL*

India is the world's most populous and Israel the Middle-East's only democracy. Judaism and Hinduism are among the world's ancient civilizations and "root faiths" that have sprouted other major religions. Their rituals are sometimes similar, which is why Indian hosts don't bat an eyelid when: Jewish guests request particular items on the menu not be cooked in particular pots or served with particular dishes. The distinctive Jewish humour resonates well in India. India's tradition of hospitality towards the Jewish people is centuries old. India's relationship with Israel, which gained independence within a year of India's in a similarly traumatic partition, was a major anomaly. One of the earliest to recognize Israel, India was one of the last to establish ambassadorial relations in 1992. Full relations were maintained with China and Pakistan, countries with which India has fought wars; but not with Israel, with whom we have no direct quarrel. The policy of stand offishness provoked resentment and cynicism about India's moral authority without materially assisting the Palestinian cause or winning Arab votes against Pakistan in international forums. The governing issue was 'Jerusalem'.

On the contrary, India adopted odd strategic choices. Having taken out Iraq's nuclear reactor in 1981, in the early 1980s apparently Israel thrice proposed to India that they should jointly attack and destroy Pakistan's nuclear plant at Kahuta. The Israeli air force was confident of achieving the pinpoint accuracy needed to destroy the facility, but needed refueling facilities in western India because of the distances involved. India thrice refused enmity should be made of sterner stuff. How things have changed. India and Israel

* Prof. Ramesh Thakur, "Reach Out Israel", *The Times of India*, New Delhi, Dec. 13, 2007, p. 14.

discovered common concerns in the growth of Islamic fundamentalism in Central and South-West Asia, which culminated in 1990s. This trauma of terrorism has become today a reality.

In the Middle-East, Israel is small, is dated vulnerable and threatened nation, but has built good political clout against fundamentalism. India can take benefit of it to solve her many problems.

In the words of General Secretary of the UN, Ban-ki-moon, Asia's time has come to influence the course of contemporary world politics. We, Asians inhabit the world's largest continent, with the world's largest population and its fastest growing economies. We have a rich history and ancient cultures. Yet our role in international affairs is far less than it could, or should be. Asia's contribution to the UN, though significant, could be grater. Its humanitarian assistance, to put it politely, is less than generous. We are the only continent where regional integration and common markets have not taken hold.*

Latin Americans and North Americans drama of creating a free-trade zone. Europeans speak of building a United States of Europe. The African Union aspires to become a United States of Africa. Why not believe in a United States of Asia? There are many reasons why Asia is different: history, cultural diversity, unresolved territorial and political disputes, a lack of multilateral experience, and the predominance of one or two centres of power. But the main reasons is what we have not tried. Asia does not do itself justice. As an Asian secretary-general, one would like to see an Asia that is both better integrated and more internationally engaged.

For more than forty years India chose not to clash Israel under the pressures from Indian Muslims and the Arab world. But once India recognized her (Israel) as a state, the prospects of cooperation between the two has been almost limitless, and it is evident from the past experience that Israel has always extended a hand of friendship to India on many crucial occasions. India discovered that it was in its interest to be

* See the text of his article published in the *New York Times*, dated 16th December, 2007.

involved in the peace process and that it was imperative to establish relations with Israel, turning down the misleading assumption on two grounds that the opinion in the Indian Muslim would got annoyed.

First, there was no hostile reaction from the Muslim community when India announced the resumption of full diplomatic relation with Israel. Secondly, a large number of Arab countries such as Egypt and Syria have developed excellent relations with the Israeli Government. Jordan and Lebanon, too, have been eager to establish cordial relations with Israel after the Gulf war. The American attack on Iraq further changed the things in the wake of the rise of religions fundamentalism *versus* nuclear weapons programme. India can effectively deal with the matters pertaining to nuclear proliferation. The Middle-East peace process is in progress and our concern should be at close-relations with both Arabs and Israelis, in order to keep the Middle-East conflict-free as this is the primary source of India's energy.

PM'S TRIP TO NIGERIA

His visit to Nigeria was historic since it was undertaken after 45 years gap. It was meant to challenge China's expedient diplomacy. History speaks how the West under the flag of colonialism exploited the African Continent (known to be a Dark Continent) and the developed world never took care of the setting it free from the grip of oppressive rulers. The case in point is of Dafar Killings by Robert Mugabe's repression in Zimbabwe.

It is China, who regarded a new era of cultural and political ties through economic cooperation in search of oil and minerals. Abandoned by the West, Beijing filled the 'vacuum', by demonstrating its influence through hosting 48 out of 53 African leaders in 2006. It was both historic and historical, as China was the *'first pre-eminent outside power'* in Africa and its second biggest trading partner. Infact, this 'vacuum' should have been filled by Indian leadership in the hunt for energy. Still there is opportunity to break China's monopoly but cautiously through investment, trade and economic cooperation to procure natural resources.*

It has to be noted that China's economic and strategic cooperation with these countries have nothing to improve the human conditions and prosperity, as China has rejected the UN plan for a peace-keeping force in Darfar and blocked UN resolutions. China never spoke against exploitation and human atrocities, as well as the western sanctions.

Since the western powers will not take a realistic view of African needs, it is up to India to counter the Chinese behemoth. India needs oil, uranium and raw materials but unlike China, New Delhi can offer Africans a mix of growth economics and political freedoms. India also enjoys the advantage of a large expatriate business community throughout Africa, Especially in South Africa, Kenya and Tanzania, that could help to realize Nehru's view that; "the whole world owes it to the African people not to hinder them, but to help them in freedom in every way".

ONE-DAY CONGRESS SESSION AND INDIA'S FOREIGN POLICY

On November 17, 2007 the Congress leadership asserted the need to underscore an independent foreign policy to be part of its Resolution, which pushed on the backfoot by the Left's charge of joining the US strategic axis in the wake of the Indo-US nuclear deal and joint Army exercised. Gladly, our Foreign Policy emerged as a stick of sorts against Congress after the Left raised its red flag against the nuclear deal while slamming it for joining the US strategic orbit. The sudden chill in relations with old ally—Russia has not helped matters either. With the Union government having agreed to roll back the nuke pact, there is a feeling that a vigorous denial is needed to shop the Left's charge from sticking. The resolution of virtues of the nuclear pact alongside its emphasis on an autonomous foreign policy.

* Deepak Datta Ray, "Don't Ignore Africa", *The Times of India*, New Delhi, Oct. 3. 2007, p. 14.

INDIA'S CONCERN IN PAKISTAN

With the declaration of emergency in Pakistan, the Indian Government was concerned of her priority *versus* the military rule in Pakistan, Chaoes in its internal politics (events like the clash of President in uniform with the judiciary) which was fully Talibanised. New Delhi was extremely worried about the prospect of Pak's nuclear warheads falling into the wrong hands if the country descended into anarchy.

Unfortunately, the country has been under military rule for more than half century of its existence, and in the foreseeable future, the military rule, even if its face appears to be a democratic appearance, is going to be the biggest player in Pakistan. Sadly, the Indian Government's response to the goings-on across the border has been far too timid. Instead of condemning the suspension of civil rights and the Constitution, New Delhi has been circumspect in the name of India's self-interest. In Pakistan the Indian government is willing to back a military dictatorship in the hope it will help control terrorism in our backyard. It has no qualms in playing footsie with a ruthless military regime in Myanmar in return for energy supplies and help in tackling insurgents in the north-east.

How different are we then from, say, the US, which wrecks a country—Iraq—in the name of spreading democracy while backing regressive monarchies and dictatorships when it suits American interests? India may be a young and evolving democracy, but has been a good example of how the contestations and claims of different sections of a society can be negotiated within the democratic framework. The day we stop standing up for democracy especially in the neighbourhood is when our interests will be compromised.

PAK'S INTEGRITY IN DOUBT

The Pentageon Centre has expressed in concern at the developments in Pakistan. The US has started believing that New Delhi, in comparison to Pakistan, is growing as a potential power with global influence and Pakistan has failed in curbing the global terrorism, specifically in search or

Osama-bin-Laden. The US has viewed the US-India strategic partnership more relevant. India is seen as a potential power with global reach.

According to the *Newsweek of New York* of 22nd Oct., 2007, Pakistan which has recently witnessed a series of suicide attacks by pro-Taliban and al-Qaida militants is 'the most dangerous country in the world', in comparison to Afghanistan and Iraq. There is no political instability. It has a trusted network of radical Islamists with an abundance of angry anti-western recruits. There is growing nuclear-programme but without stability. And most frightening fact is that, in Pakistan thousands have been retired to join the study of Madrassas about courses in compulsory technology video production relating to war against the West.

THE SECRETS OF AID OUT

On the eve of the assassination of Mrs. Benazir Bhutto, *The New York Times* highlighted the secrets that the US aid flowing to Pakistan and intended to fight Al-Qaida and Taliban, was grossly misused. Instead, the money was diverted to pay weapons systems against India, almost with the same intentions that was diverted during the Cold War period against India. The nexus of Pakistani military/ISI and jehadis based in Pakistan strengthened the Islamic tendencies across South Asia. Ironically, Washington never looked closely at the operations of this nexus, whereas President Musharraf in uniform, in the name of the war against terror. Successfully kept the US in dark of about the dual game. In fact, Islamabad never allowed to strengthen the roots of civilian democracy. Ultimately this culminated into the assassination of Mrs. Butto on the eve of elections to be held in Jan. 2008 in Pakistan.

On the other hand, on going ethnic war in Balochistan is a big challenge to Pakistan, as Pakistan's undeclared war in Balochistan is taking alarming proportions. The Punjabi settlers long resented by the local people are fleeing the provinces as the ethnic gulf widens in Pakistan's biggest province. Islamabad-locked in a bitter conflict with Baloch nationalists, demanding political and economic autonomy is now finding it hard to restore order in the region on boil since the Pakistan

Army started a military operation two years ago. The killing of tribunal chieftain Nawab Akbar Khan Bugti further infuriated Balochs and made them more determined to fight for their rights. In 1948, Pakistan annexed Balochistan against the will of the Balochs, which resulted in three wars—the first led by Karim Khan in 1948, in 1968 led by Nawab Nowroz Khan, and then in 1973-77 by a coalition of Baloch tribes. The disparities, too, are wide. Gas reserves in Balochistan supply most of Pakistan with its energy, but remain off limits to the local population.

It is believed that the visit of Mrs. Sonia Gandhi to China in Oct. 2007 was of significance in terms of an early settlement of the border issue in East sector under the principle of 'give and take', because Chinese leadership has refused to accept the Macmohan Line. In the changed political environment, China, too, is serious to a positive/acceptable settlement of issue on the basis of mutual concession. The border row has been a big obstacle between the two big nations of Asia. It is further believed that the PM's visit to China in January 2008 would make a platform for 'substantial adjustment'.

In the light of national interest, China intends to Dam rivers like Yarlung Tsangopoj in Tibet—(knownces Brahmaputra) in 2009 and divert its water to its grid North-East region. If the Gorges Dam is constructed, it will affect our source of major rivers including these Brahmaputra, the Sutlej and the Indus, i.e. 90% of the river flow will go into lower flow. This may be a new source of tension between India and China. China's plan is to have a hydropower project in the Tibet Autonomous Region.

MOVE TOWARDS EAST ASIA

In the changing political climate, it is now the turn of eastern European nations. Today, the CE-4 countries (Poland, Hungray, the Czech Republic and Slovakia) are known as 'European Tigers', because these ex-Soviet bloc countries have shown how rapidly results can be achieved by adopting economic reforms and the growth through the opportunities made available by globalization. New Delhi can grab the opportunities and learn lessons from the CE-4 countries who were, till yesterday the part of socialist economies. In short, India needs to integrate economically with neighbouring nations. That also means bringing its infrastructure on par with East Asia or China. Prime Minister Manmohan Singh has identified the poor state of roads, ports and power as a critical bottleneck for faster Indian growth. Another barrier is an increasing skills shortage brought on by an archaic educational system that's desperately in need of reform. Lending voice to east European tigers' roar is the high quality of human resources found in these countries. If New Delhi doesn't alter its laidback approach to tackling deficiencies in hard and soft infrastructure, the Indian economy could soon turn into yesterday's flavour.

The world's largest and third largest armies of China and India held their first ever joint military exercise, in a bid to counter-terrorism maneuver in China. Yet Indian Army is still warry of PLA's role in the 1962 war, because, despite several military CBMs being held, the 4,052 Km Line of Actual Control between the two remain unresolved. Our intelligence agencies have noted several events of 'incursions' by Chinese forces into our terror (nearby LoC) and built up military infrastructure in the Tibet Autonomous Region. From east of Sikkim and Arunachal Pradesh were not safe, as around 300 cases of intrusions by Chinese troops have been recorded since last two years. Likewise, India needs to keep a watch on 300 new Madrassas schools operating on Indo-Nepal border. Our Indo-Nepal border is totally open and freely accessible. They have mouchroomed in the past three years. The Sashatra Seema Bul (SSB) has already informed the Home Ministry about their suspicious activities.

The Commonwealth Summit (CHOGM-2007) held in CKampala of Uganda in Nov. 2007 was historic and unprecedented in itself as Kamesh Sharma was elected as the new General Secretary, the first Asian diplomat to win the seat. J. Hered India a good opportunity to show case at an international diplomacy and image at an international platforms when the NAM is defunct and has lost much of its sheen and importance, India should now use this platform take the Leadership role of the Afro-Asian countries, who are members of this multi-racial, multi-ethnic, multi-linguistic organization with 53 members. Many of them are still backward and under-developing stage. It is worth-recalling that the British empire created this body to facilitate its national interests and economic pursuits and India as a new Republic too joined the non-white Commonwealth in 1947 to strengthen the ties with these countries. Today, India can spread its commitment to democracy (because of our success in governance and, holding peaceful and regular elections) in the right of the fact that many of these countries are still grappling with transition to democracy after the fight against Apartheid. India's role in this fight has been laudable and active in the Cold War era. In this new era of international order, the issue like disarmament, globalization and economic reforms, human rights can be pushed by North-South dialogue through this forum. India's edge in IT offers great opportunity to forge new ties with the member-countries. Likewise, India should joint the worldwide movement for democracy through the 'UN Democracy Fund' because doing so is in India's own national interest. It would strengthen out leadership role on the world stage, to include India's permanent membership on the UN Security Council, and its inclusion in global agenda setting dialogues, such as the G-8.

APPENDIX

(I) IMAGE OF OUR JUDICIARY

Our judiciary has excellently performed in giving new direction to the country on the basis of the constitutional performance. On the contrary, some developments have tarnished its image, like that of the other constitutional bodies. For example, in the P.F. Scam, the CBI report has confirmed the fraudulent withdrawal of Rs. 6.58 crore from the P.F. fund accounts of class III and IV employees of the Ghaziabad district of Uttar Pradesh. An extensive probe of the CBI has found a former Supreme Court Justice Tarun Chatterjee, along with 23 other Judges of Allahabad High Court (both retired and sitting judges). This is the biggest ever indictment of the country's judiciary. It needs introinspection and an in-built check.

The Appointment of HC Judges in Questioned

The petition filed by former Union Law Minister Shanti Bhushan, in July 2007, challenged the appointment of a Madras High Court judge Ashok Kumar. As per the petition, a number of judges have been elevated on the recommendations of the Supreme Court Collegiums, despite facing adverse remarks. The petition questioned the powers of the CJI to appoint a judge even after the collegiums has refused to make the necessary recommendations. Such appointments were made during the tenure of Chief Justice of India K. Sabharwal in 2005.

On that basis, the Supreme Court has asked the Union Government to submit a comprehensive report on the appointment of permanent judges in High Courts since 1999, along with the cases of elevation as permanent judges. Ashok

Kumar was elevated in Jan. 2007 in disregard of the law laid down by Supreme Court in the Special Reference Judgement case of 1998 as well as of SC collegiums. It was the nine-judge bench decision which upheld that even appointments of judges were subject to Judicial Review. In this petition, the order annualling the appointment of K.N. Srivastava as a judge of the Gauhati High Court too had been referred.

Our Judges : Not above the Law

The controversy over Karnataka High Court Chief Justice P.D. Dinakaran, who is facing various allegations including land grabbing, took an unusual turn. After he refused to comply with the advice of the Chief Justice of India to go on leave until an impeachment inquiry was completed, he has been transferred to the Sikkim High Court. This immediately raised two questions. One, if the CJI found him unfit to continue duties in Karnataka, why should there be a different yardstick for Sikkim? The Sikkim Bar Association raised this issue and then decided to boycott Justice Dinakaran if he is appointed to their High Court. They also rightly objected to Sikkim being treated as a punishment posting for judges. Indeed, this is not the first time that controversial judges have been transferred to Sikkim. On at least two occasions in the recent past 'tainted' judges had been transferred to Sikkim from other High Courts. In reaction to the judge, Law minister Veerappa Moily made it clear that Karnataka High Court Chief Justice P.D. Dinakaran will have to heed the advice of Supreme Court collegiums and proceed on leave as he was not above the law. In his words: 'The hands of law are long enough to catch anyone. I don't think Justice Dinakaran is above the law, or is beyond the reach of the law', this was in response to a question on government's view about Dinkaran's defiance of the SC collegiums' advice. Moily refused to get drawn into the controversy any further. However, sources said there were no legal complications if an acting chief justice was asked to join even as the serving chief justice went on leave.

Justice Dinakaran had not been performing judicial functions after Rajya Sabha Chairman Hamid Ansari admitted a motion in December 2009 seeking his removal on charges of corruption, land grab and abuse of judicial office the impeachment motion moved by 76 Rajya Sabha members. SC collegiums asked Justice Dinakaran to go on leave since it was felt that judicial work of the Karnataka HC was suffering since he had stopped attending work.

The Dinakaran episode virtually saddened the Judiciary, specifically the former CJ of India, K.G. Balkrishnan. He admitted it on the eve of his retirement. But he was of a strong view that he has not responsible for the controversy, or the collegiums system. In many cases, while selecting judges for any High Court, the integrity of such persons is not tested and sounded. It so happens because out 3000 lawyers working in the High Courts, two-three persons are picked and there is no particular yardstick to select a person for a post of judge in the higher judiciary. Here, the Executive plays an important role as it must made a thorough inquiry about the person to be selected. The role of collegiums comes after the proposed appointment.

In short, more important issue is how to deal with misdemeanours of judges in the higher courts, impeachment is an extreme as well as cumbersome process. Not surprisingly, till date, impeachment motions against judges have proved to be non-starters. This makes it imperative to have provisions for less radical punishment for errant judges. The government has been sitting on a new legislation that is meant to supersede the Judges (Inquiry) Bill. The new legislation—the Judicial Accountability and Standard Bill—is expected to overhaul the process of appointment of judges and investigations into allegations of impropriety. There is a crying need to fine tune the process of enquiring into misdemeanours by judges and to enforce disciplinary measures. Until that happens, we could face situations where errant judges go unpunished.[1]

The above-cited episode brought the Judiciary and the Executive in clash, overtly or covertly, leading to emphasis on bringing the assets of judges under the Right of Information. In one of the orders of the Central Information Commission (CIC) stressed that making the assets of judges be made public. This

1. Shift stick: editorially, *The Times of India*, Jaipur, 12/4/2010, p. 12.

was challenged by the Supreme Court's registrar in Delhi High Court in Jan. 2009, saying that this information cannot be made public.

Improving Infrastructure of Trial Courts

Within two months of taking over as Chief Justice of India, Justice S.H. Kapadia prepared a blueprint to improve the infrastructure of trail courts groaning under a pendency of more than 250 crore cases and has spoken to Prime Minister Manmohan Singh about the need for an additional grant of Rs. 7,077 crore to make lower judiciary capable to fight the menace.

This requirement was in addition to the Rs. 70.08 crore provided under the 11th Plan. Total estimated cost of infrastructure needs of district and subordinate courts now calculated is of Rs. 7,077 crore (excluding Allahabad, Delhi and Jammu and Kashmir of which data was not provided by the respective High Courts). Rs. 2,182 crore is required in 2010-11 itself: The report was made public on 13th July, 2010.

The report presented a pitiable picture of the lower judiciary. It said that court fees were abysmally low in most cases, leading to a deluge the trial courts. Therefore, it requested the Centre and state governments to take immediate measures to revise court fees so that a balance was struck between welfare measures and commercial needs. The report underlined the need to change in Section 138 of Negotiable Instruments Act for cheque bouncing offences, as the courts of Magistrates are almost getting crushed under the weight of the above cited cheque bouncing cases in urban areas.

Judges are Accountable to Society

At a time when many feel sweeping contempt powers are stifling critical stress of the judiciary, the Supreme Court on 15th July signed a bold new approach saying judges are accountable to the society and are not scared of fair and reasonable criticism of their judgments and public actions. As per the judgment: 'In fact, fair and reasonable criticism must be encouraged as no one, including judges, can claim infallibility. . . . There is no manner of doubt that judges are accountable to the society. Any criticism of judicial system or judges which hinders administration of justice or brings the disrepute must be prevented'.

The Bench comprising Justices J.M. Panchal and A.K. Patnaik while dismissing a petition seeking initiation of criminal contempt proceedings against HRD minister Kapil Sibal for his remarks as a senior advocate 15 years ago is expressing concern over the falling standards in the judiciary and the legal profession.

The Supreme Court showed a remarkable resilience towards the Minister's statement as fair criticism of the Indian Judiciary and his constructive criticism were associated with suggestions to root out the malaise (corruption and lack of infrastructure facilities in the Judiciary). The petition against Sibal seeking initiation of contempt proceedings was filed by an advocate in the Punjab and Haryana High Court. The case was transferred to the apex court in 1997. In this judgment, the apex court projected itself as a great believer in the constitutional guarantee to the citizens on the right to freedom of expression under Article 19(1)(a) of the Indian Constitution and as any fair and reasonable criticism of a judgment/a public act of a judge is no crime.

Parallel to it, Law Minister Veerappa Moily's 'Mission Under trial Plan' should be appreciated, because it is, too, a bold step in honouring human rights languishing in jails. As per it, over two lakh under trial prisoners who had endlessly waited for the conclusion of trial and had not seen their families for years, would be released, on the ground that those they were booked for petty offences yet they had virtually, served the maximum sentence in jails, without the trial and they have caused overcrowded jails without basic facilities.

Surprisingly, Molly's efforts in sensitizing the state governments about the continuous violation of the fundamental rights of these hapless under trial prisoners for year's yielded results and Uttar Pradesh took the lead in releasing 52,843 so far under trials and settling the cases of 4,203 more.

The states which released a large number of under trials included Orissa (19,350), Andhra Pradesh (over 14,000), Delhi (13,526), Maharashtra (10,956), Madhya Pradesh (10,183), Assam (5,236), Haryana (4,963), Gujarat (4,311), Karnataka

(4,738), Jharkhand (4,320), Kerala (3,775), Punjab (4,926) and J&K (1,476)[2]

Socialism is Still a Must for all Parties

Since India, veered away from 'socialism' two decades ago (1990) in the light of loosening state's grip over the economy (that is beginning era of liberalization) and determining market forces, a PIL sought to do away the declaration of allegiance to 'socialism' enshrined in the 'Preamble' of the Constitution on July 12, 2010, the Supreme Court refused to entertain a PIL against the anomaly. Significantly, the top court cited an interesting reason to turn down the petition argued by senior advocate Fali S. Nariman. It said no political party, including those responsible for getting the state to vacate the 'commanding heights' of the economy, had objected to being required to swear by socialism.

Section 29-A of Representation of People Act mandates that no political party would be registered by the Election Commission unless it bore 'true faith and allegiance to the Constitution of India as by law established and to the principles of socialism, secularism and democracy'. The PIL was lodged by NGO : Good governance India Foundation and the Lawyer Nariman also cited the objection of Dr. B.R. Ambedkar, main architect of the Constitution, to insertion of the word 'socialist' in the 'Preamble' and how it was left out from the Constitution after a lengthy debate during the Constituent Assembly proceedings.

But Solicitor General Gopal Subramaniam said that all parties knew their duties and none had ever objected or moved the Election Commission challenging the requirement to give declaration owing allegiance to the word 'socialist'.[3]

(2) ACTIVIST ROLE OF RTI

In an important judgement, the Rajasthan High Court imposed a fine of Rs. 10,000 on the Jaipur Municipal Corporation (JMC) for not constituting various committees

2. *The Times of India*, Jaipur, July 22, 2010, p. 7.
3. *The Times of India* news, 13th July, 2010, p. 4.

required under sections 55 of the new Raj Municipalities Act, 2009, after the elections. The delay was due to the local politics, that is, Mayor-*cum*-chair person belongs to ruling Congress while 46 corporations out of 77 belong to the BJP. The JMC failed to discharge its duties. These cases put a check on the whimsical role of the administration/political leadership and compelled the public authority to disclose information. Likewise, the Chief Information Commissioner (CIS) of Rajasthan, S.D. Kaurani, imposed a penalty of Rs. 25,000 on district collector of Bikaner for failing to answer some questions under the RTI. The matter related to an application filed by Sripal Jain on December 2009, seeking information regarding deployment of election officers in Bikaner (west) assembly segment during the 2008 Vidhan Sabha polls. The applicant had sought information like names of poll duty employees, whose duties were cancelled, on what ground duties were cancelled, details of the officers who performed their duties, details of employees on duty in all the seven assembly segments of Bikaner during the 2008 assembly polls. In response top its, failure the CIS directed the Bikaner collector to deposit the amount within 30 days and extract the amount from the official responsible for the lapse. Besides, the commissioner asked the collector to give all information sought by the applicant within the next 10 days.[4]

Chief Information Commissioner (CIC) Wajahat Habibullah on 11 June, 2010 said that rural people in Rajasthan are more aware about the Right to Information (RTI) Act, as RTI is the only tool which compels politicians as well as bureaucrats to maintain transparency in their functioning. Habibullah was speaking at a seminar on 'How RTI is Useful to Eradicate Corruption from Politics' organized by Citizen Council and PUCL in Ajmer. In his words, 'the whole world is looking towards our country for its implementation; we are proving that we have the largest and best democratic set-up.' Habibullah said, Ajmer is the birth place of this act and activist Aruna Roy started the movement for it. A survey was

4. *The Times of India* news, 8.6.2009) (Also see Tanojay son's article, 'Lift the veil of Secrecy : Indian Judiciary cannot remain a closed book, *Ibid.*, 18.12.2009, p. 12.

conducted to know how many people of Rajasthan know this act. About 40% people from urban areas and 20% rural people know about it. Thirty per cent of them use RTI. He said, 'It is only Rajasthan where more rural people know about this act and they also use this power to get the information.' In his opinion, corruption can be removed from the system by making information 'public'. All the government departments should follow Section 4 of the act as it makes the Government more responsible and transparent.

Again, the Central Information Commission slapped a penalty of Rs. 15,000 on senior officials of IIT, Kharagpur, for delay in providing information to a professor of the institute. The Commission has also directed the IIT to pay a compensation of Rs. 5,000 to Prof. Rajeev Kumar for the loss and detriment suffered by him. As a matter of fact, for two simple and straight forward queries, the complainant had to wait for almost five months. This was due to the carelessness of the officials or the poor functioning of the institution. Information Commissioner Shailesh Gandhi said there was no reasonable cause for what appeared to be a joint responsibility of registrar Dr. T.K. Ghosal and his OSD T.K. Mukherjee in delaying the supply of information to Prof. Kumar. It may be recalled that Prof. Kumar, in October, 2008, had sought from the Rajiv Gandhi School of Intellectual Property Law (RGSIPL) at IIT the list of all individuals who were called for guest and invited lectures at the school from July 2006 onwards. He also sought to know the names, designation and all related details including nature of work, total amount of remuneration and honorarium paid to them.

The High Court is the appellate authority for challenging CIC's decisions—a fact that led to this unusual situation of the apex court moving a lower court over a dispute, as cited above. The apex court said that information relating to declaration of assets by Supreme Court judges to the Chief Justice of India (CJI) was not a mandatory exercise under law, but driven by an informal resolution of May 7, 1997—implying that information on judges' assets did not come under RTIs purview. The petitioner added that the CIC had committed an error by equating the Supreme Court and the CJI as one and the same authority whereas the CJI's position was quite distinct from that of the Supreme Court in terms of the RTI Act. 'CJI is not a public authority as defined under the RTI Act, and therefore, is not required to designate a central public information officer (central PIO) for it, or to supply information held or maintained by it.' It may be recalled that on Jan. 2009, the CIC had directed the Supreme Court (SC) to furnish information as to whether any declaration of assets had been filed by SC judges or not.

'There is nothing under the Constitution of India or under any other law which requires judges of the Supreme Court to declare their assets to the Chief Justice of India', said the petition which was drafted by advocate Devdatt Kamath and settled by Solicitor General G.E. Vahanhvati. Quoting section 8(1(1) of the RTI Act which imposed a ban on furnishing of personal information, the SC Registrar said any query relating to assets of judges voluntarily declared before the CJI squarely fell within the meaning of section 8(1)(1).

In support of the CIC's decision/order, Law Commission chairman Justice A.R. Lakshmanan, a retired judge of the Supreme Court, on the August 2009 came out strongly in favour of ushering in transparency in declaration of assets and liability by judges and it should be under the purview of RTI Act. In his words: 'Persons holding high public office should give details of his assets and liabilities and the public should know about it. Coming clean of the controversy stirred by the provision in the Judges (Declaration of Assets and Liabilities) Act Justice Lakshmanan said, "I declared my assets the day I became a judge of Madras High Court in 1990 and have since then declared it every year. Why should a judge have anything to hide?' He said expressing complete agreement with noted jurist Fali S. Nariman. In fact, 'If the credibility of the higher judiciary is to be restored, it is essential that every judge of the Supreme Court set an example and voluntarily make a public disclosure of his (or her) assets on the website of the Supreme Court'.

Incidentally, the Law Commission chairman submitted its 230th report to Law Minister Veerappa Moily suggesting 7-point reforms for judiciary.

Since then, the concept of transparency and accountability, too, is favoured with the functioning of the Indian Judiciary.

RTI is one of the ways to keep a check on a growing trend of corruption in our courts. On the contrary, sadly, the Centre has blocked all information on action to retrieve black money abroad illegally and invoked secret provisions of double taxation avoidable agreement (DTTA). It may be recalled that the noted Supreme Court criminal lawyer Ram Jethmalani, asked a copy of the letter dated March 16, 2009 by which the German Government had informed India that it was in a position to provide requisite information about account holders. It is believed that the petition touched upon the core of the controversy relating to the allegation against a group of elite class that black money to the tune of Rs. 70 lakh crore was trashed abroad.

After preaching transparency to the whole country Central Information Commission appears to have trouble following its own diktat. For example, over 18 months after it received an RTI query asking for wealth declaration of information commissioners, CIC continues to withhold the information on the pretext that it has sought advice from Election Commission. Incidentally, of the nine information commissioners and one chief information commissioner so far only one, Shailesh Gandhi, has made his list of assets public.

In an order passed on 2nd July, 2010, chief information commissioner Wajahat Habibullah said since Gandhi had already expressed willingness to disclose his income details, the information could be made public after getting his consent. Habibullah said as Gandhi was recognized as a 'third party' under the RTI Act, his consent was required. For the rest, the commission has sought the EC's and vice. The directions came after Pune-based Vihar Durve filed an RTI plea in 2008 asking for information relating to assets.

(3) A CHANGE OF REGIME NO GROUND FOR GOVERNOR'S REMOVAL

After a classic decision given in the S.R. Bommai case, 1994, putting a check on the abuse of Governor's discretionary power, in application of Article 356, the Supreme Court delivered once again a significant verdict against the political pattern of sacking four Governors, on 7th May, 2010. They were: The Governors of Uttar Pradesh, Haryana, Gujarat and Goa—namely Vishnu Kant Shastri, Babu Parmanand, Kallashpat Mishra and Kidarnath Sahni—who had to summarily packed off from respective Raj Bhawans, ostensibly because of their saffron affiliations.

Five judges' Constitution Bench of the Supreme Court dealt with the harsh decision of the UPA-1 Government for removing four Governors that were appointed by the previous NDA Government in 2004. The decision of the UPA-I government might be claimed politically correct, but legally, it was untenable. The court held that if the reasons for removal were irrelevant, the sync with the policies and ideologies have no sense with the removal of Governors. The Bench comprising Chief Justice K.G. Balakrishnan and Justices D.H. Kapadia, R.V. Raveendran, B. Sudershan Reddy and P. Sathasivam minced no words in registering their strong disapproval of regime-change as a ground for dismissal of Governors. This may set the stage for a more cautious approach in the future.

Justice Raveendran, writing the unanimous 56 page judgment, said: 'Governor, cannot be removed on the ground that he is out of sync with the policies and ideologies of the Union Government or the party in power at the Centre. Nor can he be removed on the ground that the Union government has lost confidence in him.' It follows therefore, that a change in government at Centre is not a good ground for removal of governors holding office to make way for others favoured by the new government', in what could pinch the conscience of the government'.

Attorney General G.E. Vahanvati had defended the decision to summarily dismiss the Governors saying in a democracy, political parties were formed on shared beliefs and they contest an election with a declared agenda. He argued that 'If a party which comes to power with a particular social and economic agenda, finds that a Governor is out of sync with its policies, then it should be able to remove such a Governor'. The AG was categorical in his submission that the Centre would have the right to remove a Governor without attributing any fault to him, if the President loses confidence in a Governor or finds that the 'Governor is out of sync with the democratic and electoral mandate'. The bench agreed with Vahanvati that no reasons need to be ascribed for the summary dismissal of Governors as they continue in their post as long as they enjoyed the pleasure of the President.

But, it sounded a caution while agreeing with former AG Soli Sorabjee, who appeared for petitioner B.P. Singhal. 'Having regard to the nature of functions of the governor in maintaining Centre-state relations, and the flexibility available to the government in such matters, it is needless to say that there will be no interference unless a very strong case is made out.' It further ruled that where the apex court feels the power to dismiss a Governor had been exercised arbitrarily, the court would intervene. In his words; 'If the Union government does not disclose any reason, or if reasons disclosed are found to be the irrelevant, arbitrary, whimsical, or malafide, the court will interfere. However, the court will not interfere merely on the ground that a different view is possible or that the material or reasons are insufficient'. The ultimate analysis of the case is that the constitutional law has survived. It is a check on the presidential activism.

(4) SECOND GUJJARS' AGITATION CALLED OFF

After keeping the state on centre books for several days the agitation of Gujjars on May 6, 2010 accepted a formula proposed by the state government to met their demand for 5% reservation in the state. The agitation was called off in the evening by Col. Kirori Singh Bainsla, leader of Gurjjars' Arakshan Sangathan Samiti.

The magic formula to end the impose emerged after a one to one meeting between chief minister Ashok Gehlot and Col. Bainsla in the morning at the former's residence.

The government has conceded to our demand. They have given us in writing that the government would fight for our cause in the court and try to get us reservation within two months, said Roop Singh spokes person of Samiti. Till then, we will continue to enjoy benefits under the OBC category in recruitments and got an additional 1% reservation under special backward classes. This 1% reservation is what is left in the state for 50% limit. Currently, the reservation in the state stands at 49%. 'After the issue is settled in the court the government will arrange us 4% reservation in a constitutional way, Singh said.

On the Maharashtra pattern special reservation was assured by the Government outside the 50% limit.

On the contrary, the Gujjar agitation was far from the end or over. A major section of the community cutting across the party lines publicly rejected the 'peace deal or agreement' and called for to continue the agitation that was began in 2007. The deal was arrived, it alleged, by the Bainsla for his personal interest that is for getting the Rajya Sabha seat, which the CM refused to provide him. According to the president of Akhil Bharatiya Gujjar Mahsabha Ramvir Singh Bidhuri.

Two days after he signed the agreement with chief minister Ashok Gehlot we held a mahapanchayat and have excommunicated him. 'Bainsla has been using this agitation to serve his personal and had betrayed the community', said Bidhuri, who resigned from the primary membership of the Congress party so as to lead the agitation from and a political front.

'According to the Constitution no community can enjoy benefits in separate categories. Therefore, the assurance that the Gujjars will get a 1% special reservation while continuing to enjoy benefits under the OBC and even the general categories is illegal. Moreover, this 1% will be shared by three other communities. Therefore, there is nothing that the community has gained from the agreement,' he added.

This act was staged by Gehlot, Jitendre Singh and Bainsla for cheating the community. How could the chief minister do this to us when last year as the leader of the Opposition he was the first to point out that the agreement being put forth by the BJP is unconstitutional? We have knowledge that Bainsla shook hands with the chief minister as his daughter Sunita Bainsla was promised a ticket to the Rajya Sabha this time, he said.

Additional Quota to Gujjars

The state government on 6th May, 2010 cleared 1% additional quota for Gujjars and three other communities in addition to the existing reservation given to them under the

OBC category as promised by chief minister Ashok Gehlot to Gujjar leader Col. Kirori Singh Bainsla. The decision was taken at a cabinet meeting.

As per it, the Gujjars would continue to get the benefits for the OBC and 1% for the special backward classes, until the legal hurdles are cleared. After that the provisions for 5% reservation for the special backward classes would be made. Gehlot said no other alternate solution was available given the fact that the 5% quota for special backward classes and 14% reservations for the economically backward is a subjudiced matter.

'As it is a pending matter in the High Court, our role is limited. However, this solution has been welcomed by Kirori Singh Bainsla and the community at large, he said. Gehlot said, 'the government would go ahead and advertise the recruitment but the process for 18% seats (14% for the economically backward and 4% for the special backward classes) would not begin now'. Youngsters who have crossed the age limit during this period will be given an extension.

The rival faction of the community was not happy at it announced to oppose the deal arrived between the Bainsla and the CM. A group of Gujjars announced to keep the agitation continued, stating that it was a 'bogus agreement' and Bainsla did it for his personal gains. The SC/ST population is growing therefore 1% quota promised to us (Gujjar community) by the CM will not be coming it would go over to the SC/ST. He alleged that the chief minister wants us to fight with the SC/ST and therefore he had settled for the agreement. But we want a 5% reservation from the 21% quota for the OBCs in the state, he added. Bidhuri also reiterated earlier demands of a Gujjar regiment in the Indian Army, withdrawal of cases against members of the community, release of Gujjars arrested during the agitation, compensation for the injured and a Rs. 500 crore deposit for the Dev Narayan Board.

He cited a similar agreement in Uttar Pradesh and Bihar where a portion of the OBC quota was taken away and given to other community. The Samiti decided to go for a placeful agitation from June 16, 2010 at district level.

The Samiti has also nominated its office bearers and MLA Hem Singh Badhana will be the president, while former MLA Gopi Chand Gujjar will be the convenor. The patrons include Nathu Singh Gujjar, Kalu Lal Gujjar, Praladh Singh Gunjal, Ram Gopal Guard and Amar Singh Kasana, Members, have also been made responsible for each district.

He referred to the observations of Israni committee and Chopra committee that have already endorsed special reservation for the community. In July 2009, the Rajasthan Government had announced of 5% quota for Gujjars and 14% for the EBCs, which took the total reservation to 68%. However, the Rajasthan High Court stayed the job and educational quota provided to the Gujjars and Economically Backward Classes (EBCs) on the ground that it exceeded the overall limit of 50% laid drawn by the Supreme Court.

On the contrary, in a significant judgment, the Supreme Court has ruled that governments cannot force the reservation policy on minority educational institutions, including those getting grant in aid, and ask them to appoint teachers from the SC and ST communities.

A bench comprising justices B. S. Chauhan and Swatanter Kumar gave this ruling while negating the applicability of Rule 64 of Delhi School Education Rules, 1973 to a school run by the Sindhi community in Lajpat Nagar. The rule insisted that minority schools have to appoint the requisite number of SC and ST candidates as teachers to receive grant-in-aid. Justice Kumar, writing the judgement said that the Government is free to frame regulations against the mal-administration in the minority linguistic or religious schools be they are public or private to ensure better organization and development of school education.

Such powers must operate within its limitation while ensuring that it does not. In any way, dilute or impair the basic character of linguistic minority its right to establish and administer has to be construed liberally to bring it in alignment with the constitutional protections available to such communities.[5]

5. *The Times of India* news, Jaipur edn., 16.7.2010, p. 9.

Is Rajasthan Government serious about youth and women quota? Who is the legal advisor to the state government? That is the question doing the rounds with the High Court striking one government decision after another? The latest in the series of legal setbacks to the government is the High Court verdict striking down 50% reservation for women and 30% for youth in panchayat bodies, almost on the same line of quota in the municipal elections.

A division bench, comprising Chief Justice Jagdish Bhatia and Justice M.N. Bhandari ruled on 20.5.10 that while the quota for women was fixed without any basis and was 'excessive', the reservation for youth violated on Constitution.

The latest order a supplementary of an earlier one quashing the reservation for women and youth in municipal bodies. The state government had already filed a special leave petition in the Supreme Court challenging the earlier order.

According to same legal experts, however, blame the government's casual approach for the setbacks. For example, 'the government should have done some home work before taking such decisions', pointed out lawyer R.D. Rastogi. The government has not followed any procedure and it seems the decision aimed only at making political profit out of it.

Advocate Hemant Nahata said, 'The state government should have some quantifiable data to support its decision. It should have done a survey to find out the percentage of women and youth in the population to support its decision.'

The judges held that the 50% reservation for women and those in the age group of 21 to 35 on certain earmarked seats is unconstitutional. The order has come as a big blow to the state government as it failed to appraise the court that the reservation for women is based on their proportionate population.

Further, it failed to appraise how the state was justified in fixing certain number of seats in the municipal and panchayat elections of the state for the young candidates belonging to the age group of 21 to 35.

It was contended before the court that the 50% reservation for women is 'excessive' and goes contrary to the mandate of Article 243 of the Constitution that provided that one-third of the total seats be reserved for women. It was further contended that without ascertaining even proportionate population of women in the state, amendment has been made to provide reservation to them.

It was given out by the petitioners that on account of excessive reservation for women as well as young persons by putting an age ceiling, ordinary citizen has been deprived to contest elections, which cannot be said to be in consonance with the spirit of the constitution. The constitution provides minimum reservation in favour of women a candidate that is, one-third of the seats in the respective category. It was argued.

If women are proportionately less than the population of men, then reservation extended in favour of women can be maintained in proportion to the population ratio. In absence of such figures, we are constrained to give a specific opinion on the aforesaid issue.

It is worth-recalling that the Supreme Court bench leded by V.J.S.H. Kapadia, agreed on 5th July, 2010 to extend one year extend to T.N. that has provided 69% reservation since 1993 and Karnataka that has provided 73% since 1994, the above 50% cap fixed by previous apex court judgements for admission and employment, but asked the government to place quantifiable data about OBC population before the Backward Commission to justify quotas exceeding the ceiling it laid down in 1992 in its verdict in the Indira Sawhney case' where it upheld the implementation of Mandal Commission's recommendation to reserve 27% of central jobs for OBCs.

Both state laws providing for quota in excess of 50% cap were challenged before the Supreme Court (SC) and even contempt petitions were filed as they violated the constitution bench's Indira Sawhney judgment. In its 2007 judgment in *I.R. Cohello* case, the SC ruled that judicial scrutiny of a 9th Schedule law was possible if it was shown that the legislation was violative of the basic structure of the Constitution. These states have sought the support of 9th schedule of the Constitution that bars judicial scrutiny of the constitutional validity of the law. The above legislations have been operating for more than 15 years extending for more than one year, but with the rider that the state governments would revisit these laws and produce quantifiable data to prove before State Backward Commission the necessity of reservation in excess of 58%.

(5) REFLECTION ON IMPLEMENTING THE MGNREGS IN RAJASTHAN

The National Rural Employment Guarantee Scheme was enacted by Indian Parliament in 2005 and Rajasthan may have gladly claimed to implement it well and thoroughly. The scheme was re-christened, on eve of fifty years of Panchayat Raj institutions (2nd Oct., 2009) as Mahatma Gandhi National Rural Guarantee Act (MGNREGA). The employment scheme is a sure as sunrise in the sense it is like a dream for the unorganized workers in the tribal/rural areas of the state for 100 days of guarantees to the poors.

As regards Rajasthan, the implementation of Act brought to fore various irregularities in the rural areas. The authorities usually get complaints of irregularities and neglect of essential provisions. The rural masses are still not aware of the law's importance. The Right to Information has yet not extensively covered the actual performance of NREGA in various areas. Therefore, corruption has spread at several places. A report by activists of the 'Suchana Evam Rozgar Ka Abhiyan' (NGO) has brought to light that workers at various sites in the panchayats were less paid wages and maintained no book, whereas according to the rules, each worker has to be given a real wage of Rs. 100 per day and entries should be made in the book. The irked workers have asked the state about the fraud done by officials.[6]

In the wake of this scenario, the Rozgar Evum Suchna Ka Adhikar Abhiyan has threatened to launch an indefinite agitation near the Statue Circle of Jaipur if the July deadline, set by the government, to correct anomalies in the MGNREGA is not met. The Rajasthan Government set the deadline after activists of the organization, including social worker Aruna Roy, along with thousands of MGNREGA workers on 23 June, 2010, staged a rally at the Statue Circle and met government officials. According to Mrs. Roy, it is true that the government of Rajasthan has made a lot of efforts in implementing the Rozgar Guarantee Scheme. But then what is the point in all

6. Based on the report prepared by Anindo Dey, *The Times of India*, 26.6.2010, p. 3.

these efforts if workers are getting Rs. 1 as wages. The government must fix accountability on persons under whom the workers have got such poor payments: Roy further said, we know it is impossible for workers to get a Re 1 wage, so the government should take the person supervising the site to task for either not ensuring that people work or for faulty measurements. She was addressing to a huge rally at Jaipur exposing several anomalies of the Scheme. Thousands of MGNREGA workers from 30 districts attended it.

Like that of the Gujaral model (as cited earlier) MGNREGA workers in Rajasthan also geared up to form their Union. To this effect, the process of legalizing its forum has begun in May, 2010 under the MKSS's guidance.

According to Shankar Singh of the Mazdoor Kisan Shakti Sangathan (MKSS) four districts—Ajmer, Rajsamand, Bikaner and Pali are represented in the union. There are around 300 members of the proposed union. He said, 'Anyone who has got a job card can become a union member. It is being formed, so that the system gets a more centralized approach to deal with the workers' problems'. . . . The union will have representation at the Gram Panchayat level, at the Block level and at the district level. The idea is not to give them a platform wherein they take a stance like 'no work but full pay'. But there are so many complaints pouring in from all parts of the state that such a system will help in the formation of a pressure group so that the problems of labourers are catered to.

The union, which will be named Rajasthan Rozgar Guarantee Mazdoor Union, will have 10-15 representatives even in the smallest of village and will have a representation at the state level. It is worth recalling that the MKSS has assisted the state government for the famous Bhilwara social audit which had unearthed hundreds of anomalies in MGNREGA Fund.[7]

According to social activist and the leader of MKSS Aruna Roy, the Gehlot Government has failed to implement of the Act in spirit and letters. The important decision of the Government are not made public through the websites of

7. *The Hindustan Times* news, 28.5.200 p. 5.

various department, thus lacking transparency on governance, nor the all information on NREGA in all gram panchayats of the state on wall is made mandatory. Likewise, little has been done by the administrative reforms department towards any more to bring in transparency.

Other drawbacks of its implementation are as follows. One, junior engineers come in a week after the work is completed. Secondly, the process of Social Audits is defect and no action is taken against the field officials. Thirdly, basic information when demanded is not supplied by the concerned officials. Fourthly, the payment is not given weeks together. Fifthly, the scope of the RTI has yet not enlarged and sounded to create awareness to cap the growing trend of corrupt at the grassroots level. Due to Hume sums of money involved in the project, the NREGA Mafia has gained ground.

In fact, Rajasthan is perhaps the only state that has just one Information Commissioner when there is scope for 11 such commissioners. The state should appoint more commissioners so that all the backlog of complaints can be cleared. There should be a commissioner in every division of the state. Even in the appointment of commissioners there has to be some clarity.

The activist also stressed the need for strengthening Section 4 of the Act that mandates all public authorities to maintain all their records duly catalogued and indexed in a manner that facilitates the RTI.

MGNREGA is a Government scheme and it is the duty of the Government to ensure its proper implementation. The faulty officials should be nabbed and punished. In this regard, one of the suggestions is that workers employed under this scheme ought to be organized and trained for its success. The first step in this direction is the formation of National Rural Employment Workers' Union (NREGWUG) as it prevails in Gujarat. This union grew out of the efforts and thinking of *'Dish: Eklavya Sangathan'*. That has exposed NREGA's irregularities for the better implementation of law. The weaker sections in our rural areas have yet to be informed about the potential of this law. Not only this, they should have a vision of sustainable livelihood based on protection of land rights, conservation of water and all round development of the region. NREGA can be useful in improving the green cover and in water conservation because of prolonged drought and adverse weather conditions prevailing in Rajasthan.

There is a need to assure employment with statutory provisions to provide social security and improved conditions of work and remuneration of contract worker at par with the employees. The NREGA report submitted to the Centre in July 2010 has stressed such a need, along with the reforms to simplify labour regulations and land reforms.

On the line of Punjab, the state Government should appoint on Ombudsman for taking up complaints relating to NREGA. This system gives a scope for preventing corrupt practices. It may be noted here that the appointment of Ombudsman comes as a directive of the Ministry of Rural Development, New Delhi, and the appointments were to be done by December, 2009. But the State Government has not lived up to the deadline. In fact, trained and experienced persons are to be appointed as Social Audit Facilitators for getting the success.

The UPA-II Government has proposed to launch an urban employment guarantee scheme on the lines of NREGA and give statutory sanctions to minimum wages. The proposal, which focuses on generating employment and enhancing employability among less advantaged, is part of the short-term strategies and targets of the government contained in the first Annual Report to the People on Employment. At present, states are under no obligations to implement revision of minimum wages by the Centre. The report released by the ministry of Labour and Employment has emphasized on achieving an employment growth rate of at least 25% per annum compatible with the 9% growth in the economy.

The working group on wages of Central Employment Guarantee Council has recommended lesser working hours (Nine hours including one hour of rest) and indexing NREGA wages under the Minimum Wages Act. It further recommends that the price rise should be linked with the real value of NREGA wages. The erosion of real wages threatens to undermine the entire programme and it is a gross injustice to the NREGA workers. Therefore, the wages fixed by the Centre should promptly revise upwards every six month in line with the Consumer Price Index and the Minimum Wages Act, 1948.

The social audit of NREGS has been a matter of concern for the state Government as the Bhilwara type audit inspection was processed by the state administration. It faced strong protests at local level. It may be called that the state government had initiated the largest social audit of its kind in Bhilwara last year, where nearly 1,700 participants went from village to village combing 11 panchayats, looking for irregularities. It also saw protests from sarpanches in the state who filed cases in courts against the process. The High Court, ultimately, stayed participation of outside agencies (NGOs) involved in the same audit process.

Meanwhile, the state Government has shot of a letter to the Union Rural Development Ministry seeking an amendment to Section 13(b) of Schedule 1 of NREGA which prevents outsiders from participants in social audit. The letter was sent to Union Rural Development Secretary B.K. Singh on February 17, 2010. The letter states, "In order to make the social audit a strong tool for transparency in transaction and expenditure incurred. Government of India may kindly consider the desirability of amending Section 13{b) of Schedule 1 to the Act." The government has already resumed the inspection of NREGA accounts of panchayats which could not be done earlier due to panchayat polls—According to State Panchayati Raj Minister Bharat Singh; 'The inspection by teams from the capital had to be suspended due to the polls. But now that the polls are over, we are resuming the inspection in the seven panchayats out of the original 16'.[8] At present, while section 15{b) of NREGA provides for the conduct of a social audit once every six months, it prevents active participation, facilitation or assistance of any outsider in the gram sabha, including civil society organizations or government agencies. In fact, it was this clause that the High Court cited and halted the participation of NGOs in the audit process. After the stay, the state conducted inspections of the NREGS accounts of various panchayats from where reports of anomalies were coming in. However, the state level inspection was not totally successful.

8. *The Times of India* report, 5/3/10, p. 4.

Minister to Visit NREGA Sites

Frustrated to constant non-adherence to departmental orders by officials, Bharat Singh, rural development and panchayati raj minister, has decided to personally visit all NREGA sites close to the capital regularity. His decision came at the recently concluded NREGA samvad, a periodical meeting of officials and villagers to discuss the scheme's progress in the state. The meeting saw about 150 villagers from 19 districts participate. He holds meetings with a pattern of NREGA Samvad (Dialogue) at district level to know about its execution and implementation problems. For this Helpline No. 1077 across the state except Bhilwara has been set-up to establish or coordination between Panchyats and administration.

To conclude, there is no harm if the NGOs are involved in social audit of schemes, and to this effect, the present section 13(b) of the NREGA should be amended to ensure the role of Gram Sabhas free from corrupt practices. Despite many problems and anomalies in the NREGA, the scheme has changed many lives in rural India, specifically in Rajasthan it has brought a sea-change in the lives of rural folk. It has empowered them by raising their income level to an extent so that they can fulfil minimum needs.

To empower them further, the RTI should be included in the curricula to create awareness and increase its application among the rural, poor masses. The section 4 of the Act should be sounded and lastly, the recommendations of the Working Group on Transparency and Accountability (WGTA) including an amendment to section 13(b) of the NREGA should be accepted to curb the role of NREGA mafia.

(6) UNIFIED COMMAND TO TACKLE MAOIST INSURGENCY

Faced with a surge in severe Naxal violence, four worst hit states—Chhattisgarh, Orissa, West Bengal and Jharkhand—agreed to form unified commands for anti-naxal operations. The decision was taken at the meeting of chief ministers and the representatives of Naxal affected states. Our Prime Minister Manmohan Singh asked them to remain 'united' and not to 'inter-personal issues' come in the way of the strategy to tackle the menace.

The agreement and deliberations marked a growing political convergence among states not to let the killings of security personnel and civilians by Maoists distract them from objective of snuffing, out the challenge. The states which have agreed to form 'unified commands' are ruled by parties of different persuasions while Chhattisgarh and West Bengal are governed by the BJP and the Left, respectively. Orissa is ruled by Biju Janata Dal, Jharkhand is under central rule. The meet was called on July 14, 2010 in New Delhi. Unfortunately, the states like Bihar, Maharashtra and AP, who attended the deliberations, said 'no' to the offer, saying that there was no immediate need for such command. Currently, similar commands exist in terror and insurgency hit J&K and Assam. Such unified commands are basically created to ensure better coordination and control among the central and state security forces. There the command is headed by the respective C.Ms. It may be noted that the states' consent is sought to create unified command, which is in consonance with the federal concept. But for the new command of four states, the respective chief secretaries will head and each of state will also appoint a retired Major General of Army as one the member of the command.

The Nature of Security Focus

Chhattisgarh, Jharkhand, Orissa and West Bengal to have united commands headed by respective chief secretaries each of the states to appoint a retired Major General of the Army as one of the members of the command.

Additional 16,000 SPOs to be appointed in Bihar, Jharkhand, Orissa, West Bengal, Maharashtra, Andhra and Chattisgarh.

More helicopters to be available for logistics support, troop movement, supplies and evacuation in Maoist-affected areas.

The Centre to fund establishment and strengthening of 400 police stations in affected districts, Rs. 2 crore to be given for each police station: additional special police officers in Maoist hit states.

Development Focus

Road connectivity in 34 Maoist-hit districts to be improved, roads and bridges to be built at Rs. 950 crore As part of development scheme, which the Planning Commission will consider special development plan for affected districts, with stress on road connectivity, primary education, primary healthcare and drinking water.

- Contrary to this more various khaps from UP, Haryana and Delhi have shown their opposition to amendments to deal with honour killings. A memorandum to effect is likely to be submitted to the President of India, stressing that the Hindu Marriage Act, 1955 should be amended to disallow marriage in the same gotra.

In yet another case, a family of Barmer (Rajasthan) had to face the caste Panchayat's ire because the man registered a case against his daughter's-in-law for presenting her for dowry. Despite the police intervention, the caste panchayat issued a draconian diktat against the family. The panchayat banished the family from community, while asking the villagers not to give them works. It forced the family to withdraw the case.

- OBC lobby is getting pressures to include caste as a category in the 2011 census. The last such exercise was taken in 1931 but fortunately, the British regime did include the caste in that census. Since the India was to move towards a casteless society, it would be a regressive more if the UPA government includes caste in the census 2011, as the reservation policy as an affirmative measure have helped Dalits and others to more towards empowerment.

(7) SOME HIGHLIGHTS OF KHAP PANCHAYATS

- It is opposed to 'sagotra' or inter-caste marriage or 'same gotra' marriages and creates spread terror in the caste community. In its enforcement, for example, Haryana C.M. Bhupinder Singh Hooda, bowed before the Khap Panchayat's clout. He accepted the legitimacy of it, describing it them as informal social organizations, like ONGs. In short, our politicians have added fuel to the fire by keeping mum over brutal killings; it is like a capital punishment/death sentence without legal justification.

- The khap panchayats has demanded an amendment in the Hindu Marriage Act to make matrimony within the gotra unlawful. This patriarchal clan dominates in the rural areas, and may spread with urban areas too.
- The police administration does not dare to take action against diktats or brutally murdered these panchayats, though they do not work in conformity with the law of the land. Likewise, the politicians to keep silence on it mainly because these khaps influence the voters to a large extent.
- Khap panchayats sanctioned honour killings in north India may have hogged all the headlines but such sordid incidents have been reported from all over the country, a recent study has concluded. For example, there has been a spate of incidents in western Uttar Pradesh, Delhi, Haryana and Punjab, incidents have also been reported from other parts of the country. We have been receiving complaints from states like Chhattisgarh, Tamil Nadu, Jharkhand and Andhra Pradesh, said Ravi Kant, president of NGO Shakti Vahini which carried out the study, another myth busted was that killing to preserve honour was mainly done by the boy's family. Preliminary analysis by Shakti Vahini showed that in 90% of the cases, the preparators of the crime were from the girl's family.

That such a paradigm shift will bring about a certain underlying tension in a socio-culture context is to be expected. It's inevitable that norms of marriage and interaction will change when women and youth are empowered. The government, however, has failed when it comes to managing the ugly backlash from patriarchal quarters that is undermining the liberal fabric of the country's Constitution. It is up to the political leadership to provide clear direction. And here, judging by the likes of Naveen Jindal and Haryana chief minister Bhupinder Singh Hooda, they have not just failed, but on occasion supported the peddlers of caste and gotra in pursuit of vote banks. This must no longer be allowed to continue. It's up to the authorities to pursue and make examples of the murderers.[9]

With khap dictated honour killings threatening to become a trend, the Centre is mulling an ordinance to the rein in the caste courts meting out extreme punishments to young couples who don't follow the diktat against marrying within the same gotra. The Centre has already discussed amendments to relevant laws, Indian Penal Code, Indian Evidence Act and Hindu Marriage Act, to deter village elders from holding kangaroo courts which call for killing of young couples who don't agree with their notion about gotras and marriages. The recommendations of various panel laws hopefully may take place in place, it is recalled that the Union Cabinet, on 17th July, 2010 referred a standalone law to deal with honour killings to a group of ministers after several members found fault with the proposal to amend the existing law to deal with the menace. The Group of Ministers will submit its recommendation after getting inputs from states so that a bill designed to deter honour killings can be introduced.

Our PM Manmohan Singh has decided to refer it to a GoM after several ministers questioned the efficacy of the home ministry drafted bill, which proposed slapping murder charges on all those participating in khap panchayat decisions to kill couples marrying against social norms. For its proper response, the Centre therefore plans to consult state governments and take their suggestions for a specific law.

In 1945, the issue was settled by the Bombay High Court which categorically declared some gotra marriages were legal. And that has been the law of the land since. According to Mrs. Jagmati Sangwan, former international player who faced the worst night more of the Khap panchayat, said so in an interview on 14th May, 2010. It is instructive to learn about the

9. Editorially, Tough questions, 26.6.10, p. 10.

vigour with which two reputed judges went into the issue. In 1945, much before Hindu personal law was codified. They consulted the writings of leading experts and delved into Hindu scriptures to arrive at their verdict.

The case, *'Madhavrao* v. *Raghavendrarao'* involved a Deshastha Brahmin couple and the two judge bench comprised Harilal Kania, the first Chief Justice of independent India and P.B. Gajendragadhar who became Chief Justice of India in the 1960s. The essence of the case whether 'sagotra' marriage within the same gotra was valid under Hindu custom, the court initially relied in a landmark 1868 case where the Privy Council had stated that 'under the Hindu system of law, clear proof of usage will outweigh the written text of the law.' However, a custom which was at variance with the written text of Hindu law, had to be ancient, certain and reasonable if it was to be recognized by the court.

With honour killings repeatedly making national headlines the Supreme Court has issued notices to Centre, Haryana and UP, Punjab, Rajasthan, Jharkhand, Bihar, HP and MP where the honour killings have been practiced. Of course, there is much scope for modifying the traditional laws. Seeking their response steps taken to protect couples from the dead of khap panchayats the Bench comprising justification. N.M. Lodha and A.P. Patnaik were initially reluctant to entertain PIL filed by NGO 'Shakti Vahiani' highlighting the reign of terror of khap panchayats dishing our extreme penalties to couples who fell in love or eloped transgressing the socially resented sagotra marital relationships. When the Bench weighed the necessity of the court's intervention then it appeared to it that the government was alive to the situation and FIRs have been registered against the brutal murder of couples.

The study commissioned by the National Commission for Women (NCW), also found that 72% of the 326 cases surveyed were, in fact, inter-caste marriage while same gotra marriages were only 3%. Marriages within the caste were 15% while only 1% was inter-religious marriages. According to the study, at the core of the conflict is a woman's fight to make her own choices. In a largely patriarchal society an educated girl's decision to choose her own life partner is seen by her family as offending their honour said Ravi Kant. There are also fears in the family that a contentious marriage may lead to the girl staking her claim on property and land holdings that belong to her father instead of forsaking her claim in return for dowry which usually happens in an arranged marriage.

Bibliography

Agrawal, C. and Chowdhry, N.K., History of Rise and Fall of Non-Congress Government of India (*Ibid*).

———, Indian Economy Crisis and Reforms, (New Delhi, Shipra Publications, 1973).

Asgar Ali Engineer, Babri Masjid and Ram Janam Bhomi Controversy, (New Delhi, Ajanta, 1990).

Austin, Granville, Indian Constitution of a Nation, (London, Clarendon Press, 1972).

Bajwa, G.S., Human Rights in India: Implementation and Violations, (New Delhi, Anmol, 1995).

Baldev Singh, Decentralisation, Panchayati Raj and District Planning, (New Delhi, Atlantic, 1996).

Basu, D.D., Comparative Federalism, (New Delhi, Prentice Hall, 1987).

———, Human Rights in Constitutional Law, (New Delhi, Prentice-Hall Pvt. Ltd., 1994).

———, Shorter Constitution of India, (New Delhi, Prentice Hall Pvt. Ltd., 11th ed.).

Bhawani Singh, Governor, Role Identification and Sarkaria Commission Report, (Jaipur, Printwell, 1991).

———, Regionalism and Politics of Separation in India, (Jaipur Printwell, 1993).

Bidyut Chakraborthy and R.K. Pandey, Indian Government and Politics, Sage, New Delhi, 2008.

Bidyut Chakraborthy, Forging Power Coalition Politics in India, New Delhi, Oxford, 2005.

Bomball, K.R., National Power and State Autonomy, (Meerut, Menakshi, 1977).

———, The Foundations of Indian Federalism, (Bombay, Asia, 1967).

Brass, Paul R., The Politics in India Since Independence, (New Delhi, Cambridge University Press, 1992).

Chadda, Maya, Ethnicity, Security and Separation in India, (New Delhi, Oxford Press, 1997).

Chakrabarty, Bidyut (ed.), Centre-State Relations in India, (Delhi, Segment, 1995).

Chatterjee, S.R., Governor's Role in the Indian Constitution, (New Delhi, Mittal Publications, 1996).

Chaturvedi, Arun and Sohanlal Mena, New Dimensions of Politics, (in Hindi), Jaipur, Printwell, 1996).

Datta, Prabath, India's Democracy: New Challenges, (New Delhi, Kanishka, 1997).

David, Butler, Ashok Lahiri and Prannoy Roy, India Decides, (New Delhi, Living Media India 1991).

Dua, B.D., President of Rule in India, 1950-84: A Study in Crises Politics, (Delhi, S. Chand & Co., 1985).

Faria, B.L., Indian Government and Politics, (Agra, Sahitya, 1996).

R.K. Menaria, Sarkaria Commision Report and Centre-State Relations, (Agra, Sahitya Bhawan, 1989).

Forsythe, David P., Human Rights and Development: International View, (London, Macmillan, 1989).

G. Ram Reddy, ed., Patterns of Panchayati Raj in India, (New Delhi, Macmillan, 1977).

Gehlot, N.S., India at Fifty: Facing Stresses and Strains (Jaipur National, 1999).

———, (ed.) Politics of Communalism and Secularism, (New Delhi, Deep and Deep, 1993).

———, Elections and Electoral Politics in India, (New Delhi, Deep and Deep Publications, 1994).

———, Indian Government and Politics, (Jaipur, Rawat, 1996).

Glannier, Marc, Competing Equalities : Law and the Backward Classes in India, (Oxford, 1991, Paperback).

Hassan, Zoya (ed.), The State, Political Process and Identity, (Delhi, Sage, 1989).

Jain, P.C., India's Economic Crises: Diagnosis and Treatment, (New Delhi, Concept, 1992).

Jalal, Bimal, India's Economic Crisis: The Way Ahead (Oxford, 1991).

Javeed Alam, Who Wants Democracy?, (New Delhi, Orient Longman, 2004).

Johari, J.C., Indian Political System, (New Delhi, Arnol Publications, 1996).

Joshi, P.C., Secularism and Development: The Indian Experience, (New Delhi, Vikas, 1997).

Kamal, K.L. and R.P. Joshi, Wither Indian Politics, (Jaipur, Printwell, 1994).

Kashyap, Subhash, C., (ed.) Reforming the Constitution, (New Delhi, UBSPD, 1992).

———, (ed.) Coalition Government and Politics in India, (New Delhi, Uppal, 1997).

Kaushik, Asha, (ed.) Democratic Concerns: The Indian Experience, two volumes, (Aalekh Pulisher, 1994).

Leslie Lipson, The Great Issues of Politics: An Introduction to Political Science, (New Delhi, 9th edn., Prentice-Hall of India, 1996).

Lislen, G.K., Development, Devolution and Democracy: Village Discourse in West Bengal, (New Delhi, Sage, 1996).

M. Govinda Rao and Nirvikar Singh, Political Economy of Federalism in India, (New Delhi, Oxford, 2005).

Madan, N.L., Indian Political System, (New Delhi, Ajanta, 1989).

Maheshwari, S.R., The Mandal Commission and Mandalisation : A Critique (New Delhi, Concept, 1993).

Markandam, K.C., Aspects of Indian Polity, (Jalandhar, ABS Publication, Two volumes, 1990).

Mukherjee, D.K., Elections and Electorate in India Since 1977, (New Delhi, Segment, 1995).

N.K. Trikha, Second Chamber of Indian Parliament, (New Delhi, Allied Publishers, 1984).

Nageshwar Prasad, (Ed.), Hind Swaraj : A Fresh Look, (New Delhi, Gandhi Peace Foundation, 1985).

Narang, A.S., Ethnic Identities and Federalism, (Simla, IIAS, 1995).

N.S. Gehlot, New Challenges to Indian Politics, (Deep and Deep Publications (P) Ltd., New Delhi, 2002).

Pannikar, K.N. (ed.), Communicalism in Indian History, Politics and Culture (New Delhi, Manohar Publications, 1992).

Pran Chopra (ed.), The Supreme Court *versus* the Constitution : A Challenge to Federalism, (New Delhi, Sage Publications, 2006).

Prasad, R.C., Preface to Ambedkarism, (Delhi, Motilal Banarasidas Publications, 1997).

Puri, G.G. and Joshi, V.T., India at Crossroads, (New Delhi, Mittal Publications, 1996).

R.K. Pandey (ed.), Right to Information: Problems and Solutions, Nainital, Uttarakhand Academy of Administration, 2007.

Ramesh Kumar, Regionalisation of Politics in India, (New Delhi, Mohit Publications, 1996).

Ramu, P.S., Eleventh Lok Sabha Elections, 1996 : Dangerous Prospects of Parliamentary Democracy in India, (New Delhi, Institute for Socialist Education, 1996).

Ravi Karan Singh, Dispensation of Justice; Role and Accountability of Judges and Advocates, (New Delhi, Deep and Deep Publications, 2004).

Reagon, Michael, D., The New Federalism, (New York, Oxford University Press, 1972).

S.K. Chaturvedi and Others, Human Development in South Asia in 21st Century, (Radha Publications, New Delhi, 2008).

Subramanian, S., Human Rights: Principles, Practices and Abuses, (New Delhi, Manas Publications).

Singh, M.P. and Saxena, Rekha, Indian Politics in Transition: From Domiance to Chaos, (New Delhi, Deep and Deep Publications, 1994).

Sharma, A., District Planning Admihistration, (Jaipur, Surabhi Publications, 1996).

Sharma, B.A.V. and Madhusudan Reddy, Reservation Policy in India, (New Delhi, Life and Light Publishers, 1988).
Sharma, B.K., Political Instability in India, (New Delhi, Mittal, 1989).
Shastre, U., Religious Converts in India, (New Delhi, Mittal, 1997).
Shivlal, Election Activity in India, 1993 (*Ibid.*, 1996).
———, Indian Assembly Polls: Data 1994-95, (New Delhi, Atlantic Publishers, 1995).
———, India Polls: 1996-97, (*Ibid.*, 1997).
Singh, M.P. and Rekha Saxena (ed.), India's Political Agenda: Perspectives on Party System, (Delhi, Kalinga, 1996).
Singh, M.P., Lok Sabha Elections, 1989: Indian Politics in the 1990s (Delhi, Kalinga, 1992).
Singh, S.N., Reservation Policy for Backward Classes, (Jaipur, Rawat, 1996).
Sinha, Sachidanand, Coalition in Politics, The New Challenge, (Muzaffarpur, Maral Prakashan, 1987).
Siwach, J.R., Dyanmics of India Government and Politics, (New Delhi, Sterling, 1990).
Special issue of the IIPA, New Delhi, on Right to Information: Present Status and Issues.
Subramanian, S., Human Rights : An International Handbook, (New Delhi, Manas, 1996).
The Report of the Commission on Centre State Relations, (New Delhi, Government of India Publications, 1988).
Thomas Blom Hansa and Others, The BJP and Compulsions of Politics in India, New Delhi, 1968.
Tiwari, O.P., Federalism and Centre-State Relations in India, (New Delhi, Deep and Deep Publications, 1996).
Tiwari, T., Issues in Indian Politics, (New Delhi, Mittal, 1996).
Varma, R.S., J&K at the Political Crossroads, (New Delhi, Vikas, 1994).
Vimla, Shukla, Indian Political System and Prime Minister, (New Delhi, Anmol, 1989).
Watts, R.I., New Federations: Experiments in the Commonwealth, (Oxford, Clarendon Press, 1986).
Zelliot Elnor, Political Thought in Modern India, (New Delhi, Sage, 1986).

Index